THE

Astrological and Numerological Keys to THE SECRET DOCTRINE

VOLUME 1

BODO BALSYS

UNIVERSAL DHARMA PUBLICATIONS
SYDNEY, AUSTRALIA

ISBN 978-0-6487877-0-9

2nd Edition, 2024

Artwork on Cover: The Magician, by the author.

Dedication

Thanks to my students, past, present and future, and in particular to those that have helped in the production of this book.

Oṁ

Obeisance to the Gurus!
To the Buddhas of the three times.
To the Council of Bodhisattvas, *mahāsattvas*.
To them I pledge allegiance.

Oṁ Hūṁ! Hūṁ! Hūṁ!

The Earth God, artwork by the author

The Earth God

The Earth God was born
into a world filled with violence,
and constant danger, the unceasing struggle
and conflict of many foes, in competition
for territorial acquisition,
and related resources to be gained.
At first his Mother's caring
protected him from harassment,
but, as adolescence developed,
so grew fears for his life
and meagre possessions.
Between him and his companions
there was much passioned turmoil,
anger, spite, and jealous resentment;
while bodily allurements
and heated sensations left him scarred
with much internal affliction.
Despite this outward struggle
his mental life was simple,
no questioning, pondering, or caring why;
the task of survival was his main motivation.
During this war-wrought period
his family were gradually vanquished,
dispersed, drowned, even forgotten,
and he found himself wandering,
like a lost sheep bleating
out its confusion in its journeying
to a chasm of hopefulness and hunger,
crying out for help in its desolation,
but no one could answer.
Yet he stayed not that way forever,
for he gradually learnt the need
of selective tasting
and the secret of non-attachment
to any scenic location
if its useful forage has been plundered.

His discriminative ability
became well developed
in the constant search for new vegetation,
in restless wandering,
and in the avoidance of the placement
of every dangerous predicament.
He had to learn the art of dissociation
from all that causes harm
or poisoned the efficacy
of body, speech, and mind, of all his senses,
if he were to travel safely
through the fearful danger-fraught wilderness
that was his habitation.
Also, reliance upon his intuition
coupled with intelligent thinking
came to be everyday stronger.
It was a voice that was silently demanding,
prompting, telling him of the presence
of all pits, traps, poisons, illusions,
and how to provision for,
and sense the coming near future,
of lean periods, droughts and famine,
or when to seek shelter; and this capacity,
when he did listen, served him well.
In this period of maturing,
his memory's imaginative understanding
of many life's seasoned cyclic changes,
continually enhanced his confidence
of the ability to handle
any fearsome trouble or upheaval
that might come his way.
In the light of his observations
he broke the earth's verdant ground,
many seeds he planted and watered,
then built an abode in which
he could live and watch them grow.
Eventually a city sprouted
around his simple dwelling,

and he become its chief counsellor,
the patron of all the arts that were started,
and was the father of many children.
As they were growing into men and women,
protected by the wisdom of their father's caring,
and while his old age was advancing,
a prolonged period of thinking was ensuing.
Then at the pinnacle of his earthly attainment
came a blissful feeling overpowering,
providing a tranquil moment's serenity,
at a time when his eyes were seeing
a sun brilliantly glowing
at the portal of his essential being,
enticing him with a mystery unthinkable,
luring him towards an unmeasurable journey,
he felt all resistance leaving,
and a will for only what the
future was certainly bringing.
Then his Heart, like a nova exploding
in an instant flash of lightening activity,
placed him in a cosmos
with countless stellar lights beaming,
each with a Fiery sphere of noetic energy,
interrelated by the radiance of their coherent gleaming.
Though they were in many diverse groupings,
each demonstrated the fruition
of the gain of many lives of progression
and which was coming, undifferentiated
in every particular notion
from that which was himself,
for they were all his Brothers.
It was an astounding, expanding passion,
here was the One Reality
behind every life's evolving history.
At once he saw the context
of many realms of being,
of every level and progressive order
of the ineffable Light-filled

world around him, consubstantiated with
the infinite universe around him,
absolute, the fount of omniscient power.
It was that which
the One vast Mind was sustaining.
Then the Sun increased its burning,
becoming even more brilliant,
its incandescence growing,
its energy inside swelling
in splendour, becoming explosive,
lighter, white whiter,
brighter than the brightest Sun,
for, to fundamental Essence he was approaching,
and it was, as many seers had stated:

'unmodified, undifferentiated, unformed',

a paradox to be known only by the Knowing,
he was as God becoming.

Contents

Preface....xiii

1. The Proem, (Pages from a prehistoric record)....1
   - Explanation of the Proem....1
   - The significance of symbols....10
   - The Advaita Vedāntic and Buddhist views on Creation....14
   - The role of *māyā*....25
   - The three *guṇas*....31
   - Continuation of the Proem....40
   - The fundamental propositions of *The Secret Doctrine*....42
2. The Numerological Key....48
   - General introduction....48
   - The Basic Meaning of the Numbers....56
3. The Method of Interpretation....78
   - The Occult Catechism....78
   - The five levels of expression to the commentary....91
   - The Parabrahman level of interpretation....94
   - The Brahman level of interpretation....100
   - The Īśvara level of interpretation....104
   - The Māyā—Trimūrti level of interpretation....114
   - The Rings....115
   - The Breath....121
   - The Mother....124
   - Fifthly, the expression of the Dhyāni Buddhas governing the three planes of human evolution. 128
   - The Vairocana level of interpretation....131
   - The Akṣobhya level of interpretation....132
   - The Amitābha level of interpretation....134
   - The Ratnasambhava level of interpretation....143
   - The Amoghasiddhi level of interpretation....148
4. Commentaries - Stanza 1 151
   - Introduction....151
   - Stanza One part One....157
   - Stanza One part Two....171
   - Stanza One part Three....186
   - Stanza One part Four....195

Stanza One part Five 208
Stanza One part Six 225
Stanza One part Seven 244
Stanza One part Eight 251
Stanza One part Nine 265

5. Commentaries - Stanza 2 275
Stanza Two part One 276
Stanza Two part Two 294
Stanza Two part Three 303
Stanza Two part Four 309
Stanza Two part Five 316
Stanza Two part Six 323

6A. Stanzas 3:1 – 3:4 331
Commentaries Stanza Three 331
The general outline of the verses of Stanza Three 333
Stanza Three part One 347
Stanza Three part Two 359
Stanza Three part Three 371
Stanza Three part Four 386

6B. Stanzas 3:5 – 3:7 422
Stanza Three part Five 422
Stanza Three part Six 434
Stanza Three part Seven 454

6C. Stanzas 3:8 – 3:12 496
Stanza Three part Eight 496
Stanza Three part Nine 510
Stanza Three part Ten 526
Stanza Three part Eleven 538
Stanza Three part Twelve 556

Appendix
Keynotes of Stanzas 1 to 3 from the *Book of Dzyan* 571
STANZA I 571
STANZA 2 573
STANZA 3 574

Bibliography 578
Index 580
About the Author 603

Figures

Figure 1. The ever-invisible robes ... 162
Figure 2. The infinite Bosom of Duration ... 179
Figure 3. The Ah-Hi ... 193
Figure 4. The cycle of Being ... 210
Figure 5: The Caduceus staff ... 231
Figure 6. The space-time continuum ... 257
Figure 7. The five tiers of the Head lotus ... 283
Figure 8. The fall of the three into the four ... 397
Figure 9. The Oeaohoo in terms of human evolution ... 432

Tables

Table 1: The Seven Eternities ... 157
Table 2. The Planetary Rulers governing the Constellations ... 346

Preface

The phrase the *secret doctrine* refers not just to the book penned by H.P. Blavatsky, but also to the esoteric doctrine professed by the Hierarchy of Enlightened Being. This doctrine is ageless, hence has also been called the *ageless wisdom* by Helena Roerich. By 'ageless' is meant that this doctrine is that known by all enlightened beings throughout the dawn of time. This not just for civilisations that appeared upon our earth, but also upon all globes that bore human life in our solar system. With sufficient insight the Initiate of high degree could also extrapolate back to the previous solar system, and telepathically communicate with advanced beings from other star systems, to find that all in our local cosmos are incorporated by the same laws and follow a singular evolutionary purpose. All Lives are but an integrated Unity directed by the Purpose of a Grand Heavenly 'MAN', a Logos Whose Thought Form for evolutionary progress conditions everything that is incorporated by the term 'universe', esoterically considered. Cosmic evolution is but that aspect of the arcane lore of the enlightened that can at any time be revealed exoterically to assist those struggling upon the Initiation path to attain their higher Initiations. It represents the 'ear whispered truths' of the Buddhists, understood only by the enlightened. The esotericism concerning these Truths has been increasingly revealed since Blavatsky first presented her monumental writings to the world.

More than a century has passed since *The Secret Doctrine* has been published yet no serious detailed esoteric study of the teachings veiled by the Stanzas of Dyzan has appeared, except that presented by

Alice A. Bailey in *A Treatise on Cosmic Fire* (T.C.F.),[1] with *Esoteric Astrology* providing astrological support. Anyone who studies these works and the others by Bailey will discover that she is the true esoteric successor of Blavatsky, and has drunk from the same source as her predecessor. Indeed she was the amanuensis of the same Masters, being part of the same major Hierarchical programme of presenting the *secret doctrine,* the esoteric lore, to those in the world who have the capacity to receive it thus. Unfortunately many exponents of the Theosophical Society would not accept the writings of the Master D.K. (Djwhal Khul, who telepathically dictated the contents of the books to Alice Bailey) as the next level of presented teachings from Hierarchy. They thereby closed the door to Hierarchy for them as a major conduit for their esoteric educative purpose amongst humanity. The Theosophical Society has consequently become effectively an exoteric organisation concerned with the distribution of the past Hierarchical dispensation for the education of aspirants, probationary disciples and some Initiates of the lower degrees. Even so, by keeping the publications and early teachings alive they have provided a valuable service that perhaps is the best that could be hoped for from the organisation that represents the third Ray, or Mother attribute, the foundation for the appearance of the major second Ray outpouring for humanity.

When the writings of D.K. were published from 1919 onwards then the Son aspect of this Hierarchical dispensation manifested. This was the second stage of a planned outpouring consisting of three main stages. The concept of a needed trinity should be obvious to all esotericists, being a major basis to esoteric lore. With this present publication of the *Astrological and Numerical Keys to the Secret Doctrine,* based on other esoteric pronouncements by Hierarchy, all of the support texts provided by D.K. and my earlier writings, the Father phase of the revealed texts has now manifested. This trinity of teachings will also stand as a Mother that will help birth the major second Ray cycle upon the planet, the new Aquarian age, to truly make it a sacred planet. Obviously, being the 'Father phase', means that the present outpouring

1 D.K. has effectively presented mainly the physiological key to *The Secret Doctrine*. For a synopsis to the various keys to esoteric texts see footnote 47 of *A Treatise on Cosmic Fire,* 109, 110.

is the synthesis of all that has preceded it, and also presents much more esoteric information relating to divinity, and of the nature of the constitution of Shambhala. The ordinary esoteric student may however be challenged by the advanced esotericism, and that it also necessitates developing more will to somewhat master Buddhist philosophy. The teachings now demand a much greater awakening of the abstract Mind than was hitherto needed, and so the way of the *dharma* leading to enlightenment progresses.

The astrological content of this book is derived from *Esoteric Astrology, A Treatise on Cosmic Fire,* and other works by Bailey, *The Secret Doctrine* itself, plus what I will further explicate. The reader should study these texts with care to gain many valuable insights as to the nature of the *ageless wisdom.* Some of the foundation, a background, for the numerological information presented here is also provided in my earlier Buddhist writings, such as my book on *maṇḍalas.*

Of necessity I will have to quote all relevant passages given by Blavatsky in her monumental work so that the necessary commentaries can be given, as much is provided in her statements, as well as veiled in the structure of the words of the Stanzas of Dzyan.

The esoteric view of planetary formation differs from the theories presently presented by modern scientists, as they do not take into account the existence of the subjective planes of perception, the *chakras,* or of the nature of Logoic Mind in its Creative aptitude. The esoteric view concerns the gradual materialisation of the globes from the subjective planes down. This view however also takes into account some of the present accepted scientific view of the agglomeration of particulate matter due to the force of gravity and the collision of bodies of matter, especially in the early formative years of solar evolution. Nevertheless thought-form construction, condensation, crystallisation and materialisation of dense substance is the method utilised throughout for the appearance of the planets and planetoids in solar evolution.

The students of Blavatsky's *The Secret Doctrine* (S.D.) need no reminders of the importance of this work to the history of the world's religious outpouring. The Stanzas of Dzyan (Stanzas of meditation) are, as Blavatsky states, 'a most archaic doctrine'. It is in fact a Shambhalic text brought to this planet with the coming of the Lords of Flame when the present humanity were Individualised.[2] The Cosmological part was consequently written as a codified teaching inherited from the Initiates of an earlier world cycle. The second part of *The Secret Doctrine,* Anthropogenesis, was part of the teaching provided to the Initiates at the Mystery Schools in ancient Atlantis at a time when those Schools were but an offshoot of Shambhala.

In these Stanzas the nature of the formation of world spheres (Cosmogenesis) and the early history of humanity (Anthropogenesis) is encoded in the language of Initiates, using various keys needed for appropriate interpretation. The symbolic, allegorical, physiological and literal keys are already well known to students of the esoteric lore. The astrological and numerological keys to the text have only ever been partly revealed, such as what is obvious from the actual wording of the Stanzas, e.g., 'the three fall into the four' (Stanza 3:4), and in phrases such as 'the one is four, and four takes to itself three, and the union produces sapta' in Stanza 3:7. The way that Hierarchy structures the intricacies of their information via the medium of words, as well as the subtleties of the astrological and numerological encoding, has thus not yet been comprehended by esoteric students. The revelation of the nature of this codification is consequently a purpose for the writing of this series. A far vaster amount of esoteric lore hidden in the wording than has been so far veiled can thereby be illuminated.

This series will initially consist of two volumes dealing with the Cosmogenesis part of the S.D. These teachings will be a continuation of what was presented in the T.C.F. and my earlier books, such as the last volume, *The Constitution of Shambhala* of the *A Treatise of Mind* series and especially *Esoteric Cosmology and Modern Physics,* to which the reader should refer for the foundational teachings concerning the genesis of the universe. The first volume of this present series provides a further explanation of the introductory postulates of the Proem, and introduces the numerological key and the methodology of its application in chapter two. The later chapters explain the process concerning the early evolution of the solar system as it emerges from a 'deep sleep' state *(pralaya).* This period of emergence constitutes the initial Stanzas of the S.D. Within the context of these Stanzas the symbolism can be

2 See *A Treatise on Cosmic Fire* for detail.

extended to include the local universe of which our sun forms a part, as well the formation of the planetary sphere that is our earth. (By 'local universe' is meant that part within the Milky Way galaxy wherein our sun is found and the companion stars with which it is travelling, which roughly corresponds to the stars visible to the naked eye on a clear moonless night. These stars are part of the Body of manifestation of the ONE that the Master D.K. states in *A Treatise on Cosmic Fire* is 'The One About Whom Naught May be Said', a concept which I shorten to THAT Logos.) To comprehend one must invoke the hermetic axiom: 'As above so below, that which is within is also without'.

Volume two of this series will deal with the Cosmological text of the S.D. from Stanzas four to seven, which are mainly concerned with earth evolution. This evolution is significant in that the earth is the fourth globe of the fourth Chain of the fourth Scheme in our solar system, which is one that is considered as of 'the fourth order'. (Meaning that our sun is an average member of the 'Atlantean' population of stars evolving in the Milky Way.) Being the 'fourth' means that our earth acts as a mirror that allows us to extrapolate information from above down and from within without, as all perspectives in our solar system and local universe are mirrored by our position in the scheme of things.

When volume three appears it will endeavour to fill in the missing gap, as much as is presently possible, in the lacunae between Stanza three and Stanza four, thus presenting the early evolution of the solar system before the formation of our earth sphere, plus showing the role that the earth plays in the schema of solar evolution. The continuing solar evolution until its *pralaya* will also be discussed, explicating the role of Mars and its relation to the earth, and the Pluto Scheme. There will also be a commentary of conditions in the former solar system before this present one, taking into account the esoteric fact that our present solar evolution is but the middle of three such star systems, which esoterically are viewed as a unity.

When I have the time I will hopefully provide further volumes dealing with the numerological and astrological coding to the Stanzas of Dzyan found at the beginning of the T.C.F. As a consequence a considerable amount of extra esoteric information concerning solar evolution will be discovered.

Hopefully also the nature of the Cosmic Paths that are provided in coded fashion at the back of the T.C.F. can also be further revealed. These Paths are those that Initiates of the fifth degree will contemplate travelling upon once they have finished their earth service work. The great majority will travel thus as Buddhas, when they have attained their sixth Initiation. There is only a limited number of positions available at Shambhala for earth service, consequently most Initiates of the sixth degree set their sights to further evolution in cosmos. Such information now needs to be provided in greater detail than hitherto because with the advent of the new era concerning the reappearance of the blue Christ, and as a consequence of the outcome of the expected period of planetary Initiation, a large number of Initiates will graduate to the higher degrees, and so will need to seriously contemplate upon what lies ahead.

1

The Proem

(Pages from a prehistoric record)

Explanation of the Proem

In the Proem Blavatsky presents a consideration of the nature of the archaic (Shambhalic) manuscript she is interpreting by explaining some of the glyphs found within it. She also provides the background of esoteric postulates that forms the basis for comprehension of the entire text. For the sake of completeness I shall quote extensively from *The Secret Doctrine,* plus add significant necessary commentary, based upon the underlying numerological coding to the text, to clarify some of the topics Blavatsky hints at. A considerable amount of supplementary information will therefore be added, which was veiled by the arrangement of the text.

I shall retain the Sanskrit style used in my other books, rather than Blavatsky's Westernised version of the script, and shall also incorporate the esoteric Buddhist philosophy from these writings into the analysis when needed. This will appropriately supplement Blavatsky's foundational mainly Hinduistic terminology. Buddhism is built upon the foundational Hindu doctrines from which it grew. Hence Buddhism should be viewed as a complementary and reformed version of Hinduism. At any rate the cosmological doctrines of the Hindu religion have never been surpassed in Buddhism, which is more a religion concerned with the process of liberation from *saṃsāra,* rather than being preoccupied with speculation of how the universe and our world system came into existence. Neither is it concerned with the nature of our earth system and its placement within the solar system, and that within the constellations of stars of which our sun is one. My concern is the *esoteric doctrines* of both religions, which needs to be utilised to properly interpret the text. Both religions manifest an overwhelming abundance of exoteric easily read, but misleading dogma, if read superficially. It is now time that the esoteric is unveiled in the exoteric. In incorporating the esoteric *dharma* the appearance of a hybrid religion shall be evidenced, as this numerological rendition of the *Stanzas of Dzyan* (Stanzas for meditation) is explained. Extensive esoteric astrological considerations are also incorporated in a veiled fashion throughout *The Secret Doctrine,* as the reader shall see.

It should be noted that everything reincarnates: humans, plants, animals, planetary and solar systems, and universes. The Laws of periodicity, of rhythmic sustainability and of *karma* govern the fundamental process of 'the great Breath' which spawned All, and it is principally the rebirth of our solar system, under the rubric of 'the universe, or cosmos' that concerns us here.

This book continues from the teachings presented in my earlier works, specifically the information published in *The Constitution of Shambhala* and *Esoteric Cosmology and Modern Physics,* which have served to lay the foundation philosophy for comprehension of what shall be herein revealed. Obviously a greater use of the ancient esoteric terminology shall be advanced than was evident in the previous publications.

The section of Blavatsky's text entitled 'The Proem' begins thus:

> An Archaic Manuscript — a collection of palm leaves made impermeable to water, fire, and air, by some specific and unknown process — is before the writer's eye. On the first page is an immaculate white disc with a dull black ground. On the following page, the same disc, but with a central point. The first, the student knows, represents Kosmos in Eternity, before the re-awakening of still slumbering Energy, the Emanation of the Word in later systems. The point in the hitherto immaculate Disc, Space and Eternity in Pralaya, denotes the dawn of differentiation. It is the Point in the Mundane Egg,[1] the germ within which will become the Universe, the ALL, the boundless, periodical Kosmos, this germ being latent and active, periodically

1 Note given here, 'see Part II., "The Mundane Egg"'.

> and by turns. The one circle is divine Unity, from which all proceeds, whither all returns. Its circumference — a forcibly limited symbol, in view of the limitation of the human mind — indicates the abstract, ever incognisable PRESENCE, and its plane, the Universal Soul, although the two are one. Only, the face of the Disc being white, and the ground all around black, clearly shows that its plane is the only knowledge, dim and hazy though it still is, that is attainable by man. It is on this plane that the Manvantaric manifestations begin; for it is in this SOUL that slumbers, during the Pralaya, the Divine Thought, wherein lies concealed the plan of every future Cosmogony and Theogony.
>
> It is the ONE LIFE, eternal, invisible, yet Omnipresent, without beginning or end, yet periodical in its regular manifestations, between which periods reigns the dark mystery of non-Being; unconscious, yet absolute Consciousness, unrealizable, yet the one self-existing reality; truly, "a chaos to the sense, a Kosmos to the reason." Its one absolute attribute, which is ITSELF, eternal, ceaseless Motion, is called in esoteric parlance the "Great Breath," which is the perpetual motion of the universe, in the sense of limitless, ever-present SPACE. That which is motionless cannot be Divine. But then there is nothing in fact and reality absolutely motionless within the universal soul.[2]

The central point within the circle ('the Mundane Egg') represents the focal point for the Thought of the Divine Thinker, the seed germ, the *bīja,*[3] wherein the entire potential of the past evolutionary cycles has been stored. The Logoic Thinker needs to activate the key elements needed for the new incarnation (Logoic Personality), and then to project them into manifestation for the new universe (or world sphere) to be breathed with Life. Everything is projected by means of the Eye of the Divine Thinker, and the central dot in the circle is but a way of symbolising such an Eye.

---

2 Blavatsky, Helena Petrovna, (H.P.B.) *The Secret Doctrine: The Synthesis of Science, Religion, and Philosophy*, (Theosophical Publishing Company, 1888), Vol. 1, Cosmogenesis, 1-2.

3 *Bīja,* seed (syllable), the seminal point, the sound (*vac*) essence of a deity. The essential part of a *mantra,* the seed germ, starting point for the display of power or creativity, for a *maṇḍala* or as a focus for meditation. It is the individual potentiality from which each *dharma* of existence is produced. The fundamental qualities of *bījas* have been aptly explained in *A Treatise on Mind.*

The *circumference* depicts that aspect of the non manifest unbounded Space that is to be delineated as a sphere of contained Activity by the Logoic Thinker, into which the *prāṇas* (energies) of the *bīja* expansion incarnate. It then becomes the vehicle via which the Eye can command movement in Space. Thus proceeds the 'abstract, ever incognisable PRESENCE'.

From this perspective the 'universal Soul' manifests in the form of the lotus of the Sambhogakāya Flower/*tathāgatagarbha*[4] upon the higher levels of the (cosmic) mental plane. For humans it is the Buddha-germ that will guarantee the long evolutionary haul of the consciousness-stream to liberation. At this stage the disc with the central dot is hidden as the Jewel in the Heart of the Lotus of the resplendent 3 + 9 petalled Flower that now takes central stage in the process of liberating its quota of allocated substance (cosmic 'dust').

This cosmic purpose (the redemption of cosmic dark matter) is depicted in the symbolism of 'the face of the disc being white, and the surrounding ground black'. The Eye exists to convey Light into a domain that is 'black', bereft of light, in the process to convert it into intelligent conscious substance, a self-generating unit of Light. (A sun thus comes into existence.) This conversion of non-radiatory dark space, into autoluminous embodied space is the purpose of the manifestation of circumscribed Space. 'Dark space' then constitutes the vast bulk of the plenitude, and within it we have the Law of Periodicity manifesting the sequence of repeating cycles of incarnation according to group cyclic purpose. This incorporates the expansion of the Conscious domains of a vast cosmic collective organism, the integrated Hierarchies of liberated Compassionate Lives. The Law of *karma* is then utilised so that all Lives are rightly interconnected, allowing substance-consciousness interactions to happen according to the Law, as every transaction must be accounted for and so the ultimate energy-balance score-sheet of the universe will equilibrise into unity. The Law of Economy thus manifests its rigour upon the appearing phenomena, and within it the energies of rhythmic sustainability are utilised to ensure that the aeonic-long process manifests its own inherent sustainable cycles. The Eye can

4 These terms, detailed in volume 3 of *A Treatise on Mind,* refer to the Soul form, the Causal Body.

then project its gaze into the night of the thickest black substance and so begin the process of its conversion to the Light. The Eye becomes a Sun that is a 'darkness-eater'.

The consumption of such darkness is then what is 'attainable by man', the seven-leafed plant[5] planted in the darkness of this cosmic black soil (the systemic mental plane) so that it can properly begin the process of conversion of the cosmic mineral kingdom into consciousness. This 'man-plant' consequently becomes the necessary middle principle in the entire milieu of being/non-being. The human unit is thus an transitory transmogrifying cyclically appearing phenomena, yet is a 'spark' of the Real. In the cyclical appearance of such 'sparks' 'the plan of every future cosmogony' is veiled, and the theogony of all world creation myths evolve. The human actor plays out the *māyā* (illusion) of that theogony upon his/her little world-stage, repeated billions of times during any cycle, to incur the plenitude of the eventual harvest of the golden grains that each man-plant has produced.

The hundreds of billions of *deva* and human units informing every star system rhythmically beat out the durations (through cycles of incarnations) of the integrated Unit, the 'one absolute attribute, which is Itself, eternal, ceaseless Motion'. These group Lives move in and out of the substance matter as mass streams and flows of energies (*prāṇas*) via the reincarnation process. The sum total is then envisioned as the 'Great Breath', projecting into manifestation each appearing star, planetary system, or even universe. Liberated streams of Life are also out-Breathed from one Scheme to other systems to manifest purposes unbeknownst to us. From the out-Breathing eventually comes an Inbreathing of all back to its originating Source, hence manifesting the *pralaya,* or termination of things. This is then 'the perpetual motion of the Universe, in the sense of limitless, ever-present SPACE'.

Blavatsky continues:

> Occultism sums up the "One Existence" thus: "Deity is an arcane, living (or moving) FIRE, and the eternal witnesses to this unseen Presence, are Light, Heat, Moisture," — this trinity including, and being the cause of, every phenomena in Nature. Intra-Cosmic motion

5 Explained in Stanza 7:3.

> is eternal and ceaseless; cosmic motion (the visible, or that which is subject to perception) is finite and periodical. As an eternal abstraction it is the EVER-PRESENT; as a manifestation, it is finite both in the coming direction and the opposite, the two being the Alpha and Omega of successive reconstructions. Kosmos — the NOUMENON — has naught to do with the causal relations of the phenomenal World. It is only with reference to the intra-cosmic soul, the ideal Kosmos in the immutable Divine Thought, that we can say: "It never had a beginning nor will it have an end." With regard to its body or Cosmic organization, though it cannot be said that it had a first, or will ever have a last construction, yet at each new Manvantara, its organization may be regarded as the first and last of its kind, as it evolves every time on a higher plane.[6]

The 'arcane, living (or moving) FIRE' brings our vision immediately to the cosmic mental plane, thus to cosmic Mind, from whence acts the Deity whom we are here considering. (This One embodies the evolutionary journeying of human Monads.) We can actually eventually know something about That Mind through a thorough analysis of the properties and functions of our own minds, and the role of *manas* (Fire) in its activities. Buddhist Philosophy has done much of this work, specifically in relation to the logic of the Yogācāra, where the principal statement is 'all is mind/Mind'.[7] In Volume 2 of *A Treatise on Mind* I analysed in depth the nature of the two principle subdivisions of mind/Mind, the rarefied, instantaneously perceptive all-knowing abstract Mind and the intellectual, logicising empirical mind. One needs to transpose the applied philosophy in a transmuted way to the domain of the Creative Ādi (primordial) Buddha at the dawn of whatever will be.

'Light, Heat, Moisture', the 'eternal witnesses to this unseen Presence', represent the conditionings which the man-plant needs to survive in the domain of the cosmic soil in which it has been planted. Light is an emanation of the enlightened domains *(buddhi),* heat is an aspect of the Fiery mental plane, and moisture the astral (Watery) domain. The man-plants are the human Monads (effectively incarnated

---

6 Ibid., 2-3.

7 Specifically dealt with in Volume 2 of *A Treatise on Mind.*

Buddhas, though yet to ascend) or as H.P.B. states, 'the Eternal Pilgrim'[8] existing upon the second of the *dharmakāyic* realms (*anupādaka*). We can also include the term '*nirvāṇee*', which refers to a liberated Buddha (Monad) in the process of travelling a cosmic Path. H.P.B. also uses the term 'Imperishable Jivas'.[9] *Jīva* means Life force, hence a Monad embodies such an imperishable force. Monads are the harbingers of the principle of Life and its purpose for the human family. Without this Life principle there would be no consciousness-stream, no successive incarnations of anything. The Soul would have no purpose. Life persists throughout the many dramas of any consciousness-stream played out in space and time, and abstracts the gain from that play, to project it towards a future (cosmic) vista.

As an eternal Pilgrim the Monad's Ray has been projected as the central point of the Shambhogakāya Flower. Its energy is protected by the triune formation of the Flower's central bud. The Monad/ Flower together take the attributes of a Pratyeka Buddha whilst this Flower is active for the period of evolutionary time that produces the Bodhisattva path and the eventual attainment of the fourth Initiation. A Pratyeka Buddha is exoterically the 'solitary contemplative' of the Hīnayānist, and the concept was later incorporated into the Mahāyāna doctrines. Therein such a one is said to possess all of the attributes of a Buddha, but is concerned entirely with its own internal self-contemplative development, the enlightenment of those involved in the general external environment being of no concern.[10] Later, as a consequence of the revelations necessary to tread the Bodhisattva path, one conceives of the final Monadic appearance on earth as a

---

8 See footnote two of *The Secret Doctrine* (S.D.), Vol. 1, 16, where H.P.B. states: '"Pilgrim" is the appellation given to our *Monad* (the two in one) during its cycle of incarnations. It is the only immortal and eternal principle in us, being an indivisible part of the integral whole — the Universal Spirit, from which it emanates, and into which it is absorbed at the end of the cycle'.

9 S.D., Vol 1, 218. There she is speaking of the fourth Creative Hierarchy.

10 Such a concept is an error, taken from the fact that the Buddhists have thought only in terms of the human personality and have not taken into account lines of development other than that along the second Ray, or comprehended the nature of the Sambhogakāya Flower. This subject has been explained in Volume 3 of *A Treatise on Mind*, 348-53.

Mānuśi Buddha.[11] The Monadic Presence is then fully incarnate in the dense form, via its *nirmaṇakāya,* a living Buddha.

After attaining *parinirvāṇa* the fully liberated One (the Monad) commences his cosmic training upon one or other of the cosmic Paths. The eternal Pilgrim therefore continues upon its pilgrimage in cosmos. It is a cosmic traveller, having many homes in various star systems, each of which becomes a school of learning for it. The drama unfolds in an increasingly expansive cosmic panorama as the Monad evolves via the *nāḍī* system of a great Logos, evolving from the petals of minor *chakras* to eventually encompass the vast spaces and qualities of the major *chakras.* The way of Monadic evolution thus enables the Monad to eventually embody the qualities of a Logos. The present earth sphere consequently represents but one step on the way to its ultimate evolutionary goal.

The 'eternal witnesses to this unseen Presence' can be thought of in these terms:

- *Light* is the radiance projected via an illuminating source. It is that portion of the cosmic Consciousness of a Monad expressed as it manifest its aeonic Pilgrimage on the road to the cosmic Initiations. The extent of the projection of that Light implies the level of Knowledge of the illuminating One. It relates to the Monad's fundamental colouring that governs its overall mode of activity on the Way. Upon a lower scale the human unit must develop a similar lighted consciousness if it is to find its way out of the maze of mind, and so acknowledge this Presence as the Real, everything else being the 'unreal'. The Monadic Light manifests as an aspect of the cosmic Law of Synthesis.

11 Belonging to or propitious to mankind. A Mānuśī Buddha, as contrasted to a Dhyāni Buddha, is one who incarnates on earth to teach humanity. Exoterically here are said to be seven human Buddhas, including Śakyamuni. Esoterically a Buddha can be considered one who has attained his sixth Initiation upon any of the Ray lines, hence the Chohans are Buddhas, but have not played a similar exoteric role as Gautama. Many more than seven have hence evolved. The number seven is symbolic for the divine embodiments of the Teachings to be given to each Root Race, hence Gautama was thus for the Aryan (fifth) Root Race. Maitreya consequently will appear to herald the Teachings for the sixth Root Race.

- *Heat* represents the emanation of the third tier of the Monadic Eye at this stage of its cosmic evolution. Heat is the experiential gain of the Monad's aeonic Sacrifice in cosmic dense space, the consequence of being 'planted' into the cosmic dense physical plane. Heat comes as a consequence of friction, through the resistance of substance to the evolutionary push of the incarnating *Jīva*. Such friction generates the Fiery Element and the way of development of mind into Mind. It is an expression of the energy needed to drive all forward to its planned goal. Heat is an attribute of the cosmic Law of Economy.
- *Moisture* represents the condensation of the Watery Element needed to sustain the growth of the man-plant in the material domain. This inevitably produces the formation of the astral plane, the consequence of the principle of desire and emotions of humanity. This causes both the agonising miasmas of the human mental-emotional life, plus is the basis for the expression of *bodhicitta*, the power of compassionate Love that manifests as the way out from the materialistic grind. The development of the way of the Heart and the pouring of its Blood to serve the all is the liberating panacea to be found by each human unit. 'Moisture' thus has a reference to the attribute of the cosmic Waters that manifests via the colouration of the second tier of the Monadic Eye. 'Moisture' is the mechanism of the pathway of the cosmic Law of Attraction.

The statement that this trinity includes and is the cause of 'every phenomena in Nature' has reference to the fact that these three expressions are causative of conditionings found within the three sub-planes of the cosmic dense physical: the familiar mental, astral and dense realms. Here the panoply of Nature finds its means of expression. We thus have the three Outpourings of Life incorporating the streams of sentience, *deva* and human lives. All inevitably bear witness to the 'arcane, living (or moving) FIRE' that is Deity. These streams of Earthy sentient, Watery-Fiery human and *deva* Lives, and Airy liberated Lives represent the cellular substance, blood stream and electrical activity of the nerves, and *prāṇic* energies of that living Deity.

The remainder of this quote refers to the high revelations that one on the path to enlightenment will inevitably realise as he/she ascends the higher way to *dharmakāya*. Then such Entities as 'the intra-cosmic soul, the ideal Kosmos in the immutable Divine Thought' can be appropriately contemplated. Such meditation necessitates application of the adage 'as above so below, that which is within is also without', and apply it in a transmuted fashion in relation to the human Sambhogakāya Flower. This allows one to infer how a Logoic Personality should be conditioned by a similar Soul Form upon the cosmic higher mental plane.

The significance of symbols

H.P.B. continues with an elaboration of the symbols introduced at the beginning:

> The first illustration being a plain disc ○, the second in the Archaic symbol shows ⊙, a disc with a point in it — the first differentiation in the periodical manifestations of the ever-eternal nature, sexless and infinite, "Aditi in THAT" (Rig Veda), the point in the disc, or potential Space within abstract Space. In its third stage the point is transformed into a diameter, thus ⊖. It now symbolises a divine immaculate Mother-Nature within the all-embracing absolute Infinitude. When the horizontal diameter is crossed by a vertical one, ⊕, it becomes the mundane cross. Humanity has reached its third root-race; it is the sign for the origin of human life to begin. When the circumference disappears and leaves only the + it is a sign that the fall of man into matter is accomplished, and the FOURTH race begins. The Cross within a circle, symbolizes pure Pantheism; when the Cross is left uninscribed, it became phallic. It had the same and yet other meanings as a TAU inscribed within a circle ⦶ or as a "Thor's Hammer," the Jaina cross, so-called, or simply Svastica, within a circle ࿕.
>
> By the third symbol — the circle divided into two by the horizontal line of the diameter — the first manifestation of creative (still passive, because feminine) Nature was meant. The first shadowy perception of man connected with procreation is feminine, because man knows his mother more than his father. Hence female deities were more sacred than the male. Nature is therefore feminine, and, to a degree, objective and tangible, and the spirit Principle which fructifies it is concealed. By adding to circle with the horizontal line in it, a perpendicular line, the Tau was formed - T┬- the oldest form of the letter. It was the glyph of the third root-race to the day of its symbolical

> Fall — *i.e.*, when the separation of sexes by natural evolution took place — when the figure became ⦶, the circle, or sexless life modified or separated — a double glyph or symbol. With the races of our Fifth Race it became in symbology the sacr', and in Hebrew n'cabvah, of the first-formed races; then it changed into the Egyptian ☥ (emblem of life), and still later into the sign of Venus, ♀. Then comes the Svastika (Thor's hammer, or the "Hermetic Cross" now), entirely separated from its Circle, thus becoming purely phallic. The esoteric symbol of Kali Yuga is the five-pointed star reversed, thus ⛧ - the sign of human sorcery, with its two points (horns) turned heavenward, a position every Occultist will recognize as one of the "left-hand," and used in ceremonial magic.[12]

There are many levels of interpretation to each of those symbols. The *plain circle* for instance always stands for the earliest epoch of any thought construct, for the circumscription of undifferentiated matter. There is also the etheric component of a planetary or solar Logos, or of a human unit, to consider. The specific symbols associated with the evolution of each Root Race of humanity become more meaningful in section two of *The Secret Doctrine,* Anthropogenesis where these Races are explained.

The *circle with the point in the centre* stands for the awakening of the central heat of a manifesting unit. The central integrating dynamo is the point of Power, of Fire, the centre of intense luminescence, the nucleus that sustains the complete activity of all the organelles of the cell or solar form. It establishes the organising Eye that can see and control the domain now to be mastered. The point can be extended to represent the central Throne, or seat of Power of an incarnate Logos, from which all else manifests.

The *horizontal line* dividing the sphere into two represents the movement outwards from the centre to the periphery of the sphere of activity. It is feminine because it represents the incorporation of substance matter into the Logoic sphere, wherewith all things are constructed. It signifies the separation between the energies of the Logos (the 'Spirit of God') and the 'face of the Waters'.[13] It concerns

12 Ibid., Vol. 1, 4 – 6.

13 See *Gen. 1:2.*

the appearance of the planes of perception, the expression of the first Outpouring[14] producing the prima matrix from which the phenomena of things emanate.

The *vertical line* represents the impregnating masculine principle (the descent of the Spirit, the Will-to-Be). This concerns the process of the awakening of sensation, hence of consciousness-expansion, the second Outpouring, the projecting of the Compassionate Will to experience the 'not self'. It produces the beginning of radiatory activity that comes as a consequence of the separation of the sexes, duality. The two then grow to experience each other to produce or discover the third that is the child of their interrelationship. Consciousness consequently evolves. This produces the concept of the trinity, or triune Logos. (Symbolised by the triangle in the circle.) There is also the etheric component of a planetary or solar Logos to consider, or of a human unit. The vertical line representing the three-fold central *nāḍīs*. From them radiate out the other *nāḍīs* and the *chakra* system, which when activated, is symbolised by the circle divided into four. This implies that all of the forces that animate the four quadrants of any manifestation have been established.

The four petals of the Base of Spine *chakra* are thus awakened and therefore the form can appear in the physical domain. This is the Seat of Power from which all else can evolve. With respect to planetary and solar evolutions we have the appearance of the four kingdoms of Nature: the mineral, the plant, animal and human. Also there is the dissemination of the four Elements whereby the Logos can control the process of the transmutation of the lowest principles and prepare for its ascension to the highest level of expression. (Represented by the fifth Element, Aether.) There are also the *devas* that administer to the evolutionary development of the four exoteric kingdoms.

The *swastika* implies that (human) consciousness has evolved to the extent that it controls the activities of substance and of the outwards expansions of all kingdoms of Nature. Fourth dimensional motion is implied, plus radiatory expansion into all directions of space. This represents the power to drive all of the wheels of manifestation onwards

---

14 See volume 6 of *A Treatise on Mind,* 276-84 for information on the three Outpourings.

and outwards upon their evolutionary paths. It is the basis to awakening the potency of the five Dhyāni Buddhas throughout manifestation.

Numerologically, the plain sphere is depicted by the cypher zero. The circle with central point is then symbolised by the number one, signifying definiteness, the establishment of a point of power, the first principle. The circle with the horizontal line through it is symbolised by the number two, from the point of view of the two hemispheres that are formed. It represents the second stage of the evolutionary process, the activation of the Mother. This concerns the process related to the differentiation of the sexes, the appearance of the forces that differentiate the all into its component parts. When the Mother appears and is impregnated with the outward Breath of the Father (the vertical line) then the triangle within the sphere is formed. Implicit here is the birth of the Son in Her Womb. The complete differentiation of the Mother, and the triune deity is symbolised by the number three.

The circle with the Tau cross (adding the masculine principle to the feminine horizontal line), is also symbolised by the number three. It signifies the birthing of the activity that inevitably awakens consciousness. Hence it relates to the early formative stages of the appearance of consciousness.

The fixed cross within the circle is symbolised by the number four, and likewise the swastika. At this stage consciousness awakens and manifests its activities via all four arms of the fixed cross.

The pentagram is symbolised by the number five. The downwards pointing pentagram concerns inversion into matter, intensifying the forces of materialistic activity, hence it symbolises the left hand path. Pointing upwards we have the awakening of the higher perceptions associated with the attributes of travelling the right hand path. The five points of the pentagram relate to the attributes of the five sense-consciousnesses, the five Elements, and inevitably the generation of the Wisdoms of the five Dhyāni Buddhas. We thus have the appearance of the Fiery Element of the mind/Mind.

The ankh cross is symbolised by the number 7, representing here the complete awakening of the consciousness principle and its ascension to enlightened states of perception, the centres above the diaphragm. The spiral motion, of the movement of energies that cycle from the

Tau to form the circle of awakened activity above it, is symbolised by the number 6.

The spiral-cyclic movement of the energies associated with consciousness unfoldment to the attainment of liberation (complete enlightenment) is symbolised by the number 8, the infinity sign.

The straight line pointing upwards is symbolised by the number 9, signifying the projection of the *antaḥkaraṇa* to divinity, and the passing of Initiation testings.

The point within the circle can also be symbolised by the number 10, signifying complete perfection. This number is sometimes also symbolised by the vertical line within a sphere, signifying the projection of a point of power of a Logos to govern space, the complete *maṇḍala* of manifestation.

When the symbols appear within a circle then the inference is cosmological, the Monadic level. It also implies that a thought construct is self-contained as a *maṇḍala* of expression, sustained by a central point of power. When outside of a circle then they relate to the human plane and forms of expression of self-conscious units. The consideration is generally upon what is empirically objectivised, though can also be considered related to liberated levels of experience.

The Advaita Vedāntic and Buddhist views on Creation

As the Proem has directed our thoughts to the physical plane, wherein the evolution of the world's religious dispensation is played out, it is appropriate that *The Secret Doctrine* now incorporates religious symbolism. The religion of choice is the Hindu, as its philosophy is accessible and effectively contains the symbolism of the entire creative process associated with cosmogenesis. It utilises esoteric tenets in its religious symbolism and myths, whilst the Sanskrit language has been evolved to be able to express the subtlest and most profound form of arcane philosophy. Blavatsky starts with the concept of Parabrahman:

> Indeed, if the Parabrahmam of the Hindus may be taken as a representative of the hidden and nameless deities of other nations, this absolute Principle will be found to be the prototype from which all the others were copied. Parabrahm is not "God," because It is not a God. "It is that which is supreme, and not supreme (paravara),"

> explains Mandukya Upanishad (2.28). IT is "Supreme" as CAUSE, not supreme as effect. Parabrahman is simply, as a "Secondless Reality," the all-inclusive Kosmos — or, rather, the infinite Cosmic Space — in the highest spiritual sense, of course. Brahma (neuter) being the unchanging, pure, free, undecaying supreme Root, the "One true Existence, Paramarthika," and the absolute Chit and Chaitanya (intelligence, consciousness) cannot be a cognizer, "for THAT can have no subject of cognition." Can the flame be called the essence of Fire? This Essence is "the LIFE and LIGHT of the Universe, the visible fire and flame are destruction, death, and evil." "Fire and Flame destroy the body of an Arhat, their essence make him immortal"[15]... In this ALL lies concealed its coeternal and coeval emanation or inherent radiation, which, upon becoming periodically Brahmā, (the male-female Potency) becomes or expands itself into the manifested Universe. Narayana moving on the (abstract) waters of Space, is transformed into the Waters of concrete substance moved by him, who now becomes the manifested WORD or Logos.[16]

Here a number of principles of the Brahmanical philosophy are introduced which are worthy to note. First there is the trinity of Parabrahman, Brahman and Brahmā to consider. *Brahman* is absolute (abstract) Consciousness (*sat*-the eternal being/non-being, *chit*-consciousness, and *ānanda*-bliss) resting of and within itself. As a consequence it needs no other support. From the text we see that Brahman the 'one true existence' (*paramāthika*) can be considered to be composed of two attributes, *chit* (intelligence) and *chaitanya* (the higher consciousness, the principle of Love that underlies all that is). Parabrahman then is that which is 'beyond' the all-pervasive principle of Consciousness. Therefore no intelligence can perceive or comprehend its nature, the 'all-inclusive Kosmos'. Thirdly we have that principle from which phenomena can appear; Brahmā, the all-knowing creative Deity. Nārāyana (a form of Vishnu, though in the earliest concept he was but *Brahmā* resting upon cosmic Waters[17]), 'the deliverer of mankind', is said

---

15 Ibid., Vol. 1, 6.

16 Ibid., Vol. 1, 7.

17 *A Classical Dictionary of Hindu Mythology and Religion,* for instance states under the heading Brahmā: According to the Satapatha Brāmana and Manu, the

to repose upon the seven-headed serpent of space (Ananta-Nāga) and has the five-headed Brahmā[18] reposing on a lotus growing from his naval.

To further clarify the above I shall use the Advaita Vedāntic view of the creation of the material universe.

> How can we explain the universe by limiting our discourse to Brahman alone? The Advaita Vedānta has adequate metaphysical provision for explaining the universe. When we descend from the absolute (*pāramārthika*) level to the empirical (*vyāvahārika*) level, we leave the neutral entity and deal with a feminine entity and a masculine entity. These two metaphysical beings are *Māyā* and *Īśvara*. We use the pronoun *tat* (that) for Brahman, *sā* (she) for *Māyā*, and *saḥ* (he) for *Īśvara*[19]...The *Mūla-Prakṛti Māyā* (the Primordial Nature) is the Power (*Śakti*) of *Brahman*. If *Brahman* is compared to fire, *Māyā* is the heat of that fire. Both are inseperable. *Brahman* being eternal and timeless, *Māyā* is coeternal with *Brahman*. *Māyā* does not constitute an entity second to *Brahman*. Hence, the non-duality of *Brahman* is not violated at all...[20]
>
> *Māyā* is uncreated. She has no beginning. She has no end. She does not decay. She is imperishable (*akṣara*). She is undifferentiated (*avyākṛta*). She exists in an unmanifested condition and, hence, is *avyakta*. She is indescribable (*anirvacanīyā*). It cannot be said that she is real (*sat*); it cannot be said that she is unreal (*asat*); it cannot be said that she is both real and unreal (*sadasat*). She is not an independent entity (*asvatantrā*) separate from and second to *Brahman*. Her existence depends upon *Brahman (brahmāśrayā, Īśvarāśrayā)*. Due to such dependent existence, she is said to be different from *Brahman*, non-different from *Brahman*, and neither different nor non-different

---

supreme soul, the self-existent lord, created the waters and deposited in them the seed, which seed became a golden egg, in which he was born as Brahmā, the progenitor of all the worlds. As the waters (*nara*) were "the place of his movement, he (Brahmā) was called Nārāyana." Here the name Nārāyana is referred distinctly to Brahmā, but afterwards became the name of Vishnu. (John Dowsen, *A Classical Dictionary of Hindu Mythology, and Religion, Geography, History and Literature*, [Munshiram Manoharlal, 2000], 57.)

18 At this stage Brahmā is five-headed rather than four-headed.

19 Panda, N. C., *Cyclic Universe*, Vol. 2., (D.K. Printworld (P) Ltd., New Delhi, 2002), 773-774.

20 Ibid., 774.

> from *Brahman*. She is made up of three strings (*guṇas*), viz., *sattva* (serenity), *rajas* (activity), and *tamas* (inertia), kept in equipoise. She is undifferentiated and at the same time has three constituents. She is said to be with, without, and with and without parts. There is no way to describe her with any degree of precision.
>
> By virtue of the constitution of *sattva, Māyā* exercises her *jñāna-śakti* or *cit-śakti* (the power of knowledge) and her creative power (*sarjanā-śakti*). By her constituent of *rajas*, she exercises her generating power (*janana-śakti*), activating power (*bala-śakti*), strong propensities (*pravṛtti-śakti*), will-power (*icchā-śakti*), and projecting power (*vikṣepa-śakti*). By her constituent of *tamas*, she exercises her concealing power (*āvaraṇa-śakti*), and deluding power (*mohinī-śakti*) [21]... *Māyā* is the substantial cause (*upādāna kāraṇa*) of the universe. This is a Vedāntic statement; but it needs an explanation so that the Vedāntic metaphysics is not misunderstood. Both the Sāṅkhya and the Vedānta reject the idea that something can be created out of nothing and that something can be converted into nothing. So the Sāṅkhya says that the universe evolves from *Pradhāna*, the Primordial Nature, and the Vedānta says that the universe manifests from the Unmanifest *Māyā*, and subsequently evolves. Thus, according to the Vedānta, the material or substantial cause of the universe is *Māyā*, the *Mūla-Prakṛti*. Here lies a difference, however, between the Sāṅkhya and the Vedānta. The Sāṅkhya accepts the doctrine of transformation (*pariṇāma-vāda*). When wood is transformed into a chair, it is wood that is the material cause of the chair. The Vedānta, for the cosmogonical purpose, does not accept the doctrine of transformation. It rejects *brahma-pariṇāma-vāda* (the transformation of *Brahman* into the universe) and *māyā-pariṇāma-vāda* (the transformation of *Māyā* into the universe).[22]

The Buddhists (especially the Mādhyamika) do not espouse the 'creation' of anything, except maybe via the Yogācāra doctrine that

---

21 Ibid., 774-775.

22 Ibid., 776. One can presume here that the difference between the Advaita and the Sāṅkhya views is that the Advaita are thinking similar to the Buddhists that perceive *śūnyatā* as a finality. (One needs but to transpose *śūnyatā* with Brahman here.) The Sāṅkhya on the other hand are viewing more in terms of *dharmakāya*, of the mechanism that transforms *saṃsāra* into *dharmakāya*.

everything is an attribute of mind, therefore created by mind, sustained by mind and dissolved again by mind at the end of its usefulness. However my *A Treatise on Mind,* which sets to reform Buddhist logic, presents a better account of the nature of things, incorporates also the subject of the 'creation' of things, even of universes. At any rate the cosmological notions the Buddhists possess are generally directly taken from Hinduism, oft with very little alteration. However, Buddhism eschews the concept of (personal) gods and the God concept, and also the concept of a permanent Soul *(ātman).* These subjects have been properly analysed in my Treatise, and so we can proceed.

The Buddhist concept of the creation of things (the formation of *saṃsāric* activity in relation to the Void) can be gleaned from the first chapter of Nāgārjuna's *Mūlamadhyamakakārikā.* One can transpose concepts related to the appearance of phenomena in relation to the human condition to that of the local universe. (As was explained in detail in my book *Divine Cosmology and Modern Physics.)* This subject is dealt with in volume 1 of my *Treatise on Mind,* where I state:

> The Buddha-germ[23] energises Void Element *bījas*[24] with its compassionate thought of what is to be (or rather, 'must be'). The energisation attracts to the *bījas* the appropriate substance (*citta*) from the consciousness-store (*ālayavijñāna*), which then moves according to the inherent constitution of the *bīja* and the quality of the substance attracted. This movement concerns the conveyance of the winds/*prāṇas* of the *nāḍīs* incorporating the 'I'[25] that manifests in *saṃsāra.* The *nāḍī* system is the real or true corporeal form of a human unit,[26] the physical body is but an automaton of the *prāṇas* that flow within the *nāḍīs.* The *nāḍī* system is constituted of the Earthy Void Elements, and the elementary Winds (*prāṇas* in the form of the Void Elements) are the Breath of compassion of the downward focussed Mind of the

23 The *tathāgatagarbha,* which I have explained in terms of the Sambhogakāya Flower, the human Soul, which from the present view can be equated with the 'One true Existence, Paramārthika', when conceived of cosmologically.

24 Here taken as seeds, seed syllables, the focal point of a *yogin's* meditation, and for every act of creative endeavour.

25 The 'I' here can cosmologically be correlated to Īśvara.

26 Similarly for any incarnate Logos.

tathāgatagarbha. The Winds (of which there are five) are then utilised by a personal-I as the base energies for the conscious volitions that interrelate with *saṃsāra* via the five sense-perceptors to produce the *saṃskāras* manifesting as elementary mind, and the *karma*-formations that perpetuate the wheel of Dependent Origination.[27] The unreal is thereby produced that constantly changes according to the vicissitudes of the play of the *māyā* of which it is a part.

This is an outline of the process of the formation of *saṃsāric* activity in relation to the Void. Nāgārjuna's opening statement in his *Mūlamadhyamakakārikā* can now be analysed, which is concerned with the conditions of existence.

> No existents whatsoever are evident anywhere that are arisen from themselves, form another, from both, or from a non-cause.[28]

'Existents' here refers to 'things' pertaining to *saṃsāra*. They do not arise from themselves, nevertheless, when the subject is analysed appropriately one must conjecture a primal substance *(mūlaprakṛti, svabhāva)* that is the foundational matrix that is utilised by an originating Mind to start the process of *karma*-formations in Nature. This substance has not 'arisen from itself', rather is a pre-existing primordial matrix of elementary inchoate and universally prevalent substance, which is incorporated into the *maṇḍala* of that which must be. Therefore it does not arise 'from another', except in the way that phenomena interrelates in the cause-effect paradigm explained above, all of which is bound in illusionality. In establishing the pre-existing matrix of substance, there can be no 'other'. From the point of view of conventional truth, one thing arises from causes generated by other things, but from the point of view of ultimate truth inevitably all things are 'empty', thus there is no such 'arising'. Things therefore cannot

---

27 This is another important consideration in endeavouring to try to correlate Buddhist concepts with that of the Advaita Vedānta philosophy. The concept concerning the wheel of Dependent Origination *(pratītyasamutpāda)* is that everything in *saṃsāra* is dependent upon everything else, and that the entire cycle of this wheel of rebirth has its basis in ignorance. The *saṃskāras* are predispositions called forth from former incarnations *(manvantaras)* of a cosmos or of Logoic evolution.

28 David J. Kalupahana, *Mūlamadhyamakakārikā of Nāgārjuna, The Philosophy of the Middle Way,* (Motilal Barnasidass, Delhi, 1999), 105.

arise 'from both'. The last point of this quaternary relating to arising from a 'non-cause' is obviously true from a conventional point of view, because the cause of something cannot arise from that which is not a cause. However, from the point of view of ultimate truth this both is and is not the case, as 'a non-cause' can be considered the Void, via which the impetus to produce phenomena has emanated. However, by definition, the Void is void of the phenomenal, of things that can produce *saṃsāric* interaction of their own accord. Thus Nāgārjuna's statement is correct from this viewpoint. However, something must account for the phenomena, for its appearance, and thus we must look to the *dharmakāya* for this impetus. Here we have our answer, as explained above. So this realm produces both the cause of the origination of *saṃsāra* and the clause for its annulment. From another viewpoint it is 'a non-cause'. This is because the originating source is a Buddha-Mind, so the effect remains karmaless, or rather, it concerns the rectification of the *karma* still inherent in *saṃsāra*. In such a way a Buddha-field is enriched. Such a Mind works effortlessly with the law of cycles in order to activate that which already exists, the *bīja* of what is to be. It is therefore not 'a cause', but rather part of the process of the continuum of driving the all to Buddhahood.

In the second verse Nāgārjuna presents 'four conditions':

> There are only four conditions, namely, primary condition, objectively supporting condition, immediately contiguous condition, and dominant condition. A fifth condition does not exist.[29]

From the perspective of my presented philosophy the 'primary condition' refers to the prima-matrix from which all emanated, or else to the Void Elements utilised by the *tathāgatagarbha*. The 'objectively supporting condition' represents establishing the *bīja* of what is to be. The 'immediately contiguous condition' refers to the substance of the *ālayavijñāna,* the abstract Mind from which the driving impetus to manifests phenomenal activity originates. The 'dominant condition' concerns the conditionings of *māyā* wherein all is enacted.

Verse three states:[30]

> The self-nature of existents is not evident in the conditions, etc.
> In the absence of self-nature, other-nature too is not evident.

29 Ibid., 106.

30 Ibid., 107.

This is evident from the point of view of the entire activity stemming via the Void, which is freed from such a nature, and also an expression of a Buddha-Mind, which is likewise freed. From the point of view of conventional truth however, a form of such a 'self-nature' is seen in the *bīja,* and from another perspective the *ālayavijñāna,* and we have already seen that various 'selves' abound in the *māyā,* if one interprets 'self-nature' as the limited duration of the existents that manifest as appearing phenomena. Being transient there is however no true 'self-nature' of this phenomena. Kalupahana however points out that the phrase the 'self-nature of existents' refers to *svabhāva.* I had earlier stated, quoting from Napper,[31] that there are 'two meanings to the word *svabhāva'*: 'one is inherent existence, the object of negation, which does not exist in the least; the other is emptiness, the final nature of each and every phenomenon'. So if the first meaning is intended, then Nāgārjuna is correct, but if the second, (which I elaborated in terms of five Void Elements), then not so.

'Other nature' can be considered to refer to the substance of the phenomenal world, and which clothes the physical body. Once we have a state (i.e., *śūnyatā)* where 'self' is not evident, then there is nothing to register the existence or otherwise of form, of the substance that constitutes the *mayāvirūpa* of people's lives. This too then 'is not evident'.[32]

In continuing this correlation between Buddhist and Hindu concepts, where though the Advaita philosophy appears closest to the Buddhist mindset, nevertheless the Sāṅkhya conception of transformation is the more esoteric. Thus a comparison to the concept of *Brahman,* ('absolute abstract Consciousness, *sat* - the eternal Being/Non Being, *chit* - consciousness, and *ānanda* - bliss'), can be made. There is no direct correlation, but effectively the integration can be seen as follows, if we extend the general Buddhistic concepts to be inclusive of cosmogenic levels. We can equate Brahman with the consciousness-store *(ālayavijñāna),* from whence all seed *bījas,* causative and expressive of the phenomena of consciousness (mind) emanate. They are activated at

31 Napper, Elizabeth. *Dependent Arising and Emptiness* (Wisdom Publications, Boston, 1989), 127.

32 *A Treatise on Mind,* Vol 1, 295-7.

the appropriate time by the 'Creator King' (Vajrasattva/Ādi Buddha).[33] This is an evolved Buddha from a past cycle, who's new role is to now manifest a world sphere as His zone of compassionate endeavour.

Vajrasattva here therefore takes the role of Īśvara, whilst Māyā is the feminine 'substance store' that consciousness must utilise to manifest the formed space into which the principle of mind can incarnate and utilise as a mechanism of increasing its knowledge base as a foundation for gaining enlightenment. The originating level of knowledge is the seminal point of ignorance that must be eliminated by means of incarnating into the great wheel of *pratītyasamutpāda.*

Once the rebirthing process has been instigated by Īśvara then spontaneously there is the sprouting of the five heads of Brahmā. (Note that he originally had five heads, but one was destroyed by Śiva because Brahmā had 'spoken disrespectfully'.[34])

These 'heads' are representative of the Wisdoms of the five Dhyāni Buddhas that set the conditionings within manifest space whereby knowledge can be gained by the 'man-plant'. Thus there is the appearance of the five senses and sense-consciousnesses. Vairocana represents the head that was destroyed by Śiva, as he appears as the central point of the *maṇḍala* of the Dhyāni Buddhas, the remaining four delineate the four directions in space.

The symbolism of the *trimūrti*: Brahmā, Viṣṇu and Śiva, are accounted for in that they represent 'the three times' via which *saṃsāra* must play itself out. Brahmā represents the past, of all that was formerly accomplished (created) and which must now be improved upon. This concerned the creation of everything that was and exists now, the appearance of *manvantara.* Viṣṇu represents the present, the eternal Now, wherein consciousness is sustained, and via which it must move to become more expansive and inclusive of the all. We thus have the sustainer and preserver of the universe. Śiva represents the future, therefore is expressive of the *yogin's* path, wherein everything that was in the past must be transformed or destroyed to enter into a new more enlightened cycle of expression. With the termination of phenomena

33 See the section entitled 'Does a God exist' in *A Treatise on Mind,* volume 2, chapter 7, 195-203, for further detail.

34 Dowson, 57.

all then enters into the store-consciousness, hence we have *pralaya,* or in Buddhist terms, the manifestation of *śūnyatā.* Śiva is considered the destroyer.

The three attributes of time are also symbolised by the Wrathful Deity Mahākāla (meaning 'great time', hence stands beyond time or death). His three faced form signifies the three times, as personified by Brahmā, Viṣṇu, and Śiva.

The attributes of the above entities can also be seen expressed via the five Jinas, thus:

a. The energies and qualities of Brahman is found in Vairocana, the one who exists at the centre of the *maṇḍala* of the Jinas, from whom emanates the power and ineffable radiance that sustains the united purpose of all five Jinas. Vairocana's Dharmadhātu Wisdom represents the omnipresent reservoir of their attributes.

b. Akṣobhya, in the form of Īśvara, reflects the attributes of Brahman into manifestation via *māyā,* the illusional mirror of substance/phenomena. Akṣobhya's Mirror-like Wisdom manifests in the form of compassionate concern to rightly organise what manifests via *māyā* so that what does consciously evolve eventually expresses the Dharmadhātu Wisdom.

c. Amitābha manifests the functions of Brahmā, by embodying the Fires of the Mind, therefore its discriminative, segregative and hence creative qualities. He expresses the functions of the 'Creator King' into/as *saṃsāra.* From mind/Mind all phenomena proceeds and into which it is absorbed again. Reflecting the qualities of Brahmā within himself he is the creative (therefore discriminative) light of wisdom that is boundless and ineffable.

d. Ratnasambhava as Viṣṇu becomes the mechanism whereby the qualities of Akṣobhya can manifest in phenomenal space, to produce the equanimity of all things (the Equalising Wisdom). It shows all to be but an emanation of Love. (The embodiment of Kṛṣṇa, an Avatar of Viṣṇu in the Hindu myths.) That Love concerns following the path to enlightenment and consequent liberation.

e. Amoghasiddhi reflects the centralising power of Vairocana into the formed realms, allowing the development of *siddhis* (Śiva's prowess) that signify the All-accomplishing Wisdom of an enlightened one. Similarly Śiva is the embodiment of yogic power of the kingdom of the Hindu gods.

Alex Wayman cites a somewhat different arrangement from Buddhist Tantric sources:

> Certain Buddhist Tantras replace those names [of the Dhyāni Buddhas—my note] with others. For example, the *Hevajatantra* has the appellation Brahmā, etc. Mkhas grub rje explains the progenitors in terms of those names as follows:
>
> The Buddha Vairocana is called Brahmā. The Tibetan *saṅs rgyas* translates the Sanskrit "Buddha". Because he enters the elimination of defilement, he establishes the part of freedom from defilement. Moreover, the Tibetan *tshaṅs pa* (Brahmā) is equivalent to entrance into Nirvāṇa; hence the name is used with the meaning of 'Nirvāṇa of no fixed abode' (*apratiṣṭhitanirvāṇa*).
>
> Akṣobhya is called Viṣṇu. The reason for using this term is that Akṣobhya establishes the "Dharmadhātu knowledge" and by means of this knowledge enters the reality of the intrinsic nature (*svabhāva*) which pervades all things.
>
> Amoghasiddhi is named Śiva, because through the nature of "knowledge of the procedure of duty" (*kṛtyānuṣṭhāna-jñāna*) he continually provides all sentient beings with mundane and supramundane goods.
>
> The term Sarva is used for Ratnasambhava because, through his "equality-knowledge" (*samatā-jñāna*), he establishes in this equality the full comprehension of the nature of all things.
>
> Amitābha is referred to Tattva, because he establishes the part of "discriminative knowledge" (*pratyavekṣaṇa-jñāna*) which comprehends reality (*tattva*), and with sublime joy is like the sky.
>
> Vajrasattva is termed Vibuddha ("expanded") because he has expanded to the states of the "great co-natal joy" (*sahajānanda*) while fully comprehending them.[35]

---

35 Alex Wayman, *The Buddhist Tantras: Light on Indo-Tibetan Esotericism*, (Motilal Barnasidass, New Delhi, 2005), 46-47.

The consideration here is that the entire *maṇḍala* of the Jinas emanates from Vairocana, who can thus be equated with Brahmā, 'the creator', from whom the phenomena of *saṃsāra* emanates. From this perspective he expresses the attributes of Vajrasattva. Amoghasiddhi can then be equated with Śiva, because Śiva is the god of the *yogin,* that develops the powers (*siddhis*) that controls the manifestation of all forms of phenomena. Amitābha is referred to as *tattva* (the principles or five Elements, of existence) because he embodies the functions of the Mind which can discern reality, whilst Ratnasambhava projects the potency of the Jinas equally to all *(sarva).*

It should also be noted that the Buddha-germ (*tathāgatagarbha*) is a form of the Mundane Egg (*hiraṇyagarbha*), and from one perspective the entire story of creation happens within it (the human Soul/Sambhogakāya Flower). This introduces the philosophy of the *Ratnagotravibhāga,*[36] which was adequately explained in Volume 3 of my *Treatise on Mind.* The story of the concept of the 'I' (around which the creative process is woven) continues with each out-breathing by this Flower of an incarnate personality. As stated earlier, because the *tathāgatagarbha* has been seeded with purpose and conscious volition the cycles of births and deaths can ensue.

The role of *māyā*

In order to comprehend the nature of the manifestation of phenomena in the Advaita Vedānta system the function of Māyā *(māyā)* in the scheme of things needs to be analysed. Once established then everything else becomes comprehensible. Panda stated above that:

1. *Māyā* is uncreated.
2. She has no beginning.
3. She has no end.
4. She does not decay.
5. She is imperishable (*akṣara).*
6. She is undifferentiated (*avyākṛta*).
7. She exists in an unmanifested condition.
8. She is indescribable (*anirvacanīyā*).

36 See *The Uttaratantra of Maitreya* trans. E. Obermiller (Sri Satguru, New Delhi, 1991).

9. It cannot be said that she is real (*sat*).
10. It cannot be said that she is unreal (*asat*).
11. It cannot be said that she is both real and unreal (*sadasat*).
12. She is not an independent entity (*asvatantrā*) separate from and second to *Brahman*. Her existence depends upon *Brahman*, therefore:

a. She is said to be different from *Brahman*.
b. Non-different from *Brahman*.
c. Neither different nor non-different from *Brahman*.

The first seven of these statements describes *māyā* in the form of the Void Elements. They are defined as the Elements stripped of their ephemeral conditionings, so that all that remains is the primordial Element that is Void of *saṃsāric* attributes (therefore equated with the concept of *svabhāva*). They can then act as seed-germs for the later manifestation of the phenomena attributable to *saṃsāra*. Being Void (*śūnya*) then *māyā* in this form cannot be created, cannot have a beginning or end, cannot decay, or be destroyed, and is unmanifest, held as potential only within the confines of that state we call *śūnyatā*. Therefore it is 'coeternal with *Brahman*'. (Brahman here representing the Buddha-nature.) The concept of being 'undifferentiated' refers to the inherent unity of all that is Void. Differentiation only comes into manifestation in the Mind's Eye when the five types of emanations of energy states become defined in terms of phenomena of some type.

Normally the consideration of the Void Elements is for the five Elements governing the planes of perception associated with the emanation and resolution of *karma*. Here however the originating substance for the seven planes of perception is implicated. The first three statements can be considered a unity, the three in One, the substance of *dharmakāya*, which is uncreated, has no beginning nor end. These terms are depicted in relation to absolute time, hence beyond the consideration of cyclic time, which conditions the phenomena of *saṃsāra*. They relate to the highest three planes of perception.

That which is 'uncreated' refers to the substance of the plane *ādi*, which embodies the *bījas* of the rest of the *māyā* of things. It is the primordial state from which all that manifests as *māyā* ensues. From it emanates the driving will to cause the differentiation of phenomena. The statement 'no beginning' relates to the substance of the second plane of perception, *anupādaka,* meaning 'parentless', or 'self born of the divine essence', as it has no progenitors. Herein the Monad (Spirit) finds its place of residence and is the cause of the energy of *bodhicitta,* the driving force of compassion that pushes the sum of *saṃsāra* to liberation. This is the energy of Love-Wisdom, which is all-pervasive, eternal.

The next term 'has no end' relates to the plane *ātma,* from whence we have the emanation of the phenomena of *māyā,* as far as the world of human evolution is concerned. The term *ātma* means 'to pervade with breath, or eternal movement', which literally has no end, as it pervades all space, the 'boundless all'. This is the Mother of whatever is to be, the plane of the emanation and resolution of *karma.* The Void Element is Aether and is expressed by the third Ray of Mathematically Exact Activity.

The next four statements relate to the attributes of the substance, the Void Elements that emanate from *ātma* (the third *dharmakāyaic* level). First we have the Airy Element embodying the fourth plane of perception, *buddhi,* implied in the term 'does not decay'. This plane is also conceived in terms of *śūnyatā,* the Void, which is not corruptible (hence is unchangeable). It differs thus from the lower three states, associated with the three worlds of human livingness, the mental, astral and dense physical planes. The Ray governing this fourth plane is the fourth of Beautifying Harmony overcoming Conflict.

The term 'imperishable' refers to the fifth plane of perception and the Fiery Element embodying the substance of mind/Mind. Though it causes the modifications of the phenomena of *saṃsāra,* however when this Fiery substance is also considered inclusive of the Mind of 'God', then its imperishability is exemplified. It is the prime creative differentiating force, and is governed by the fifth Ray of Science.

The term 'undifferentiated' refers to the Watery Void Element, not viewed in terms of the astral plane created by human desire-minds, but rather as a field of pure radiant energy that is utilised to sustain the efficacy of *mantra* and the emanation of phenomena. This energy is governed by the sixth Ray of Devotion and Idealism.

Finally we have the phrase 'She exists in an unmanifested condition', which refers to the seventh (normally the fifth) Void Element. This Element is viewed as the etheric substratum (the true substance of *māyā)* underlying the manifestation of the material phenomena we experience with our senses. It is governed by the seventh Ray of Ceremonial, Cyclic or Rhythmic Activity, materialising Power.

The remaining five points stem from the fact that a consciousness has arisen that can discern the real from the unreal, truth from falsity, etc. The analysis is therefore from within the precincts of *saṃsāra* and via the consciousness of a human unit, rather than to the planes of perception. (Which, in the descending order, can be considered planes of increasing materialisation of *māyā.)*

Māyā represents the etheric substance or substratum of 'matter'. It is the substance from which is built the *nāḍīs* that are the carrier of the *prāṇas* that sustains all Life and via which the *saṃskāras* governing the manifestation of phenomena are derived. The *saṃskāras* condition all that we are and the qualities of the universe that has come to be. *Māyā* thus also forms the substance of the *chakras* that regulate the expression of all that is. *Māyā* manifests as the energy field that instantaneously clothes the thoughts and ideas that one generates and which can manifest in the field of action. Consciousness then perceives the effects of thoughts in variegated ways. These often manifest illusionally, as day-dreams, wish-fulfilling images of the mind, and the like. Being transient such thoughts are therefore also generally considered as *māyā.*

With respect to the human personality and the expression of the five sense-consciousnesses that are the foundation of the empirical mind the phrase: 'She is indescribable *(anirvacanīyā)'* relates to the sense of *smell* (governed by the Element Ether). The perceptions derived from this sense (in its subjective connotations) are most subtle and often barely discernable, generally producing 'indescribable' effects upon consciousness, as they are attributes from the *dharmakāya.*

The phrase 'It cannot be said that she is real *(sat)'* relates to the sense of *taste* (the Airy Element), and the subtle discernments called intuition, derived from the domain of the abstract Mind, or from *śūnyatā.* Such subtle discernments are beyond what the empirical mind considers real, thus are often quickly dismissed by the ordinary person. The Airy Element is the carrier of all the *prāṇas* and of their propensity to manifest the phenomena around us by which we experience things, which can be considered illusional, hence not real. The attributes of this Element are most difficult to perceive, virtually undetectable, similar to the air on a windless day, thus can be considered 'not real' from this perspective.

The phrase 'It cannot be said that she is unreal (*asat*)' relates to the sense of *sight* (the Fiery Element), hence everything the intellect experiences and discerns to be real, because visually seen and cognised by the empirical functions of the mind. As the Fiery Element embodies the substance of our thoughts, the field of consciousness that will eventually produce enlightenment, so we can say that of everything associated with the phenomena of *saṃsāra* such thoughts alone pertain to the 'real'.

The phrase 'It cannot be said that she is both real and unreal *(sadasat)'* relates to the illusional Watery astral zone of experience (the sense of *touch),* where desire-mind produces a mixture of valid and also imaginary, desire-filled imagery. The substance of our desires and emotions thus either pertain to the 'real', because helping to build the character of our consciousness, or to the 'unreal', because of their undoubted ephemeral nature. They can produce one or the other at any time, hence it is neither real nor unreal.

The final phrase 'She is not an independent entity *(asvatantrā)* separate from and second to *Brahman'* relates to experiences upon the dense physical plane (the sense of *hearing),* hence to the empirical comprehension of the sum of *saṃsāra*. The statement therefore states that whatever is experienced therein is 'not an independent entity' from Brahman. Brahman hence incorporates everything from the highest to the lowest strata of experiences. From *saṃsāra* the Buddha-nature evolves, which can be equated with Brahman.

With respect to *saṃsāra* one must differentiate *prakṛti* (substance matter) from *māyā*. *Prakṛti* is that aspect of *māyā* that covers it with what can be perceived, subtly or objectively. It is the stratum of concretised substance that clothes the empirical universe, and which we perceive as tangible, 'real', or else it informs the body of our emotions and desires, likewise 'real' for the normal empirical mind that experiences it. *Prakṛti* is transformed by means of the Fires of consciousness into enlightenment vectors.

We saw that *saṃsāra* and Brahman are made to be identical in the Advaita Vedānta philosophy, similarly *saṃsāra* and *śūnyatā* are said to be identical in Buddhism, as Chapter XXV, verse 19 of Nāgārjuna's *Mūlamadhyamakārikā* states:

> There is not the slightest difference
> Between cyclic existence and nirvāṇa.
> There is not the slightest difference
> Between nirvāṇa and cyclic existence.[37]

From this one can equate the Advaita concept of Brahman (or *parabrahman,* implied also in the mantric statement: *Oṁ tat sat,*[38] to *nirvāṇa-śūnyatā. (Nirvāṇa* being defined as a state of residing in *śūnyatā.)*

The final statements given concerning *māyā* is that:

a. She is said to be different from *Brahman*—when manifesting illusionally to the consciousness that perceives.
b. Non-different from *Brahman*—when embodying the substance that pertains to the real, such as enlightened perceptions.
c. Neither different nor non-different from *Brahman*—when manifesting in the form of the *saṃsāra,* which depends upon the way one perceives it and builds it into the structure of one's consciousness.

As stated above, the movement of the mind concerns the conveyance of the winds *(prāṇas)* of the *nāḍī* system incorporating that form in *saṃsāra.*[39] The *nāḍī* system is the real, from the perspective that it underlies the appearance of phenomena and its essence is derived from the Void Elements, of which the *prāṇas* become reified through the actions of consciousness. The elementary Winds are the real, being the expression of the Breath of the act of compassion of the absorbed

---

37 Garfield, Jay L., *The Fundamental Wisdom of the Middle Way,* (Oxford University Press, Oxford, 1995), 75.

38 *Oṁ* (signifying the liberations of consciousness). *Tat,* (neuter pronoun), the immutable, the unfathomable, the essence of all being/non-being. *Sat,* existent, reality, being. The eternally existing principle, Be-ness, the immutable, the ever present, changeless and eternal root, from and through which all proceeds.

39 The mantric sound *Oṁ* is also termed *praṇava,* or that which resonates the essence of the *prāṇas* ('winds').

Buddha. The manifesting phenomena is the unreal, as it constantly changes according to the vicissitudes of the play of the *māyā* of which it is a part. The process of the formation of *saṃsāric* activity in relation to the Void is hence outlined.

The three *guṇas*

Next to be considered is the fact that *māyā,* according to Panda above: 'is made up of three strings (*guṇas*), viz., *sattva* (serenity), *rajas* (activity), and *tamas* (inertia), kept in equipoise. She is undifferentiated and at the same time has three constituents. She is said to be with, without, and with and without parts'.

The three *guṇas* are the three aspects of motion, as D.K. states in *A Treatise on Cosmic Fire:*

> Motion is characterised, as we know, by three qualities:
>
> 1. Inertia,
> 2. Mobility,
> 3. Rhythm.
>
> These three are experienced in just the above sequence and presuppose a period of slow activity, succeeded by one of extreme movement. This middle period produces incidentally (as the true note and rate is sought) cycles of chaos, of experiment, of experience and of comprehension. Following on these two degrees of motion (which are characteristic of the atom, Man, of the Heavenly Man or group, and of the Logos or the Totality) comes a period of rhythm and of stabilisation wherein the point of balance is achieved. By the force of balancing the pairs of opposites, and thus producing equilibrium, pralaya is the inevitable sequence.[40]

These *guṇas* can also be viewed in terms of *Life,* referring to the intensity of Monadic/*dharmakāyic* Life, thus is *sattvic.* Next is *Consciousness,* referring to the cyclic or rhythmic activity of the Soul/*tathāgatagarbha* (when compared to the dynamism of the Monad) hence is *rajaistic.* Finally we have *Form,* referring to the comparative inertia of the life of the personality vehicle, wherein changes in attitude

---

40 Bailey, T.C.F., 129-130.

and awareness of the true nature of things happens very slowly, thus is *tamasic* in nature. One can also consider the perception of the three times (of the evolution of consciousness, or of the various kingdoms in Nature), where the *past* can refer to *tamas* because the cycles of activity are comparative sluggish, of long duration, and governed by inertia. Next is the *present*, the epoch of cyclic activity, which happens at a comparatively brisk pace (*rajas*). Finally there is the *future* wherein all of the gains in consciousness have been taken into account, making further progress quite rapid (*sattvic*). Units of measurement can here be applied, such as periods of evolutionary time, *kalpas*, and the duration of various cycles (of experiential growth). When concerned with 'non-unit terms' in the analysis of the *guṇas* then *māyā* can be said to be without parts. When analysed in terms of measurable units, then we can say that *māyā* is with parts, and when consciousness is involved then 'She' is 'with and without parts'.

Panda then elaborates and introduces the differences between Vedāntic and Śaṅkara's philosophy, which is of value to add here.

> How is *Māyā* the material cause of the universe then? Śaṅkara, in his Introduction to the *Brahma-Sūtra (Adhyāsa-bhāṣya),* has defined the word *adhyāsa* as perceiving or understanding something as something else (*atasmiṁs-tadbuddhiḥ).* He considers the universe as an illusory appearance of Brahman that is the substratum (*adhiṣṭhāna*). Later Advaita Vedāntists gave a similar doctrine known as *vivarta-vāda.* This *vivarta-vāda* regards the world-appearance as an *adhyāsa* or false appearance in place of the *Brahman*-substratum, thereby reducing the world to an unreal appearance.
>
> Despite the declaration of *adhyāsa-vāda*, Śaṅkara does recognise the creation (*sṛṣṭi*), sustenance (*sthiti*) and dissolution (*pralaya*) of the universe. The *Vedānta-Sūtra* also recognises the universe as *empirically real*, although not absolutely real. It is the general consensus of the Vedāntic scriptures that the universe is not nothing and that it is not a mere illusion. The empirical universe has a beginning. It evolves. It has a grand design. It evolves purposefully. It works in a co-ordinated way. It will undergo involution in a systematic reverse way. It will be reabsorbed into *Māyā*. This completes a cycle. Such cycles are infinite in number. All these processes cannot go hand in hand with the concept of illusion only. We have to clarify the concept of the *empirical universe.*

> The *sattva* constituent of *Māyā* generates the empirical substance of the universe. Its generation does not involve *de novo* creation or creation out of nothing. It causes the unmanifested entities to manifest (from *avyakta* to *vyakta*). The *rajas* constituent makes the manifest entities active. The *tamas* constituent renders inertia to the manifested entities. The activities of the manifested entities are results of action and inertia.[41]

Next Panda presents detail of the nature of the manifestation of the knowable universe from the Hindu perspective. This is important because it brings to the fore the concept of Mahat, which is a fundamental esoteric term, referring to cosmic (empirical) Mind, from which effectively all phenomena known in the systemic planes is caused to appear. This happens in a sense similar to the Yogācāra philosophy, that states all is mind, resides in mind and is created by mind.

> What is the exact nature of the manifestation? The last state of the involution of the universe is the *Virāḍ* or *Mahat*. All the matter and energy of the universe pass through the reverse processes from gross to subtle states and finally become *Ākāśa* (Space). The path of involution from *Ākāśa* to *Virāḍ* involves three steps, viz., *Ākāśa* → *Prāṇa* → *Āpaḥ* → *Virāḍ*. This *Virāḍ* or the Supermind of the universe is the cosmic audio-cum-video tape. It stores the whole universe in the form of memory traces. The dissolution of *Virāḍ* in *Māyā* or *Prakṛti* is the *prākṛta pralaya* or total dissolution. Like the salt in sea-water, *Virāḍ* remains in a dormant state in *Prakṛti*. When the equipoise state (*sāmyāvasthā*) of the three constituents (*sattva, rajas, tamas*) of *Prakṛti* is disturbed, the universe is recreated by the manifestation of *Virāḍ* in the analogy of the crystallisation of salt in its solvent. The subsequent processes of manifestation traverse the path from a more subtle state to a less subtle state and from subtle to gross states. The first three steps are from *Virāḍ* to *Āpaḥ*, from *Āpaḥ* to *Prāṇa*, and from *Prāṇa* to *Ākaśa*. Particles appear from *Ākaśa* and the universe evolves in a creative way. From *Avyakta* (Unmanifested) to *Vyakta* (Manifest) and from *Vyakta* to *Avyakta* is the cyclic course of the universe. The manifestation of the universe is a continuous process in a cosmic period. It begins in one step in a single moment.

41 Panda, op. cit., 776-777.

> But the creative work of *Māyā* is not over in a single instant; it continues throughout the first half of the cosmic period.
>
> The stuff of the universe, including unmanifested and manifested, is transient, always changeable, and has no independent existence. It is a becoming stuff, entirely dependent upon the Being *(Brahman)* for existence and functioning. Its existence is empirical; its functions are empirical.
>
> In the empirical creation of the universe, none of the three constituents of *Māyā* are transformed. *Māyā* has magical power. God is the magician (*Māyāvī)* and the world is a magic-show. The magical performance is done through *Māyā*.[42]

From the *guṇas* therefore come the four constituents, 'from *Virāḍ* to *Āpaḥ*, from *Āpaḥ* to *Prāṇa*, and from *Prāṇa* to *Ākaśa*',[43] which happen when the *guṇas* come to be 'disturbed', i.e., energy is activated. This can only happen by means of the seed Thought *(bīja)* directed from the abstracted Consciousness, Brahman. Though Brahman can be considered abstracted or aloof from the Creation, nevertheless the original projection to disturb the serene energy dispensation of Māyā caused the manifestation of the above sequence. *Virāḍ/Mahat* then represents the empirical Logoic Mind wherein all forms of manifestation are possible. The generation of the Thought-Forms of awakening of perceptions, of the appearance of 'things', as the *saṃskāras* of past cycles of activity come to the fore, and are then activated.

Āpaḥ here represents the cosmic Waters of space, the fluid substance of the cosmic astral plane which clothes and animates (cosmic) Thought, so that it can become tangible, eventually manifesting as the fluid ever-changing forms of *saṃsāra*. *Āpaḥ* is said to be the 'subtle, primordial Cosmic Plasma (Fluid). The Ṛg Veda (VI.50.7) states that it is the *first* Mother (*mātṛtamāḥ*) of all movable and immovable entities in the universe'.[44] Hence we have the particularisation (energisation of the awakening *saṃskāras*) of the five Void Elements with the qualities to

---

42 Ibid., 778-779.

43 Note that the *prāṇa* indicated here is cosmic *prāṇa* manifesting via the cosmic Waters, whereas *ākaśa* represents that *prāṇa* manifesting via the four cosmic ethers plus the systemic higher mental plane.

44 Ibid., 552, *fn*. 10.

be expressed by that Incarnation of the Logos (the embodiment of the Creative Word) of all that is to be. This Logos is then considered to be Nārāyaṇa. Panda states that:

> The word *Nāra*[45] means subtle Cosmic Plasma, and *ayana* means *patha* or way. God or Nārāyaṇa reclines on the *Āpaḥ* or *Nāra* and, hence, He is known as Nārāyaṇa...The reclining God was supported by Himself, His *bala-śakti* (the Power of His Vigour), which was a Cosmic Helix or the Cosmic Serpent (the mechanics of the Cosmic Spring). God emerged through His own umbilicus as Brahmā or Hiraṇyagarbha under whose Chairpersonship the universe evolved.[46]

The doctrine of the five *prāṇas* (though here in the form of *ākāśa*), as an emanation of that Creative Word or Breath, taking the form of the attributes of the five Dhyāni Buddhas and the inevitable expression and development of their wisdoms (*prajñās*) has been explained in my previous books, therefore only needs to be mentioned here. It is now possible to consider the constituency of what embodies all that is, and which can be mastered by means of yogic austerities (*tapas*). Such mastery is technically accomplished by means of the control of breath. Thus the creative process comes full circle, being imitated by the consciousness bearer in the illusional word (*saṃsāra*) provided for this purpose. The five breaths *(prāṇas)* are termed *prāṇa, apāna, udāna, samāna* and *vyāna.* I have explained them in my earlier works, but the more exoteric account can be found in *The Yoga Sūtras of Patanjali.*

Ākaśa can be considered the primordial substance of systemic[47] (manifested) space. It manifests via the four cosmic ethers, the etheric substratum of the cosmic dense physical plane, that are the carriers of the five cosmic *prāṇas* in the form of *ākaśa.* It is the elementary (plastic) substance of the *dharmakāya* wielded by a Buddha-Mind to convey the expression of his Wisdom. Without the *ākaśa* the spontaneity of the enlightened Mind could not be expressed. From it also comes

---

45 Another rendering of this word, or in the form of *Nāra,* is that it means man, human, bodily form, the incarnation of Viṣṇu, sometimes equated with Puruṣa. Nāra is also the primeval Waters upon which Viṣṇu rests upon Śeṣa, the seven-headed serpent.

46 Ibid.

47 Technically the space enclosed by the solar Logos, via which all therein evolve.

all of the Elements, atoms, and attributes of phenomenal life. It is the medium that allows the *saṃsāra-śūnyatā* nexus to exist. *Ākaśa* therefore also veils Mahat (cosmic Mind), *āpaḥ* (cosmic Waters), that manifests as cosmic *prāṇa,* the streams of energy qualifications that vivify consciousness via the cosmic ethers. This then makes a sevenfold differentiation, which from one perspective represents the seven-headed serpent[48] upon which Nārāyaṇa rests as he floats upon the Waters of cosmic space. Viṣṇu reclines upon Śeṣa (seven-headed serpent) as his couch in Nāra the primeval (milky) Waters. This signifies the primal manifestation of the consciousness aspect of the Deity that spreads outwards to encompass absolute space. (Hence the name Nārāyaṇa for Viṣṇu.) The seven-headed serpent symbolises the seven planes of perception, the seven spirals of the Logoic permanent atom and subsidiary spirillae.[49] Viṣṇu therefore signifies the Consciousness aspect or Lives that incarnate into those planes.

Nārāyaṇa then is the Divinity who rests upon the ocean of consciousness and that moves into humanity *(nara).* He is a Logos, from whose naval rises Brahmā who qualifies or circumscribes abstracted (cosmic) space (*āpaḥ*) in terms of a world-sphere (be this sphere that of a solar system, planetary system, a galaxy, universe), so that consciousness can evolve. Nārāyaṇa represents cosmic Love-Wisdom (as an embodiment of Viṣṇu), the principle that acts for compassionate reasons, hence awakens to the Thought of the need of a world-sphere so that the All can progress into higher consciousness states.

Śiva is an embodiment of the first Ray of Will or power, that instigates the appearance of the Logoic permanent atom, via which all can arise. Brahmā expresses the third Ray (hence the subsidiary Rays) that with mathematical exact Activity causes the appearance of the categories of phenomena. Śiva is thus the Father, Viṣṇu the Son and Brahmā the Mother aspects of deity.

---

48 This serpent is but a version of Śiva, as we then have the *trimūrti,* with Brahmā rising from the naval of Viṣṇu. Note also the symbolism of the serpent around Śiva's neck relates to the arousal of *kuṇḍalinī,* the serpent power, and that he is generally portrayed in meditation, via which the potency of the serpent can be rightly directed.

49 The nature of the Logoic physical permanent atom is explained in my *Esoteric Cosmology and Modern Physics* and Bailey's *A Treatise on Cosmic Fire,* to which the reader can refer for detail.

In Buddhistic terms we have the expression of the formation of a Buddha-sphere by a primordial Ādi Buddha (Vajrasattva). Hence there is no such thing as a 'Self' that does this 'creating'. Essentially there is but a projection of a Thought-Construct that has temporal illusional appearance, whilst appearing units of consciousness evolve to experience it. As such the Buddhist logic is quite congenial with the concept of Brahman. However in Hinduism the concept of the creation process becomes increasingly deified and particularised via the mind until they rationalise in terms of a 'permanent' Soul (*ātman*). This *ātman* (or *paramātman)* when conceived in terms of a Logos becomes Īśvara (or Puruṣa, the Heavenly Man as pure Consciousness).

From the domain of cosmic Mind however the creative process must be visualised, and the laws of Mind considered. This Mind in Buddhist terms is considered the *dharmakāya*.

The particularising agent (Īśvara) can be equated with an Ādi Buddha, if one has the concept of the nature of a Buddha in mind. The Ādi Buddha is the Monadic form that has undergone further cosmic journeying and gained the results of that education via attaining higher cosmic Initiations, and consequently has returned to play a role in world or solar formation as a Logos. Human units evolving within that body of manifestation then conceive of such a One as a Divine Personality (Īśvara or 'God').

Īśvara is the Mind that directs and moulds the *ākaśa* within *saṃsāra*. Īśvara stands as the Logoic Personality that is an emanation of Brahman (the Logoic Soul). Being the evolving Personality of a Logos, so Īśvara embodies the Life within the periodical vehicles (globes, Chains, Schemes). Īśvara can be considered to be the *sambhogakāya* form that the Ādi Buddha takes so that it can direct the evolving streams of consciousness within the Logoic Personality. Īśvara works to transform consciousness-streams into their liberated cosmic expression. Panda can again be quoted for the Advaita viewpoint. He introduces the term *jīvātmā* and places this 'vital life of the self' in the scheme of things.

> *Brahman*, the fundamental Consciousness, is reflected on its own power, *Māyā*. This reflected Consciousness is *Īśvara* or God. The fundamental Consciousness, reflected on a non-living entity, is *bhūtātmā* (the self of the non-living entity such as atoms, molecules, stars, and planets). The fundamental Consciousness, reflected on a

living entity, is known as *jīvātmā* or *jīva* (the self of a living entity, both plants and animals). *Māyā* as such is insentient. She becomes conscious by virtue of the reflection. Such reflection is known as *cidābhāsa*. The reflected consciousness is induced and empirical. The fundamental Consciousness is absolute; it is transcendent and, for its pervasiveness in all, is also immanent.

The Advaita Vedānta uses a term *upādhi* (limiting adjunct). We may take the example of the Great Space (*Mahākāśa*). In the absence of limiting adjuncts, Space is *Mahākāśa*. When *Mahākāśa* is limited in a pot, it is *ghatākāśa* (space in a pot) and distinguished from the *Mahākāśa*. On breaking the pot, the distinction between the *ghatākāśa* and the *Mahākāśa* disappears. In the same analogy, the absolute Consciousness (*Brahman*), with *Māyā* as the limiting adjunct, is *Īśvara* (God), and, with a created entity as the limiting adjunct, is *bhūtātmā* or *jīvātmā* (individual self).

Brahman is attributeless *(nirguṇa)* and functionless (*niṣkriya*). *Īśvara* has attributes and is otherwise known as *saguṇa* (with attributes) *Brahman*. *Māyā* is the Power (*Śakti*) of *Brahman*. *Brahman* and *Īśvara*, being non-different, *Māyā* is also the Power of *Īśvara,* who becomes possessor of *guṇas* (attributes) by the virtue of the three *guṇas,* viz., *sattva, rajas* and *tamas*, of *Māyā*. It is not correct to say that *Īśvara* is non-functional. But is also not correct to say that He functions in the ordinary sense of the word 'function'. *Māyā* the *Śakti* of *Īśvara*, is the direct agent, the doer (*kartrī)* of creation (*sṛṣṭi*), sustenance (*sthiti* and *pālana*), and dissolution (*pralaya*). The Chairpersonship of *Īśvara*, His simple presence in everything of the universe and the whole universe, is enough to induce activity in *Māyā*. *Īśvara* cannot be the doer without *Māyā*. Thus, she is very meaningful (*arthavatī sā*) in the total cosmology.

Like *Brahman, Īśvara* and Māyā are formless. But, unlike *Brahman Īśvara* can take any form through his *Māyā-Śakti* (Magical Power). These forms of *Īśvara* are empirical, not transcendental, however.

Īśvara is the architect of the universe *(vidhātā)*. He prepares the blueprint. He is the engineer of the Cosmic Edifice. He is the controller and ruler of the entire cosmos.[50]

It should be noted that in our esoteric philosophy *bhūtātmā* 'the self of the non-living entity' and *jīva* 'the self of a living entity', are not so

---

50 Ibid., 780-781.

easily distinguished, because the Life force (*jīva*) manifests through all of the kingdoms of Nature. All is sentient, but almost imperceptibly so in the mineral kingdom. Note that the word *bhūta* (of *bhūtātmā*) refers to 'that which exists', the five great Elements. The *jīva* of the first of these Elements, Earth, activates the evolutionary direction of the mineral kingdom, so that it eventually evolves into the plant kingdom. The *jīva* of the plant kingdom utilises the Water Element. The *jīva* animating the animal kingdom utilises the Fiery Element, that propelling the human kingdom utilises the Airy Element, and liberated beings are vitalised by the *jīva* of Aether.

The extract also introduces the three times (past, present and future) of any thought construction, be it from the mind of a human or of Deity: 'the doer (*kartrī*) of creation (*sṛṣṭi*), sustenance (*sthiti* and *pālana*), and dissolution (*pralaya*)'. The functions of these three times and the integration of the way they work, for instance, with the qualities of the associated *guṇas*, become personified as Gods in the literature. We thus have the appearance of the *trimūrti*. Note that the Hindu concept of *ātman* or the *jīvātmā* for a human unit is effectively an integration of the attributes of the Sambhogakāya Flower (the Soul) and the Monad.

> *Īśvara* or the Cosmic Self is one only. The One is named as Three (Trinity), viz., Brahmā or Hiraṇyagarbha, Viṣṇu or Nārāyaṇa and Rudra or Maheśvara[51]. The creation of the universe started when the Cosmic Egg appeared, or even before when *Virāḍ* or *Mahat* was born. That was the beginning of creation. It is still now in process and will continue throughout the Cosmic Cycle. *Īśvara,* with reference to His creative activity is known as Brahmā. The universe is sustained by Viṣṇu who is the same *Īśvara.* Both in the micro- and the macro-world, annihilation is a continual process during the whole period of the Cosmic Cycle. Finally, the entire Cosmos will be dissolved (*mahāpralaya*) in *Māyā. Īśvara,* with reference to all these annihilative processes, is known as Rudra. Sarasvatī, Lakṣmī, and Gaurī or Kālī are the *Śaktis* (Power or Consorts) of Brahmā, Viṣṇu, and Rudra, respectively. All these three are essentially *Māyā*, the one and only one *Śakti* of God.[52]

51 Names for Śiva.

52 Ibid., 782-783.

Continuation of the Proem

Having divulged this cosmological background we are now in a better position to comprehend Blavatsky's statements in the Proem section of *The Secret Doctrine.*

> The Occultists are, therefore, at one with the Adwaita Vedantin philosophers as to the above tenet. They show the impossibility of accepting on philosophical grounds the idea of the absolute ALL creating or even evolving the "Golden Egg," into which it is said to enter in order to transform itself into Brahmā — the Creator, who expands himself later into the gods and all the visible Universe. They say that Absolute Unity cannot pass to Infinity; for Infinity presupposes the limitless extension of *something*, and the duration of that "something"; and the One All is like Space — which is its only mental and physical representation on this earth, or our plane of existence — neither an object of, nor a subject to, perception. If one could suppose the Eternal Infinite All, the Omnipresent Unity, instead of being in Eternity, becoming through periodical manifestation a manifold Universe or a multiple personality, that Unity would cease to be one. Locke's idea that "pure space is capable of neither resistance nor motion" — is incorrect. Space is neither a "limitless void," nor a "conditioned fullness," but both: being, on the plane of absolute abstraction, the ever-incognisable Deity, which is void only to finite minds, and on that of *mayavic* perception, the Plenum, the absolute Container of all that is, whether manifested or unmanifested; it is, therefore, that ABSOLUTE ALL[53]..."What is that which was, is, and will be, whether there is a Universe or not; whether there be gods or none?' asks the esoteric Senzar Catechism. And the answer made is—'SPACE'.[54]

Nowadays it is best to use the term 'esotericists' rather than 'occultists' because of the derogatory assertions in the popular imagination of occultists being followers of black magic or those interested in pursuing the development of the lower psychic powers. The purpose being to bewilder or to amuse onlookers, or else to demonstrate psychic superiority to an otherwise spiritually numbed audience.

53 *The Secret Doctrine,* Vol. 1, 8.

54 Ibid., 9.

Leaving the 'Absolute All' aside, and looking to the phenomenal universe, then what is known as 'space' is depicted as *ākāśa,* which also veils Mahat (cosmic empirical Mind), *āpaḥ* (cosmic Waters), and *prāṇa* (or *māyā*), the streams of energy qualifications that vivify consciousness via the cosmic *nāḍī* system for our earth Scheme. Blavatsky now introduces a major source of revelation to humanity, which can be directly perceived by means of the Clear Light of Mind. This source is the Hierarchy of liberated enlightened Beings that those who undergo the necessary meditative and Initiation training will contact, and from whom revelatory instructions will come in the form of telepathic and visual impressions. The most esoteric teachings will be communicated thereby, and the secrets of this most sacred science will be safeguarded from the concretisations, unwise distortions and scornful projections from the empirical minds of the unworthy. This Hierarchy are not only subjective directive agents but are Bodhisattvas that continuously incarnate to further advance the course of human civilisation.[55]

Blavatsky continues:

> The Occultist accepts revelation as coming from divine yet still finite Beings, the manifested lives, never from the Unmanifestable ONE LIFE; from those Entities, called Primordial Man, Dhyani-Buddhas, or Dhyan Chohans, the "Rishi-Prajāpati" of the Hindus, the Elohim or "Sons of God," the Planetary Spirits of all nations, who have become Gods for men. He also regards the Adi-Sakti — the direct emanation of Mulaprakriti, the eternal Root of THAT, and the female aspect of the Creative Cause, Brahmā, in her A'kásic form of the Universal Soul — as philosophically a Maya, and the cause of human Maya. But this view does not prevent him from believing in its existence so long as it lasts, to wit, for one Mahamanvantara; nor from applying A'kās'a, the radiation of Mulaprakriti, to practical purposes, connected as the World-Soul is with all natural phenomena, known or unknown to science.[56]

55 The nature of this Hierarchy of enlightened Beings were explained in my book *The Constitution of Shambhala,* volumes 7A and 7B of *A Treatise on Mind.* See also *The Externalisation of the Hierarchy* and other books of A.A. Bailey.

56 Ibid., Vol 1., 9-10.

Blavatsky therefore states that all manifesting forms in the universe, and indeed that the universe itself, is transient, though having substantiality for the duration of its existence.

The fundamental propositions of *The Secret Doctrine*

Blavatsky now provides the 'three fundamental propositions' of *The Secret Doctrine*, the ageless wisdom of the esoteric lore. Because of their importance they need to be quoted verbatim.

> (a) An Omnipresent, Eternal, Boundless, and Immutable PRINCIPLE on which all speculation is impossible, since it transcends the power of human conception and could only be dwarfed by any human expression or similitude. It is beyond the range and reach of thought — in the words of Mandukya, "unthinkable and unspeakable."
>
> To render these ideas clearer to the general reader, let him set out with the postulate that there is one absolute Reality which antecedes all manifested, conditioned, being. This Infinite and Eternal Cause — dimly formulated in the "Unconscious" and "Unknowable" of current European philosophy — is the rootless root of "all that was, is, or ever shall be." It is of course devoid of all attributes and is essentially without any relation to manifested, finite Being. It is "Be-ness" rather than Being (in Sanskrit, *Sat),* and is beyond all thought or speculation.
>
> This "Be-ness" is symbolised in the Secret Doctrine under two aspects. On the one hand, absolute abstract Space, representing bare subjectivity, the one thing which no human mind can either exclude from any conception, or conceive of by itself. On the other, absolute Abstract Motion representing Unconditioned Consciousness. Even our Western thinkers have shown that Consciousness is inconceivable to us apart from change, and motion best symbolises change, its essential characteristic. This latter aspect of the one Reality, is also symbolised by the term "The Great Breath," a symbol sufficiently graphic to need no further elucidation. Thus, then, the first fundamental axiom of the Secret Doctrine is this metaphysical ONE ABSOLUTE — BE-NESS — symbolised by finite intelligence as the theological Trinity...[57]
>
> Parabrahm (the One Reality, the Absolute) is the field of Absolute Consciousness, *i.e.,* that Essence which is out of all relation to

57 Ibid., 14.

conditioned existence, and of which conscious existence is a conditioned symbol. But once that we pass in thought from this (to us) Absolute Negation, duality supervenes in the contrast of Spirit (or consciousness) and Matter, Subject and Object.

Spirit (or Consciousness) and Matter are, however, to be regarded, not as independent realities, but as the two facets or aspects of the Absolute (Parabrahm), which constitute the basis of conditioned Being whether subjective or objective.

Considering this metaphysical triad as the Root from which proceeds all manifestation, the great Breath assumes the character of precosmic Ideation. It is the *fons et origo* of force and of all individual consciousness, and supplies the guiding intelligence in the vast scheme of cosmic Evolution. On the other hand, precosmic root- substance *(Mulaprakriti)* is that aspect of the Absolute which underlies all the objective planes of Nature.

Just as pre-Cosmic Ideation is the root of all individual consciousness, so pre-Cosmic Substance is the substratum of matter in the various grades of its differentiation.

Hence it will be apparent that the contrast of these two aspects of the Absolute is essential to the existence of the "Manifested Universe." Apart from Cosmic Substance, Cosmic Ideation could not manifest as individual consciousness, since it is only through a vehicle[58] of matter that consciousness wells up as "I am I," a physical basis being necessary to focus a ray of the Universal Mind at a certain stage of complexity. Again, apart from Cosmic Ideation, Cosmic Substance would remain an empty abstraction, and no emergence of consciousness could ensue.

The "Manifested Universe," therefore, is pervaded by duality, which is, as it were, the very essence of its EX-istence as "manifestation."

But just as the opposite poles of subject and object, spirit and matter, are but aspects of the One Unity in which they are synthesized, so, in the manifested Universe, there is "that" which links spirit to matter, subject to object.

This something, at present unknown to Western speculation, is called by the occultists Fohat. It is the "bridge" by which the

58 Blavatsky's footnote here: 'Called in Sanskrit: "Upadhi"'.

"Ideas" existing in the "Divine Thought" are impressed on Cosmic substance as the "laws of Nature." Fohat is thus the dynamic energy of Cosmic Ideation; or, regarded from the other side, it is the intelligent medium, the guiding power of all manifestation, the "Thought Divine" transmitted and made manifest through the Dhyan Chohans,[59] the Architects of the visible World. Thus from Spirit, or Cosmic Ideation, comes our consciousness; from Cosmic Substance the several vehicles in which that consciousness is individualised and attains to self — or reflective — consciousness; while Fohat, in its various manifestations, is the mysterious link between Mind and Matter, the animating principle electrifying every atom into life.

The following summary will afford a clearer idea to the reader.

(1.) The ABSOLUTE; the *Parabrahm* of the Vedantins or the one Reality, SAT, which is, as Hegel says, both Absolute Being and Non-Being.

(2.) The first manifestation, the impersonal, and, in philosophy, *unmanifested* Logos, the precursor of the "manifested." This is the "First Cause," the "Unconscious" of European Pantheists.

(3.) Spirit-matter, LIFE; the "Spirit of the Universe," the Purusha and Prakriti, or the *second* Logos.

(4.) Cosmic Ideation, MAHAT or Intelligence, the Universal World-Soul; the Cosmic Noumenon of Matter, the basis of the intelligent operations in and of Nature, also called MAHA-BUDDHI.[60]

The ONE REALITY; its *dual* aspects in the conditioned Universe.

Further, the Secret Doctrine affirms: —

---

59 Blavatsky states here that they are 'Called by Christian theology: Archangels, Seraphs, etc., etc.' However they are also liberated Buddhas, Initiates of the sixth degree and greater. In our literature the term is simplified to Chohan.

60 In terms of the above philosophy these three Logoi can be considered to be Brahman as the first Logos, Nārāyaṇa (taking the form of Īśvara) then becomes the second Logos, with Māyā and Mahat, integrated as the feminised form of Brahman, Brahmā as the third Logos. (Cosmic Intelligence emanating from the 'naval', Solar Plexus centre, of Viṣṇu, floating upon the Waters of Space.) This third Logos then reflects the expression of the qualities of the three Logoi via the cosmic Egg (Hiraṇyagarbha, a form of Brahmā) as the *trimūrti*: Śiva, Viṣṇu, and Brahmā. Via them the rest of the manifested universe springs.

(b.) The Eternity of the Universe *in toto* as a boundless plane; periodically "the playground of numberless Universes incessantly manifesting and disappearing," called "the manifesting stars," and the "sparks of Eternity." "The Eternity of the Pilgrim"[61] is like a wink of the Eye of Self-Existence (Book of Dzyan.) "The appearance and disappearance of Worlds is like a regular tidal ebb of flux and reflux." (See Part II., "Days and Nights of Brahmâ.")

This second assertion of the Secret Doctrine is the absolute universality of that law of periodicity, of flux and reflux, ebb and flow, which physical science has observed and recorded in all departments of nature. An alternation such as that of Day and Night, Life and Death, Sleeping and Waking, is a fact so common, so perfectly universal and without exception, that it is easy to comprehend that in it we see one of the absolutely fundamental laws of the universe.

Moreover, the Secret Doctrine teaches: —

(c) The fundamental identity of all Souls with the Universal Over-Soul, the latter being itself an aspect of the Unknown Root; and the obligatory pilgrimage for every Soul — a spark of the former — through the Cycle of Incarnation (or "Necessity") in accordance with Cyclic and Karmic law, during the whole term. In other words, no purely spiritual Buddhi (divine Soul) can have an independent (conscious) existence before the spark which issued from the pure Essence of the Universal Sixth principle, — or the OVER-SOUL, — has (a) passed through every elemental form of the phenomenal world of that Manvantara, and (b) acquired individuality, first by natural impulse, and then by self-induced and self-devised efforts (checked by its Karma), thus ascending through all the degrees of intelligence, from the lowest to the highest Manas, from mineral and plant, up to the holiest archangel (Dhyani-Buddha). The pivotal doctrine of the Esoteric philosophy admits no privileges or special gifts in man, save those won by his

61 Here Blavatsky gives a footnote: '"Pilgrim" is the appellation given to our Monad (the two in one) during its cycle of incarnations. It is the only immortal and eternal principle in us, being an indivisible part of the integral whole — the Universal Spirit, from which it emanates, and into which it is absorbed at the end of the cycle. When it is said to emanate from the one spirit, an awkward and incorrect expression has to be used, for lack of appropriate words in English. The Vedantins call it Sutratma (Thread-Soul), but their explanation, too, differs somewhat from that of the occultists; to explain which difference, however, is left to the Vedantins themselves.'

own Ego through personal effort and merit throughout a long series of metempsychoses and reincarnations. This is why the Hindus say that the Universe is Brahma and Brahmâ, for Brahma is in every atom of the universe, the six principles in Nature being all the outcome — the variously differentiated aspects — of the SEVENTH and ONE, the only reality in the Universe whether Cosmical or micro-cosmical; and also why the permutations (psychic, spiritual and physical), on the plane of manifestation and form, of the sixth (Brahmâ the vehicle of Brahma) are viewed by metaphysical antiphrasis as illusive and Mayavic. For although the root of every atom individually and of every form collectively, is that seventh principle or the one Reality, still, in its manifested phenomenal and temporary appearance, it is no better than an evanescent illusion of our senses. (See, for clearer definition, Addendum "Gods, Monads and Atoms," and also "Theophania," "Bodhisatvas and Reincarnation," etc., etc.)

In its absoluteness, the One Principle under its two aspects (of Parabrahmam and Mulaprakriti) is sexless, unconditioned and eternal. Its periodical (manvantaric) emanation — or primal radiation — is also One, androgynous and phenomenally finite. When the radiation radiates in its turn, all its radiations are also androgynous, to become male and female principles in their lower aspects. After Pralaya, whether the great or the minor Pralaya (the latter leaving the worlds in *statu quo*[62]*)*, the first that re-awakes to active life is the plastic A'kâs'a, Father-Mother, the Spirit and Soul of Ether, or the plane on the surface of the Circle. Space is called the "Mother" before its Cosmic activity, and Father-Mother at the first stage of re-awakening. [63]

A *fourth postulate (or proposition)* can now be provided, which concerns the principle of evolution out of matter, the appearance of the middle principle, *consciousness,* and its PURPOSE, via which all forms struggle to escape from the bondage that life in form

62 Here Blavatsky's footnote states: 'It is not the physical organisms that remain in statu quo, least of all their psychical principles, during the great Cosmic or even Solar pralayas, but only their Akâsic or astral "photographs." But during the minor pralayas, once over-taken by the "Night," the planets remain intact, though dead, as a huge animal, caught and embedded in the polar ice, remains the same for ages'.

63 Ibid., Vol. I, 15-18. See also the Introductory postulates form Bailey's *A Treatise on Cosmic Fire*, 3 – 7.

signifies. This ensues the liberation of consciousness and its eventual abstraction into the Void that is the plenitude. By struggling with its attachment to matter (*mūlaprakṛti)* that has been incorporated as its base expression, consciousness transforms and then transmutes that originating substance into superconsciousness. This lucid state of conscious awareness then liberates itself totally from what formerly was (the attainment of *śūnyatā),* and hence awakens to the experience of Parabrahman. Brahman (in the form of Īśvara) and the sum of the causative forces that originally integrated *mūlaprakṛti* into a form now come into view. The transcended (enlightened, liberated) Consciousness can then travel upon the pathways of the creative forces back to the Source (a Logos), bringing with it the gain of the experiences gained through the transformation of its quota of *mūlaprakṛti.* The *gain* is the integration of transformed *mūlaprakṛti* with Brahman, so that the two become one in the appearance of the Dhyāni Buddha (Buddha of Meditation), rather than facing each other (as in the opening statement of the Book of Genesis, where 'the Spirit of God moved upon the face of the waters'.[64]) The returning *nirvāṇees* bring the future to the past, by transforming it upon a higher cycle of expression, and so the serpent of time consumes itself with the gain of its movement through space. The serpent thus spirals ever upwards into increasingly higher, more refined dimensions of space, whilst that serpent evolves into a Dragon of Wisdom.

Oṁ

64 *Genesis 1:1.*

2

The Numerological Key

General introduction

The *numerical code* that is used for esoteric texts written by enlightened beings in the English language is based on the alphabet, to which there are 26 letters, each letter having a numerical correspondence. It was first formulated under the auspices of Francis Bacon[1] in relation to work on the translation of the 1611, authorised King James version of the Bible. Obviously as the language changed over time, so also the numerological system was modified, allowing it to be expressed in the way it stands today, utilising modern grammatically correct English.

We thus have:

1	2	3	4	5	6	7	8	9
A	B	C	D	E	F	G	H	I
J	K	L	M	N	O	P	Q	R
S	T	U	V	W	X	Y	Z	

Many key phrases and the Old Commentaries, for instance, presented by D.K.'s books are always numerically coded, and he has throughout his books hinted at this coding. Any genuine communication from the Masters are generally similarly coded. The coding is one way to distinguish a communication from a genuine Master from an imposter

1 He later became the Count of St Germain, and Rakoczi as the Mahāchohan.

(of which there are many), always willing to beguile a desire-filled aspirant. Genuine communications are generally quite terse, and often enigmatic, as are the *Stanzas of Dzyan* for instance, hence veil many more levels of meaning via this means than what can be analysed by interpreting the words alone. Such communications are only given to advanced students when they are under direct instructions from a Master, or to a group undergoing group Initiation processes with view of group testings. The Masters are extremely prudent, but compassionate, and hence only present pertinent, timely instructions in this fashion. The gullible, spiritually foolish, the devotionally desirous, those ensconced in opinion of 'I', thus focussed upon themselves as the centre of their world, are not so instructed. The teachings come only in relation to those that have offered themselves genuinely for world service, and are part of a group in training to thus serve, in line with the laws of group evolution. These laws were introduced in D.K.'s books and elaborated in volumes 6 and 7 of my *Treatise on Mind* series.

Words can easily form in the mental bodies of disciples that are desirous of 'communications', taken from the disciple's own thought-field, their own desire-minds, or wafted into the mind from the general mental environment of humanity. Also there are many astral imposters posing as Masters feeding nice sounding words, but spiritually trite, often platitudes and erroneous. Sometimes there is a mixture of sources, where some information may be genuinely from an enlightened being, but aspects are often intercepted by members of the dark brotherhood, thus changing the entire meaning or tone of the communication. Interceptions are especially dangerous. Hence the Hierarchical amanuensis, such as were Alice Bailey and Mme Blavatsky, had to be trained appropriately to ensure that what was telepathically received was accurate. Others, the channelers, are not so trained, and are astrally focussed, or else astral-mental, in which case the 'communications' are invariably of the intercepted variety, with oft many nice general level spiritual platitudes to sweeten the tone for the gullible. There is however rarely any real content of true in-depth esoteric meaning. They may serve the aspirants and low level disciples, but not those upon the Initiation path. The coded brevity and multi-levelled meanings of the Master's words are missing.

The 'channelers' feed glamour and spiritual desire for sensationalised esoteric or occult knowledge. They often are aimed at placating or vibrantly stimulating the emotions of some personality or the group in question. Exhilarated emotions may make aspirants happy, but the Master's are more interested in bringing to the surface hidden faults needing working upon and eliminating altogether out from the psyche. Channeled information may and often do speak of the Christ or other lofty beings, or are purported to come from the great Ones, but are rarely, if ever, so. *Beware of long-winded utterances* designed to make people 'feel good'. The Masters *never* feed the emotions or subtle glamour. The development of the mind and awakening the attributes of the abstract Mind by way of the evocation of group evolution is their *modus operandi*. Do not be fooled by the channelers or by mediumistic utterances. The Masters focus upon the need of the hour in relation to the ways of group Initiation, and if instructions are to be given to a wider audience, then the numerological coding is normally applied. Within the instructions the esoteric lore, as presented in my works, D.K.'s, Blavatsky's, and Helena Roerich, is always evident. Without this foundation in the communication then what is provided is suspect. Every word is carefully weighed by a Master to provide the precise meaning intended. They are skilled word-smiths and waste not their thoughts in careless suggestions and thought-projections. With their telepathic instructions come the associated images needed for appropriate interpretation of the communication.

In the coding each number veils a type of force associated with the qualities of the number. The number can be considered to be the central life (or Monad) to its component parts (if it is greater than 1). It can be viewed as a unit which is inclusive of a number of individual members constituting that unity (unless the number is 1 or 0). The number 6 for instance is 2 x 3 and thus has veiled within it attributes of the second and third Rays. In this number system we are concerned with positive whole numbers, the cypher zero, and often the associated symbolism associated with a particular number. For example, the number 8 symbolises the concept of infinity, or of spiral-cyclic motion leading to infinity.

A compound number (a number greater than the number 9) is also considered to be the product of its component parts and can be analysed accordingly. For instance, the number 23, which has no direct numerological significance on its own, has two numerals, the number 2 (or 20) and the number 3, and in such a case the sum of these numerals (the number 5) is part of the analysis.

Sometimes a number, such as the number 12, can also be regarded as the sum or product of other numbers, e.g., 7 + 5 = 12, where the numbers seven and five constitute a special consideration of the overall number twelve. In this case we have the significance of the seven sacred planets and the five non-sacred ones, or the seven Rays and the five *prāṇas* or Elements, the seven sacred petals, and five non-sacred petals, to the Heart centre. Obviously a large amount of esoteric knowledge is a precondition to properly interpret each number. There is also the product 3 x 4 = 12, which relates to the four quadrants of three petals (each oriented to the four cardinal directions) of the Heart centre, or of the twelve signs of the zodiac, to which the number 12 also refers. We also have 2 x 6 = 12, which refers to two basic hemispheres of this lotus, orientated in either the north-south direction or the east-west direction, or else we have the six polar opposites of the zodiac. These products are a major component of the numerological consideration.

The simple mathematical rule that addition and multiplication are commutative in that the sum or product of two numbers is the same in whatever order they are added or multiplied, are obviously factors in this system of numerology. The other rules such as multiplication and addition are both associative and that multiplication is distributive with respect to addition can also be used.

The number to be analysed can theoretically be placed on the cross and 'crucified' for analysis. The direction *north* represents the whole number of a word, giving us the fundamental integral quality of any word we are analysing. Here we can also analyse any key components of the individual numbers of the word. For instance, the numbers of the word 'will' add to 20, signifying the expression of the second Ray energies of Love-Wisdom, however all of the component numbers of the word are along the third Ray line (5. 9. 3. 3.). Here the dictionary meaning of the word will is paramount, whilst the number 20 indicates the close relation between the first and second Ray lines, with the third Ray attributes indicating that which the will acts upon or qualities to be generated. However the numbers of individual words are rarely analysed by themselves, unless there is some specific significance there, such as three ones, exemplifying the force or will attribute of the word in consideration. The numbers but provide added insight into the meaning of a word, phrase, or sentence under consideration. The basic interpretation is therefore the dictionary definition, supplemented by the esoteric considerations.

The numerical interpretation is specifically concerned with the combination of words constituting the meaningful phrases of a sentence. In the analysis commas, colons and semicolons are regarded as the end of a numerological statement. The numbers of the sentence as a whole are thus only added when such entities do not exist. This represents the *western* direction of outwards into the field of service. For instance, the numbers of the phrase 'the will' add to 35 (7 x 5), 8, implying that 'the will' in question manifests via the five Rays of Mind, projecting the forces of mind, specifically of the abstract Mind (being the fifth sub-plane of the mind/Mind), via forward progressive spiral-cyclic energies (8). Here we see that the focus of the interpretation (the direction *east* into the Heart of Life) concerns the way that the numbers can be divided (7 x 5). Finally the addition of the individual numbers (3 + 5 = 8) provides supplementary information, here of the mode of manifestation of this will energy via spiral-cyclic motion. Here the direction *south* is implicated, the most confined or limited mode of interpretation. Sometimes this direction is the best that can be derived from the interpretation of a particular phrase, in the absence of any meaningful divisible components of the larger number in question. For instance the number 19 has no specific numerological significance, hence the numbers 1 + 9 must be added = 10, thus the interpretation relates to that which tends towards or produces perfection.

The meanings ascribed to each number, as obtained from its relationship to the presented esoteric philosophy, finds its basis in the results of the numerical and geometric considerations of esoteric geometry. This geometry is an extension of the *maṇḍalas* derived from a consideration of the *chakras,* as was shown in volumes 4 and 5A of *A Treatise on Mind.* These volumes, plus volume 7A and 7B contain significant numerological information, which can be found via their indexes. Further significant numerological deductions from cosmological considerations, as provided in the esoteric lore, will be revealed in *The Secret Doctrine.* Pertinent compilations can be made by an earnest student of numerological correlations found in key phrases derived from that lore as they work to interpret genuine numerological writings of the Masters. Such information will assist the students to derive further meaning in later decoding work. The basic more important meanings of the numbers are given in the list presented below, which the earnest student can build upon. More meanings can be added to the list as they are discovered.

In the analysis of the numbers to any phrase the basic meaning of the number as a whole is first analysed, followed by the implications of what it is divisible by, which might be called its 'Soul expression', and then the implications when the numbers are added. Generally the most important deductions from the numbers are discussed and the remainder either omitted because being self-evident, or curtly discussed as secondary indicators, to prevent the tedium of undue repetition.

In numbers greater than 100 we look first to the significance of the hundreds unit, as this gives us the major determinant of the number, e.g., the number 200 refers to a major second Ray cycle or Ray dispensation, the number 300 a major third Ray cycle or Ray dispensation. We then have the remaining two numbers to consider, such as the number 49 of the number 249, which then is interpreted in the usual way, thus 49 = 7 x 7, and in this case within the context of the meaning of the number 200. We can also look to see if the number is divisible. The number 249 is divisible by 3 x 83, which has no specific interpretable meaning, hence is discounted. Finally one needs to analyse the subsidiary interpretation of the numbers added together, thus 2 + 4 + 9 = 15 = 3 x 5. This final addition can be dispensed with as trivial, if the main number has factors, which in this case is the number 7 x 7. This number can relate to the Rays and subrays, Races and sub-Races, the planes and sub-planes, etc., depending upon the context of the overall meaning of the phrase in question. If the overall number has no factors then the numerals added together must be taken into account.

If the number is divisible, such as the number 242 = 121 x 2 = 11 x 11 x 2, then we must analyse the most important factors. In this case it is 11 x 11 x 2. This is interpretable as the reflection (2) into manifestation of the *nāḍī* system (11) of Deity (11 x 11). Hence the complete *nāḍī* system of the integrated greater and lesser bodies of manifestation must be countenanced. (Because of the number 200 the focus would normally be upon a the body of manifestation of a Logos.) Alternatively one could think in terms of the reflection from Deity into manifestation of intensified first Ray energies (11 x 11) through the sum of the *nāḍīs*. Here the number 11 x 11 x 2 is primary to the secondary consideration of 242 = 200 + 6 x 7, which relates to the appearance of the manifest form (6 x 7). The reflection of the *nāḍī* system into the appearing form is the major numerological significant point made. One can also consider that there are consciousness-links *(antaḥkaraṇas,* also symbolised by the number 11) within that form that integrate its various aspects within the appearance of a major second Ray cycle (200) that reflects the energies of the greater *nāḍī* system of Deity into that form. Here whether or not the interpretation relates to such a cycle depends upon the context of the words the number is derived from.

In practice only the most obvious component parts of large numbers such as the number 102 = 100 + 2 (the second Ray dispensation of a major cycle of expression, the number 100) provides the most useful esoteric information. The most obvious divisors of a number thus give us more esoteric information concerning the intended meaning of the word or phrase that we are interpreting than when the numerals are added. The number 102 for instance = 51 x 2 = 17 x 6, which signifies the Desire principle (6) of a Logos (17). Such a principle is in fact but the expression of the energy of Love into manifestation, because such a Logoic Desire is Divine Love. (Hence it has a similar meaning to the number 102.) According to the actual wording of the phrase in question one would then choose which of the different renderings of the numerology are most applicable.

Though the above may be somewhat complicated to the reader, how the system works will become clearer when the numerological analysis is read. The various meanings given to the numbers will be explained as the appropriate sections of the writings dealing with the numerological interpretation is read. In the later chapters I shall use a more streamlined approach, overriding the relative cumbersome, tedious nature of treating every trivial number for the phrases. This will make the account more readable.

The interpretation of the numbers always depends upon the context of the word, phrase or sentence in which they are found. This provides us with the specific angle of vision to interpret and what quality associated with the number is to be emphasised, or is most relevant. For instance, the viewpoint may be from the angle of the evolution of the various Races of humanity, to the particular Ray energies that are involved, to Planetary evolution, a Monadic or cosmic perspective, or from the angle of the struggling personality in *saṃsāra*.

It should be noted that the word 'and' appearing after commas, colons and semicolons is generally not included in the numerological discussion, because it is a bridging term. If it appears in the middle of a phrase then it is counted. If a number appears twice in a row, but more specifically three times consecutively then it has special significance. For instance, the number 7.7. is a shorthand version of the number 777 (meaning 'the 777 incarnations' and its ramifications). The number 7.7. also exemplifies seventh Ray purpose, the expression of all septenaries and their cycles of activity. If a number appears twice in a row then discretion should be used as to if it is needed for the interpretation.

The information concerning symbols in *A Treatise on Cosmic Fire* is useful here, as everything we are trying to interpret is symbolic in nature:

1. *Symbols are intended for: —*

    a. The little evolved. They teach great truths in a simple form.

    b. The bulk of humanity. They preserve truth intact and embody cosmic facts.

    c. The pupils of the Masters. They develop intuition.

2. *Symbolic books in the Master's archives used for instruction.* These books are interpreted: —

    a. By their colour.

    b. By their position, i.e. above, on and beneath a line.

    c. By their connection with each other.

d. By their key. One page may be read four ways: —

1. From above downwards involution.
2. From beneath upwards evolution.
3. Right to left greater cycles, etc.
4. Left to right lesser cycles.

3. *The three keys:* —

1. Cosmic interpretation. The symbols standing for cosmic facts, i.e., Darkness. Light. The cross. The triangle.

2. Systemic interpretation. Dealing with evolution of system and all therein.

3. Human interpretation. Dealing with man himself. The cross of humanity. Seven-branched candlestick.

4. *Four kinds of symbols:* —

1. Symbols of extraneous objects	physical plane things.
2. Symbols of emotional nature	astral plane things; pictures.
3. Numerical symbolism	Lower mental. Man used himself to count by.
4. Geometrical symbolism	abstract symbolism, higher mental.[2]

Below is a list of the main numbers that have definite meanings assigned to them.

The Basic Meaning of the Numbers

The numbers 1 – 12 can be briefly explained. The numbers 1 – 7 relate to the seven Ray qualities, planes of perception, Rounds, Schemes, etc. in their numerical order. Thus the number four can refer to the fourth Ray, Round, Racial cycle (the Atlantean), globe, Scheme, etc., depending upon the context of the phrase being analysed. The number

2 Alice Bailey, T.C.F., 1140.

8 refers to the spiral-cyclic energies that interrelate and energise the seven, driving their qualities onwards via repetitive cycles of expression (incarnations). The number 9 relates to the process of Initiation into the mysteries of the sum of the implications of everything implied here (by way of praxis and meditation). The multiples of nine indicate the level of Initiation implied. Hence 18 = 2 x 9 implicates the second Initiation. The number 10 refers to evolutionary perfection or mastery of anything, the ending of a cycle. The number 11 refers to adeptship, the complete expression of that mastery as practical application. It also relates to the *nāḍī* system, or to the projection of the *antaḥkaraṇa,* normally upwards (or the *sūtrātmā* downwards). The number 12 refers to the awakening of the petals of the Heart centre, thus it represents the way of compassionate activity, from whence enlightenment (*bodhicitta*) ensues. The permutations of this number relate to the signs of the zodiac, or to one or other of the twelve Creative Hierarchies. Thus 24 = 2 x 12 refers to the second sign of the zodiac, Taurus the bull, or to the second Creative Hierarchy, counted from either from below upwards, or from above down, depending upon context in the text.

Obviously some proficiency in comprehension of the basic tenets of the esoteric doctrine needs to be gained before one can properly utilise the numerical coding.

- **Hundreds and thousands** always refer to large scale events, large cycles, be they planetary or solar, for example a 250,000 year great astrological cycle, to things pertaining to Monadic or cosmic levels. They can also refer to that pertaining to the appearance of *pralaya.*
- **Decades (10-100)** have many meanings depending upon the number. They bring one's focus to an individual theme.
- **Units (1-10)**, generally refer to a specific Ray, depending upon the number. The seven Rays can also be symbolised by the number 7, as well as the septenaries in Nature. The numbers can refer to things pertaining to personality evolution, if our angle of vision is from below up. They can also refer to what pertains to Deity, if interpretation is from above to down. All numbers can be numerologically reduced to units and therefore the meanings associated with them is basic to any interpretation, and are normally disregarded as trivial.

The meanings to specific numbers can now be presented. The list is not exhaustive. More meanings to the numbers will be gleaned when the esoteric texts are analysed.

1 This relates to the beginning of all things; to the first Ray of Will or Power, to what is first or primordial. It can refer to the projection of an *antaḥkaraṇa.*

1, 2, 3 The numbers 1 – 3, as well as referring to the first, second and third Rays, represent the trinity in manifestation: Father, Son, Mother, or to the first three stages of the evolutionary process.

2 The second Ray of Love-Wisdom. The second Person of the Trinity. It relates also to the Son in manifestation, and occasionally to the second plane of perception, *anupādaka.* This Ray can also veil the energies of Jupiter.

3 The third Ray of Mathematically Exact Activity. The third Person of the trinity. It is the basic number for the Mother's department upon any system, of any of the various triads in Nature. Saturn, the lord of *karma* might be implied.

4 The fourth Ray of Harmony overcoming Strife. Occasionally it relates to the *buddhic* plane and to the Airy Element. It symbolises the fourth principle in nature; the quaternary of *buddhi, manas,* the astral and dense physical plane. It also refers to what is material in nature, the four concrete mental sub-planes for instance, to the square of manifestation. It may refer to the 'four Beasts' supporting the throne of God, the 'four corners of the Universe', the four Lipika Lords, etc. It is a number also relating to the fourth kingdom of Nature, humanity. Mercury, the planetary ruler governing the fourth Ray might be implied.

5 The fifth Ray of Science, governing the expression of the mind in general, and of the Element Fire. This number, and its permutations, has many relationships. We have the nature of Brahmā (who had five 'mind-born' Sons, the Kumāras), the five senses, the five instincts, the five organs of action as well as those of sensation, the five *prāṇas*, the five *chakras* (esoterically understood), the wisdoms associated with the five Dhyāni Buddhas, the pentagram, and the five races of humanity

so far developed (especially the present Aryan Root Race). It sums up the empirical or intellectual attainment of humanity or 'God'. The energies of the five *vayus*. Venus, the ruler of the fifth Ray could be implied.

6 The sixth Ray of Devotion-Aspiration, all of the qualities associated with the hexagram, and with the expression of the desire principle that underlies emotional phenomena, as well as to the forces of Nature. It can refer to the driving energies or forces impelling thoughts to their conclusion, to be clothed in formed substance. It can symbolise the astral plane and the Element Water. Also Mars, governing the sixth Ray, and Neptune, as the god of the Waters might be implied.

7 The seventh Ray of Ceremonial Aptitude, of Magic and of Material Power. Generally also relates to any of the septenaries in Nature. There are thus the seven Races, seven *chakras*, seven planetary Schemes, seven planes of perception, etc., governing evolutionary space. Occasionally it relates to the dense physical plane, the Element Earth. Uranus, governing the energies of the seventh Ray might be implied.

8 This number indicates the nature of the evolution of the Christ-consciousness (Love-Wisdom) by means of the expression of spiral-cyclic motion which awakens the petals of the various *chakras*.

9 The number of the first Initiation, the birth into the cave of the Heart. It can also refer to the Initiation process generally. The multiples of this number indicates the level of Initiation implied.

10 This is the number of perfection, of completion, the end attainment of evolution. It also signifies the first differentiation of the Creative process and the projection of the *antaḥkaraṇa* to fulfil the creative purpose, expressed thus: ⦶.

Also the entire etheric body, with its intricate *nāḍī* system can be implied, but the number 11 more specifically relates to this. The vertical line represents the central spinal column (symbolising the three-fold chord of *iḍā, piṇgalā* and *suṣumṇā nāḍīs).* It is the masculine principle in application and can also refer to the *antaḥkaraṇa*. The sphere indicates the basic ovoid shape of all such beings (e.g., the human form viewed etherically), thus the totality of any body of manifestation.

100 The *great perfection,* thus the end of a major cycle of evolution e.g., of a planetary system or a great astrological year.

1000 Cycles associated with a solar evolution or what concerns an immense number of beings. It is irrelevant how many noughts follow the one. (Similarly if the first numeral is say a 2, which then shifts our focus to an immense number related to the second Ray dispensation.) Note that the Head centre has a symbolic number of 1,000 petals, thus this number can relate to its level of expression, and when related to the earth to the planetary Head centre, Shambhala.

11 10 + 1. The number of adeptship. (One who has perfectly mastered the expression the purpose of any Ray disposition colouring their Souls, via the development of the first Ray capabilities.) This concerns the attainment of the perfection associated with the number 10, then the ability to project purpose into manifest expression. Note that in this solar system the first Ray is *always* modified by the second Ray. (The number 2.) The number also relates to the *nāḍī* system. In the form of the number 11 x 11 the complete vivification of the *nāḍīs* is implied. The number also symbolises the projection of the *antaḥkaraṇa* in any of the directions of space, according to the wording of the phrase being interpreted. The *antaḥkaraṇa* utilises the *nāḍīs* in its approach from here to there.

12 Signifies the signs of the zodiac in general, and to the first sign (Aries) in particular. Also relates to the twelve Creative Hierarchies, or specifically to the first Creative Hierarchy. It is the number of the major petals to the Heart centre, which it thus specifically symbolises, and of which the twelve signs of the zodiac are expressions. Multiples of 12 relate to the twelve signs of the zodiac according to the number of its divisor, e.g., 60 = 5 x 12, hence referring to the fifth sign, Leo the lion.

13 Numbers that are not divisible by other numbers often have a special significance of their own. The number 13 for instance has a special reference to the moon and moon Chain happenings. There

are 13 lunar months to one year of 12 solar months. The number 13 is also 1/4 of the number 52 (= 13 x 4), the number of weeks to a year, and therefore can occasionally be interpreted to mean the first season or quadrant of a new year (spring) or zodiacal cycle. This number normally refers to a sphere (the number 12) with the central dot added, thus to a sphere of activity.

14 **2 x 7**. Refers to the second Root Race, and the second (astral) plane of perception, cosmically or systemically (meaning within our solar system).

15 **3 x 5**. The empirical mind, intelligence and its activities via the domain of mind. It can also refer to *kāma-manas,* the emotional or desire-mind of any incarnate personality, as most people think emotionally. This number can signify the Lords of Flame, (though very rarely), as they manifest in groups of 15 (7 x 15 = 105). Such Lords are effectively Masters of Wisdom, esoterically called 'fivefold points of light', and embody the energies of the pentagram (or of Brahmā) in terms of the three major levels of expression (Monadic, Causal, or concrete). Each point can be considered triune, making the number of energies that the Master perfectly embodies and expresses. The usual interpretation however relates to the empirical mind.

16 **2 x 8**. Note that 16 = 2 x 2 x 2 x 2 (2^4), the foundation or base enthroning the second Ray of Love-Wisdom, allowing its complete expression in manifest space. Thus this number signifies the Power of the Christ, the Master of Masters, on the second Ray line. It can also refer to the Throat centre, to which there are 16 petals, if the phrase indicates that this is the focus of interpretation, however the major interpretation is that of the Christ principle.

17 This number has the distinction to be the sum of the numbers of the word 'God,' and can be interpreted accordingly, as referring to Deity. It is one number past the number 16 that signifies the Christ, hence can be considered to signify his 'Father'. This number can also be considered in terms of the potency of the five Dhyāni Buddhas manifesting through each of the twelve main petals of the Head lotus in turn, taking each of these

petals to represent one turning of the zodiacal wheel, hence the demonstration of the potency of one or other of the signs of the zodiac. In effect this summarises the expression of 'God' in this solar system. See also T.C.F.: 'the forty-nine groups of solar fires concerned in the great work are those spoken of, and they become the forty-nine Planetary Logoi...In them is hid the mystery of the three who become the sixteen—united or synthesised by the seventeenth'.[3]

18 **2 x 9**. Signifies the second Initiation, the Baptism. Can also refer to the nine-headed Hydra in its two division of right and left hand *prāṇas* or heads.

101 **100 + 1**. Basically similar meaning as the number 11, but the effects are on a more universal scale: the end of one major cycle of evolution (the number 100) and the beginning of another, associated with the number 1 (the first Ray). It can be expressed as the projection of the *sūtrātmā* from the highest to the lowest aspect of manifest life (100 + 1). The 0 of the number 101 interrelates the two ones, signified by what is above and below the cypher zero thus:

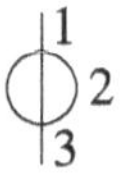

The number 1 relates to what is projected from the kingdom of God (Shambhala). 2 refers to the cipher zero, here the cycle of manifestation of a world sphere from the *pralaya* condition and the process of its awakening, producing all of its ramifications. The line through the sphere is the *sūtrātmā,* interrelating what is above to the below, and *vice versa*. (The *sūtrātmā* then becomes the *antaḥkaraṇa,* after manifesting in the form of the *nāḍī* system.) 3 refers to what is projected downwards into the realms of activity, the ephemeral domains *(saṃsāra).*

102 The emanation of the second Ray of Love-Wisdom on a higher (Shambhalic) level than normally considered.

3 Alice Bailey, T.C.F., 879.

103 The emanation of the third Ray from a Shambhalic level, or of the divine Activity of the Mother, that pertaining to the *deva* kingdom.

104 Normally the number pertains to the fourth kingdom (and Creative Hierarchy) in Nature, the human. It can therefore refer to a member of cosmic Humanity. It can also refer to the emanation of the fourth Ray from the Shambhalic level, but is a minor consideration. Similar to the number 40 this number can symbolise the function of a mirror reflecting the principles of the abstract Logos into manifestation. This number is sometimes taken as 52 x 2, which refers to the duration of the great cosmological years *(manvantaras)* within a *mahāmanvantara.*

105 The number of the 'Lords of Flame' that came with Sanat Kumāra at the time of the Individualisation of humanity to establish Shambhala. Together they make the 105 Kumāras informing a Logoic Head Lotus and its empowerment. The demonstration of the energy of Mind into the planetary manifestation. 105 = 3 x 35, 7 x 15 are numbers relating to the expression of the Lords of Flame in the disposition of a Head centre. This centre is explained in volume 5A of *A Treatise on Mind.*

106 The energy of Logoic Desire. The sixth Ray expression cosmically.

107 The ending of one large cycle of evolution and the beginning of another one associated with the number 7: the 7 planes, the 7 planetary cycles and Regents, the seven Rays, etc.

108 **9 x 12**. This is a very important number for a number of reasons, e.g., it is the number of Kumāras to a Planetary Scheme (105) plus three for the abstract triune Deity. It therefore relates to the sum of the petals of a Head lotus. (A shortened version of the number 1080, explained in my book *An Esoteric Exposition of the Bardo Thödol*[4]*)*. It has other esoteric implications, such as being the number of *nāḍīs* below the diaphragm and similarly above it. The number is also interpreted as the ninth sign of the zodiac, Sagittarius, and also the corresponding Creative Hierarchy. It can signify the twelfth Initiation, here taken to

4 Balsys, *An Esoteric Exposition of the Bardo Thödol, Volume 5A*, 428.

be the degree of attainment of our solar Logos, the bearer of all the zodiacal energies to our solar system. It is a most sacred number in the Buddhist and Hindu religions.

109 Signifies the process of Initiation generally (the number 9) on a large scale, hence planetary Initiation.

110 **100 + 10**. The relation of one Logoic sphere (100) to a lesser sphere (10). Can signify the empowerment of a first Ray cycle, hence a new cycle of expression. When interpreted in terms of 11 x 10 has a similar meaning as the number 111, referring to the complete *nāḍī* system of a Logos.

111 **100 + 10 + 1**. The expression of first Ray energies on all three levels of Being. Will or power as it is expressed in:

> Shambhala—Father—Spirit, the number 100
> The Hierarchy—Son—Soul, the number 10
> Humanity—Mother—Matter, the number 1

Together they embody the trinity (the number 3) as the empowerment of the Will in any sphere of attainment, thus the manifestation of a major first Ray cycle, or else the projection of a new cycle of expression on all levels of being. Normally interpreted as the projection of the *sūtrātmā* (or *antaḥkaraṇa* from below up) from one Logoic sphere (100) to a lesser sphere (10). The Will to bring all forward, or to produce *pralaya*. Can refer to the complete *nāḍī* system (11) of an entity, which is but an extension of the *sūtrātmā,* but thought of in terms of an integrating whole with other such systems

112 **7 x 16**. The expression of the Christ's energies (16) on all seven planes of perception (x 7). Normally interpreted as the Ray Ashrams of Hierarchy. In the form of the number 100 + 12 it signifies the onset of a cycle of the dissemination of the energies of Love-Wisdom, of the awakening of the Heart centre.

120 **12 x 10, 5 x 24, 6 x 20**. Specifically the tenth sign of the zodiac, Capricorn and also the corresponding Creative Hierarchy. This is the mount of material plane *karma*. Also, the expression of zodiacal energies into the material form, the spiritualisation of the dense form. The number 12 x 10 also relates to the ten signed zodiac (effectively at the stage when a Logos manifests as a Solar Plexus centre). The divisors 5 x 24 and 6 x 20 have obscure meanings overruled by the significance of the rendering as the sign Capricorn.

121 **11 x 11**. The sum of the *nāḍī* system, the reticulation of lines of energies of the *nāḍīs,* thus also indicating the *prāṇic* vitalisation of any body of manifestation.

124 **31 x 4, 100 + 24**. The 100 + 24 relates to the expression of the sign Taurus the bull. Can signify a Throne or Seat of Power of a Logos (Shambhala), whereby the potency of the directed energy of the Will governing manifestation emanates.

125 **25 x 5, 5^3**. This number signifies that which incorporates the energies of cosmic Mind (or Mahat), thus that associated with the Mind of a Logos incarnated in a dense physical Body. The number can indicate the five liberated Hierarchies (25 x 5), the custodians of cosmic Mind for this solar system, or else the five Kumāras (Dhyāni Buddhas) associated with the expression of Mahat for a planetary system. The number 25 is that which en-Souls (the sum of the mental plane) through the dissemination of the principle of Mind— x 5: the five Beings that thus embody the five planes of Brahmā. The number 125 signifies the number of major and minor *chakras* incorporated within the *maṇḍala* of the Causal form empowering a Logoic Head centre (Shambhala), needed for the reception of Mahat. The number 5^3 refers to the three transmuted correspondences for the expression of the principle of Mind: cosmic, systemic and human.

128 **32 x 4, 2^7**. The establishment of the Seat of Power for the Christ principle, thus the power base of Hierarchy. Also, the Shambhalic or Logoic expression of Love-Wisdom. The number 2^7 relates to the manifestation of the second Ray to all seven planes of perception or the seven Ray Ashrams of Hierarchy.

130 **13 x 10**, signifies the central point and the circumference of a sphere of activity, thus this number refers to the Activity aspect of Deity, the Womb of the great Mother that governs the evolutionary impetus of all forms in Nature.

131 **100 + 31**. The emanation of the first Ray purpose by Deity.

132 **11 x 12**. The eleventh sign of the zodiac, Aquarius and also the corresponding Creative Hierarchy. Also the emanation of the second Ray purpose by Deity (100 + 32).

133 **100 + 33**. The emanation of the third Ray purpose by Deity. Also symbolises the Creative Intelligences in general.

135 **15 x 9, 45 x 3, 100 + 7 x 5**. The number 15 x 9 refers generally to the Lords of Flame, perfected Sons of Mind, who have been Initiated into the mysteries of cosmic Mind (Mahat). They are Masters (5 x 9) of the three levels of *dharmakāya*. The number 100 + 7 x 5 relates to the expression of Mahat into manifestation, which is the standard interpretation of the number 135.

144 **12 x 12, 6 x 24, 16 x 9**. The number 144 exemplifies all of the signs of the zodiac, and anything that is governed by the signs, thus the 144,000 of the tribes of the 'Children of Israel' (*Rev. Ch 7:4),* referring to a major way of categorising the kingdom of Souls, according to their zodiacal signs. The number can also refer to the twelve Creative Hierarchies. The number 16 x 9 indicates the Initiation process for the making of a cosmic Christ (via the repetitive turning of the Wheels of Life). The divisor 6 x 24 relates to the expression of cosmic Desire to turn the zodiacal Wheel via the Taurean impetus. (The meaning of the divisors 6 x 24 and 16 x 9 are rarely used in interpretations, they are simply implied.) The number 144 can also refer to the twelfth sign of the zodiac, Pisces and also the corresponding Creative Hierarchy.

150 **5 x 30, 10 x 15, 25 x 6, 50 x 3**. The most important consideration here is 3 x 50, referring to the expression of cosmic Mind (50) on the three major levels of expression, thus en-Souling the sum of formed (manifested) space. The complete perfection of the principle Mind, (10 x 15) e.g., the qualities of a planetary Logos, or a Lord of Shambhala, and of His entire Body of manifestation (the number 60). One can also consider the principle of Mind as it is expressed by a solar Logos.

151 **100 + 51 (17 x 3)**. A great cycle (100) of Activity (3) by Deity (17). Also, the activity of the third Logos = 17 x 3 (+ 100).

152 **100 + 52**. A major zodiacal cycle or epoch, a great year

(mahāmanvantara), or a Day of Brahmā. (The number 52 being the number of weeks to a year.)

155 **31 x 5, 100 + 55**. Bearers of the first Ray attributes from Shambhala (31) by way of cosmic Mind (5). Hence the number can refer to the five Dhyāni Buddhas (the five Kumāras). The number 100 + 55 relates to the expression of the energies of cosmic Mind *(dharmakāya)* at the level indicated by the phrase in question.

160 **10 x 16, 100 + 5 x 12**. The manifestation of the energies of the cosmic Christ (10 x 16). A great cycle for the dissemination of Leonine (solar) energies (100 + 5 x 12), the energisation of the fifth major petal of the Head centre.

165 **33 x 5**. The cycle of the activity of Mind on a vast scale. Thus effectively the activity of the *deva* kingdom, the (feminine) Consorts of the Dhyāni Buddhas. The effect of the work of the Creative Intelligences on the five planes of manifestation of Brahmā, or of the fifth Creative Hierarchy. The activity of the Mother's department.

166 **100 + 66**. The symbolism of the number 66 on a solar or cosmic scale.

175 **25 x 7**. The seven Ray Ashrams, or the seven Spirits before the Throne of God. That which governs the seven planes, or Rays of planetary manifestation by way of the expression of (cosmic) Mind.

180 **2 x 90**. The enactment of the planetary second Initiation, specifically for a Logos, hence planetary Initiation, or the cosmic second Initiation. The interpretation of the other factors of this number (3 x 60, 18 x 10, 5 x 36) are rarely if ever used.

20 **2 x 10**. The perfected expression of the second Ray of Love-Wisdom, which is the function of the Hierarchy of enlightened Being, thus this number symbolises the energies of that Hierarchy.

21 **3 x 7**. Generally it refers to the three densest planes of perception (the worlds of human livingness, mental, astral and physical). Can refer to the qualities of the spiritual triad (*ātma-buddhi-manas*). Can also refer to the third (Lemurian) Root Race.

22 **2 x 11, 10 + 12**. Generally taken to represent the manifestation of the 10 planetary plus 12 zodiacal energies into the world of form. Can also symbolise the second Ray purpose, or be taken to represent the kingdom of Souls (as distinct from the Hierarchy), who convey the planetary and zodiacal energies into manifestation. Hence this number can refer to the world Soul, the Womb of time and space from which all material forms and forces are moulded. This Womb can either relate to the macrocosm or else to microcosmic scale of events. The number also signifies the mastery of the second Ray energies (2 x 11) as an adept. D.K. also presents twenty-two methods of group interplay.[5] The number can be considered as a shorthand version of the number 222.

Esoteric Psychology I states:

> We study the seven ray Lives with their seven psychological types, and the twelve creative Hierarchies, as outlined for us in *The Secret Doctrine*. The 7 + 12 = 19, and if you add to these 19 expressions of the Life the 3 major aspects of Deity, which we call the life of God the Father, the love of God the Son, and the active intelligence of God the Holy Ghost, you arrive at the mystic number 22 which is called (in esotericism) the number of the adept.[6]

24 **2 x 12, 4 x 6**. The second sign of the zodiac (Taurus), and the corresponding Creative Hierarchy. The Bull drives the zodiacal wheel through its course in the heavens. Taurus is the Bull of Logoic Desire, carries the Pleiades on its back, as well as symbolising the function of the Ājñā centre. (Cosmically the Hyades star cluster, the forehead of the Bull.) The number also refers to the 'four and twenty Elders' of Ch. 4 of *The Revelation of St. John*. This refers to the basic *maṇḍala* upon which is derived the floral shape of the *chakras*. Note that the number 'four and twenty' is really 4 + 20, which gives a different arrangement of the number 24, one that provides a *maṇḍala* based upon the pentagram (4 + 4 x 5), rather than that of a hexagram (e.g., the number 24 = 4 x 6).

---

5 See T.C.F., 1222-23.

6 Alice Bailey, *Esoteric Psychology I*, 155.

25 **5 x 5**. The interpretation of this number is based on the fact that 25 = 5 x 5, where the number 5 refers to the fifth plane or Root Race, and the other 5 to the respective sub-plane or sub-Race. It can refer to the fifth sub-Race of the fifth Root Race (out of seven), to those who can fully use their minds. Often it is taken to refer to the Soul (Sambhogakāya Flower) residing on the fifth sub-plane of the mental (fifth plane). Thus it specifically refers to the plane of perception (the higher mental) whereon the Soul resides, and to the 'Clear Light' that the enlightened resides upon this causal or abstract mental plane. It can also relate to cosmic Mind (Mahat), or One who bears that principle.

27 **3 x 9**. Signifies the third Initiation, the Transfiguration, as well as the number associated with the Laws of Fire[7] wielded by the One who sits on the Throne (of God).

28 **7 x 4**. Refers to the fourth Root Race (the Atlantean), the fourth plane of perception (*buddhi*), to the ability of *buddhi* to relate the highest to the lowest. The number can refer to the sum of the quaternary—dense physical, etheric, astral and lower mental planes. It can also refer to the four planes of perception wherein a human Soul finds its expression—*buddhi, manas,* astral and dense, or else to the four cosmic, planetary or human ethers. It is also a number signifying the fourth Creative Hierarchy (humanity), or to a complete personality cycle.[8]

200 **2 x 100**. The great perfection of second Ray energies.

202 **200 + 2**. The perfected expression of the second Ray in a planetary system. plus a re-enactment of the second Ray cycle on a higher octave of expression.

222 **111 x 2, 200 + 20 + 2**. The perfected expression of the second Ray energy on all three levels of being (Monadic, Causal and concrete). The impetus of a major second Ray cycle into the planetary manifestation.

30 Divine activity, the forces of the Mother aspect of deity. The manifestation of the third Ray as it emanates from Shambhala.

---

7 See T.C.F., 427.

8 See Alice Bailey, *The Externalisation of the Hierarchy*, 112.

31 **30 + 1**. The energies of deity as a manifestation of the Will.

32 **4 x 8, 2 x 16**. The energy of deity as a manifestation of Love-Wisdom,[9] the Love aspect of Shambhala. Also, the ability of the Christ (the number 16) to act as a mediator (the number 2) of the cosmic Christ to the dense realms.

33 **30 + 3, 3 x 11**. The energy of deity as a manifestation of Activity. The third Ray potency as it emanates from Shambhala. There are said to be 330,000,000,000 Gods (Creative Intelligences) in the Hindu pantheon, the number of entities that can be considered to be intelligently active within the boundaries of a planetary Scheme. The number 33 signifies the energies of the Mother's department, where the Creative Intelligences can be considered Her *deva* agents. Often this number is interpreted as one or other of the Creative Hierarchies.

35 **7 x 5**. Refers to the fifth Root race (the Aryan), the fifth plane of perception (the mental), specifically the abstract Mind.

36 **4 x 9, 3 x 12**. Signifies the fourth Initiation, the Crucifixion-Renunciation. It generally also refers to the third sign of the zodiac, Gemini the twins, or the corresponding Creative Hierarchy. Gemini governs the *nāḍī* system, which is often an important significant of this number.

39 **13 x 3**. This number can refer to 3/4 of a zodiacal year, or cycle of evolution, to a full cycle of materialistic evolution before the onset of the second Ray cycle proper. The number normally relates to divine activity, the activity aspect of manifestation.

333 **3 x 111, 300 + 30 + 3**. The expression of the third Ray on all three levels of expression (Monadic, Causal, and personality), hence the major output of the third Ray cycle of the Mother. The first Outpouring. This number can refer to the flow or awakening of Logoic *kuṇḍalinī*.

40 **4 x 10**. This is the number of humanity, the fourth Creative Hierarchy. (They are the perfected expression of the quaternary, embodying the energies of *buddhi*.) It also signifies our particular

---

9 See also T.C.F., 1223, where D.K. states that there are 'thirty-two vibrations necessary to produce, as far as man is concerned, the five planes of evolution'.

planetary cycle, which is in its fourth Round, in fact to any perfected entity that embodies the quaternary or *buddhic* energies. The number also symbolises the function of a mirror that reflects the principles of the abstract Logos into manifestation.

42 **6 x 7**. Refers to the sixth Root Race, Round, or the sixth plane of perception (the astral), thus to the expression of the Waters, the desire/emotional principle in *saṃsāra*. It can refer to the energies of the planet Mars. It also signifies an expanded form of the Seal of Solomon, signifying the Son in incarnation, thus is a number concerned with general evolution in the material world, wherein the Desire of the Logos finds its fulfilment. The sixth Ray and its subrays can also be implicated.

44 **4 x 11**. The number symbolises adeptship or mastery of the processes associated with human evolution on all levels, the mastery of the fourth plane of perception, or the emanation of the fourth Ray cycle. It also refers to this particular incarnation of the solar Logos, as the solar system is said to be 'of the fourth order' in T.C.F. This number generally relates to a human kingdom, cosmic or systemic, being the fourth kingdom in Nature. It differs from the number 40, in that here we are concerned more specifically with all cycles of expression of the fourth Round, and specifically to our earth Scheme and globe, as this Scheme is the fourth in solar evolution.

45 **9 x 5**. Signifies the fifth Initiation, the Ascension/Revelation. It can also refer to the mode of action of the adepts of the black Hierarchy, as they are ruled by the number 5 of the mind, and are organised according to the constitution of the nine-headed Hydra.

48 **4 x 12**. The fourth sign of the zodiac, Cancer, and also the corresponding Creative Hierarchy. This represents the Doorway into incarnation, thus the start of a new cycle of endeavour for any perspective Logos or being.

49 **7 x 7**. Refers to the seventh Root Race, the seventh plane of perception (the dense physical), to the complete emanation of the seventh Ray. It also can refer to the totality of all planes of perception, Root Races, to all of the various septenaries

and their subdivisions associated with the various categories of manifest Life.

400 Any great cycle that concerns the perfection of the fourth principle in Nature.

444 **400 + 40 + 4**. Generally signifies cosmic Humanity, but can also signify the fourth Round and Scheme in our solar system. It refers to the Seat of Power upon which any member of cosmic Humanity sits, from which emanates the fourth kingdom in Nature.

50 **5 x 10, 5**. Perfection of the principle of *manas,* the expression of Fire on the mental plane, hence the demonstration of the abstract Mind *(dharmakāya).* Can refer to the fifth Creative Hierarchy, the *devas* that embody mind/Mind.

51 **17 x 3**. Refers to the activity aspect of Deity, the cycles actively manifesting within the body of a Logos, hence the means whereby divinity expresses itself in the formed realms. The active expression of the will of Deity into manifestation. Can refer to the third Logos.

52 **13 x 4**. The number of weeks to a year, thus any complete zodiacal cycle. The number 13 x 4 refers to the four quadrants of a *maṇḍala.* The number 52 generally refers to a great evolutionary cycle, a great year *(manvantara* or *mahāmanvantara).* Refer to page 792 T.C.F. for information concerning a 100 years of Brahmā, one year of Brahmā, one week of Brahmā etc. One year of Brahmā equals the period of seven Chains, where the seven planetary Schemes are concerned.

54 **6 x 9**. Signifies the sixth Initiation, the Decision. Also a reference to Monadic Life, because they are residents of the second plane of perception (the sixth from below up) *(anupādaka).* Initiates of the sixth degree are fully integrated with the Monad.

55 **5 x 11**. Complete mastery, the perfect expression of the fifth principle (*manas*, and the Fiery Element) on all levels of perception, hence the experience of the *dharmakāya* attained by a Master of Wisdom. It also signifies the fifth planetary Scheme (Venus) as well as the fundamental quality of the *deva* kingdom, as this kingdom is primarily Intelligence, whilst humanity is

primarily Love. It can refer to the energy of Mind as it emanates from Shambhala.

56 **7 x 8**. This number is concerned with the mode of vitalisation of a form (the seven planes of perception, seven *chakras*, etc.) by means of spiral-cyclic/*kuṇḍalinī* energies. There are seven types of spiral-cyclic energy.[10] Also the seven Ray energies. D.K. states that: 'The language of the prism, of which "the seven Mother colours have each seven sons," that is to say, forty-nine shades or "Sons" between the seven, which graduated tints are so many letters or alphabetical characters. The language of colour has, therefore, fifty-six letters for the Initiate. Of these letters each septenary is absorbed by the mother colour, as each of the seven mother colours is absorbed finally in the white ray, Divine Unity symbolised by these colours.'[11]

555 **500 + 50 +5**. The expression of *manas* on all three levels of expression:

a. The number 500, the secret of Fire on the Cosmic mental plane, to which the Lord of the World (Sanat Kumāra) is responsive. He is a Kumāra, whose symbol is the five pointed star, being the fruit of the type of evolution engendered in the past solar system when this fifth Ray quality was the object of evolution. This concerns the Shambhalic level of expression.
b. The number 50, the secret of Fire on the mental plane and that which rules the kingdom of Souls, the cells in the body of 'God'. This is the Hierarchical level of expression.
c. The number 5, the secret of Fire on the physical plane and its permutations as electricity and that cohesive force that holds atoms together, giving them a form. The level of expression associated with Humanity.

60 **6 x 10, 5 x 12**. This number principally refers to the fifth sign of the zodiac (Leo), the corresponding Creative Hierarchy, and petal of the Heart centre (5 x 12). Leo embodies self-consciousness,

---

10 See T.C.F., 1035-36.

11 See T.C.F., *fn*. 14, 1091.

pride, as well as the Soul in manifestation (the embodiment of the energies of the sun). The number can also concern the perfection, or perfected expression, of the principle of desire (6 x 10), the sixth Ray.

62 **31 x 2**. The projection, or reflection, of the first Ray energy of Deity into manifestation.

63 **7 x 9**. Signifies the seventh Initiation.

64 **8 x 8, 16 x 4, 32 x 2**. The perfected expression of the Christ energies into the four lower planes of perception, or the Logoic quaternary. It expresses Love-Wisdom (32) into manifestation. It also refers to the projection of spiral-cyclic energies (hence carrying the energies of Love-Wisdom) throughout the body of manifestation of any Being.

65 **13 x 5**. The complete cycle of expression for the manifestation of Mind within a planetary or solar system, or for a human unit. Literally the cycle for the activity of the energies of mind/Mind. Can refer to the five planes of Brahmā associated with the *karma* of *saṃsāric* manifestation.

66 **6 x 11**. The evolution or expression of the psychic (Watery) constitution in the material world and its mastery. Signifies the ramifications of the *maṇḍala* based on the hexagon, hence a number therefore signifying the incarnation of any being (via the empowerment of the Sacral centre). Usually taken as a shorthand form of the number 666.

666 **600 + 60 + 6, 18 = 2 x 9**. The number of the 'beast' which 'is the number of a man'.[12] This number signifies the entire creative and evolutionary period on all realms of perception, especially in relation to the making of humanity or of the incarnate form of a Logos. It deals with the Body of manifestation (hence a 'beast') of an entire Planetary evolution, its constitution and qualities, thus everything concerning the material and psychic manifestation of humanity and 'God'. (The ramifications of the *maṇḍala* based on the hexagon and the potency of the Sacral centre on the three main levels of expression.) The 6 + 6 + 6 interpretation refers to the mode of manifestation of the dark

---

12 *Rev 13:18.*

brotherhood, who are arranged in *maṇḍalic* groupings based on the number six. They embody the powers of Watery aspect of the nine-headed Hydra (18 = 2 x 3 x 3) in its two divisions of the right and left handed *nāḍīs*.

70 Generally signifies the septenaries in Nature (similar to the number 77). The demonstration of the seventh Ray purpose, especially as an emanation from Deity. This number can also relate to the seven incarnate Creative Hierarchies.

72 **9 x 8, 6 x 12**. Signifies the eighth Initiation. This is an important number for it symbolises the ideal age of the life span of a person, and therefore signifies that the Initiate has journeyed the complete gamut of the evolutionary process. Yogic texts generally state that there are 72,000 *nāḍīs* to the human body, though the number has some basis to truth, it is technically incorrect, as the actual number of *nāḍīs* is based on the number 96.[13] The number 72 also relates to the number of heartbeats per minute. The normal interpretation of 6 x 12 refers to the sixth sign in the zodiac (Virgo) and the corresponding Creative Hierarchy. This sign governs the evolution of the feminine (*deva*) principle in Nature, the embodiment of the forces of the Mother.

75 **25 x 3, 5 x 15**. The number 25 refers to that which en-Souls, thus to the levels of en-Soulment (the *anima mundi* or world Soul). The number 25 x 3 thus specifically implicates the three Buddhas of Activity, who en-Soul the three lower kingdoms of Nature. The number can also refer to the three planetary executives of Hierarchy: the Manu, Christ and the Mahāchohan. The number 25 x 3 can refer to the three *dharmakāyic* levels and therefore indicates a Master's subservience to the energies derived from cosmos. (Ultimately from the cosmic mental plane.) The number 15 x 5 can refer to a Lord of Flame or to the five Dhyāni Buddhas, though the number 85, or 25 x 5 is more appropriate for them. The symbolism can also refer to an adept of the dark brotherhood, having utterly mastered the vicissitudes of *manas*/Mahat, hence the potency of a sorcerer.

13 This subject is explained in detail in Volumes four and five of my *A Treatise on Mind* series.

77 **7 x 11**. The symbolic 777 incarnations undertaken by any Soul, human or Logoic to obtain evolutionary perfection.[14] Thus we have the perfection of the Rounds, globes, Chains, Schemes of evolution, and all of the septenaries of Nature associated with the awakening of the seven *chakras* in Nature. The number can also exemplify the outpouring of the seventh Ray purpose and the energy of transmutation.

80 **8 x 10, 16 x 5, 4 x 20**. The number 16 is a number signifying the conveyance of the Christ's energies, here via the five planes of Mind (*ātma, buddhi, manas,* astral, and dense). The Minds (5) that embody the Christ principle (16), literally the Masters of Wisdom, but more specifically this is a number that symbolises the Mahāchohan's department. The number 8 x 10 signifies the vitalisation of all of the *nāḍīs* associated with an incarnate being by means of spiral-cyclic energies, inevitably producing the foundation for the perfected embodiment of Love-Wisdom. The number 4 x 20 relates to the Seat of Power of this energy, thus for the Hierarchy of Love.

81 **9 x 9**. Signifies the ninth Initiation.

84 **7 x 12**. The seventh sign of the zodiac Libra, and the corresponding Creative Hierarchy.

85 **17 x 5**. The Minds (5) that embody the Sense-Consciousnesses of Deity (17), hence refers to the five Dhyāni Buddhas.

88 **8 x 11**. The perfected expression of *kuṇḍalinī*-spiral cyclic energies throughout the kingdoms of Nature, or in any body of manifestation. It also refers to the 88 visible constellations in the Body of THAT Logos. As the number 11 relates to the *nāḍī* system, so this number relates to the circulation of these energies *(prāṇas)* throughout the *nāḍīs* of any incarnate being, cosmic or systemic.

90 **9 x 10**. Signifies the tenth Initiation, here taken to be the degree of attainment the Logos of a sacred planet, a member of cosmic Humanity, rather than being of the cosmic animal kingdom.

---

14 See T.C.F., 306, 776, 825-26, 829-30.

93 **31 x 3**. The activity aspect of the Will energy emanated from Shambhala, the *antaḥkaraṇas* projected between such centres, or into manifestation. This energy drives forward Logoic Purpose.

95 Signifies the period that stands between Initiation (90) and evolutionary perfection (100). Therefore it refers to what is evolving towards perfection (enlightenment), the conditionings pertaining to *saṃsāra*.

96 **8 x 12**. The eighth sign of the zodiac (Scorpio) and also the corresponding Creative Hierarchy. This number is important also because it represents the actual number of minor petals to any tier of petals of a major *chakra*. Thus it represents the number associated with the petals of a *chakra* and consequently with their mastery. As the *nāḍīs* interrelate the petals of the *chakras*, so this number can relate to this factor. The trials and tests associated with the mastery of the *nāḍīs*, thus the awakening of *chakras*, is governed by the sign Scorpio. Hence Scorpio signifies the process of testings for Initiation, specifically of the desire principle. The number 96 also refers to the Ājñā centre, which has 48 petals to each of its lobes.

99 **9 x 11**. Signifies the eleventh Initiation, here taken represent the further attainment of a Logos of a sacred planet, who therefore is an Adept of all that the Initiation process symbolises and confers.

999 **900 + 90 + 9**. The number for the attainment of the Initiation process upon all three major levels of expression.

1,000 Complete evolutionary perfection of a *mahāmanvantara*. This is the symbolic number of petals to a Head lotus, hence refers to the complete awakening of such a centre, producing the attainment of the *dharmakāya*, or the *Dharmadhātu* Wisdom of Vairocana.

Other numbers could be considered, especially in relation to the emanation of the *deva* kingdom, with many further technical notes given to the numbers treated. The reader however can glean these esoteric nuances later in this series and also when the numerological information from Hierarchy in my later books are studied.

3

The Method of Interpretation

The Occult Catechism

By way of illustration of the numerological methodology I shall utilise an extract from *The Secret Doctrine*, 'The Occult Catechism', which acts as an introduction to the cosmological section of the teachings. At first numbers are assigned to each letter, the numbers are then added for the words concerned and finally added for the complete phrase or sentence. A 'complete phrase' is terminated by any comma, colon, semicolon, or full stop. Generally the word 'the' added to any phrase particularises it, effectively making it a 'self'. As earlier stated the numbers for the word 'and' are disregarded if it follows a comma, colon, or semicolon, as it represents a joining word, a bridge between two phrases. If it is part of a list or an essential part of a sentence then its numbers are counted. Words in brackets are disregarded because they act as an explanation of the intended meaning. All Old Commentaries, both in *Secret Doctrine* and T.C.F. are similarly coded. For each phrase there is normally a number of interpretations, often taken from different levels of perception.

The Catechism begins thus:

> *"What is it that ever is?" "Space, the eternal Anupadaka." (Footnote: 'Meaning "parentless"'). "What is it that ever was?" "The Germ in the Root." "What is it that is ever coming and going?" "The Great Breath." "Then, there are three Eternals?" "No, the three are one. That which ever is is one, that which ever was is one, that which is ever being and becoming is also one: and this is Space."*

"Explain, O Lanoo (disciple)."—"The One is an unbroken Circle (ring) with no circumference, for it is nowhere and everywhere; the One is the boundless plane of the Circle, manifesting a diameter only during the manvantaric periods; the One is the indivisible point found nowhere, perceived everywhere during those periods; it is the Vertical and the Horizontal, the Father and the Mother, the summit and base of the Father, the two extremities of the Mother, reaching in reality nowhere, for the One is the Ring as also the rings that are within that Ring. Light in darkness and darkness in light: the 'Breath which is eternal.' It proceeds from without inwardly, when it is everywhere, and from within outwardly, when it is nowhere — (i.e., maya, one of the centres). It expands and contracts (exhalation and inhalation). When it expands, the Mother diffuses and scatters; when it contracts, the Mother draws back and ingathers. This produces the periods of Evolution and Dissolution, Manwantara and Pralaya. The Germ is invisible and fiery; the Root (the plane of the circle) is cool; but during Evolution and Manwantara her garment is cold and radiant. Hot Breath is the Father who devours the progeny of the many-faced Element (heterogeneous); and leaves the single-faced ones (homogeneous). Cool Breath is the Mother, who conceives, forms, brings forth, and receives them back into her bosom, to reform them at the Dawn (of the Day of Brahmā, or Manvantara)...[1]

The first two phrases are presented as:

'What is it that ever is? 'Space, the eternal Anupadaka.'

The numbers of the meaningful phrases are:

What is it? (37, 10), *ever is* (33, 6), *it that ever is* (57, 12), *What is it that ever is?* (83 = 11, 20), *Space* (17, 8), *the eternal Anupadaka* (70, 16).

For all the phrases in the Stanzas, and all other numerologically coded work, the phrases are first assigned their respective numbers, as explained in chapter two. The clearest layout for the phrases are shown as below:

---

1 H.P. Blavatsky, *The Secret Doctrine*, (Theosophical Publishing, New York, 1888 and the 2005 version), 11-12. One reason why the Old Commentary was italicised was to indicate that it has been numerically coded, therefore to interpret it accordingly.

What	*is*	*it*	*that*	*ever*	*is?*	
16	10	11	13	23	10	= 83 = 11
7	1	2	4	5	1	= 20

Because the number 83 has no special numerological meaning, the numbers are then added together (8 + 3) to make 11, whilst the number 20, which is the product of the result of the first line of numbers added together, does have significance, so it is analysed accordingly. Each meaningful sub-phrase is also treated similarly. Similarly with the phrase:

The	*eternal*	*Anupadaka.*	
15	30	25	= 70
6	3	7	= 16

Here both the numbers 70 and 16 have numerological significance and are analysed accordingly. Of all such interpretations the first line of numbers possess the greater significance, whilst the numerological meaning of the second line is often insignificant, or trivial, and so may be disregarded, unless there is important information that is conveyed by this number. To treat both lines of numbers with equal importance is generally quite tedious and unnecessary, thus often only the product of the first line is explained. Throughout the analysis I will present the numbers of all the important phrases which are explained in my text.

The number 10 of the phrase '*What is it?*' simply informs us that the query concerns the completeness, wholeness, or universality of 'what it is'. The number 33 of the phrase '*ever is*' informs us that we are essentially concerned with that *deva* substance (of the Creative Intelligences) that is expressed as the (inherent) Activity aspect of a Logos, part of the Womb of the great Mother, which is yet to be activated so that it can be transformed, to cause the appearance of a 'child'. The number 12 of the phrase '*it that ever is*' refers here to the expression of the Heart, as the Heart is Life. Note here that the concern is with manifest space ('that' or a 'something' that exists) which the Heart sustains, rather than that which is not, the Void, *śūnyatā*).

The complete phrase can now be analysed: '*What is it that ever is?*' (83 = 11, 20). These numbers indicate that all is an expression of the

Will and Love-Wisdom of Deity, and by extension, the *nāḍī* system (11) by means of which these energies manifest.

By the number 17 we see that *Space* is the Body of manifestation of a Logos. Space normally refers to *ākāśa,* which is defined as the subtle and ethereal fluid pervading the totality of the universe, and a vehicle of life. It is its higher cosmic correspondence of *prāṇa.* Much was given concerning Space in chapter one, thus does not need further explanation.

Anupādaka is defined as 'parentless', or 'self born of the divine essence'. This may also be described as the essence of Consciousness, rarefied *bodhicitta.* It refers to the second of the seven systemic planes of perception, the second *dharmakāya* level, wherein resides the Monad. The numbers 70 and 16 of the phrase *'the eternal Anupadaka'* refer to the fact that we are here concerned with one of the seven planes of perception, which help to produce evolutionary perfection for those evolving through these planes. This plane is concerned with the expression of the energies of the Christ principle (16), hence is the second plane, via which this principle manifests. This plane eternally stands above or beyond the five planes of Mind (*ātma, buddhi, manas,* astral and dense) that are concerned with cyclic manifestation, with the emanation and resolution of the *karma* associated with the cycles of *manvantara.*

Anupādaka stands beyond *ākāśa,* to which the term Space normally refers, hence we are concerned with the doorway of the passage of all the *nirvāṇees* from the earth Scheme to destinations in the cosmic astral plane. *Anupādaka* is the home of all Monadic Life, which is our primary investigation with respect to understanding the functions, purpose and placement of humanity, if *manvantara* has ensued. From this the domain the cosmic Christ (the embodiment of the Heart) can impregnate *saṃsāra* with the principle of *bodhicitta.* Upon this domain the Lords of Life establish the Logoic Head centre, Shambhala. This then is what 'ever is'. The implication however is that rather than *manvantara* a state of *pralaya* is manifest.

Having established the primacy of the plane *anupādaka,* we are now in a position to analyse the phrases:

> *"What is it that ever was?" "The Germ in the Root." "What is it that is ever coming and going?" "The Great Breath."*

The numbers for these sentences are:

> *it that ever was* (54 = 6 x 9, 18 = 2 x 9), *What is it that ever was?* (80 = 16 x 5, 26), *The Germ* (40, 13), *the Root* (38, 11), *in the Root (52, 16), The Germ in the Root* (92 = 11), *ever coming and going* (101, 20), *coming and* going (78 = 13 x 6, 7.1.7), *it that is ever coming and going* (135 = 27 x 5, 27), *What is it that is ever coming and going?* (161 = 7, 35), *The great Breath* (66, 21 = 7 x 3).

The numbers of the phrases *'it that ever was', 'ever was'*, and *'What is it that ever was?'* add to 6 x 9, 30, and 80 = 16 x 5.[2] The number 6 x 9 refers to the Monads that establish themselves upon the plane *anupādaka* at the onset of a new *manvantara* wherein a human kingdom can gain their evolutionary experiences. The number 6 x 9 would normally relate to an Initiate of the sixth degree (that have consequently mastered the plane *anupādaka),* but in the case of the beginning of the evolutionary experience our focus is upon the Monads that exist upon that plane. The entire gamut of evolution, as explained in the second section of the Secret Doctrine (Anthropogenisis), can then come into play. The conditions associated with the ending of *pralaya* therefore concerns us here. The implication is that one *manvantara* has just passed and the gain absorbed in the major centres of abstraction prior to the new incarnation. The conception of seed or germ of all that is to be can now be considered as a consequence.

Continuing along this vein number 16 x 5 implies that the Monads are units (of Mind) bearing the Christ principle (16), effectively Monads of Love-Wisdom, who had gained such in former evolutionary cycles in cosmos, hence the appellation 'it that ever was'. This Monadic Life governed by the second Ray are the main ones that have come to inform our earth sphere. The other two Ray lines possible are first and third Ray Monads. They are also hinted at in the number 10 of the phrase *'What is it'*, and the number 30 of the phrase 'ever was' (signifying also the activity of the *devas).* The number 16 x 5 also refers to the

---

2 The insignificant numbers are as per usual omitted in one's reckoning.

dhyānis, those that will inform and govern the new planetary evolution via a Shambhala that is to be established. They are symbolised by the activity of the five Dhyāni Buddhas (Jinas), who govern the process whereby the five sense consciousnesses are expressed in Nature so that a human kingdom ultimately evolves the five wisdoms (*prajñās*) of the Jinas. Such development happens during the major second Ray cycle in evolution. The entire process of Monadic evolution on earth is therefore hinted at.

Literally therefore, all that there ever was (and will be) for the governance of systemic space for the driving forward of all that is towards evolutionary perfection are human and *deva* (symbolised by the number 30) Monadic Life. Incarnate humans become the wielders of the consciousness that registers the fact of the existence or non-existence of anything. Their minds therefore differentiate, segregate, organise and create the forms of phenomena seen all around us. The number 30 refers to all of the activity that will produce the driving forth of experiences of knowledge into wisdom, and finally to liberation. Each *manvantara* represents a cycle for such opportunity. Inevitably a major cycle governed by the second Ray of Love-Wisdom, demonstrating loving Bodhisattvic activity by the great majority will appear, signifying the beginning of the period of dissolution.

The answer given to this question in the commentary is *'the Germ in the Root'*. The numbers of the associated phrases being 40 (*'the Germ')* and 11 (*'the Root'),* which is also the number for the entire phrase. Also the numbers 52 and 16 inform us what is *'in the Root'*. The number 40 indicates that this Germ is the root or seed of the human unit, taken as the Monad. This is one interpretation, however we must also look to a broader perspective, which concerns the entire process of *manvantara* (symbolised by the number 52, the number of 'weeks' to a great evolutionary year), hence to *hiraṇyagarbha,* 'the golden embryo'.[3]

---

3 *Hiraṇyagarbha,* literally the 'golden womb, embryo' or 'Golden Egg', the 'universal germ'. From it comes the universe or the world sphere. Technically the womb of space-time, from which all evolution sprang. A name of Brahmā, he who was born from the radiant golden egg (*hiranya*), or womb (*garba*), of the self-existent Brahman (the unborn, immutable, absolute ground of the universe). See Stanza 3:4 for a detailed explanation of *hiraṇyagarbha* in terms of the phrase 'the luminous egg'.

Cosmologically the focus is upon the womb of space-time, from which all evolution sprang. *Hiraṇyagarbha* is a name of Brahmā, he who was born from the Golden Egg. He is the creative Deity whose animating principle is the activity of the *devas,* the feminine principle in Nature. At any rate the objective of this entire creative paean is humanity, the fourth kingdom in Nature. 'The Root' therefore is the Creative Logos, the feminine principle, embodying the universal substance matter (*mūlaprakṛti*) the 'Womb' from which came the entire material universe.

The number 11 here refers to the etheric substratum of space, thus the *nāḍī* system of Deity, which persists during the *pralaya* period, and which is 'the Root' from which the universe sprang. It is not conditioned by the laws of formed space, therefore is also that 'which ever was'. We find therefore that 'the Germ' (*hiraṇyagarbha*) exists *in* 'the Root' that is the *nāḍī* system of periodical cyclic manifestation. The *nāḍīs* and the *chakras* are esoterically part of a plant kingdom, hence another interpretation of the concept of 'the Germ in the root'. From this root and the plant associated with it we have the flowers *(chakras)* that draw forth the *saṃskāras* conditioning evolutionary being. The number 11 here also refers to the process of the informing deity (Brahmā) projecting the *sūtrātmās,* the Life links, into manifest space so that the lives can appear therein that undergo their evolutionary cycles.

The number 16 simply informs us that the Love-Wisdom or Christ principle is veiled, hidden 'in the root', and must yet see its 'light of day'.

Having analysed the pre-existing conditionings governing the process of inevitable *manvantara* the meaning of what 'is ever coming and going' can now be interpreted in the form of the question: '*What is it that is ever coming and going?'* That is, the concern now is the nature of the constitution of *saṃsāra.* This question is answered by the numbers of the phrase *'it that is ever coming and going'* (15 x 9, 3 x 9). The pronoun 'it' defines the subject matter, hence is included in the analysis. The numbers imply the concept of Initiated ones, the Lords of Flame that are the average population of Shambhala (15 x 9) at the time of the Individualisation of humanity. We must also consider the members of humanity that will evolve to become Initiates (3 x 9) as a consequence of Individualisation. The Lords of Flame are perfected Sons of Mind, for the number 15 x 9 implies one who has been fully initiated into the mysteries of Mind. This Mind refers to the lowest level of *dharmakāya* (*ātma*), making them Masters of Wisdom (though some at first may be third degree Initiates). They are either 'coming or going', according to the necessity of the service work of the Initiate status that they have evolved, and then their further evolution to accomplish higher arenas of service.

The number 3 x 9 also refers to the human Soul, which is technically an Initiate of the third degree. What is therefore implied is that the members of humanity, continuously 'come and go' systemically via consequences of the rebirthing process, according to the meditation of the Lords of *karma* in relation to Ray and other cyclic calculations. It should be noted that one of the appellations given to the human or fourth kingdom in Nature is 'the Initiates'.

The numbers of the phrase *'coming and going'* are 15, 7.1.7. These numbers connote this process, as the number seven of 'coming' refers to a complete cycle of incarnations in *saṃsāra,* of the manifestation of a septenary of manifestation, and also with respect to the number seven of 'going'. Literally it implies the undertaking of the symbolic 777 Incarnations. The number one links the incarnations, it strings them together, hence symbolises an incarnation between the successive 'sevens' representing groups of incarnations. It signifies the consciousness link (*antaḥkaraṇa*) that interrelates the lives. The number 15 informs us that the activity of the mind, consciousness, is what perpetually 'comes and goes' with each new incarnation, and indeed with each new thought. One here can also use the Yogācāra philosophy of 'everything is mind'.

The number 7 x 5 of *the complete phrase* reinforces this idea, signifying the coming and going of the cycles of mind, and of the 'man-plant' that is the bearer of this principle.

The numbers 101, 20 of the phrase *'ever coming and going'* refer here to the Monads, as they are embodiments of the first and second Ray purpose. This Ray combination is always interpretable as referring to Monadic Life. They bring forth the existence of the human Souls for the new *manvantara*. These Souls have 'come', and as they evolve the necessary Initiation level, then inevitably they must leave evolutionary space.

The commentary then answers, from another perspective, the question it poses as to what is ever coming and going, not alluded to in the former numbers, namely '*The great breath*'. The breathing process implies the existence of an Entity that is engrossed with the in and outflowing of the *prāṇas* constituting phenomenal life. From a Logoic perspective these *prāṇas* are the streams of Life that 'come and go'. Appropriately the numbers of this phrase add to 66, 7 x 3. It was stated above that the number 66 relates to the evolution or expression of the psychic (Watery) constitution in the material world and its mastery. Therefore it signifies the incarnate expression of any being (which becomes animated by the informing *prāṇas*). The Waters of the cosmic astral plane presently concern us here, whereon the Creative Logos is 'slumbering', because in a *pralaya* state. The number 7 x 3 refers to the eventual out-breathing of the three planes of human evolution (the systemic mental, astral and dense realms) at the time of the new *manvantara*.

The numbers for the rest of the first paragraph are:

> *Then (20, 2), there are three Eternals* (104, 32), *three Eternals (60, 15), there are three (73 = 10, 28, 11.6.11), No* (11, 2), *the three are one* (75 = 25 x 3, 30), *the three (44), That which ever is* (79, 16), *That which ever is is one* (105, 24), *that which was is one (102, 30), that which was (76, 22), being and becoming* (79, 16) *that which is ever being* (107, 26 = 8), *that which is ever being and becoming* (158, 32), *ever being and becoming* (102, 21), *becoming* (41, 5), *is also one* (37, 10), *that which is ever being and becoming is also one* (195, 42), *this is Space* (47, 11).

The next question presented is: *'Then, there are three Eternals?'* The 'eternals' referred to here are '*the eternal Anupadaka, the Germ in the Root, and the great Breath.*' They represent the qualities of the three primordial Logoi.

- The first Logos manifests the function of the Will or Father aspect, which is parentless as it has no progenitor for the entire system of expression that concerns us here. Everything is inevitably drawn into this One at the dissolution of whatever was. This One in the form of Parabrahman is *anupādaka*.

- The second Logos embodies the Son or Consciousness principle, the vast expanse of the ocean of Love-Wisdom. This is the *'great Breath'*, which sustains the rhythmic cyclic activity of *pralaya* and *manvantara*, from whence comes the Hindu concept of the Days and Nights of Brahmā. (In Hinduism this is symbolised by Brahmā sitting upon a lotus blossom that arises out of the naval of the sleeping Viṣṇu.)

- The third Logos embodies the Activity or Mother aspect, from which the entire panoply of *saṃsāra* comes into play. This is '*the Germ in the Root'*, the germ being *hiraṇyagarbha*, and the 'Root' here represents the 'ocean' that nourishes the germ or seed of the man-plant (the consciousness bearer), at whatever level one wishes to observe the process.

We are told however, that though seemingly distinct, the three are One, an inseparable unity. This represents the triad that is the eternal Logos, the esoteric version of the Hindu *trimūrti* of Brahmā, Viṣṇu and Śiva.[4] (Interpretable as the number 25 x 3 of the phrase *'the three are one'*.) That which 'ever was' represents the function of Śiva, who instigates the appearance of the phenomena to be, as well as being 'the destroyer' of it in the future. Śiva ever causes the process of birthing and deaths of universes. The function of Viṣṇu is held by that which 'ever is' (Space, *ākāśa),* because the Love-Wisdom principle embodies the duration of Space. The function of the past (of Brahmā the Creator) is held by that which is 'ever coming and going', the illusional play of *saṃsāra*. Śiva sets the Wheel of activity in motion, Brahmā causes the appearance of the diversity of the evolving forms, Viśṇu sustains that activity for its appointed duration, then Śiva terminates all cycles after they have played their rightful roles. We saw previously that the three are One in the form of Brahman-Īśvara.

The numbers of the phrase *'there are three eternals'* (104, 32), refer to the constitution, the 'Humanity' informing the Head centre of a cosmic Logos, the correspondence of Shambhala. The Father (Śiva)—Son (Viṣṇu)—Mother (Brahmā) embody the triune expression of the three major tiers of such a Head centre (signified by the number

---

4 They are in reality a secondary emanation that come into expression once *manvantara* has commenced, the embodiment of the process of its emanation, sustaining and dissolution.

105 below). The *trimūrti* is but an expression of the way that the Mind of Īśvara is organised. We are reminded here that all is an emanation or expression of cosmic Love (32).

With respect to our earth, the numbers 104, 32 refer to Monadic Life (the human kingdom, 104), appearing under the auspices of Shambhala, bringing about a new evolutionary cycle wherein a new humanity flourishes as it pursues its journeying along the path of developing Love-Wisdom (32). They then also are One, Lords of Love (32), though manifesting in a seemingly plurality of Ray colourings and qualities. The Monads are either along the first, second or third Rays, which also can be symbolised by the term 'three eternals'.

The number 60 (5 x 12) of *'three eternals',* relates to the sign Leo the lion, hence of individuation (thus the concept of three entities, here considered 'eternals'), the power of the ego, or the demonstration of the Soul upon the higher mental plane, also the powers of a sun in its glory. This sign governs human (Monadic) evolution in the realms of form. (We can similarly posit such rulership for the average population of suns, cosmic Humanity evolving via the cosmic astral ocean.) With reference to Leo then, the concept of 'eternals' relates to the Soul aspect underlying manifestation, which is eternal with respect to the appearing forms, which undergo the 777 incarnations governed by the Soul.

In relation to this apparent diversity the question first posits that then there are three such 'Individuated' Entities, embodied forms (60). To this inference the answer is 'no'. The word *Then'* (20) relates to the consciousness principle (Love-Wisdom) that acts as a bridging mechanism between the 'three eternals'. They are one through the expression of Love-Wisdom but manifest as three via the establishment of a Head centre (105), which is fundamentally triune, and the appearance of form (60), whereby consciousness can evolve. Thus we have the trinity of Spirit (the Head centre, Shambhala), the kingdom of Souls or Hierarchy (the Son), and the manifest form *(saṃsāra),* the domain of the great Mother administered to (symbolised by the number 60).

The numbers of the phrase *'there are three'* (10, 7 x 4, 11.6.11) sums this up quite succinctly, where the number 10 refers to the Spirit, the number 7 x 4 relates to humanity and the *buddhic* plane, their esoteric 'home', whilst the numbers 11.6.11 hints at the principle of desire (6),

Logoic or human, extending the *antaḥkaraṇas* from One to the other (the number 11), so that all come to know and to incorporate the other via the attribute of the appearing form (6), the domain of the Mother.

The exclamation *'No'* acts similarly as an *antaḥkaraṇa*. The associated number 11 is essentially a linking number, and also implies that we are concerned with the constitution of cosmic etheric Space. (*Māyā,* as explained in Chapter One, manifesting in the form of *ākāśa* or with the Buddhist concept of *svabhāva.*) All etheric bodies are interrelated, hence from the plane *buddhi* (the fourth cosmic ether) one can travel into cosmic space. Cosmic *nāḍīs* extend from one planetary or stellar sphere to the next. The human *nāḍī* system reflects the attributes of *buddhi* into manifestation.

The remaining part of this first paragraph presents further detail as to the nature of the *trimūrti* with respect to the 'three times'. However it looks at the relationship between the three from a different perspective: that from the point of view of manifest space and of those that are incarnate therein, rather than purely cosmologically.

The first phrase given is that *'the three are one'* (25 x 3, 30). By the numbers of the phrase *'the three'* (44, 17) we see that we are concerned with cosmic Humanity, emanations of Logoic Mind from the cosmic mental plane (25 x 3), literally with the Sambhogakāya Flowers (Souls) of these Logoi (symbolised here by the number 25). They are personified in the Hindu mythology as Śiva, Viṣṇu and Brahmā, the Father, Son, and Mother.

The next phrase: *'that which ever is is one'* (105) relates to the eternal Now, wherein the three of the *trimūrti* are One. The concept of 'ever is' relates to what exists, whether there is a *pralaya* or *manvantara*, hence remains abstracted (*viz.* the concept of Brahman). This can be conceived of as the *first Logos.* Whether there is abstraction of the appearance of multiplicity, all are integrated as 'One'. That One bears the potency of the Will or Power of the first Ray, however it manifests via the principle of Love-Wisdom (which must be interpreted in terms of its first Ray attribute here). This is signified by the number 16 of the phrase *'that which ever is'*. Thus this 'One cosmic Life' is but a cosmic Christ. This energy sustains the All needed for the evolution of the consciousness principle within the duration of Space (the manifestation of the Mother) that is the pulsation of the Heartbeat of the One cosmic Life.

The number 105 refers to the manifestation of Logoic Mind, that 'ever is' with respect to the evolution of the Monadic Life that constitute the 'brain cells' of such a Mind (whose embodied expression is Dynamic Love). This number thus signifies the constitution of Shambhala, the planetary Head centre from which emanates the first Ray energy of Will, the Commands governing all manifest space via Compassionate Purpose. The Monadic Lives then bear the Thought-streams of the great Presiding One that embodies them. The associated number 24 of this phrase refers to the second sign of the zodiac, Taurus the bull. Taurus governs the expression of the cosmic astral plane, wherein the abstracted Logos *('that which ever is')* resides. The number 8 of the phrase *'is one'* refers to the spiral-cyclic motion that integrates the 'three times' into unity (the Father). The Head centre possesses five tiers of petals, but three are major and are directly concerned with the phenomenon of manifestation and garnering the results of the evolutionary process. Their attributes were aptly explained in my book *The Esoteric Exposition of the Bardo Thödol.* These three main tiers manifest the functions of the 'three' that are 'one'.

What remains after every evolutionary cycle can now be analysed, thus to the function of the *second Logos.* In this solar system this is literally the Love-Wisdom principle, signified by the number 22 of the phrase '*that which ever was'*. Love-Wisdom is the gain of the *manvantaras* (the coming and going of cycles) manifesting within our solar system. The number 22 also refers to the Womb of space-time, governed by the 10 Planetary Rulers and 12 zodiacal expressions, which consequently conditions solar evolution.

This evolution is also implied by the number 102 of the phrase '*that which ever was is one*'. This number reminds us that the Logoi of the three times are integrated, 'One', under the auspices of the second Ray of Love-Wisdom. The principle of dynamic Love unites the All into one ocean of Consciousness-Bliss. The number 30 of this phrase refers to the Activity of the past that produces the Love-Wisdom of the Now, which 'ever was' in the sense that such cycles have unfolded seemingly forever.

Next we are to analyse work of the *third Logos,* the Mother, in the phrase *'that which is ever being and becoming is also one'* (100 + 95, 6 x 7). The substance of Her Womb (6 x 7) is evolving to a future perfection. Here the number 6 x 7 refers to the planes of perception in general and to the Waters of the astral plane specifically. The number 100 + 95 refers to the process of becoming enlightened, the evolutionary period before the great perfection, of *'that which is ever being and becoming'* (32). The number 32, as well as the number 16 of the phrase *'being and becoming'* refer to the Love-Wisdom principle, which is what evolves during this period, yet it is that which is 'ever being'. It simply IS the nature of the Logoic Presence. This is also implied by the number 102 of the phrase *'ever being and becoming'*, whilst the associate number 7 x 3 refers to the three worlds of human livingness (the mental, astral and physical planes) that are ever becoming.

The number 107 of the phrase *'that which is ever being'* refers to the sum total all of the septenaries of Nature, to the cycles of Life governing the entities constituting *saṃsāra* which are working towards evolutionary perfection. All are evolving within the embrace of the Ken of the triune Logos, the Lord of Love that guarantees their ultimate perfection.

The concept of the three times are implicit in *the complete phrase*, where *'that which is ever being'* refers to the eternal Now. The process of *'becoming'* (5) relates to the actions wherein the past becomes the future by means of the action of consciousness, the activities of the mind (5) that can think clearly in terms of what happened and what must be. Through the mind the *saṃskāras* must be processed and transformed as they move from the past towards the progressively evolving future. The phrase *'is also one'* refers to the present-future, because consciousness must evolve the perception to identify with the One.

This section ends with the statement *'This is space'* (11), which reminds us that the Compassionate aspect of the Logos ever manifests His/Her Love throughout space. The number 11 relates to the cosmic ethers, the *nāḍīs* via which this 'space' manifests within the solar system. Identification with 'space' is attained at the fourth Initiation via the experience of *śūnyatā*.

The five levels of expression to the commentary

Having analysed what might be considered the introduction to this commentary we can now proceed to the main body of the text. This entices the disciple to think esoterically, enlighteningly, hence to explain the central principles of Logoic manifestation.

The first phrase is: *'Explain, O Lanoo (disciple)'*. The numbers of the word *'Explain'* add to 36 = 4 x 9, 3 x 12 (Gemini), whilst those of the phrase *'O Lanoo'* add to 27 = 3 x 9. By this we see that the disciple who is asked to explain the meaning of the commentary is either a third or fourth degree Initiate. Consequently he/she has the capacity to comprehend the esotericism of the commentary. By the number 4 x 9 of the word *'Explain'*, which precedes this section, the Initiate is also asked to meditate upon the attributes needed to undertake the fourth Initiation, or if such an Initiate, to stand within the precincts of the Temple of the Lord upon cosmic ethers signified by the sign Gemini the twins, who rules their expression. The meditative endeavour to explain therefore signifies the testings needed for the Initiate to attain the Initiation, or to bring into consciousness the awareness related to cosmos. Proper esoteric interpretation of the meanings of this commentary can then be made. One must thus be fully liberated, to be able to view things from the stance obtained at the *śūnyatā-saṃsāra* nexus, the bridge between the mental plane and *buddhi* (the fourth cosmic ether).[5]

The sign Gemini the twins represents the temple (of Initiation) wherein the disciple is appropriately trained to comprehend the nature of esoteric cosmogony via direct internal perception *(pratyakṣa)*. The implication is that the disciple needs to evoke the links to cosmic etheric space to do so.

There are *five levels of expression* to the paragraph following this statement concerning the necessity of the disciple to show comprehension of what was learned through his/her explanation. The first four are indicated by the phrase *'The One'* at the beginning of the statements for each section. They are essentially a commentary of the opening parts of the Proem, where Blavatsky presents the symbols of the archaic manuscript.

The numbers of the phrase *'the One'* add to 31, signifying that this One possesses the Will to penetrate deep into the Mysteries of being/non-being. A Throne or seat of Power must be established with which to utilise the Will to circumscribe *māyā* with intelligent Purpose. The relevant section of the Proem related to this is given below.

---

5 The significance of this nexus was explained in the first three volumes of *A Treatise on Mind.*

The first illustration being a plain disc ○, the second in the Archaic symbol shows ⊙, a disc with a point in it — the first differentiation in the periodical manifestations of the ever-eternal nature, sexless and infinite, "Aditi[6] in THAT" (Rig Veda), the point in the disc, or potential Space within abstract Space. In its third stage the point is transformed into a diameter, thus ⊖. It now symbolises a divine immaculate Mother-Nature within the all-embracing absolute Infinitude. When the horizontal diameter is crossed by a vertical one, ⊕, it becomes the mundane cross.[7]

The levels of interpretation are:

- **First the Parabrahman level of interpretation.**
  This is governed by the attributes of Vairocana (boundless Light) and his Dharmadhātu Wisdom.[8]

  The One is an unbroken Circle (ring) with no circumference, for it is nowhere and everywhere;

- **Second the Brahman level of interpretation.**
  This is governed by the attributes of Akṣobhya, the great Mirror-like Wisdom reflecting cosmos into the solar or planetary system.

  The One is the boundless plane of the Circle, manifesting a diameter only during the manvantaric periods;

- **Thirdly the Īśvara level of interpretation.**
  This is governed by the attributes of Amitābha, whose Discriminating Inner Wisdom demonstrates the methodology of expressing cosmic Mind in manifestation.

  The One is the indivisible point found nowhere, perceived everywhere during those periods; it is the Vertical and the Horizontal, the Father

---

6 *Aditi,* the free, unbounded feminine personification of the created universe, specifically in its infinite fluxial essence. The infinite Mother. The boundless all, eternal Space, infinite, abstracted, containing the potential of formed space. The endless expanse of the universe, hence is the Mother of the Gods and all that proceeds in manifestation.

7 S.D., Vol. I, 4-5.

8 Much information concerning the Dhyāni Buddhas and their wisdoms are explained in *A Treatise on Mind* series, especially volume 5A, where the reader can look for detailed explanation.

and the Mother, the summit and base of the Father, the two extremities of the Mother, reaching in reality nowhere,

- **Fourth the Māyā—*trimūrti* level of interpretation.**
  This is governed by the attributes of Ratnasambhava, the Equalising Wisdom infusing the cosmic astral (Watery) Breath as the *māyā* of the centres, whose activity expands and contracts according to the way of cosmic Mind in action.

  For the One is the Ring as also the rings that are within that Ring. Light in darkness and darkness in Light: the 'Breath which is eternal.' It proceeds from without inwardly, when it is everywhere, and from within outwardly, when it is nowhere—(i.e., maya, one of the centres). It expands and contracts (exhalation and inhalation). When it expands, the Mother diffuses and scatters; when it contracts, the Mother draws back and ingathers. This produces the periods of Evolution and Dissolution, Manwantara and Pralaya.

- **Fifth the sum of the expression of the five Dhyāni Buddhas.**
  This is governed cosmically by the attributes of Amoghasiddhi, whose All-accomplishing Wisdom synthesises the potency of the five Jinas.

  The Germ is invisible and fiery; the Root (the plane of the circle) is cool; but during Evolution and Manwantara her garment is cold and radiant. Hot Breath is the Father who devours the progeny of the many-faced Element (heterogeneous), and leaves the single-faced ones (homogeneous). Cool Breath is the Mother, who conceives, forms, brings forth, and receives them back into her bosom, to reform them at the Dawn (of the Day of Brahmā, or Manvantara).[9]

The Parabrahman level of interpretation.

Parabrahman was earlier said to be 'beyond' the all-pervasive principle of Consciousness. Parabrahman, according to Advaita Vedānta, is the timeless, spaceless existence supporting the entire manifestation of cosmos. It is infinite, attributeless, possessing no name or form. The self-enduring, eternal, self-sufficient cause of all, the essence

9 S.D., Vol. I, 11-12.

of everything in the cosmos. It thus sustains any Logoic body of manifestation. Parabrahman can relate to the Dharmadhātu Wisdom of the Dhyāni Buddha Vairocana. The term *dharmadhātu* means the 'suchness' or 'thusness' of being. It is the pristine cognition of reality's transcendental expanse or sphere of empowerment. *Dharmadhātu* is pristine cognition, the fundamental essence or realm *(dhātu)* of the *dharma,* hence is almost synonymous with *dharmakāya. Dharmakāya* is the body *(kāya)* of the *dharma,* whilst *dharmadhātu* is the realm within which this *dharma* resides. *Dharmatā* manifests as the force that projects *dharma* into manifestation via the spaciousness of the abstracted Mind. *Dharmatā,* in the form of *tathatā* (the Buddha-essence) becomes the mechanism of containment of that *dharma* in the form of the *tathāgatagarbha* (the Sambhogakāya Flower, or Buddha-Womb).

The associated phrases are:

The One is an unbroken Circle (ring) with no circumference,
for it is nowhere and everywhere;

The numerical breakdown:

The One (31, 13), *an unbroken Circle* (75, 21), *The One is an unbroken Circle* (116, 35), *no circumference* (80, 17), *with no circumference* (104, 23), *an unbroken Circle (ring) with no circumference* (220, 58), *it is nowhere* (64, 10), *for it is nowhere* (85, 13), *nowhere and everywhere* (115, 16), *it is nowhere and everywhere (136, 19), for it is nowhere and everywhere (157, 22).*

The numbers 25 x 3, 7 x 3 of the phrase *'an unbroken Circle'* relate to the plain disc of the quote from the Proem, in which case here the disc is also dark (Space). The main analysis here concerns the importance of using the adjective 'unbroken' to qualify this circle. It means that the sphere of containment is complete for whatever is included within the circle. It is a boundless, unfathomable, ring-pass-not preventing escape of that contained within it. The Logos (Mind) that circumscribes the sphere of attainment can thereby concentrate all energies upon the growth and development of what has been circumscribed until the appropriate time of release. It is therefore a completed Thought

Form that has the property of expansion or contraction, as well as internal growth or rearrangement of the Landscape, the Mindscape contained within. This is symbolised by the number 25 x 3, referring to the demonstration of Thought pertaining to the Father-Son-Mother aspects of Deity, or the manifestation of the forces of Mind on three levels of expression.

This ring-pass-not is the outer containment of a *maṇḍala* of unknown potency that has yet to fulfil its potential. Within it therefore the entire evolutionary paean of what is yet to be must eventually flower within a circumscribed or defined purpose. Both the numbers 25 x 3 and 7 x 3 inform us that there is an intrinsic or inherent trinity of circles to consider contained within 'the One'.

This 'One' is:

a. The first Ray expression—the indivisible point found nowhere.
b. The second Ray expression—the boundless plane of the circle.
c. The third Ray expression—an unbroken circle.

There are other 'rings' (circles) within that One, which represent the *laya*[10] seeds of Logoi to be. All are abstracted in Parabrahman, which though being attributeless, timeless, spaceless, having no name or form, has the capacity to support whatever comes to be in the cosmic landscape. Thus the logic proceeds. The spheres of influence of the Logoi of the three times must inevitably be accommodated in the concept analysed. This implies the three Logoic levels (25 x 3), and inevitably in the field of *māyā* the three levels of the systemic *manasic*, astral and dense spheres of containment (7 x 3) that are enclosed by the circumference. These three being inferred by 'that is not'. They are 'not' because illusional, *if* there was a consciousness existent at that stage to perceive anything. From this perspective 'an unbroken circle' refers to the expression of Brahman, taking this term to refer to the expression of the abstracted Logoic Mind upon cosmic mental levels. The 'boundless plane of the circle' of the Brahman level of interpretation then becomes the first differentiation—that associated with the cosmic astral plane. The 'indivisible point found nowhere' consequently refers

10 Point of primal receptivity.

to the *bīja* of the eventual solar or world sphere that will manifest upon the cosmic physical plane.

The *'three rings'* can refer to the tiers of the Monadic Eye for a Logos, however the three Logoic levels (25 x 3) can also refer to the three main whorls of petals to the Soul (Sambhogakāya Flower) aspect of the universe, which in this case has withdrawn the attributes of the previous incarnation into the constitution of its whorls of petals, or projected them in *bīja* form into the permanent atoms. One must here look cosmically to Parabrahman as a Soul aspect, in the similar sense to what a Soul represents to a normal human incarnate human mind. It is something totally abstract, and yet absorbs the all of his/her being. The 'boundless plane' then represents, by analogy, the mind of an incarnate human, wherein thought forms can be constructed, whilst the 'invisible point' represents the personality structure, the concept of an 'I' that is 'found nowhere' because constantly moving, changing, hence illusional.

The trinities (25 x 3) can also refer to the 'Spirit' of Deity, the brooding Mind (Mahat), and the substance matter *(mūlaprakṛti)* of the Mother. One can also incorporate the Shambhalic (the *dharmakāya),* the Solar or Hierarchical level *(sambhogakāya),* and that pertaining to the mundane or human level *(nirmaṇakāya)* levels of interpretation.[11]

The *dharmakāyaic* level relates to the numbers of the phrase *'The One is an unbroken Circle (ring)',* which add to 116, 7 x 5. This means that such an 'unbroken Circle' is in fact a boundless, though also 'bounded' Lord of Compassion (100 + 16) existing upon the abstract domains of the cosmic mental plane (7 x 5), hence to the Soul aspect of whatever is, later to incarnate as a cosmos, or any other cosmic entity. The implication is that 'the One' (31, 13), Whose Will (31) governing the sum of what was, is and will be, is such a Lord. The term 'unbroken' here hints at the fact that the 'bounded-ness' of this Lord is not limited to the 'circle', which is produced by the activity of the Mother aspect of Deity, causing the appearance of the *nirmaṇakāya.* This Soul, that this One manifests as, is responsible for instigating the formation of

11 These three bodies of a Buddha are integrated into a fourth body, the *svabhāvikāya,* the Self-born body, literally the absolute body of a Buddha as it exists in cosmos and integrated with all other Buddha-forms. From this perspective Parabrahman may also be equated with *svabhāvikāya.*

the various levels of the 'unbroken circle', as well as delineating the bounded unboundedness or esoteric limits to the expression of the Lords of Sacrifice that will incarnate into cosmic space to establish Shambhalas, Head centres for the manifestation of 'form' for them. We see that by the number 100 + 16 here, the numbers 220, 16 x 5 and 22 below, that the principle of Love-Wisdom is the common thread ruling all three levels of expression for this incarnation of the solar Logos.

The *sambhogakāya* level is presented in the number 220 of the complete phrase: *'The One is an unbroken Circle with no circumference'*, where the Love-Wisdom principle that incarnates into the Womb of space-time is implied. The 'unbroken' circle represents the parameters of that 'Womb' (of the Mother) from the point of view of a miniscule individual viewing from the inside. This Womb is impregnated with the cosmic version of the twelve zodiacal and ten astrological energies, of the Ray Lives, the Creative Hierarchies and the energies of the triune Deity that are encapsulated.

The phrases *'no circumference'* and *'with no circumference'* also relate to this level of expression, to the expanse of consciousness (the Love-Wisdom principle) contained by this 'unbroken circle'. This is limitless, hence has 'no circumference', in contradistinction to that associated with cosmic Mind (the Father-Mother), which has a feasible 'boundary' – of the Thought construct contained by Mind, even if that 'Thought' is of vast duration. Hence the term 'unbroken circle' for this *sambhogakāya* level of interpretation. The important numbers of the two phrases are 80 = 16 x 5, 17 and 104. The number 17 refers to Deity, a Logos, whereas the number 16 x 5 refers to the Hierarchies of Life embodied by such a Deity. The number 104 similarly refers to members of cosmic Humanity. This level of expression therefore relates to the liberated Hierarchies of beings, Logoic Lives, contained within the sphere of the Logoic Thought (of 'the One'), who effectively have no limitation to the expansion of their Consciousnesses, to the experience of what is termed Love. There is thus technically no circumference to their 'circles'. The nature of the ineffable, unbounded Wisdom (*prajñā*) of these Lives therefore causes these 'circles' to have 'no circumference'. Enlightenment has no bounds. The five liberated Hierarchies reside outside of the confines of the cosmic dense physical form, which is here incorporated within a sphere of activity. That 'sphere' then represents the Thought-Form of the creative Logos.

The anomalous statements of there being 'an unbroken circle' as well as this circle having 'no circumference' can be solved when we look to the two main levels of interpretation of the complete phrase:

1. From the point of view of liberated beings, there is 'no circumference' or bounds to the vision and scope for the enlightenment of the established Dhyānis. The circle is 'broken', or more appropriately manifests in the form of spiral-cyclic motion (80). The nature of the Waters of cosmic astral space is literally implied.
2. From the point of view of those incarnate in *saṃsāra, manvantaric* space, in which case we have a bounded, 'unbroken circle'. Similarly the vast Mind-Space of the cosmic Logos has circumscribed a Thought-Form for Incarnation, which from this perspective is an 'unbroken circle'.

The next phrase *'for it is nowhere and everywhere'* (22) relates to the level of interpretation associated with physical incarnation, the *nirmaṇakāya* level of interpretation, with the establishment of 'circles', Logoic spheres of activity, which are *'nowhere and everywhere'* (100 + 3 x 5, 16). The other subsidiary phrases are; *'it is nowhere'* (8 x 8), *'for it is nowhere'* (85 = 17 x 5), *'everywhere',* (31 x 2, 8). When it is 'everywhere' it exists in the mind/Mind that observes 'everywhere', and everywhere it looks there it sees the boundaries of all forms and the limitations of their existential lives. The moon, earth, all planets, sun and every component in the universe has fixed orbits and arenas of space within which to travel. The number 100 + 3 x 5 thus refers to this vast or universal scale expression of the active Mind utilised to analyse all that is. All have their circumscribed spaces of activity (8, 8 x 8). When it is 'nowhere' then our observation is from the point of view of *śūnyatā,* which is Void of all attributes of mind. This view then necessitates the development of the Christ-consciousness (enlightenment), symbolised by the number 16.

The number 13 x 5 above refers here to the zones of activity of the Dhyāni Buddhas, which can also be considered to exist 'nowhere' because established in *śūnyatā,* but which is also everywhere, because 'everywhere' is where the spread of their influence can be found. Their energies represent the fount of the dissemination of the evolution of mind/Mind in *saṃsāra.* The number 22 refers to zodiacal and planetary energies (cosmic energies) that manifest through and via the One, which is *'nowhere and everywhere'.* One can also look to the locus of each sphere of activity (circle or Womb, the number 22), that are moving in space, and because all is in constant motion within the space of a *manvantara,* so each locus can be found anywhere and is nowhere in particular, except existing in the mind, as part of the illusionality of the thought forms contained therein. Similarly the enlightened Mind can be *'nowhere and everywhere'* for all of the reasons mentioned above.

The Brahman level of interpretation.

Continuing with the earlier information we see that this level of interpretation relates to the cosmic astral plane, wherein the concept of Brahman gains its validity. As earlier stated Brahman is the neutral form of Brahmā. It is the essence from which all things emanate and into which all things return, hence is unborn, immutable, the absolute ground to the universe. In the symbolism of the Proem it can be illustrated by the plain disc, now illumined, hence not in darkness. The cosmic astral plane can be considered boundless because literally we are concerned with the Waters of Space, for which there appears no end to its duration.

This Brahman level of interpretation can also be viewed in terms of the attributes of Akṣobhya, whose Mirror-like Wisdom reflects the qualities of the abstracted cosmos (Parabrahman) into whatever manifests as solar or planetary systems. Though there is an appearance of separation, differentiation everywhere, in fact everything is an aspect of the one fundamental essence, viewed as Brahman, or in Buddhism as the *dharmakāya.* Brahman represents the Waters of Space, conditioned by cosmic Mind.

> *The One is the boundless plane of the Circle, manifesting a diameter only during the manvantaric periods.*

The numerical breakdown:

> *The One* (31, 13), *the boundless Plane* (66, 12), *boundless plane of (3.3.3), the Circle* (47, 11), *The One is the boundless plane* (107, 26), *the boundless plane of the Circle (125, 26), The One is the boundless plane of the Circle* (166, 40), *manifesting a diameter* (94, 22), *the manvantaric periods (100, 19), during the manvantaric periods* (137, 29 = 11), *only during the manvantaric periods* (158, 32), *manifesting a diameter only during the manvantaric periods* (252, 54).

The numbers 66 and 100 + 66 of the phrases *'the boundless plane'* and '*the One is the boundless Plane of the Circle*' here refer to the Watery aspect of this cosmic astral plane, rather than incarnate existence per se. (The number 6 refers to the sixth plane of perception, the astral.)

One must also ascertain what a *'boundless plane'* actually represents. Here we are effectively asked to look to the two dimensional view of the circle, as if we are observing a circle on a sheet of paper. This represents a plane of perception (level of existence), which esoterically has a spatial thickness, as the planes of perception are likened to the layers of an onion, one overlapping another. One can look to any plane, but specifically the focus is upon the mental plane, to the realm of thoughts, which are bounded by a sphere of limitation and can also be considered 'unbounded' in the case of an enlightened One. (However, even so, there is always a limitation to the thought, even if embracing the Mind of 'God'.) The sum total of the mental plane can be considered bounded but endless, because there can be no end to the realm of ideas and concepts one may have. The Thought process circumscribes the astral substance to manifest an existent form, here implying the material universe. This produces the concept of the three times with respect to Logoic Thought, and has its focus on the *ātmic* plane, the plane of expression of the Third Logos. (Producing the Brahman – Brahmā relationship explained in chapter one, where the separation of Brahmā from Brahman is symbolised by the appearance of a diameter.) From this plane all *karma,* and hence *saṃsāra,* comes into existence (the subsidiary significance of the number 66 above). This *karma* manifests via the three planes of human livingness, which is headed by the mental plane.

This process is symbolised by the number 3.3.3. (of the words 'boundless plane of'). The third Ray of Mathematically Exact Activity governs the activity of the Mind of the Mother, which produces *'a diameter'* (40), signifying the separation of the 'Waters' from 'a firmament',[12] or the activity of Brahmā *(hiraṇyagarbha* the cosmic golden Egg), from which all evolution sprang within the self-existent Brahman.

The numbers 125 and 107 of the phrases *'The One is the boundless Plane'* and *'the boundless Plane of the Circle'* continue along this vein concerning the manifestation of phenomena, of world or solar spheres that appear to contain differentiated entities within 'the boundless Plane'. The number 107 refers to any of the seven planes of perception in the solar system, of which the mental plane is but one. Each of these can be viewed in terms of being unbroken circles, where only the physical domain is exoterically viewed to have a circumference—signifying the earth upon which we reside. One can also consider the seven globes to a planetary Chain, or the seven Chains to a solar sphere. The number 125 (25 x 5) refers to the establishment of a planetary or solar Head lotus (Shambhala), the governing principle that organises that substance, according to the way of manifestation of the five Dhyāni Buddhas and the great Lords that embody their principles (25 x 5).

Next is the phrase *'manifesting a diameter only during the manvantaric periods'* (200 + 52, 6 x 9, 3 x 12, Gemini) in relation to this plane of the Circle that is 'the One'. A diameter esoterically represents the feminine principle in Nature, which is to be bisected by the vertical masculine principle. Essentially this refers to the establishment of the seven spirals (planes of perception) of the primal atom that is the cosmic or mundane Egg (of the earth sphere for instance). The number 22 of the phrase *'manifesting a diameter'* informs us that such a diameter literally concerns establishing the Womb of space-time whereby everything can come into being. This is because this number refers primarily to the ten planetary and twelve zodiacal energies and qualifications conditioning the Womb, needed by the child within the Womb to evolve. This diameter thus signifies the activity within the Womb wherein all

---

12 *Genesis 1:6*, 'And God said, Let there be a firmament in the midst of the waters, and let it divide the waters from the waters'.

forms evolve.[13] The number 6 x 9 here simply refers to the opportunity for Monads to gain their evolutionary perfection during *manvantara.*

The number 200 + 52 refers to the new *manvantara* of Love-Wisdom (in the case of our present solar system), a great year (52) of Brahmā wherein Viṣṇu manifests his purpose. In relation to this, Gemini concerns the establishment of the *nāḍī* system within the Womb of time-space, via which the manifestation of all phenomena must proceed. The four cosmic ethers flow via these *nāḍīs.* These ethers convey the zodiacal and planetary energies that condition the evolution of the material universe. '*A diameter*' (40) therefore principally refers to the *nāḍīs* underlying all of space. From the diameter the various *nāḍīs* radiate outwards to form the body of manifestation. The number 40 here refers to the mirror aspect that reflects what exists in the subjective universe into/as the formed universe. This then represents the function of this diameter.

The numbers of the phrase '*the manvantaric periods*' add to 100, referring to the great Year of the *mahāmanvantara,* a 100 years of Brahmā. It concerns the process that will produce complete evolutionary perfection for the Jīvas that will incarnate during this solar year. When the numbers of the word '*during*' are added, producing the number 11, then the purpose of the *nāḍī* system is implied. A *mahāmanvantara* contains many lesser evolutionary periods (*manvantaras*).

When this phrase is particularised by the numbers of the word 'only' then the resultant numbers 32 and 14 inform us that this diameter is principally concerned with the Watery dispensation (14) of the Mother. (The astral plane, cosmically and systemically.) The Waters of Life and Love (32) then become the energies manifesting as streams of vitality nourishing the multitudes of Lives that play their roles in the new *manvantara. Saṃsāric* evolution for humanity is primarily Watery (astral) in nature, as even when the mind is awakened it is mostly influenced or controlled by people's desires and emotions, producing the consequent attachments to ephemera, all forms of sensation and sensual pleasures.

---

13 Exoterically it relates to the splitting of the fertilised egg into two during mitosis. The place of separation between the two forming cells is such a 'diameter'.

The Īśvara level of interpretation.

This level of interpretation relates to the formation of solar and planetary spheres (Īśvaras) in the universe. The associated section of the Proem consequently concerns the archaic symbol of a disc with a point in it, 'the first differentiation in the periodical manifestations of the ever-eternal nature, sexless and infinite, "Aditi in THAT"'. It is 'the point in the disc, or potential Space within abstract Space', etc.

This process is governed by the attributes of Amitābha, whose Discriminating Inner Wisdom demonstrates the methodology of expressing cosmic Mind into manifestation. The point with the disc, plus all of the variegations of the manifestation of the Thought-Forms of the Logoi, are governed by the natural segregative, discriminative, analytical functions of the Mind.

> *The One is the indivisible point found nowhere, perceived everywhere during those periods; it is the Vertical and the Horizontal, the Father and the Mother, the summit and base of the Father, the two extremities of the Mother, reaching in reality nowhere.*

The numerical breakdown:

The One (31, 13), *the indivisible point* (104, 23), *The One is the indivisible point* (145, 37), *found nowhere* (67, 13), *the indivisible point found nowhere* (171, 36 = Gemini), *The One is the indivisible point found nowhere* (212, 50), *perceived everywhere* (113, 14), *those periods* (63, 9), *during those periods* (98, 17), *perceived everywhere during those periods* (211 31), *the Vertical and the Horizontal* (131, 32), *the Vertical* (51, 15), *it is the Vertical* (72, 18), *the Horizontal* (70, 16), *it is the Vertical and the Horizontal* (152, 36), *the Father and the Mother* (105, 24), *the Father* (46, 10), *the Mother* (49, 13), *the summit and base of the Father* (115, 34), *base of the Father* (67, 22), *the summit* (38, 11), *the summit and base* (57, 21), *the Father* (46, 10), *the two extremities of the Mother* (146, 38 = 11), *the two extremities* (85, 22), *the Mother* (49, 13), *of the Mother* (61, 16), *extremities of the Mother* (118, 28), *two extremities of the Mother (131, 32),*

> *reaching in reality nowhere* (140, 32), *in reality* (50, 14), *reaching in reality* (97, 25), *in reality nowhere (93, 21).*

Having analysed the conception of 'the One' as a cosmic Egg when it manifests 'a diameter', the implications of this concept can now be further scrutinised from the beginning to the ending of this process. This introduces the Logoic source or focal point of all that is to be: '*The One is the indivisible point found nowhere*' (212, 50). An '*indivisible point*' (17) refers to one dimensional space, from which all the other dimensions stem. It is the point of power of a Logos (17), the *bīja* that contains the potential of all that is to be, from which therefore can be derived the *saṃskāras* of the activities from past lives. A point can also be considered a sphere (of attainment) when viewed at a great distance, as for instance are the stars in the night sky. We can also look to this point to be the ultimate atom (*aṇu*) found in Nature.

The term *indivisible* refers to what cannot be divided into parts, meaning therefore that the entire sphere of attainment that derives from the *aṇu* is a unity, a whole, even though there are many component parts to it. The entire progress of the sphere of attainment evolves together in a unified fashion; as the One that embodies their purpose and guides them thereto. The mind is what divides and segregates, whilst the Heart unifies to embrace the All. We see therefore that this 'point' or sphere of attainment is indivisible when directed by the Heart of the Logos (200 + 12), and divisible when the associated substance is manipulated by mind/Mind (50). The phrase therefore relates specifically to the period of time before humanity evolved from out of the morass of substance. However, when the numbers of the subsidiary phrases (5, 100 + 9 x 5, 50) are investigated we see that what relates to the analytical processes of the human mind (5) will eventually produce the perfection of Mind (the *dharmakāya*, 50) via the Initiation process. A Master of Wisdom (9 x 5) thereby evolves. During this process 'the One' becomes divisible then indivisible again.

The 'point' is found 'everywhere' when the individualities appear that are the representative egos, 'selves' of human consciousness. This is the mainstay of *saṃsāra*. The 'point' is 'found nowhere' in the enlightened Mind, for there the concept of the ego is eliminated, there is only unity, oneness, *śūnyatā*. (The number 13 of the phrase '*found nowhere*' refers to the unitary point within the sphere. Similarly for the number 100 + 13 of the phrase '*perceived everywhere'*, signifying the Seat of Power of any Logos, or those that manifest as individualities.)

The number 104 of the phrase '*the indivisible point*' refers to the middle between extremes (the fourth Ray or plane of perception), to the establishment of the Seats of Power of members of cosmic Humanity upon the quaternary of the four lower planes of perception of systemic space. It therefore signifies points of Power from which the entire dispensation of the Logos emanates. This 'point' also acts as a 'mirror' that reflects the principles of the abstract Logos into manifestation.

The number 200 + 12 of the phrase *'the One is the indivisible point found nowhere'* implicates the way of the Heart, of the major second Ray dispensation, wherein all of the separative attributes of mind become unified into the Clear Mind of Reason (50) by way of the Heart centre. Within such a Mind the 'point' is found nowhere, as all becomes one coherent unified expanse of events, of being/non-being. The 'point' cannot be found when *saṃsāra* does not exist to individualise it, as there is no phenomena whereby it can be taken account of. This then describes *pralaya*, a period of abstraction *(śūnyatā)*. The number 100 + 9 x 5 of the phrase *'the One is the indivisible point'* refers to a Logos, here viewed as being a cosmic Master of Wisdom who establishes the Seat of Power of His/Her Logoic manifestation. As such the Seat of Power can be viewed as *indivisible* because from it manifests the unified whole.

Concerning a new *manvantara* we are told that this point is '*perceived everywhere during those periods*' (33). The meaning of such perception has already been described with respect to the evolution of the mind that discriminates and its development into a super-Mind. We can now more minutely analyse the significance of Mind in Nature's domain because the number 33 refers to the cycles of Activity and to the Creative Intelligences,[14] the Creative Hierarchies that manifest the sum of phenomena during *manvantara*. Human intelligence is also creative, with respect to the 'things' that it manipulates, the 'points' in time and space (as are the atoms of Nature), and accumulations of them, consisting of the various objects constituting human civilisation.

14 Symbolically 330,000,000,000 deities of the Hindu pantheon.

Wherever one perceives a thing, there can be considered a moving point in the mind's eye, which moves from point to point to create pictures, moving images of the transient phenomena people interrelate with.

The numbers of the phrases '*those periods*' and '*during those periods*' add to (98 = 49 x 2, 17). The periods concerned refer to *manvantara*, wherein the various septenaries in Nature (7 x 7 x 2) manifest upon all levels of perception. Even the Logos (17) manifests via seven Creative Hierarchies, Rounds, Chains, Schemes, Root Races of humanity, to lead all into higher states of Revelation, the purpose of any new *manvantara* to achieve. The demonstration of the effects of *manvantara* is *'perceived everywhere during those periods'* (211, 31). The number 200 + 11 here refers to the intricate *nāḍī* system of the Logos, which though is found 'nowhere' as far as empirical manifestation is concerned, because not seen by the physical eyes, nevertheless is 'perceived everywhere' through the development of the inner vision, as it encompasses the sum of manifest space. From it all phenomenal objects appear, or can be made to appear through the demonstration of the Will (31), hence the manifestation of *siddhis*.

We saw above that '*the indivisible point*' is *'perceived everywhere'* (113, 14, 5) during *manvantara* because of the innumerable number of individualities (egos, units of consciousness, 5) that come to exist and who are able to see everywhere with their consciousnesses. They can deduce the intricate nature of the meaning of such points and of their interrelatedness in the world with its great biodiversity, and in cosmos, with its innumerable 'points' in space (100 + 13): stars, and other interstellar objects. The number 2 x 7 here implies that such perception also happens psychically, astrally, for similar individualities can be found existing upon the inner realms.

'The Vertical and the Horizontal' arms of a sphere of manifestation (131, 32) would normally represent the fixed cross of the Heavens that conveys the complete expression of a *manvantara,* in terms of the four cardinal directions of space. By the numbers 100 + 31 and 32, however, what we are considering is in fact a *cardinal cross* of the projection of the power of the Will of Deity (100 + 31) to drive the process of *manvantara* and *pralaya,* of the appearance and recession of phenomena. This manifests nominally via the downward arm of the cross, to produce *manvantara* and an upwards direction to produce

pralaya. The east-west direction, or horizontal arm, concerns what will evoke Love-Wisdom (32) from out of the manifest evolving forms.

The vertical arm represents the dynamical forceful, penetrative masculine principle in Nature. This expresses the projection of the energies from the Logos (the *suṣumṇā nāḍī)* that fertilised the mundane Egg and which sets the entire dynamo of the evolutionary process into motion, inevitably causing the appearance of a human kingdom. Human Souls represent the dynamism of Love for the planetary sphere (the *piṅgalā nāḍī*) and are therefore the carriers of the consciousness-principle. They are secondary creators, being responsive to the qualities of the civilisations which they build via their incarnate personalities, and the associated *karma*.

The vertical and the horizontal arms therefore represent the mechanism whereby the entire Womb of space-time can give birth to all of the denizens that must appropriate substance and evolve therein. (At this stage the vision is upon the manifestation of a *mutable cross*.) The objective being to ultimately develop Love-Wisdom via the Initiation process undertaken by humanity, signified by the numbers 8 x 9, 18 of the phrase *'it is the Vertical'*. The associated number 72 = 6 x 12 here refers to the qualities of the sixth sign of the zodiac, Virgo. She holds an ear of wheat, signifying the procreative, nutritive forces of Nature. Implied is the work of the entire feminine *deva* evolution embodying the functions of the Womb of space-time that is impregnated (the vertical line) with the dynamic purpose of the new *manvantara*. The implication therefore is that this cardinal cross aspect exists in that Womb.

Once the mundane Egg has been fertilised then the attributes of the great Mother come into play (the *iḍā nāḍī),* as symbolised by the qualities of the sign Virgo and the numbers of the phrase *'the Vertical',* which add to 51 = 17 x 3. The number 17 x 3 informs us that the expression of the Creative aspect of Deity descends down this line of orientation during *manvantara*. This relates to the first Outpouring of the substance informing a sphere of activity. The entire Womb thus comes under the domain of the formative forces of the Mother, the *(deva)* substance that builds the purpose for any evolving form to be. The *devas* nurture and evolve that form to bring out the fruition of that purpose. *'The Horizontal'* (70, 16) line then manifests as the planes of substance, of the dimensions of perception (70), wherein the Christ-child (16) is made to grow.

The numbers of the complete phrase *'it is the Vertical and the Horizontal'* add to 152, 36. First we have the implication of a complete year of Brahmā (100 + 52), then the etheric body of the Logos (36 = 3 x 12), as governed by Gemini, the third sign of the zodiac, wherein 'the Vertical and the Horizontal' are manifest in terms of the established *nāḍī* system. (The *nāḍīs* manifest in this vertical and horizontal fashion, both in a human and Logoic body of manifestation.) There is also the subsidiary implication of Initiation (17 x 9, 4 x 9), which implies that the Womb exists so that all can evolve their evolutionary purpose and thereby gain the higher Initiations. Be this for the Logos (17 x 9), being a purpose why such a One manifests a new incarnation, or for a human kingdom, that must gain the ability to overcome the thrall of matter, to gain liberation, *śūnyatā,* (4 x 9). The entire evolutionary process must be rightly directed according to Logoic Will to produce such a consequence.

The commentary continues with a sequence of statements further explaining the meaning of the vertical and horizontal lines, to add to the basic meaning of the phrase *'the Father and the Mother'* (105, 24) that has already been provided. The number 10 indicates that '*the Father*' (the vertical line) is already perfected. The numbers 7 x 7, 13 inform us that '*the Mother*' (the horizontal line) represents the totality of the spheres of attainment (13) established by the Father. All of the septenaries and related subdivisions governing Nature and of the way that all in cosmos evolve (7 x 7) is then the function of the Womb of time-space of the Mother.

The numbers (105, 24) inform us that the interrelation between 'the Father' (the Dhyānis from a former evolutionary cycle) and 'the Mother' (the Deva kingdom embodying the substance of manifestation) together establish a planetary Head centre (105), a Shambhala, that manifests so that the dissemination of the forces of the Mind can eventually govern the sum of *manvantara* via the human bearers of mind. The number 24 refers to the second sign of the zodiac, Taurus the bull, signifying the continuous cycling wheels of Life in the zodiac, wherein wisdom can be evolved. Taurus is the power driving that entire zodiacal wheel forward in space.

The phrases *'the summit and base of the Father'* (100 + 3 x 5, 17 x 2) and *'the summit and base'* (12, 7 x 3) refer to the line of energy that stretches from the highest empyreal heaven (the Heart in the Head, the twelve petals of the Head lotus (12), to the foundation or support of manifest space, the concrete dense physical sub-planes (7 x 3) governed by the Base of Spine centre. The highest and lowest realms of attainment are thus linked by means of the Thought projection of the Father. Thought literally circumscribes the universe of forms and binds it together in one comprehensive, integrally united sphere of attainment. There also lies the significance of the phrase *'the One'* that integrates all, *'the summit and base'* into unity as 'the Father'. The number 100 + 3 x 5 informs us that this 'summit' concerns the mode of the active dissemination of the Mind (specifically the Intellect, Mahat) of the Logos from *dharmakāyic* realms, expressed as the Power (17 x 2) of the Logos reflected into the base, so as to govern the realms of manifestation. The Divine Thought discriminates to rightly determine the ordering and formation of all the particulars of manifest space.

When looking to a *summit* one's vision is directed to a mountain, or an extremely high place, to which our thoughts and idealism are directed. It often implies what is to be attained in the future. The number 11 of the phrase *'the summit'* informs us that this highest point of attainment, literally the established Throne of the Father, consists of intensified first Ray energy, which sustains the *nāḍī* system of all that is manifest. Esoterically this refers to the highest of the four cosmic ethers *(ādi)* associated with systemic space, to which evolving humanity must aspire. Also, viewing the number 11 as an *antaḥkaraṇa,* one can presume that it can be extended as far into cosmic Space as possible, so in fact there is no ending to this summit of the Father.

The numbers of the phrase *'base of the Father'* (22, 13) represent the 'base' or lowest level of expression, (the Base of Spine-Sacral centre interrelation), the sphere of activity (13, 4) upon which the Logos 'Sits'. From this foundation evolves the Womb (22) that the Logos has fecundated, allowing the reception and incorporation of zodiacal and planetary energies into the enclosed sphere (12). From this base all other *chakras* (factors of evolutionary expression), stem. The Womb is embodied by the next *chakra* up, the Solar Plexus centre.

By the numbers of the phrases *'the two extremities of the Mother'* (11) and *'the Mother'* (7 x 7, 13) we see that these extremities also incorporate *'the summit and the base of the Father'*. What distinguishes the Father from Mother is that the Mother is concerned with the factor of substance (the ethers), the manifestation of the *māyā-mūlaprakṛti* that encompasses space, whilst the Father is concerned with the Life principle that incarnates into the *māyā*. The substance of all of the seven planes of perception, wherein Mind constructs Thought-forms and consciousness evolves, is entirely the Mother's domain. Her agents (the *devas*) embody that substance in its entirety, hence all modifications of that substance are registered as part of their bodies of manifestation. They then reconstruct the modifications within substance so that beneficial results for the whole ('the One') are produced, which become the modifying *karma* of the denizens of the fields of Life. The *devas* utilise that substance as their bodies of manifestation, incorporated as the *prāṇas* in the *nāḍīs* (11).

We saw that the main line of interrelation is the *east-west horizontal line,* which has its source in the eastern direction, the Way of the Heart, that projects outward to the western direction of the expression of human activities. The focus therefore concerns the modifications of human *karma* nurturing people's hearts, as well as the outward expression upon the battlefields of strife, so that eventually humanity evolve compassionate understanding as to the true nature of the way all Life must travel. The numbers 13 x 5, 22 of the phrase *'the two extremities'* indicate this, where the number 13 x 5 refers to the expression of the five Jina Wisdoms that delineate the way of evolution of consciousness-space (of humanity). This represents the eastern extreme of the Way of the Heart of enlightenment-consciousness. Thus there is a boundless duration of being/non-being, where the 'indivisible Point' is 'found nowhere'. The number 22 on the other hand refers to the western direction of the bounded universe, the containment of the energies from the zodiacal conditionings, stars, constellations, galaxies, atoms, and planets etc. They can be observed and defined by the empirical mind and the effects of their energies experienced. Together all that produces the awakening of intelligence represents the Womb of space-time.

From or *'of the Mother'* comes the divine Christ-child (16) of the enlightened consciousness that is the objective of it all.

By the numbers 100 + 2 x 9, 4 x 7, 100 + 31 and 32 of the phrases *'extremities of the Mother'* and *'two extremities of the Mother'*, we see that they are similar to the 'extremities' of the Father, however the analysis is now from below up. The lower extremity represents the three planes of human evolution (the cosmic dense physical), of the mental, astral and the dense physical planes. They are part of the five planes of Brahmā, where the highest two planes are *ātma* and *buddhi* (4 x 7), the lowest of the four cosmic ethers. The lower three represent the Womb of consciousness-space wherein the kingdoms of Nature evolve the fundamental characteristics of mind, whilst *buddhi* represents the mode of release from that Womb.[15] This necessitates mastering the substance of its space via the Initiation process, specifically by mastering the Watery astral plane (100 + 18). Everywhere there is substance of some sort to be properly expressed by the *deva* evolution according to the impacts of energies upon them.

By the numbers 100 + 31 and 32 we see that the other extremity of the Mother represents the Will and Love-Wisdom aspect of Deity, that the Mother is also endowed with these qualities, but they are directed towards vitalising the substance and lives contained in Her Womb. Therefore all planes of perception and energies are included, because all comes within the scope of the nurturing embrace of the great Mother. The *devas* are cooperatively worked with via developed Love-Wisdom (32) and directed through mastery of Divine Will (31) by humanity.

The term 'reality' of the phrase *'in reality'* (50) esoterically refers to the *dharmakāya* level of interpretation (the domain of Mind, 50). The 'reality' here therefore is the expression of cosmic Mind. The numbers of the word 'nowhere', to which the 'extremities of the Mother' reach add to 7, whilst the phrase *'in reality nowhere'* provides the number 3 x 7 (as well as 31 x 3). The number 3 x 7 refers to the three lower planes of perception associated with *saṃsāra,* which are completely illusional because the substance is ever-changing. The term 'nowhere'

---

15 Note that *śūnyatā* is the realm of Emptiness, the Void expressing pure Love-Wisdom, but not the activity of the *devas*. *Śūnyatā* proper is the fourth sub-plane of *buddhi*.

refers to this perspective. Even the physical globe is moving through space at a constant velocity. Hence its locus is 'nowhere' because not fixed, always moving. The number 25 = 5 x 5 of the phrase *'reaching in reality'* refers to the mental plane, which is in reality the dense physical plane of a Logos, literally the substance upon which such a One 'walks'. Hence this is the lowest plane wherein the Mind of the Logos reaches. When the word 'nowhere' is added to the phrase it refers to what is below the Threshold of Consciousness of such a One, hence 'nowhere'.

The numbers of the complete phrase *'reaching in reality nowhere'* add to 14 x 10, and 32, 5, to which we can add the 31 x 3 of the phrase *'in reality nowhere'*. These numbers refer to the attributes of the Mind of the Logos that does this 'reaching out', by means of Love-Wisdom (32) and the active Will (31 x 3) from the cosmic astral plane (14 x 10), whereon the Logos resides, and which is the 'reality' herein referred to. It is the source of the consciousness associated with the systemic evolutionary impetus, whilst the Love-Wisdom principle (*bodhicitta, 32)* integrates cosmic Space (or cosmic Mind) with the empirical mind (5), which *'in reality'* is nowhere, because temporal, illusional. All however come within the embrace of the Mother's care. The cosmic astral energy, accessed through one-pointed devotion to Divinity so that the little ones evolving in systemic space can be nurtured, becomes the highest form of Love in our solar system. This energy reaches down to fecundate manifest space *('nowhere')* with its beneficence, to unite all consciously separative units within *saṃsāra* so as to be embraced by the One. The phrase *'reaching in reality nowhere'* therefore refers to the relation of the *dharmakāya* level (which 'reaches out to') to *saṃsāra.* From this perspective *'nowhere'* can also refer to *śūnyatā,* because it is 'nowhere', not a thing, nothing, Void, with respect to the evolving lives in *saṃsāra.*

The next section deals specifically with the level above what is titled 'nowhere', and which is more conventionally known as Māyā, or the etheric substratum of space. This becomes the focus of expression for the *trimūrti*, the triune Deity responsible for the evolution of any body of manifestation.

The Māyā—Trimūrti level of interpretation.

This level of interpretation is governed by the attributes of Ratnasambhava, the Equalising Wisdom infusing the cosmic astral (Watery) 'Breath' as the *māyā* of the centres, whose activities expand and contract according to the way of cosmic Mind in action. Our vision descends generally to the four cosmic ethers wherein exist the *nāḍī* and *chakra* system of the Logoi, whereon they establish their Seats of Power to produce their bodies of manifestation ('Rings'). Ratnasambhava's energy can be conceived of as the *bodhicitta* that drives each Logos to manifest as a Bodhisattva, to bring to liberation all lesser Lives constituting the forms via which they have incarnated. The phrase associated with this level is presented below.

> *For the One is the Ring as also the rings that are within that Ring. Light in darkness and darkness in light: the 'Breath which is eternal.' It proceeds from without inwardly, when it is everywhere, and from within outwardly, when it is nowhere—(i.e., maya, one of the centres). It expands and contracts (exhalation and inhalation). When it expands, the Mother diffuses and scatters; when it contracts, the Mother draws back and ingathers. This produces the periods of Evolution and Dissolution, Manwantara and Pralaya.*

The numerical breakdown:

The One (31, 13), *the One is the Ring* (86, 23), *for the One is the Ring* (107, 26), *the Ring* (45, 9), *the Rings* (46, 10), *within that Ring* (81, 18), *also the rings* (57, 12), *the Ring as also the rings* (104, 23), *the One is the Ring as also the rings* (145, 37), *the rings that are within that Ring* (155, 38), *the One is the Ring as also the rings that are within that Ring* (254, 65), *For the One is the Ring as also the rings that are within that Ring* (275, 68), *as also the rings that are within that Ring (168, 42), Light in darkness (71, 26), darkness in Light* (71, 26), *Light in darkness and darkness in Light* (152, 53), *the 'Breath* (42, 15), *Breath which is eternal* (100, 19), '*is eternal*' (40), *the 'Breath which is eternal'* (115, 25), *from without inwardly* (103, 22), *It proceeds from without* (111, 21), *It proceeds from without inwardly* (154,

28), *it is everywhere* (83, 11), *when it is everywhere* (106, 16), *from within outwardly* (103, 22), *from within* (63, 18), *when it is nowhere* (87, 15), *it is nowhere* (64, 10), *When it expands* (63, 18), *the Mother* (49, 13), *the Mother diffuses* (84 = Libra, 21), *diffuses and scatters* (69, 15), *the Mother diffuses and scatters* (118, 28), *when it contracts* (66, 12), *it contracts* (43, 7), *the Mother draws back* (77, 23), *draws back and ingathers* (85, 22), *the Mother draws back and ingathers* (134, 35), *the periods of Evolution* (111, 21), *Evolution and Dissolution* (102, 21), *produces the periods of Evolution and Dissolution* (208, 46), *the periods of Evolution and Dissolution (170, 35), This produces the periods of Evolution* (169, 34), *This produces the periods of Evolution and Dissolution* (228, 48), *Manwantara and Pralaya* (73, 10).

There are three main sections to this phrase. The first shall be titled 'the Rings', relating to the activity of the Father, the first Logos that utilises the Will to cause all to come to be. The second section relates to the second Logos and the Breath that sustains. The third section is that of the activity of the Mother, within which all is contained.

The Rings

The section opens with the sentence *'for the One is the Ring as also the rings that are within that Ring'* (275 = 11 x 25, 200 + 3 x 25, 17 x 4). We saw above that *'the Ring'* (9 x 5) refers to *'the unbroken circle'*, a sphere of manifestation (incarnation). This number refers to the fact that each circle is a sphere of initiatory undertaking bound by the Mind of a cosmic Master of Wisdom. What is incarnate within a 'Ring' therefore effectively represents the manifestation of such a Being's 'Ashram'. This Ring is a Thought-Form of the Logos (Īśvara), a sphere of limitation that has circumscribed an area of space. Therein the *maṇḍala* of the *manvantara* manifests. This is signified by the number 5 (signifying the Mind or Mahat) and its permutations of the phrase *'the One is the Ring'*. We thus also have the numbers 11 x 25, 200 + 3 x 25, 9 x 5. This entire passage needs to be interpreted from this perspective. The numbers of *the complete phrase* refer to the Logoic One who has perfectly mastered cosmic Mind, allowing that One to en-Soul all Life (25). This One thereby embodies all streams of Lives, boundaries of self-contained activity within these Rings, so that the Lives thus circumscribed can complete their evolutionary goal. The Logoic constraints are put thereby upon the cosmic forces and entities that could harm the progress of the *maṇḍala* containing the Lives. The Rings thus help to protect, much like the skin that delineates a cell, that allows the right nutrients to enter, excluding as much as possible that could harm the development of the life contained within. The number 17 x 4 reminds us that such Rings, as ‘boundaries of attainment’, are also Thrones, Seats of Power of any Logos, whose Meditation-Mind necessitates their establishment for the sake of those who must follow in the wake of the Way that the One has travelled.

The number 11 x 25 links the incarnate Souls (25) manifesting within the Rings to all similar Souls in cosmos via established *antaḥkaraṇas,* pathways, Consciousness-links in Space, incorporating the cosmic *nāḍī* system (11). All become One within the bounds of a solar system, and to all solar Logoi such a One has affiliations with. Such pathways allow group Souls to disincarnate and enter into *pralaya,* to travel to their appointed destinations, according to cyclic and Ray law, before manifesting again in a Logoic sphere at the appointed cycle of opportunity. The number 11 x 25 also implicates the Dhyānis (25), the great Ones Who incarnate into a Logoic Head centre. Each posses cosmic links (11) to similar Ones incarnate in other zones of cosmic activity (‘Rings’). The number 200 + 3 x 5 refers to the ability of a Lord of Love (200) to manifest divine Activity (3 x 5) of the Mind to accomplish Logoic Purpose via a body of manifestation. This is the higher cosmic correspondence to the way a human unit uses his/her empirical mind to produce the forms of desired activity in the world of the personality.

The numbers of the phrase *‘for the One is the Ring’* add to 107, informing us that this Ring circumscribes all of the septenaries associated with manifest space. *‘Within that Ring’* exist the high Initiates, the Lords of Life (9 x 9) that have established themselves within the Logoic Head centre, who thereby can guide the sum of the beings evolving through evolutionary space.

‘The rings’ contained within the one fundamental Ring are perfected zones, spheres of self-contained activity (10). They represent, for instance, the planetary spheres evolving within the solar sphere of

activity. Each such sphere of activity (a planetary or solar Scheme) contains lesser 'rings' of the Chains, Rounds and globes of experience[16] for those incarnate within them.

Concerning *'the rings that are within that Ring'* (31 x 5) there are two ways that these Rings can be analysed. First in the form of concentric circles. There are five such circles to a planetary Head Lotus, equable with the five levels of Shambhala explained in part A of my book *The Constitution of Shambhala.* These Rings are expressions of the energies of the Dhyāni Buddhas constituting the *maṇḍala* of manifest being/non-being. From them manifests interlaced rings of energies vivifying all embodied Lives. The number 31 x 5 here relates to these spheres of attainment in terms of the expression of emanatory Wills of these Jinas. The number 31 thus informs us that this way of cosmic Mind (5) is but an expression of the Divine Will of the Logos that sustains the duration of activities of all that manifest within the Rings for as long as there is a Purpose. When that Purpose has been fulfilled then the Divine Will abstracts the five streams of evolutionary expression,[17] producing the ensuing dissolution *(pralaya).*

The Rings can also be analysed in terms of the Schemes, Chains etc., manifesting in a sequence of cyclic events *(yugas)* within evolutionary space. They manifest in terms of 7 x 7 cycles of expression, or as the 777 Incarnations, explained in volumes 4 and 5A of my *A Treatise on Mind* series.

The numbers of the phrase *'the One is the Ring as also the rings that are within that Ring'* add to 254, 65 = 13 x 5. The number 13 x 5 has a similar connotation as above, wherein there are spheres of activity (13) governed by the expression of Mind (5). The number 200 + 6 x 9 is similar to the number 100 + 5 x 9 explained below, however, here we are concerned with a higher cosmic Initiate (the eleventh or higher Initiations),[18] hence has evolved to the level of a solar Logos, wherein other Logoi are included within such a One's Body of Manifestation.

---

16 These will be explained in detail in the following volumes. See also the introductory information presented in S.D., vol. 1, 152*ff* and the information presented in T.C.F.

17 The mineral, plant, animal, human and the divine (incorporating also the *devas).*

18 See the section on the higher Initiations in volume 7B of *A Treatise on Mind.*

The number 100 + 5 x 9 of the phrase '*the One is the Ring as also the rings*' refers to the fact that the Ashrams of the Masters of Wisdom, here viewed as members of cosmic Humanity (rather than being esoterically considered members of the cosmic animal kingdom), and all other zones of enlightened activity they embody, are similarly Rings of attainment within the Shambhalic domains of the Logoi concerned. All great Ones limit their zones of possible activity to appropriately assist those evolving within their care.

The number 104 of the phrase '*the Ring as also the rings*' refers to the ring-pass-nots of all Who play roles within the Shambhalic domain. All have evolved through the human kingdom (symbolised by the number 4). Also the number 104 = 52 x 2, which refers to the duration of the great cosmological years *(manvantaras),* the great years of evolution that delineate the progress of each Ring within the duration of a *mahāmanvantara.*

The number 12 of the phrase *'also the rings'* relates to the Heart centre, or to the twelve main petals of the Head lotus, which governs the evolution of each of these rings. There are also subsidiary connotations, such as the turning of the wheel of the zodiac, and the expression of all associated cycles as the rings revolve and undergo their journeys through space.

The numbers of the phrase *'as also the rings that are within that Ring'* (168, 42) refer to the establishment of Logoic Seat of Power ('that Ring') of the central Head lotus, from which all of the lesser 'rings' *(chakras)* derive their power (100 + 17 x 4) and accommodate the vicissitudes of the evolving forms (6 x 7), the spheres of attainment built by the Logos for the lesser Lives to evolve within. The number 168 when divided by 2 produces 84, relating to the sign Virgo the virgin, and when divided by 24 (signifying the attributes of Taurus the bull) produces the number 7. The number 7 relates to the seven Chains, Schemes and globes associated with these 'rings', whilst Taurus provides the substance that informs them, as well as assisting in turning the Wheels of their cycles of expression. Virgo governs the expression of the *devas* that embody the substance of the rings.

The next statement: *'Light in Darkness and Darkness in Light'* (100 + 52) is somewhat of an enigma, because 'how can light abide in darkness, or darkness in light', we might query, arguing that 'because where there is light there can be no darkness?' However it is all a question of the nature of the intensity of the light generated. The flame of a candle shines brightly enough to dissipate the darkness of night for a certain spherical distance from it. This is viewed as a light in darkness, but then the darkness in light can be construed to represent the shadows that are cast when a solid opaque object is placed in front of a light source. Also that candle light when placed in front of a 1,000 Watt beam of light is relatively seen as darkness. Similarly the sun's disc when viewed in a telescope shows dark and lighted patches, even though the coolest part of the surface of the sun is about 3,000 degree Celsius.

The different intensities of darkness (shades of grey, various types of shadows) indicate the differing intensities, states of consciousness, of those evolving within the enclosed spaces of the 'rings'. They indicate the various degrees of Initiation status, of the ability to contain and project the relative intensities of Light of the Initiates working to serve the Plan of the Logos. One can also look to the mode of manifestation of *manvantara* and *pralaya*. Both of these periods of the evolutionary process are symbolised by the number 52, which refers to a great Day, Year or Night of Brahmā. *Manvantara* contains the different eras *(yugas)*, from Satya Yuga, the golden age, to Kali Yuga the dark or iron age.

Light manifesting in the darkness of ignorance is another way of describing the way consciousness manifests in *saṃsāra*. Here darkness is but a term for ignorance, and the light is the light of reason, of knowledge, then of esoteric perception, the wisdom that sheds light in that darkness. This esoteric fact is symbolised by the stars in the night sky, which are light bearers dispelling the darkness of absolute space. The degree of the intensity of light is the measurement of the nature of the consciousness that has been generated to dispel the darkness of what is unknown.

At the ending of the evolutionary process the remaining darkness, the units of darkened resolved (or dark brotherhood), and that portion of the evolutionary impulse that have not attained perfection (enlightenment), must be recycled. They are abstracted into the intensity of the Light of the higher strata of being/non-being that qualifies the period of *pralaya*. Though *pralaya* is depicted as the darkness of night, it can actually signify a period of intense light that manifests at the ending of things. The concept of darkness is given for *pralaya* because it is likened to a deep sleep, which is the onset of darkness to consciousness, and generally happens in the darkness of night. However, it would be better to equate the *pralaya* period with the light of liberated consciousness. Within that *pralaya* there are spheres of darkened space wherein units of ignorance are contained.

The numbers of all the subsidiary phrases, plus the main phrase all add to 8, indicating that all happens as a natural consequence of the unfoldment of spiral-cyclic motion. The evolutionary process is spiral-cyclic, which indicates the way of the evolution of consciousness as time spirals through the expanding space of awakening consciousness.

The phrase *'Light in darkness'* relates to the effects of the Lords of Compassion to educate the ignorant, the mentally sleeping ones, as to the significance of what light reveals. This signifies a process of descent from above and can register in consciousness as illumination or the intuition. The corollary phrase *'darkness in Light'* relates to the ascending spiral of evolution, where the sleepers are awakening and developing the light of reason. Therefore the extent of the darkness that still exists there relates to the extent of their remaining ignorance. Inevitably we need to look to the level of Initiation status. This then represents the evolutionary process of ascent from matter, from the darkness of ignorance.

There are two types of energisation for these 'rings', centripetal (from without to within) and centrifugal (from the centre to the circumference of the sphere). First the centripetal type of motion is described, which relates to the processes of the Logos that leads to the creation of individualities, of unities, the 'self' around which individual *karma* can be woven, and who become bearers of the principle of mind. In their turn they become lesser creative agents. Such atomic unities are found everywhere in Nature. The centrifugal motion relates to the process of expansion of the consciousness of those ones gaining enlightenment, to produce their eventual release from the limitations of the 'rings'. Breaking free from the unit, to become all-encompassing they then can be considered 'nowhere', because they are 'no-thing', nothing whereby one can assign a locality to. Yet they become identified with the All, the One, which is everywhere.

The Breath

Next to consider is the phrase *'the "Breath which is eternal"'* (100 + 3 x 5, 25). In and out breathing refers to the coming and going of the cycles of *manvantara* and *pralaya*, but if the Breath '*is eternal*' (40), then the concern is with the eternal Now. This is the function that the second Logos (Viṣṇu), the Son aspect of Deity, provides. He sustains the universe. The qualities of the second Logos are therefore personified, whereas earlier, in the phrase 'Light in Darkness' the functions of the Creative deity (Brahmā), the third Logos (the Mother) are expressed. She embodies the Womb of materiality, the substance of manifestation (the 'darkness'). Therein the Light is poured, but the darkness must also be made to generate light. Light bearers must evolve, to eventually become the Light supernal of the first Logos (Śiva), who conditions the ending of things, the onset of *pralaya*.

The number 40 refers to the result of having established a Seat of Power that includes a *maṇḍala* of expression wherein a humanity evolves consciousness. The conditions must therefore be maintained to allow consciousness to flower into enlightenment. For this reason *'the Breath'* (6 x 7) regulating the cycles of Life must manifest eternally, for the duration of the existence that will allow consciousness to thus flower. The concept of breathing is synonymous with energisation, vitalisation and oxygenation of a living being. The reference here relates directly to the activity that vitalises consciousness. The number 6 x 7 thus implies that this eternal Breath lasts for the duration of the evolution of the Root Races as far as human evolution is concerned. Each Root Race is out-breathed and inbreathed, with the final Root Race signifying the process of 'inbreathing' or abstraction of the Breath of cyclic manifestation.

The numbers 100 + 3 x 5, 25 imply that this eternal Breath vitalises the cycles of activity of mind (3 x 5) for the duration of the great cycle of activity (100) of the kingdom of Souls (25). The entire world Soul *(anima mundi)* is thereby implied.

The number 100 of the phrase *'Breath which is eternal'* refers to vitalisation of the entire period of a great *manvantara* or Year of Brahmā. Within the scope of this *mahāmanvantara* the countless groupings and diversifications of the little Lives 'thrill' into activity. They evolve and progress along their appointed paths until the period of transcendence (termed *pralaya)* appears for them. *Pralaya* appears at the ending of the evolutionary accomplishment of any species of Life, regardless whether or not the major period of *pralaya* has ensued for the whole.

The numbers of the phrases '*It proceeds from without*', '*from without inwardly*' and '*It proceeds from without inwardly*' add to 111, 7 x 3, 103, 22, 2 x 77, and 4 x 7. The number 111 refers to the demonstration of the Will of Deity by means of this cyclical Breathing process upon all possible levels of expression to produce the purpose of the entire *maṇḍala* of the material domain (7 x 3). The strong force of Divine Will is thus applied upon all levels of expression via *antaḥkaraṇas* from various Logoic sources (stars, constellations) bearing the needed energies at the opportune times. Each sphere of evolutionary attainment is conditioned by external forces (environmental, solar, and Logoic) that help mould the shape of the form concerned and to direct its outward course to future purpose. The energies are woven inwardly via the Heart of the integral Life by means of the intricate *nāḍī* system (111, 4 x 7) as a consequence of being properly 'digested' by the Beings embodying the form. (The number 4 x 7 here symbolises the four cosmic *nāḍīs* wherein all of this is enacted.)

The number 2 x 77 reminds us that this is the mechanism whereby all beings, from Deity down to the smallest sentience, can undergo their '777 incarnations' to evolutionary perfection. What is expressed in the above is reflected in that below. The numbers 103, 22 refer to the active expression (103) of the energies from the starry Lives in the cosmos impacting upon the Womb of manifest Life (22). The energies direct the sum of the purpose of those incarnated in the realms of form. The number 103 also has a reference to the *deva* kingdom that help mould the evolving forms from within that Womb, as the sum of the environmental conditionings within which those forms live and develop is constituted of *deva* substance. This reminds us that the without to within motion essentially relates to the involutionary process, the formative period of any evolving entity. Literally it concerns the process of the Mother nurturing the child.

It is *'everywhere'* because what proceeds from without within are the cosmic energies directed by a Logos, the One that is everywhere. The form that comes into expression and is consequently vitalised is an effect of the Desire (106) or Love (16) of the Logos (the numbers of the phrase *'when it is everywhere')*. This phrase also implies that there is a timing process involved, when related to the consequent appearance of the little 'selves'. They are not 'everywhere' all at once, rather it refers to the dissemination of atomic unities (evolving Lives) appearing here and there as a evolutionary sequence, of stages of appearances of 'selves'. However the Breath blows upon all such 'selves' as integrated groups in the One body of manifestation. Group evolution is the way of the Breath; the units are part of organelles and organs in the composite body, and when the Breath blows upon them it is thus everywhere. Those that develop group consciousness consequently directly experience this Breath. The phrase thus indicates that the Breath manifests 'everywhere' within the ken of enlightened beings (16) that have appeared from out of *manvantaric* space (106). They have developed the Will *('it is everywhere'* = 11) to emulate the processes that Deity has established in impelling the great Breath that sustains the All. The enlightened ones project the *antaḥkaraṇas* of return along the pathways of approach manifested by the Breath (11). As an 'inbreathing' the Breath returns along the path it has travelled outwardly.

The phrase then continues with the words *'from within outwardly'* (103, 22), *'when it is nowhere'* (15). From the central point of each 'self', Soul form, or Logos (which together constitutes the constitution of the womb of time and space, 22) manifests the centrifugal motion (103) which is the returning Breath. This cycle of activity from the central point of the sphere of the manifesting divinity liberates that unity. It literally tears asunder the confining form of the ring-pass-not of the 'ego', which then no longer exists. Evolutionary purpose has been attained, and consequently the 'Breath' then is 'nowhere', as it exists in *śūnyatā,* the Void. The number 3 x 5 above refers to the activity of this Breath that now is 'nowhere'. 'Nowhere' in this particular case refers to the mind, the domain of thoughts, which do not have a specific locale in space. The enlightened Mind becomes expansive inclusive Reason, inclusive of the All, hence can be both everywhere and nowhere in the process of breathing in an out the thoughts. This is symbolised by the numbers 7 x 9 and 2 x 9 of the phrase *'from within',* which relate to the enlightenment process, that makes the consciousness 'nowhere' because it becomes inclusive of everything, everywhere at once.

The numbers 8 x 8 and 10 of the phrase *'it is nowhere'* refer to the spiral-cyclic energy that is generated by the *nirvaṇees* as they gain the evolutionary perfection (10) that liberates them. H.P.B's note here is that this refers to 'Māyā, one of the centres'. The source of generation of such substance is the Sacral centre *(svādiṣṭhāna chakra),* whilst the *māya* refers to etheric space, which, because it is not formed, a physical 'thing' per se, is 'nowhere'. It is not perceived by means of the five sense-consciousnesses, which are used to locate a thing in time and space, to name and assign a particular locality to that thing.

The Mother

This section is concerned with the attributes of the appearing form, of the Womb of time and space governed by the third Logos, the Mother. The next phrase to consider with respect to this is: *'It expands and contracts' (10).* We are told that this phrase refers to 'exhalation and inhalation' of the great Breath. When we look to the expansion process *('It expands',* 40, 13) then we see that it concerns the entire sphere of activity (13) from the centre to the circumference, and that circumference grows outwardly with each outbreathing of the Logoic Breath and then contracts. The number 40 informs us that the Logoic Seat of Power similarly expands and contracts. The numbers of the phrase '*expands and contracts*' (17) simply refers to the entire body of manifestation of Deity that moves in this way. The number 10 of the complete phrase refers to the complete *maṇḍala* of expression.

The numbers 7 x 9 and 2 x 9 of the phrase '*when it expands*' indicate that the expansion process of the entire *maṇḍala* of time and space concerns the methodology whereby its constituency passes Initiation testings along the way to higher sentient states, conscious awareness and then enlightenment for humans. Perception becomes more rarefied and subtle as Initiation proceeds. Contact with the higher planes signifies an expansion process. Consciousness expands to experience the All, hence '*the Mother diffuses and scatters*' (100 + 2 x 9, 7 x 4). The hold of the Mother is increasingly lessened upon the upward Way as the Son returns to the Father. The Initiation process (2 x 9) signifies the growth of the Son/Suns (units of Consciousness) who eventually supersede the epoch of the Mother. Her forces, the highlight being the potency of human intelligence, become more diffuse and scatter (are transcended) through the development of Mind upon the yogic path. Enlightenment and liberation from *saṃsāra* then come to the fore. The number 7 x 4 at first refers to the quaternary, which is superseded when the human unit integrates with the triad of the abstract Mind, *buddhi* and *ātma*. It also refers to the fourth plane, *buddhi,* wherein the Mother is effectively non-existent. The Initiation process offers the complete flower of the Son in incarnation and then liberation from all of the trammels of the form.

The numbers of the phrase *'the Mother diffuses'* add to 7 x 12 (Libra) and 7 x 3, whilst those of the phrase *'diffuses and scatters'* add to 3 x 5. Libra the Balances governs the meditative process associated with in and out-breathing, whether upon a human or a Logoic scale. All karmic factors, *skandhas* and *saṃskāras,* are thus breathed in and out as the process of life unfolds. The energies of the Mother are diffused as the attributes of the Son increasingly appear in *saṃsāra* (7 x 3). The karmic factors also appear to *scatter* when they are carried by the individualities that are units of inertia; average humanity that are primarily conditioned and swayed by the (mental-emotional) forces around them (3 x 5). They are not masters of their own destiny (as are the awakened) hence are swayed by the streams of group *karma* of the societies of which they are a part. When viewing mass or group interrelationships a random chaotic mess of such karmic factors appears to the enlightened Mind. The Bodhisattvas working within that mess try to bring order to the chaos and to refine the substance so that it becomes more vibrant and expansive via directed spiritual purpose.

The role of Libra is to equilibrate the available *karma* so that it too can be refined and consequently be eliminated. As this is being effected the attachment to the forces of the Mother wanes, becomes more diffuse.

The phrases *'When it contracts'* (66, 12) and *'it contracts'* (7) refer to the contraction of the circumference of the circle of manifestation back into the sphere of the central Eye from which all originally emanated.

This concerns the 'inbreathing' action of the Father. The 'it' here relates to the sum of the Body of Manifestation of the Logos (66), of all the septenaries in Nature (7), which are also conditioned by the twelve great zodiacal potencies (12).

The numbers of the phrases *'the Mother draws back'* and *'draws back and ingathers'* add to 77, 22, 13, and 13 x 5. We see therefore that what 'ingathers' is:

a. The circumference of the sphere of activity (13)
b. The Womb of space-time (22), and the associated septenaries of evolving Lives undergoing their cycles of incarnations (77).
c. The Dhyānis, or rather, the Rāja Lords governing the five planes of Brahmā (13 x 5) associated with the *karma* of the manifestation of *saṃsāra*.

The numbers 134 = 100 + 17 x 2 and 35 of the complete phrase, *'the Mother draws back and ingathers'* refers to the Son developing the Logoic Will (17 x 2) by abstracting His consciousness so as to travel to the Father. Abstraction, ingathering of the attributes of the Mother (7 x 5), is the consequence. The Will of the Father is reflected into *saṃsāra* to help accompish this process. This Will manifests upon all four pillars of the quaternary of manifestation governing the Mother's domain to cause it to draw all back to the central Logoic Eye (the source of it all).

'The periods of evolution and dissolution' (170, 35) have been described above. We see that the form of evolution explained here is not as depicted by the deductions of scientific materialism, which teaches natural selection via survival of the fittest. Rather we have guided embodied evolution, Intelligent Design, where the *devas* (the constituency of the Mother's department) guide the entire process via carefully selecting the genetic material of each species concerned, according to a pre-planned schema for their evolution. The *devas* embody the sum of Nature's domain, where the three lower kingdoms in Nature are the physical forms (vehicles) for the *devas*.

The number 7 x 5 refers to the sum of manifestation associated with the evolution of mind and thence its transcendence into Mind, which is then followed by the period of dissolution. Note that the phrase *'the periods'* refers to cycle after cycle of in and out-breathing of Life and of the streams of lesser lives. All happens as a consequence of the Logos also marching towards a comparative evolutionary perfection (17 x 10). One after another species of Life goes through its respective cycle of out-breathing and then the period of dissolution, to be re-emanated as a new entity (species) upon a higher cycle of the ever turning wheel.[19] The form is eliminated, or rather sublimated, to be rearranged so that it can bear a higher sentience or state of consciousness. Thus evolution proceeds.

The number 200 + 8 of the phrase *'produces the periods of Evolution and Dissolution'* refers to the spiral-cyclic motion (8) causing such evolutionary development in the field of consciousness (200).

The numbers of the phrases *'the periods of Evolution'* and *'Evolution and Dissolution'* are 111, 7 x 3, and 102. The number 7 x 3 refers to the three planes of human evolution (the mental, astral and dense physical, otherwise known as *saṃsāra),* as the domains wherein these periods of evolution and dissolution occur. The number 111 refers to the Wills of the Creative and Destroyer Logoi that produce the periods of evolution and then the dissolution (abstraction) of the cycle of evolution of each species, Races of humanity, and for the entire *manvantara* of opportunity. This number can also refer to the appearance of the *nāḍīs* throughout the Bodies of manifestation of the Logoi and then their eventual dissolution, The number 102 refers to the activity and work of the second Logos to sustain the entire process with the principle of Love-Wisdom (which allows karmic adjudication), so that the variegation of all the species can play out their anointed roles.

The numbers of *the entire phrase* add to 200 + 7 x 4, 4 x 12 (Cancer). Cancer represents the door to incarnation for all of the lives that must incarnate into *saṃsāra*, and technically also the period of dissolution, as its polar opposite is Capricorn, the mount of Initiation. The number 200 + 7 x 4 refers to the demonstration of the Seat of Power of a Logos (7 x 4) that sustains the *manvantara* with Love-Wisdom (200) for the duration of the great Year wherein all periods of dissolution and

19 As all species are interrelated the action happens concurrently for them, as well as individually for one or other of the species over a sequence of time.

consequent evolution of species must occur. This then is '*Manwantara and Pralaya*' (73, 19 = 10), the gist of which has been outlined above, concerning complete cycles of expression (10).[20]

This ends the section concerned with the Māyā—Trimūrti level of interpretation, and we can now concentrate upon the mode of manifestation of the *maṇḍala* of the five Jinas that cause the evolution of the Mind within the domain of being/non-being. 'Being' here referring to what exists in the domain of *manvantara*, and non-being referring to conditionings associated with *pralaya (śūnyatā).*

Fifthly, the expression of the Dhyāni Buddhas governing the three planes of human evolution.

This fifth level is governed cosmically overall by the attributes of Amoghasiddhi, whose All-accomplishing Wisdom synthesises the potency of the five Jinas, especially as they manifest their combined Power upon physical plane happenings *(saṃsāra).* The complete mastery of *saṃsāra* causes the perfection of this Wisdom.

> *The Germ is invisible and fiery; the Root (the plane of the circle) is cool; but during Evolution and Manwantara her garment is cold and radiant. Hot Breath is the Father who devours the progeny of the many-faced Element (heterogeneous), and leaves the single-faced ones (homogeneous). Cool Breath is the Mother, who conceives, forms, brings forth, and receives them back into her bosom, to reform them at the Dawn (of the Day of Brahmā, or Manvantara)...*

The numerical breakdown:

---

20 Note that here Blavatsky uses the term *Manwantara* whereas elsewhere she uses *Manvantara.* The term *Manwantara* is a phonetic rendition of the Sanskrit, and is correct from that perspective, however the modern transliteration is *manvantara,* and which was standardised ('corrected') as such in for instance the later fifth Adyar Edition of *The Secret Doctrine* (1962). The numbers of the phrase '*Manwantara and Pralaya*' add to 73, 19 = 10, which simply refers to 'perfection', which is the objective of the process. Another interpretation can be gained when the phrase uses the term *'manvantara',* which gives us the numbers 9 x 8 and 2 x 9 relating to the Initiation process producing that perfection.

> *The Germ* (40, 13), *is invisible* (1.11), *invisible and fiery* (93, 21), *The Germ is invisible* (97, 25), *The Germ is invisible and fiery* (143, 35), *the Root* (38, 11), *the plane of the circle* (95, 24), *the Root is cool* (66, 21), *during Evolution* (80, 17), *Evolution and Manwantara* (87, 15), *during Evolution and Manwantara* (124, 25), *her garment is cold* (81, 18), *her garment* (55, 10), *cold and radiant* (57, 12), *her garment is cold and radiant* (122, 23), *during Evolution and Manwantara her garment is cold* (205, 43), *but during Evolution and Manwantara her garment is cold* (212, 50), *during Evolution and Manwantara her garment is cold and radiant* (246, 48), *but during Evolution and Manwantara her garment is cold and radiant* (253, 55, 7.10.71.7), *Hot Breath* (43, 16), *the Father who devours* (97, 25), *Hot Breath is the Father* (99, 27), *devours the progeny* (93, 21), *the Father who devours the progeny* (158, 41), *Hot Breath is the Father who devours* (150, 42), *Hot Breath is the Father who devours the progeny* (211, 58), *the many-faced Element* (80, 35), *the progeny of the many-faced Element* (153, 54), *devours the progeny of the many-faced Element* (185, 59), *the Father who devours the progeny of the many-faced Element* (250, 79), *Hot Breath is the Father who devours the progeny of the many-faced Element* (303, 96), *(heterogeneous), the single-faced ones* (81, 27), *leaves the single-faced ones* (100, 37), *(homogeneous), Cool Breath* (45, 18), *the Mother* (49, 13), *Cool Breath is the Mother* (104, 32), *who conceives* (60, 15), *forms* (26, 8), *brings forth* (64, 10), *her bosom* (41, 14), *into her bosom* (63, 18), *back into her bosom* (71, 26), *receives them back* (68, 23), *receives them back into her bosom* (131, 41), *to reform them* (66, 30), *the Dawn* (30, 6.6), *at the Dawn* (33, 15), *to reform them at the Dawn* (99, 45), *the Day of Brahmā* (64, 19), *of the Day of Brahmā* (76, 22), *or Manvantara* (48, 6.6).

This paragraph can be interpreted in terms of referring to the mode of manifestation of the attributes of the five Dhyāni Buddhas. First we have the *Vairocana level of interpretation.* This is the most abstracted level, related to the Dharmadhātu Wisdom[21] and the expression of the Aetheric Element from the Domain of the presiding Logos. Hence it represents that into which all is abstracted. Cosmic *karma* is activated to begin the process of the formation of the Logoic sphere (universe, solar or world form) of activity. This level of interpretation is concerned with the phrase:

The Germ is invisible and fiery.

Next is the *Akṣobhya*[22] *level of interpretation.* This level of Logoic Activity reflects the abstracted into the manifested domains via the Mirror-like Wisdom, and the Airy Element upon His/Her Domain. The Logos meditates upon what is to be and ingathers His/Her forces so that the work can be accomplished. There is but one sentence associated with level of interpretation:

The Root (the plane of the circle) is cool.

The third level of interpretation is that of *Amitābha.*[23] Here the Fiery Element of the Logoic Mind is expressed to effect the actual manifestation of phenomena via the onset of *manvantara* via the Discriminating Inner Wisdom. The sentences to this level of interpretation are:

---

21 The Dharmadhātu Wisdom is the wisdom of superlative qualities. It is the pristine cognition of reality's transcendental expanse or sphere of empowerment. The fundamental essence or realm of the *dharma*, the *dharmakāya*. Vairocana is presented as the intensely luminous one, the illuminator. He represents the totality of all Buddhas, the centre of the *maṇḍala* of the Jinas. His colour is white, expressing the pure radiant or spotless consciousness, and manifests the teaching gesture. His consort (*prajñā*) is Ākaśadhātvīśarī.

22 The 'unshakable or immutable One', who possesses the Mirror-like Wisdom. The emanatory colour is dark blue. He manifests the earth-touching gesture (*bhumisparśa mudrā*) and establishes *bodhicitta* to achieve enlightenment. The direction is east, the vehicle is an elephant. Akṣobhya presides over the *vajra* family. The Consort (*prajñā*) is Locanā.

23 Amitābha, the Dhyāni Buddha of limitless or boundless light, red in colour. He manifests the Discriminating Inner Wisdom, and governs the western direction of outwards to the service of humanity. He is depicted in a meditation gesture (*dhyāna mudrā*). His vehicle is a peacock, and his symbol is the lotus blossom and Element is Fire. When presiding over the blissful land (Sukhavati), then is known as Amitāyus. His Consort is Pāṇḍaravāsinī.

But during Evolution and Manwantara her garment is cold and radiant. Hot Breath is the Father who devours the progeny of the many-faced Element (heterogeneous), and leaves the single-faced ones (homogeneous).

The Ratnasambhava[24] *level of interpretation.* Here the Equalising Wisdom is applied, ensuring that what issues forth is totally conditioned by the principle of Love, cosmically the Watery Element, from which the form is precipitated. The sentence for this level is:

Cool Breath is the Mother, who conceives, forms, brings forth, and receives them back into her bosom.

The Amoghasiddhi level of interpretation.[25] Here the All-accomplishing Wisdom is applied to the evolving form manifesting via the Earthy Element (the seven systemic planes of perception), to ensure that the outcome goes according to the originating Plan. The final sentence demonstrates this level of interpretation.

to reform them at the Dawn (of the Day of Brahmā, or Manvantara).

The Vairocana level of interpretation

The *maṇḍala* of the five Jinas begins with the construct of *'the Germ',* (40, 13) the seed point (13) whereon the Logos (Vairocana) establishes His Seat of Power (40). From this *bīja* the entire *maṇḍalic* expression will emanate. It contains *saṃskāras* and associated *karma* from past incarnations of Logoic activity.

---

24 Ratnasambhava's name means 'jewel-born' or 'source of the precious jewel', and governs the southern direction of the *maṇḍala* of the Jinas. His potency is the Equalising Wisdom *(samatā jñāna,* the equality of all phenomena), yellow in colour. Ratnasambhava's symbol is the jewel, the source of all precious things, and governs the dissemination of the Watery Element. His Consort is Māmakī. The gesture is of bestowal *(varada mudrā),* and his vehicle (*vāhana*) is the horse.

25 Amoghasiddhi, 'Unfailing success, unlimited accomplishment', the Dhyāni Buddha of the All-accomplishing Wisdom, manifesting the *abhaya mudrā,* demonstrating fearlessness. His colour is green and he occupies the northern position of the *maṇḍala.* His vehicle is Garuda and the emblem is the *viśvavajra* or sword. His Consort is Tārā, the mother of compassion. The Element he governs is Earth.

We are told that this germ *'is invisible'* (1.11), which means that it is beyond the reach of the sense of sight. What will make it visible, in the line of sight, is the development of the penetrative perception of the first Ray (1.11), utilising the Divine Will to awaken the third, All-seeing Eye (Ājñā centre) that can project the *antaḥkaraṇas* (11) thereto with the necessary potency to activate the Germ. Once its attributes are awakened, then they are brought into the light of the new cosmic Day wherein they can be 'seen'. What is 'invisible' exists as a point of latency within the cosmic *nāḍīs*. To 'See' necessitates one awakening the Eye of Vision via the appropriate meditation.

The numbers of the phrase '*The Germ is invisible*' add to 25, 16, informing us that this Germ can be considered a 'permanent atom', stored within the Soul aspect (Sambhogakāya Flower) of the Logos (25). The Germ is the Son (16) when the Logos reincarnates.

The numbers of the phrase '*invisible and fiery*' add to 31 x 3, 7 x 3. The number 31 x 3 indicates that at the appropriate cycle this Germ is activated by the Will of Deity to make it Fiery. The projection of this Will energises the spirals and spirillae of the atomic unit that is the Germ (7 x 3). The Germ will inevitably become the central point of Power of a new Shambhala, a manifesting Head centre. The Logoic Will infuses the Germ with the energies of cosmic Mind (Mahat) that awakens its activity. The Germ then becomes the zone of immutable Fire for solar or planetary Life. This zone becomes the Source of Mind for all Lives that will evolve within the cosmic dense physical plane via the spirals and spirillae of the Logoic physical permanent atom. The numbers of the *complete phrase* (7 x 5) informs us that this Germ is responsible for the manifestation of all attributes of Mind in Nature (via the *ātmic* plane), that will allow the evolution of the five kingdoms of Nature, senses, instincts, sense-consciousnesses, and inevitably the five types of Wisdoms of the Jinas. With such empowerment the Fiery Element works to transmogrify the dense physical plane. The numbers 31 x 3 and 7 x 5 here can also symbolise the first Outpouring of the *deva* lives incorporating the substance of the planes of perception.

The Akṣobhya level of interpretation

The next phrase to analyse, *'the Root (the plane of the circle) is cool'* (66,

7 x 3), concerns demonstration of the attributes of the Dhyāni Buddha Akṣobhya. We are told that *'the Root'* (11) represents *'the plane of the circle',*[26] which consequently manifests as 'the Mirror' that reflects the highest Wisdom, the Dharmadhātu, into manifestation via the qualities of the remaining three Jinas. All is therefore governed by the Mind of the abstracted Logos, whereas the remaining Jinas particularise the attributes of that Mind and process what must Be to effect its happening.

The Root that grows from 'the Germ' is that of the world or cosmological Tree. This Tree has its roots in the Waters of the cosmic astral plane, hence is inverted. Its trunk and branches symbolise the intricate *nāḍī* system of the earth (11), via which all of the nutrients, the five aspects of *ākāśa* that are the integrated Wisdoms of the Jinas, flow to feed the myriad Lives experiencing the ebb and flow process of *manvantara* and *pralaya*. There are myriads of smaller cycles of such coming and going within each major cycle. (The birth and death of each human unit for instance.)

'The Root is cool' (66) because the roots of this Tree emanate from the Waters of cosmic astral space, which provides the nutrients for the entire *manvantara*. By implication therefore these Waters are cool, and we can conceive this to be so because it is constituted of the consequences of the meditation Minds of the *nirvāṇees* travelling through this Space. The rootlets are 'grounded', integrated into the trunk, the main stem of this 'plant' on the plane *anupādaka* (that interrelates the Monadic groupings that come into manifestation) and extends to the *buddhic* plane, which channels the cooling Waters of the cosmic astral plane. The number 66 here has reference to these cosmic Waters, Logoic Desire (60 + 6), which then nourishes or vitalise the Lives manifesting within *saṃsāra*. Humanity reflects this attribute in an aberrant way through their desire-emotions, that has caused the appearance of the systemic astral plane. This phrase therefore specifically concerns the manifestation of the Logoic *piṅgalā nāḍī* system, rather than that of the *iḍā,* which will tend to be Fiery. (The disseminator of Mahat rather than the Waters of Love.)

---

26 The number 24 of this phrase refers to Taurus, which governs the general attributes of the cosmic astral plane.

The Amitābha level of interpretation

Akṣobhya's Mirror-like Wisdom is the essence of the *samādhi* attained by a *yogin*. This meditation-Mind is *'cold and radiant'* when serenely residing naturally in its own domain of the Clear Light, or of *śūnyatā*. When meditating upon *saṃsāra* (the conditionings of *manvantara)* the attributes of that Mind flow through to influence the manifest form *('her garment')*. The discriminating attributes determining the particulars of such a meditation is then an expression of Amitābha's Discriminating Inner Wisdom. All aspects of what must be are then carefully scrutinised so that the right outcomes will be produced.

From the statements related to the interpretation concerning Amitābha's function one can see that there are two levels to His meditation, in a similar manner that the mental plane is divided into an abstract (the higher mental plane) and a concrete portion (the lower mental plane). The meditation upon *'her garment'* is that upon the *deva* kingdom, whereas the expression concerning the manifestation of *'Hot Breath'* relates to the human kingdom. The *devas* effectively embody the attributes of the concrete portion, whose manifestation is therefore 'cool', only becoming perturbed (hence 'hot') when incorporated as aspects of human mental-emotions. The statement here is generalised, idealised, because the *devas* actually embody all substance, even that of the higher mental plane, however the *solar devas (dhyānis)* embodying human Souls are specialised to appropriately accommodate this *'Hot Breath'*.

The choice of terminology again confronts us, as to the difference between *'Manwantara'* and *'Manvantara'* numerologically speaking. Because the focus of the *manvantara* here is upon *'her garment'*, which relates to the attributes of the *devas,* who are *manasic* in their constitution, so the numbers with the powers of five are appropriate. This is provided by the use of the term *'Manwantara'*, which HPB uses, whereas if we used the term *'Manvantara'* then there would be a number of phrases, providing versions of the number four, such as 44, which relates to the human kingdom, therefore inappropriate.

When analysing the phrase *'her garment'* (5 x 11) we see that it refers to the 'garment' or sheath that clothes the Mother of this world. This 'garment' is governed or conditioned by the intensity of Mind (5 x 11). This then means that Her Mind's Will is *'cold and radiant'*

(12), and which thereby keeps the entire evolutionary impetus in thrall. This Mind represents the entire *deva* evolution, which are conditioned, in fact embody, the qualities and functions of mind/Mind in cosmic and systemic space. Such a Mind can be esoterically defined as being Space itself. Mind is the fundamental *deva* Intelligence that permeates space with its own essential nature. This Intelligence then diversifies everything in terms of atomic and subatomic unities, infusing the all with elementary sentience (or elemental wills). By its very nature this sentience will inevitably develop into consciousness, as borne by a human vehicle.

The nature of this garment is 'cold' because the *devas* do not have the human emotions that 'warm' thoughts up, often to emotional boiling points, such as in arguments, warfare, fanaticism, and critical assertions. The mode of activity of the *deva* kingdom can thus be considered to be cool, clearly perceived thought direction. Logical application of directed purpose is the way they travel. When the radiance (which connotes the nature of the emanatory colourings of the substance they embody) is added then the quality and extent of the related radiatory energy connotes the degree of direct connection to the Heart of Life (12). This concerns what might be described as the spiritual age of the *deva* in question.

When 'her garment' is just 'cold' then the pristine nature of the *deva* kingdom is implied, which relates to the expression of their Intelligences working abstractly in their own domains. There is no heat or passion in the mode of *manasic* activity of the *devas,* they work with cool, reflective Flame, with the need as it exists at any particular time. When the term 'radiant' is added, then the focus is upon the way they work via substance, the Womb of time and space, as signified by the number 100 + 22 of the phrase *'her garment is cold and radiant'*. Radiance is the effect of mind/Mind modifying elementary substance to produce evolutionary progression, the gain being viewed as 'radiance'. The number 22 relates to the planetary and zodiacal energies that impact upon and modify the substance of that Womb. The intrinsic nature of these energies is radiance indeed.

The numbers of the phrase *'during Evolution'* add to 16 x 5, 17. During the evolutionary process the emanatory qualities of the five Jinas (16 x 5) come to condition the sum of the evolutionary impetus manifested so that the attributes of mind/Mind can be evolved. All is directed by Logoic Mind (17).

The numbers of the phrase *'during Evolution and Manwantara'* (100 + 24 = Taurus, 5 x 5) refer to the evolution of wisdom from out of the principle of Logoic Desire, which is consistent with the symbolism of the sign Taurus the bull. Taurus turns the wheel of the zodiac upon its path, hence all of the lesser wheels come into manifestation and revolve under the auspices of the Eye of the Bull (the directed gaze of the Logos), which is concomitant with the evolutionary process. The type of evolution within Nature's domain concerning us here is guided evolution by means of the *deva* kingdom. They are the Intelligences (5 x 5) directing the entire course of the evolution of the species, which they embody in their entirety.

The number 124 also equals 31 x 4, which refers to the directive purpose of the Will of Deity (31) to impetus the entire course of evolution to its purposeful completion, via the establishment of a Throne (Seat of Power) upon which a Logos sits. This happens at the time of the Individualisation of humanity (within our earth Scheme). Thus *'evolution and Manwantara'* (15 = 3 x 5) can proceed, rightly guided and directed by the Creative Hierarchies of divine Beings and *devas* that have incarnated to make it so. The bearers of mind (3 x 5) can then evolve and play their appointed roles.

The world of the form wherein they evolve are governed by the Lunar Fathers *(lunar pitris),* who embody the substance of the three words of human livingness. The entire course of the evolutionary process is for the human unit to break free from the influence of the *lunar pitris,* hence to gain the experience of the liberated domains, the 'cold Flame' (clear Cold Reason), of the enlightened Mind.

The sequence 7.10.7.1.7 appears in the numbers of the phrase *'but during Evolution and Manwantara'.* This is but a version of the symbolic 777 Incarnations, which all lives incarnating into a *mahāmanvantara* must undergo as the lesser cycles *(yugas)* therein come and go. The number 200 + 5 of the phrase *'during Evolution and Manwantara her garment is cold'* simply informs us as to the 'cool and radiant' nature of the Minds of the greater *devas* that literally are the Consorts of the Dhyāni Buddhas and the other great Beings that embody a manifesting Head centre of a planetary or solar Logos. The Great Ones are conditioned by the second Ray, which 'cools' the Mind.

The numbers of the phrases associated with the Mother's garment being 'cold' add to 81, 18, 205, 7, 212 and 50. The numbers 81 = 3 x 3 x 3 x 3, and 18 = 2 x 9, here refer to the three main divisions of the *devas* (Agnichaitans, Agnisuryans and Agnishvattas) that are organised by Amitābha's Mind to produce the appearance of the *manvantara.* We are concerned therefore with the mode of reflection of the three orders from the abstract mental domain for instance into the lower concreted ones. The number 7 is self-explanatory with respect to the *devas,* as they embody the sum of the form nature, and are organised according to the law of Cycles and governed by ritualised Magic, as ordained by the seventh Ray. The numbers 205 and 50 remind us that we are here concerned with what is inherently Intelligent. The number 212 informs us that the way of the Heart (12) is described as 'cold clear Reason', because it is devoid of emotional considerations, therefore the epoch of Love-Wisdom (200) is 'cool' or cold by definition. Similarly the description of the meditation Mind, which is crystal clear, fresh and cool, like a snow-bound landscape. This number hence refers to the solar *devas,* those that are responsible for building the Soul aspect of all manifest Life *(anima mundi),* including that of the kingdom of the Sambhogakāya Flower.

The number 212 also equals 106 x 2, which relates to the process that reflects the energies ('cool Waters') of the cosmic astral plane into the systemic domains via the *anima-mundi,* which can also be considered the Womb of Life.

When the numbers of all the phrases containing the word *'radiant'* are grouped then we have the numbers: 12, 48 = Cancer, 5 x 11, 100 + 22 appearing, to describe the processes of the effect of the work of the *devas* in the formed realms. The numbers 5 x 11 and 100 + 22 have already been explained, hence it but remains to delve into the significance of the sign Cancer the crab and the number 12. The number twelve simply reminds us that in this solar system everything comes under the embrace of the Heart of Life, of the way of unfoldment of the twelve petals of the Head centre, and hence of the conditionings of the twelve signs of the zodiac. In the case of the *devas* one must interpret the influence of these signs in terms of their effect upon material substance. (The manifestation of the energies of mind/Mind.) The garment of the great Mother remains 'cold and radiant', especially after the appearance of the major second Ray period, whence evolution speeds up greatly as the evolving Lives begin to free themselves from the constraints of *deva* substance, in preparation to be born ('ejected') out of the Womb.

Cancer governs the conditionings within that Womb, the sum of the Waters therein, hence what in reality 'radiates', once the murkiness of human activity generated by people's emotional-minds have been clarified, refined, and transmogrified into the Airy Love-Wisdom principle. Cancer is the sign of mass incarnation, of mass sentience and the consciousness that develops when streams of Life first incarnate into, and hence identify with, the substance that forms their periodical sheaths, and the world around them.

Having delved into the 'garment' of the incarnating Logos, the Breathing process of such a One can be investigated. The second part of the statement re the *devas* and Amitābha's function is therefore focussed upon the Fiery nature of human evolution,[27] symbolised by the phrase *'Hot Breath'* (16, 7). The term 'hot' here literally concerns the intensity of the nature of the energies expressed in order to effect the evolutionary purpose of humanity. This is because the purpose of human evolution is to develop the Will via Love-Wisdom. (The Will being the most intense of the energies available.) Humans must evolve to be Logoi, and hence command (utilising Secret Mantra[28]), whereas the *devas* are receptive and build in response to what has been planned and Commanded. The numbers 16, 7 of the phrase '*Hot Breath*' here refers to the activity of the Logos, Īśvara, the cosmic Christ (16) breathing Life into all of the (seven major) groupings of Lives incarnating via the seven planes of perception (7).

---

27 One could question the nature of Fiery activity, such as volcanoes, the heat of a sun, ordinary terrestrial fire, which the *devas* are responsible. The effect may be hot, fiery, upon the physical plane, nevertheless the nature of the greater *deva* Minds that govern such effects is 'cool Fire', a controlled intensity of energy expression.

28 See the Buddhist volumes of *A Treatise on Mind* series for a proper explanation of the meaning of this term.

This is the background to the interpretation of the phrase '*Hot Breath is the Father who devours the progeny of the many-faced element*' (303, 96 = Scorpio). The nature and relation of the Monadic Life governing the expression of the human evolutionary process, to the kingdom of 'God' (Shambhala) is also implied. The emanatory energy of the Breath is also hot from the perspective that it is the expression of the Fiery cosmic Mind (Mahat). Fire is the Element that governs the mind/Mind. The number 303 informs us that at the beginning of the evolutionary process this Mind is actively Intelligent and manifests with the precision of the third Ray (3). It directs the panoply of the entire material manifestation of the Mother (300). Though the Mother's substance is cool the Fiery Wind blows through it to organise this substance according to Logoic Purpose.

The sign Scorpio, which governs strong energisation, martial activity, sexuality and testings in the field of Life, thus indicates that initially the Father impregnates the 'Seed' or 'Germ' of the Mother with vitalising purposeful Life that awakens the *bījas* of all the Life forms that are to be. This is heterogeneous because there are many different Life streams to be thus activated. The number 96 also relates to the Eye (the Ājñā centre) that directs the Fire that 'devours'.

The number 303 here also refers to the resultant evocation of *kuṇḍalinī* energies by the prospective *nirvāṇees* who will come into manifestation to preside over much of the activity. This Fire is imbued into all of Nature as a result of the primordial union between Father and Mother. The Fire manifests as the internal Heat sustaining all that is, and is also seen as result of the fusion of the primordial quarks of substance that bond together the nucleus of atoms (released in nuclear explosions or in radioactive decay of the elements of science). Thus this energy is causative of the nuclear furnace fuelling the radiance of a sun. The Fiery energy of the Logoic Will-to-Sustain integrates all forms into unity within the Womb of the Mother.

Kuṇḍalinī is the latent heat of the Mother, 'hot Breath' is the energy of the Father that will liberate it later in a Fiery conflagration. The Mother's garment (substance of her sheaths) may be 'cool' but her vital Life is warm, as this heat is necessary for the organisation of the separated forms into unities and coherent organisms. Life gradually evolves through the generation of an increasing amount of internal heat. From cold blooded animals to warm blooded ones, and from the warm blooded to those that can bear the Fires of intelligence, until finally the liberating furnace of awakening *kuṇḍalinī* is generated, so the story goes.

Kuṇḍalinī is properly awakened when the Monadic Word or Sound (i.e., of 'the Father') is called forth by the activity of the Son (the meditative *yogin* or *yoginī)* to travel down the spinal cord, thence to fuse with this latent heat stored in the Base of Spine centre. The many layered serpent is thereby awakened, which evolves to become the Fiery Dragon of Wisdom. For general humanity this happens slowly at first, with individuals here and there gaining the necessary internal heat to escape the bounds of form, but later entire groups will similarly accomplish their liberation.

Scorpio also projects the energy that causes the trials and testings of the Initiation process that will inevitably 'devour' the *'progeny of the many-faced Element'* (17 x 9, 6 x 9). This necessitates cleansing the *karma* that sustains all attributes of *saṃsāra* in those undergoing these testings. As each individual unit passes the required grade then it becomes absorbed into Shambhalic Life, hence 'devoured' by that kingdom. In this way eventually the entire kingdom of God is also inevitably Initiated into higher energies and Purpose (17 x 9) when enough streams of embodied spiralling Lives gain their liberation, and become *nirvāṇees.* These Lords of Life gain their release from the limitations of the Incarnation they have manifested for the duration of the planetary or solar Life. They can break the bonds of the ring-pass-not of the planet to play more exalted appointed roles in cosmos. The number 6 x 9 relates to the human Monads that stand as the 'devourers' for the kingdom of Souls that have been projected for the purpose of enlightening the human 'predicament', meaning here the mechanism of transforming the base substance of matter, hence making it Fiery.

The numbers of the phrase *'Hot Breath is the Father'* add to 9 x 11, 3 x 9. We see that this 'Hot Breath', in the form of the energy of the Father, manifests as the intensified Will to instigate the process of Initiation for all beings in our planetary or solar system, including the Lords of Shambhala (9 x 11). The Father's Breath (the third Outpouring[29]) starts

29 See Figure 3, of my book *Meditation and the Initiation Process,* 280, for explanation.

at the liberation of *kuṇḍalinī* at the third Initiation and persists for the higher Initiations. The invocation of the Father (the Will) to produce the higher Initiations is the way that liberation from the realms of form occurs.

The numbers of the phrase *'the Father who devours'* add to (16, 5 x 5). The number 5 x 5 here refers to what en-Souls all forms, whereas the number 16 simply informs us that this Father is a Lord of Compassion. This is also further exemplified by the numbers of the phrase *'Hot Breath is the Father who devours'* (6 x 25). Here we have that which en-Souls (25) all of the kingdoms of Nature in the planetary system. (The subsidiary number 6 x 7 of this phrase refers to the septenaries of the progeny that are 'devoured'.)

The 'Hot Breath' also assists humanity to produce their heaven and hell states, through their crass anger, fears, hatreds, etc. This astral zone of activity 'devours' or consumes humanity for many evolutionary epochs, whereby they have to suffer the resultant *karma,* until they learn not to pervert the available energies in a way that causes them and others suffering.

'The progeny' refers to those who are enlightened—Christs (16). They are Bodhisattvas, the Sons in incarnation who undergo the Initiation process. They can thus withstand the 'Hot Breath' of the Father, and so be 'devoured'. This is but a way of saying that they can then enter into the kingdom of Shambhala. The devouring process thus concerns the 'digestion' of the Initiates concerned so that their input into the planetary service can be properly processed, and their progress monitored, for them to be eventually expelled, ejected out of the system altogether into cosmos as *nirvāṇees.*

The numbers of the phrase *'the Father who devours the progeny'* add to 158 = 14 (2 x 7). The number 2 x 7 here simply implies that this Father is a member of the cosmic astral Humanity. Also that He draws the energy from the cosmic astral to intensify the Wills of the Initiates that are to be Initiated into the mysteries of this plane. When we add the phrase '*Hot breath is*' to this statement then we get the number 200 + 11, meaning that this Breath is the application of the Will as a consequence of the major second Ray cycle appearing in a body of expression, human, planetary or solar. The entire *nāḍī* system (11) becomes vivified with this Fiery Breath that liberates.

The numbers of the phrase *'the many-faced Element'* add to 16 x 5, 7 x 5. Here we see that there is an 'Element', a form that has many faces to it. The first major interpretation refers to the five Elements (5 x 7), and their 'many faces' or sub-Elements, manifesting ultimately as the plenitude of the forms encompassing Nature's kingdoms. These Elements are Ākāśa, Air, Fire, Water and Earth. H.P.B.'s commentary here is that they are heterogeneous. The Elements therefore represent what sustains the existence of *saṃsāra.* As the relation between the Elements, *skandhas* and *saṃskāras* have been adequately treated in my earlier books they need no elaboration. The number 16 x 5 refer to Dhyāni Buddhas (or the corresponding Rāja Lords) that are the major agents of *karma* responsible for the dissemination of the five Elements, *prāṇas,* sentience and consciousness-streams in Nature.

The *'the many-faced Element'* can also refer to the globes and Chains to an evolutionary Scheme, where each such sphere of activity (a 'head') can be considered to possess a 'face', with sub-attributes governed by the number seven, as are for instance the two eyes, two ears, two nostrils and mouth of a human face.

The numbers of the phrase *'devours the progeny of the many-faced Element'* add to 100 + 17 x 5. This number also refers to the functions of the five Dhyāni Buddhas, the five Kumāras responsible for the expression of the dissemination of these heterogeneous Elements. When the numbers of the phrase *'the Father who'* are added then the number 25 x 10 is obtained, which refers to the complete constitution of the kingdom of 'God', of the Lords that en-Soul the entire ten petals of the Logoic Solar Plexus centre. (This centre effectively is the way Shambhala appears to their Peers in cosmos.) This is so because it is primarily a centre for reception of cosmic astral energies and Impressions, for our system is a system of Love, and the source of all Systemic Love comes via these Invigorating Waters.

The numbers of the phrases *'Hot Breath is the Father who devours the progeny'* and *'devours the progeny'* add to 200 + 11 and 31 x 3. Both of these numbers relate to the expression of Logoic Will to 'devour' the All at the appropriate cycle. Here the number 31 x 3 refers to the Activity or third Ray aspect of this Will, which directs the general evolutionary Purpose and awakens *kuṇḍalinī* when appropriate. The number 200 + 11 relates to the second Ray aspect of the Will, which nurtures the awakening of the consciousness principle in humanity and the development of the Hierarchy of Enlightened Being. The number 11 also relates to the utilisation of the *antaḥkaraṇa* to incorporate sources of Love from other constellations in cosmos.

By the numbers 9 x 9 and 100 of the phrases *'the single-faced ones'* and *'leaves the single-faced ones'* we see that 'the Father' leaves the high level Initiates that are already perfected (100) and are also Lords of Shambhala to manifest activities on their own accord. They are the executive directors, co-workers with this Great Lord, and thus pass not through His Body of manifestation in the sense of being 'devoured'. They already are totally liberated from *saṃsāra,* members of the cosmic fraternity of *nirvāṇees.* They are thus 'single-faced', one-pointed as far as the evolutionary impetus is concerned and the direction of energies and Purpose they wield to those that form their bodies of manifestation within the planet. They are 'homogeneous' because there is no duality within them. They travel with the singleness of Purpose of Monadic evolution.

The Ratnasambhava level of interpretation

The Equalising Wisdom of Ratnasambhava here manifests in such a way via the Breath of the Mother so as to 'cool', harmonise the *manvantara* with the logic of the Clear Mind of pure Reason. Such a Mind therefore governs the entire evolutionary process within the Womb of the Mother. The progress of all Life streams is carefully weighed so that there is an integral harmony, a careful balance found throughout Nature, wherein all lives find an ecological niche, rightly playing out their appointed role with respect to all other Life forms within the environment of which they are a part.

Here the concept of *'Cool Breath'* (9 x 5) esoterically refers to the nature of the manifestation of the five *prāṇas* ('Breath') throughout the Mother's domain. It is the energy that produces the Initiation process of the five kingdoms of Nature, considered esoterically as the mineral, plant, animal, human and divine (the *devas,* plus the Initiated members of humanity). In its five main subdivisions the Breath, and Elements conveyed by the *prāṇas* sweep through the respective kingdom that each main *prāṇa* conditions. The Earthy Element mainly governs the evolutionary progress of the mineral kingdom, the Watery Element mainly conditions the evolution of the plant kingdom, and so on, with the Fiery for the animal kingdom, Airy for the human and Aether for the divine kingdom. The overall sweep of these conditioning influences is *'Cool Breath'*.

There are seven statements associated with this section concerning the phrase *'Cool Breath is the Mother, who conceives, forms, brings forth, and receives them back into her bosom'*. Five specifically concern the process of descent and two upon the path of ascent, for which the 'Hot Breath' of the Father is also utilised to assist in the abstracting process.

We therefore have:

Cool Breath	*anupādaka*
the Mother	*ātma*
who conceives	higher mental plane
forms	lower mental plane
brings forth	astral plane
her bosom	etheric double and *buddhi*
receives them	physical plane
back into her bosom	liberation from *saṃsāra*

The creativity of the Mother is ensconced upon the plane *ātma*. The creative Word emanates from there. The Airy Element ('Cool Breath') manifests via the plane *anupādaka*. Air is the governing *prāṇa* that conveys the five cosmic ethers, which the Mother utilises as Her Breath. (What is signified as Air here is the reflected Airy aspect of the cosmic Waters.) The forms to be are conceived upon the higher mental plane, as that which en-Souls Life. The forms consequently appear upon the lower mental plane as empirical consolidated shapes. This plane is cosmic dense from the Logoic perspective. The astral plane, a realm of energisation, 'brings forth', precipitates into activity the Idea-forms conceived Mentally. Here the Bosom of the Mother is the etheric double wherein exist the *chakras* and *nāḍīs* that sustain manifest Life. The higher correspondence to the fourth ether for humans is the plane *buddhi,* wherein the Logoic *nāḍī* system is found. The physical plane receives all of these energies in the form of concretised or materialised aspects of the originating Thought Forms. Upon this plane of perception the activities manifest via an appearing human kingdom that liberates the sum of what has been expressed in *saṃsāra* onto the plane *buddhi (śūnyatā).* This necessitates generating the Fires of the Father.

The path of descent concerns the movement of the energies from the plane *ātma* to the etheric. The dense physical plane is the plane of externalisation of all the energies and forces, as well as being the plane of ascent, wherein the Fires must be generated. To do so the attributes of both the higher and lower mental plane must be engendered, drawing forth the Creative Fires from *ātma* and also liberating *kuṇḍalinī.* These Fires must be fanned by the Cool Breath streaming from *anupādaka.* Such attainment concerns treading the Initiation path. What is here presented as 'Cool' is therefore only relatively so, it is still a form of Fiery energy needed to sustain manifestation, but which has its basis in the cosmic astral ocean. The *ātmic* Fires draw energies from the cosmic mental plane, being the effect of the interrelation of Father-Mother, to give birth to attributes of the form.

The descending Fire coming to liberate during the process of the attainment of the third Initiation onwards is the 'Hot Breath' from the Father, which has its originating Source upon the cosmic mental plane. This Breath transmogrifies the physical plane liberating its inherent Life, drawing all into the cosmic ethers. In utilising the Fire of the dynamic energy of the Will the prospective *nirvāṇees* find their placing upon the Monadic domain *(anupādaka)* in preparation for their ascent to cosmos. This plane therefore becomes 'Hot' in the process. There is a spiral-cyclic dance in relation to the interrelation between the Cool and Hot Breaths.

Having presented this outline it can also be said that the general energies via the Mirror-like Wisdom of Akṣobhya manifests as the *'Cool Breath'* upon *anupādaka.* The Mother utilises the Dharmadhātu Wisdom of Vairocana in terms of the regulation of this Breath and its effects in the manifest domains via the *ātmic* plane. Amitābha's Discriminating Inner Wisdom is then utilised to 'Conceive' upon the higher mental plane and materialises the Thoughts upon the lower mental plane. Ratnasambhava's Equalising Wisdom then brings forth what is to come into manifest expression, whilst Amoghasiddhi's All-accomplishing Wisdom grounds it all upon the physical plane. (His is the Power by means of which phenomena is actualised in dense manifestation.) The process that 'receives them back into her bosom' is also governed at first by Amoghasiddhi's power and then in turn by the evocation of all of the Wisdoms of the Dhyāni Buddhas. Liberation happens upon the plane *buddhi* via embodying the Mirror-like Wisdom and the complete expression of the Airy Element to produce the Clear Light of Mind.

The numbers of the phrase *'the Mother'* add to 7 x 7, 13, where the number 7 x 7 refers to all of the septenaries in Nature for which she is responsible. The 13 is but a numerological form of *'her bosom'* (14). It symbolises the Logoic sphere with the central dot, which is but a depiction of a breast or 'bosom'. The number 2 x 7 indicates that the 'milk' that is expressed through this 'bosom' is what emanates from the Waters of the cosmic astral plane, here styled as *'Cool Breath'*.

The numbers of the phrase *'Cool Breath is the Mother'* add to 104, 32. The number 32 indicates that this Breath is cooled through the energies of Love-Wisdom generated through the Mother's nurturing care and compassion for her children. The number 104 here refers to the harmonising energies of Ratnasambhava manifesting via this Bosom. (The fourth Ray implicated here being the middle between extremes.) The Creative Fiery energy must be carefully monitored by the Love-Wisdom principle so that it doesn't distort the evolutionary process, the birthing of the Son (the kingdoms of Nature, symbolised here by the number 104). Once humanity appears then the energy of the Breath can easily distort the emotions, or unduly facilitate the development of *kliṣṭamanas,* defiled mind, creating the murkiness of the systemic astral plane. The Mother's department consequently must evolve the varying degrees of sentience and consciousness within the evolving forms with tempered Breath, subdued Fire.

The numbers of the phrase *'who conceives'* add to 5 x 12 (Leo). The number 5 x 12 also refers to the five types of *prāṇas* that course through the *nāḍīs* of the Mother, the purpose of which is to give birth to humanity, here represented by the sign Leo the lion. This 'Son' is the carrier of self-consciousness, a human Soul. Therefore the human

Causal Body (Sambhogakāya Flower) is specifically what is conceived. Generally all that is born in the Womb of the Mother, the entire *anima mundi,* finds its conceptual framework (blueprint) upon the *ātmic* plane. All is conceived within the placid Minds of the great Deva Lords who are the main creative forces within that Womb. They work generally with Amitābha's energies, via which are moulded the Concepts that produce the conception of the forms that are to be.

The spiral-cyclic energies of the *prāṇas* (8) appear via the fourth cosmic ether, *buddhi,* and are directed to the conceived images that will manifest ('forms') upon the higher domains of Mind. The desired *manasic* shapes then appear, to complete the *maṇḍala* of what is to be, preparatory to the action of parturition. The entire *maṇḍala* is harmonised (energised) by means of Ratnasambhava's Equalising Wisdom, that then *'brings forth'* (8 x 8), condenses, the desired forms preparatory for manifest expression upon the physical domain. The Earthy-Fiery energies of Amoghasiddhi's All-accomplishing Wisdom is brought to bear to eventually precipitate the mental construct into the physical domain. Cool Flame mainly energises the astral plane, the Watery Womb, which for the *devas* is but a body of energies, a zone of energisation needed to precipitate the lives that come forth into objectivity. Humanity utilises the formative energies of this Flame and add mental-emotional input, which creates their astral plane heaven and hells.

The remainder of the phrase: *'receives them back into her bosom'* concerns the entire process of the evolutionary progression of Life from the smallest forms of sentience to humanity. We then have the march of the civilisations, and the actors therein, until the Initiates appear that can gain their release via the nexus between *saṃsāra* and *śūnyatā,* to enter the *dharmakāya.* (Which is the true Bosom of the Mother of the World.)

The phrase *'receives them back'* (68 = 17 x 4, 14) brings our focus to the astral plane (14 = 2 x 7) and its Watery substance, which from one perspective represents the Watery Loving embrace of the Mother, and from another, the hell-like battle zones of people's emotions. The entire battle with, and mastery of, the mental-emotions manifests here, hence we have the path of discipleship to the attainment of the second

Initiation. They are received back to this plane after having experienced the happenings upon the dense physical plane, wherein the grip of *saṃsāra* is strongest. Here therefore we are concerned with the upward arc of the evolutionary process. Mastery of the astral domain must be accomplished before one can come back to the Mother's Throne (17 x 4). Such ones have developed the Fiery attributes of 'the Father' (17) by becoming Shambhalic recipients. (Another interpretation of the number 17 x 4.)

The phrase *'into her bosom'* (7 x 9, 4.4.) refers to returning the fourth cosmic ether *(buddhi),* according to the above formula. Therein 'her bosom' sheds its cosmic astral milk via the plane *anupādaka*. The number 7 x 9 here simply refers to the process related to the attainment of the higher Initiations that will allow the associated Initiates to thereby enter through the central point of the Logoic sphere as a way of escape from the ring-pass-not of our planetary space. The number 4.4. effectively refers to the human *jīvas* (humanity being ruled by the number 44) that have their release, the Initiation status, that will allow them to pass through that 'bosom'.

The number 8 of the phrase *'back into her bosom'* refers to the spiral-cyclic motion that produces the evolutionary movement of the sum of *saṃsāra* towards 'her bosom', back to the central point of the sphere of all Life. All *saṃsāric* activity will have been brought to conclusion, and *pralaya* (disincarnation of the worldly sphere) will consequently manifest, in preparation for a new cycle of activity *(manvantara).*

She therefore *'receives them back into her bosom'* (100 + 31) as they develop the Fiery Will (31) to overcome all obstacles to complete liberation. Thus is achieved the great perfection (100), which is accomplished as a consequence of the entire *mahāmanvantara.*

The Amoghasiddhi level of interpretation

Amoghasiddhi's All-accomplishing Wisdom governs the manifestation of the entire Earthy Element, hence the general expression of the processes associated with the evolution of the cosmic dense physical plane, whereon the new *manvantara* is enacted. It also concerns the Initiation process whereby one gains mastery of the sum of manifestation.

The final phrases of the text: *'to reform them'* (66, 30), *'to reform them at the dawn'* (99, 45), *'at the dawn'* (33, 3 x 5), and *'the dawn'* (30, 6.6., 12) refer to treading the entire Initiation path that allows high Initiates to master the thraldom of the form and to enter through the Mother's Bosom upon the upward arc of gaining evolutionary perfection.

Here is also implied a recycling of the failures of previous epochs of evolutionary attainment (30) at the dawning of each new *manvantara.* They are the dark brotherhood and the humans that had not passed the necessary grade of achievement, as well as the denizens of the lesser kingdoms. They will continue the gist of their past evolutionary process within the context of the new educational conditionings, drawing forth *saṃskāras* that were formerly generated. *Karma* works to propel them along the road to enlightenment and consequent liberation from *saṃsāra.*

The number 6.6 or 66, is but a shortened version of the number 666, which refers to the entire corpus of entities that must evolve along the path of sex to produce the principle of desire, so to become a humanity, and then to move on, including that which is considered 'evil'. The number 3 x 5 refers to the evolution of intelligence. The numbers 30, 33, and 12 refer to the activity cycle of the new wheel of Love (12). The number 33 also has the subsidiary interpretation of referring to the Creative Intelligences that administer to the needs of the new evolutionary cycle, which is but a way of symbolising the mode of activity of the *devas.* They are the principle workers in the Mother's Bosom, ensuring that the *karma* of all that is will unfold as designed by the Father. Thus is the Son born, who transforms material substance into Love and Light.

One can also look to the numbers of the words parenthesised: *'of the Day of Brahmā, or Manvantara'.* The numbers of *'the Day of Brahmā'* add to 8 x 8, whilst those of the complete phrase add to 22. Also we have the numbers 3.6.3.3.7 presented, which emphasise the demonstration of a new cycle of activity (governed by the third Ray of Mathematically Exact Activity). The numbers of the phrase *'or Manvantara'* add to 48, referring to the sign Cancer the crab, which signifies mass incarnation and mass consciousness, the entire rebirthing process. We also have the number 6.6., explained above. The number 8 x 8 relates to the many cycles of expression *(yugas)* that will produce the evolutionary purpose, whilst the number 22 refers to the great Womb of the Mother wherein all this is to happen.

In conclusion I shall add here H.P.B.'s commentary following this Occult Catechism:

> For clearer understanding on the part of the general reader, it must be stated that Occult Science recognizes *Seven* Cosmic Elements—four entirely physical, and the fifth (Ether) semi-material, as it will become visible in the air towards the end of our Fourth Round, to reign supreme over the others during the whole of the Fifth. The remaining two are as yet absolutely beyond the range of human perception. These latter will, however, appear as presentments during the 6th and 7th Races of this Round, and will become known in the 6th and 7th Rounds respectively. These seven elements with their numberless sub-elements (far more numerous than those known to Science) are simply *conditional* modifications and aspects of the ONE and only Element. This latter is not Ether, not even Ākāsa, but the *Source* of these.[30]

Many are the planes of perception that one must master upon the upward way to cosmos, and as one does so an increasingly number of the Mysteries veiled by the night sky will become revealed. Until then the Mother's Womb is our benevolent home.

Oṁ

---

30 Ibid., 12.

4

Commentaries - Stanza 1

Introduction

We are now in a position to analyse the stanzas of *The Secret Doctrine* numerologically, to derive the veiled meanings hidden within them. The advanced esotericism of the causation process will then be comprehended. It should be emphasised that though the stanzas are said to relate specifically to the evolution of our earth Scheme, information can be extrapolated relating to the rest of cosmos because of the 'mirror-like' position of our earth in the local universe. The term 'universe' in *The Secret Doctrine* generally refers to the evolution of our solar system, from which one can extrapolate the attributes of the universe in general. Stanza one refers to the general conditionings within our solar system during *pralaya*, of which our earth is a part.[1]

In the interpretation of the following stanzas I shall somewhat dispense with the cumbersome 'long method' of dealing with every numerological statement. The interpretation will nevertheless be comprehensive by providing an explanation of every important number that illustrates the commentary, but will eliminate the tedium of repetitious statements necessitated by alluding to each number that appears.

Stanza one is divided into nine statements. This stanza relates generally to the plane *ādi*, which contains the 'blueprint' of the attributes

1 Stanzas 1 – 3 are primarily concerned with the general evolution of the solar system, whilst the earth Scheme is the focus from Stanza four onwards.

of the stanzas that follow, according to numerical affiliation. This 'blueprint' is an expression of the energies of the five liberated Creative Hierarchies associated with the first five stanzas that impact upon *ādi* and then from *ādi* to condition the remainder of the cosmic ethers. Upon this plane of perception exist the seeds *(bījas)* of all that will follow, once activated. Here specifically the main spirals of the Logoic physical permanent atom become abstracted. They will incorporate everything concerning Logoic manifestation when reactivated during *manvantara*. The presumption is that the universe that is to awaken will carry forward *saṃskāras* developed in a former incarnation.

Stanza 1:1 provides a general overview of the seven Eternities. Pisces the fishes, the sign of death and of termination of cycles, generally governs the import of this stanza. The glyph for this sign is of the two fishes united by a band. Here 'the eternal Parent' signifies one fish and 'her ever-invisible Robes' another fish, whilst that which wraps them is the uniting band. Effectively Stanza 1:1 relates to the *ātmic* sub-plane of the cosmic astral plane, from whence will emanate the *karma* that will cause the outpouring of the seven Eternities. Normally active upon this plane is the first of the Creative Hierarchies (termed 'Intelligent substance' in *Esoteric Astrology*[2]) who veils the manifestation of the rest under the guise of the phrase 'the eternal Parent'. This stanza is governed by the third Ray of Mathematically Exact Activity, hence is given a feminine gender.

Stanza 1:2, which relates to time and the 'infinite Bosom of Duration', is governed by the fourth Ray of Beautifying Harmony overcoming Strife and concerns the *buddhic* (fourth) sub-plane upon the cosmic astral plane. The fourth Ray here reflects the energies of Love-Wisdom, as all is conditioned by the principle of Love. From this Bosom will flow the cosmic 'milk' of the second Ray dispensation, projected via the fourth Ray,[3] to propel primal substance so that it spreads 'in milk white Curds' (Stanza 3:4). All Life is sustained thereby.

---

2 See Alice Bailey, (Lucis Press, London, 1968), *Esoteric Astrology*, 34-5 for the terms for all of these Creative Hierarchies.

3 Note that all of the Rays governing the liberated Hierarchies upon the cosmic astral plane are effectively subrays of the first Ray from the perspective of human consciousness.

The flow of this nutritive Compassionate 'milk' is the focus of our present solar incarnation. Here normally active is the second of the Creative Hierarchies (termed 'Unity thro' effort' in *Esoteric Astrology).*

The sign Aquarius the water bearer rules Stanza 1:2[4] and concerns the general abstracted non-differentiated state of the energy flow of the seven Eternities. Aquarius governs the emanation of cosmic Love, of the inevitable activities of a Logoic Bodhisattva when He/She awakens. The glyph of this sign symbolises the curdling of the substance of the 'Depths of Mother' when time awakens. This will happen when the central dot ('nipple') of this 'Bosom' moves in spiral-cyclic motion from the centre to the periphery of the bounded sphere.

D.K. states:

> In this solar system the vibration of the cosmic astral plane is becoming dominant, and through that vibration, travelling via the fourth cosmic ether (whereon as earlier stated are the etheric centre of the planetary Logoi) and our systemic astral plane, certain eventualities become possible. The "Sons of desire," logoic or human, can learn certain lessons, undergo certain experiences, and add the faculty of love-wisdom to the intelligence earlier gained.
>
> Our solar Logos, and the Heavenly Men, are polarised on the cosmic astral plane, and the effect of Their life energy as it flows through the systemic "Heart" can be seen in the activity of the astral plane, and in the part sex and passion play in the development of man. At the close of this mahamanvantara there will be ready for manifestation in the coming third system nirvanis who will be, in very essence, "active intelligent love"; they will have to wait until the five lower planes of the system have reached a stage of vibratory development which will permit them to enter, as the nirvanis in this system waited until the three lower planes became adequate in vibratory response. We are here speaking in terms of the Heavenly Men.[5]

Stanza 1:3 deals with the first Eternity upon the fifth (mental) cosmic astral sub-plane via which manifests the Intelligent attributes (Mahat)

4 We are consequently concerned with the reversed zodiac in this analysis, which generally conditions the mode of travel of those ensconced in *saṃsāra.*

5 T.C.F., 687.

of the Father aspect of Deity. The fifth Ray of Science comes into dominance here. The bearers of Mahat into manifestation are collectively denoted here as 'Universal Mind'. The expression of Mahat is governed by the attributes of the sign Capricorn the goat. The concept of 'eternity' here relates to the function of the Mind that recognises the durations of Being, once cyclic time is awakened. On each level of these Eternities 'slumber'[6] the self-conscious Lives (Creative Intelligences) that had evolved in the former evolutionary expression, and who are to play definite roles in the new cycle. The first two of the liberated Hierarchies in our present solar system, veiled in the Stanza 1:1 and Stanza 1:2 are effectively abstractions. The third of the liberated Hierarchies 'Light thro' knowledge' is veiled in the symbolism of Stanza 1:3, and hence is an emanation of the first Eternity. The fourth of the Liberated Hierarchies, titled 'Desire for duality', 'slumbered' in the second Eternity (Stanza 1:4). The fifth of the Liberated Hierarchies, titled 'Mass life. Veiling the Christ', 'slumbered' in the third Eternity (Stanza 1:5). Of the seven Creative Hierarchies that will actively incarnate in the cosmic dense physical plane only four are effectively self-conscious, the remainder relate to the substance that needs to be liberated. First we have the 'Divine Flames' manifest upon the plane *ādi,* the fourth Eternity (Stanza 1:6), then the 'Divine Builders' upon the plane *anupādaka* and the fifth Eternity. The 'Lesser Builders' 'slumber' upon the plane *ātma* in the sixth Eternity, and the 'human Hierarchy, Lords of Sacrifice' find their home upon *buddhi* within the context of the seventh Eternity. This schema is of course only a rough outline in terms of the existence of the Creative Hierarchies of conscious Lives, but the stanzas themselves only indirectly relate to them, being more concerned with the general esotericism of the nature of the levels of *pralaya.*

---

6 I am using the concept of 'slumbering' here for the Creative Intelligences that would be normally active upon the respective plane of perception, however in *pralaya* an entity 'slumbers' upon a higher dimension than they would be normally active upon. For example most humans will 'slumber' on the astral plane during the sleep of the human personality upon the physical plane. To transpose such concepts to Creative Hierarchies, whose functioning already is very abstruse is not done in the stanzas *per se,* rather they relate to the forms of appearance and activity that would be in *manvantara,* however the view is now upon the non-existence of such activity, implied by the concept of 'slumbering'.

Stanza 1:4 refers to the 'seven Ways to Bliss' and the 'causes of misery'. Continuing from the above, this stanza therefore refers to the second Eternity upon the sixth sub-plane of the cosmic astral wherein the fourth of the Liberated Hierarchies, titled 'Desire for duality', 'slumbered'. These 'Ways of Bliss' are embodied by the Son aspect of Deity, bearing the energy of cosmic Love associated with the Waters of this sixth astral sub-plane. They are the *nirvāṇees* from the former solar evolution, and will administer to the new streams of humanity that will evolve in the forthcoming solar incarnation, who will get ensnared by the causes of misery. The duality that is 'desired for' is here indicated by the juxtaposition of the concept of 'Bliss' to the 'causes of misery', which will manifest upon the appearance of *saṃsāra*. Logoic Desire expressed via the sixth Ray of Devotion-Aspiration will eventuate the appearance of the Schemes and globes wherein the manifesting Lives will play out their appointed roles. Sagittarius the archer will direct the *karma* of the evolving human kingdoms at the appointed time.

Stanza 1:5, concerned with 'Darkness alone', relates to the third Eternity upon the seventh sub-plane of the cosmic astral wherein 'slumbered' the fifth of the Liberated Hierarchies, 'Mass life'. This 'Darkness' is ruled by the seventh Ray of cyclic Power and Ritual activity of the Mother, who embodies the substance of what is to appear. Naught yet is manifested within Her Womb, hence the Father-Son-Mother aspects of the triune Logos, of those incorporated in the first three Eternities, are still waiting for the cycle of corporeal manifestation into the cosmic dense physical plane. This Trinity will consequently be reflected into the attributes of the lower three Eternities via the mirror-like aspect of the fourth Eternity. This will represent the 'fall of the three into the four' for the new Wheel. Because Consciousness had not yet appeared to register Light, so 'Darkness' ruled. The Creative process for the new *manvantara* will properly begin via the auspices of Scorpio the scorpion. Scorpio will ensure that the tests, trials and tribulations for the new world sphere will manifest to rightly progress the entire *manvantara*.

Stanza 1:6 relates to the fourth Eternity upon the first systemic plane, the first cosmic ether *(ādi)*, where the focus is upon the 'Son of Necessity', the new Logoic Form that will soon manifest. Therein 'slumbered' the

'Divine Flames', the first of the Hierarchies that will incarnate. The emanation of the first Ray of Will or Power will ensure that this 'Son' (the new Logoic *maṇḍala)* will reflect into manifestation the attributes desired by the Logos. Libra the balances will regulate the cycles of the in and out-Breathing of what is to be and to rightly incorporate the *karma.* Via Libra therefore the Logoic physical permanent atom, and the cycles of expression governing the appearance of the septenaries of manifestation (Rāja Lords, etc.) will come into being. *Ādi* represents the demonstration of the Will of the Father in systemic space.

Stanza 1:7 therefore relates to the fifth Eternity upon the second cosmic ether *(anupādaka)* where 'slumbered' the 'Divine Builders', from which emanates the causes for Existence, Monadic Life and the appearance of a Logoic Head centre. They govern the manifesting streams of Life into dense physical incarnation.

The functions of the Son (governed by the emanation of the second Ray of Love-Wisdom) in systemic space first happens upon the second plane of perception, *anupādaka.* At first however the Mother must give birth to the forms via which the Son evolves, but Her functions are reflected via *anupādaka* from the fifth cosmic astral, which draws upon the emanative cosmic *karma.* The Mother's energies impact upon the next plane of perception, *ātma.* This causes the first Outpouring that empowers the five planes of Brahmā. The 'causes of Existence' that emanate from the Mother's Bosom are the *devas,* and for our world system they flow through the second plane *(anupādaka)* to effect their work, colouring their substance with the principle of Love, with which everything in this solar system is conditioned by. This Outpouring comes under the directive Eye of Virgo the virgin, who rules the Mother's department.

Stanza 1:8 relates to the sixth Eternity upon the third cosmic ether *(ātma)* whereon the abstracted Life broods, stretching boundlessly, existing in 'dreamless Sleep'. Upon this plane 'slumber' the 'Lesser Builders'. From this domain emanates the *karma* that will propel the 'one form of Existence' into manifestation when the awakening is to happen. The general characteristics of this Existence is governed by the attributes of the sign Leo the lion, who governs the self-conscious individual, Logoic or human. This represents the Son aspect of deity that is reflected into manifestation and will evolve from out of the substance emanated via the first Outpouring.

Stanza 1:9, the final verse of the first stanza refers to the Soul aspect of all Life (the 'alaya of the Universe') that must awaken in evolutionary space if manifestation is to proceed. The sum of cosmos is veiled by the fourth cosmic ether *(buddhi),* bringing our vision also to the higher correspondence of *buddhi* in Stanza 1:2 ('the infinite Bosom of Duration'). The concern is now with the seventh Eternity and the direct Will of the Father aspect of Deity, which empowers the formation of the *nāḍīs* and the evolution of the kingdoms of Nature upon the dense physical plane. This allows the appearance of Dangma (the Initiate) and the opening of his/her Eye. The forces within this Soul-form prepare the Lives for incarnation into the three lower sub-planes of the cosmic dense physical via the impetus of the sign Cancer the crab, who governs mass incarnation. Upon *buddhi* 'slumber' the 'human Hierarchy', the 'Lords of Sacrifice'.

These *seven Eternities* can be tabulated thus:

5th cosmic astral	Domain of the Father	first Eternity
6th cosmic astral	Domain of the Son	second Eternity
7th cosmic astral	Domain of the Mother	third Eternity
Ādi	The Mirror (Darkness Alone)	fourth Eternity
Anupādaka	Son of Necessity	fifth Eternity
Ātma	Causes of Existence	sixth Eternity
Buddhi	One Existence	seventh Eternity
Higher mental	Alaya of the Universe	Reflecting the seven
Lower mental	Dangma – the Eye	Māyā to be mastered

Table 1: The Seven Eternities

Stanza One part One

Stanza 1:1 states:

> **The eternal Parent *(Space)*, wrapped in Her ever invisible robes, had slumbered once again for seven Eternities.**[7]

7 This statement is from the 1888 edition of *The Secret Doctrine,* 35, where H.P.B. begins her actual commentary. I have changed throughout the upper case that H.P.B. uses for the text to lower case, and presented appropriate capitalisation, as this makes for a better presentation of the text.

Keynotes: Pisces, cosmic astral *ātmic* sub-plane, the first Creative Hierarchy, the third Ray.

The numerical breakdown of the first phrase:

The eternal (45, 9), *The eternal Parent* (74, 20), *Space* (17, 8).

Stanza 1:1 begins with the sign Pisces the fishes, which brings to a conclusion the *manvatara* of the earlier activity, and projects all of its Life into a deep sleep state *(pralaya).* The cord that united the 'fishes' swimming in the Waters of *saṃsāra* is broken, and 'The eternal Parent' is abstracted into the cosmic astral plane, whereon it consequently 'slumbers'. This can be likened to a personality on earth, who goes to sleep at night, and 'slumbers', the brain consciousness is not awake, but the astral body is quite active. Similarly for a cosmic Logos. Hence the viewpoint of these stanzas relates to one being incarnate and 'sleeping', rather than disincarnate. Consequently the concern is with the periods between *manvantaras,* rather than that of a *mahāmanvantara,* which can be likened to complete death, hence sleepless abstraction. For a period of complete dissolution of the life of a *mahāmanvantara* for a solar Logos however, the third *ātmic,* cosmic astral sub-plane is indicated, signifying the abstraction of all of the *karma* concerning the former activity.

H.P.B.'S essential commentary.

> The "Parent Space" is the eternal, ever-present cause of all—the incomprehensible DEITY, whose "invisible robes" are the mystic root of all matter and of the Universe. Space is the *one eternal thing* that we can most easily imagine, immovable in its abstraction and uninfluenced by either the presence or absence in it of an objective Universe. It is without dimension, in every sense, and self-existent. Spirit is the first differentiation from THAT, the causeless cause of both Spirit and Matter. It is, as taught in the esoteric catechism, neither limitless void, nor conditioned fulness, but both. It was and ever will be.[8]

The numbers of the phrase *'The eternal'* add to 5 x 9, which informs us that cosmically speaking, what manifests eternally is a Master of

8 Ibid.

Wisdom, one who has perfectly evolved the cosmic Mind (Mahat) and has transcended the concreted reflection, the empirical mind.[9] Transcending the mind (wherewith the cycles of time are derived) produces an eternal state of being/non-being, not limited by the durations or categories of phenomena formulated by mind. Such an entity (on a human, planetary or cosmic scale) can manipulate primordial substance and circumscribe it into a sphere of activity, a zone of time reckoning. This substance can then be imbued with the right qualities, and finally be dissolved at the appointed cycle.

By virtue of the number 5 x 9 we can also look to the great Mother as this Parent, because the Space that will inevitably be incorporated in Her Womb will be conditioned by Mind and will undergo Initiation progression. She is the cosmic Master that will form the new sphere of activity. The Mother bears the energies of the third Ray of Mathematically Exact Activity needed to rightly categorise and organise the contents of that Womb when the time comes for its activity. The Mother evolved aeons ago from the status of being a Mahāchohan, governing the dissemination of the five Rays of Mind for an earth-like sphere.

The numbers of the word *'Space'* (it is in parenthesis partly to separate it from the rest of the phrase numerically), add up to 17 or 8, the number associated with the word 'God',[10] to whom we can equate the concept of a Parent. *Space is an entity,* a fundamental occult postulate. By the number 8 we see that Space is also fundamentally an expression of cosmic electricity, manifesting as spiral-cyclic motion. Space is viewed via the fourth cosmic ether *(buddhi),* the cosmic etheric

---

9 A Master of Wisdom has evolved from a previous cycle of evolution which He/She has completely mastered (the three planes of human livingness) and now commands all of the Words of Power governing these planes via the *ātmic* plane upon which the Master resides. Such a One becomes a 'parent' or Father to the *jīvas* that will incarnate into the new *manvantara.* Note that the terms Master and Adept are often interchangeable, because though an adept is technically an Initiate of the fourth degree, the term also signifies one who has mastered the phenomena of the three planes.

10 I normally parenthesise this term because the word is open to considerable interpretation, from that given to by various theists and philosophers, to the esoteric view presented in my books of a 'God' being a Buddha that has evolved into a Logos (meaning 'embodied Word').

double, which conveys *prāṇic* energy in the form of *ākāśa*. *Ākāśa* is the higher correspondence to the *prāṇa* that vivifies our etheric forms.[11] *Ākāśa* is that subtle supersensuous essence that pervades the Space of the four cosmic ethers, our higher planes of perception. The term is derived from the Sanskrit root *'kas'*, meaning to radiate, shine. The word *ākāśa* also directly translates as 'space', where space is that through which things must manifest in order to make a visible appearance. Through this 'space' things thus come into being. *Ākāśa* can also be considered the Space of the Consciousness that resonates the eternal Sound. This 'Space' can also be considered an emanation of the 'Intelligent substance' that D.K. denotes to be the attribute of the first of the Creative Hierarchy, which now 'slumbered' at this level of expression. This is the 'intelligent substance' of the Mother, but which also veils the attributes of the triune Logos.

The word *eternal* means without beginning and without end, existing throughout all time, a state of timelessness. It constitutes the activity of the entire life-span, the full hundred years (*mahākalpa*) of the Life of Brahmā. Brahmā is the eternal prototype of all Masters. He is the Creative Deity and therefore the Parent of all manifested Life.

The numbers of the phrase *'The eternal Parent'* add to 11, 20. The numbers 11, 20 and 30 (of the word 'eternal') denote this Parent to be the embodiment of the triune Logos:

- *The Father*, symbolised by the number 11, informing us that He is the embodiment of the first Ray energy of Will or Power. He is able to extend the *antaḥkaraṇas* of Purpose in all directions of space, which must be done if He is to be a Parent and instigate (impel) the creation of a form (the manifest universe).

- *The Son* (the number 20), implying what will evolve from the Womb created and impelled by Father-Mother is the consciousness principle, thence the perfected embodiment of Love-Wisdom.

- *The Mother* (the number 30), the perfected embodiment of the third Ray of Mathematical Activity, which conditions the Womb of time and space, and that causes the phenomenal interrelation of

---

11 See *Esoteric Cosmology and Modern Physics* for detail.

all manifested life. At first the third Ray of Activity (the Mother) is latent, but soon becomes the primary procreative agent.

The attributes of these three are integrated as 'the One'—also viewed as the *Monad*. The Monad, signifying, 'singular, unity', the Spirit aspect of whatever is to BE can also be viewed the eternal Parent, the Adept Who is 'God' (Space) and Who at present is abstracted into the fundamental triune Ray expression, as indicated by the numbers of the phrase *'the eternal parent'*.

When the time comes for *manvantara* the Father projects a solitary Ray of Power (symbolised by the number 11) that becomes the cord that unites the 'fishes' swimming in the Waters of *saṃsāra,* and so Pisces, the entire wheel of the zodiac, is activated. That cord differentiates into manifold diversity (the Activity of the Mother), integrating various manifesting Life forms into a unified whole, hence there is but One Life and that is of the Father, but which becomes Father-Mother when the Son is to be born. At first the 'fishes' represents the Monad-Soul interrelation and later the Soul-body interrelationship.

The numerical breakdown of the second phrase:

> *wrapped in* (52, 16), *ever invisible* (70, 16), *Her ever invisible robes* (100 + 3 x 5, 5 x 5), *in Her ever invisible robes* (12, 30), *ever-invisible robes* (31 x 3, 21), *wrapped in Her ever invisible robes* (167, 14).

The word *wrapped* means covered or concealed. The number 16 of the phrase '*wrapped in'* (52, 16) here refers to the robes of the Christ, the Love-Wisdom principle in cosmos. This directs our vision to the plane wherein the cosmic Sambhogakāya Flower resides. There the set of robes that wraps a cosmic Christ (here our planetary Logos) emanates. During *pralaya* everything is abstracted within the embrace of this cosmic Soul form, from which they must re-emerge at the appropriate time. The number 52 refers to the life span of a great cosmic year (of Brahmā), or because of 'slumbering', the inference concerns a night of Brahmā. This night is divided into seven Eternities (5 + 2 = 7). There are seven sub-planes (sheaths) to each plane of perception, and as an entity must evolve through seven sheaths, planes, *lokas*, or spheres of manifestation, so this can be said to take 'seven Eternities' or *yugas*. Because of the sleeping process these 'seven Eternities' can relate to the seven cosmic astral sub-planes. This is symbolised by the number 14 = 2 x 7 of the phrase *'wrapped in Her ever invisible robes'*. Therein the Lives embodied by the Logos are 'wrapped' during the *pralaya* period.

Note that a robe can conceptually be depicted by the plain disc:

which is motionless and dark. When all the robes are taken into account then we have a series of interrelated layers of substance. They enclose slumbering Space within the symbolic walls of a Womb for seven Eternities. This can be symbolically depicted in the form of seven concentric circles:

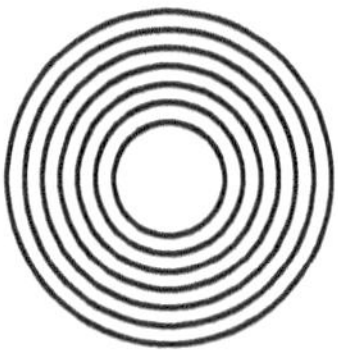

Figure 1. The ever-invisible robes

The number 22 of the word *Her* is of interest as it is the number associated with the planetary and zodiacal forces that vitalise the kingdom of the Soul, which gives birth to the pilgrim that evolves through all the Rounds of manifested life. The feminine in Nature builds with these forces, which thus organise the substance of Her Womb. The prime concern here are the forces (manifesting *saṃskāras)* of the Soul that have been abstracted back into pristine Oneness during a great *pralaya*. This Soul is an Adept on its own domain, but needs to gain dominion over the cosmic physical plane and so must eventually awaken from its slumber.

The phrase *'ever invisible'* (70, 16) means what is never visible to the physical *eyes,* therefore to the empirical mind. The empirical mind's eye is directed one way only, downwards into the material domain, hence the inner Eyes *(chakras)* needed to perceive the 'invisible' are not awakened. The physical eyes are concerned with visualising material forms that are conditioned and controlled by the mind for cycle after cycle. (The esoteric meaning of the word 'ever'.) The mental-emotions and desires of humans condition and cloud their little world view, obscuring any possible image of the 'ever-invisible'. The robes are only invisible whilst the mind is conditioned by time and its cycles (signified by the word 'ever'). Once one enters a timeless zone to view via the *chakras* then these 'ever invisible robes' become visible because the limiting cycles have been superseded.

Each cycle represents a day or waking period of visual perception. What is 'ever invisible' therefore is what is 'immaterial', subjective, non-perceptive to the visual sense-consciousness for any cycle of material activity. Upon the abstracted higher mental plane the Soul, for instance, is certainly imperceptible to physical sight as well as to lower clairvoyance. The Soul is not a material form cognisable by the eye of the empirical mind, yet acts as a window, a higher Eye that can look towards the Monad, as well as to the embodied form.

The number 70 of this phrase relates to the septenaries of material expression of the cycles that come and go. The number 16 signifies the number of the Christ-principle (Hierarchy) and its activities, which is 'ever-invisible' to the materialistically focussed.

Note that the phrase 'ever invisible' manifests a dual significance:

a. The word *ever* (meaning always, constantly, at any time), which relates to cycles of sustaining mental concepts that never materialise, always remaining abstracted.

b. The word *invisible*, signifying what is not perceived by the conscious mind, is not mentally or physically apparent.

When linked to the concept of 'robes' then the implication is that these robes manifest cyclic activity not apparent to the empirical mind. This process has a similar significance as the meaning of the phrase *'the fall of the three into the four'*, which concerns the way that the triune Deity is reflected into the physical world, allowing the qualities of the subjective realms to materialise into/as the formed realms. The triangle of divinity becomes a square as soon as matter is formed and regulated, for when another factor is added to the triangle it must geometrically become a square so that it can keep the resemblance of form. The prodigy, the resultant form, is thus objectively differentiated from the Cause. The process of manifestation therefore proceeds from the third—the Mother (the lowest expression of the abstract triune Deity) and She expresses Herself as the fourth principle—the manifested universe. This principle is symbolised by a square. As the creative process unfolds to form the material world, so this world tends to reproduce itself as countless different forms, all reflecting (in differing degrees) the triune qualities of Deity. The square is illusory and though it has a momentary reality, it has no permanence in the scheme of things. It symbolises the transitory material world, and is an arbitrary medium between the archetypal and what is projected into objectivity. Whilst consciousness resides within the domain of the 'square' then the formative forces that caused its appearance is invisible.

The dual implication of the statement *'ever invisible'* can thus also be viewed in terms of:

a. The material world, which can be considered metaphorically ever-invisible to the enlightened, for it is illusionary, *(māyā),* hence effectively 'non-existent', though is a field of service. Logoi have transcended the ability to see into the three lower sub-planes of the cosmic physical. They are dense physical to them, and so below their threshold of Awareness. From this perspective the planes of *saṃsāra* can be considered 'ever invisible' to them.

b. To those focussed upon the dense material world, the subjective domains are 'ever invisible', specifically the four higher planes. The physical senses have not the ability to contact, touch or see them.

These subjective domains are planes of abstraction, into which all Life is incorporated during *pralaya*. They constitute what might be considered the energy body of the cosmic Christ where the potency of the energies are such that they would destroy the mechanism the form would utilise to see. Once the substance of the eyes have become sufficiently refined to withstand the energy impact, then they will perceive the awakening *chakras*. The process necessitates transformation and transmutation, which inevitably causes the fourth Initiation, where through a process of complete renunciation the Initiate is freed from all material identification. (This concerns undertaking an individual *pralaya* by the Initiate concerned, termed *śūnyatā* in Buddhism.) The transforming energy produces the radioactivity and destruction of all atomic Lives and also eventually the Soul-form.

A *robe* is a long outer garment that clothes and can be taken off or put on at will. The esoteric implication is that of a sheath or coat of skin. H.P.B. states:

> Thus, the "Robes" stand for the noumenon of undifferentiated Cosmic Matter. It is not matter as we know it, but the spiritual essence of matter, and is co-eternal and even one with Space in its abstract sense. Root-nature as also the source of the subtle invisible properties in visible matter. It is the Soul, so to say, of the ONE infinite Spirit. The Hindus call it Mulaprakriti, and say that it is the primordial substance, which is the basis of the Upadhi or vehicle of every phenomenon, whether physical, mental or psychic. It is the source from which Akāsha radiates.[12]

The 'ever invisible robes' are essentially the result of the projection of Mind by the Creative Deity, and are constituted of *deva* substance. They are consequently an aspect of the Mother's domain. The human Soul similarly builds the sheaths of the personality into which it incarnates, and these sheaths are also appropriated from the *devas*. In a sense all mind/Minds build 'robes', which are but the thought-forms conveying ideas. A robe is a veil that hides what it covers from viewers. It becomes invisible if the eyes are not focused upon it, and this idea underlies the various interpretations of the meanings of this stanza.

The numbers of the phrase *'ever invisible robes'* add to 31 x 3, 7 x 3, 12. Such 'robes' could be considered to be enigmatical, as they must be seen by those who can 'put them on'. For these robes to exist it thus implies the existence of 'invisible' agents that can utilise them. All such beings (as are Lords of Shambhala) have evolved over aeons of time from what can be viewed by the physical senses to the invisible. The number 7 x 3 here refers to the robes of the spiritual triad, *ātma, buddhi, manas,* which are veiled to normal physical perception. The number 31 x 3 concerns the robes of the triune Logos, which are embodiments of the first Ray of Will or Power (31), hence beyond the vision of all but

12 Ibid., Vol. 1, 35.

the highest Initiates. The number 12 here implies the energies of the twelve signs of the zodiac, or to the twelve Creative Hierarchies, where the nine highest embody the substance of these ever-invisible robes. The zodiacal energies vitalise that substance with twelve different potencies. The robes that clothe the body of Logoi are so rarefied as to be not seen by anyone but those who can view via the spiritual triad, because without the All-seeing Eye awakened such substance is ever invisible. Initiates greater than the fourth degree, who reside within the four cosmic etheric sheaths are enlightened, hence freed from the lethargic effect of the cosmic dense plane and so are capable of seeing such robes. Their Eyes can withstand the intensities of the associated energies. Logically also, once in *pralaya* it is possibly to see such 'robes' because the being is residing within the plane or planes wherein they exist.

With respect to the phrase *'Her ever invisible robes'* (100 + 3 x 5, 5 x 5) we see that these robes are an expression of the activity (3 x 5) of the Intelligent Mind (Mahat) of 'the eternal Parent' (100). The concept of 'the eternal Parent' is also dual in that this Parent is at first androgynous, Father-Mother, hence eternal. It manifests as the Mother for the process of a *manvantara*, yet remains eternally abstracted as the Father (the Monadic aspect of this Parent - 100). The triadic sheaths ('Her ever invisible robes') of the Mother aspect also manifests to embody the empirical form, once 'the three' fall into 'the four'. The numbers 100 + 7 x 5 refers to the Mahatic activity of the Mother, which produces the expression of the five Dhyāni Buddhas in Nature. The numbers 7 x 5 and 5 x 5 also refer to the activity of the *devas*, who embody mind/Mind *in totia*. The Mother en-Souls the angelic triads.

The number 25 also relates to the higher mental plane, which constitutes the substance of the three tiers of petals of the Sambhogakāya Flower (the Soul form). From the viewpoint of a human personality the higher mental plane is incorporeal. It is the realm of abstraction and of archetypes, of energy and energy patterns. The lower mental plane is empirical and formed (concrete), being where the archetypal patterns of the higher mental plane manifest in the form of symbols and images, which can be seen, defined and utilised by the concrete mind. This is not so on the higher mental plane, therefore its sub-planes (robes) can be considered ever-invisible from the perspective of the lower planes.

The numbers of the phase *'in Her ever invisible robes'* add to 30 or to 12. These numbers relate to the Life of the Mother (the number 30), plus all the Lives associated with the twelve Creative Hierarchies that will incarnate during the next out-Breathing of the solar or planetary Logos. They exist within these robes.

The numerical breakdown of the third phrase:

> *had slumbered* (7 x 7, 13), *once again* (42, 6 x 7, 3 x 5), *slumbered once again* (78 = 15, 2 x 12 = Taurus), *had slumbered once again* (91, 28), *for seven Eternities* (31 x 3, 12), *seven Eternities* (6 x 12 = Virgo, 9 x 8), *slumbered once again for seven Eternities* (171 = 9, 3 x 12, 4 x 9, Gemini), *had slumbered once again for seven Eternities* (100 + 7 x 12, Libra, 40).

The *'seven Eternities'* (72 = 6 x 12—Virgo, 9 x 8) do not just refer to seven durations of cyclic slumbering 'Breath', but also to seven planes of perception into which the Life of a former solar system abstracted into. As cosmic Mind, which was the objective of the former solar Logos to achieve, rules all of these Eternities, so their focus was the mental sub-plane of the cosmic astral. The gain of this present solar system is Love-Wisdom, hence the focus of the sheaths is upon the fourth and second cosmic ether, and inevitably the fourth cosmic astral sub-plane. The number 72 refers to the complete duration of the ideal age of the life-span of a person (or Deity), similarly for these Eternities. They concern the subjective levels of perception (such as the cosmic astral plane) whereon the necessary experiences and material can be gathered in preparation for dense physical incarnation, allowing the actual descent and awakening. Virgo embodies the store of primal *deva* substance *(mūlaprakṛti)* that the Logos (Īśvara) must utilise as the basis for incarnating into His/Her periodic sheaths. Such substance also constitutes the store of *saṃskāras* to be incorporated into the new Day.

The number 9 x 8 symbolises the nine stages of the gestation process. The properties associated with the Virgoan disposition and the qualities to be gained by the child She is to bear, was the object of meditation of the Logos. Within Virgo's Womb the divine Christ child (the present planetary system) is formed. The number also reminds us that the purpose of the incarnation of a Logos is similar to the process that eventually makes a Buddha (presently an Initiate of the eighth degree) when birth into the dense form will no longer be necessary.

To *slumber* is to be to be asleep, in an inactive or quiescent state as far as external activity is concerned. The number 36 of the phrase *'slumbered once again for seven Eternities'* implies the sign Gemini the twins, which governs the four cosmic ethers, within which the Mother slumbered for these 'Eternities'. This number also refers to the subjective framework via which the Creative Deity can manifest a form, the temple of the Lord. The twins can also symbolise the male-female interrelation, of the entire evolutionary process that leads to 'union'. Gemini governs the energy body of the 'slumbering' manifest form. The Logoic Thought will eventually direct the *prāṇas* to awaken the sum of the male and female cellular constituents of the body. By the time the sexes in planetary evolution are differentiated then a significant way has been travelled towards the condensation of the physical form via the etheric framework. Thus:

The mental conception and first beginnings - the sign *Aries.*
The projection of desire - the sign *Taurus.*
The establishment of the etheric framework - the sign *Gemini.*
Finally, the physical incarnation - the sign *Cancer.*

This *manvantaric* process was yet to manifest, as all Life was abstracted into the innermost etheric recesses of this 'Temple'. All Life was absorbed into the Logoic *dhyāna,* wrapped in the robes of the four cosmic ethers. During *pralaya* a Soul is focused upwards towards the spiritual triad and the *buddhic* plane, and not downwards into the realms of form.

Being a member of the main sequence of stars, common cosmic Humanity, the solar Logos is polarised upon the cosmic astral plane. The planetary Logos would also be abstracted onto that plane, which is here likened to a sleep state. Similarly a normal person is at first abstracted into the etheric body before travelling to the astral plane for the duration of a night during sleep. This Logoic interlude is said to last for 'seven Eternities'—for seven periods of internal growth, acquiescence to the new conditions, before eventual awakening to a new Day of activity.

The numbers of the phrase *'slumbered once again'* add to 2 x 12, 3 x 5. The number 2 x 12 refers to the sign Taurus, which signifies the principle of (cosmic) Desire (for objects of the senses, etc.), which is non-active during this slumbering process. Taurus governs the general attributes of the cosmic astral plane, whereon three of the sub-planes of these 'Eternities' manifested. Together therefore, Taurus-Gemini govern the planes and sub-planes of the 'seven Eternities' within which the Logos 'slept'. Note that this phrase is in past tense, and when likened to a person's sleep where the astral body journeys into subjective space, we see that it gleans information and prepares for the next day's accomplished. A personality sometimes remembers this experience in the form of dreams. The Logos draws upon similar experiences (upon a vast scale) in this homology to what a person experiences in the domains of the life after death. Such experiences are incorporated into the subconscious mind before awakening from sleep.

The number twenty-four also refers to the twenty-four Elders that constitute an important part of the Head centre of a Logos, and who condition the integrating *maṇḍala* of an entire embodied form. All such great Ones, the entire constitution of a Head Lotus, also 'slumber' with the sleeping Logos. The number 3 x 5 here has a specific reference to the attainment of the past cycle (Day or Incarnation) with respect to what the activity of Mind had gleaned. All associated units of memory (the entities that embody Logoic *saṃskāras)* also 'slumbered once again'.

The number 4 x 7 of the phrase *'had slumbered once again'* here refers to the (cosmic) *buddhic* plane, or to the four cosmic ethers, wherein the dense substance of the planetary System had been abstracted during the *pralaya* period. The number also indicates that a member of cosmic Humanity had 'slumbered'.

The number 7 x 7 of the phrase *'had slumbered'* refers to this period of seven Eternities, each eternity being divided into seven sub-periods or aeons.

For an average deceased person these seven Eternities can refer to the five higher astral sub-planes (the lowest two sub-planes are not places of human habitation), the lower mental plane and then absorption into the petals of the Soul before reincarnating. For purely mental types the seven Eternities can refer to the seven sub-planes of the mental, there being four concrete and three abstracted. For liberated enlightened beings these Eternities can refer to the four cosmic ethers plus the three lowest levels of the cosmic astral plane.

H.P.B's essential commentary on the seven Eternities:

> By the Seven "Eternities," aeons or periods are meant. The word "Eternity," as understood in Christian theology, has no meaning to the Asiatic ear, except in its application to the ONE existence; nor is the term sempiternity, the eternal only in futurity, anything better than a misnomer. Such words do not and cannot exist in philosophic metaphysics, and were unknown till the advent of ecclesiastical Christianity. The Seven Eternities meant are the seven periods, or a period answering in its duration to the seven periods, of a Manvantara, extending throughout a Maha-Kalpa or the "Great Age" – 100 Years of Brahmā – making a total of 311,040,000,000,000 of years; each Year of Brahmā being composed of 360 "days," and of the same number of "nights" of Brahmā (reckoning by the Chandrayana or lunar year); and a "Day of Brahmā" consisting of 4,320,000,000 of mortal years. These "Eternities" belong to the most secret calculations, in which, in order to arrive at the true total, every figure must be 7^x (7 to the power of x); x varying according to the nature of the cycle in the subjective or real world; and every figure relating to, or representing all the different cycles from the greatest to the smallest – in the objective or unreal world – must necessarily be multiples of seven. The key to this cannot be given, for herein lies the mystery of esoteric calculations, and for the purpose of ordinary calculation it has no sense...In the Secret Doctrine the figure and number 4 are the male symbol only on the highest plane of abstraction; on the plane of matter the 3 is the masculine and the 4 the female: the upright and the horizontal in the fourth stage of symbolism, when the symbols become the glyphs of the generative powers on the physical plane.[13]

Note also that the numbers of the word *Eternities* add to 52 which signifies the number of weeks to a great zodiacal year, or even 100 years of Brahmā, as explained above in H.P.B's commentary. There are seven of these great zodiacal years, and all these cycles are governed or regulated by the energies emanating from the great (astrological) constellations. This is indicated by the numbers of the phrase *'for*

13 Ibid., Vol. 1, 35-36.

seven Eternities' which add to 12, 31 x 3. The number 12 relates to the energies of the twelve signs of the zodiac, as well as of the twelve Creative Hierarchies. Together they constitute the environment of a Womb, the energies and entities from which the new cosmic Child is to be fashioned. The Eternities are therefore stellar or cosmic zones of influences, via which our Logos must travel whilst slumbering and from which the material and energies needed for the forthcoming incarnation is gathered by the necessary cosmic contacts.

The number 31 x 3 refers to the evocation of the energy of the Will of the Logos that sustains the duration during the seven Eternities.

The phrase *'once again'* (6 x 7, 3 x 5) informs us that this Logos had slumbered (many times) before. The number 6 x 7 implicates the cosmic astral plane wherein the Logos is abstracted during this sleep. It can also imply the sixth, or second last cycle, before reawakening. The number 3 x 5 informs us that it is the concrete mind that slumbers. Its sleep produces the period of abstraction from (cosmic) dense involvement.

Finally the numbers of the complete phrase *'had slumbered once again for seven Eternities'* add to 4 x 10. The number 40 refers to the fact that our planetary Logos is that of the fourth Scheme, and the earth is the fourth globe of the planetary Chain. It also refers to the Logoic quaternary, or Logoic Personality, who is a member of cosmic Humanity, who slumbered again for seven Eternities.

Stanza One part Two

Stanza 1:2 states:

> **Time was not, for it lay asleep in the infinite Bosom of Duration.**

> *Keynotes:* Aquarius, cosmic astral *buddhic* sub-plane.

This stanza is governed by the sign Aquarius the water bearer, from whom emanates the Waters of cosmic Love, hence the activities of Logoic Bodhisattva. Once the *sūtrātmā* was broken in the former sign, Pisces the fishes, then the former manifestation is abstracted into a state of pure energy, symbolised by the two wavy lines of the glyph for Aquarius. One line represents the Life of the Soul aspect, and the other the energy field of the incarnate being, which is now withdrawn into its slumbering state. Thus time has nothing to work with, as time only relates to cycles of material activity. The energy streams are boundless, and infinite in their duration.

The numerical breakdown of this statement:

> time was (3 x 9), was not (20, 11), time was not (40, 13), lay asleep (33, 6), it lay asleep (44, 8), in the infinite (79, 16), the infinite (65, 11), asleep in the infinite (101, 20), it lay asleep in the infinite (123, 24 = Taurus), The infinite Bosom (84 = Libra, 21), in the infinite Bosom (98 = 49 x 2 = 17, 26 = 8), asleep in the infinite Bosom (120 = Capricorn, 30), it lay asleep in the infinite Bosom (142, 34), for it lay asleep in the infinite (144 = 12 x 12 = Pisces, 3 x 9), for it lay asleep in the infinite Bosom (163 = 100 + 7 x 9, 37 = 10), of Duration (51 = 17 x 3, 15), Bosom of Duration (70, 25), the infinite Bosom of Duration (135, 36 = Gemini), in the infinite Bosom of Duration (149, 41), asleep in the infinite Bosom of Duration (171, 45), it lay asleep in the infinite Bosom of Duration (193, 49), For it lay asleep in the infinite Bosom of Duration (214, 52).

Time is defined as that in which events are distinguishable with reference to before and after, a beginning and end, a relation in reference to concurrence or succession. It concerns the measurable aspect of duration within which change is determined. It therefore relates to the world of changes, of ceaseless transmutation and activity, of transience, impermanence, death and decay and all of the various illusions associated with the dense material world. Time can therefore be considered to exist in *saṃsāra*. It exists only in terms of the cycles of transience of this world, and is therefore, an illusion, as H.P.B. points out in her commentary:

> Time is only an illusion produced by the succession of our states of consciousness as we travel through eternal duration, and it does not exist where no consciousness exists in which the illusion can be produced; but "lies asleep." The present is only a mathematical line which divides that part of eternal duration which we call the future, form that part which we call the past. Nothing on earth has real duration, for nothing remains without change – or the same – for

> the billionth part of a second; and the sensation that we have of the actuality of the division of "time" known as the present, comes from the blurring of the momentary glimpse, or succession of glimpses, of things that our senses give us, as those things pass from the region of ideals which we call the future, to the region of memories that we name the past. In the same way we experience a sensation of duration in the case of the instantaneous electric spark, by reason of the blurred and continuing impression on the retina. The real person or thing does not consist solely of what is seen at any particular moment, but is composed of the sum of all its various and changing conditions from its appearance in material form to its disappearance from the earth. It is these "sum-totals" that exist from eternity in the "future," and pass by degrees through matter, to exist for eternity in the "past." No one could say that a bar of metal dropped into the sea come into existence as it left the air, and ceased to exist as it entered the water, and that the bar itself consisted only of the cross-section thereof which at any given moment coincided with the mathematical plane that separates, and, at the same time joins, the atmosphere and the ocean. Even so of persons and things, which, dropping out of the to-be into the has-been, out of the Future into the Past – present momentarily to our senses a cross-section, as it were, of their total selves, as they pass through time and space (as matter) on their way from one eternity to another: and these two eternities constitute that "duration" in which alone anything has true existence, were our senses but able to cognize it there.[14]

The numbers of the phrase '*time was*' add to 3 x 9, which informs us that when time does exist then it's purpose will produce the mastery of the mind, which happens by the time the third Initiation is taken. The objective of the various cycles associated with time provides the 'time' for a human kingdom to conquer all the cycles associated with the material world (*saṃsāra*), and undertake the third Initiation. Time thus exists for every person possessing the type of consciousness wherein illusion can be produced. After the third Initiation has been attained the law of cycles takes precedence, wherein time is viewed in terms of unfolding cycles. The realm of true timelessness is reached with the attainment of *buddhic* perception.

14 Ibid., 37.

The numbers of the phrase '*was not*' (20, 11) refer to the appearance of the first and second Ray cycles that will incur the manifestation of 'timelessness' to the victorious ones that will escape from the throttle of *saṃsāra* as a consequence. Once the first or second Ray energies, with their penetrating and transmutative abilities, manifest and bear on the form then this produces an ending to all cycles and conditionings associated with that form, thus an end to time as we understand it. The first and second Rays produce abstraction by bringing everything back to the emanating source of being (the Monad). This process makes all 'invisible'. An objective of time therefore is to effect the demonstration of second Ray cycle, which then will produce the dissolution of time, to make it 'not'.

The numbers of the phrase *'time was not'* add to 4 x 10. Here the number 40 refers to the energy of the fourth plane *(buddhi).* This plane is the realm of the intuition and of timelessness, where the three times, the past, present and the future are one, where all is seen as it essentially is in the immense duration of being/non-being. *Buddhi* is the plane of at-onement, the formlessness that is Void. There is only steadfast identification to ultimate Beingness *(śūnyatā)* and an immutable adherence to Purpose, the ceaseless persevering Devotion that knows not the bounds of time. Nor is it conditioned or limited by its cycles. Time was not, for the Logos was absorbed into His/Her fundamental *Buddhic* expression, and was thus in 'the fourth eternity'. It was earlier stated that the 'infinite Bosom of Duration', is governed by the fourth Ray of Beautifying Harmony overcoming Strife and concerns the *buddhic* (fourth) sub-plane upon the cosmic astral plane. See also my section 'The Examination of Time in the *Mūlamadhyamakakārikā'*[15] for a further esoteric explanation of the nature of time.

The numbers of the phase *'lay asleep'* add to 33, indicating that what also lay asleep with time is the totality of the third Ray aspect of Deity, the principle of Intelligence, and the symbolic 33,000,000,000 Creative Intelligences, the Creative Hierarchies, that constitute all of the Lives in the solar system. Time could not be 'awake', hence active, because these Intelligences were not incarnate to record it. Without the recording in some way of the manifestation of time the account of the

15 Chapter 11, volume 2 of *A Treatise on Mind,* 319-39.

duration of the seven Eternities for instance is meaningless. Time has no meaning if minds do not exist to denote its passage.

To *lay* is to lie (the body) on something solid, dense or material, implying the dense physical plane, or any of the seven planes of perception. (As they are also sheaths, robes of matter, wherein one can abide via a tangible form with respect to them.) What actually lies 'asleep' however is the principle of Intelligence (the third or Brahmā aspect of Deity) lying upon a bed of the substance of the mind/Mind. That relating to the second and first Ray aspects have consequently been liberated, freed from bondage to form. They are not conditioned by time.

The numbers of the phrase *'it lay asleep'* add to 4 x 11, indicating what it was that slumbered. As this number also signifies a member of cosmic Humanity, so then we can look to a similar occurrence when the entirety of a Logoic Body of manifestation was slumbering. If the focus is limited to the earth Scheme, then this number refers to our planetary Logos, being the fourth in the system. Time was asleep, because the entire planetary system was asleep.

The *bosom* refers to the breast and chest area in the body, especially of a woman. It veils the heart and lungs and is said to be a seat of passions, emotions and feeling. The main emphasis here is that it embodies the life-sustaining factor (milk) that is to feed the future child. The 'bosom' also takes the guise of Aquarius the water bearer, which in this case bears nourishing milk, therefore here Aquarius is feminine. This is especially the case in relation to the term 'duration', which relates to the two wavy bands for the glyph of this sign. They can be extended to any length to signify the nature of a duration.

'The infinite Bosom of Duration' is thus governed by the general attributes of the sign Aquarius, which signifies the abstraction of the consciousness (self-conscious Lives) that is the 'milk' contained by this 'Bosom'. Consciousness is of infinite duration, and though the intelligence principle slumbers, the Consciousness-bearers, the liberated ones from the former aeon, are freed to fully explore cosmic astral or etheric space. Aquarius and Virgo are related here in that the Consciousness-bearers vitalise the Mind of the Virgin (Virgo). The two constellations are linked symbolically in that Virgo's hair can be seen flowing in the wind (the Airy Element governing Aquarius) forming

many strands of the Aquarian glyph. Consequently Virgo thinks as an Aquarian, the compassionate Bodhisattva.

The sign Virgo relates to the feminine qualities of this 'infinite Duration of Being', but the function that nurtures the form is at this stage in abeyance. Because a bosom has an inference to human emotions we see that the 'infinite Bosom' is more directly related to the *Solar Plexus centre* than the Heart centre. It causes the vitalisation of the cosmic etheric body (ruled by Gemini). This vitalisation process is also regulated by the *prāṇic triangle,* which has its focal points in the chest area, and is directly related to the Heart centre. The other major aspect to consider with respect to the Solar Plexus centre is the feminine polarisation of our planetary Logos. The Solar Plexus centre is the abdominal brain, ruled by the qualities of the pentagram, and is the lower reflex of the Head centre.

The word *infinite* refers to what is boundless, immeasurable, immense, without any conceivable limit. It only has meaning in reference to that which is finite (and thus conditioned by the mind). An abstracted or universal Mind can however be 'infinite', from the perspective of the bounded concrete mind, and is so because it has transcended the time concept and has included in its embrace the immense duration of Space. (See also Stanza 1:8.) As Stanza 1:2 relates specifically to the cosmic *buddhic* (fourth) sub-plane of the cosmic astral plane, so the term 'infinite' also has a direct reference to the attributes of *buddhi,* or *śūnyatā,* cosmically considered.

The number 11 of the phrase *'the infinite'* refers to the essential identification of the Infinite to the Spirit or Monadic aspect (governed by the first Ray), and which is eternally unmanifest, unmodified, unmade, etc. It also refers to the cosmic *nāḍī* system, within which the All resides, and which certainly can be considered 'infinite'.

Because the significance of the word infinite is considered in terms of the 'Bosom' then what is hinted at is the Universal Mind (Aquarius). This Mind is concerned with the formation (creation) and nurturing of the Divine cosmic Child, and provides the qualities needed for its survival in the dense physical world.

The numbers of the phrase *'the infinite Bosom'* add to 7 x 12, 3 x 7. The number 7 x 12 refers to the sign Libra the balances, which is the hub of the entire wheel of the zodiac, around which all the other signs revolve. Libra manifests the great Law that sustains all being/non-being. It is also the sign of contemplation, of meditative abstraction, of the in and out-breathing of cyclic Breath. This sign therefore subjectively conditions the appearance of Space and the various cycles associated with time, that govern the birth and death of all wheels (*chakras*) and entities within that Space. It is fitting therefore that at the end of any cycle of endeavour that time should once more go to 'sleep'. As the sign Virgo was equated with the word 'bosom', therefore in the phrase 'the infinite Bosom' both signs are directly related, fused in the form of Virgo-Libra. This is to be expected, as time and its various cycles must be equally conditioned by the quality of the substance of Space, the activities of Virgo's Womb, plus the greater Laws regulating the progression of all forms within that Womb, to parturition. Virgo-Libra represents the duration of the substance absorbed in the great Wheel. That substance is conditioned by the cyclic impulse governed by Libra that determines its appearances and abstraction back into the universal pool of substance *(mūlaprakṛti).* Though time does not exist *per se,* the law of cycles does, which conditions this 'pool' of substance.

Note that three of the four signs so far mentioned represent the Airy triplicity (Aquarius, Gemini and Libra), which governs the process of dissolution associated with *pralaya.* The material forms are governed by Virgo the slumbering Mother, and they do so within the embrace of the Air (the *prāṇas* incorporated within the cosmic *nāḍīs,* Gemini), and the *dhyāna* of the Logoic abstracted meditation (Libra) which sustains their state of abstraction.

With respect to the number 3 x 7 we see that the qualities of the spiritual triad *(ātma-buddhi-manas*) represents the Bosom of being/non-being for the human unit. For humanity such a 'Bosom' is indeed infinite.

D.K. states in relation to human evolution that:

> It is only at what is called the "final judgement" that another fusion will take place and Virgo-Libra will form one sign, for then man's sense of antagonistic dualism will be ended and the scales will have been turned finally in favour of that which the virgin-Mother has hidden from expression for aeons...
>
> Eventually in some mysterious way, there will be only ten signs of the zodiac again; Aries and Pisces will form one sign, for "the end is the beginning". This dual and blended sign is called in some

> of the ancient books "the sign of the Fish with the head of the Ram." We shall then have:
>
> | | |
> |---|---|
> | 1. Aries-Pisces | 6. Virgo-Libra |
> | 2. Taurus | 7. Scorpio |
> | 3. Gemini | 8. Sagittarius |
> | 4. Cancer | 9. Capricorn |
> | 5. Leo | 10. Aquarius |
>
> Fire and water will then blend, veiling the past which has gone instead of the future as is now the case. Earth and air will then fuse and in this way the old prophecy repeated in the Bible, that "there will be no more sea" will be proved correct. Air (heaven) will then have "come down to Earth" and fusion will be established.
>
> In the cosmic sense then and not in the individual sense, the unfoldment of the Cosmic Christ will be manifested for which "the whole creation waits"; thus will come the consummation of desire as a result of dedicated aspiration.[16]

The numbers of the phrase *'in the infinite Bosom'* add to 98 = 49 x 2, 17. The number 49 x 2 refers to all of the septenaries that formerly existed in a *manvantara,* and which are now 'asleep'. The number 17 implies here the nascent germ of the cosmic Christ child, the Logos (17) of a new solar or planetary system.

The numbers 10 x 12, 30 of the phrase *'asleep in the infinite Bosom'* refer to the sign Capricorn the goat. Capricorn is the most material, hard, rocky of all the signs. It governs the mountain load of *karma* (30) associated with the three dense planes of perception as well as the angelic kingdom responsible for the manifestation of the various forms that are to evolve within the confines of the cosmic mental, astral and dense planes. Its governance also extends to all who are associated with the left hand path. Everything concerning material evolution thus lay asleep in the infinite Bosom. The associated *karma* and the related cycles of time are held in abeyance until a cycle appears for their manifestation.

The number 10 x 12 here also has an indirect reference to the ten signs of the zodiac governed by the manifestation of a Solar Plexus centre that conditions Life before the advent of mind by a humanity.

---

16 Alice A. Bailey, *Esoteric Astrology,* (Lucis Publishing House, New York 1979), 230-231.

All associated beings were likewise asleep. The other permutations of the number 120 such as 6 x 20, 60 x 2, 30 x 4 and 5 x 24 are generally associated with the appearance of the form (6, 60, 30 x 4) and the computation of the cycles of time associated with that form. The number 5 x 24 refers to the Lords (Dhyān Chohans) that administer to these lives. The number 30 relates to the perfected expression of the third Ray, the Brahmā or activity (matter) aspect of deity that governs the cycles of activity in the material world. All lay asleep in the infinite Bosom because they were abstracted back to the one eternal cycle of Duration after completion of all lesser cycles of events.

The numbers of the phrase *'it lay asleep in the infinite Bosom'* add to 100 + 6 x 7, 17 x 2, referring to the sum of formed space (6 x 7), or the major divisions of time conditioning that space, governing for instance the evolution of the Rounds of the various Schemes of a solar system. All such cycles of activity thus lay asleep. The number 17 x 2 refers to this activity as the reflection of the attributes of a Deity, which also slumbered.

Figure 2. The infinite Bosom of Duration

The above figure of the circle with the central dot presents the idea of the abstract Deity that has established a central Throne or Seat of Power, thereby organising space by means of a circumference or limit of expression, defining the domain of what is governed. (The central point represents the nipple of the Bosom.) The potential of extended Being and continuous new birth has been abstracted into the nipple, the seed *(bindu)* or centre point of the Bosom, from which all manifestation will later come.

The term *infinite* refers to the entire constitution of the cosmic Logos, the absolute abstracted Deity, the One consummating Source (Parabrahman), and not just that aspect associated with the Bosom (Īśvara or Māyā), which is related to rebirth, thus the re-emergence of the cycles of time (governed by Brahmā). When the word 'Bosom' and thus the concept of what leads to a new birth, or which vitalises an already established form (Child), is removed from the phrases, then we have the statements: *'in the infinite'* (79, 16), *'asleep in the infinite'* (101, 20), *'it lay asleep'* (44, 8), *'it lay asleep in the infinite'* (123, 24 = Taurus). The term 'it' thus refers to the attributes of Īśvara or Māyā, but before the focussed collectivisation of the attributes of this Entity in the 'nipple' just prior to recommencing a *mahāmanvantara.*

The numbers 101, 10, 20, and 123 refer to the first, second, and third Ray aspects of Deity (Father-Son-Mother), the triad of being/non-being, all of which are therefore 'slumbering'. It refers to That which is able to extend the cosmic *antaḥkaraṇas* (101) in all directions in time and Space when the purpose admits it. That One therefore is truly Infinite, however lies 'asleep' because not thus manifesting. No Thought-Forms concerning embodied Being are extended or projected anywhere, space has not been encompassed by a ring-pass-not, the Logos is Self-absorbed within Him/Herself and not otherwise occupied. Even the perfected expression of the second Ray energy, the Son of God, lies asleep therein—everything was motionless and dark, nothing existed to experience 'time'. These numbers refer to the ability of the Builders (a second Ray function) to project Their energies (the number 100 + 1) into (as) manifest space in such a way that forms can be made an accomplished fact. These Builders are the cosmic equivalent of the Hierarchy of Enlightened Being (the number 20). This ability also lies dormant, but must awaken once the 'Bosom' manifests its function.

The number 16 refers to the cosmic Christ, the integral Love-Wisdom aspect (the cosmic Hierarchy of Love and Light), the Consciousness-bearers within the Absolute. They are the expression of the expression of the Deified 'Son' that are similarly not in active manifestation, hence 'slumbering'. They are however active upon the subjective domains preparing for the next incarnation.

The number 2 x 12 signifies the second sign of the zodiac, Taurus the bull, thus the Eye of illumination (the All-seeing Eye) that was similarly 'asleep', closed with respect to active manifestation. All energies that lie asleep in the Infinite must inevitably be directed by this Eye. Because there is no Personality existing to project force, so there was no cosmic Desire to use the Eye as a focal point of the creative Will. This was the cause for the non-existence of time. The

Logos desired it not, being absorbed into an immeasurable Identification with That Beyond. Similarly all Lords (44) that embody the principle of Logoic Desire (symbolised by the number 24 = 6 x 4) did not focus their collective Eyes downwards into manifestation.

The number 2 x 12 can also symbolise the second of the Creative Hierarchies ('Unity thro' effort'), abstracted upon the fourth cosmic astral sub-plane, Who's Eye was not actively projecting cosmic energies into manifestation, as there was nothing to energise.

The numbers of phrase *'for it lay asleep in the infinite'* add to 12 x 12, and to 3 x 9. A meaning of the number 144 here is that it refers to the twelfth sign of the zodiac (Pisces the fishes) and thus to the completion of one major cosmic zodiacal cycle. We are therefore concerned with the *pralaya* period before the commencement of the next zodiacal cycle. As stated, Pisces is the sign of *death*, being governed by Pluto both esoterically and Hierarchically. It symbolises the utter death of all cycles associated with the form nature, and ultimately the form of the Soul itself. Such death being an effect of the energies of Pisces. Pluto is a Lord of the first Ray of Will or Power. The demonstration of this energy allows the abstracting quality associated with Pisces. The other major meanings of the number 144 relate to the turning of the entire zodiacal wheel and of the groupings of Lives conditioned by the twelve signs that tread that wheel. The number 9 x 3 implicates the third degree Initiate, thus the Causal forms of those Lives, Souls that were not incarnate, hence were 'slumbering' in *pralaya*. Accordingly time was non-existent for them.

The phrase *'of Duration'* (17 x 3, 3 x 5) immediately hints at the duration of the months of gestation (Eternities) in the Womb of the cosmic Mother (17 x 3). The number 3 x 5 refers to the utilisation of the energies of the active Mind (Mahat) needed to produce the eventual birth. This Duration is determined by the expression of the third Ray of Mathematically Exact Activity, which must be used if 'the seventh Eternity' is to appear and the new Logoic Personality be born. Note the relation of time to the word duration, for the word duration signifies the portion of time during which anything exists. The gain is the quality or attribute evolved by an entity living through such a duration of time. Time does not exist, but duration, the vehicle (or cycles) that carries or holds it, does. The consequence of such a duration is to eventually give birth to the intelligences (3 x 5) that can record time and thus awaken it by means of the light of conscious recollection.

The number 100 + 7 x 9 of the phrase *'for it lay asleep in the infinite Bosom'* signifies that the cycles of Initiation attainment (conditioned by time) 'lay asleep' for seven Eternities. The conditionings were not existent for such activity to manifest.

The word *'Duration'* here is numerologically significant. The numbers add to 13 x 3, 12. The number 12 informs us that this duration is astrologically conditioned, whilst the energies from the constellations together constitute the Womb or foetal bed for slumbering 'time'. The number 13 x 3 indicates that the extent of the duration during which time sleeps is for a symbolic three quarters of the *pralaya* period, after which the awakening pains of the labour begins, during the sixth and seventh Eternities. (The number 13 x 3 is three quarters of the number 52, which signifies such a period, a great cycle, of being/non-being.)

The numbers of the phrase *'Bosom of Duration'* add to 70, 5 x 5. The number 5 x 5 refers to the higher mental plane and the Soul thereon. The reference is to the Soul as a Bosom, the source of nourishment, the Life engendering factor of this Duration. It causes the downward arc (of these seven Eternities) that eventually results in the formation of manifested space (the formed Universe). The number 7 x 10 indicates the divisions of the substance of this Bosom, its seven major cycles of expression.

When the meanings and qualities of 'the infinite' are added to the phrase 'Bosom of Duration', then the view is to that aspect of the Bosom of Duration (of the Soul) that is infinite. This implicates the qualities of the spiritual Triad, as implied by the numbers of the phrase *'the infinite Bosom of Duration',* which add to 9 x 15, 4 x 9, and 3 x 12. The number 9 x 15 informs us that this infinite Bosom contains the forces of the Ah-Hi, the Initiated Lords of Life that condition time and space. They were obviously not actively engaged in a cycle of activity (15) during the duration of *pralaya,* when 'time is asleep'. When 'time awakens' then the Ah-Hi actively manifest (3 x 5) the conditionings of the appearing *manvantara* that will produce the adeptship (4 x 9) of Mind, or rather, an eventual complete liberation from *saṃsāra* by the appearing *jīvas* (Life forms). During *manvantara* the number 9 indicates the nine Initiation stages or months (literally of gestation) through which the Lives must evolve before they can enter a vaster world (universe) that is completely freed from all material involvement. (The entrance thereto is the attainment of *śūnyatā* by the Initiate of the fourth degree, the number 4 x 9.) The Ah-Hi are the factors working upon the matrix of the Womb to produce the enlightenment of the lives within it, and their consequent liberation from it.

Here however the concern is with the stages of the seven Eternities, which includes evolution through the etheric and dense material realms. They are included as part of the Infinite Bosom of Duration, for the word 'infinite' refers to all spheres and planes of perception possible, inclusive of the dense physical as well as the subjective realms. However, from the esoteric viewpoint only the subjective realms, the cosmic ethers, are 'Real'. For the liberated Lives the planes of transience are invisible, non-existent at this stage. Their residence starts with the fourth plane of perception, *śūnyatā,* the Void wherein this Duration can be experienced. 'The Infinite Bosom of Duration' concerns the complete duration of the solar system from the end of one Incarnation by the solar or planetary Adept, the cosmic Christ, to the next Incarnation. The attainment then is similar to that gained by the Initiate of the fourth degree. The seven Eternities within this Infinite Bosom are experienced after disincarnation, or the complete enlightenment by an Initiate of high degree,.

How the constitution, the conditioning in the Womb (or Bosom), of the Logos changes when 'time is not' is also indicated by the number 3 x 12, which implicates the sign *Gemini the twins.* Gemini rules the etheric body and the relationships between all the pairs of opposites in the (local) universe. The concept of 'Duration' therefore but describes the nature of the existence in etheric space. Therein the Consciousness principle (the Ah-Hi) governing solar evolution are abstracted, though meditatively active for the duration of the *manvantara.* The Ah-Hi are self-absorbed whilst in *pralaya,* preparing for the next cycle of activity. (Similarly the astral body of a normal human is active during the sleep of the person concerned.) Being the containment of this Consciousness principle Gemini is the sign of the cosmic Christ. The solar or planetary Logos is highly sensitised to these etheric energies because:

a. Its direct relationship to the cosmic *buddhic* plane.
b. The *chakra* system is contained in the ethers, wherein if energies are conditioned by the spiritual triad then *pralaya* ensues.
c. If energies are wilfully directed via the ethers by the Soul in preparation for rebirth then there is a consequent *manvantara*.

In relation to this conditioning the Tibetan states:

> Because the Ray of Love-Wisdom, the second Ray, pours through Gemini it becomes apparent how true is the occult teaching that love underlies the entire universe. God is Love, we are assured, and this statement is both an exoteric and an esoteric truth. This underlying Love of Deity reaches our Solar System primarily through Gemini, which forms, with the constellation of the Great Bear and the Pleiades, a Cosmic triangle. This is the triangle of the Cosmic Christ and is the esoteric symbol lying behind the Cosmic Cross.[17]

The reason why the second Ray 'pours through Gemini' is because of it being the zone of expression for the Consciousness principle within the 'Infinite Bosom of Duration'. D.K. further states that Gemini is related to the Heart of the Sun (Sirius),[18] and when this esoteric fact is coupled with knowledge that our present solar system is one that embodies the second Ray of Love-Wisdom, then the importance of Gemini becomes clear.

Though time was 'asleep' because the material world did not then exist, however, in That which governs the Infinite Bosom of Duration, a form of it can be considered to be active through the cycles of duration, but such cycles are not determined by our world of cause and effect. Effectively, timelessness is the complete conditioning of past, present and future, as the eternal NOW. The length of a cycle reckoned in terms of human years is immaterial, what is of importance are the cycles of accomplishment, called 'Durations'.

The numbers 10 x 12, 30 of the phrase *'asleep in the Infinite Bosom'* refer to the sign Capricorn the goat. The interpretation here is similar, though the obverse of that given previously. Here Capricorn refers to

17 Bailey, *Esoteric Astrology*, 348.

18 Ibid., 351.

the summit of the mount of Initiation, where the new order of being/ non-being exists, and from which the new cycle of activity (30) can be initiated. The symbolic unicorn has taken wings and flies into the infinitude of Space. More specifically however the number 10 x 12 here relates to the ten signed zodiac that conditions the attributes of this 'Infinite Bosom'.

The numbers of the phrase *'in the Infinite Bosom of Duration'* add to 100 = 7 x 7, 5, whilst those of the phrase *'it lay asleep in the Infinite Bosom of Duration'* add to 7 x 7. We are thereby informed that what is 'in' this Infinite Bosom are the seeds (Lives, 7 x 7) of what will later be expressed in a *manvantara.* They are all part of the demonstration of cosmic Intelligent Mind (Mahat). When Mahat awakens then the Creative process will proceed and produce a new material world wherein these streams of Lives will play their roles. Capricorn also represents Mahat, which at the appropriate time will activate the ten signed zodiac to condition the ordering of the newly appearing Space *(manvantara).*[19] Time lay asleep for the 'Seven Eternities', and also the various sub-periods or aeons, into which these Eternities can be subdivided (7 x 7), as explained earlier in relation to the phrase *'had slumbered'.*

The numbers of the phrase *'asleep in the Infinite Bosom of Duration'* add to 5 x 9. This number here refers to the (cosmic) Master, the Logos that will be overseeing the creative process via Mahat, but who now slumbers. All aspects constituting the empirical Mind of the Logos are consequently similarly 'slumbering'. All the factors concerning the manifestation of 'time' thereby lay asleep for the duration needed for the Logos to develop the Thoughts of the new Day to Be. We have the new Vision, mantras, energy directions and contacts needed for the new *manvantara* to manifest upon a slightly higher cycle than before and to cleanse redundant *karma* (stored by Capricorn).

Finally, the number 52 of the complete phrase *'for it lay asleep in the Infinite Bosom of Duration'* indicates that time lay asleep for one great cosmic Night. This is 'infinity' indeed when related to the minute time scale reckoned by those on the earth.

---

19 Note that Capricorn is ruled esoterically and exoterically by Saturn, the Lord of *karma*, and Hierarchically by Venus, who governs the fifth Ray of Science.

Stanza One part Three

Stanza 1:3 states:

> **Universal Mind was not, for there were no Ah-Hi** *(celestial beings)* **to contain** *(hence to manifest)* **it.**

Keynotes: Capricorn, fifth cosmic astral sub-plane, the fifth Ray, the third liberated Hierarchy, the Father, the first Eternity.

The numerical breakdown:

Universal Mind (62 = 31 x 2, 8), was not (20, 11), Mind was not (42, 15), Universal Mind was not (82, 19 = 10, 4.4.7.4), there were no Ah-Hi (90, 36 = Gemini), for there were no Ah-Hi (111, 39), to contain it (50, 14), no Ah-Hi to contain it (87 = 15, 33), there were no Ah-Hi to contain it (140, 50), For there were no Ah-Hi to contain it (161 = 8, 53 = 8).

The zodiacal wheel now turns to the sign Capricorn the goat, hence the substance that is the mountain of Mind, or rather to the Entities that are the bearers of Mind (cosmic Intelligence, Mahat). Neither the cosmic nor the systemic bearers of Mind at this stage were able to cognise phenomena. Mind was absorbed in itself, and naught was that could be utilised by way of Thought structures (limited spheres of mentation). All bearers of mind/Mind existed in a deep sleep or meditation state.

We are also brought to the fifth (mental) cosmic astral sub-plane in our consideration, hence must consider the quality of Mind (Mahat) derived therefrom. The bearers of Mahat into manifestation are collectively denoted here as 'Universal Mind'. This Mind then manifests as the Father aspect of Deity, as it reflects into manifestation the attributes of the Logoic Mentation upon the cosmic mental plane.[20] Being the plane of the reflection of cosmic Mind, so here manifests the first 'Eternity', as the concept of 'Eternity' relates to the function of the Mind that recognises the durations of Being, once cyclic time is awakened.

---

20 The term 'Father' here is relative, as we are really viewing the first Ray attribute of the Mother's department, being the creative aptitude of Mahat that brings all into manifestation, which here lies 'asleep'. Perhaps a better term to use is 'Father-Mother', Logoically the form of activity associated with the Saturn synthesising Scheme.

Upon this cosmic astral sub-plane the third of the liberated Hierarchies 'Light thro' knowledge' undergo their form or *pralaya.* From this perspective in relation to the term Ah-Hi, the 'Ah' therefore relates to Them, and the remainder of the Creative Hierarchies that had gained self-consciousness relate to the 'Hi'. Being the first or Father aspect of the Creative Process the actual schema of manifestation starts from here (hence is the 'first Eternity'), as all emanates from Mahat. From this perspective then there are seven Creative Hierarchies that are responsible for the appearance of a Logoic Form. The lowest three Creative Hierarchies simply represent the substance of the forms built into the planes of illusion. The three liberated Hierarchies upon the fifth, sixth and seventh cosmic astral sub-planes manifest as a spiritual triad and the four manifesting in the four cosmic ethers representing the quaternary. This then expresses a higher significance of the phrase 'the fall of the three into the four' than what is commonly thought of by esotericists. Via the four cosmic ethers cyclically appears the transient phenomena known as *saṃsāra*, and which humans take to be 'real'. The Lives constituting these seven Creative Hierarchies are what 'slumber' in the 'seven Eternities'.

The word 'universal'[21] generally refers to what is unlimited, all-pervading, all-reaching, pertaining to the whole, the totality. This totality is here inclusive of the entire universe.[22] The universal Mind is a phrase denoting the abstract Mind applied universally. It produces a universal, all-embracive state of identification with the qualities of the entire multi-dimensional universe. The collective Mind embraced by all enlightened beings is here hinted at. Another term that could be used here is *dharmakāya*. The *dharmakāya* is defined as 'the body or vehicle of the *dharma'* (the *dharma* being the spiritual law that governs all that is). It is the ultimate body of Truth, the primordial, eternally self-existing essentiality of *bodhi* (enlightenment). It is the highest of the three-fold bodies (*trikāya*) of a Buddha, or of any Initiate of the fifth degree or greater'. It can be considered cosmic Mind. From the

---

21 *Buddhic* perception can also be perceived in terms of universality, where such perception describes the annihilation of what is known as mind.

22 Note that when I use the term 'universe' it generally means the local universe, consisting of the portion of the galaxy wherein our sun is placed, and of its associated stars and constellations.

Theosophical perspective the *dharmakāya* can be called *triadal (ātmā-buddhi-manas)*, or what manifests via the *śūnyatā-saṃsāra* nexus, explained in my Buddhist books. The type of consciousness obtained by intelligent units on the earth can be likened to a speck of dust in an enormous dust storm, but viewed as a tiny cloud by the universal Mind.

The numbers of the phrase *'Universal Mind'* add to 31 x 2, (and to 8), which refers to what is a direct expression or reflection (2) of the Logoic Will (31) to condition the manifest form. The number 8 signifies the spiral-cyclic energy that sustains all being/non-being. Here this energy is a carrier of the *dharmakāya*. Mind is inherently dual:

a. The empirical mind conditioned by the world of form and of material involvement wherein time exists, therefore of what is finite, limited, conditioned, transient and impermanent. These attributes are associated with the non universal worlds of human involvement: the mental, astral and dense physical planes.
b. The infinite, abstracted Mind of the Logos (the Monadic aspect), the One consummating Source of Mind, which is universal in its scope. An enlightened Mind can be considered an awakened, active portion of the universal Mind.

The numbers of the phrase *'Universal Mind was not'* add to 10, signifying here the completion of the ten stages to perfected evolution, where all aspects of consciousness evolve into the circle of abstract Deity. These stages of evolution were non-existent, therefore That Mind was not being expressed, there was no externalised means whereby it could be comprehended. At that stage, before the conception of the new world order (the cycle of being/non-being when the Word of Power for the new cycle is communed to the Soul) the Soul and the Monad ('Universal Mind') are at-oned and the embodied Word, the personality to perceive was non-existent. If there was no means of perception of it, then 'Universal Mind was not'. Note the significance of this in relation to the statement in *John 1:1:* 'In the beginning was the Word, and the Word was with God, and the Word was God'. 'The Word' is but an embodiment of the Thought of the 'Universal Mind'. This phrase has reference to:

a. The state of abstraction of the Lord of Hosts, the solar or planetary Logos, whose Mind encompasses the duration of the Minds consisting the sum of the Body of manifestation of such a One. ('The Word was God'.) Because manifestation (the expressed Word) was not, so for the Minds that support it. At the end of all evolutionary attainment no state of consciousness identification with forms exists, for then there is naught, as all is abstracted into That about which Naught can be said, 'Naught was' (c.f., Stanza 1:6).

b. The slow emergence ('in the beginning was the Word') of the solar or planetary Logos back into the realms of form to complete the journey through 'seven Eternities', aeons of evolutionary expression. At this stage 'Universal Mind' was in the process of consolidating its Images, bringing together the Thought Form of the new Idea consisting of the myriad Lives (Minds) that would embody the processes of *manvantara*. This allowed the vehicles to evolve that could actively contain the 'Universal Mind' in that material evolution.

c. We see therefore that 'Universal Mind' *(dharmakāya)* is existent 'the Word was with God', once the appropriate vehicles had evolved they could perceive. It is however considered 'not' when consciousness is inwardly focussed and abstracted into *śūnyatā* (the Void). Such Emptiness is a state of abstracted Awareness, wherein Mind as such has no meaning, because there is no point of application.

These three times of the Word are One in the Eternal Now that is 'Universal Mind', it is only the existence or non-existence of a perceiver that made the distinction of what was or was not.

What has been described in the *ślokas* so far is the effect of the process of a period of sleep on a universal, cosmic scale, which is effectively but a form of death. Similarly, the human unit leaves the body in sleep (and thereby dies to it) and awakens in the incarnation of the next new day. There is no fear, pain or resentment, but simply a loss of consciousness in one world and an awakening in another, the being leaving the former dense vehicle, to reside in 'ever-invisible robes' (the subtle sheaths) for the symbolic duration of 'seven Eternities'. The first thing noticed by the indwelling consciousness, now residing within the embrace of the higher Self, is the loss of identity with time and therefore with material involvement, as we understand it. Eventually even consciousness is lost when it is abstracted back into the One consummating Source (the Soul). There is then experience of an eternal moment of Identification (the Ineffable White Light) when all robes are cast aside, before the Ray is again projected into manifestation.

The numbers of the phrase *'was not'* add to 11 or 20, signifying that nothing existed because of the effect of the abstraction process of the first and second Ray cycles, the combined Will and Love-Wisdom aspect of Deity. The 'Universal Mind' necessitates the outpouring of the third Ray to again manifest its expression.

The numbers 6 x 7, 3 x 5 of the phrase *'Mind was not'* inform us that this Mind (Mahat = 3 x 5) did not exist because the conditionings, the embodied forms (6 x 7) that could support it were not in manifestation. They were abstracted into the domain of the cosmic astral plane (6 x 7) for the duration of the expression of *pralaya* of the solar or planetary Logos. The Logoic Mind was abstracted from *saṃsāra,* hence 'was not'.

H.P.B. states concerning 'Mind':

> Mind' is a name given to the sum of the states of Consciousness grouped under Thought, Will, and Feeling. During deep sleep, ideation ceases on the physical plane, and memory is in abeyance; thus for the time-being "Mind is not," because the organ, through which the Ego manifests ideation and memory on the material plane, has temporarily ceased to function. A noumenon can become a phenomenon on any plane of existence only by manifesting on that plane through an appropriate basis or vehicle; and during the long night of rest called Pralaya, when all the existences are dissolved, the "UNIVERSAL MIND" remains a permanent possibility of mental action, or as that abstract absolute thought, of which mind is the concrete relative manifestation.[23]

The number 4.4.7.4. refers to the human bearers of that Mind, cosmic Humanity (the Ah-Hi) or humanity in general. As they were not empirically active, therefore there was no means for the expression of the 'Universal Mind'.

The term Ah-Hi can be interpreted differently, depending upon whether one is interpreting from the point of view of below-up or

23 S.D., Vol. 1, 38.

above-down. The view here is from above-down. Ah then refers to the expiration of the great Breath that produced the involutionary process, and Hi to the inspiration, the abstraction process back to the primeval Source of the entire evolutionary Paean. With the expiration comes the great Lords, Logoi, Dhyān Chohans (Heads of Shambhala) that were responsible for all that we see. With the inspiration comes the process that leads to the evolution of Dhyān Chohans from out of the material domains by the humanity of each of the various Schemes evolving in the solar system.

Concerning the Ah-Hi H.P.B. states:

> The AH-HI (Dhyan-Chohans) are the collective hosts of spiritual Beings – the Angelic hosts of Christianity, the Elohim and "Messengers" of the Jews – who are the vehicle for the manifestation of the divine or universal thought and will. They are the Intelligent Forces that give to, and enact in Nature her "laws," while themselves acting according to laws imposed upon them in a similar manner by still higher Powers; but they are not "the personifications" of the powers of Nature, as erroneously thought. This hierarchy of spiritual Beings, through which the Universal Mind comes into action, is like an army – a "Host," truly – by means of which the fighting power of a nation manifests itself, and which is composed of army corps, divisions, brigades, regiments, and so forth, each with its separate individuality or life, and its limited freedom of action and limited responsibilities; each contained in a larger individuality, to which its own interests are subservient, and each containing lesser individualities in itself.[24]

From the *deva* perspective the Ah represents the greater Builders that embody all manifest Life. They are the *inward inspiration* of the Breath that keeps them manifest upon the abstract domains of Life, being 'too pure' to come into active manifestation. They embody the Soul aspect of all that is manifest, of the dual *deva* kingdom. Here the Hi represents the *outward expiration* of the Lesser Builders that embody the formed attributes (e.g., the human personality) of manifestation.

H.P.B. states that the term Ah-Hi means 'celestial beings'. The major significance of this term is derived from the fact that it is divided into two portions:

---

24 Ibid.

1. *Ah*—concerned here with *expiration*, the outward Breath of Life, the expiration of the Fiery Lives (solar *prāṇa)* that sustains the entire body of manifestation. These are the Creative Intelligences stemming from the archetypal Mind causing manifestation. This concerns the science of evocation. The numbers of the letter A add to 1, which relates to the first Ray of Will or Power, which is the driving Will behind the manifestation of Breath. The numbers of the letter H add to 8, which is the swirling cyclic motion that sustains all of the activities of Being and which causes the evolution of enlightenment (*bodhi*). Together the numbers add to the number nine of Initiation, signifying here Initiation into new cycles of attainment, which cause the evocation of higher principles from out of the evolving Lives.
2. *Hi*—concerned with *inspiration,* the *inbreathing* of Consciousness, the enlightenment-principle that comes as a result of evolution, the passing of Initiation testings. Initiates respond to the originating outward breathing motion upon the path of return. They can identify with their Monads with respect to the evolutionary Paean of a Logos, or for the evolving personality with respect to the evolutionary impetus of the human Soul. (The development of the higher Mind being the objective.) These ones bear the gain of what was originally breathed out, which is now directed inwards as conscious realisation. We thus have the science of invocation, the consequent vitalisation of the entire internal constitution, and its growth to maturity. Eventually enlightenment is attained, for which purpose there is also an outward expression. Thus the spiral turns in upon itself. Upon *the path of return* therefore *inspiration* concerns the drawing forth of the inward Breath of enlightenment, by invoking the potencies and forces from the higher domains. This path necessitates passing all of the Initiation testings along the upward Way, and the eventual making of Dhyān Chohans who leave upon their cosmic paths. (The numbers of Hi add to 17, concerning the eventuation of the attributes of a Logos.)

The Ah-Hi thus represent the outward (Ah – *rūpa*) and inward (Hi – *arūpa*) manifestations of the Hierarchy of life. Ah (Āḥ) here represents the beginning of the mantric sound Aūṁ, the sound of creation. The

Hi here represents the mantric sound of abstraction, where the 'H' is aspirated soundlessly, producing a resonant 'eee' sound that is drawn upwards to the higher strata of Mind, thereby liberating consciousness.

The inward manifests outwardly and the outward manifests inwardly.

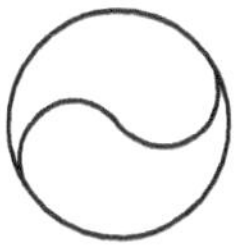

Thus the yin-yang is indicated, the nature of the interrelation between the parallel streams of Life: the human, masculine stream (Hi) and the *deva*, feminine stream (Ah). The numbers of the two H's each add to 8, indicating the nature of the spiral-cyclic motion between the two groups, the dual evolutionary process.

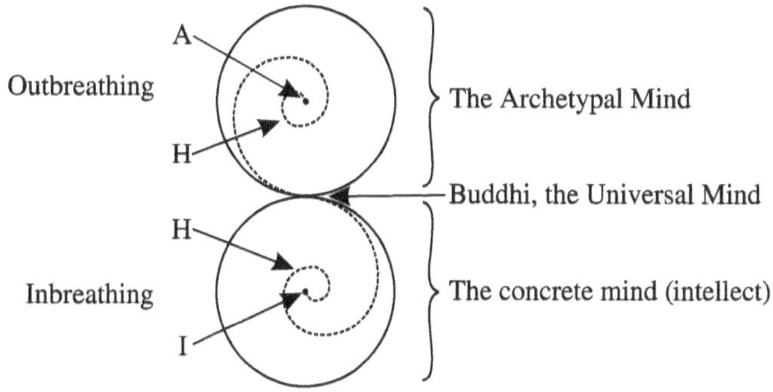

Figure 3. The Ah-Hi

The viewpoint of the Ah-Hi in this diagram is from above-down, from the position of the creative forces governing solar evolution, not from the point of view of an aspiring human unit. The aspiring person breathes in the result of the breathing out of the Lords of Shambhala, producing a resultant conscious knowledge of the true nature of phenomena. There is an eventual transmutation of that into enlightenment once the person learns to breathe out on his/her own tiny scale the gain of the inbreathing process. This concerns the esoteric science of *prāṇāyāma*.

The Ah-Hi are also comprised of two major groups of angelic beings, one group being responsible for the archetypal, energising the

Logoic Plan. They build the blueprint of the *maṇḍalic* construct. The other group are responsible for the expression of the archetype as the corporeal realms. They embody the form.

The numbers of the phrase *'there was no Ah-Hi'* add to 9 x 10, 4 x 9, 3 x 12. The number 9 x 10 is the number of the perfected Initiate (Ah-Hi seen as an integrated unit) who is responsible for the process of the manifestation of a planet, or of the entire Initiation path. The number refers to the Greater Builders. Such were not active at this time. The number 3 x 12 refers to the sign Gemini the twins, hence the etheric body into which all were abstracted. (The cosmic ethers and the cosmic astral plane are here viewed as one integral unit.) Effectively, the number 90 refers to the *Ah*, greater Initiates (Monads) that represent the prime Causative agents in manifestation, and the 4 x 9 to the *Hi*, the lesser Initiates, the returning *nirvāṇees*. Those embodying the *Ah* were aloof from manifestation, whist the *nirvāṇees* had not yet evolved.

When the numbers of the word 'for' are added to this phrase, then the reason why there are no Ah-Hi (*'For there were no Ah-hi')* is indicated, in the number 111 (100 + 10 + 1). This number informs us that the first Ray of Will or Power (the destroyer Ray) was in active demonstration on all levels, planetary, solar, or cosmic. All of the major cycles of activity had therefore run their course and all Life had abstracted back to the one consummating source via developed *antaḥkaraṇas* to liberation. With the first Ray cycle being dominant the material domain would cease to exist.

The numbers of the phrase *'to contain it'* add to 50, which refers to the *manasaputras* or angelic kingdom. They are Lords of the creative force, the intelligent Minds responsible for the manifestation of form. Collectively they are the receptors of universal Mind and are responsible for its distribution via the Lesser Builders. As neither were in manifestation, nothing could be contained by minds, thus nothing could exist. All forms in the universe are in fact mind/Mind-born and borne.

The numbers of the phrase *'no Ah-Hi to contain it'* add to 33, 3 x 5, signifying the Creative Intelligences (Hierarchies), the Lesser Builders, who distribute the potency of the universal Mind into manifestation. They embody the Ah aspect of the Ah-Hi and also were in *parinispanna*. The number 3 x 5 refers to the 'Hi' part, embodied by the *mānasaputras* that are 'to contain' the embodied form, and all attributes of mind. It thus also refers to the intelligences (humans) who evolve and demonstrate mind in the manifest realms.

The numbers of the phrase *'There were no Ah-Hi to contain it'* add to 140 = 2 x 70, 7 x 20, and to 50 (explained above). The number 2 x 70 refers to the refection of the archetypal form into/as the manifested realms. This form, in its various septenaries associated with manifest space, did then not exist. More specifically, the number 7 x 20 refers to the seven Creative Hierarchies (20) associated with systemic space. They are the Ah-Hi manifesting via various septenaries. Consequently they did not exist in a materialised space. There was no established Shambhalic expression that could house these Creative Hierarchies, nor the spiritual gold (wisdom) tried in the Fires of the Mind with which to build the temple of a Logoic Head centre. Therefore there was no universal Mind to contain any manifestation. The Sun-Sons did not exist in active manifestation (with respect to solar beginnings). As there were no solar or cosmic Lords incarnate from which anything else could evolve, so everything was still in a *nirvāṇa* state.

The numbers of the complete phrase *'For there were no Ah-Hi to contain it'* add to 8, the spiral-cyclic energies sustaining the activities of the yin-yang depicted above were not manifest, hence 'nought was'.

Stanza One part Four

Stanza 1: 4 states:

> **The seven Ways to Bliss** *(Moksha or Nirvana)* **were not. The great causes of misery** *(Nidana and Maya)* **were not, for there was no one to produce and get ensnared by them.**

Keynotes: Sagittarius, the sixth cosmic astral sub-plane, the Son, the second Eternity.

Following from Capricorn this stanza is governed by the qualities of the sign Sagittarius the archer, which fires the arrows of one-pointed aspiration to a goal. In the case of a Logos, the arrows are those of directed Thought to create the forms of all-that-must-Be. The Archer then marshals all resources to achieve that goal: be these Creation, 'the seven Ways of Bliss', or to be ensnared by the 'causes of misery' (once a human kingdom appears). The focus is now via the sixth cosmic astral sub-plane, wherein the pure Waters of cosmic Love that sustains the evolution of solar and planetary systems are expressed. This energy is here designated as 'The seven Ways to Bliss'.

The numerical breakdown of the first phrase:

> The seven Ways (49 = 7 x 7, 13), The seven Ways to Bliss (73 = 10, 28), Ways to Bliss (38 = 11, 20), The seven Ways to Bliss were not (110, 11), Ways to Bliss were not (75, 30).

'The seven Ways' (7 x 7) at first are the *seven Ray paths,* which concern absorption into one or other of the seven Ray Ashrams of the Masters of Wisdom. The higher correlation is seen in the form of the seven cosmic Paths (though they are not governed by the Rays), or the Ways of the seven planetary Logoi governing the Rays for the solar system. The number 7 x 7 indicates the sub-divisions of each of the seven Ways.

Bliss is an attribute of the Spirit-Monad, just as joy is an attribute of the Soul, and happiness is a personality attribute. Bliss is the way of progress of those constituting a planetary or solar Head centre from place to place in the solar or cosmic landscape.[25] Bliss represents the most intense form of the energy of Love that is sustainable by the human unit. These pathways were not then in existence, because obviously no beings were incarnate to apply them. Both Bliss and the expression of misery are experienced by those who embody the Son in incarnation, referring to the highest and lowest connotations of the concept of 'Son'. The highest being the liberated streams of Life, who experience Bliss and the lowest being a humanity struggling in the spheres of sensation, and who are subject to the causes of misery. The cosmic Waters, the Love expressed via this sixth cosmic astral sub-plane, feeds both streams of Life. The difference being that one stream fully imbibes these energies, and the other is resistant to their influx. The fourth Creative Hierarchy that are responsible for the dissemination of this energy, titled 'Desire for duality' now 'slumbered' upon the second Eternity, hence the energies of cosmic Love was not being expressed, nor were those who could evolve by means of this expression. As stated,

25 See also Stanza 2:1, where Bliss is also equated with 'non-being'.

the duality that is 'desired for' is here indicated by the juxtaposition of the concept of Bliss to the 'causes of misery', which will manifest upon the appearance of *saṃsāra*. Logoic Desire expressed via the sixth Ray of Devotion-Aspiration will eventuate the appearance of the Schemes and globes wherein the manifesting Lives will play out their appointed roles. The Thought, impelled by Logoic Desire for the appearance of such Schemes, etc., had not yet appeared, hence naught was.

The *'Ways to Bliss'* are the seven cosmic Paths explained in T.C.F. by A. A. Bailey:

1. The Path of Earth Service.
2. The Path of Magnetic Work.
3. The Path of training for the Planetary Logos.
4. The Path to Sirius.
5. The Ray Path.
6. The Path on which a Solar Logos is found.
7. The Path of Absolute Sonship.[26]

Concerning *'The seven Ways to Bliss'*, (7 x 4, 10) H.P.B. states that:

> There are Seven "Paths" or "Ways" to the bliss of Non-Existence, which is absolute Being, Existence, and Consciousness. They were not, because the Universe was, so far, empty, and existed only in the Divine Thought.[27]

Once a person has attained *buddhic* perception *(śūnyatā,* the fourth cosmic ether) (7 x 4,11), then these cosmic pathways can be perceived. Here the intricate cosmic *nāḍī* system is discovered, as well as the various *chakras,* the suns (etc.) to which liberated beings can travel. *Buddhi* is the doorway to cosmic space.

The numbers of the phrase *'Ways to Bliss'* add to 11 or 20, signifying the combined first and second Ray energies that liberate one from the realms of form, to travel to the Lords of Life and the Heart of all Being. The 'Ways to Bliss' are the many paths thereto. Blavatsky states that these Ways are 'Moksha or Nirvana', both of which are symbolised by the numbers 11 and 20. *Mokṣa* (from the root *mokṣ* to release, liberate) means liberation, release from suffering of *saṃsāra*, hence

---

26 See T.C.F., 1241-82.

27 *The Secret Doctrine,* Vol. 1, 38-39.

gaining complete enlightenment. *Mokṣa* literally relates to the state of awareness gained at the 'other shore' of manifest being (*śūnyatā*). *Nirvāṇa* is defined as the state beyond sorrow, literally 'blowing out', as 'suchness', the great Peace, the final attainment of the evolutionary process, the state of abiding in *śūnyatā*. Esoterically, *nirvāṇa* signifies the mode of travel from *śūnyatā* to cosmic astral space via one or other of the cosmic Paths.

The numbers of the phrase *'The seven Ways to Bliss were not'* add to 11 x 10, 100 + 10. The number 110 has a similar meaning as the number 10 (evolutionary or cyclic perfection), but here indicates the attainment of one after another cycle of activity within a major sphere of evolution (the number 100), indicating happenings on a cosmic scale. It signifies that the Ones who could travel upon the Paths (*antaḥkaraṇas,* the number 11) of cosmic Compassionate Activity (the 'Ways to Bliss') had already done so, after gaining liberation from a earth sphere. The Doors thereto (symbolised by the number 11 x 10) were closed *('were not')* until the next cycle of activity.

This phrase presents further information concerning the process of 'dying', via a comprehension of the nature of the first Ray aspect of Deity and how it abstracts the All back into the undefinable 'Darkness', as indicated by Stanza 1:5. The Father, Son and Mother aspects of this cosmic abstraction process are to be accounted for:

a. *'Time was not'*. This refers to the third Ray, the Mother or Activity aspect, concerned with the cyclic appearances and endings of things.

b. *'Universal Mind was not'*, which refers to the second Ray, the Son or consciousness aspect, concerned with the expression of the twelve Creative Hierarchies in time and space.

c. *'The Seven ways to Bliss were not'*. Here the first Ray, the Father aspect, is implicated. This is concerned with Monadic evolution in cosmic space.

The three are One, and what underlies the One is the 'Naught' that 'was' (Stanza 1:6). Obviously very little can be actually said about this first Ray aspect to those are still residing in the form and bonded by time, yet to develop the Universal Mind.

The numbers of the phrase *'Ways to Bliss were not'* add to 75 (25 x 3). At first this number refers to the spiritualisation of the mental plane by responding to the energies of the spiritual Triad, thence to the evolution of the great Ones, the Chohans who demonstrate the attributes of cosmic Mind *(dharmakāya).* They can then find the specific Way to Bliss applicable to them within the Logoic Mind. It also refers to the three Buddhas of Activity, who disseminate Mind to the Body of manifestation of a globe, Chain, or Scheme of evolution. They help constitute the Doorways to these Ways to Bliss. However all this was not possible because no being was incarnate.

The numerical breakdown of the second sentence:

> The great causes (53 = 8, 17, 6.6.5.), causes of misery (61 = 7, 16), The great causes of misery (100, 28), causes of misery were not (98 = 49 x 2, 26 = 8), The great causes of misery were not (137, 38 = 11).

The numbers of the phrase *'The great causes'* add to 17, 8, 6.6.5. The number 17 relates to Deity, informing us that these causes are concerned with the spiral-cyclic activity (8) in the realm of form that governs Logoic evolution, whereby the *saṃskāras* of past planetary *karma* are projected into planetary manifestation causing the evolutionary process. What was created in the past, and needing transformation by a human kingdom constitutes 'great causes' of misery. These causes concern the evolution of human consciousness in such a way that they contribute to that kingdom evolving the attributes of a Logos, once the *saṃskāras* have been transmuted into enlightenment vectors.

The number 6.6.5. here relates to the principle of desire-attachment (6.6.), coupled with mind (5), hence the manifestation of desire-mind (*kāma-manas*), for all things pleasurable and pertaining to *saṃsāra*. Such attachment, coupled with ignorance and residing in *māyā* (illusion), are the foundation causes for all misery obtained by humanity. The Logos has manifested a world sphere so that humanity could learn from this desire principle and to master it by appropriately developing mind/Mind.

In Buddhism these causes of misery are called the twelve *nidānas*, (*pratītyasamutpāda*) or causes of being, as H.P.B. points out in her footnote[28] as well as the commentary. *Pratītyasamutpāda* is translated as 'dependent arising, dependent origination, the links of interrelationship that cause the treading of the wheel of rebirth'. Blavatsky states:

> The twelve Nidanas or causes of being. Each is the effect of its antecedent cause, and a cause, in its turn, to its successor; the sum total of the Nidanas being based on the four truths, a doctrine especially characteristic of the Hīnayāna System. They belong to the theory of the stream of catenated law which produces a merit and demerit, and finally brings Karma into full sway. It is based upon the great truth that re-incarnation is to be dreaded, as existence in this world only entails upon man suffering, misery and pain; Death itself being unable to deliver man from it, since death is merely the door through which he passes to another life on earth after a little rest on its threshold –Devachan.[29]

The twelve *nidānas* are the underlying cause and determining factor, the cause-effect relation (dependent origination) for our rebirthing process, they are the twelve causes of existence, or twelvefold chain of causation. They progressively arise out of each other. The order given is: 1. Ignorance *(avidya)*, the root cause of them all. 2. Action producing attachment to form *(saṃskāra)*. 3. The development of consciousness (*vijñāna*). 4. The ability to name the various forms (*nāmarūpa*). 5. The development and use of the senses and sense objects *(sadāyātana)*. 6. Physical plane contact by means of the sense of touch *(sparsa)*. 7. Feeling perceptions, sensation next appear *(vedanā)*. 8. Thirst or desire for things *(tṛṣnā)*. 9. Clinging onto objects of desire *(upādāna)*. 10. Becoming, clinging, or being content with mundane existence *(bhāva)*. 11. Producing birth, or rebirth *(jāti)*. 12. The ageing process, sorrow, pain *(duhkha)* and death (*jarāmaraṇa*).

The aversion to pain and suffering eventually leads one to the realisation of the Buddha's Four Noble Truths and treading the Eightfold Path.[30]

---

28 The footnote given by Blavatsky being: 'The "12" Nidanas (in Tibetan Ten-brel chug-nyi) are the chief causes of existence, effects generated by a concatenation of causes produced.' Ibid., 38.

29 Ibid., 39.

30 See chapter 8 ('The Maṇḍala and the Eightfold Path') of volume 4 of *A Treatise on Mind*, for an appropriate explanation of this path.

The numbers of the word *causes* are interesting, for they are upon the first Ray line (3.1.3.1.5.1., which add to 5). This implies that the implementation of these causes is via first Ray abilities, the will to overcome all obstacles in the process of causation. The theme of the first Ray is further provided in the numbers of the complete phrase *'The great causes of misery were not'*, which add to 11, also referring to the *nāḍīs* through which all energies associated with this misery must flow. The cause of the sum of the *māyā* of all the phenomena seen around us is here implied. It also refers to the projection of desire and attachment, the *antaḥkaraṇas* from 'here to there', that are the causes of anything. Finally, there are the major abstracting processes associated with the first Ray that will inevitably bring all into the Darkness of abstraction.

In the phrase *'The seven Ways to Bliss were not'* and *'The great causes of misery were not'* there is a division similar to what the term Ah-Hi had with respect to Universal Mind. The first phrase refers to the archetypal, the expression of the first Ray in terms of the manifestation of enlightened Being, the constitution of Shambhala, wherein reside the Heavenly Men, the Dhyān Chohans (symbolised by the Ah). The second phrase is concerned with the expression, development and final purpose of the energy of the Will in the formed realms, which manifests via its lower reflux, the energy of desire (the personal will) and consequent attachment to things desired. It thus concerns the evolution of a human kingdom (the Hi).

The numbers of the phrase *'causes of misery'* add to 16, 7, informing us that these causes of misery are concerned with the evolution of a Christ (16) within the formed realms (7). The number 7 is the important number here, which pertains to life in the material domain. It also refers to the seven Ray qualities which categorise the causes of misery. These Rays concern the active expression of the Plan in the material domain to overcome attachments to all forms of activity (the third Ray). There is also the production of harmony in the midst of strife (the fourth Ray), intelligent activity to comprehend why the phenomena exists wherein there is so much pain, suffering, and also happiness (the fifth Ray). The desire-mind unfolding via desires and ambitions of all types, whereby one learns from one's mistakes, is governed by the sixth Ray.

The seventh Ray concerns the ritualistic, circuitous, repetitious activity of life in *saṃsāra,* which produces much scope for learning. There is also the conversion of desire into Love (the second Ray), and the first Ray development of the Will. The reason for it all is comprehended via the development of compassionate awareness (16).

The number 7 x 7 x 2 of the phrase *'causes of misery were not'* refers to the various planes and sub-planes of perception that must be mastered if these 'causes of misery' are to be eliminated, to make them 'not'. This causes the approach of *pralaya.*

The numbers of the phrase *'The great causes of misery'* add to 100, 7 x 4, informing us that these causes are associated with the attainment of a complete Round (*manvantara*) of evolution, right to the time of the great perfection (100). This incorporates the myriad renunciations needed to obtain the fourth Initiation and to experience conditionings upon the fourth plane *(śūnyatā),* thereby eliminating the causes to misery. Such renunciations can also be considered causes of misery for one upon the path of Return. Painful indeed, at first, is this path of detachment, renunciation and transmutation of desire, of dispassion, and the ability to dispel illusions at all associated levels.

The numerical breakdown of the third phrase:

> there was no one (63 = 7 x 9, 27), no one (27, 9), for there was no one (84 = 7 x 12, 30), no one to produce (72 = Virgo, 27), get ensnared (49, 13), to produce and get ensnared (104, 32), there was no one to produce (45, 108 = Sagittarius), no one to produce and get ensnared (131, 41 = 5), For there was no one to produce (129, 48 = Cancer), For there was no one to produce and get ensnared (188 = 100 + 88, 62 = 31 x 2), get ensnared by them (77, 32), to produce and get ensnared by them (132 = 66 x 2, 51 = 17 x 3), no one to produce and get ensnared by them (159 = 15, 60 = Leo), There was no one to produce and get ensnared (167, 59 = 14), There was no one to produce and get ensnared by them (195 = 100 + 95, 78 = 15), For there was no one to produce and get ensnared by them (216 = 108 x 2, 24 x 9, 81 = 9 x 9).

The word *one* means 'that which is singular, indivisible', and esoterically to the first or Father aspect of all manifested Life. It appears, for instance, in Ch 4:2 of *The Revelation of St. John* in the phrase: 'behold, a throne was set in heaven and One sat on the throne'. Such a 'One' refers to a planetary Logos, the direct incarnate representative of the 'first and the last', the cause and consummation of the entire pageant of Creation. The concept of 'One' concerns establishing an 'I Am' principle that allows complete assertion of an identity that distinguishes such a One from all other beings. It signifies the embodiment of a Creative Logos that has evolved from massed consciousness to the central point of a sphere of attainment.

The phrase *'no one'* (3 x 9) therefore indicates that no such entity existed. There was no *One* that produced a Throne (or Base *chakra*) to sit upon, from whence manifest space could emanate. The various planetary or solar spheres were not in existence—'Naught was'. The number 3 x 9 informs us that there were no Initiates of the third degree (human Souls), or their cosmic equivalents, that built Thrones of self-conscious activity, to thereby manifest personalities that could 'get ensnared' by the causes of misery. Also, those that have attained the third Initiation or greater cannot get ensnared by the causes of misery, for such tendencies have been left far behind, because they no longer possess a separative personality. Personality and Soul are then integrated into a unity upon the higher mental plane.

The numbers 3 x 9 and 7 x 9 of the phrase *'there was no one'* also signify that no Initiates were incarnate to manifest the compassionate activity of trying to salvage those living in misery. All were in a state of *pralaya*.

The number 7 x 12 of the phrase *'For there was no one'* relates to Libra the balances, which indicates that no being existed because the great Wheel of the Law had run its course, the cycles of activity were not manifesting. *Karma* was not, and therefore manifest being was not. The manifold wheels (*chakras*) of manifest Life were not turning to produce the phenomena of *saṃsāra*. The 'causes of misery' therefore could not exist. Nobody existed to identify with, or be attached to the vicissitudes of ever changing phenomena.

The numbers of the phrase *'no one to produce'* add to 6 x 12 (Virgo), 8 x 9, 3 x 9. Because the great cosmic Mother (Virgo) was not manifest, so there was 'no one to produce' anything. The child was not yet existent in her Womb so there was no one, not even Initiates (8 x 9, 3 x 9) to produce and get ensnared by the *māyā* of phenomena. Here specifically the *deva* triads are implicated. The number 72 also indicates the ideal life-span of any incarnate entity, human, planetary, or solar. No such beings existed that could create or produce forms, manipulate energy, etc., consequently ensnarement was not possible.

The number 9 x 5 of the phrase *'there was no one to produce'* refers to Masters of Wisdom, hence the constituency of Hierarchy. The accompanying number 108 is the sacred number, referring to the complete Head Lotus (Shambhala) of any incarnate Logos or a person. As there were no bearers of such a Head lotus, or the existence of Hierarchy, so nothing else could be. The number 108 also refers to *Sagittarius the archer,* who fires arrows of aspiration to the mountaintop of Initiation, and esoterically starts each new cycle of endeavour upon the reversed wheel, by projecting the energies that turn the wheels in Libra. No one existed to walk the path to liberation, neither was it time for the Logos to fire Sagittarian arrows of Creative Thought, thus signifying the new cycle of activity. Similarly a Sagittarian personality fires arrows of desire and of selfishness that ensnare aspects of *māyā* needed to be experienced. However 'Naught was'.

The numbers of the phrase *'For there was no one to produce'* (material incarnation) add to 4 x 12, referring to Cancer the crab, the gateway to birth, to mass incarnation, and therefore of material involvement, the primal cause of misery in a solar system. The doorway into incarnation ruled by Cancer was closed. The claws of the crab, holding the Diamond Mind, was focussed upwards to cosmic astral space, assisting in the development of new attributes that would manifest in the next *manvantara.*

The number four refers to the qualities associated with human evolution and which ensnare people. We have the quaternary—the mental, astral, etheric and dense physical substance that constitute one's form nature, the illusional body of appearance, and which together constitute the domain of *māyā*, as H.P.B. explains in her commentary:

> Maya or illusion is an element which enters into all finite things, for everything that exists has only a relative, not an absolute, reality, since the appearance which the hidden noumenon assumes for any observer

depends upon his power of cognition. To the untrained eye of the savage, a painting is at first an unmeaning confusion of streaks and daubs of colour, while an educated eye sees instantly a face or a landscape. Nothing is permanent except the one hidden absolute existence which contains in itself the noumenon of all realities. The existences belonging to every plane of being, up to the highest Dhyan-Chohans, are, in degree, of the nature of shadows cast by a magic lantern on a colourless screen; but all things are relatively real, for the cognizer is also a reflection, and the things cognized are therefore as real to him as himself. Whatever reality things posses must be looked for in them before or after they have passed like a flash through the material world; but we cannot cognise any such existence directly, so long as we have a sense-instruments which bring only material existence into the field of our consciousness. Whatever plane our consciousness may be acting in, both we and the things belonging to that plane are, for the time being, our only realities. As we rise in the scale of development we perceive that during the stages through which we have passed we mistook shadows for realities, and the upward progress of the Ego is a series of progressive awakenings, each advance bringing with it the idea that now, at last, we have reached "reality;" but only when we shall have reached absolute Consciousness, and blended our own with it, shall we be free from the delusions produced by Maya.[31]

We saw in the Proem that *māyā* embodies the aggregates of forces controlling one's *chakras,* by excluding the controlling impressions from the realms of enlightenment. The perceptions derived from the three planes of human livingness are then viewed as real rather than that obtained from the higher planes. *Māyā* incorporates the sum of the energies working through the *nāḍīs* that at first cause an individual to identify unduly with *saṃsāra* and its allurements. *Māyā* thereby embodies impressions that veil the real. In the Advaita Vedānta it is the beginningless cause that produces the illusion of the world, a power of the Brahman that is neither real or unreal.

To 'ensnare' is to catch in a snare, to entangle. Here it implies emotional-mental entanglements, which produce the causes of misery associated with the desire-mind which everyone knows so well. To

31 Ibid., Vol. 1, 39-40.

'get ensnared' (49, 13) numerologically means to be involved in cycles of activity (13) within the planes and sub-planes (7 x 7) of material involvement with phenomena of any type: psychic, subjective, or objective.

The numbers of the phrase *'no one to produce and get ensnared'* add to 5 and to 100 + 31. The number five signifies the mental principle of the human units who both produce their own *māyā* and get ensnared by it. The number 100 + 31 refers to the bearers of Logoic Will, the producers of the world sphere, hence of the universal *māyā*. The numbers 188 = 100 + 88, 17, 31 x 2 of the phrase *'For there was no one to produce and get ensnared'* refer to the various Logoi (17), or embodiments of Deity, that reflect the first Ray Purpose (31 x 2) into manifestation. Because neither spiral-cyclic motion (88) nor the Will to manifest such cycles of activity (31 x 2) were active, so there was *'no one'* to *'get ensnared'*.

The number 77 of the phrase *'get ensnared by them'* refers to the 777 incarnations of any incarnate entity, to the turning of the various wheels of incarnate being. Obviously no being was undergoing any of their 777 incarnations at this stage, as all was in *pralaya*.

The number to 66 x 2 of the phrase *'to produce and get ensnared by them'* is but a version of the number 666, referring to the manifestation of a material body of manifestation, which did not exist for anyone to get ensnared. The other number (17 x 3) refers to the activity cycle of an incarnate Logos, hence of the Mother, which likewise was not manifesting at this stage. No one was incarnate to produce and get ensnared by any form of activity.

The number 14 of the phrase *'There was no one to produce and get ensnared'* refers to the astral plane, hence the forms of desire and emotionality that are the causes of misery for humanity. This plane and the associated heaven and hell states were not vitalised because there was no humanity existing.

The numbers of the phrases *'There was no one to produce and get ensnared by them'* add to 100 + 95, 15, whilst those of *'no one to produce and get ensnared by them'* add to 15, 5 x 12. The number 5 x 12 refers to the sign *Leo the lion*, who represents the dominant individual, the bearer of the empirical mind (15) which produces the illusion of material plane living which people are 'ensnared' into believing to be reality. The sign Leo also refers to the Individualisation process of an entire kingdom of Souls. The forming of the 'snare' of consciousness (the Soul) allows the principle of mind to be evolved and stored, as the entire process of material evolution is undertaken. As a human Hierarchy was not yet existent so there was no ensnarement. The number 100 + 95 refers to the time period when the evolutionary process is in full play, preceding evolutionary perfection (here the number 200). As evolution was not happening, so nothing else could.

The numbers of *the complete phrase* add to 216 = 200 + 16, 108 x 2, 24 x 9, and to 9 x 9. The number 9 x 9 refers to the Initiate of the ninth degree, the Planetary Regents governing planetary evolution (with all of the attendant causes of misery). All of the permutations of the number 216, which refer to a Lord of Love (200 + 16) manifesting a planetary Head lotus (108 x 2), initiating the zodiacal cycles (24 x 9) were not in active manifestation. Without their existence the Ways to Bliss also could not evolve.

Once could also look to such phrases as: *'one to produce'* (61, 25), *'one to produce and get ensnared'* (120 = Capricorn, 39), *'one to produce and get ensnared by them'* (148 = 100 + 48 = Cancer, 58), *'to produce and get ensnared'* (104, 32), and interpret them in terms of the conditionings whereby active manifestation is possible. Such an exercise is obviously redundant here, hence shall be omitted.

In summary we see that the causes of misery and of those that get ensnared by them are manifold and can be viewed from many different levels of perception. Basically they are concerned with the many changes associated with material involvement, via the evolution of the mental principle and of desire-attachment. This is borne by the instruments that must contain that evolution; the various Logoi, the Soul and the human personality. Also, specifically, the objective of all this misery in the world is to help humans to develop first Ray qualities (via the path of overcoming materialism). This concerns gaining the sword-like adamantine qualities that pierce all obstacles and eliminate illusions and so help blaze the way along the Initiation path to liberation.

Stanza One part Five

Stanza 1:5 states:

> **Darkness alone filled the Boundless All, for Father, Mother and Son were once more one, and the Son had not awakened yet for the new Wheel and his pilgrimage thereon.**

Keynotes: Scorpio, seventh cosmic astral sub-plane, the Mother, the third Eternity.

The numerical breakdown of the first phrase:

> Darkness alone (48 = Cancer, 12), the Boundless All (49, 22), filled the Boundless All (79, 25), Boundless All (34, 16), Darkness alone filled the Boundless All (127, 37).

As earlier stated 'Darkness alone' relates to the third Eternity upon the seventh sub-plane of the cosmic astral wherein 'slumbered' the fifth of the Liberated Hierarchies, 'Mass life'. This Darkness is ruled by the seventh Ray of cyclic Power and Ritual activity of the Mother, who embodies the substance of what is to appear. Naught yet is manifested within Her Womb, hence the Father-Son-Mother aspects the triune Logos, those incorporated in the first three Eternities, are waiting for the cycle of corporeal manifestation into the cosmic dense physical plane. This Trinity will be reflected into the attributes of the lower three Eternities via the mirror-like aspect of the fourth Eternity. This will represent the 'fall of the three into the four' for the new Wheel. Because Consciousness had not yet appeared to register Light, so Darkness ruled. The projection of this massed Life is first in the form of the substance that will inform the cosmic dense physical plane. Strong first Ray energies (under the auspices of Vulcan) will be needed to accomplish this task. These energies are applied via the four ethers and *nāḍī* system of the Logos, in order to cause the precipitation of cosmic dense physical substance (the three planes of *saṃsāra*). 'Gravitational' forces from this seventh cosmic astral sub-plane will therefore condition the sum of the cosmic dense physical. These forces are effectively the energy of Mahat utilised to project the substance of what is to Be ('Mass Life') into dense physical incarnation. The force of gravity then is the energy of the Logoic Mind needed to control and regulate the dense physical appearance.[32]

This foundational Creative process for the new *manvantara* will set the stage for the outpouring of the Consciousness principle (the Son) via the auspices of Scorpio the scorpion. Scorpio governs all of the trials and tribulations of the Son's pilgrimage so as to rightly progress upon the Wheel of birth and death during the entire *manvantara*. The trials incorporate the testings associated with overcoming the attributes of the dark brotherhood. They must be defeated if the Pilgrim is to travel rightly upon the Wheel to liberation from the darkness of ignorance.

Darkness is not necessarily darkness as we understand it. It can also be clear, cold Light of such intensity that it turns into shadow all other types of light, as D.K. explains:

> darkness is pure spirit....each contact with the Initiator leads the Initiate closer to the centre of pure darkness – a darkness which is the very antithesis of darkness as the non-Initiate and the unenlightened understand. It is a centre or point of such intense brilliance that everything else fades out.[33]

He further states that it is the expression of the demonstration of the Will aspect (by the custodian of that energy) that:

> adds darkness unto light so that the stars appear, for in the light the stars shine not, but in the darkness light diffused is not, but only focussed points of radiance.[34]

Darkness therefore is that condition that cannot be properly defined or understood by the empirical mind (but which allows the light of all manifest suns to appear). It is that Divine Will into which all forms of existence have been abstracted. (As explained by the three previous *ślokas.)* It is the integral essence of the triune cosmic Logos; the Father (Ray 1), the Son (Ray 2) and the Mother (Ray 3). This Essence represents the Unmanifested God (Brahman) appearing in the form of the Darkness of unconditioned Space, as indicated by the figure below:

---

32 My book *Esoteric Cosmology and Modern Physics* delves into this subject in some detail.

33 Bailey, Alice, A. *The Rays and the Initiations,* (Lucis Press, New York), 174.

34 Ibid., 170.

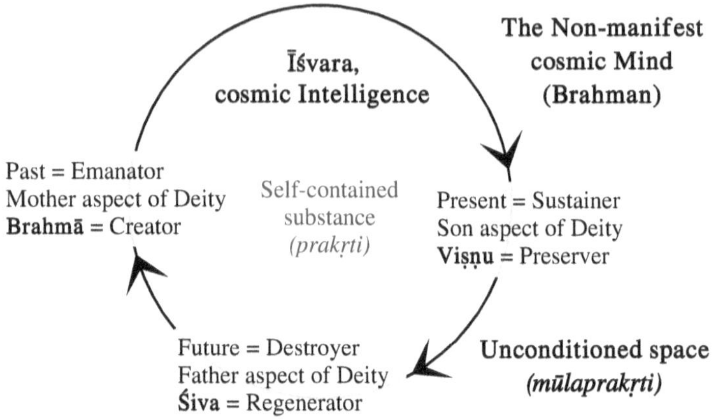

Figure 4. The cycle of Being[35]

Within the Darkness of unconditioned Space 'the stars appear' (here represented as the cycle of being) at the appointed time when a Logos (a cosmic Intelligence) circumscribes an arena of Darkness to generate a sphere of light. The Logoi manifest 'focussed points of radiance' as they establish Head centres (Shambhalas) and a Base of Spine centre upon which they sit.

Interestingly the numbers of the word *darkness* add to 7 x 4, indicating that this Darkness is synonymous with the type of light associated with the *buddhic* plane (*śūnyatā,* Emptiness, the Void), which is darkness indeed to the empirical mind. From a lower perspective, darkness refers to the substance of the four material planes of human evolution, the quaternary or 'square' associated with That which was before anything was, the particles of cosmic 'black dust' that were the prototypes of the human Monads emanating from the cosmic mental plane at the beginning of their duration of being/non-being.

H.P.B.'s essential commentary:

> "Darkness is Father-Mother: light their Son," says an old Eastern proverb. Light is inconceivable except as coming from some source which is the cause of it; and as, in the case of primordial light, that source is unknown, though so strongly demanded by reason and logic,

35 This appeared as Figure 1 in my book *Esoteric Cosmology and Modern Physics.*

> therefore it is called "Darkness" by us, from an intellectual point of view. As to borrowed or secondary light, wherever its source, it can be only of a temporary mayavic character. Darkness, then, is the eternal matrix in which the sources of light appear and disappear. Nothing is added to darkness to make of it light, or to light to make it darkness, on this our plane. They are interchangeable, and scientifically, light is but a mode of darkness *and vice versā*. Yet both are phenomena of the same noumenon – which is absolute darkness to the scientific mind, and but a grey twilight to the perception of the average mystic, though to that of the spiritual eye of the Initiate it is absolute light. How far we discern the light that shines in darkness depends upon our powers of vision. What is light to us is darkness to certain insects, and the eye of the clairvoyant sees illumination where the normal eye sees only blackness. When the whole universe was plunged in sleep – had returned to its one primordial element – there was neither centre of luminosity, nor eye to perceive light, and darkness necessarily filled the boundless all.[36]

The numbers of the phrase *'Darkness alone'* add to 4 x 12, referring to the sign Cancer the crab, which generally embodies the Watery substance of the Womb of manifest Life. This 'Womb' thus stood 'alone', was not impregnated and therefore was in Darkness. Cancer is one of the signs that comprise the Cardinal cross, the cross determining the qualities of the Spirit or Life principle. It is the polar opposite to Capricorn, who governs the mount of material substance governed by mind/Mind. Capricorn embodies the mode of the crystallisation of the Watery darkness into consolidated forms. Via Capricorn the Creative Logoic Mind produces the appearance of the substance of the seven planes of systemic space. Cancer governs the massed instinctual consciousness of the incarnate Lives, and later the Waters expressing the qualities of the astral plane. It is the major Water sign in the zodiac, therefore it logically also governs the depths of the Watery substance of undifferentiated, non manifest Space, the cosmic astral substance from which the corporeal universe emanates. In the book of Genesis the associated statement is the 'face of the waters' upon which 'the Spirit of God' moved.[37]

---

36 Blavatsky, Vol. 1, 40-41.

37 *Genesis 1:2:* 'And the earth was without form, and void; and darkness *was* upon

Having discussed the virtually incomprehensible abstraction process concerning the three aspects of Being, the Cancerian vision directs us to the conditions inside the Great Womb upon the cosmic astral plane from whence space-time will emerge. Therein forces manifest that will fluidly organise the Waters before the appearance of formed space. D.K. states that in Cancer:

> lies hid the whole problem of the Law of Rebirth. Reincarnation is implicit in the manifested universe and is a basic and fundamental theme underlying systemic pulsation.[38]

The Watery signs Cancer and Scorpio have a direct interrelationship in the reincarnation process, where Scorpio conditions the Lives ('the Son'), preparing their consciousness for rebirth. Cancer represents the mass-movement of the Lives as they come into objectivity. The energies of Scorpio projects the Lives into manifestation (starting from the sixth cosmic astral sub-plane) via turning the Wheels that will condition evolutionary space in the new *manvantara.* Scorpio (the polar opposite of Taurus, who in many ways governs the cosmic astral plane as a whole) energises the movement of the Waters within systemic space via the dynamics of the turning *chakras.* This sign conditions, via the Law of Attraction, the integrated energies of the next five signs presented below.[39] This Law plays upon and through the evolving Watery Lives as they undergo their evolutionary journey in *manvantara.* These five signs can be considered to directly embody this Darkness, where Darkness represents the primeval substance of the Waters of Space, and which convey the attributes of the Womb of the Mother. By 'Waters' here is considered that which is fluidic, having the characteristics of a flux, and can be easily changed and manipulated by Thought.

- Sagittarius represents the directive Will of the Logoic Thought that initially impels the Watery motion.

---

the face of the deep. And the Spirit of God moved upon the face of the waters.'

38 Bailey, *Esoteric Astrology,* 312.

39 The significance of Scorpio as the bearer of the Law of Attraction into manifestation is seen in the fact that it is the sign of the testings for the Initiation process, which is the mode of return of the successful Initiates that become *nirvāṇees* back to cosmic space.

- Scorpio governs the evolutionary movement of the Lives (the 'Son') in the Waters, hence manifests a second Ray function.
- Virgo signifies the overall control of the energies of the Mother's Domain, the Womb wherein the Waters play their role. She governs the third Ray organisational motion of the Waters. This represents the Aetheric attribute of the cosmic Waters.
- Taurus generally governs the substance of the cosmic astral plane via the function of the fourth Ray, which conveys the *nāḍīs* of the Watery sphere (the four cosmic astral ethers). The All-Seeing Eye attributed to Taurus manifests via this Ray. Taurus governs the Airy aspect of the cosmic Waters.
- Pisces, signifies the fifth Ray dispensation of this Watery Darkness, from whence comes the reappearance and disappearance of cycles within the Mother's Womb. Pisces governs the Watery 'swamp' that is the containment of the Lives during *pralaya*. Pisces embodies the Fiery attribute of the cosmic Waters.
- Cancer governs mobility of the Waters and hence the process (gyration) of their 'condensation', the projection downwards into formed space. Here the materialising function of the sixth Ray comes into play. Pisces represents the Watery depths, and Cancer the motion within the Deep. The activity of Cancer brings to light what must appear. Cancer embodies the Watery aspect of the cosmic Waters.
- The sum of the Waters are poured by Aquarius the water bearer according to the cyclic need. Aquarius thus manifests a seventh Ray function. Aquarius represents the Earthy aspect of the cosmic Waters.
- Gemini is the house (the field of expression of the *nāḍīs)* that contains the sum of the Watery flow in systemic space.

Sagittarius, Scorpio and Virgo here are abstractions, they wield the functions of the three major Laws for the cosmic astral plane. Sagittarius the Law of Synthesis, Scorpio the Law of Attraction, and Virgo the Law of Economy. Taurus, the milk-giving cosmic Cow, the great nurturing universal Mother, governs the substance of the cosmic astral generally.

Pisces represents the Watery Darkness, as an expression of Mahat upon the cosmic Waters. Cancer, whose esoteric and Hierarchical rulers are Neptune, the god of the Waters, represents the movements of the Watery forms of activity. Aquarius differentiates the Waters in terms of various streams (Rays) that are poured into manifestation.

Gemini is the containment of the Waters in the systemic realms (cosmic dense space). Libra regulates the cyclic mode of activity of these Watery *prāṇas*. Aries instigates the activity of their condensation and crystallisation into dense form. Capricorn embodies the sum of what is precipitated from the Waters, and governs the mode of expression of the associated *karma*. From Aries to Capricorn turns the ten signed zodiac that dispenses the Waters as a function of the *devas*.

The first Ray aspect of Vulcan, the esoteric and Hierarchical planetary ruler of Taurus, empowers the directive one-pointed focus of the Logoic Eye. The Eye directs the Myriad arrows (Thoughts and Lives) fired by Logoic Archers into the forms (planetary and solar spheres) that are built in systemic space. These Fiery arrows, expressing Will, can thus be viewed as great Lives moving from one part of cosmic space to another.

Pisces represents the Individualised Logoic Mind upon the cosmic astral plane that receives these directive Thoughts and adapts them to its own Thought-space. Cancer signifies the adaptation of that Thought-space to the Desire to build what must be in order to accomplish Logoic Purpose. The Logos then builds an etheric Temple (Gemini) to contain the energies of that Desire, and Aquarius pours Watery streams to the Temple. Gemini then regulates the pulse of the movement of the Watery *prāṇas* from sign to sign with the turning of the zodiacal wheel (regulated by Libra).

In order to build the Logoic sphere the Individuating energy of Leo is generated to circumscribe a sphere in space and to blaze out the luminosity of the conversion of primal substance (the 'cosmic dust' inherent in systemic space) into Mind. The Lion roars out its Sounds of accomplishment. The Divine Flames take the Notes, to vivify the awakening permanent atom with the vibrant movement of the Incarnating Watery Lives. A new sphere of Activity thus comes into being and the play of *manvantara* ensues. This may be so, however our present consideration is the expression of Darkness, before the Leonine energies generated the light of the Son/Sun.

The relationship of the signs possessing two identical esoteric and Hierarchical rulers is shown below. There we see the progression from the greater Will directing Thoughts into a Watery Logoic Mind that eventually organises spheres of containment for Logoic Purpose.

Taurus	Vulcan	Vulcan	The cosmic Will.
Pisces	Pluto	Pluto	The organising Watery Mind.
Cancer	Neptune	Neptune	The directed Desire.
Aquarius	Jupiter	The Moon[40]	The streams of Loving Purpose.
Leo	The Sun	The Sun	The Light of the containing Spheres.

This Darkness, 'the "dark light" of matter, the diffused light of substance',[41] of the form, when incorporated by the light from the Soul aspect of the cosmic Logoi allows the stars of light to appear, once they are committed to reincarnate.

Darkness is at first 'alone', bereft from relationship with any other quality or principle, because the animating Life had merged with its Essence by means of a process of abstraction. The primal substance was remaindered, which physically was Darkness itself. The astral substance is abstracted from the previous dense form. Eventually also the astral body is cast aside, allowing the indwelling entity to fully participate in the *devachan* experience of the Thought Body.

The phrase *'Darkness alone'* can also refer specifically to the cosmic mental plane into which the Mind of the ineffable Logos is abstracted during the deepest part of *pralaya*. It is 'Dark' because not comprehended by those upon the lower strata of being. The great Ones upon the cosmic astral plane are abstracted in Their Thought (Meditation) processes and will not awaken from there until the next *manvantara*, when those Thoughts will be utilised as the karmic propensities for the next cosmic Personality.

The beings constituting the 'cast off shell' of the former planetary or solar incarnation, who are therefore manifest upon the cosmic etheric

---

40 Note that the Moon here veils Jupiter. Vulcan and Pluto are governed by the first Ray, Neptune the sixth Ray, Jupiter and the Sun the second Ray and the Moon the fourth Ray. See Tabulations VI and VII of Bailey, *Esoteric Astrology*, 68.

41 Ibid., 329. The quotation is from a listing of the signs of the zodiac in terms of the quality of Light they bear. The phrase given for Cancer is: *'The Light within the form.* This is the diffused light of substance itself, the "dark light" of matter, referred to in *The Secret Doctrine*. It is the light awaiting the stimulation coming from the soul light'.

levels, await the call to awaken their former activities upon the material domain. The karmic propensities will then drive all forward through the Darkness of the cosmic dense physical plane. The darkness (ignorance) of that substance must be converted and through evolutionary gain directed to the cosmic realms of Light. For our solar evolution many such beings will constitute the Lives stored in the Pluto and Mars Schemes that will be projected there at the ending of the solar *manvanatara*. They will be awakened in the Womb (here represented as 'Darkness alone') of the next solar system.

The cosmic dense physical plane was effectively in Darkness between the two solar incarnations, for the Eyes of the cosmic Logos were not focussed thereon, and all other lesser Eyes were 'asleep', thus for them it did not exist. Darkness therefore was 'alone'. It is unconditioned by time and the various cycles that modify the world of the senses, for the realms of *māyā* and the various entities therein have yet to evolve. Their *bījas* were not yet activated.

It should also be noted that the lower levels of the astral plane of our planet can be visualised as a dark, murky cloud hovering over it and which is almost impenetrable to light. This is the 'darkness' that is equable with the 'hell' often mentioned in the Bible—'the darkness shall cover the Earth' *(Isaiah 60:2)*, the 'mists of darkness' mentioned in *II Peter 2:17*, the 'outer darkness' *(Matthew 8:12)*, etc. A purpose of the Christ, the Son in incarnation, is to dispel all forms of darkness, the fogs, mists and glamour that keep people bound to the prison of this earth.[42] Christ is the 'Light that shineth in the darkness and the darkness comprehended it not' *(John 1:5)*. The 'darkness' here is the darkness of ignorance, and converting ignorance to light is the purpose of the entire evolutionary impetus. The darkness of ignorance within any incarnating Logos is conquered through following one of the five basic instincts—the instinct towards knowledge, which guides the entire path of evolution.

The entire course of Monadic evolution concerns the process of incarnating into this Darkness to illuminate it. This concerns the conversion of the dark substance of Space in such a way that eventually luminous suns are born.

42 The Christ has his corollaries in an awakened universe, solar system, Scheme or globe of evolution.

The word *boundless* means 'unlimited, vast, without boundaries or confines, immeasurable, infinite', which then is the motion of the Darkness that filled this *'Boundless All'*. Consequently the 'Darkness alone' is revealed to be boundless, unlimited, when the Light of Day gradually awakens the consciousness principle that can reveal the true nature of the Darkness. When the *manvantara,* the cycle of Activity, ceases then the Darkness again consumes the All, much like the approach of nightfall on the earth, which becomes the period of sleep or rest. That which is Boundless must be considered so in relation to what is finite, conditioned by activity via the three-dimensional world of the senses. *'The Boundless All'* (49, 22) can be considered to be something even greater than Darkness. It is the All (7 x 7), the seven layered container (e.g., as 'the Seven Eternities') of that Darkness and everything else that could come to be for 'the moment' of its appearance. However at this stage Darkness was all there was, and therefore it 'filled' this All. (Be this the 'All' of cosmic Mind, or the material domain.) The number 22 here refers to the zodiacal and planetary energies that condition Space.

The word *Boundless* also has a similar meaning to the phrase *'Infinite Bosom of Duration'*, except that the word Duration is related to the concept of time, and the word Boundless with Space. Space (the Eternal Parent or cosmic Mother) is the 'container' of this Darkness. This phrase is therefore really a continuation of Stanza 1:1, which can accordingly be rewritten thus:

> The eternal Parent (Space), wrapped in Her ever-invisible robes, had slumbered once again for seven Eternities, (in) Darkness (that) alone filled the Boundless All.

Note that *Darkness* can relate not only to cosmic dense physical conditionings, but also to the effect of the ineffable spiritual Light (emanating via *buddhi),* which turns into shadow all other types of light. This state of being/non-being is also symbolised by the phrase 'the Boundless All'. It should therefore not be too presumptive to say that the Boundless All, in the form of ineffable spiritual Light, is also a container of Darkness, from the point of view those incarnate in dense material space. The withdrawing activity of the Mind of the cosmic

Adept 'filled' the former manifestation with Darkness, for Ineffable Life was inevitably absorbed back into the Soul of cosmic Being. What was remaindered was 'stored' in the astral or physical permanent atoms, as *bījas* to be Breathed out in a later cycle.

The numbers of the phrase *'filled the Boundless All'* add to 16, 25. Here the number 16 refers to the Christ principle which filled this 'All', whilst the number 5 x 5 refers to cosmic Mind, which similarly 'filled the Boundless All'.

The number 100 + 3 x 9 of the phrase *'Darkness alone filled the Boundless All'* refers to the Soul aspect of the universe, which had absorbed all Lives into its embrace as *bījas* for a future *mahāmanvantara,* hence all was ins Darkness. The number 10 of this phrase signifies the completeness, the totality of all Space, thus also of the Darkness that filled it.

The numerical breakdown of the remaining phrases:

> For Father (52, 17), Mother and Son (56 = 7 x 8, 11), were once more one (83 = 11, 29 = 11), once more one (59 = 14, 5, 23 = 5), Mother and Son were once more (123, 33), Mother and Son were once more one (139 = 100 + 13 x 3, 40), The Son (27, 9), not awakened yet (55, 19 = 10), The Son had not awakened yet (95, 32), the new Wheel (56 = 7 x 8, 20), for the new Wheel (77, 23), not awakened yet for the new Wheel (132, 42), not awakened yet for the new Wheel and his pilgrimage thereon (261, 63), had not awakened yet (68, 23), his pilgrimage (79 = 16, 16), had not awakened yet for the new Wheel (145, 46 = 10), had not awakened yet for the new Wheel and his pilgrimage thereon (274, 67), the Son had not awakened yet for the new Wheel (172, 55), pilgrimage thereon (101, 11), The Son had not awakened yet for the new Wheel and his pilgrimage thereon (301, 76).

The meaning of *Father, Mother and Son* in terms of the triune Deity, were explained in Stanza 1:1 in relation to the phrase 'The Eternal Parent', thus needs no further explanation.

The numbers of these words have numerological significance. The number 31 of the word *Father* refers to the first Ray quality, which indeed is the Father of all manifest life. The numbers of the word *Mother* add to 7, informing us that 'She' is responsible for the various septenaries found in the appearance of things, the manifestation of the seven planes of perception, hence the appearance of the manifest universe. The number 12 of the word *Son* signifies the twelve Creative Hierarchies that constitute the Son in incarnation, the Consciousness aspect within the body of manifestation of a Logos.

The numbers of the phrase *'For Father'* add to 17 (the number relating to 'God') and to 52, indicating that this One is the Will instigating *manvantara* and *pralaya*.

Numerologically, the integration of *'Mother and Son'* indicates the spiral-cyclic energy (7 x 8) associated with the consciousness aspect (the Son) evoked on all seven levels of Being (the Mother). The numbers 11, 2 of this phrase indicate the combined first and second Ray energies that is the product of the at-onement of the Mother and Son. The Son has been born and was the dominant factor in evolution within the Mother's Bosom, but has now projected *antaḥkaraṇas* (11) to the Father, carrying the Mother with him via developing first Ray attributes, thus *pralaya* has ensued. Consequently there is only One supernal Light, not three.

When the numbers of the phrase *'Mother and Son'* are added to those of *'For Father'* (here disregarding the comma), completing the trinity: Father-Mother-Son, the result is the number 108, which signifies the powers associated with the Head centre of a Logos, wherein the three attributes of Deity reside. All is absorbed into the One, Shambhala.

The numbers of the phrase *'Mother and Son were once more'* add to 123, 33, indicating the integration of the first three Rays (123), as well as the Activity aspect of Shambhala. It refers to when *manvantara* is active, via the symbolic 33,000,000,000 Creative Intelligences (Masters, *devas* and intelligent humans) that condition the phenomena appearing via the evolution of a solar system (or of any Logos). Such was not however, because all were abstracted into the One.

The numbers of the phrase *'were once more one'*, as well as those of the phrase *'Mother and Son'* add to 11, explained above in terms of the projection of *antaḥkaraṇas*. The Will has generated conditions to cause the unification of Mother to Son, and thence Mother-Son to the Father. This number is also found for the complete statement: *'For Father, Mother and Son were once more one'*. It signifies the *nāḍīs* of the cosmic rainbow bridge that link two different states of

Awareness, localities of existence, or planes of perception. This can be either upwards or downwards to and from abstract space. It also refers to the first Ray, the destroyer of all that is, causing the abstraction into the One. The number 11, as an *antaḥkaraṇa*, links the three times:

That of the past – 'were once', the Mother.
That of the present – 'once more', the Son.
That of the future – 'were once more one', the Father.

The Son is the result of the evolution of the form in the Womb of the Mother. The Son eventually evolves into a Father, who has absorbed the qualities of both the Mother and the Son, and possesses the seeds for the birth of a new Son (solar system). That Son has inherent capabilities for the evolution of a future Father.

The numbers of the phrase *'Mother and Son were once more one'* add to 100 + 13 x 3, 4 x 10, indicating the perfection of the form nature (via divine Activity, 13 x 3) as a consequence of a future birthing of a Son (a humanity, the number 40). They were now integrated and abstracted into the Father, 'the Boundless All' that is Darkness, the ONE, the Indivisible in His Unmanifest, Unmodified, Unformed state.

H.P.B.'s essential commentary:

> The Father-Mother are the male and female principle in root-nature, the opposite poles that manifest in all things on every plane of Kosmos, or Spirit and Substance, in a less allegorical aspect, the resultant of which is the Universe, or the Son. They are "once more One" when in the "Night of Brahmā," during Pralaya, all in the objective Universe has returned to its one primal and eternal cause, to reappear at the following Dawn – as it does periodically. "Karana" – Eternal Cause – was alone. To put it more plainly: Karana is alone during the "Nights of Brahmā." The previous objective Universe has dissolved into its one primal and eternal cause, and is, so to say, held in solution in space, to differentiate again and crystallize out anew at the following Manvantaric dawn, which is the commencement of a new "Day" or new activity of Brahmā – the symbol of the Universe. In esoteric parlance, Brahmā[43] is Father-Mother-Son, or Spirit, Soul and Body at once;

43 Here H.P.B. is referring to the Brahman, which is of neutral gender, and which is the Causeless Cause of all manifest Life.

> each personage being symbolical of an attribute, and each attribute or quality being a graduated efflux of Divine Breath it its cyclic differentiation, involutionary and evolutionary. In the cosmicophysical sense, it is the Universe, the planetary chain and the earth; in the purely spiritual, the Unknown Deity, Planetary Spirit, and Man – the Son of the two, the creature of Spirit and Matter, and a manifestation of them in his periodical appearances on Earth during the "wheels," or the Manvantaras.[44]

The meaning of *'the Son'* (3 x 9) was explained previously regarding the phrase *'were once more'*. The Son must undergo this 'pilgrimage' and not the Father-Mother, for the Son is both the reason for and the result of evolution. The number 3 x 9 informs us that this Son is essentially an Initiate of the third degree, i.e., a Soul in incarnation.

To be *awakened* means to have been roused from sleep, and consequently to be able to *see* (here not just physically, but also psychically, occultly) so as to undertake a normal day's activity. The numbers of the word 'awakened' add to 7 x 4, indicating the esoteric significance of being 'awake', which is being enlightened by having *buddhic* perception. There are two directions to which one can wake. (Though esoterically there are also the eight directions of a compass, plus the two directions of the axel of a wheel.)

1. Downwards to the realms of form, which is here implied.
2. Upwards into the realms of light.

This 'awakening' (the opening of the *Eyes*) is directly related to the thought process, the evocation of the will to engender (spiritual) Creativity. The awakening can be via the Mind of a Logos, an enlightened being, or a normal human. This is indicated by the numbers of the phrase *'not awakened yet',* which add to 5 x 11. The number 55 signifies absolute mastery of the use of the Mind, making thus a Master of Wisdom, which is an objective of the evolution of a 'Son'. The time for such evolution, of a new planetary or solar Personality, or the manifestation of a human Soul, has not yet appeared. The number 55 of the phrase *'The Son had not awakened yet for the new Wheel'*

---

44 Ibid., 41.

has a similar connotation. Masters had not yet appeared because no entity was awakened. The Mind is the prime creative agent used by the Masters to control the sum of material manifestation in time and space. Because the creative aptitude of the Mind was not manifest, so nothing could appear.

The numbers of the phrases *'had not awakened yet'* and *'the Son had not awakened yet'* both add to 5, indicating the functioning of the mind. The numbers of the first phrase also add to 17 x 4, signifying that the Seat of Power for the manifestation of new personality of 'God' (4 x 17) had not yet awakened. Those of the second phrase also add to 32, 95, signifying that this Son (the solar Personality) had not yet awakened to embody the second Ray attribute of Love-Wisdom (32). The time for undertaking the evolutionary path (95) had not yet appeared.

Regarding the Wheel, H.P.B. states in a footnote that:

> That which is called "wheel" is the symbolical expression for a world or globe, which shows that the ancients were aware that our Earth was a revolving globe, not a motionless square as some Christian Fathers taught. The "Great Wheel" is the whole duration of our Cycle of being, or Maha Kalpa, *i.e.,* the whole revolution of our special chain of seven planets or Spheres from beginning to end; the "Small Wheels" meaning the Rounds, to which there are also Seven.[45]

There are other explanations of the meaning of the word Wheel:

1. It refers to the *chakras* (psychic centres), of which there are seven major ones. These are depicted as wheels with various spokes of energy in the human etheric body, or that of deity. They are also depicted as lotus blossoms, the petals of which can be seen as the radiating out from a central point or hub of a sphere ('wheel'). Note that the word *chakra* means 'wheel' and that there are a differing number of spokes according to the *chakra* concerned.
2. The Sambhogakāya Flower, which according to D.K. can be viewed: 'As nine spokes of a wheel, converging towards a central hub which is in itself threefold, and which hides the central energy or dynamo of force – the generator of all the activity'.[46]

45 Ibid., 40.

46 Bailey, *A Treatise on Cosmic Fire*, (Lucis Press, New York, 1973), 818.

3. The great Wheel of the zodiac.
4. The Wheel of the Law *(dharmacakra),* which is governed by the sign Libra the balance.
5. As Blavatsky mentions, the Wheels of the planetary or solar Rounds, Chains, globes, Root and sub-races within a Scheme.

It is perhaps needless to say that all these Wheels are interrelated, effectively being attributes of each other.

The numbers of the phrase *'the new Wheel'* add to 7 x 8, informing us that the qualities of this Wheel bears spiral-cyclic energy, sustaining the activity of all the *chakras* associated with any of the above-mentioned Wheels. Indeed, these Wheels exist to convey energy and Consciousness-attributes, *saṃskāras* or *prāṇas* from one plane, globe, *chakra,* or state of being to another.

The numbers of the phrase *'for the new Wheel'* add to 77, referring to the 777 Incarnations, revolutions or cycles, that this new Wheel must undergo to manifest the complete cycle of its evolutionary Purpose. This is needed to eventually awaken the complete potency of a Head lotus.

The numbers of the phrase *'not awakened yet for the new Wheel'* add to 66 x 2, 42. The number 66 x 2 refers to the sum of the *maṇḍala* of the formed realms, which had not yet awakened, whilst the number 6 x 7 refers to the septenaries, the Root Races etc., constituting the new Wheel.

The numbers of the phrase *'not awakened yet for the new Wheel and his pilgrimage thereon'* add to 7 x 9, those of the phrase *'had not awakened yet for the new Wheel'* add to 100 + 9 x 5. These numbers refer to the Masters and high Initiates yet to awaken, who will be the Causative agents turning the motion of the new Wheel. The other phrases numerologically presenting this Initiation process are: *'The Son had not awakened'* (9 x 9, 3 x 9), *'had not awakened'* (6 x 9, 2 x 9), and *'The Son had not awakened yet for the new Wheel'* (100 + 9 x 8, 55). The treading of the entire Wheel by the 'pilgrim' (the Son) necessitates the ability to eventually pass Initiation testings. At each step of the way these testings are ruled by Scorpio the scorpion. Whether it concerns mastery of the physical plane apparatus during the Lemurian epoch, the emotional body for the Atlantean period, or the mind for the Aryans, Scorpio sets the parameters of the testings at each stage of the turning Wheels *(chakras)*. The pilgrims must then manifest actions that will hopefully produce a successful outcome. All left hand traits must be overcome along the way, to successfully resist the scheming and machinations of the dark brotherhood.

The numbers of the phrase *'had not awakened yet for the new Wheel and his pilgrimage thereon'* add to 13, which refers to a Logoic sphere of accomplishment, a ring-pass-not of enclosed space wherein a Logos manifests a Seat of Power, symbolised by the circle with a central dot. Such had not yet been manifested, thus the pilgrim could not progress upon the associated Wheels.

The word *pilgrimage* refers to the oft long and weary journey of a person who normally seeks a sacred place or temple. Esoterically it has reference to the aeonic journey of the Soul or Monad in the formed realms to gather the needed experiences to gain Initiation and to liberate the embodied Elementary lives.

The numbers of the phrase *'his pilgrimage'* add to 16, the number of a Christ, the true Son or Soul, the *anima mundi* within the planet, with whose pilgrimage we are here concerned.

The numbers 20, 11, 101 of the phrases *'his pilgrimage thereon'* and *'pilgrimage thereon'*, refer to the needed development of first and second Ray qualities that are the purpose of this 'pilgrimage', as well as to the *nāḍī* system (11) of a Logos, through which the Son must travel upon the upward Way that constitutes the pilgrimage. The *nāḍīs* lead from Chain to Chain, Scheme to Scheme, and later from star to star of cosmic evolution (101).

The numbers of the complete phrase *'The Son had not yet awakened for the new Wheel and His Pilgrimage thereon'* add to 300 + 1. This number signifies the ending of one large cycle of evolution associated with the third Ray or Mother aspect of Deity (the number 300) and the beginning of a new one (the number 1) whereon the Son can evolve and undertake his Pilgrimage back to the Father. (The Source of His Being.) Note that the objective of the third Ray cycle (material evolution) is to give birth to the second Ray cycle of the Son, the manifestation of Love-Wisdom, which in turn must birth the first Ray cycle, the expression of the Will of 'God', the destroyer Ray.

Stanza One part Six

Stanza 1:6 states:

> **The seven Sublime Lords and the seven Truths had ceased to be, and the Universe, the Son of Necessity, was immersed in Paranishpanna** *(absolute perfection, Paranirvana, which is Yong-Grub)* **to be out-breathed by that which is and yet is not. Naught was.**

Keynotes: Libra, first cosmic ether – *ādi,* the fourth Eternity. The focal point of Stanza one.

The numerical breakdown of the first phrase:

> Sublime Lords (50, 14), seven sublime Lords (70, 16), The seven sublime Lords (85, 22), the seven Truths (60 = Leo, 15), The seven sublime Lords and the seven Truths (155 = 100 + 55, 31 x 5, 38 = 11), ceased to be (34, 25), had ceased to be (47, 29, = 11), the seven Truths had ceased to be (107, 44), the seven Truths had ceased (92 = 11, 29 = 11), The seven sublime Lords and the seven Truths had ceased (187 = 16, 52), The seven sublime Lords and the seven Truths had ceased to be (202, 67 = 13).

This Stanza brings to light the functions of Libra the balances, which governs the meditation process, here of the interlude between the Breaths of the septenaries of Life. All is abstracted in contemplative absorption, by the Meditative rhythms of a Logoic Mind. Inevitably the focus of this Meditation will be upon the first, or 'atomic' sub-plane of the cosmic dense physical, *ādi,* which demonstrates the Will of the Father in systemic space. Libra will then regulate the major and minor cycles of the in and out-Breathing of what is to be and to rightly incorporate the *karma.* Via Libra the Logoic physical permanent atom and the cycles of expression (the movement of the *prāṇas* within the spirals and spirillae) governing the appearance of the septenaries of manifestation will come into being.

Ādi is the focal point of Stanza I because the *mahāmanvantara* begins upon awakening the Logoic physical permanent atom whose *bindu*[47] is stored upon this first of the seven systemic planes. Within

47 A bundle of seeds *(bījas).*

the *bindu* are stored the seeds *(bījas)* for systemic evolution. *Ādi* is 'the fourth Eternity', allowing the attributes of the abstracted three lower liberated Hierarchies to 'fall into the four' of cosmic etheric space. The focus is upon the 'Son of Necessity', the new Logoic Form that will soon manifest, once the Divine Flames, the first of the Hierarchies that will incarnate are awakened. The emanation of the first Ray of Will or Power will thus cause the appearance of the Logoic *maṇḍala* that will reflect into manifestation the attributes desired by the Logos via the awakening Son. Initially the Son refers to the great Ones, the liberated beings (Lords) who govern the creative process. They are Contemplatives, predisposed to meditation and who regulate the appearance of the seven Ray aspects of *'the seven Truths'* that will govern the seven Creative Hierarchies who will incarnate in systemic space. As all had disincarnated, so then everything else *'ceased to be'*. 'Naught was', because the Logoic Contemplator was focussed upon *nirvāṇic* peace rather than upon *saṃsāric* activity. No Wheels were turning, neither was the karmic Law wielded by Libra expressed.

The numbers of the phrase *'ceased to be'* (17 x 2, 5 x 5) refer to all embodiments of Divinity (17 x 2) and to the various vehicles of mind/Mind, such as the 'seven Sublime Lords', that could ascertain Truth (5 x 5).

The word *Lord* signifies one who has power and authority, a ruler or governor (over a feudal estate), any person of rank and authority, a titled nobleman. Esoterically Lords are high Initiates, the 'Nobility' within the ranks of Hierarchy, such as Chohans (Initiates of the sixth degree) and greater. They are Lords over vast spiritual estates, Ray departments, and other offices at Shambhala. The word *sublime* means to be lifted up into exaltation, expressing a joyous or exhilarating emotion, concerning an elevated sense of beauty, grandeur, or what is transcendent in nature. It is associated with sentiments of awe and reverence, a sense of vastness and power beyond human comprehension. Physically it means to pass from the solid to the gaseous state without apparently liquefying.

A *'sublime Lord'* therefore is an exalted Ruler of a large spiritual estate (a planetary or solar system), who possesses beauty, grandeur and power far beyond human comprehension. Such a One directly embodies many states of being, non-being or planes of perception, and has complete dominance over the entire material realm. An example being a Logos or an Avatāra, such as Sanat Kumāra, the virgin Youth, Melchesidek, described in *Hebrews 7:3*: 'Without Father, without mother, without descent, having neither beginning of days, nor end of life, but made like unto the Son of God'.

Concerning *the Seven Sublime Lords* H.P.B. states:

> The seven sublime lords are the Seven Creative Spirits, the Dhyan-Chohans, who correspond to the Hebrew Elohim. It is the same hierarchy of Archangels to which St. Michael, St. Gabriel, and others belong, in the Christian theogony. Only while St. Michael, for instance, is allowed in dogmatic Latin theology to watch over all the promontories and gulfs, in the Esoteric System, the Dhyanis watch successively over one of the Rounds and the great Root-races of our planetary chain. They are, moreover, said to send their Bodhisatvas, the human correspondents of the Dhyani-Buddhas (of whom *vide infra)* during every Round and Race.[48]

The numbers of the phrase *'Seven Sublime Lords'* add to 70, 16. The number 7 x 10 informs us that these Lords are perfected Beings, Sons of 'God', Christs in all respects (16), each being responsible for the evolution of a sphere of activity (10). Depending upon the angle of vision they are the planetary Regents, a solar Lord, a group of seven solar Logoi, or the Creative Hierarchies. Regarding our earth Scheme they are the Regents of the Chains, the seven esoteric Kumāras.[49]

The numbers of the phrase *'The Seven Sublime Lords'* add to 17 x 5, 22. The number 17 (the number of 'God') x 5 implies that they are essentially Mind-born Sons of Brahmā, Kumāras. (Or from a Buddhist perspective, the five Dhyāni Buddhas, from whence emanate all of the pentads governing Nature.) The number 22 refers to the fact that that they can also be styled zodiacal and Planetary Lords, the Dhyānis governing the entire Womb of time and space.

'The seven Truths' (5 x 12 = Leo the lion) are effectively the seven Words of Power that govern the manifestation of any planetary or

---

48 Ibid., 42.

49 The nature of the Kumāras are explained in The S.D., 89, 457 and elsewhere, as well as in T.C.F. by A.A. Bailey, 188, 412-3, 702-4, 751-3, 887-8. For detail see also *A Treatise on Mind,* Volumes 7A and B.

solar system, the Schemes or planes of perception. They have their ramifications or reflections on any locality of existence. It can be imputed that each of these Lords is a custodian to a different Truth, or Ray quality, Word of Power, than his Brother/Sister. The Truths *(mantras)* must be correctly ascertained and utilised to sustain any particular body of manifestation. Leo is the fifth sign of the zodiac and governs the self-conscious individual (systemic or cosmic). Only self-conscious units can awaken to the Truths controlling the manifestation of the material world (60). From the above we can also infer that these 'Truths' here relate more specifically to the nature of the manifestation of the seven incarnate Creative Hierarchies.

A person is Initiated to one or other level of esoteric Truths when standing at the portals of Initiation. They constitute the Words of Power that become part of the equipment embodied, and to be used to work Creatively in the various manifested realms, as explained by D.K.

> These seven Words of the solar system, which form the Logoic Word which we only know in its triple form as AUM, are revealed at the seven initiations.
>
> At the first initiation is given the Word for the physical plane.
> At the second initiation is given the Word for the astral plane.
> At the third initiation is given the Word for the lower mental plane.
>
> At this initiation, in which, as earlier said, the Hierophant is the Lord of the World, not only is the Word given for the lower mental plane, but a word which synthesises the three Words for the three worlds is also committed. It is given to the initiate as a topic for meditation, until he takes the fourth initiation, but he is forbidden to use it until the final liberation, as it gives entire control on the three lower planes.
>
> At the fourth initiation the Word for the higher mental plane is imparted.
> At the fifth initiation the Word for the buddhic plane is given.
> At the sixth initiation the Word for the atmic plane.
> At the seventh initiation the Word for the monadic plane is given.
>
> At the sixth initiation the Word which synthesises the fourth, fifth and sixth Words is given by the Hierophant, and thus the initiate wields complete control, through the power of sound, over the substance of

> the five planes of human evolution. At the seventh Initiation the triple AUM, in its true character, is revealed to the illumined Buddha, and he can then manipulate energy in the six worlds or planes.[50]

It is therefore only after the seventh Initiation that these Seven Truths regarding the dense body of manifestation of a solar Logos are known in their entirety. The Logoi also have correspondences to these Words for the Initiations that they have attained.

Concerning these Truths, H.P.B. states:

> Out of the Seven Truths and Revelations, or rather revealed secrets, four only have been handed to us, as we are still in the Fourth Round, and the world also has had only four Buddhas, so far. This is a very complicated question, and will receive more ample treatment later on.
>
> So far "there are only Four Truths, and Four Vedas" – say the Hindus and Buddhists. For a similar reason Irenæus insisted on the necessity of Four Gospels. But as every new Root-race at the head of a Round must have its revelation and revealers, the next Round will bring the Fifth, the following the sixth, and so on.[51]

Note that there were three fundamental Truths (postulates) so far discovered and predominantly upheld by humanity, which are given in the Proem of the S.D., whilst I have subsequently provided the fourth for this Round in chapter one. Concerning this fourth fundamental postulate D.K. states,

> It will be apparent, therefore, that the real and esoteric astrology will deal with four kinds of force, when it seeks to explain the nature of the Energies which influence any human being:
>
> The quality of the solar system.
> The quality of the Logos of the planet as it pours through the chains and globes and rounds in a sevenfold differentiation.
> The quality of our earth's complementary planet.
> The quality of the attraction of our earth's polar opposites.

---

50 Bailey, A. A., *Initiation, Human and Solar,* (Lucis Press, New York) pages 160-61. See also T.C.F., 926-929 for a further indication of the nature of these Seven Truths regarding the production of the form of a solar system.

51 Blavatsky, Ibid., 42. See also Bailey, T.C.F., 879-80.

> This involves information as yet veiled in deepest mystery, but which will unfold as the true psychology is studied, and which will eventually embody itself in a fourth fundamental of the *Secret Doctrine so* that later students will have the three as they are now found in the Proem to that book, plus the fourth. This might be expected in this fourth round. The true astrology will reveal the nature of this fourth proposition at some later date.[52]

What D.K. speaks of in terms of 'quality' above I explain in terms of consciousness and its evolution into superconsciousness, to gain liberation from *saṃsāra*. I stated in chapter one that 'the returning *nirvāṇees* bring the future to the past, by transforming it upon a higher cycle of expression, and so the serpent of time consumes itself with the gain of its movement through space. The serpent thus spirals ever upwards into increasingly higher, more refined dimensions of space, whilst that serpent evolves into a Dragon of Wisdom'. In relation to this statement the 'quality of the Logos of the planet as it pours through the chains and globes and rounds' is expressed in the phrase 'so the serpent of time consumes itself with the gain of its movement through space'. The quality of 'our earth's complementary planet' referred to here is Mars. Mars governs the sixth Ray of devotion, aspiration, desire and emotion (the Watery Element), and is a planet covered by red sands. Earth is ruled by the third Ray of Activity, which is feminine in nature. The martial energy of Mars is masculine. Its energies are Scorpionic, governing the trials and tribulations in the deserts of materialism and Initiation testings. The earth on the other hand, being feminine, is covered by the green verdure and the watery oceans, symbolising the desire-emotions that are the main challenges people must overcome to master the path. Most people are also governed by the glamours of the astral plane, ruled by Mars. Consequently the attributes of one planet compliments the other.

The earth's 'polar opposites' referred to are Mercury and Venus. They are sacred planets, whereas the earth and Mars are non-sacred. Mercury embodies the functions of the caduceus staff. This staff has two serpents entwined around a central column (the *suṣumṇā nāḍī),* where the serpents signify the *iḍā* and *piṇgalā nāḍīs*. As the serpents ascend

52 T.C.F., 1191.

through the dimensions of perception they transform and liberate the substance of the periodical sheaths. The nature of the spiral movement and the process of the ascent is governed by the energies of Mars, but the battle ground, the place of ascent, of refinement and transmutation of the energies is the earth. Mercury therefore governs the nature of treading the path to liberation. The caduceus is surmounted by the winged disc, where two wings protrude on either side of the disc (which symbolises the 'quality' or potency of the sun). The two wings represent the lobes of the Ājñā centre, which here signifies the potency of the other polar opposite hinted at, which is Venus, the 'Earth's alter ego'[53] or primary, the higher Self (the Soul), which guides the process of the liberation of consciousness for humanity. The Lords of Flame from Venus came to bequeath mind (consciousness) to humanity at the time of their Individualisation from the animal kingdom.

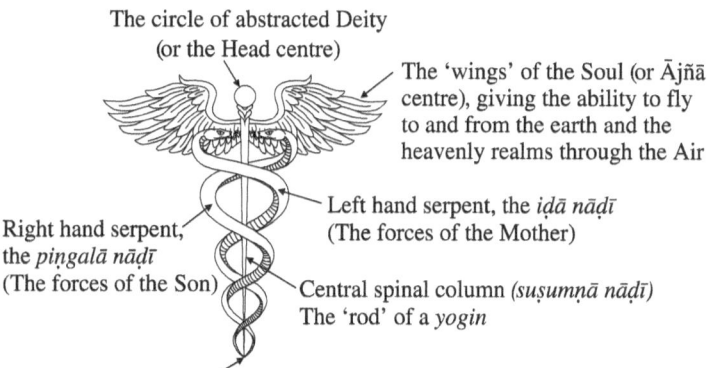

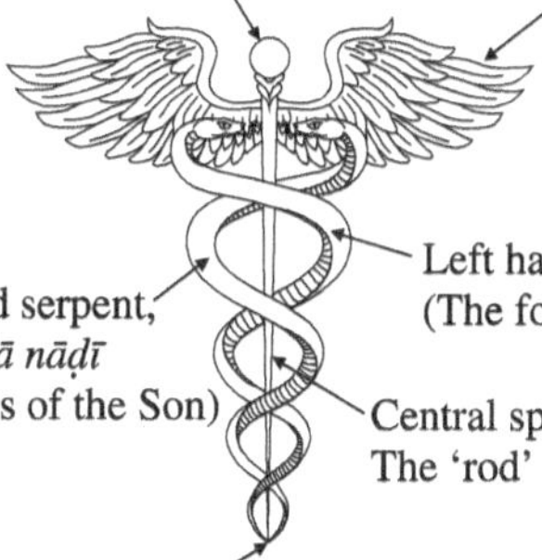

Figure 5: The Caduceus staff

Concerning the relation of the abovementioned planets to our earth, D.K. states:

> It is not permissible to say much about this mystery, that "*Venus is the Earth's alter ego*," nor is it advisable, but certain ideas may be suggested which - if brooded on - may result in a wider grasp of the beauty of nature's synthesis, and of the wonderful correlation of all that is in process of evolution.

53 T.C.F., 298.

> Perhaps some idea may be gained if we remember that, in an occult sense, Venus is to the Earth what the higher Self is to man.
>
> The coming of the Lords of Flame to the Earth was all under law and not just an accidental and fortunate happening; it was a planetary matter which finds its correspondence in the connection between the mental unit and the manasic permanent atom. Again, as the antahkarana is built by individual man between these two points, so - again in a planetary sense - is a channel being built by collective man on this planet to its primary, Venus[54]...We might consider - *from the standpoint of the present* - that Venus, Jupiter and Saturn might be considered as the vehicles of the three super-principles at this time. Mercury, the Earth and Mars are closely allied to these three, but a hidden mystery lies here. The evolution of the inner round has a close connection with this problem.[55]

Mercury is the polar opposite of the earth in the sense that most of humanity is primarily presently Watery, functioning via their emotional body, which is their major objective to master in this cycle. Mercury stands for the intuition *(buddhi),* which is obtained once the Watery aspect is completely transcended. Venus embodies the Fiery Element, the earth is Earthy, but more specifically, being the 'alter ego' of the earth Venus stands as a polar opposite because the relationship is that between the Soul and personality. Mercury and Venus together represent the qualities of the super-principles for those upon our planet.

The Words provided for Initiation are more than simple mantras, because each Word is a key that unlocks a tome of Revelation concerning the hidden Mysteries of the associated plane of perception and the nature of the command of the related substance. Modern empirical scientists have exoterically discovered the Word for the physical plane related to

---

54 Ibid.

55 Ibid., 299. A little more information concerning the relation between the triangle of the earth, Mars and Mercury can be gleaned from *Esoteric Astrology.* The relationship is exemplified by the fact that the planetary School upon Mercury ('The points of yellow Life') is upon the plane *anupādaka,* that of the earth ('The School of Magnetic Response') upon *buddhi,* and Mars ('The School for Warriors') is upon the astral plane. Here there is a 2-4-6 interrelation associated with the manifestation and mastery of the Consciousness principle. See T.C.F., 1177-80 for more information concerning these Schools.

the first Initiation when they formulated the doctrines of nuclear physics and gained the keys for the transmutation of substance.

The number 31 x 5 of the phrase *'The seven sublime Lords and the seven Truths'* informs us that these Seven Sublime Lords and the Truths they embody are really the Mind-formed aspects of the first Ray (the number 31). This is but a way of numerologically depicting the qualities of the five Dhyāni Buddhas, or the emanation of the five Kūmaras, which were explained in my *Treatise on Mind.* In volume 7A the fifth Kumāra was revealed to be the *Mother of the World.*[56] These Buddhas are the expression of the Will of the Creative Logos, the Ādi Buddha (Vajrasattva), the result of His Creative endeavours via Mind (the number 5), which is needed to sustain the manifest world. These Truths express the Wisdoms (*prajñās*) that they convey throughout manifested space. We can here deduce that five of these Truths are exoterically expressed and two are veiled by means of the union between the primordial Buddha (Logos) and His Consort. (For our earth this pair are Sanat Kumāra and the Mother of the World.) The Truths can also relate to Revelations associated with comprehending the nature of the seven Root Races, Chains, Rounds, etc., of evolution.

The numbers of the phrase *'had ceased to be'* add to 11, as also do the numbers of the phrases *'The seven Truths had ceased'*, and *'seven Truths had ceased to be'*, indicating that these Truths were no longer conveyed in the *nāḍīs* sustaining manifestation. They did not exist because the potency of first Ray energies ended the previous *manvantara.* Also the *antaḥkaraṇas* linking all of the Truths, Lords and their permutations in manifestation had ceased. The esoteric links still existed, but there were no incarnate beings to ascertain them.

The numbers of the phrase *'The seven Truths had ceased to be'* add to 100 + 7, 4 x 11. The number 100 + 7 here signifies the seven Ray categories of these Truths that effect the seven planes of expression with consciousness-attributes 'ceased to be'. Also, once sufficient number of *nirvāṇees* discover the seven cosmic Paths to cosmos after finalising their experiences in evolutionary space, then this process causes the onset of *pralaya.* The number 4 x 11 signifies the adeptship of Logoi or of humans. Such ones become *nirvāṇees* at their respective level,

---

56 The other three are Sanat Kumāra and the three Buddhas of Activity.

taking with them the gain of their incarnate evolution. These Truths are consequently no longer existent (related as they are to the totality of manifest space). Humanity (4 x 11) were not incarnate, hence there were no Truths to be discovered.

The numbers of the phrase *'The Seven Sublime Lords and the Seven Truths had ceased'* add to 52, 16, 7. The number 52 refers to a great cosmic year, or a period of *pralaya*, the duration of the great Night wherein everything had ceased, hence these Lords, cosmic Christs (16), the seven planetary Regents, Truths, etc., did not exist.

The numbers of *the complete phrase* add to 200 + 2, referring to the second Ray cycle associated with these Lords and their Truths, which 'ceased to be', as all was abstracted back into the One. All that remained was the first Ray Purpose.

The numerical breakdown of the final phrases.

> the Universe (56, 11), the Son (27), of Necessity (50), the Son of necessity (77, 23), in Paranishpanna (74 = 11), immersed in Paranishpanna (115, 16, 7), was immersed in Paranishpanna (122, 23 = 5), to be out-breathed (62, 26 = 8), out-breathed by that which is (112 = 7 x 16, 31), that which is (56, 11), to be out-breathed by that which is (127 = 100 + 3 x 9, 46 = 10), yet is not (37 = 10), is not (23 = 5), yet is (24 = 6), that which is and yet is not (103, 22), out-breathed by that (69 = 15, 24 = Taurus), to be out-breathed by that (84 = Libra, 39), to be out-breathed by that which is yet is not (174, 57), immersed in Paranishpanna to be out-breathed (177, 42), was immersed in Paranishpanna to be out-breathed (184, 49), out-breathed by that which is and yet is not (159, 42), immersed in Paranishpanna to be out-breathed by that which is (242, 62), immersed in Paranishpanna to be out-breathed by that which is and yet is not (289, 73), was immersed in Paranishpanna to be out-breathed by that which is (249, 69), was immersed in Paranishpanna to be out-breathed by that which is and yet is not (296, 80), Naught was (33, 15).

The word *universe* means 'turned into one, combined into one whole, a closed system or self inclusive and independent organisation'. It signifies the totality of all Space containing myriads of stars, galaxies, and atoms. Scientific investigation has greatly expanded our horizons and understanding of this subject in the past few centuries. Esoterically it also includes the multidimensional Space associated with the various planes of perception.

The numbers of the phrase *'the Universe'* add to 7 x 8, 11. The number 11 refers to the underlying *nāḍī* system, whilst 7 x 8 refers to the manifold petals of the opened *chakras* that a universe esoterically emanates from and is organised by.[57] More specifically however, these numbers refer to the spiral-cyclic motion, the potent energy of the Will, that organises the manifestation of a universe.

The universe can be esoterically related to:

a. That associated with the internal constitution of a human unit.
b. The 'universe' contained within the body of manifestation of a solar or planetary Logos.
c. The universe associated with a group of seven solar systems (esoterically 10), constellations, galaxies, etc. Specifically however, we are concerned with that grouping of constellations constituting of the stars viewed in the night sky: the 88 constellations, plus the subjective ones, that form the Body of manifestation of *The One about Whom Naught May be Said,* mentioned in T.C.F by A.A. Bailey. Beyond that the Adept cannot know, but can only speculate by means of the use of the Law of Correspondences, and by utilising a vast body of knowledge, being the result of enlightened contacts.
d. The ineffable universe, the totality of all the galaxies etc, in manifest and multidimensional, non manifest space.

Note that the universe normally relates to what is material, the incarnate 'something', therefore on the planes of abstraction and of at-onement it loses its identity, it becomes 'no-thing'.

H.P.B. states:

> The Secret Doctrine teaches the progressive development of everything, worlds as well as atoms; and this stupendous development has neither conceivable beginning nor imaginable end. Our "Universe"

57 See also my book *Esoteric Cosmology and Modern Physics* for detail.

> is only one of an infinite number of Universes, all of them "Sons of Necessity," because links in the great Cosmic chain of Universes, each one standing in the relation of an effect as regards its predecessor, and being a cause as regards its successor.[58]

We saw how the previous stanzas dealt with:

1. The Eternal Parent, the Synthesis.
2. The Mother aspect of Deity (Time).
3. The Son aspect of Deity (Universal Mind).
4. The Father aspect of Deity (the Seven Ways to Bliss).
5. The union of the Trinity as One (Darkness).

Stanza six is primarily concerned with the constitution of the Trinity, and in turn with the Septenary ('the Seven Sublime Lords'), the totality of Their combined bodies of manifestation, the universe and all of the entities therein. All were 'Sons....of Necessity'.

The word *necessity* here refers to what is absolutely needed, and an irresistible force to obtain it. We are concerned with a first Ray quality, as also indicated by the numbers of this word, which add to 11. One can consequently conclude that this period of sleeping and waking, of birth and death, is necessary for the entire universe, if its evolutionary goal is to be achieved—if first and second Ray qualities (Will and Love-Wisdom) are to be obtained by every associated being.

Necessity therefore, can be a name given to the effect of the Will of the great Ineffable cosmic Deity, of which the entire universe is the Son, the manifest progeny. Necessity is the original Cause, whilst the universe is the effect. Birth and death is necessary, as every form (no matter originally how perfect) gradually evolves characteristics that cannot be adequately expressed or conveyed by the old form. It becomes too limited, inert, crystallised and therefore it must be changed, resulting in its death. A new form must consequently appear that can adequately express the evolved characteristics. Necessity therefore signifies *change*, nothing in the universe is static, everywhere we see the continuous work of the triune Abstract Deity—the Creator (the Mother), the Sustainer (the Son) and the Destroyer (the Father) in the great interdependent chain of Being-Non Being.

---

58 Ibid., Vol. 1, 43.

If this chain of cause and effect producing change did not exist, then the universe could not be; there could not be any conscious awareness of existence, nor any vehicle to store and collect the information associated with that awareness. In effect Naught would be, all would be 'immersed in Paranishpanna'.

That which is *'of Necessity'* (50) is the demonstration of the perfected manifestation of Mind (50), but mind is illusionary, as is all else manifesting in time and Space. It is the cause of the *māyā*, the impermanent, fleeting, transient universe. Paradoxically however, transience is the foundation that eventually produces the perfection of the Mind. All phenomena is mind-caused, mind-sustained, and mind-resolved, the objective of which is the perfected Mind. Mind is essentially all there is, and the universe is the necessary, the result of its activity. Mind governs the rhythms of the pulsations of the manifesting cycles *(yugas),* it demonstrates the way of the manifestation of the custodian of the Law (Libra).

The numbers of the phrase *'the Son of Necessity'* add to 77, referring to the 777 incarnations through which any entity must evolve, if the experiences and qualities needed to be a perfected Soul are to be gained by way of the evolution of mind/Mind and the Love-Wisdom principle. The objective of the journey in the world of form has then been gained. Completing the evolutionary requirements of the 777 incarnations is therefore 'a Son of necessity' for the Soul concerned, which is a Son in manifestation. (The numbers of the word *'the Son'* = 3 x 9, referring here to the Soul.)

To have *immersed* is to have plunged into or have placed something into a liquid. This instantly directs our eyes to the (cosmic) astral plane, wherein the various component parts of the form nature of the universe must necessarily be abstracted during this *pralaya* period. (As was explained in the previous stanza regarding the word 'darkness'.) The universe is effectively the incarnate body of any being, therefore is a 'son of necessity' as far as incarnation in the formed realms is concerned. The numbers of the phrase *'immersed in Paranishpanna'* add to 100 + 15, 16, 7, implying that all of the Sons of mind/Mind (100 + 15), the entire consciousness-principle (16), plus all of the septenaries of manifest expression (7) were thus 'immersed', abstracted in *pralaya.*

Concerning 'Paranishpanna'[59] H.P.B. states:

> *"Paranishpanna"* is the absolute perfection to which all existences attain at the close of a great period of activity, or Maha-Manvantara, and in which they rest during the succeeding period of repose. In Tibetan it is called Yong-Grub. Up to the day of the Yogāchārya school the true nature of Paranirvana was taught publically, but since then it has become entirely esoteric; hence so many contradictory interpretations of it. It is only a true Idealist who can understand it. Everything has to be viewed as an ideal, with the exception of Paranirvana, by him who would comprehend that state and acquire a knowledge of how Non Ego, Voidness, and Darkness are Three in One and alone Self-existent and perfect. It is absolute, however, only in a relative sense, for it must give room to still further absolute perfection, according to a higher standard of excellence in the following period of activity – just as a perfect flower must cease to be a perfect flower and die, in order to grow into a perfect fruit, – if a somewhat Irish mode of expression may be permitted.[60]

The 'Three in One' of 'Non-Ego, Voidness, and Darkness' presents a triad of Father-Son-Mother with respect to the abstraction process. The aspect of Non-Ego is permanently abstracted, therefore relates to the Father (Will) aspect. Voidness is *śūnyatā,* and relates to what is Void of attributes of mind (as explained in my Buddhist books). The Love-Wisdom or Son attribute works to abstract consciousness into *śūnyatā* as part of the process of gaining enlightenment, as is well explained in Buddhist philosophy. Darkness relates to incarnation into substance (*mūlaprakṛti*), an expression of the Mother's department, which clothes all appearing forms. Philosophically it is the demonstration of ignorance.

The word *nirvāṇa* is the state of abiding in *śūnyatā,* absorption into the *buddhic* plane, the fourth cosmic ether, which happens at the fourth Initiation when the person has 'journeyed to the other shore' (of *saṃsāra),* as the *Heart Sūtra* styles it. When enquiring into this subject

59 *Paranishpanna,* correctly spelt *parinispanna,* meaning: beyond the finished, perfection, absolutely ripened, fully fulfilled accomplishment that supersedes all discrimination. A fully accomplished state, thus thoroughly established absolute reality. It is that which issues or comes forth from the Absolute.

60 Ibid., Vol. 1, 42-43.

one need to comprehend the nature of the *śūnyatā-saṃsāra* nexus, explained in my *Treatise on Mind*. Evolution in the realms of material form is thereby transcended. *Parinirvāṇa* signifies that beyond *nirvāṇa*, hence to the sub-planes of the cosmic etheric, our higher systemic planes (*buddhi, ātma, anupādaka, ādi*). *Mahāparinirvāṇa* is even beyond *parinirvāṇa,* and from this perspective it refers to that beyond experience in the cosmic dense physical realms, hence identification with the cosmic astral plane.

The number 11 of the phrase *'in Paranishpanna'* here signifies the etheric body of a Logos, the four cosmic ethers. The number 11 can also simply refer to being abstracted into the first Ray aspect of Deity.

The number 100 + 22 of the phrase *'was immersed in Paranishpanna'* refers to all of the beings and energies constituting the cosmic Womb, which were abstracted in *parinispanna.*

To be *'out-breathed'* means to have been expulsed with the air from the lungs. The purpose is to expel waste Airy-Watery products from the system, preparatory for the inbreathing of fresh life-sustaining vitality. The Element Air relates to the *buddhic* plane. It is the carrier of the life-giving vitality *(prāṇa)* which is conveyed by the etheric body. Esoterically, out-breathing is an outward going activity via which one is expelled into the external environment or universe. It relates to an expansion into a larger domain (of experience), immersion into the immensity of what exists outside of the former body of manifestation. It can therefore signify a consciousness-expanding factor.

To have out-breathed means that one had previously inhaled, where the process of 'inhalation' is associated with an inward focussing of a cosmic Logos, abstracting His/Her constitution into the vast domains of cosmic Mind. This cyclic rhythmic Breathing is governed by the sign Libra the balances. We thus have a concept of the laws governing the disincarnation, interlude and rebirthing of the Life principle *(jīva).* In relation to the meditation process the right regulation of the breath produces an abstraction into the fundamental centre (or centres) of consciousness and vitality, an inevitable absorption into the central Heart of Being. Inward concentration produces a *dhyāna* state, where the external activity (of outward expansiveness) ceases. The Air (*buddhi*), the conscious-engendering factor, then pervades the vast reaches of the meditation Mind-space.

Out-breathing signifies a renewed activity with the external environment, giving birth to the conclusions of the previous period of inwardly focussed activity. The process of in and out-breathing thus produces the sleeping and awakening process of *pralaya-manvantara.* The substance (Lives) of the consciousness-engendering factor is accordingly breathed in and out.

Concerning this process H.P.B. states:

> The appearance and disappearance of the Universe are pictured as an outbreathing and inbreathing of "the Great Breath," which is eternal, and which, being Motion, is one of the three aspects of the Absolute – Abstract Space and Duration being the other two. When the "Great Breath" is projected, it is called the Divine Breath, and is regarded as the breathing of the Unknowable Deity – the One Existence – which breathes out a thought, as it were, which becomes the Kosmos. (See "Isis Unveiled.") So also is it that when the Divine Breath is inspired again the Universe disappears into the bosom of "the Great Mother," who then sleeps "wrapped in her invisible robes." [61]

'To be out-breathed' (31 x 2, 8) refers to the projection of the Will of Deity to cause manifestation (31 x 2) via spiral-cyclic motion (8). The numbers of the phrase *'out-breathed by that which is'* add to 7 x 16, 31, referring to the various Planetary Logoi (Christs). They are a cosmic Hierarchy that together produce the outward expansion of the consciousness principle in manifest space via the respective *chakras* that are activated by means of the Will (31). The concept of *'that which is'* concerns comprehension of the nature of the central Throne of Deity, upon which such a One sits. The number 7 x 8 of this phrase refers to the spiral-cyclic energy that sustains manifestation via the seven major *chakras* through which the energies emanate.

The meaning of the word THAT as the Square, the quaternary that is the foundation stone, the central throne or base *chakra* of all manifest Being, the embodiment of the qualities of the divine Personality, was given in *Esoteric Cosmology and Modern Physics.* The qualities of this Throne therefore needs little further commentary. When viewing the word 'that' in this light the numerological interpretation must take

61 Ibid., Vol. 1, 43.

this into consideration, hence we can include the phrases *'out-breathed by that'* (3 x 5, 2 x 12 = Taurus) and *'to be out-breathed by that'* (7 x 12 = Libra, 3 x 13) in our analysis, where the word *'that'* refers to the seat of Power (That) of a presiding Logos.

Taurus the bull embodies the Eye of illumination, the Eye of Vision and of Power, which must be utilised to direct the Creation ('exhalation') of the universe. Taurus constitutes the substance of the cosmic astral plane and clothes the Divine Thought form, cosmically or systemically considered. It is thus identified with the Great Mother, the cosmic Egg of the creation myths, and assists in the formation of the Christ Child in the womb of Virgo and the birthing in Capricorn. This cosmic or world Egg is out-breathed by 'That', a function of Taurus. The number 24 also symbolises the great enlightened Beings that are responsible for the evolution of the consciousness (the Son) of an entire Logoic manifestation. The number 3 x 5 refers to the activity aspect which causes this breathing out process.

The number 7 x 12 refers to the seventh sign of the zodiac, Libra the balances, which governs the entire wheel of the Law, the wheel of the universal *dharma* and of the zodiac. It incorporates all of the cycles of being-non being, the various wheels within wheels (*chakras*) that regulate all manifest Life. All this will also be brought into activity by the enthronement of the 'I am That I am'.[62] The number 3 x 13 indicates the Activity or Mother cycle in evolution, from which the Son or consciousness aspect evolves.

The numbers of the phrase *'to be out-breathed by that which is'* add to 100 + 3 x 9, 10. Ten is the number of perfection and of completion, signifying the totality of any body of manifestation, the entire world or cosmic sphere, which is to be breathed out. The number 100 + 3 x 9 refers to the Sambhogakāya Flower, the Soul of *'that which is'*, which breathes out the new Day of manifestation.

The numbers of the phrases *'immersed in Paranishpanna to be out-breathed'* and *'was immersed in Paranishpanna to be out-breathed'* add to 177, 42, 1 + 7 x 12 = Libra, 49. The significance of Libra to this entire verse has already been explained. The numbers 100 + 77, 6 x7 and 7 x 7 all relate to the septenaries governing the manifestation of

62 *Ex. 3:14-15.*

formed space and the 777 incarnations via which all evolve through. The seven spirals of the Logoic physical permanent atom via which the Lives could manifest their activity were not awakened and so nothing else could exist. *Paranishpanna* here thus principally refers to *ādi,* or the cosmic astral sub-planes veiled by it.

The numbers of the phrases *'immersed in Paranishpanna to be out-breathed by that which is'* and *'was immersed in Paranishpanna to be out-breathed by that which is'* add to 200 + 7 x 6, 31 x 2, 200 + 7 x 7, 15, also refer to the cycles of material involvement of the septenaries, but now the emphasis is upon the bearers of the consciousness, the manifestation of Love-Wisdom (200), and to the Will, Destroyer aspect (31 x 2), which causes *pralaya* after the major second Ray cycle has manifested.

The numbers of the phrase *'yet is not'* add to 10, signifying that the sum of this cyclic manifestation (10) was not. Also all manifest things, all forms, everything visible, is transient, impermanent and illusory. They undergo constant mutable change, disease, decay and death with consequent cyclic rebirth. Therefore all that seemingly 'is' is not. All is *māyā,* an illusion, and this illusoriness is caused by the empirical mind through perception of the transient universe in terms of its image making faculty. This incorporates images stored in the subconscious mind that can be distorted or altered by the imagination. Naught is, except for the transient appearance of whatever is considered to 'be'. This is sustained by the will of the thinker via the impetus of desire. When such a thinker no longer thinks of this creation, or the universe around, then for all practical purposes that universe ceases to exist. The thinking process manifests in the form of internal dialogue and visualisation, seeing a thing with the mind's Eye. The number 24 of the phrase *'yet is',* refers to the sign Taurus the bull and the all-seeing Eye that must be directly utilised by a creator to sustain the creation. All 'is' as long as the Eye is actively focussed.

The term *'is not'* (5) implies that no thinking entities (5) exist to register any activity. This introduces the question of the three times: the past, the present and the future and their illusory nature. Esoterically there is only the One eternal duration of being-non being.

This is explained by H.P.B thus:

> By "that which is, and yet is not" is meant the Great Breath itself, which we can only speak of as absolute existence, but cannot picture to our imagination as any form of existence that we can distinguish from Non-existence. The three periods – the Present, the Past, and the Future – are in the esoteric philosophy a compound time; for the three are a composite number only in relation to the phenomenal plane, but in the realm of noumena have no abstract validity. As said in the Scriptures: "The Past time is the Present time, as also the Future, which, though it has not come into existence, still is"; according to a precept in the Prasanga Madhyamika teaching, whose dogmas have been known ever since it broke away from the purely esoteric schools. Our ideas, in short, on duration and time are all derived from our sensations according to the laws of Association. Inextricably bound up with the relativity of human knowledge, they nevertheless can have no existence except in the experience of the individual ego, and perish when its evolutionary march dispels the Maya of phenomenal existence. What is Time, for instance, but the panoramic succession of our states of consciousness?[63]

The numbers of the phrase *'that which is and yet is not'* (103, 22), refer to everything conditioned by the cycles of activity (103), or what exists in the womb of space and time (22). They are and yet are not for the reasons explained above concerning the consideration of time, and the phrase 'yet is not'. We also have the significance of the word 'That' explained earlier, the Logoic Seat of Power, 'which is', but 'yet is not' *manvantarically* manifest.

The remaining phrases, concerned with having yet to be out-breathed from his Seat of Power and *'which is and yet is not'*, provide the numbers 12, 6 x 7 and 10.[64] The numbers 10 and 6 x 7 have already been explained, whereas the number 12 here refers to the complete zodiacal wheel conditioning the formed realms, which still needs to be established, plus the petals of a Head lotus or Heart centre, which are to receive their energies. The Heart as the centre of Life is not yet vitalised, hence nothing could be.

---

63 Blavatsky, Ibid., 43-44.

64 These phrases are: *'out-breathed by that which is and yet is not'* (159, 42 = 6 x 7), *'immersed in Paranishpanna to be out-breathed by that which is and yet is not'* (289, 73 = 10), and *'to be out-breathed by that which is yet is not'* (174, 57 = 12).

The numbers of *the complete phrase* add to 200 + 96, 16 x 5, which refer to all of the entities constituting the petals of the various *chakras* (which are governed by the permutations of the number 96). They are the Hierarchies of Life (16 x 5), bearing the consciousness-principle (200), which still need to be out-breathed.

The word *nought* means 'nothing, non-existence', as well as referring to the cypher zero. Its qualities are explained in Stanza 1:2 in relation to the phrase *'the Infinite Bosom of Duration'*, to which we must again focus our vision. The numbers of this word add to 8, which indicates the spiral-cyclic motion that sustains manifestation, which 'was not', therefore *'Naught was'* (33). The number 33 signifies the myriads of Creative Intelligences that are responsible for sustaining the manifest universe. They embody the third Ray or activity aspect of Deity and as Their divine Creativity was not active nothing could exist.

Stanza One part Seven

Stanza 1:7 states:

> **The causes of Existence had been done away with; the visible that was, and the invisible that is, rested in eternal non-being, the one Being.**

Keynotes: Virgo, second cosmic ether – *anupādaka,* the fifth Eternity.

The numerical breakdown of the first phrase:

> The causes of Existence (82, 19 = 10), done away with (58 = 13, 13), had been done away with (88, 25), Existence had been done away with (129 = 12, 30), The causes of Existence had been done away with (170, 44).

We now come to a consideration of the sign Virgo, the great Mother, who embodies the great 'causes of Existence' in Her Womb. The agents of the Mother's department, the *devas,* embodying both the subjective and objective universe 'rested in eternal non-being' *(śūnyatā* and beyond). Thus there were no actors and nothing to act upon in the great Womb of Mother Nature, the 'one Being'.

Our vision is also focussed on the fifth Eternity and the plane *anupādaka,* the second cosmic ether, whereon Shambhala would be externalised as a cause of Existence, but which 'had been done away with'. Because the Divine Builders, from which emanates the causes for Existence, were in *pralaya,* so also Monadic Life and the Logoic Head centre that governs the Lives manifesting in dense physical incarnation.

As earlier stated the functions of the Son (governed by the emanation of the second Ray of Love-Wisdom) in systemic space first happens upon the second plane of perception, *anupādaka.* At first however the Mother must give birth to the forms via which the Son evolves, but Her functions are reflected via *anupādaka* from the fifth cosmic astral sub-plane, which draws upon the emanative cosmic *karma.* The Mother's energies impact upon the next plane of perception, *ātma.* This causes the first Outpouring that empowers the five planes of Brahmā. The 'causes of Existence' that emanate from the Mother's Bosom are the *devas,* and for our world system they flow through the second plane *(anupādaka)* to effect their work, colouring their substance with the principle of Love, with which everything in this solar system is conditioned by. This Outpouring comes under the directive Eye of Virgo the virgin, who rules the Mother's department.

Most of these *'causes of Existence'* were explained in the previous verse, so verse 1:7 simply states that 'they have been done away with'. Concerning the *'causes of Existence'* H.P.B. states:

> "The Causes of Existence" mean not only the physical causes known to science, but the metaphysical causes, the chief of which is the desire to exist, an outcome of Nidana[65] and Maya. This desire for a sentient life shows itself in everything, from an atom to a sun, and is a reflection of the Divine Thought propelled into objective existence, into a law that the Universe should exist. According to esoteric teaching, the real

65 *Nidāna* is the underlying cause and determining factor. It is the cause-effect relation, Dependent Origination, the twelve causes of existence, twelvefold chain of causation. They progressively arise out of each other. The order given is: 1. Ignorance *(avidya),* the root cause of them all. 2. Action producing attachment to form *(saṃskāra).* 3. The development of consciousness (*vijñāna*). 4. The ability to name the various forms (*nāmarūpa*). 5. The development and use of the senses and sense objects *(sadāyātana).* 6. Physical plane contact by means of the sense of touch *(sparsa).* 7. Feeling perceptions, sensation next appear *(vedanā).* 8. Thirst or desire for things *(tṛṣnā).* 9. Clinging onto objects of desire *(upādāna).* 10. Becoming, clinging, or being content with mundane existence *(bhāva).* 11. Producing birth, or rebirth *(jāti).* 12. The ageing process, sorrow, pain *(duhkha)* and death (*jarāmaraṇa*).

> cause of that supposed desire, and of all existence, remains for ever hidden, and its first emanations are the most complete abstractions mind can conceive. These abstractions must of necessity be postulated as the cause of the material Universe which presents itself to the senses and the intellect; and they must underlie the secondary and subordinate powers of Nature, which, anthropomorphized, have been worshipped as God and gods by the common herd of every age. It is impossible to conceive anything without a cause; the attempt to do so makes the mind a blank. This is virtually the condition to which the mind must come at last when we try to trace back the chain of causes and effects, but both science and religion jump to this condition of blankness much more quickly than is necessary; for they ignore the metaphysical abstractions which are the only conceivable causes of physical concretions. These abstractions become more and more concrete as they approach our plane of existence, until finally they phenomenalise in the form of the material Universe, by a process of conversion of metaphysics into physics, analogous to that by which steam can be condensed into water, and water frozen into ice.[66]

The word *existence* means 'reality' as opposed to the appearance of some phenomena. Existence is fundamentally concerned with the qualities of the mind, as all phenomena is mind-conceived, according to the Yogācāra philosophy explained in volume 2 of my *Treatise on Mind* series.

The number 13 of the phrase *'done away with'* indicates the spheres of Logoic attainment, which do not exist at this stage. The number 10 of the phrase *'the causes of Existence'* signifies everything that constitutes a sphere of attainment and which produces evolutionary perfection. The numbers also refer to the concept of Existence as referring to the principle of Life, hence the human *jīvas* (Monads), that had no reason to yet appear in the formed realms. Neither could manifest the angelic triads of the Mother's department. All were *'done away with'* in the conditionings of the *pralaya*.

The numbers of the phrase *'had been done away with'* add to 88, 25, indicating the cycles (88) sustaining the activities of mind/Mind (5 x 5) which no longer exist. Without the appearance of mind/Mind there is no possibility for any 'causes' to manifest.

---

66 Ibid., 44-45.

The numbers of the phrase *'Existence had been done away with'* add to 12 and to 30, where the number twelve here relates to the *nidānas,* and the number 30 to the activity that sustains them. Because such activity did not exist, so Dependent Origination had no foundation for its existence.

The numbers of *the complete phrase* add to 170, 44, referring to the Creative Logoi (17 x 10), cosmic Humanity (44). The number 44 can also refers to the lesser creative agents, humanity, who manifest the factors of existence via the *nidānas,* but as the Logoi have not created the conditions for the appearance of phenomena, the substance of *māyā,* so nothing else could be. All Shambhalic correspondences had been done away with and thus nothing could exist.

The numerical breakdown of the remaining phrases:

> the visible (48 = Cancer, 12), the visible that was (68 = 17 x 4, 23 = 5), the invisible (62 = 31 x 2, 17), the invisible that is (85 = 17 x 5, 22), eternal non-being (74 = 11, 20), 'in eternal non-being', (88, 25), rested in eternal non-being (100 + 14, 33), the one (31, 13), the one Being (14, 5), one Being (44, 17).

The word *visible* has a direct reference to the use of the eyes, and the brain-mind coordination of what has been seen. A thing can only be visible when the eyes are focussed upon it. Esoterically, the eyes refer to the various *chakras* in the body, through which one can focus on the objects on any of the planes of perception. (If that faculty for perception has been opened.) What this word means however, in relation to the term invisible, is that what was formerly visible no longer is, as no one exists to view such an object. Also, the material world (related to the third aspect of Deity) is considered to be directly associated with the *past* ('that was'). The second aspect of Deity is related to the present ('that is'), and the first aspect to the future ('the one Being').

As Stanza 1:7 is governed by the sign Virgo the virgin, so then these phrases refer primarily to the manifestation of the *deva* hierarchy. The *deva* kingdom is primarily dual, whilst the human kingdom manifests as a triplicity. The phrase *'the visible that was'* therefore refers specifically to the *rūpa devas,* who embody the substance of the forms of the three worlds of human evolution, whilst the phrase *'the invisible that is'* refers primarily to the *arūpa devas,* who embody the substance of the subjective domains, specifically to the substance of the higher mental domain and the four cosmic ethers. The term 'was' directly relates to the third aspect of Deity, hence associated with the incarnate form, whereas the term 'is' refers to its advancement to the 'present', relating to the second aspect of Deity, who works to abstract itself out of form, to become formless.

The numbers of the phrase *'the visible'* add to 4 x 12, 6.6., refer to the fourth sign of the zodiac, Cancer the crab, who governs the doorway into incarnation, hence makes visible. The subjective that was formerly invisible incarnates into formed objectivity. The Creative Builders, the lunar *pitṛ,* the 'Fathers' of all that formed is, come into manifestation to create the attributes of *saṃsāra* (symbolised by the number 6.6.).

The numbers of the phrase *'the visible that was'* add to 17 x 4, referring to the quaternary that is the Logoic Seat of Power (the That) governing all manifest Being. Via this Seat the formed attributes of space appear, the tangibility experienced by the Lives that will incarnate into it.

The word *invisible* refers to what is not seen (the *arūpa* universe), and therefore not an embodied dense form. The assumption being that physical eyes are needed do the seeing. What is invisible therefore refers to the subtle bodies of a being, or to the planes of perception one enters after dying, or in the sleep state. The word invisible therefore refers to the lower mental, astral and etheric sheaths, but can also refer to the spiritual triad (*ātma-buddhi-manas*), or to the qualities of the Monad-Soul. The invisible forms become increasing intense and radiant as one climbs up the dimensions of perception. Such forms become visible to one who is liberated from dense incarnation, or who has developed the inner eyes to see.

When it comes to seeing the *arūpa* forms existing upon the plane *buddhi*, then even the form of the Soul enters dissolution in the process that leads to its liberation at the fourth Initiation (*śūnyatā*).

The number 31 x 2 of the phrase *'the invisible'* refer to the reflection of the first Ray energy, the destroyer Ray, into the manifest realms. This energy destroys the forms that did 'see', so that only what was formerly invisible remains. One must consequently develop first Ray attributes to see the invisible. The *arūpa devas* utilise this energy during the *pralaya* process to abstract the lesser *deva* lives back into the subjective domains of the Mother's Bosom.

The numbers of the phrase *'the invisible that is'* add to 17 x 5, 22, where 17 x 5 refers to the Kumāras, the Dhyāni Buddhas that are an attribute of the Creative Deity (Brahmā), the Mother's department. The inference therefore refers to the planetary Head centre, Shambhala, and the sum of the inner domains, the cosmic ethers. The lower mental plane is considered cosmic dense physical. The higher mental or abstract realm of the Mind, wherein resides the Sambhogakāya Flower, and the four cosmic ethers, (our higher four planes of perception) are thus 'the Invisible that is'. The number 22 here refers to the greater *devas,* the Divine and Lesser Builders and the Rāja Lords, thence the archangels, landscape *devas*, angels, nature spirits, and so forth that embody the Womb of the Mother. They 'breathe out' the visible forms that 'see' and are the bearers of the zodiacal and planetary energies (22) to the sum of the constituency of the form. The constitution of Shambhala and the domains whereon exists the Soul, or of the *devas* that embody the sum of substance, are never seen by those that rely upon the physical eyes to see.

When we talk of energy, or of bodies of manifestation that exist only in high energy states, then the conception concerns what is normally invisible to human perception. The empirically minded only know the effects of such expression through experiencing colour, sound, feeling, sensation, pain, etc. The *devas* embody the substance of those experiences, of the manifesting *saṃskāras,* hence are the bearers of the related *karma* when they rectify the imbalances in their forms caused by the humanity that are blind to causative energies and the entities existing upon the subjective domains.

Concerning the nature of the *'eternal non-being, the one Being',* H.P.B. states:

> The idea of Eternal Non-Being, which is the One Being, will appear a paradox to anyone who does not remember that we limit our ideas of being to our present consciousness of existence; making it a specific, instead of a generic term. An unborn infant, could it think in our acceptation of that term, would necessarily limit its conception of being, in a similar manner, to the intrauterine life which alone it

> knows; and were it to endeavour to express to its consciousness the idea of life after birth (death to it), it would, in the absence of data to go upon, and of faculties to comprehend such data, probably express that life as "Non-Being which is Real Being." In our case the One Being is the noumenon of all the noumena which we know must underlie phenomena, and give them whatever shadow of reality they possess, but which we have not the senses nor the intellect to cognize at present. The impalpable atoms of gold scattered through the substance of a ton of auriferous quartz may be imperceptible to the naked eye of the miner, yet he knows that they are not only present there but that they alone give his quartz any appreciable value; and this relation of the gold to the quartz may faintly shadow forth that of the noumenon to the phenomenon. But the miner knows what the gold will look like when extracted from the quartz, whereas the common mortal can form no conception of the reality of things separated from the Maya which veils them, and in which they are hidden. Alone the Initiate, rich with lore acquired by numberless generations of his predecessors, directs the "Eye of Dangma" toward the essence of things on which no Maya can have any influence. It is here that the teachings of esoteric philosophy in relation to the Nidanas and the Four Truths become of the greatest importance; but they are secret.[67]

The word non-being is dual, indicating the latent, or nascent duality of all existence. Even the Existence that is 'non-being, the one Being' is effectively hermaphrodite, male-female. Thus we have Spirit-Matter, Father-Mother, Monad-Soul, human and *deva* Hierarchies.

The meaning of the word *eternal* was explained in Stanza 1:1, whilst the numbers of the phrase *'eternal non-being'* add to 11, 20, indicating the etheric body and *nāḍīs* of the Logos. This indicates the state of existence of this 'non-being', as well as the Consciousness (20) that resides within the *nāḍīs* after the corporeal form has been discarded. The number 8 x 11 of the phrase *'in eternal non-being'*, has a similar meaning as the above, referring to all levels of existence within the etheric body of the greater Logos, of the field of energies that the *devas* embody to sustain all phenomenal life. The *devas* are the vitality Breathed out by the solar Logos to nourish all that is and is not. The associated number 25 of this phrase refers to the Soul aspect

67 Ibid., Vol. I, 45.

of manifest Life, but specifically to the embodiments of mind/Mind in all of its permutations.

The numbers of the phrase *'rested in eternal non-being'* add to 100 + 14, 33. The number 100 + 14 refers to the cosmic or systemic astral plane, whereas the number 33 refers to the Intelligences *(deva* and human) that were abstracted into this plane. Because there was no form in active manifestation, so the creative Builders (33), the *devas,* 'rested' from such activity, until they are again called to appropriately manifest activity upon a higher cycle than previously.

The numbers of the phrase *'the one'* add to 31, 13, signifying the central point within a sphere of activity, the Bosom of the Mother (13), and the emanating source of the energy of Will or Power (31). *'The one Being'* is the One residing in a sheath of cosmic astral substance (14). In relation to this the numbers of the phrase *'one Being'* add to 44, 17, refer to a Logos (17), a member of cosmic Humanity.

Stanza One part Eight

Stanza 1:8 states:

> **Alone, the one form of Existence stretched boundless, infinite, causeless, in dreamless sleep; and Life pulsated unconscious in universal Space, throughout that All-Presence which is sensed by the 'opened Eye' of the Dangma.**

> *Keynotes:* Leo, third cosmic ether – *ātma,* the sixth Eternity.

> The numerical breakdown of the first phrase:

> Alone (20, 2), the one form of Existence (109, 28), one form of Existence (94, 22), stretched boundless (69 = 15), one form of Existence stretched boundless (163 = 100 + 63 = 7 x 9, 37 = 10), the one form of Existence stretched boundless (178 = 16, 43 = 7), form of Existence (78, 15), Existence stretched boundless (110, 20).

The previous stanza mainly focussed upon the functions of the feminine *deva* kingdom via the auspices of the sign Virgo. Stanza 1:8 brings our view to the bearers of the Consciousness principle (systemic and cosmic

Humanity). As earlier stated, this Stanza relates to the sixth Eternity upon the third cosmic ether *(ātma)* whereon the abstracted Life broods, stretching boundlessly, existing in 'dreamless Sleep'. Upon this plane the Lesser Builders are normally active. From this domain emanates the *karma* that will propel the 'one form of Existence' into manifestation when the awakening is to happen, as well as that of material plane activity, and also of its final abstraction.

The general characteristics of this Existence is governed by the attributes of the sign Leo the lion, who governs the self-conscious individual, (the ego basking in the sun of accomplishment) Logoic or human. This represents the Son aspect of deity that is reflected into manifestation that will evolve from out of the substance emanated via the first Outpouring. Because this 'form of existence' pulsed unconscious in universal space so Naught was, yet there appears some stirrings in preparation for awakening, which was sensed by the '"Opened Eye" of the Dangma'.

Note that the plane *anupādaka* associated with the previous phrase normally relates to the function of a human kingdom, the Monads, (being along the even Ray line 2-4-6) and *ātma* to the domain of the Mother, the *deva* kingdom. During *pralaya* however, one moves to a higher dimension of perception than when functioning in manifest space. This concept is thus exemplified in these two stanzas.

The numbers of the phrase *'the one form of Existence'* add to 109, 7 x 4, whilst those of the complete phrase, *'the one form of Existence stretched boundless'* add to 16, 7. This form of Existence is therefore a Christ (16), the Lord of Love, the Love-Wisdom principle, the Consciousness attribute, the expression of a Hierarchy of enlightened Being, the correspondence of the Christ's department upon the earth. They are members of a human kingdom (4 x 7) resting or merged into its own essential Self, its own sphere of Being. We are therefore concerned with the Son aspect of the trinity: Father-Son-Mother. The term 'Alone' (that which is solitary, apart from others, by itself) therefore indicates that the Father-Mother were incorporated into the Son.

The number 109 also refers to the fourth Creative Hierarchy, which are called 'The Initiates'.[68] Here one should visualise that such a Creative Hierarchy encompasses the limitless expanse of the universe.

68 Bailey, *Esoteric Astrology*, 35.

The use of the word *form* is important here. It refers to the shape or structure of anything, a body as distinguished by its external appearance. It concerns a particular disposition or arrangement of matter, whereby individuality is gained. Such an orderly arrangement or shape (symbolised by the number 7) is a property of the Soul, the Son aspect on the higher mental plane.[69] (From the angle of vision of those on the higher formless planes of perception the mental plane is material, formed.) The form of the Causal Body of the Universe therefore, is what 'stretched boundless'. Everything is therefore absorbed back into its constitution.

Though it is 'One, alone' from the viewpoint of those who represent factors of its expression, the Logoic Soul is in fact part of a grouping of such entities upon the cosmic higher mental plane. The Causal Forms of our planetary or solar Logoi are virtually unimaginable abstractions to us. We can only get some comprehension through exercising the law of Correspondences. The true nature therefore of the Soul of a universe is but the vaguest of conceptions.

Concerning the word *Existence*, it was previously stated that existence means reality as opposed to appearance, and that existence is fundamentally concerned with the qualities of the mental plane (thus the number 3 x 5 for the phrase *'form of Existence'),* for only the mind/ Mind can cognise what it is.

The number 22 of the phrase *'one form of Existence'* here indicates the entire constitution of this existence, as governed by the zodiacal and planetary energies conditioning the Womb of space and time.

Concerning *'the one form of Existence'* H.P.B states:

> The Secret Doctrine....postulates a "One Form of Existence" as the basis and source of all things. But perhaps the phrase, the "One Form of Existence," is not altogether correct. The Sanskrit word is Prabhavapyaya,[70] "the place, or rather plane, whence emerges the origination, and into which is the resolution of all things," says a commentator. It is not the "Mother of the World," as translated by Wilson (see Book I., Vishnu Purana); for Jagad Yoni (as shown by FitzEdward Hall) is scarcely so much the "Mother of the World" or

69 It is the middle of the trinity of Monad (Father) – Soul (Son) – Mother (appearance).

70 The term *prabhavāpyaya* means 'birth, creation, origination'.

> the "Womb of the World" as the "Material Cause of the Universe." The Purānic commentators explain it by Karana – "Cause" – but the Esoteric philosophy, by the *ideal spirit of that cause.* It is, in its secondary stage, the Svābhāvat[71] of the Buddhist Philosopher, the eternal cause and effect, omnipresent yet abstract, the self-existent plastic Essence and the root of all things, viewed in the same dual light as the Vedantin views his Parabrahm and Mulaprakriti, the one under two aspects. It seems indeed extraordinary to find great scholars speculating on the possibility of the Vedanta, and the Uttara-Mimansa especially, having been "evoked by the teachings of the Buddhists," whereas, it is on the contrary Buddhism (of Gautama, the Buddha) that was "evoked" and entirely upreared[72] on the tenets of the Secret Doctrine, of which a partial sketch is here attempted, and on which, also, the Upanishads are made to rest. The above, according to the teachings of Sri Sankarāchārya, is undeniable.[73]

To be *stretched* is to be extended in length or breadth, expanded or distended, especially by force. It concerns moving from point to point in space, in a continuous line, surface or space measured over time. The associated elasticity allows a Logos to expand and contract in *manvantara* and *pralaya*, inbreathing and out-breathing, sleeping and waking. It includes the cycles of being and non-being. What is stretched (expanded) is the substance composing a form, specifically the substance of the mind/Mind. The substance of the Mind, its Thoughts, can expand to fill the boundaries of any universe, so as to experience the fullness of it. The substance of the lesser planes are directly manipulated by the Mind and respond automatically to its impulses. The substance of the higher planes is 'eternally ever-present', hence effectively does not stretch or contract. (This statement however is only relatively

71 See volume 1 of *A Treatise on Mind* for detailed explanation of the Buddhist meaning of the term *svabhāva*. *Svabhāva* is derived from *sva* self + *bhū* to become, grow into; hence self-becoming into something, self-generation, self-directed evolution. It is the unfolding of the individual essence by inner impulse, rather than by mere mechanical activity in Nature. There are two distinct meanings, the first being inherent existence, self-essence, individual being, thus is transient, hence illusory. The second being emptiness *(śūnyatā)* the final nature of all phenomena.

72 This word logically should be 'reared'.

73 Ibid., Vol 1, 46-47.

meaningful, because ultimately all is an aspect of the One MIND, which obeys the laws conditioning Mind.)

The number 3 x 5 of the phrase *'stretched boundless'* signifies the Activity aspect of the Mind (of God), which causes the stretching process to encompass all of Space.

The word *boundless* means being immeasurable, possessing no boundaries or limitations. Esoterically this signifies a limitless sphere of circumscription, that of a greater Logos, within which our particular Logos resides. When viewed multidimensionally it concerns the ability to rise from one plane of comparative limitation to another that offers greater freedom of movement. This is similar to the extension of the silver cord of a person that rises through the various sub-planes of the astral. The concept of such stretching, by a silver cord for instance, is indicated by the number 100 + 10 of the phrase *'Existence stretched boundless'*. Also one can consider the process of the projection of *antaḥkaraṇas* from one dimension or realm to the next.

The numerical breakdown of the next four statements:

> infinite (50), causeless (23 = 5), dreamless sleep (54 = 6 x 9), in dreamless sleep (68 = 17 x 4, 14), Life pulsated (49 = 7 x 7), Life pulsated unconscious (94, 22), in universal Space (71 = 8, 17 = 8), Universal Space (57 = 12, 12), unconscious in universal Space (116, 26), Life pulsated unconscious in universal Space (165, 39).

The meaning of the word *infinite* (50) was explained in Stanza 1:2 in relation to the phrase *'the infinite Bosom of Duration'*. The infinite cannot be regulated or delineated by the (divine) geometry that governs manifested Space; it knows no boundaries, certainly none that the mind could comprehend. It becomes known only after the mind has been perfectly developed and then superseded, made 'below the threshold of consciousness' by Mind. The number 50 refers to the expression of such a Mind.

The number 5 of the word *'causeless'* refers to the mind/Mind, thus this 'sleep' of 'the one form of Existence' was within the domains of cosmic Mind, where that Mind was not active, hence not expanding, as all was simply absorbed in it. With the Mind not actively focussed upon anything no 'causes' were produced. The word causeless also means ‘karmaless’. As *karma* is mind-conditioned, caused by means of the free-will to act, as either dark or white brotherhood in the realms of form, so the need or means for such action did not exist. The word ‘cause’ effectively refers to origination and the karmic causes thereby of the manifest universe. What is causeless therefore is that beyond the volitions of mind, and thus not conditioned by its analytical and constructive qualities. Here is also implied the concept of *buddhi* or *śūnyatā*, Emptiness, the Void. When there are causes *śūnyatā* acts as a pure unstained mirror that reflects the Archetypal, the Ideal, into the concrete manifest world via the agency of a mind that sees, recollects, and directs.

When there are ‘causes’ however then it implies the functioning of the plane *ātma,* from whence comes the first Outpouring of the *deva* substance and the *karma* that conditions manifestation via the work of the Lesser Builders. Also the directive focussed Leonine Will focuses the energies of the mind/Mind via the Eye of the Dangma, or else that of the Logos. Leo governs the appearance of the units of consciousness that can ‘sense’ the ‘All-Presence’.

The meaning of *sleep* and its relation to the meditation state (*dhyāna*) has been explained previously in Stanza 1:1, regarding the phrase ‘the Eternal Parent’ that had ‘slumbered once again’. The word ‘slumbered’ relates to a sleep that can be interrupted by dream periods, the ‘seven Eternities’. Here the sleep is dreamless, which verifies that this phrase is concerned with the period when the ‘one form of Existence’ was absorbed into the ‘fourth eternity’, into the boundless confines of *buddhic* non-being.

The number 6 x 9 of the phrase *‘dreamless sleep’* signifies the Monadic state,[74] implying that fundamental identification with Monadic perception is causative of such a ‘sleep’ because all is abstracted into it.

The nature of this ‘dreamless sleep’ is indicated by the number 17 x 4 of the phrase *‘in dreamless sleep’,* referring to the personality nature of the Logos concerned (those constituting the Logoic Seat of Power) that was absorbed in deep sleep *(dhyāna).*

To have *pulsated* means to have expanded and contracted, throbbed, with regular movements, as in the beating of the heart or of an artery.

74 The Monad being technically an Initiate of the sixth degree.

A *pulse* is any short quick regularly repeated motion, such as of light and sound. We see therefore that though the personality nature was in 'dreamless sleep', Life—the *esseence* of all Being, still pulsated via the cosmic Heart, which regulated the various cycles associated with the cosmic Night, the *pralaya* period of the yet to be accomplished 'seven Eternities'. Accordingly the numbers of the phrase *'Life pulsated'* add to 7 x 7, indicating the 7 x 7 subdivisions of all manifest and non-manifest Life, the seven Eternities and their respective sub-cycles. This 'Life', the Consciousnesses that were regulated by the Heart centre, as governed by the sign Leo the lion, was moved by the act of pulsation throughout the *nāḍīs* of the Logos. Streams of Lives moved from *chakra* to *chakra* in cosmic space, to undergo various forms of experience, development of Awareness states. Such however was not associated with material plane activity, but rather directly concerned with the domains of Mind.

Concerning the numbers of the phrases *'unconscious in universal Space'* (116, 8) and *'in universal Space'* (17, 8), we see that the number 8 indicates spiral-cyclic motion, which can then be extended to the eight directions in space. This spiral-cyclic motion is associated with the pulsations of Life (the units of Consciousness, 100 + 16) in and out of manifestation. The spiral associated with the number 8 represents the space-time continuum, as was explained in *Esoteric Cosmology and Modern Physics.*

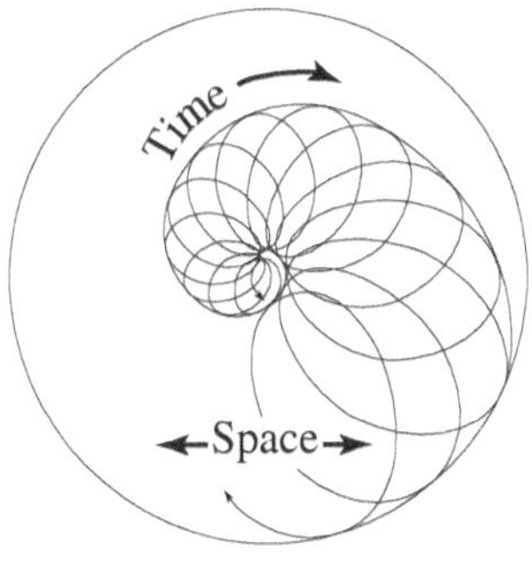

Figure 6. The space-time continuum

When projected to the four directions of space then manifests the four petalled lotus (Base of Spine centre), from whence evolves the flowers of the other *chakras*. These directions can also be viewed as the four ventricles of the cosmic Heart, which 'pulsates unconsciously'.

The phrase *'unconscious in universal Space'* is thus not just concerned with the description of the 'one form of Existence', (the cosmic Soul) but also with the relative inactivity of the myriads of beings that together constitute the substance of this 'form of Existence'. They embody the Life or vitalising Blood of the spiritual triad, as well as the constitution of the subjective sheaths upon the cosmic astral and etheric planes. (Zones of residence for many prior to rebirth.) The concern therefore is with understanding the totality of the 'sleeping' Logos and the process of awakening to incarnate life at the end of the seventh Eternity.

Note the difference in meaning between unconsciousness, and being in deep sleep. Being unconscious means not being aware, having no conscious experience. The mental equipment may exist, but there is a lack of memory, intelligence, or awareness of self for an indefinite period. Sleep, on the other hand, is a relatively regular period of rest or repose, which allows consciousness to leave the body and then to return when the body has sufficiently rested. The concept of 'Unconsciousness' for the great cosmic Deities concerns a period of complete abstraction of Mind from *manvantara*. They can be considered 'Unconscious' from the perspective of there being no form to be conscious of. Everything exists in potential, awaiting the new Day of Activity, reactivated by the out-breathing of the Logoic Meditation. The word 'unconscious' therefore refers specifically to the 'after death state' of the Entities constituting the dense form (the body) of the 'sleeping' Logos. They are manifesting in an *arūpa,* formless state. *'Dreamless sleep'* (54, 9) thus refers to the activity of the indwelling consciousness, the Soul aspect (9) that periodically inhabits the dense form. (The number 9 here referring to the petals of the Sambhogakāya Flower, and the number 6 x 9 to the energies of the Monad vivifying them.) The Soul is responsible for the pulsations or cycles (the 777 incarnations) associated with the body of manifestation.

Concerning 'dreamless sleep' H.P.B. states:

> Dreamless sleep is one of the seven states of consciousness known in Oriental esotericism. In each of these states a different portion of the mind comes into action; or as a Vedantin would express it, the individual

> is conscious in a different plane to his being. The term "dreamless sleep," in this case is applied allegorically to the Universe to express a condition somewhat analogous to that state of consciousness in man, which, not being remembered in a waking state, seems blank, just as the sleep of the mesmerised subject seems to him an unconscious blank when he returns to his normal condition, although he has been talking and acting as a conscious individual would.[75]

The number 22 of the phrase *'Life pulsated unconscious'* refers to the conditioning cosmic energies (and the Lives bearing them) that pulsated in the cosmic *nāḍīs.*

The numbers of the word *Space* add to 17, as also those of the phrase *'in universal Space'*, signifying that 'Space is an Entity', and also a series of interrelationships associated with an abstracted Logos and lesser Logoi within His/Her body of Manifestation. There are a succession of such Logoi from the greater to lesser ones, in much the same manner as a human being can be considered to represent an absolute Logos with respect to the constitution of the organs of the dense body, and they in turn to their cellular constituency. Comprehension of such Life comes via the means of sense contact, subjective or objective, coordinated by the rational mind. If that mind is unconscious then what is known as Life is unknown to it, but Mind can still be aware of the conditionings upon the domain it is abstracted upon, and so Know the nature of what is 'pulsating'.

The meaning of the word *universal* was explained earlier in relation to the phrase *'Universal Mind was not'*. There it was related to the awareness of the spiritual triad, and when associated with the word Space (the numbers of which add to 17) then the implication is that the phrase *'Universal Space'* (12) can be rephrased as a Universal Logos, that constitutes the totality of the Monad-Soul Identification. The number 12 here signifies the cosmic Heart centre (or Soul) into which all is abstracted, and which pulsates the circulating Lives during *pralaya.*

The numbers of the phrase *'Life pulsated unconscious in universal Space'* add to 33 x 5, 13 x 3. The number 33 x 5 refers to the sum of the Creative Intelligences embodying the Head centre (or else the

75 S.D. Vol. 1., 47.

Sambhogakāya Flower) of a Logos. They represent the Creative forces organising Logoic Thought. Because the Logos was not Creatively active so these Lives were technically 'unconscious' in terms of such activity, but were of course Conscious within the self-absorbed streams of Logoic Dhyāna that 'pulsated' in *pralaya*. Such activity (13 x 3) manifests spontaneously and automatically within the *nāḍīs* of the sleeping form. Whatever can be considered 'Life' is protected and nourished, despite the lack of the material body. All of these Beings are preparing for a reawakening of Life into active manifestation at the appointed cycle. They will then energise the seeds of the lesser Hierarchies of Life incorporated in the astral and physical permanent atoms, as well as the mental unit.

The numerical breakdown of the last phrase:

> All-Presence (47 = 11), that All-Presence (60 = Leo, 15), throughout that All-Presence (114 = 100 + 2 x 7, 24 = Taurus), which is sensed (64, 10), the 'opened Eye' (64 = 8 x 8, 19 = 10), sensed by the 'opened Eye' (94 = 13, 31), the 'opened Eye' of the Dangma (113, 32), 'the Dangma (37, 10), sensed by the 'opened Eye' of the Dangma (143, 44), that All-Presence which is sensed (124, 25), throughout that All-Presence which is sensed (178, 34), that All-Presence which is sensed by the 'opened Eye' (197, 53), that All-Presence which is sensed by the 'opened Eye' of the Dangma (246, 66), throughout that All-Presence which is sensed by the 'opened Eye' (251, 62), throughout that All-Presence which is sensed by the 'opened Eye' of the Dangma (300, 75).

The word *presence* relates to 'being present, an existent, something that is known, what is immediately near'. Esoterically it refers to the Soul or Monad that is the Life or Divinity within. The immediate nearness of this Life principle is absolute, instantaneously effective and clear to all who are meditatively or intuitively aware of that Divinity. The Monadic Presence can also be synonymous with one's concept of 'God'.

The numbers of the word *'All-Presence'* add to 11, which here signifies the qualities of the Monad, which is the All-Presence of one's integral being. Another interpretation relates to the *nāḍīs,* which can also be considered all-present. This is especially so in a recently deceased or reincarnating individual. For one that is deceased, the principle of Life is retained in the *nāḍīs* constituting the etheric body, and for the reincarnating one the *nāḍīs* must first be established to make incarnation possible. When the word 'that' is added to this phrase then we particularise the qualities of the seat of Power of the cosmic Logos, providing another interpretation as to the nature of the all-embracing extent of this Presence.

The numbers of the phrase *'that All-Presence'* add to 5 x 12 (Leo), 3 x 5, which completes the description of the nature of this 'All-Presence' by directing our vision to what it causes, the material universe and the perfection of the Mind, as associated with the sign Leo the lion. Here Leo refers to the Divine Personality, the expression of the manifestation of Mind, in the form of the mode of expression of the five Dhyāni Buddhas, plus also the 'All-Presence' that can be considered an incarnate Logos. It relates to self-consciousness viewed on all levels of expression.

The numbers of the phrases *'that All-Presence which is sensed'* and *'throughout that All-Presence'* are 124, 25, 100 + 14, 24. The numbers 100 + 24, 24 refer to the second sign of the zodiac, Taurus the bull. The activity of wisdom and the functioning of the third Eye is governed by this sign, as well as the general attributes of the cosmic astral plane, the substance of this All-Presence (100 + 2 x 7). This is sensed by the opened eye of 'the Dangma', of the Seer (the Leonine Presence) residing in the cosmic ethers. Here specifically the *ātmic* plane is implied, from whence this Eye will direct the karmic forces of the new *manvantara* when it commences. Taurus also carries on its 'back' the Pleiades, the Mothers of any newly forming solar system, who are yet to produce a new *manvantara*.

This 'All-Presence' is not seen by the third Eye of 'the Dangma', but is *sensed* by it, meaning 'to have apprehend, intellectually perceived or discerned via a sense perception, or having felt'. One can 'sense' by means of the 'sixth sense' (the intellect), the intuition or even by abstract *manasic* apperception. To have sensed can refer to the use of any or all of the senses. Cosmically the five 'senses' involve the general qualities of the entire constitution of Brahmā. (The focus then is upon cosmic astral orifices of a Logos). That *'which is sensed'* (10) represents perfected evolutionary Being. The 'All-Presence' is however of such subjective magnitudinous vastness and subtlety that it is beyond the direct ability of the awakened Eye of the Adept to perceive directly. The implication therefore is that 'the Dangma' exists upon the cosmic etheric sub-planes, from whence what exists upon the cosmic astral can be 'sensed'.

With respect to 'the opened Eye', it can be said that there are varied meanings of the eye, and in many ways it is one of the most profound symbols of the entire esoteric philosophy, which will only be explained briefly here. It should be noted also that the sense of sight has reference to the mental plane, for as we see so we think. What we see causes changes in our mental imagery and often comprehension as to the nature of things. All images of thought are created in the mind's Eye.

In its singular connotation an Eye also has reference to an organ of clairvoyance (*chakra*). Specifically 'the Eye' refers to the All-seeing Eye (Ājña centre), which enables those that have gained spiritual perception to see the true nature of Being. This is the most direct meaning of 'the opened Eye of the Dangma'. In its higher connotation the Eye refers to the Eye of the Soul, or even to the Monadic Eye. The eye is the doorway to the entrance of light, which is registered and analysed by the brain, the thinking mechanism in the body. All divine centres (*chakras*) in the body of a Logos are 'Eyes', doorways to the entry of Light. The petals of a Head centre (Shambhala) of a Logos will also be arranged in the form of an ineffable Eye.

The eyes are composed of the most rarefied atoms of a person's constitution, and are the symbols of the enlightenment of an Initiate. In the form of the *chakras* they provide access to multidimensional perception and experiences, allowing one to either 'see, sense, or feel'. The various types of 'eye' are:

1. The two physical eyes of normal vision.
2. The eye of reason (the left eye, synthesising the *iḍā nāḍī*).
3. The eye of wisdom (the right eye, *piṇgalā nāḍī*).
4. The Eye of vision, or intuition, (the Heart centre).
5. The Eye of Fiery conflagration, of creation (the Throat centre).
6. The Eye of power (Solar Plexus centre).
7. The third Eye, the one-pointed Eye of direction, or All-seeing Eye (the Ājña centre).

8. The Eye of revelation and of enlightenment (the Head centre).
9. The directive Eye of the Soul.
10. The Monadic Eye.

Above them all stands the Eye of 'God'.

Concerning *'the opened Eye of the Dangma'*, H.P.B. States: in the S.D., Vol. 1:

> Dangma means a purified soul, one who has become a Jivanmukta, the highest adept, or rather a Mahatma so-called. His "opened eye" is the inner spiritual eye of the seer, and the faculty which manifests through it is not clairvoyance as ordinarily understood, *i.e.*, the power of seeing at a distance, but rather the faculty of spiritual intuition, through which direct and certain knowledge is obtainable. This faculty is intimately connected with the "third eye," which mythological tradition ascribes to certain races of men.[76]

The numbers of the phrase *'the "opened Eye"'* add to 8 x 8, which indicates that an awakened Eye has the ability to see and 'sense' the fields of energy that sustain all being/non-being, hence this Eye receives and transmits energies, specifically in the form of Light. We also have the concept of the spiral-cyclic motion associated with the 'slumber' of the abstracted Logos, of all the Lives. The energy field of such motion sustains the activity of this Eye. The opened Eye is really an opened Door whereby the Initiated Seer can enter or leave at will into the abstracted domains, to travel and experience cosmos. Note that the Eye is symbolised by a series of concentric circles arranged around a central sphere (the pupil).

Upon attaining sleep the consciousness of an intelligent person leaves through the door or Iris of the 'Eye' that is the 1,000 petalled lotus, a lower correspondence to the exit of a solar or planetary Logos during the commencement of *pralaya*. Through this Door the enlightened One travels to consciously experience higher dimensional perception. Because of the similarity between the death process, sleeping and meditation the enlightened seer (Dangma) can sense the 'All-Presence'

76 Ibid., footnote, page 46.

via the opened Eye, and also View the *pralaya* process and the eventual *manvantara* on a solar or cosmic level.

The number 8 of the phrase *'that All-Presence which is sensed by the 'opened Eye'* refers to the energy field (spiral-cyclic motion) of the 'All-Presence' experienced by this Eye. The intensity of the directed motion of this energy awakens the Eye to see.

The number 100 + 13 of the phrase *'the "opened Eye" of the Dangma'* refers to the sphere of activity of the Eye, whereas the associated number 32 informs us that the activity of this Eye is governed by Love-Wisdom, which is the prime attribute of the Seer, *'the Dangma'* (10, signifying perfection). This second Ray energy, in combination with an opened Eye, makes one enlightened, expressive of the Power to See. Such a Seer has fully awakened his/her Head centre to properly know all via this Ray, yet still being incarnate only senses the conditions associated with the *pralaya,* dissolution, as it concerns cosmic astral space. Such a One cannot experience it in full.

The numbers 200 + 17 x 3, and 31 x 2 of the phrase *'throughout that All-Presence which is sensed by the "opened Eye"'* further characterise the attributes of the 'All-Presence', in that such an entity manifests the divine Activity of a cosmic Christ (200 + 17 x 3) that cosmically reflects the force of Love-Wisdom (31 x 2) in terms of the first Ray energy of the Will. At first this force manifests as a generalised energy field, but will later become the driving energy propelling the spheres of phenomena. (For our present solar system.)

The number 31 of the phrase *'sensed by the "Opened Eye"'* refers to the first Ray aspect of Deity, to using the Will to 'sense' the nature of the abstracted domains which would normally be beyond the Seer's ken. The first Ray pierces the obstructions to the higher domains.

The number 44 of the phrase *'sensed by the "Opened Eye" of the Dangma'* refers to a perfected member of humanity (44), an awakened Adept who can experience the energy body (Presence, or Light body) of the Logos, who is a cosmic Christ, a member of the Humanity upon cosmic astral realms.

The numbers of the phrase *'that All-Presence which is sensed by the "opened Eye" of the Dangma'* add to 12, 66. The number 66 refers to the complete Logoic Body, the sum of the Lives existing in *pralaya,* or, specifically in active manifestation during *manvantara*. The number 12 refers to the manifestation of the petals of the Logoic Heart centre.

The numbers of the complete phrase *'throughout that All-Presence which is sensed by the 'Opened Eye' of the Dangma'* add to 300, 75. The number 300 refers to the perfection of the Activity aspect, but here to the sum of the subjective Form of the 'All-Presence', which can only be 'sensed' because of the extreme subtlety of the *arūpa* levels of the *deva* Lives, the Hierarchies of Builders existing in *pralaya*. The number 3 x 25 normally relates to the Buddhas of Activity, which are representative of the types of Entities that we are here considering. These numbers implicate the perspective of a Seer abstracted upon the *ātmic* plane, because such a one's prime focus would allow proper comprehension of the Creative forces that would awaken a new *manvantara* and its forms of activities.

Stanza One part Nine

Stanza 1:9 states:

> **But where was the Dangma when the alaya of the Universe** *(Soul as the basis of all, Anima Mundi)* **was in paramartha** *(Absolute Being and Consciousness which are Absolute Non-Being and Unconsciousness)* **and the great Wheel was anupadaka?**

Keynotes: Cancer, fourth cosmic ether – *buddhi,* the seventh Eternity.

The numerical breakdown of the first phrase:

where was the Dangma (76, 22), But where was the Dangma (83, 29), the alaya (28 = 7 x 4, 10), the alaya of the universe (96 = 12 x 8, 24), in paramartha (57 = 12), the alaya of the universe was in paramartha (160, 43 = 7), the universe was in paramartha (120 = Capricorn, 30), when the alaya of the universe was in paramartha (183, 48 = Cancer), where was the Dangma when the alaya of the universe was in paramartha? (259, 70), But where was the Dangma when the alaya of the universe was in paramartha (266, 77), the great Wheel (65, 20, 6.6.), was Anupādaka (32, 14 = 2 x 7, 7.7.), The Great Wheel was Anupādaka (97 = 16, 34), the alaya of the universe was in paramartha and the great Wheel was anupadaka (267, 78), when the alaya of the universe was

> in paramartha and the great Wheel was anupadaka (290, 83), where was the Dangma when the alaya of the universe was in paramartha and the great Wheel was anupadaka? (366, 105), But where was the Dangma when the alaya of the universe was in paramartha and the great Wheel was anupadaka? (373, 112).

This stanza brings our vision to the plane *buddhi,* the fourth cosmic ether, hence the domain of abstraction for all the lives that constitute the three worlds of human evolution. As earlier stated the concern is with the Soul aspect of all Life (the 'alaya of the Universe') that must awaken in evolutionary space if manifestation is to proceed. The sum of cosmos is veiled by the fourth cosmic ether, bringing our vision also to the higher correspondence of *buddhi* in stanza 1:2 ('the infinite Bosom of Duration'). The focus is upon the seventh Eternity and the direct Will of the Father aspect of Deity, which empowers the formation of the *nāḍīs* and the evolution of the kingdoms of Nature upon the dense physical plane. This allows the appearance of Dangma (the Initiate) and the opening of his/her Eye. The forces within this Soul-form prepare the Lives for incarnation into the three lower sub-planes of the cosmic dense physical via the impetus of the sign Cancer the crab, who governs mass incarnation through the gateway of birth, hence the act of parturition. This verse informs us that such activity was not yet. Those with the opened Eye to see and to direct were still in *nirvāṇic* space *(paramārtha).* Much was yet to be organised, the Creative Builders had yet to manifest their activity, and the Word to be sounded for the bearers of 'the ears' (the *pitris,* the Fathers of the form) who were still 'sleeping'. Upon *buddhi* 'slumber' the 'human Hierarchy', the 'Lords of Sacrifice'.

The question *'where was the Dangma?'* (13, 22) is not just a rhetorical question implying the non existence of the seer when the universe was in *paramārtha,*[77] nor is it only posed as a mental or intuitive exercise to the reader to open his/her eyes, or even for the Eye of the Dangma to open and See or 'sense' the All-Presence. It also refers to the first Thought of the Creative Deity that must occur if the Universe

---

77 *Paramārtha,* ultimate purpose, absolute existence, the most sublime supreme truth, reality. Here the term relates to the period of abstract absorption into the absolute, or 'the supreme'.

was to be reawakened. Before this prime organ of Creative Endeavour, and the opened Eye of the Dangma can be utilised, the cosmic Logos must first become aware of the Need. The Logos must find all of the energies and Entities that constitute this Eye (symbolised by the number 22) to awaken the Head centre and the Door to incarnate Being. The rest of those constituting the periodic vehicle that is to be resuscitated or reconstituted must also be found and be reawakened. They are the fully enlightened Beings (Jīvanmuktas[78]) at the level of being Grand Heavenly Men, planetary, solar or cosmic Logoi, via which the energy of Love-Wisdom must be made corporeal. The ineffable Logos must summon them, thus the question of where the Dangma was becomes the summons commanding them to make themselves Known, be present to the Vision of the Logos, Who will then again See into the Darkness (of the *kāma-manasic* realms) by projecting these Lives therein. All Lives then become part of the new creative endeavour (the *mahāmanvantara*).

The numbers 13, 22 of this phrase thus asks: 'where are the Creative beings that will circumscribe spheres of existence (13), the Wombs of time and space (22), wherein the consciousness principle (20 + 2) can function, so that a new epoch of conscious awakening can occur?'

The number 11 of the phrase *'But where was the Dangma'* refers here to the cosmic *nāḍi* system (the four cosmic ethers) wherein one must look to find them. Logoically it refers to those that will vivify a new etheric body of a Logos, via which a new manifestation could occur. Here 'the Dangma' implies the existence of Initiates of the fourth degree, who empower the attributes of the fourth cosmic ether. Their work was needed to bring into manifestation the lives of the concreted planes of perception. 'The Dangma' can also refer to human Souls that are vitalised from *buddhi*.

The meaning of the phrase *'the universe'* was given in Stanza 1:6, where it was said to refer to a cosmic Christ, 'the Son...of Necessity'.

Concerning the terms *ālaya* and *paramārtha* H.P.B. states:

> The two terms "Alaya" and "Paramārtha" have been the causes of

---

78 *Jīvanmukta*, one who has attained the highest state of realisation (*mukta*), whose consciousness has identified with the One fundamental Source. An Adept who can project the gain of that identification through his/her body of vitality, which becomes a healing or compassionate radiance.

dividing schools and splitting the truth into more different aspects than any other mystic terms. Alaya is literally the "Soul of the World" or Anima Mundi, the "Over-Soul" of Emerson, and according to esoteric teaching it changes periodically its nature. Alaya, though eternal and changeless in its inner essence on the planes which are unreachable by either men or Cosmic Gods (Dhyani Buddhas), alters during the active life-period with respect to the lower planes, ours included. During that time not only the Dhyani-Buddhas are one with Alaya in Soul and Essence, but even the man strong in the Yoga (mystic meditation) "is able to merge his soul with it" (Aryasanga, the *Bumapa* school). This is not Nirvana, but a condition next to it. Hence the disagreement. Thus, while the Yogāchāryas (of the Mahāyāna school) say that Alaya is the personification of the Voidness, and yet Alaya (*Nyingpo* and *Tsang* in Tibetan) is the basis of every visible and invisible thing, and that, though it is eternal and immutable in its essence, it reflects itself in every object of the Universe "like the moon in clear tranquil water"; other schools dispute the statement. The same for Paramārtha: the Yogāchāryas interpret the term as that which is also dependant upon other things (*paratantra);* and the Madhyamikas say that Paramārtha is limited to Paranishpanna or absolute perfection; *i.e.,* in the exposition of these "two truths" (out of four), the former believe and maintain that (on this plane, at any rate) there exists only Samvritisatya or relative truth; and the latter teach the existence of Paramārthasatya, the "absolute truth"...[79]

Esoteric philosophy teaches that everything lives and is conscious, but not that all life and consciousness are similar to those of human or even animal beings. Life we look upon as "the one form of existence," manifesting in what is called matter; or, as in man, what, incorrectly separating them, we name Spirit, Soul and Matter. Matter is the vehicle for the manifestation of soul on this plane of existence, and soul is the vehicle on a higher plane for the manifestation of spirit, and the three are a trinity synthesized by Life, which pervades them all. The idea of universal life is one of those ancient conceptions which are returning to the human mind in this century, as a consequence of its liberation from anthropomorphic theology...[80]

---

79 Ibid., 48.

80 Ibid., 49.

> "Alaya" has a double and even a triple meaning. In the Yogāchāraya system of the contemplative Mahāyāna school, Alaya is both the Universal Soul (Anima Mundi) and the Self of a progressed adept. "He who is strong in the Yoga can introduce at will his Alaya by means of meditation into the true nature of Existence." The "Alaya has an absolute eternal existence," says Arayāsanga – the rival of Nagārjuna.[81]

The numbers of the phrase *'the alaya'* add to 7 x 4, referring to the fourth plane of perception, *buddhi*, which in the esoteric sense is the Over-Soul of all manifest Life, for the entire material universe comes from it—consciousness, light, and the primordial substance (energy). The Soul on the higher mental plane exists to convey its expression into manifestation. From this perspective we can conceive of the *ālaya* to stand as the substance of the *saṃsāra-śūnyatā* nexus, to embody the consciousness-attributes of the Sambhogakāya Flower.

The *ālaya* is effectively the universal storehouse of consciousness (in the form of the *ālayavijñāna*[82]), which an enlightened Being (the Dangma) visualises via the opened Eye and directs its expression into the manifest world, if the embodied form (the Son) is to be born.

The statement by H.P.B. concerning the *ālaya* that: 'though eternal and changeless in its inner essence on the planes which are unreachable by either men or Cosmic Gods (Dhyani Buddhas)' is a little problematic, because though 'unreachable' by normal human consciousness, can be 'reached' by the enlightened, and certainly is reachable by the Dhyāni Buddhas. She may be referring to *śūnyatā* as a type of store (of *dharmakāya),* and by its definition as a Void, Emptiness, may from one perspective be considered 'unreachable' (unknowable). Certainly however it is experienceable. The *ālaya* that 'alters during the active

---

81 Ibid.

82 *Ālayavijñāna,* universal storehouse of consciousness, the mind as basis of all in the Yogācāra philosophy. *Ālayavijñāna* is *ālaya* + *vijñāna,* where *ālaya* is a place of storage of mental images. *Ālaya* indiscriminately harbours what flows into it through the *vijñānas* (the faculty of discriminating). The attributes of consciousness perform actions, hence evolve, however the *ālaya* always abides in its self-nature. The *vijñānas* may cease evolving by not acting out thought impressions, but the *ālaya* always remains as a store. C*itta* (basic mind substance) as a cumulative mental faculty is identified with the *ālayavijñāna.*

life-period with respect to the lower planes, ours included', refers to the expression of *ālaya* as the *ālayavijñāna,* hence also the embodied Soul (the Sambhogakāya Flower) upon the higher mental plane. Cosmically the *ālaya* of the universe may indeed be 'unreachable' by Dhyāni Buddhas at the present stage of their evolution on our earth system. There are many orders of transmuted correspondences of transcendence to consider. All in the universe is relative.

The numbers of the phrase *'the alaya of the Universe'* add to 8 x 12 (Scorpio), 2 x 12 (Taurus). Scorpio refers to discipleship and the passing of the tests that allow mastery of the nine-headed hydra, to attain Initiate consciousness ('the Eye of the Dangma'). The *ālaya* is then revealed in its entirety. The number 96 also refers to the constitution of the various petals of the *chakras*, which relate to the unfolding consciousness of any entity, and esoterically this 'unfolding consciousness' constitutes the *ālaya* of space. The *chakras* are the store of the consciousness attributes of any manifest being. When extended to the level of a universe then we can consider that such a universe is but a vast *chakra.*[83]

As there is a store of the consciousness (the attributes of mind/Mind, *vijñānas)* for humans, so also during the *pralaya* period being considered there is a similar store of consciousness units (human Souls, liberated Lives and *devas*) in cosmos. This 'store' is not localised, but rather is spread throughout the various etheric planets and star systems *(chakras).* Such consciousness-units are effectively the *saṃskāras* of the 'slumbering' Logos, which will be called into expression when *manvantara* ensues, according to the *karma* to be enacted as the appropriate cycles unfold. From this perspective the *ālaya* relates to the *nāḍī* system, wherein the cosmic *Chakras* are found. There are astral as well as etheric *chakras.*

Three astrological signs can be considered to embody the attributes of the *ālaya,* Aquarius for the Consciousness attributes under the auspices of cosmic Mind, Taurus, the universal store of substance upon the cosmic astral ocean, and Gemini for those contained within the cosmic etheric body. A fourth sign, Capricorn, can be considered to be the repository for the substance of Mahat, the cosmic correspondence of *citta.*

83 This theme was explored in my book *Esoteric Cosmology and Modern Physics.*

The second sign of the zodiac, *Taurus the bull*, more than any other sign (except maybe Aquarius) embodies the qualities of the *ālaya* of the universe. The symbolism of Taurus expresses the Light of the Soul hidden in the darkness of matter. Then we also have the Eye of the Bull, through which the *ālaya* manifests as the Light that makes itself visible in the darkness.

Taurus and Scorpio are polar opposites that together form one of the arms of the *fixed cross* of the Heavens, the cross of the crucified Christ. This cross expresses the consciousness aspect that is the *ālaya* in its fourfold attributes, as symbolised by the qualities of its four signs. The qualities of the four arms of the fixed cross are explained elsewhere and need no further elaboration here. The north-south arms are represented by Aquarius-Leo, and the east-west arms by Taurus-Scorpio. The fixed cross of the cosmos therefore can thus be considered the 'alaya of the Universe'. Gemini is the temple of the manifest Christ wherein consciousness-attributes, the Christ aspect, can be discovered by those incarnate in systemic space. The Initiates manifest the rituals and *dhāraṇīs* that will invoke the energies from the Presence of the cosmic Christ.

The number 24 also refers to the 'Elders' incorporated into a Logoic Head centre (as the second tier of its petals, and their ramifications throughout the remainder of the lotus). The collective Minds of these liberated beings constitute this *ālaya*.

The numbers of the phrase *'where was the Dangma when the alaya of the Universe was in paramartha?'* add to 259 = 16, 70. When the numbers of the word 'but' are added the result is the numbers 266, 77. The number 16 here can be considered to refer to 'the Dangma', as a cosmic Christ, whilst the numbers 70, 77 and 200 + 66 refer to the great cycles, spheres and Chains of evolution, that contain all attributes of the evolutionary process, the substance (200 + 66) of this *ālaya*. The question therefore poses 'where was the Christ principle when the store of Consciousness was abstracted, not actively manifested?' The answer therefore is that the cosmic Christ was similarly abstracted, not manifesting compassionate activity.

The numbers 12 x 10 and 16 x 10 of the phrases *'the Universe was in paramartha'* and *'the alaya of the Universe was in paramartha'* verifies that our concern is with the Consciousness-principle. The absolute Truth *(paramārtha)* is embodied as the cosmic Christ, the principle of Love in the universe. *Pralaya* and *manvantara* are but necessary aspects of the process that further develops and awakens this principle. The abstraction of a Christ signifies the *mahāparinirvāṇa* of a completely liberated Buddha, the true expression of which defies our comprehension. The Son is now one with the Father.

The number 12 x 10 also refers to the tenth sign of the zodiac, Capricorn the goat, the high point of material attainment, the polar opposite of Cancer. (The sign of incarnation.) It is the last sign of the zodiac of the ten signed zodiac, signifying completion. However, the main implication here is that Capricorn refers to the mount of *karma*, and it is the sum total of the *karma* of the Logos that was in *paramārtha*, waiting for the time of its recycling when the universe was to be reawakened.

The numbers of the phrase *'when the alaya of the Universe was in paramartha'* add to 48, referring to the sign Cancer the crab, hence the gateway to birth, which was closed. The sign also refers to the massed consciousness of the lesser Lives, which are in *paramārtha,* thus not physically active. Their collective consciousness was accordingly stored in the *ālaya.*

The meaning of the *wheel* was explained in *Stanza 1:5,* whilst *'the great Wheel'* (3 x 13, 12, 6.6.) is the one major wheel (of the Law, *karma*) of the universe which unites the motions of all the lesser wheels (*chakras*) in a grand consummating motion. Each Wheel is a Scheme of evolution. The number 3 x 13 refers to evolutionary time in which the cyclic motion of the great Wheel is dominant and unfolding. The inference is specifically with the first three quarters of the great Year of Brahmā, in which the material or Mother aspect reigns supreme.[84] After that the motion becomes increasingly spirally, and then fourth dimensional, as the abstraction process proceeds. The number 12 implies that this Wheel is essentially an unfolding Heart centre with 12 main spokes. The number 6.6. implies that the manifestation of this Wheel sustains the existence of the form.

Concerning the term *anupādaka* H.P.B. states:

---

84 As the number 52 signifying that Year is divided by 4 x 13.

> The term Anupadaka, "parentless," or without progenitors, is a mystical designation having several meanings in the philosophy. By this name celestial beings, the Dhyan-Chohans or Dhyani-Buddhas, are generally meant. But these correspond mystically to the human Buddhas and Bodhisattwas, known as the "Mānushi (or human) Buddhas," the latter are also designated "Anupadaka,' once their whole personality is merged in their compound sixth and seventh principles — or Atma-Buddhi, and that they have become the "diamond-souled" (Vajra-sattvas), the full Mahatmas. The "Concealed Lord' (Sangbai Dag-po), "the one merged with the absolute," can have no parents since he is Self-existent, and one with the Universal Spirit (Svayambhu), the Svābhāvat in its highest aspect. The mystery of the Hierarchy of the Anupadaka is great, its apex being the universal Spirit-Soul, and the lower rung the Mānushi-Buddha; and even every Soul-endowed man also is in Anupadaka in a latent state. Hence, when speaking of the Universe in its formless, eternal, or absolute condition, before it was fashioned by the "Builders" — the expression, "the Universe was Anupadaka."[85]

Anupādaka also represents the second highest plane of perception, wherein the human Monad (Spirit) is said to reside. The Monad is 'parentless, without progenitors' as far as the Soul-personality is concerned. It is a true child of the universe and its mode of expression is the way of evolution of the Logoi embodying all of the stars in the universe.

The numbers of the phrase *'the great Wheel was anupadaka'* add to 16, 17 x 2, whilst those of the phrase *'was anupadaka'* add to 2 x 16, 2 x 7, 7.7. These numbers essentially imply that this Wheel was absorbed in the *ālaya* that was *anupādaka,* the Monadic perception of abstracted Deity (17 x 2) prior to being breathed out again during the next 'day-be-with-us'. The Monad is considered 'parentless' and 'without progenitors' because it is completely beyond the domain of cause and effect. The Monad was abstracted into the principle of the cosmic Christ (16, 2 x 16), within the cycles of expression of *pralaya,* signified by the numbers 2 x 7 (the cosmic astral) and 7.7.

The cosmic Christ is the prototype of all the Dhyān Chohans in the universe. Generally therefore, the term *anupādaka* refers to the plane

---

85 Ibid., 52.

of perception from whence emanates all enlightened Being (during the second Outpouring of Life).

Regarding this verse the term *anupādaka* refers to the transition period associated with the Son after He has been abstracted as the Father, who then later projects His purpose via the Mother to form a new Son in incarnation via the second Outpouring. When the Father thus acts, the manifestation of the universe again becomes possible, and the Monad appears upon the plane *anupādaka.*

The important numbers of the remaining phrases concerning the statement *'But where was the Dangma when the alaya of the universe was in paramartha and the great Wheel was anupadaka?'* are 11, 105, 112 = 7 x 16 and 366. The meaning of the number 11 here has already been given. The number 105 refers to the Head centre of a Logos or a human. As such a centre comes into activity for the purpose of the manifestation of the Consciousness principle, so the question asked is 'where has the constitution of this centre been abstracted to when the great Wheel of solar or cosmic evolution was *anupādaka?'* The answer was provided above as referring to either the four cosmic ethers or cosmic astral or mental space. The number 7 x 16 refers to the Hierarchy of Light (a cosmic Christ, 'the Dangma') that informs such a centre, that were likewise abstracted. They were in *paramārtha.* The number 300 + 66 refers to the form nature of the universe, which constitutes 'the great Wheel' that was *anupādaka. Paramārtha* in terms of Monadic expression is an inconceivable concept for human minds to consider, as it is essentially synonymous with being abstracted into the great abstracted Will that is the Mind of a cosmic Logos. Monads are but cells within the Brain of such an Entity during *manvantara,* which is difficult enough to contemplate, but what a Monad represents in a discarnate Logos is another order of abstraction altogether.

5

Commentaries - Stanza 2

There is a hiatus from stanza 1:9 and 2:1, nevertheless the account picks up in a section governed generally by the sign Gemini the twins and the question as to the whereabouts of the (greater and lesser) Builders. They are needed to produce form (the *rūpa* universe) from no-form (the *arūpa* universe). This concerns the movement from the formless to the formed domains that Gemini governs, where the immortal brother governs the expression of the formless universe and the mortal brother the formed one. Stanza two is concerned with analysing the forces that a Logos needs to activate and organise in order to produce the appearance of the Wheels that revolve within the turning of the great Wheel. These forces come into manifestation via the plane *anupādaka,* which therefore generally governs the import of this stanza.

The Greater Builders manifest via the plane *anupādaka* to incarnate, and the Lesser Builders via the *ātmic* plane, hence to answer the question as to where they are during *pralaya* would make one hazard a guess that they were abstracted to the corresponding cosmic astral sub-planes *('in their Ah-Hi paranishpanna'),* from where we must start to analyse this stanza.

Stanza Two part One

Stanza 2:1 states:

> **.....Where were the Builders, the luminous Sons of manvantaric dawn?.....In the unknown Darkness in their Ah-Hi** *(Chohanic, Dhyani-Buddhic)* **paranishpanna, the Producers of form** *(rupa)* **from no-form** *(arupa),* **the root of the world—the Devamatri and Svabhavat, rested in the bliss of non-being.**

> *Keynotes:* Gemini, *anupādakā-ātmic* plane.

> The numerical breakdown of the first two phrases:

> Where were the Builders (107, 26 = 8), the Builders (51, 15), the luminous Sons (62, 17), Sons of manvantaric dawn (84 = Libra, 21), the luminous sons of manvantaric dawn (133 = 7, 34 = 7), manvantaric dawn (59 = 14, 14), the unknown Darkness (74 = 11, 20), In the unknown Darkness (88, 25), Ah-Hi paranishpanna (86=14, 14 = 5), their Ah-Hi paranishpanna (119 = 11, 20), in their Ah-hi paranishpanna (133 = 100 + 33, 25), the unknown Darkness in their Ah-Hi paranishpanna (207, 45), in the unknown Darkness in their Ah-Hi paranishpanna (221 = 200 + 7 x 3, 50).

The qualities of the sign Gemini are expressed in the attributes of the Ah-Hi, who represent the immortal and mortal brothers of this sign. They are in *parinişpanna,* not yet awakened, but must unite in service ('hold hands') to help build the new form in due time. The etheric portion is built by the immortal brother, and the dense form by the mortal brother. With respect to the Ah-Hi D.K. states:

> In the preceding system[1] the cosmic physical plane attained a certain vibratory capacity, and the devas of the internal furnaces became (relatively speaking) highly evolved, the "fires of matter" then blazing forth. Certain Existences attained self-consciousness in that earlier

1 The reference here is to the last solar system, which was ruled by the third Ray, thus was an embodiment of the Mother's department. There the activity of the *devas* reigned supreme, with the human kingdom only properly appearing near the end of that great evolutionary Wheel.

> system, and are the "nirvanis" spoken of by H. P. B.[2] As might be expected, they are characterised by active intelligence, achieved and developed by means of material evolution during a previous mahamanvantara. They are the Manasa devas and in their totality are the vehicles of the Divine mind, the dhyan-chonanic forces, the aggregate of the Ah-hi.[3]

This aggregate of liberated active Manasic Lives (Kumāras) and their *deva* counterparts from the former solar system, governed by the third Ray, are summoned in the early stages of solar or planetary evolution, allowing the new form be awakened. The second Ray Builders manifest from the *anupādaka* level of expression. They build the Soul aspects (the *anima mundi)* of the informing Lives that will inhabit the new form. This concerns the *arūpa* level of expression.

The numbers of the phrase *'the Builders'* add to 3 x 5, referring to the activity of mind. Here the concern is with the secrets of the Fires of the Mind, the prime creative energy in the cosmos. The lesser angelic Builders use this energy to produce form from no-form. Everything material is sustained by and is resolved back in the Mind. In order to build the dense physical form, the Lesser Builders[4] work with cosmic Mind via the *ātmic* plane and then with mental substance. The Greater and Lesser Builders are the second and third groups of entities that the cosmic Deity must Summon into activity. The first group are the great Entities Who are the integral Life, the Monad-Soul of the forthcoming form (the 'Divine Flames' or 'Divine Lives'[5]). They can be considered the various planetary Regents constituting a solar form, as well as the Lords of the spheres (Chains, globes, Rounds) governing manifest Life.

Concerning the Builders, H.P.B. states that:

> The "Builders," the "Sons of Manvantaric Dawn," are the real creators of the Universe; and in the doctrine, which deals only with our Planetary System, they, as the architects of the latter, are also

---

2 Footnote given: See S.D. II, 83, 84, 243.

3 T.C.F., 686-687.

4 See *Esoteric Astrology,* Tabulation II, page 35, for a summary of the main qualities of the Divine (Greater) and Lesser Builders.

5 Ibid.

> called the "Watchers" of the Seven Spheres, which exoterically are the Seven planets, and esoterically the seven earths or spheres (planets) of our chain also. The opening sentence of Stanza I., when mentioning "Seven Eternities," is made to apply both to the *Maha-Kalpa* or "the (great) Age of Brahmā," as well as to the Solar *pralaya* and subsequent resurrection of our Planetary System on a higher plane. There are many kinds of *pralaya* (dissolution of a thing visible), as will be shown elsewhere.[6]

H.P.B's phrase: 'this doctrine, which deals only with our Planetary System' indicates that the focus is specifically upon the prenatal stage of our own planetary Scheme, (the fourth in the solar system) rather than with the universe as a whole. This makes comprehension of the process easier and it is more relevant to us on the earth. The section omitted of the Stanzas therefore deals with solar evolution to the time when the appearance of the Logos of our planetary Scheme was ready to summon the Builders. This immediately follows after the stage depicted by stanza 1:9. The missing information shall be presented in volume three of this series, which is concerned with the evolution of the various planetary Schemes in this and the previous solar system.

The law of Correspondences when rightly applied allows us to relate the qualities and processes associated with the formation, evolution and liberation of the one (humanity) to the Other (ineffable or cosmic Man). The same principles concern the formation of our particular solar system, planetary Scheme, Chain, human being, or the formation of the cosmos (though in a transmuted sense). This is because the fourth or earth Scheme reflects the qualities of all the others. Our earth Scheme (hence the earth) therefore acts as a mirror whereon the imagery of the remainder of cosmos is reflected. This Law is one of the basic pillars that supports the entire edifice of the esoteric philosophy.

The numbers of the phrase *'Where were the Builders'* add to 107, which signifies a septenary, that the Builders build the seven-fold nature of formed space. They project the *karma* (or *saṃskāras)* associated with the ending of one major cycle of evolution into the new one, as governed by the significance of the number 7—the seven planes, solar cycles (etc.).

---

6 S.D. Vol. 1, 53.

Here we can also look to the *'seven eternities'*, which explains where these Builders *were* at that time. The septenary signifies the seven steps by which they were to build the material universe.

This phrase started with a lacunae between this Stanza and the end of Stanza one, stating that 'the great wheel was anupadaka', and another lacunae follows after calling for the Builders. We can only guess that there were processes involved within the *pralaya* period that the manuscript explains, mantric Sound for instance, as well as the manifold orders and sub-orders of these *deva* lives, the ontology of which H.P.B. could not reveal to us.

The meaning of the 'Son' in terms of referring to the Christ, the second Ray, or Soul aspect needs no further reiteration. These *'luminous Sons'* therefore embody the Christ principle. The word 'luminous' refers to that which shines, reflects or emits light, is bright or brilliant, and in the field of consciousness, one who is keenly intelligent or enlightened. *'The luminous Sons'* (31 x 2, 17) are therefore members of the Hierarchy of fully enlightened Beings that embody and bring the energies of Love-Wisdom, Light and Consciousness in terms of the seven Rays manifesting in the form. They are Sons (31 x 2) of the Father-Mother that have evolved out of the womb of time and must now add Their qualities and experiences to the new Awakening, fashioning it into a resplendent Sun. They express first Ray energies from the Head centre of the abstract Deity via Love-Wisdom into or as manifest space. This allows them to build the forms desired.

These Builders were Luminous Sons in two ways:

a. Those Builders that are fully liberated and who will manifest into our earth Chain via *anupādaka*. This is also indicated by the numbers of the phrase *'The luminous Sons of manvantaric dawn'*, which add to 100 + 33. These are the Greater Builders, 'the Burning Sons of Desire'.[7] They can be considered Lords of Flame at Shambhala, who build the solar form, and the Monadic aspect of manifest life. Their 'luminosity' here concerns the fact that they are essentially attributes of the cosmic Mind of the creative Logos (Brahmā). Note that *Esoteric Astrology* relates these 'Burning Sons' to the Greater

7 T.C.F., 1197, *Esoteric Astrology*, 35.

Builders, whereas T.C.F. relates them to the first of the Creative Hierarchies. This is because this is a generic term for the four higher Creative Hierarchies that 'rushed into the spheres'. This relates to the second Outpouring of the Lives bearing the Consciousness principle, who are the 'longing of the Father for the Mother'.[8] The attributes of the Greater Builders upon the plane *anupādaka* however qualifies the general attributes of these Hierarchies.

b. Those that are to enter into incarnation ('to fall') and are accordingly Rayed down to the *ātmic* plane, from whence cosmic dense physical manifestation emanates. They are the *'Sons of manvantaric dawn'* (84 = Libra, 66), the Lesser Builders or angelic triads embodying all of the *devas* that embody the sum of manifest Life (66), of the evolutionary progress and processes of the kingdoms of Nature. Libra governs the law of *karma* conditioning this Life, which emanates from the *ātmic* plane, and into which it is all resolved.

The word *manvantara* refers to the duration of any new cosmic, solar or planetary cycle of activity. It is effectively the period of one *manu*, containing 4,320,000 human years, or specifically a Day of Brahmā.

The word *dawn* signifies the appearance of the Light associated with a new Day of Brahmā that dispels the darkness of the night (of *pralaya)*. It is this Light that is brought by the Builders.

The numbers of the phrase *'manvantaric dawn'* add to 2 x 7, indicating that the approach of this Dawn concerns the first two periods of any evolutionary cycle, after which incarnation into dense material involvement happens. An example is the first two Root Races of humanity before the material appearance of the third, Lemurian epoch.

The numbers of the phrase *'Sons of manvantaric dawn'* add to 7 x 12 (Libra the balances) and to 7 x 3. Libra is the great wheel of the Law, from which a new cycle of karmic activity emanates. Libra is thus the adjudicator that dispenses *karma,* the cause of the dawning of the new *manvantara*. The Builders manifest the attributes of this sign by invoking the karmic attributes (effectively the *saṃskāras*) from a former *manvantara* of Logoic activity and incorporate them into the new Logoic construct. They are the mediators between being and non-

8 See T.C.F., 1197 for the Old Commentary from whence these quotes are extracted.

being, form and no-form. The number 7 x 12 here specifically refers to the seven Creative Hierarchies that are to inform systemic space, as explained in the previous chapter. The question technically thus asks, 'where, or in what Schools of Learning (planetary or solar domains) can they be found during this *pralaya* period, and from which they are to be recalled?' In *pralaya* they developed further needed qualities to be expressed in the new wheel of activity. The number 7 x 3 here indicates the triune attributes of these Sons.

The nature of the *Ah-Hi* were explained in Stanza 1:3, whilst *Paranishpanna* (correctly spelt *parinispanna)* was explained in Stanza 1:6, where it was stated that *parinispanna* means perfection, fully fulfilled wisdom (*prajñā*) that supersedes all discrimination. It is the fully accomplished state, thus thoroughly established absolute reality, and issues, or comes forth, from the Absolute.

H.P.B. has this additional note concerning the meaning of *parinispanna*:

> Paranishpanna, remember, is the *summum bonum,* the Absolute, hence the same as Paranirvana. Besides being the final state it is that condition of subjectivity which has no relation to anything but the one absolute truth (Para-mārthasatya) on its plane. It is that state which leads one to appreciate correctly the full meaning of Non-Being, which, as explained, is *absolute* Being. Sooner or later, all that now *seemingly* exists, will be in reality and actuality in the state of Paranishpanna. But there is a great difference between *conscious* and *unconscious* "being." The condition of Paranishpanna, without Paramārtha, the Self-analysing consciousness (Svasamvedana), is no bliss, but simply extinction (for Seven Eternities). Thus, an iron ball placed under the scorching rays of the sun will get heated through, but will not feel or appreciate the warmth, while a man will. It is only "with a mind clear and undarkened by personality, and an assimilation of the merit of manifold existences devoted to being in its collectivity (the whole living and sentient Universe)," that one gets rid of personal existence, merging into, becoming one with, the Absolute,* and continuing in full possession of Paramārtha.[9]

9 Ibid., Vol. 1, 53-54. The footnote (*) presented is: 'Hence *Non-being* is "ABSOLUTE BEING," in esoteric philosophy. In the tenets of the latter even Adi-Budha (first or primeval wisdom) is, while manifested, in one sense an illusion, Maya, since all the gods, including Brahmā, have to die at the end of "the Age of Brahmā"; the abstraction called Parabrahm alone — whether we call it Ensoph, or Herbert

The meaning of the word *Darkness* was explained in Stanza 1:5, regarding the phrase 'Darkness alone filled the Boundless All'. When viewed from below up it refers to the *buddhic* plane (and what it veils, such as the cosmic astral plane), which is dark because of being imperceptible to normal human consciousness. When viewed from above down then this darkness refers to the concrete mental substance of the cosmic dense physical plane. What it veils is similarly imperceptible to the great liberated Lords that have long ago transcended its corporeality.

We saw also earlier that the Ah-Hi are dual and signify those entities that embody the archetypal Mind, plus those that are the expressions of the empirical mind. Darkness was also seen to be basically dual, particularly referring to the substance of the form that consciousness must utilise; whilst *pariniṣpanna* refers to absolute perfection and therefore is singular.

The phrase *'in the unknown Darkness'* (8 x 11, 5 x 5) refers to being abstracted in the higher mental plane and to the Soul therein. This phrase also answers the question as to where the Builders were during this *pralaya* period, and implicates the Logoic Causal Body into which all Creative forces (Logoic *saṃskāras*) were abstracted during *pralaya*. It also implicates the essential identity between the *'unknown Darkness'* and the *Ah-Hi pariniṣpanna*. The focus is upon the domain of cosmic Mind (which is the Unknown). From here all of the Laws governing cosmic manifestation emanate and are resolved. All is an expression of Mind. Therefore when trying to establish the causes for things we must proceed to analyse the concept of Mind. The Builders (*Ah-Hi*) are the Creative Forces of that Mind when it is awake, but are inactive when the Logos is 'asleep'. The significance of Mind with respect to the darkness of Ignorance, or what produces illumination, as well as the quiescence of the Mind when asleep is all important. The Soul resides upon the higher mental plane, which is the *pariniṣpanna* between rebirths. The number 8 x 11 here relates to the abstraction of all spiral-cyclic energies, back to the Source, the 'slumbering' process.

Spencer's Unknowable — being "the One Absolute" Reality. The One secondless Existence is ADWAITA, "Without a Second" and all the rest is *Maya*, so teaches the Adwaita philosophy.'

One can also consider the constitution of a Head centre that must be constructed by a planetary or solar Logos, or the Soul of a person, if that entity is to incarnate into a physical body and actively utilise it as an instrument for perfection. The five main tiers of the Head centre, omitting the petals, are outlined in figure 7. The tiers of petals relate to the expression of the manifestation of the Ah-Hi, when viewed as the embodiments of the Manasic forces of a Logos (or a human). The 'Ah' part of the mantra Ah-Hi signifies the three innermost tiers of petals, where the focus is the construct of the Throat in the Head tier of 96 petals. The two innermost tiers of petals are concerned with the attainment of Initiation and the projection inwards to the Soul of the gain of life's experiences. There is also the Breathing out of the *prāṇic* commands from the Soul.[10] From here the energies flow to the *chakras* constituting the corporeal body, thus the consciousness-producing factors of the empirical manifestation of an embodied form are vivified and integrated into a unity.

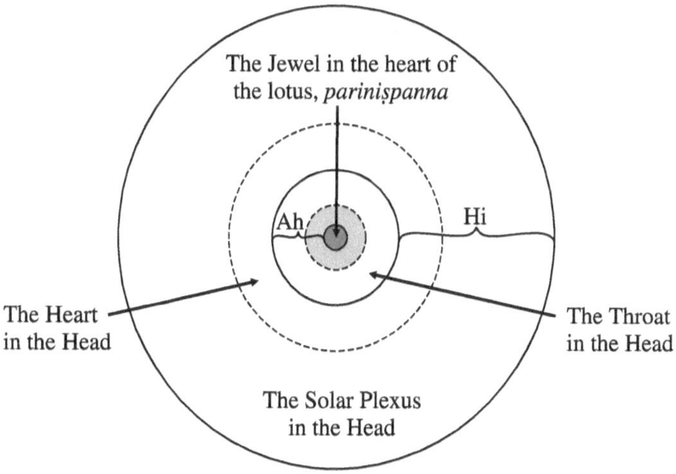

Figure 7. The five tiers of the Head lotus

10 These are effectively of the twelve signs of the zodiac, and when this number is added to the 96, then the sacred number 108 is produced. These twelve energies govern the twelve main petals of the Head lotus. The number twelve can also be considered in terms of the five *prāṇas* and the seven Rays.

The two outer tiers of petals (the Heart and Solar Plexus in the Head, 960 petals altogether)[11] are expressed by the 'Hi' part of the mantra Ah-Hi. They are concerned with the development of all attributes of consciousness to produce the empowerment of the Love-Wisdom principle. This part of the mantra therefore concerns the bulk of the evolutionary process, as it controls the major *saṃskāras* developed as a consequence of the course of unfolding the 777 incarnations. All of the *prāṇas* developed by the *chakras* below the diaphragm are processed within these outermost tiers.

The innermost Sacrifice petals relate to the expression of the Darkness of *parinișpanna,* the central abstracting sphere (the jewel in the heart of the Lotus).

The number 14 of the phrase *'manvantaric dawn'* here refers to awakening from the conditionings of the cosmic astral plane, whilst the numbers 11, 20 of the phrases *'the unknown Darkness'* and *'their Ah-Hi paranishpanna'* refer to the four cosmic ethers, the energy fields from where the *'Sons of manvantaric dawn'* will emanate. The Greater Builders are the controlling factor of the three innermost tiers of the Logoic Head centre and govern the energies stemming from the cosmic astral plane. (In this guise they establish themselves upon the second plane, *anupādaka.)* The Lesser Builders govern the factors associated with the two outermost tiers of petals of the Logoic Head lotus. They thus manifest via the third plane *ātma,* which is the plane of causative *karma*. Together the Greater and Lesser Builders *'in their Ah-Hi paranishpanna'* (100 + 33, 25) manifest the attributes of the Creative Intelligences (100 + 33) that embody the functions of a planetary Head centre (Shambhala). They also en-Soul the Consciousness principle (5 x 5). Taking transmuted correspondences into account, much could be transposed here from the information in volumes 5A and 5B of *A Treatise on Mind* concerning the method of awakening of the petals of the Head centre and the factors constituting them. This however lies outside this present work.

The number 200 + 7 of the phrase *'the unknown Darkness in their Ah-Hi Paranishpanna'* refers to 'the seven eternities', whilst the

11 These terms, plus detail concerning the constitution of the Head lotus, are explained in volume 5A of *A Treatise on Mind.*

associate number 5 x 9 here refers to the cosmic Masters, which these Builders can be considered to be, and the *parinișpanna* into which they are abstracted. The number here can also refer to the greater *deva* Lords.

The numbers of the entire phrase *'In the unknown Darkness in their Ah-Hi Paranishpanna'* add to 221, 50. The number 200 + 3 x 7 can refer to the three lower cosmic astral sub-planes, into which these Builders would be abstracted, whilst the number 50 here refers to the cosmic mental plane, which is *'the unknown Darkness'* from this perspective. From this plane they receive their Instructions to manifest their creative Activities in a new *manvantara.* (This happens via the third of the liberated Creative Hierarchies, 'Light thro' knowledge'.)

The numerical breakdown of the next phrase:

> The Producers (31 x 2 = 62, 17), The Producers of form (99, 27), form from no-form (86 = 14, 23 = 5), Producers of form from no-form (145 = 100 + 9 x 5, 37 = 10), The Producers of form from no-form (160, 43), producers of form (84 =7 x 12, Libra, 21 = 3 x 7).

The previous phrase was mainly concerned with the constitution of the Logoic Head centre, from where emanates the creative energy to organise Space into Thought Constructs. Now more detail concerning the production of the form within that Space is provided.

The numbers 31 x 2, 17 of the phrase *'The Producers'* refer to the Beings (the Greater and Lesser Builders) that reflect the energy of the Will (31) of Deity (17) into manifestation in the form of Love-Wisdom (2). They thereby precipitate the activity of the evolving Lives via the spiral-cyclic energies (8) that the Producers of the form utilise. They extend *sūtrātmās*[12] from the realm of the Creative Deity to the realm of form via which these energies manifest themselves. This statement mainly concerns the Greater Builders that endow the Soul aspect of Life (governed by Love-Wisdom) with the forms they must inhabit. Here the Causal form of the Soul is considered dense substance. We therefore have the appearance of the *anima mundi,* the world-Soul, the collective Sambhogakāya Flowers of humanity, and of the greater Lives

12 The links into the embodied form from divinity, the Monadic or Life aspect.

overshadowing them. The Blinded Lives constituting the dense material realms that need uplifting, transformation and eventual enlightenment are then organised into the forms, the human personality, these Souls will incarnate into.

The number 9 x 11 of the phrase *'The Producers of form'* refers to the Greater Builders, the high Initiates, from solar and planetary Logoi down, who are the supreme Producers of everything within any solar environment. They build the greater planetary spheres and Wheels of attainment wherein Monadic Life incarnates. The number 3 x 9 of this phrase implies the Lesser Builders constituting the embodied Souls of all Life.

The phrase *'no-form'* is dual, signifying the formless *arūpa* universe of the higher dimensions of perception. They are perceived as such by those incarnate in the formed realms because of the high energetic state of the embodiments of the enlightened beings and *devas* alike that are found upon the higher domains. They use the power of the Will *(icchāśakti)* to emanate, condense and crystallise form. Consequently, from no-form comes form, as well as the inevitable forces that cause the destruction or disintegration of form. The Will then says 'no' to form, the illusional appearance *(māyāvirūpa)* of the phenomena all around. This energy is an attribute of *ākāśa* manifesting upon the cosmic ethers and via the plane *buddhi,* to which the number 36 of this phrase refers. This number also implicates the sign Gemini the twins, who governs the temple of Life, and the entire etheric construct of whatever is to be. Out of the four cosmic ethers ('no-form') manifests the dense form of any world sphere.

The phrase *'form from no-form'* numerologically constitutes an interesting sequence of numbers. The numbers are: 25, 25, 11, 25, or 7, 7, 2, 7. The latter sequence directly implicates the number 777, referring to the 777 incarnations of any being, incorporating also the turning of the petals of the Head lotus. This number also veils the 777 Incarnations undertaken by a Logos as form is produced 'from no-form'. Here the work of the Lesser Builders is implied, whose efforts produce the inevitable appearance of the embodied forms. The numbers 25, 25, 11, 25 indicate that these Builders cause the appearance of the human Souls (25). These Souls represent the 'no-form' attribute for the evolving streams of sentient lives embodying the human personality and the world wherein such personalities reside. These Builders utilise the energies of Mind (5 x 5) to manifest the appearance of 'things' in the material domains.[13] The number 11 relates to the *sūtrātmās* of Logoic Will, as well as that of the Builders, projected from cosmic Mind to the *ātmic* plane and then to the mental plane in order to cause the appearance of the forms. The repetition of the same number three times implies the expression of the attribute via three levels of being: Father-Son-Mother, from cosmic to systemic to formed space.

The numbers 7, 7, 2, 7 indicate the septenary division of everything manifesting upon three levels of expression: that pertaining to the Head and the Chest regions, and to the centres lying below the diaphragm of the grand Heavenly Man. The activity of the Builders will 'fill the boundless All' with their Minds to mould the manifest world via Logoic Compassion (Love-Wisdom – 2). The objective of the 777 Incarnations is to generate this Love-Wisdom principle throughout the Logoic body of manifestation. The number 11 signifies the *sūtrātmās,* the Life-links, directed from one level of creative expression to the next, to produce the central jewel in the Heart of each appearing lotus from which the *mayāvirūpa* of these Incarnations emanate. The *sūtrātmās* become extended as the intricate *nāḍī* system of the evolving being in the formed *(rūpa)* domains.

The numbers of this phrase *('form from no-form')* add to 14, 5. The number 2 x 7 here refers to the substance of the cosmic astral plane, via which the various forms that manifest upon the systemic levels emanate. The number 5 indicates that this production of form, as well as the resolution of that form, occurs totally in the Mind as the process of the unfolding Mind (the constitution of Brahmā) of the Logos. In terms of the symbolism of the sign Gemini the twins, the phrase 'no-form' relates to the attributes of the immortal brother and 'form' relates to the appearance of the transient phenomena that is experienced as form.

The numbers of the complete phrase *'the Producers of form from no-form'* add to 16 x 10, 7, informing us that these Creative Hierarchies

---

13 The mode of such manifestation was provided in my book *Esoteric Cosmology and Modern Physics.*

are also relatively perfected (10) Christs (16),[14] existing in their seven orders preparing to undergo the next higher cycle of expression for them. They are the *'Sons of manvantaric dawn'*. These septenaries are beings of Mind-substance, who en-Soul the forms of Life.

The subsidiary phrase *'Producers of form from no-form'* (100 + 9 x 5) refers to humanity, 'the Initiates', the ninth Creative Hierarchy, who as human Souls are also Builders, that produce the forms of the human personality from the matrix of the *lunar pitris* and the Elemental Lives, which can initially be conceived as 'no-form'. It was also earlier stated that the phrase 'the producers of form' refers to the activity of various high Initiates (cosmic Humanity) that were the directing Wills responsible for the appearance of the phenomena of a planetary or solar system.

The numbers of the phrase *'Producers of form'* (7 x 3 and 7 x 12) relate to the qualities of the feminine *deva* hierarchy, whose cyclic appearance is governed by Libra the balances, the seventh sign of the zodiac. Libra specifically governs the forces of the Lesser Builders. These Builders exist as angelic triads (7 x 3) that organise the substance incorporated into all of the forms of incarnate life. They form the dense body of manifestation of a Logos. Without strict adherence to the mathematical and geometric ordering of cosmic law and the law of *karma* provided by the *deva* Hierarchies, causing the laws of physics, nought could be formed. Therefore this sign is a major determinant for the activity of these angelic Builders. The number 7 x 12 also has reference to and has the same meaning here as was provided with respect to the phrase *'Sons of manvantaric dawn'*.

The numerical breakdown of the final phrases.

> the root (38 = 11, 11), the world (42, 15), the root of the world (92, 29 = 11), root of the world (77, 23 = 5), the Devamatri (54, 18), Devamatri and Svabhavat (73, 19 = 10), the Devamatri and Svabhavat (88, 25), The bliss (31, 13), in the bliss (45, 18) the bliss of non-being (87 = 15, 33), in the bliss of non-being (101, 38 = 11), rested in the bliss (71, 26 = 8), rested in the bliss of non-being (127 = 10, 46 = 10).

14 From the human perspective they are liberated *nirvāṇees*, hence utterly perfected, but from their own perspective they have something yet to gain from incarnating in the systemic realms.

The phrase *'the root'* implies the source from which all else stems. These Builders therefore are the roots of the world Tree, the emanating source of Life from which the nourishment and strength must come to support the life of the entire world system, to anchor it firmly in cosmos. This Tree' is effectively the intricate *nāḍī* system which underlies and supports the appearance of the phenomena all experience. It is not surprising therefore that the numbers of this phrase, as well as those of the phrase *'the root of the world'* both add to 11, 2, which indicates the *nāḍīs* and the first and second Ray energies that manifest this function.

The phrase *'the world'* refers to our earth system, but it is also a symbol of manifest space, the totality of the entities and organisms that constitute an integral entity or evolving unit in cosmos. The numbers of this phrase add to 6 x 7, 3 x 5, where 6 x 7 signifies an expanded form of the Seal of Solomon that represents the procreative forces, thus evolution in the material world, wherein the Desire of the Logos finds its fulfilment. It also signifies the womb of Nature, the Angelic kingdom (the *devamātri)* from which all forms are constructed, thereby producing the attributes of the manifestation of 'the world'. The number can also symbolise the planes *(lokas)* through which the sum of manifest Life can incarnate, specifically the sixth plane of perception, the astral, whose Watery aspect signifies this Womb. The first of the sub-planes, *ādi,* bears the primal atomic substance (the permanent atoms) from which the subsidiary six planes are condensed. It thus manifests in the centre of the hexagram. The number 3 x 5 here relates to the activity of the Logoic Mind that causes the appearance of this world-sphere, and from which the human mind evolves.

The number 77 of the phrase *'root of the world'* refers to the 777 incarnations of the Logos, the completion of which is the motivation force, the root or basis, causing the formation and evolutionary unfoldment of the world. This number also refers to the various septenaries in Nature (made manifest by the Builders), which can also be considered to be the 'root of the world', especially via the emanation of seventh Ray purpose.

Blavatsky states that the *devamātri* is the '"Mother of the Gods," Aditi, or Cosmic Space. In the *Zohar,* she is called Sephira the Mother of the Sephiroth, and Shekinah in her primordial form, *in abscondito'*.[15] Elsewhere she states that:

> In the Rig Veda, Aditi, "The Boundless" or infinite Space, translated by Mr. Max Müller, "the visible infinite, visible by the naked eye (!!); the endless expanse beyond the Earth, beyond the clouds, beyond the sky," is the equivalent of "Mother-Space," coeval with "Darkness." She is very properly called the "Mother of the Gods," DEVA-MATRI, as it is from her Cosmic matrix that all the heavenly bodies of our system were born—Sun and Planets. Thus she is described, allegorically, in this wise: "Eight Sons were born from the body of Aditi; she approached the gods with seven, but cast away the eighth, Martanda," our sun. The seven sons called the Aditya are, cosmically or astronomically, the seven planets; and Sun being excluded from their number shows plainly that the Hindus may have known, and in fact knew, of a seventh planet, without calling it Uranus. But esoterically and theologically, so to say, the Adityas are, in their primitive most ancient meanings, the eight, and twelve great gods of the Hindu Pantheon.[16]

Being the Mother, *devamātri* also incorporates the twelve zodiacal energies, which are the conditioning forces governing the Lives manifesting in her Womb. The numbers of the phrase *'the Devamatri'* add to 6 x 9. In this context the number 6 refers to the matrix *(saṃsāra)* pertaining to Her Womb, which is catered for by the various combinations of the angelic Triads that manifest as the Soul aspect of the lesser kingdoms of Nature. Within this Womb will evolve the sixth degree Initiates (Chohans), who can exit it as *nirvāṇees* to embark upon their cosmic journey.

The meaning of the word *svabhāvat* was already basically explained in Blavatsky's commentary in Stanza 1:8 and elsewhere. She further states that:

> Svabhavat, the "Plastic Essence" that fills the Universe, is the root of all things. Svabhavat is, so to say, the Buddhistic concrete aspect of the abstraction called in Hindu philosophy *Mulaprakriti*. It is the body of the Soul, and that which Ether would be to Akasa, the latter

15 Ibid., Vol. 1, 53.

16 Ibid., Vol. 1, 99-100.

> being the informing principle of the former. Chinese mystics have made of it the synonym of "being."[17]

The term *svabhāva* was stated to be the self-existent, self-becoming, which develops its essential self from within outwardly by emanation or evolution. *Svabhāva* is the essence of cosmic world-stuff, the universal world-forming substance; the 'plastic essence' of both manifest and unmanifest matter underlying the existence of things. It can be equated with etheric substance, specifically the fourth cosmic ether, thus viewed in terms of being the conveyor of *akāśa*. It is the cosmic reservoir of Being, therefore of consciousness, of light and Life. *Svabhāva* may also be considered as Parabrahman-*mūlaprakṛti*, the one underlying cosmic substance, the divine source; the self-existent. In volume 1 of my *A Treatise on Mind,*[18] I state that an 'inherently existent essence' *(svabhāva)* does not necessarily prevent the appearance of 'causally produced phenomena'. It can be conceived of as a stratum of elementary substance (or energy field) that embodies forms by adapting and changing to accommodate each new appearance of phenomena. There is no reason why a matrix of elementary particles (such as the atoms discovered by science, and the quarks they are constituted of) cannot accommodate those changes as per the rearrangement of atoms for every physical change. The plastic essence may represent a Void Element (or Elements) that accommodates the characteristics of the appearance of phenomena and congeal or condense an aspect of itself to do so, which can then revert back to its primal state, as per the implications of the formula $E = mc^2$ (energy equals mass times the speed of light squared). Here energy can be considered such an 'essence', from which phenomena (mass) can appear, and recede again. Also the substance conveying thoughts or an idea allows a mental continuum to exist after the death of an individual.

The number 2 x 12 of the word *svabhāvat* is elucidating as it implicates the sign Taurus the bull, which was explained in relation to the phrase *'the Alaya of the Universe'*. This *alaya* represents the plane that is the

17 Ibid., Vol. 1, 61.

18 See *The 'Self' or 'Non-self' in Buddhism*, 97-98, 188-89.

store of this primal substance. Taurus is the sign from where the Building forces of the material universe stem, where Logoic Desire governs the fundamental Laws of group evolution, the forces of the 'homestead' (the domain of *svabhāva),* cosmically and systemically. The 'devamatri and svabhavat' constitute aspects of the *alaya.* The *devamātri* utilise the energies of the first of the signs, Aries the ram, to Mahatically instigate the beginning of what must be and the second sign, Taurus, to clothe the Ideation with form by utilising *svabhāva* to do so.

The Divine Ideation to instigate this creative Impulse emanates from the cosmic mental plane, hence it is the birthplace of the Devas and all the Creative Intelligences, the powers and forces sustaining all that IS. The energy then passes through the cosmic astral plane, wherein the Taurean impetus builds the desired forms. The *devas* then become expressed in their greater *(devamātri)* and lesser (*svabhāva*) ranks. Here *svabhāva* is viewed as the substance of the Lesser Builders, via which the *devamātri,* the Mothers, the Greater Builders can direct the building of all forms. (The *devas* are seen as being fundamentally dual.[19]) From *svabhāva* emanates all things material. *Svabhāva* can thus be considered the substance of the cosmic astral plane, whose energies are expressed in the cosmic ethers via the sum total of the associated entities. *Svabhāva* can be equated with the *ākāśa* utilised by the Lesser Builders via the plane *ātma* to produce the material universe. (See also stanza 2:5.)

Svabhāva (or *svabhāvat)* and *ākāśa* are synonymous, considered as the subtle and ethereal fluid pervading the totality of the phenomenon of the universe. *Ākāśa* is a vehicle of Life and is the higher correspondence to the *prāṇa* that vivifies our etheric forms, as was explained in my book on Cosmology:

> *Ākāśa* is that subtle supersensuous essence that pervades the space of the four cosmic ethers, our higher planes of perception. Specifically it carries the 'electricity' associated with *buddhi.*
>
> *Ākāśa* is the plastic essence that is the vehicle of a Creative Logos expressing itself as the formative forces conditioning the manifestation

---

19 As all substance is *deva,* so the concept here is that the *devamātri* represent the great directing Archangels, whilst *svabhāva* represents the great mass of lesser *deva* lives being directed, or molded as the manifesting forms.

> of all phenomena in systemic space. As such it is the transmuted correspondence of the five *prāṇas* manifesting in a human *nāḍī* system, hence there are five levels or degrees of *ākāśa* relating to the five higher planes of perception. The plane *ādi* conveys the Aetheric aspect of *ākāśa, anupādaka* conveys the Airy aspect, *ātma* the Fiery aspect, *buddhi* the Watery aspect, and the abstract domain of the Mind, the Earthy. The Aetheric, Airy and Fiery aspects can be considered the emanations from the domain of cosmic Mind, the Watery conveys the *prāṇas* from the cosmic astral ocean and the Earthy aspect is intrinsic to the cosmic dense physical plane. From this perspective *ākāśa* therefore is conveyed in terms of the Wisdoms of the five Dhyāni Buddhas, or rather, the expression *(prajñā)* of their Consorts, where Vairocana's Consort embodies the *ākāśa* of *ādi,* and so forth to Amoghasiddhi's Consort conveying the *ākāśa* of the higher mental plane. *Ākāśa* consequently is the conveyor of the force of compassion *(bodhicitta)* emanating from the cosmic Waters (the cosmic astral plane), hence the sum of the zodiacal and planetary energies that modify space. Thus it is the vehicle of the enlightened Mind, and experienced from the third to the seventh Initiations.[20]

The numbers of the phrase *'Devamatri and Svabhavat'* add to 10, the number of perfection, completion, of the whole, as well as symbolising the etheric constitution of a being *(svabhāva),* the various *chakras* and their forces *(devamātri)* that manifest via it.

The number 8 x 11 of the complete phrase *'the Devamatri and Svabhavat'* refers to the dynamic propulsion (11) of spiral-cyclic energies (8) that project the activity that will cause all to come to be. The number 8 relates to the energy field *(svabhāva)* underlying the etheric body. The *devamātri* utilise this energy field to build the various forms, the *anima mundi,* or the human Soul (5 x 5).

The meaning of *non-being* was explained in Stanza 1:7 with regards the phrase *'rested in eternal non-being—in the One being',* which thus has a similar meaning as the phrase *'rested in the bliss of non-being'* (which is the One being).

The meaning of the word *bliss* was explained in stanza 1:4, in the phrase *'The seven ways to bliss were not',* therefore needs no further

---

20 B. Balsys, *Esoteric Cosmology and Modern Physics,* (Universal Dharma, Sydney, 2020), 18.

explanation here. By the number 31 of the phrase *'the bliss'* we see that this bliss is a direct expression of the first Ray quality emanating from the Head Centre of Deity. The number 13 refers to the point within the circle of manifestation from whence this bliss emanates.

The number 9 x 5 of the phrase *'in the bliss'* indicates that those that pass the testings of Initiation will increasingly know of this bliss, whilst the Initiate of the fifth degree resides continuously in the 'bliss-field' of the *ākāśa*.

The phrase *'in the bliss of non-being'* (101, 11), provides the added information that to be 'in' this 'bliss' is to have completed one major cycle of evolution (the number 100, to thereby reside in the one fundamental Ray into which all the others have been abstracted). Then another can begin by directing the *antaḥkaraṇas* towards the *devamātri* to produce the manifestation process. Bliss involves experiencing intense first Ray energies.

The number 3 x 11 of the phrase *'the bliss of non-being'* refers to the energies from the outer tier of the Head centre of the kingdom of 'God' into which one must be abstracted if this bliss is to be experienced. The new Creative Ray (3 x 11) emanates from this place of abstraction.

Finally, the numbers of the phrases *'rested in the bliss'* and *'rested in the bliss of non-being'* add to 8 and 10 respectfully, which refer to pure energy, and to the perfection of Being by becoming non-being with respect to phenomenal existence. The One Being as well as the All-Being are experienced in this bliss. Such bliss is first experienced upon the plane *buddhi,* but the experience is exemplified in its higher correspondence, *anupādaka*.

Stanza Two part Two

Stanza 2:2 states:

> **.....Where was Silence? Where were the ears to sense it? No! There was neither Silence, nor Sound. Naught save ceaseless, eternal Breath** *(Motion),* **which knows itself not.**

Keynotes: Taurus, *buddhic* plane.

The numerical breakdown of the first few phrases:

> Where was Silence (70, 16), where were the ears (87, 24 = Taurus) the ears (31, 13), to sense it (36, 18), the ears to sense it (67 = 13, 31) Where were the ears to sense it? (123, 42). No! (11, 2), neither Silence (74, 11), neither Silence, nor Sound (113 = 100 + 13, 23 = 5), There was neither Silence (110, 29), There was neither Silence, nor Sound (149 = 100 + 49, 41 = 5).

Stanza 2:1 was generally conditioned by the planes *anupadāka* and *ātma.* They can be considered to represent the two pillars of the symbolism of Gemini, and are the two planes wherein the Greater and Lesser Builders are externalised. The point of view was also in relation to the mode of manifestation of energies from the cosmic astral plane into systemic space via these planes. There is another hiatus at the beginning of Stanza 2:2, which effectively focuses our vision to the four cosmic ethers proper, and specifically to the *buddhic* plane, wherein can be heard the Voice of the Silence, which liberates. The human ears to sense this Voice were not yet incarnate because the work of the Builders had not yet precipitated the process of the 'fall of the three into the four'. In the distinction between silence and sound this stanza at first continues with the type of dichotomy associated with the sign Gemini. The Sound of Silence is the sound of being/non-being whereby all of the modifications of existence can become known for what they truly are. The One that can command this Voice is a Master of manifest Life. The silence is an expression of the *buddhic* plane *(śūnyatā),* whilst sound and the ears to hear it relate to the dense physical plane, the ears being the most limiting of the senses.[21]

Because the sense-perception of *hearing* is an expression of the ears and the dense physical plane it brings the attributes of the seventh Ray of Ceremonial Magic, of cyclic and material Power into focus. The question of where the ears to sense it are therefore directly relates to the forces needed to create the dense physical plane, hence *saṃsāra* in general, just as the previous verse concerned the forces needed to construct its etheric prototype *(svabhāva).*

21 The sense of sight relates to the mental plane, that of touch to the astral plane, smell to the *ātmic* plane and taste to *buddhi.*

The sense of hearing consequently introduces those that will compose the form, directed by the sign Taurus the bull, the earth sign that on the reversed wheel follows Gemini in the zodiac. Taurus also relates to the potency of Logoic Desire which normally works to precipitate the form. That Desire however is not yet expressed. Taurus consequently governs the general building forces of a solar or planetary Logos, as well as the manifestation of the substance with which the forms are built. All Lives were inactive because the mantric Sound, the Aūṁ of creative Activity, had not yet been sounded to awaken them. There was no sound to detect for those with 'ears', the *deva* listeners, because the commands that would direct their building work did not exist. They are given the generic term the Pitris[22] ('Fathers'), of whom D.K. speaks at length in T.C.F. in relation to those that are the Builders of the forms of the earth sphere. We have to work with transmuted correspondences in order to comprehend their qualities in the solar system. These great Builders are later elaborated in Stanza 3:7 from that perspective.

D.K. speaks of three groups of lunar Pitris, or Fathers of the human form:

a. The Pitris who see, but touch nor handle not.

b. The Pitris who touch but see not.

c. The Pitris who hear but neither see nor touch.

> As they all have the gift of occult hearing, they are characterised as the "Pitris with the open ear"; they work entirely under the influence of the egoic mantrum.[23]

The Universe was created by means of Sound, as indicated by the first verse of John's Gospel.[24] Therefore it is logical for the Creative Deity to seek out the cause of all Sound and the Entities that were responsible for its reverberation for the manifestation of empirical space before the new *manvantara* could begin. The significance of the question 'where?' in relation to this has been discussed earlier.

---

22 Correctly spelled *pitṛ*.

23 T.C.F., 783. The term 'egoic mantrum' refers to the emanatory Word of the Sambhogakāya Flower (for which D.K. often uses the term 'ego').

24 In the beginning was the Word, and the Word was with God, and the Word was God.

The question *'Where was Silence?'* (70, 16) is one that is asked by a person that is approaching deep meditation and is ready to gain receptivity to impressions from the higher planes of perception. In Silence the inner plane work is commenced in the space of the meditation-Mind. Only therein can the soundless Sounds be heard and mantric Commands be spoken. Silence is necessary because any other sound vibration when the mantra is uttered would distort, hence destroy its purpose. This phrase therefore refers to the Logos gathering together the forces needed to meditate upon the creative process associated with world formation.

The number 70 relates to the dimensions of perception, to the sheaths via which a being incarnates. The question therefore asked is 'where was the silence of the *deva* workers that underlie these sheaths'. Mantra, not sound as we understand it, conditions their world, and all of their activity is enacted in profound quietude. To register silence there must be an accompanying zone of sound (the three worlds of human livingness) to compare it to. There was neither, simply Being existing in a state of non-being and its 'ceaseless eternal Breath'. The Being that 'slumbered' was the cosmic Christ, as indicated by the number 16, and in that sleep there was no need of either Silence or Sound, until the time of reawakening.

The numbers of the phrases *'the ears', 'the ears to sense it'* and the word *Silence* all add to 31, informing us that these 'ears' with which to *sense* (rather than 'hear') silence, as well as the silence itself, were emanations of the Will, necessitating evoking the highest aspect of Being. (The first Ray energy embodied by the Head centre of Deity.) D.K. states that hearing is: 'the first sense to be manifested; the first aspect of manifestation is that of sound, and necessarily we would expect sound to be the first thing noticed by man on the physical plane, the plane of densest manifestation, and of the most marked effects of sound, regarding it as a creating factor'.[25] The conditionings and qualities associated with the dense physical plane is a direct expression or reflection of the Will of Deity. The lowest and the highest planes of perception, the lowest and the highest principle, as well as the first and

25 *A Treatise on Cosmic Fire*, 190. D.K. also relates it as an expression of the third (Creative) Logos (196).

seventh Rays are direct expressions of each other. (As are the second and sixth, the third and the fifth, whilst the fourth is the mirror.)

One should also note that Hearing is the paramount sense for the cosmic dense physical plane. It primarily conditions the *devas* as they work to build the forms of all that is. For humans the primary sense developed is that of Touch, which allows them to contact the planes of Divinity and to express the energies of the Waters of cosmic Love. Sight is common to all, whilst the esoteric attributes of taste and smell await a future *manvantara* to be fully expressed by a human kingdom.

When the most High awakens to the 'Breathing' Sounds of the 'sleeping' Ones and Visualises the necessary resultant gain of their dreaming activity then the Command to descend into forms will echo through their interrelated ranks. The resounding mantric Sound will reverberate through via a palpable Silence, automatically assuring the appearance of the dense physical plane. The dense form then being renewed from the remnant of the past, because the material plane is the residue of the past incarnation and yet also contains the seeds for the future.

The ear manifests in the form of a *trumpet* to help amplify sound. A trumpet can also be viewed as a funnel that allows the right projection and precipitation of the substance of the Waters of space. The wide end of this trumpet constitutes the door to incarnation, according to the information provided in chapter 4:1 of the *Revelation of St. John.*[26] The smaller end relates to accessing the source of the sound by those upon the upward arc of evolution, to gain Initiation and liberation.

The numbers of the phrases *'Where were the ears to sense it?'*, *'Where were the ears?'* and *'to sense it'*, add to 123, 6 x 7, 24, Taurus and to 8.8. These numbers refer to the wide end of this trumpet, thus of material manifestation (6 x 7), caused by the expression of Logoic Desire (Taurus), via the emanation of the first three Rays of Deity (123) and spiral-cyclic motion (8.8.). The dense material world lays the foundation for the Initiation process that will be trod once people hear the Voice of Silence from the higher realms that impels them to move forwards to master the physical form that traps them in *saṃsāra*. The *devas* also evolve by means of a graded series of Initiations. Therefore

26 See also the diagram in *Rays and Initiations*, page 525.

stanza (2:1) was principally concerned with preparing to call forth the *deva* lives, the Builders *(devamātri* and *svabhāva)* that will organise the appearance of the Logoic form, whilst stanza 2:2 is principally concerned with those that will constitute its substance.

Sound is the result of the various inter-relationships between the forms in the dense material world. (The lower mental, astral and physical planes.) It is the result of 'the whole creation as it groaneth and travaileth in pain together until now'.[27] It is an effect of the third Ray of activity, of energy impacting upon what is inert. Silence (the Soundless Sound) on the other hand is associated with buddhic perception, it is the Voice of the Spirit as it relates to matter. From one perspective the higher mental plane, wherein exists the *śūnyatā-saṃsāra* nexus, is the realm where there is neither silence nor sound, for there the two meet and interrelate, causing the one to negate the other.

The numbers of the exclamation *'No!'* add to 11, 2. This determinant is placed preceding the phrases below as a clause on its own, to assert that this interrelation between silence and sound did not yet exist because though the potent first Ray cycle was manifest, the energy of the Will was not directed to cause the appearance of things, and the *nāḍīs* were not activated. The *sūtrātmā* had not yet been projected downwards for the manifestation of phenomena. Therefore naught could be 'save ceaseless, eternal Breath'.

The numbers of the phrases *'neither silence'* (11), *'nor sound'* (13 x 3) and *'There was neither silence'* (110) relate to the abovementioned projection of the Divine Will, or to the awakening of the *nāḍīs*. The Divine activity that would produce such activity (13 x 3) had not yet manifested. The phrases can also be considered with the commas removed between 'silence, nor sound', producing the numbers 100 + 13 and to 100 + 7 x 7 respectfully. Both of these numbers refer to the manifestation of a sphere of activity and of the septenaries that will inform it. As neither of these were manifest, so no beings existed that could appreciate either silence or sound. The condition of *śūnyatā* was therefore prevalent, which is Void of all such considerations. (Here viewed as the central sub-plane of the buddhic plane.)

---

27 *Romans 8:22.*

The numerical breakdown of the final phrases:

> ceaseless, eternal Breath (82, 110), eternal Breath (12), naught save ceaseless, eternal Breath 11), knows itself not (13, 22), which knows itself not (10, 28), which knows itself (78 = 15, 24 = Taurus).

The meaning of the *'ceaseless, eternal Breath'*[28] has been explained in stanzas 1:6 and 1:8 in such phrases as *'to be outbreathed by'* and *'Life pulsated unconscious in universal Space'*, where we saw that it was associated with the in and out-breathing of the 777 incarnations, plus that associated with the duration of the seven Eternities. This phrase therefore needs little further explanation.

The word *ceaseless* means never-ending, and relates to the Logoic Soul upon the cosmic higher mental plane that thus 'Breathes' as it projects the forms of which it is the progenitor into and out of incarnation. The word *eternal* esoterically refers to the Monadic or Soul aspect of Life, depending upon the duration of the eternity in question.

The number 10 of the phrase *'ceaseless, eternal Breath'* relates to the state of abstraction at this stage of the expression of cosmic Being. The *'eternal Breath'* (12) here indicates the Heart centre's own rhythm in expressing the pulsations of the energy of *buddhi,* into which the 'sleeping' one is abstracted. The Breathing manifests subjectively via the twelve cycles of the zodiac, signifying an internal clock for the duration of each of the Breaths of the solar and planetary Logoi.

The number 11 of the phrase *'naught save ceaseless, eternal Breath'* signifies the combined first and second Ray energy that causes the accomplishment of the process of inhalation and exhalation during this *pralaya* period. This concerns the transmission of energy, of internal motion within the slumbering One.

Concerning the meaning of *Breath,* of *Being* and *non-being,* H.P.B. states that:

a. The idea that things can ease to exist and still BE, is a fundamental one in Eastern psychology. Under this apparent contradiction in terms there rests a fact of Nature to realise which in the mind, rather than to argue about words, is the important thing. A

---

28 Note that the later editions remove the comma, which is numerologically correct here.

familiar instance of a similar paradox is afforded by chemical combination[29]....Existence as water may be said to be, for Oxygen and Hydrogen, a state of Non-Being, which is "more real Being" than their existence as gases; and it may faintly symbolise the condition of the Universe when it goes to sleep, or ceases to be, during the "Nights of Brahmā" – to awaken or re-appear again, when the dawn of the new Manvantara recalls it to what we call existence.

b. The "Breath" of the One Existence is used in its application only to the spiritual aspect of Cosmogony by Archaic esotericism; otherwise, it is replaced by its equivalent on the material plane – Motion. The One Eternal Element, or element-containing Vehicle, is *Space,* dimensionless in every sense; co-existent with which are – endless *duration,* primordial (hence indestructible) *matter,* and *motion* – absolute "perpetual motion" which is the "breath" of the "One" Element. This breath, as seen, can never cease, not even during the Pralayic eternities...

But the "Breath of the One Existence" does not, all the same, apply to the *One Causeless Cause* or the "All-Be-ness" (in contradistinction to All-Being, which is Brahmā, or the Universe). Brahmā (or Hari) the four-faced god, who, after lifting the Earth out of the waters, "accomplished the Creation," is held to be only the instrumental, and not, as clearly implied, the ideal Cause. No Orientalist, so far, seems to have thoroughly comprehended the real sense of the verses in the Purāna, that treat of "creation."

Therein Brahmā is the cause of the potencies that are to be generated subsequently for the work of "creation."... If, in the Vedanta and Nyaya, *nimitta* is the efficient cause, as contrasted with *upadāna*, the material cause, (and in the Sankhya, *pradhāna* implies the functions of both); in the Esoteric philosophy, which reconciles all these systems, and the nearest exponent of which is the Vedanta as expounded by the Advaita Vedantists, none but the *upadāna* can be speculated upon; that which is, in the minds of the Vaishnavas (the Vasishtadvaita), as the ideal in contradistinction to the real – or Parabrahm and Ishvara – can find no room in published speculations, since that ideal even is a misnomer, when applied to that of which no human reason, even that of an adept, can conceive.[30]

29 Blavatsky, *The Secret Doctrine,* Vol. 1, 54.

30 Ibid., Vol.1., 54-56.

To *know* necessitates the existence of consciousness and its ability to cognise objects of perception, thus that *'which knows itself not'* (7 x 4) is a mind/Mind that possesses no objects of perception by means of which it can revel in its own awareness. The number 7 x 4 here refers to the quaternary of the personality (consisting of the mental, astral, etheric and dense forms), which is not incarnate. Thus there is no way to know itself. Also, because consciousness is abstracted into the fourth plane of perception, *buddhi (śūnyatā,* 7 x 4*)* during the fourth Eternity, so the quaternary, the agent that is ceaselessly breathed in and out, can have no conscious perception, thus 'knows itself not.' This number refers collectively to a disincarnate humanity, abstracted in *śūnyatā.* Human Souls had no means of expressing the need to Know with respect to manifesting reincarnating forms.

The number 22 of the phrase *'knows itself not'* refers to the various zodiacal and planetary energies that together constitute and motivate the evolving form. When the quaternary does 'know itself', as indicated by the numbers of the phrases *'which knows'* and *'which knows itself'* (which add to 52, 16, 3 x 5 and 2 x 12 respectively), then we see that in a new *manvantara* (52) where the Christ principle is active (16) the evolution of the mind (3 x 5) allows one to learn and so Know. The twelve Creative Hierarchies, plus the zodiacal potencies projected into the Womb of time and space by Taurus the bull (2 x 12) will then be manifest.

Concerning consciousness (the ability to know oneself) and its relation to Absolute consciousness ('unconsciousness'). Blavatsky states:

> To know itself or oneself, necessitates consciousness and perception (both limited faculties in relation to any subject except Parabrahman), to be cognized. Hence the "Eternal Breath which knows itself not." Infinity cannot comprehend Finiteness. The Boundless can have no relation to the bounded and the conditioned. In the occult teachings, the Unknown and the Unknowable MOVER, or the Self-Existing, is the absolute divine Essence. And thus being *Absolute* Consciousness, and *Absolute* Motion – to the limited senses of those who describe this indescribable – it is unconsciousness and immovableness. Concrete consciousness cannot be predicated of abstract, Consciousness, any more than the quality wet can be predicated of water – wetness being its own attribute and the cause or the wet quality in other things. Consciousness implies limitations and qualifications; something to

be conscious of, and someone to be conscious of it. But Absolute Consciousness contains the cognizer, the things cognized and the cognition, all three in itself and all three *one*[31]...We call Absolute Consciousness "unconsciousness," because it seems to us that it must necessarily be so, just as we call the Absolute, "Darkness," because to out finite understanding it appears quite impenetrable, yet we recognize fully that our perception of such things does not do them justice. We involuntarily distinguish in our minds, for instance, between unconscious absolute consciousness, and unconsciousness, by secretly endowing the former with some indefinite quality that corresponds, on a higher plane than our thoughts can reach, with what we know as consciousness in ourselves. But this is not any kind of consciousness that we can manage to distinguish from what appears to us as unconsciousness.[32]

Stanza Two part Three

Stanza 2:3 states:

The hour had not yet struck; the Ray had not yet flashed into the Germ; the Matri-padma *(mother lotus)* **had not yet swollen.**

Keynotes: Aries, mental plane.

The numerical breakdown of the verse.

The hour (41 = 5, 14), had not yet struck (60 = Leo, 15), not yet struck (47 = 11), The hour had not yet struck (101, 29 = 11), the Ray (32, 14), not yet flashed (55, 19), had not yet flashed (68 = 17 x 4, 23 = 5), the Ray had not yet flashed (100, 37 = 10), the Germ (40, 13 = 4), flashed into the Germ (90, 27), not yet flashed into the Germ (117 = 13 x 9, 36), had not yet flashed into the Germ (130, 40), The Ray had not yet flashed into the Germ (162 = 18 x 9, 100 + 31 x 2, 54), The Matri-padma (57 = 12), had not yet swollen (68 = 14, 23 = 5), not yet swollen (55, 19 = 10), The Matri-padma had not yet swollen (125, 35 = 7 x 5).

---

31 Ibid., 56.

32 Ibid.

Stanza 2:3 relates to Aries the ram where the martial, impulsive energy of the Ram is signified by the eventual flashing of the Ray (the procreative energy of the Father) into the Germ, which would cause the pregnancy of the *mātripadma*. But the time was not yet. In our visioning we are also brought to the conditionings of the higher mental plane, wherein this Germ finds opportunity to 'swell'.

Though Aries here follows immediately after the sign Taurus and is part of the zodiac that retrogresses from Pisces to Aries via Aquarius, it is also the start of another (rectified) zodiacal wheel that has changed direction, moving from Aries to Pisces via Taurus. This is important to note, because Stanzas 2:3-6 deal with the process that immediately precedes the awakening of a solar system, where the procreative forces are preparing to incarnate via the rectified wheel.

The word *hour* again introduces the question of time, which was explained in Stanza 1:2. We saw that when time does exist then it is the result of the activities of the Soul in the realms of form, which it creates. The consideration of time concerns the development of the mind/Mind by a humanity, allowing it to conquer all the cycles associated with the material world. An hour is one twelfth part of the day, and then of the night. Esoterically therefore it relates to a twelfth part of the journey of the Sun through the heavens, thus to the signs (or a sign) of the zodiac, which are hours in the great Day in the Life of Brahmā. The specific sign that would start this new day has therefore not yet appeared.

The numbers of the phrase *'had not yet struck'* add to 60, 15. This hour therefore had not yet struck for the commencement of a new cycle of material evolution (60) and the evolution of the mind therein (15). The number 60 also refers to the fifth sign of the zodiac, Leo the lion, who controls the evolution of self-consciousness, individualised humanity, as well as the conditionings of the Sambhogakāya Flower upon the higher mental plane. The number 14 of the phrase *'the hour'* indicates that the cycle for material plane involvement had not yet begun, as the energy from the cosmic astral had not yet 'struck' the dense physical plane.

The numbers of the phrases *'not yet struck'* and *'the hour has not yet struck'* add either to 11 or to 101. These numbers indicate that the first Ray energies of the Will of Deity had not yet projected the *sūtrātmās* that would initiate the beginning of the new *manvantara*. This Ray is the one primordial Ray that synthesises the qualities of the seven major Rays. By the number 32 of the phrase *'the Ray'* we see that this Ray is a second Ray emanation (which produces the evolution of consciousness) from the Head centre of the (solar) Deity. Accordingly it is the Ineffable central store of Light (the Son aspect) in our solar or planetary system.

Concerning this Ray H.P.B. states:

> The ray of the "Ever Darkness" becomes, as it is emitted, a ray of effulgent light or life, and flashes into the "Germ" – the point in the Mundane Egg, represented by matter in its abstract sense. But the term "Point" must not be understood as applying to any particular point in Space, for a germ exists in the centre of every atom, and these collectively form "the Germ;" or rather, as no atom can be made visible to our physical eye, the collectivity of these (if the term can be applied to something which is boundless and infinite) forms the noumenon of eternal and indestructible matter.[33]

To have *flashed* is to have produced a brief sudden burst of bright light, as in lightning. This light will activate the Germ of the World Egg within the Womb of the cosmic Mother, becoming that Womb's central dynamo. This Germ is the seed *bīja* that lays the foundation for the *maṇḍala* to come. The *bīja* can also be viewed as the permanent atom. The 'flash' thereby becomes the Logoic or Monadic Word instigating the seed quality for the birth of a new world system.

The numbers of the phrases *'the Germ'* and *'had not yet flashed into the germ'* add to 4 x 10, which here relates to our particular earth Chain and also its fourth globe, which is in its fourth Round. It can also refer to the solar system which is of the fourth order.[34] The numbers of the latter phrase also add to 13 x 10, which indicates that the time for the instigation of a new cycle of activity (13 x 10), of the great year of Brahmā, had not yet appeared.

By the numbers 17 x 4, 5 of the phrase *'had not yet flashed'* we see that the Ray that emanated from the seat of Power (Throne) of the Logos (17 x 4) had not yet been emitted by that Mind (5). This is

---

33 Ibid., Vol. 1, 57.

34 See also Stanza 2:5-6.

further exemplified by the number 55 of the phrase *'not yet flashed'*, which implicate the attributes of such a Mind, of the use of its Will to project energy into the Germ to cause its awakening.

The number 100 of the phrase *'the Ray had not yet flashed'* is the number of the great perfection, indicating here that the Ray that will produce evolutionary perfection had not yet flashed because the universe was still in its *pralaya* period. The time for a new *manvantara* (symbolised also by the number 100) has not yet begun.

The numbers 4 x 9 and 3 x 12 of the phrase *'not yet flashed into the Germ'* indicate that the matrix for the temple of the Lord (Gemini the twins – 3 x 12) had not yet formed for the Ray to vitalise it with the initiating energy of Life (4 x 9). The four cosmic ethers had not yet been prepared to receive the energy that initiates the purpose of the fourth Round.

That such activity concerns the process whereby opportunity to undertake Initiation by the Logos is possible, and for all concerned with the awakening of the Germ, is indicated by the numbers 4 x 9 above, 9 x 10, 3 x 9 of the phrase *'flashed into the Germ'*, also to the numbers 6 x 9 and 100 + 31 x 2 of the complete phrase, *'The Ray had not yet flashed into the Germ'*. The Monad can be considered an Initiate of the sixth degree, hence the hour for the Ray that emanates from it to impregnate the Germ of the Soul was not yet. Neither was it time for the Logos (9 x 10) to generate the Will-to-Manifest (31 x 2). Therefore the Logos (the Monad being an aspect of the Mind of such a One) remains 'alone', 'boundless', in its *parinirvāṇa,* the summation of all there was. The number 3 x 9 here refers to the Soul, which is considered an Initiate of the third degree. It was similarly not ready to 'flash' its periodical Ray into the germ of the physical permanent atom.

The *mātripadma* is the mother Lotus, which refers to a major *chakra* in the body. There are three *chakras* in contention here. First, the Head lotus, because its activity governs all, and is activated by the Soul when it incarnates into a new form. Next, the Sacral centre, because it is the organ of physical generation, governing all forces of procreation and the vivification of the entire *nāḍī* system. It governs the Gonad centres and hence the energies that condition the Womb. The main interpretation however is the Solar Plexus centre that governs all of the forces of the *chakras* below the diaphragm, which are activated at the beginning of new cycle of evolution. They sustain by far the greater part of the evolutionary Day, until the time comes for the awakening of the Head lotus via the Heart and Throat centres. The process of such awakening will be described in the later stanzas. All of stanza two is a preview of what is to come, by calling forth all of the energies and forces that will enact and sustain the forthcoming *manvantara*.

H.P.B. provides a good description of some of the symbolical meanings of the lotus in Her commentary, as well as throughout *The Secret Doctrine.*

> One of the symbolical figures for the Dual creative power in Nature (matter and force on the material plane) is *Padma,* the water-lily of India. The Lotus is the product of heat (fire) and water (vapour or Ether); fire standing in every philosophical and religious system, even in Christianity, as a representation of the Spirit of Deity, the active, male, generative principle; and Ether, or the Soul of matter, the light of the fire, for the passive female principle from which everything in this Universe emanated. Hence, Ether or Water is the Mother, and Fire is the Father[35]...The Lotus, or Padma, is, moreover, a very ancient and favourite symbol for the Kosmos itself, and also for man. The popular reasons given are, firstly, the fact just mentioned, that the Lotus-seed contains within itself a perfect miniature or the future plant, which typifies the fact that the spiritual prototypes of all things exist in the immaterial world before these things become materialised on Earth. Secondly, the fact that the Lotus plant grows up through the water, having its root in the Ilus, or mud, and spreading its flower in the air above. The Lotus thus typifies the life of man and also that of the Kosmos; for the Secret Doctrine teaches that the elements of both are the same, and that both are developing in the same direction. The root of the Lotus sunk in the mud represents material life, the stalk passing up through the water typifies existence in the astral world, and the flower floating on the water and opening to the sky is emblematical of spiritual being.[36]

The *mātripadma* is synonymous with the 'Womb' of all Being, as indicated by the numbers of this word which add to 6 x 7 and of

---

35 Ibid., 58.

36 Ibid., 58-59.

the phrase *'the Matri-padma'* which add to 12. As previously stated, the number 6 x 7 signifies an expanded form of the Seal of Solomon, representing the procreative forces, thus evolution in the material world, wherein the Desire of the Logos finds its fulfilment, plus the Womb of Nature, the Angelic kingdom (the *devamātri).* Here the number 12 implies that this *mātripadma* is in the form of a twelve-petalled Lotus, of which each petal is embodied by one or other of the twelve Creative Hierarchies that are responsible for the appearance of all forms in the solar system. This relates to the Head lotus, the first of the three above interpretations of this *padma.*

All of the numbers of the rest of the phrases associated with *'The Matri-padma had not yet swollen'* add to powers of 5 (5 x 11, 5 x 5 x 5, and to 7 x 5) which indicate the supreme importance of the Mind in the Creative process (here the formation of a world-sphere). The number 5 x 11 refers to the complete mastery of the mental process that allows this swelling or Creation to proceed. The number 5 x 7 implies that this activity will proceeded until the major fifth Round of the planetary or solar cycle when the third Ray of Mathematically Exact Activity will have fulfilled its function (to be superseded by the second Ray cycle and then the first or destroyer Ray) because the constitution of Brahmā will have evolved to its fullest capacity. It also has a similar significance as the number 25 x 5, but here more specifically to the Rays of Mind being expressed into manifestation, to cause this expansion of mind/ Mind in manifestation.

The number 5 x 5 x 5 (25 x 5) refers to the complete evolution of the principle of Mind on all three major levels of perception (the cause of this swelling of the *mātripadma:* that associated with the kingdom of 'God', the Hierarchy of enlightened Being, humanity and the world of illusion. The number 25 x 5 has a direct relationship to the five Kumāras (Dhyāni Buddhas) that govern the five planes of Brahmā and to the five Schemes that are responsible for the development of Mind in the solar system. (Or Their correspondence in the earth Scheme.) The number 125 also relates to the complete *maṇḍala* of the Sambhogakāya Flower-Head lotus interrelation, to the complete awakening of the Head centre.

The number 25 refers to the Soul on the higher mental plane. The place for the 'swelling' of the *mātripadma* begins upon the *ātmic* plane, but its full expression is upon the higher mental plane wherein the Sambhogakāya Flowers of a human kingdom are established. When multiplied by 5 it implies that which constitutes the Soul-attribute of the five lower kingdoms in Nature, Hierarchies or planes of perception. They are governed by the Dhyāni Buddhas. All this did not exist, for the *'The Matri-padma had not yet swollen'*.

Stanza Two part Four

Stanza 2:4 states:

> **Her Heart had not yet opened for the One Ray to enter, thence to fall as three into four in the lap of Maya.**
>
> *Keynotes:* Taurus (rectified), *buddhic* plane.
>
> The numerical breakdown of the first phrase:
>
> Her Heart (47 = 11, 11), not yet opened (59 = 14, 14), had not yet opened (72, 18), Her Heart had not yet opened (119 = 11, 29 = 11), The One Ray (48, 21), to enter (34, 16), for the One Ray to enter (103, 40), Her Heart had not yet opened for the One Ray (188 = 17, 53 = 8), had not yet opened for the One Ray to enter (175 = 7 x 25, 58 = 13), Her Heart had not yet opened for the One Ray to enter (222, 69 = 15).

In this stanza the sign Taurus the bull upon the rectified wheel is implicated. Here Taurus embodies the opened Eye that projects the One Ray into 'the lap of Maya'. This represents the energies from the cosmic astral plane (systemic Love), which will consequently awaken the Heart centre of whatever is to be in the new solar system. The Heart centre circulates the *prāṇas* that vitalises the evolving form. It is the source of Life to any incarnate being. The focus therefore is upon the Logoic *nāḍī* system, and consequently the plane *buddhi* upon the upward way of this rectified Wheel. For a Logos these *prāṇas* manifest in the form of *ākāśa*. Logoic Desire had not yet awakened, as such a One contemplates what forces need to be generated to produce the awakening of new Life.

The Heart centre can be conceived as the heart of the *mātripadma* manifesting as a twelve petalled lotus, where each petal bears one or other of the twelve Creative Hierarchies that are responsible for the appearance of all Lives in the solar system. By the number 11 of the phrase *'Her Heart'* we see that the energies of the Logoic *nāḍī* system is implicated.

As this centre had not yet opened, so it is closed in a bud-like fashion, as symbolised by the cypher zero, and when we include the germ this produces the circle with the dot in the centre (⊙). The central dot here represents the Heart as this Germ, and is a 'Door' through which the 'One Ray' can pass. The *mātripadma* however, being feminine and quiescent, is symbolised by the circle with the plain stroke across it (⊖), esoterically signifying the cosmic Waters. Upon awakening, as a consequence of being fertilised by the masculine 'One Ray' (⦶), the *sūtrātmā,* which grows the *nāḍī* system and from this the *chakras.* From an energy viewpoint the petals of the *mātripadma* then awaken in ordered sequence from the centre of the sphere to the periphery. (The *mātripadma* can thereby be conceived as any of the *chakras* of an embodied system.) When viewed in terms of the four directions of space we then have the symbol of the plain cross in the circle (⊕), which presents an idea of materiality, of energy travelling in the four directions in space, or of the Base of Spine centre. As more of the petals of this Flower awaken, so the intermediate positions of this cross appear, making the eight-armed cross of direction, then the twelve petalled lotus and eventually the 1,000 petalled lotus.

The number 14 of the phrase *'not yet opened'* refers to the cosmic astral Waters that have not yet been poured upon this Flower to open its petals. The meaning of this with regards the 'swelling' and consequent 'opening' of the *mātripadma* was explained earlier.

In this light we see that the number 11 of the phrase *'Her Heart had not yet opened'* signifies the *sūtrātmā* that is projected by the Mother, who bears her version of the first Ray energy that is needed to awaken the petals of creative unfoldment.

The numbers of the phrase *'had not yet opened'* add to 72 (6 x 12). This number refers to the average number of beats per minute for the coursing of Life's blood, and in terms of years, the ideal life-span of a person, of evolution in the realms of form. 'Her Heart had not yet opened' for such activity. We also have the sixth sign of the zodiac, Libra the balances, that governs the *karma* of the great wheel of the Law and of the lesser wheels that control Life. The main implication here however refers to the Sacral centre (a six petalled lotus), which is the organ of the containment of the directed *prāṇas* from the Heart centre as it works to vitalise the form. The *prāṇas* flow from the Sacral centre through the *iḍā* and *piṅgalā nāḍīs* to vitalise the various *chakras* and the sum of the form. Thus the *chakras* of the entire *prāṇic* triangle are here implicated, being the Heart, Diaphragm and Sacral centres.

The Heart is the hub of the wheel of Life, which at this stage was not activate, thus was not turning, consequently the cycles governing the rate of expansion (awakening) of the petals of the *chakras* governing appearance of things had not yet begun.

The meaning of a Ray was explained in Stanza 2:3. Here it is qualified by the word 'One', implying singular, primal. The number 3 x 11 of the phrase *'One Ray'* add to 33 and to 15. The number 33 refers to the activity aspect of the kingdom of 'God', the formation of the outer boundaries of that kingdom, the Head centre from whence emanate the symbolic 33,000,000,000 Creative Intelligences responsible for the totality of all manifested Life. The number 33 also signifies the ring-pass-not of the Creative Deity, within which His/Her Personality is confined. Its Mahatic activity (15) thereby makes the planetary or solar Logos 'the One', the Singular, apparently 'separate' from all other solar or planetary Personalities and Their respective spheres of influence.

The numbers of the phrase *'the One Ray'* are 4 x 12 and 3 x 7. The number 4 x 12 refers to the fourth sign of the zodiac, Cancer the crab, signifying the open gates of the incarnation process, which this Ray causes—the fall of Spirit into matter and of all the related cycles of experience. Then number 3 x 7 refers to the three dense material sub-planes *'for the One Ray to enter'* (100 + 3, 4 x 10), to commence a new great cycle of activity of the totality of Being (100 + 3), governed by the third or Mother aspect of Deity. The number 4 x 10 here implies the beginning of the fourth Round, or the fourth globe, or Chain of the fourth Scheme, being the focus of the stanzas in relation to the formation of our solar Logos.

The numbers of the phrase *'to enter'* add to 17 x 2, 16, signifying that it was not yet time for the Christ, the Son (16), reflecting the attributes of Deity (17 x 2) to enter into the germ of the *mātripadma.*

The number 17 of the phrase *'Her Heart had not yet opened for the One Ray'* indicates that the time had not yet come for the active demonstration of the Creative Deity to awaken the Heart of incarnate being.

It was previously stated that the number 7 x 25 of the phrase *'had not yet opened for the One Ray to enter'* refers to the seven Creative Hierarchies that are to inform the planetary or solar form. The number can also refer to all seven Chains of a planetary system (or seven Schemes associated with a solar system), each of which are in the form of a *mātripadma* that had not yet awakened, because the creative process had not actively begun.

The numbers of the complete phrase *'Her Heart had not yet opened for the One Ray to enter'* add to 222. This number refers to the fact that this incarnation of the solar Logos is that of the second, the Son aspect of Deity, of the major second Ray cycle, which is the purpose of this Heart's activity to awaken on all levels of being. The opening of the Heart is thus the expression of the Love and Compassion of the Logos from the highest Logoic level (200) to the manifestation of the expression of the Creative Hierarchies (20), and then the embodied form (2). Consequently, the cycle for the appearance of the Logoic Christ-principle had not yet begun.

The numerical breakdown of the second phrase:

> thence to fall (49, 22), to fall (21, 12), three into four (75, 21), as three into four (77, 23 = 5), the lap of Maya (51 = 17 x 3, 15), of Maya (25, 7), in the lap of Maya (65, 20, 11), thence to fall as three into four (126, 45), to fall as three into four (98 = 49 x 2, 35), to fall as three into four in the lap of Maya (163, 55), thence to fall as three into four in the lap of Maya (191, 65).

Esoterically, *'to fall'* means the descent into incarnation, of dense material involvement into cyclic time and embodied form. The numbers 7 x 7 and 22 of the phrase *'thence to fall'* infer that falling involves incarnating into and embodying all the sheaths (robes), the planes of perception, Schemes, Chains, Rounds and Races of a planetary or solar Logos (7 x 7). The number 12 + 10 implies the Hierarchical and planetary energies that embody the totality of the substance of these sheaths, of the Womb of space-time. As the numbers of the phrase *'to fall'* add to (7 x 3, 12) so this falling is into the three dense (cosmic) sub-planes of perception, via the twelve petals of the *mātripadma*. Another great Round of evolution thereby commences, governed by the constellations of the zodiac, starting with Aries the ram (12).

The numbers of the phrase *'as three into four'* add to 77, implying the undertaking of the 777 incarnations, into which the Logos is to 'fall' again. Geometrically the reference is to the triangle, symbolising the spiritual triad, that is in the process of becoming the square of the manifestation.[37] As the meaning of this sentence will also be elaborated in Stanza 3:4, therefore it is not necessary to provide detail here. The 'four' is effectively an illusion and always tends to revert back to the triad. The interrelation between the two produces the Seal of Solomon. Note that the numbers of the phrase *'into four'* add to 10, indicating the totality of Being, of completion.

The numbers of the phrase *'three into four'* also add to 7 x 3, 25 x 3. This number 25 x 3 refers to the spiritualisation of the mental plane by response to triadial energies. Specifically it refers to the three Buddhas of Activity, the activity aspect of the Five Kumāras (or their cosmic correspondences) that disseminate the energy of Mind to the entire body of manifestation of a planetary or solar Logos. The entire mode of the evolution of consciousness can thereby begin.

The *lap* is the front part of the human body, from the waist to the knees when in a sitting position, and also metaphorically, an area of responsibility and control. Esoterically, it includes all of the psychic centres below the diaphragm, the Solar Plexus, Sacral and the Base of Spine centres, plus the minor centres (the Inner Round). These centres are particularly concerned with the act of physical and emotional activity, the birth of a 'Son'. A Logos must therefore return to incarnate Life via these centres. These *chakras* are also used by an incarnate being during the early formative years of development, which

37 See chapter 7 of my book *Esoteric Cosmology and Modern Physics* for detail concerning the geometric view of the manifestation of space.

is dominated by the Mother (the third Ray aspect of Deity). A major function of *'the Lap'* (8) is to assimilate, store and transmit energy (food-*prāṇa)* throughout the system via the Splenic and Sacral centres and the *nāḍīs* that stem from them.

Māyā is the principle of illusion, specifically the ability of matter to veil the light of divinity, the Spirit. It is the glamour that is expressed on etheric levels by the highly vitalised forms built therein by the desire-mind. It is consequently the cause of the transient phenomena of the world that we see around us. As far as the Logos or a humanity is concerned physical involvement *is* incarnation into the etheric plane (cosmic or Systemic), because the dense physical realm is not considered a principle. It is simply an automation controlled by the energies manifesting through the etheric body.

The numbers 5 x 5 and 7 of the phrase *'of Maya'* indicate that *māyā* is controlled by the thinker on the higher mental plane, which governs its effects on the dense physical plane (7). The entire quaternary is generally dominated by *māyā*. The purpose of *māyā* is to allow the thinker to master the attributes of mind (5 x 5).

The numbers of the phrase *'the lap of Maya'* add to 17 x 3, 15. The number 17 x 3 refers to the activity aspect of the Logos which incarnates into this 'lap', whilst the number 3 x 5 refers to the activity of the mind, which causes this *māyā* to be.

The numbers 11, 20, 13 x 5, of the phrase *'in the lap of Maya'* indicate the first (11), second (20), and third Ray (13 x 5) activities that will manifest in this 'lap' at the appropriate cycle to effect the totality of the body of manifestation of the Logos that will fall into incarnation.

The numbers of the *remaining phrases* add to 9 x 14, 5 x 9, 100 + 7 x 9, 49 x 2, 7 x 5, 55 and 13 x 5. These numbers imply that a Logos (9 x 14) plus the Creative Hierarchies (100 + 7 x 9, 5 x 9) are thus to fall into generation, the Rounds, planetary Schemes, Chains, etc. (7 x 7 x 2), and also that this falling process implicates cycles of Initiation attainment (9) for them. Also, what falls or manifests in time and space, is the principle of mind/Mind (7 x 5, 55 and 13 x 5) that experiences the evolutionary process and the conversion of the primary substance of 'the four' into the principle that evolves.

H.P.B's essential commentary of Stanza 2:4:

The Primordial Substance had not yet passed out of its precosmic latency into differentiated objectivity, or even become the (to man, so far) invisible Protyle of Science. But, as the hour strikes and it becomes receptive of the Fohatic impress of the Divine Thought (the Logos, or the male aspect of the Anima Mundi, Alaya) – its heart opens. It differentiates, and the THREE (Father, Mother, Son) are transformed into four. Herein lies the origin of the double mystery of the Trinity and the immaculate Conception. The first and Fundamental dogma of Occultism is Universal Unity (or Homogeneity) under three aspects. This led to a possible conception of Deity, which as an absolute unity must remain forever incomprehensible to finite intellects...[38]

The idea of *Absolute* Unity would be broken entirely in our conception, had we not something concrete before our eyes to contain that Unity. And the Deity, being absolute, must be omnipresent, hence not an atom but contains IT within itself. The roots, the trunk, and its many branches, are three distinct objects, yet they are one tree. Say the Kabalists: "The Deity is one, because It is infinite. It is triple, because It is ever manifesting." This manifestation is triple in its aspects, for it requires, as Aristotle has it, three principles for every natural body to become objective: privation, form, and matter. Privation meant, in the mind of the great philosopher, that which the Occultists call the prototypes impressed in the Astral Light – the lowest plane and world of Anima Mundi. The union of these three principles depends upon a fourth – the LIFE which radiates from the summits of the Unreachable, to become an universally diffused Essence on the manifested planes of Existence. And this QUATERNARY (Father, Mother, Son, as a UNITY, and a Quaternary, as a living manifestation) has been the means of leading to the very archaic Idea of Immaculate Conception, now finally crystallised into a dogma of the Christian Church, which has carnalized this metaphysical idea beyond any common sense[39]... The "Son" of the Immaculate Celestial Virgin (or the undifferentiated cosmic protyle, Matter in its infinitude) is born again on Earth as the Son of the terrestrial Eve – our mother Earth, and becomes Humanity as a total – past, present, and future – for Jehovah, or Jod-he-vau-he is androgyne, or both male female. Above, the Son is the whole KOSMOS; below, he is MANKIND. The triad or triangle becomes

38 Ibid., Vol. 1, 58.

39 Ibid., Vol.1, 58-59.

Tetraktis, the Sacred Pythagorean number, the perfect Square, and a 6-faced cube on Earth. The Macroprosopus (the Great Face) is now Microprosopus (the lesser face); or, as the Kabalists have it, the "Ancient of Days," descending on Adam Kadmon whom he uses as his vehicle to manifest through, gets transformed into Tetragrammaton. It is now in the "Lap of Maya," the Great Illusion, and between itself and the Reality has the Astral Light, the great Deceiver of man's limited senses, unless Knowledge through Paramarthasatya comes to the rescue.[40]

Stanza Two part Five

Stanza 2:5 states:

> **The Seven *(Sons)* were not yet born from the Web of Light. Darkness alone was Father-Mother, Svabhavat; and Svabhavat was in Darkness.**

Keynotes: Gemini, *ātmic* plane.

The numerical breakdown of the first phrase:

The Seven (35, 8), not yet born (49, 13), The Seven were not yet (86 = 14, 23 = 5), The Seven were not yet born (108, 27), not yet born from the web (101, 29 = 11), the web (27, 9), born from the web (74 = 11), from the Web (52, 16), the Web of Light (68, 23 = 5), The Seven were not yet born from the Web (160, 43 = 7), from the Web of Light (93, 30), born form the Web of Light (115 = 23 x 5, 34), not yet born from the Web of Light (142 = 100 + 42, 43 = 7), were not yet born from the Web of Light (166 = 100 + 66, 49), The Seven were not yet born from the Web of Light (201, 57 = 12).

Gemini Twins is implicated in this stanza via the symbolism of the Father-Mother and the building of the 'Web of Light', because Gemini rules the bloodstream, the *nāḍīs* and the etheric web. It also governs the dualities in the zodiac, hence those found in this Stanza: Light and Darkness, Father-Mother, Svabhāvat and Darkness. *(Svabhāva* can consequently also be conceived of in terms of Light.) At this stage therefore the plastic substance *(svabhāva)* informing the cosmic ethers

40 Ibid., Vol.1, 60.

that was to be used to form this web was now in the process of being organised by the Logos prior to the externalisation of a concrete form. Upon the rectified wheel we are brought to *ātmic* plane, the plane of the Creative aptitude of the Mother.

The meaning of *'the Seven'* was explained in Stanza 1:6, in reference to the phrase *'the Seven Sublime Lords'*. They are the planetary Regents, or Logoi to a group of seven solar systems, planetary Schemes, Chains, globes, races, planes of perception, kingdoms in Nature, Rays or Hierarchies, depending upon ones angle of vision. With regards to our earth Scheme they are the Regents, the five exoteric Kumāras (that support the throne of 'God', plus the One that sits upon it (Who is triune in His essential nature), or seven when the totality of Deity is considered. Each of the Seven is a Regent of one or other of the seven Chains to our planetary Scheme. Blavatsky states that in these Stanzas *The Secret Doctrine* is concerned 'chiefly, if not entirely, with our Solar System, and especially with our planetary chain. The "Seven Sons," therefore, are the creators of the latter. This teaching will be explained more fully hereafter.'[41]

The numbers of the phrase *'not yet born'* add to 7 x 7, as also do those of the phrase *'were not yet born from the Web of Light'* (also 100 + 66), whilst the numbers of the phrase *'not yet born from the Web of Light'* add to 7. Those of the phrase *'born from the Web of Light'* add to 7 and to 17 x 2. Those of the phrase *'The Seven were not yet born from the Web'* also add to 7 and to 16 x 10, whilst those of the phrase *'from the Web'* add to 7, 16 and to 52.

The meaning of the number 7 here, as referring to the primary seven is obvious, whilst the number 7 x 7 indicates that these 'Seven Sons', the 'Sun Sons' and their respective septenaries, were not yet born. The number 17 x 2 implies the reflection of the attributes of the Logos via these Sons, whilst the number 16 x 10 refers to the perfected expression of the Christ (hence as Logoi and the constitution of the Love-Wisdom department of a Shambhala), of which 'the Seven' are embodiments. As they were not yet born, so consciousness could not manifest, which is what is 'Born from the web of Light'. Nothing could be because material phenomena, the substance into which they were to

41 Ibid., Vol 1, 60.

incarnate (100 + 66) was not manifest. The *ātmic* plane, as the place of birthing of the *karma* of whatever is to be was not yet functioning so, as the *karmic* seeds have not yet been sought. Nothing therefore could be born.

The number 52 refers to a great zodiacal year consisting of 52 weeks of seven day cycles of activity. The cycles of the new *mahāmanvantara* were therefore not manifest, within which the web of the *nāḍīs* could generate Light (the seven Rays of manifestation). The Web of Light is the expression of the intricate *nāḍī* system that underlies the totality of the form. There are thousands of these *nāḍīs,* and where they intersect there are formed points of light, the *chakras.* Where twenty-one or more intersect the major *chakras* are formed and where a lesser number intersect we have the minor ones. Each of the *nāḍīs* convey the *prāṇas* that are the carriers of the different hues, attributes of light. The *prāṇas* are also the expressions of the consciousness used by the Thinker to create thoughts. Neither the Thinker, the thoughts, the energies of the *prāṇas* utilised by the thoughts, or the light that the thought-forms convey were existent, there were no Wheels manifesting to contain them, as 'nought was'.

'The Seven' here therefore refers particularly to the seven major *chakras* in the body of Deity, whilst the major interpretation of this 'Web of Light', as indicated by the associated numbers, is the web of the *nāḍīs* that stem from the *sūtrātmā* projected by the Causal Form of the Logos (the Light upon the cosmic higher mental plane). The number 3 x 9 of the phrase *'the Web'* here refers to the *deva* triads governing the substance of all that will be. They are not appropriately organised by the Logoic Sambhogakāya Flower. The stored *saṃskāras* within these petals and the three permanent atoms are yet to flow via the projected *sūtrātmā* to build the form into which the Logos can incarnate, but this was not yet.

Each of 'the Seven' can also be considered Logoi in their own right, existing within an intricate *nāḍī* system that interrelates all planetary Schemes in the body of the solar Logos.

The number 17 x 4 of the phrase *'the Web of Light'* informs us that this web is primarily concerned with the quaternary nature of the Logos, the seat of Power of the Divine Personality. The primordial, *Ādi*

Buddha sits upon this lotus Throne, signifying the Base of Spine centre, the foundation for the eventuation of the manifest form. Because this centre was not yet activated, so the sum of manifest being, the rest of the *chakras* and *nāḍī* system, could not come into active expression. The web from the four cosmic ethers (the four higher Systemic planes of perception) was not yet vitalised by the Thought and the mantric Sound of the divine Thinker.

The number 11 of the phrase *'born from the Web'* symbolises the *nāḍī* system, the web of Life. The number 20 of this phrase indicates the second Ray attributes (of the *prāṇas)* which were yet to be born from this web. This Ray is supreme in this solar system, and with it we have the evolution of the Hierarchy of enlightened Being, the seven Ray Ashrams (or the planetary Regents, the Logoi of the seven Rays) Who are the perfected dispensers of this Light to the dense world. All of these agents for the dissemination of Light were yet to be born from this Web.

The numbers 30 and 31 x 3 of the phrase *'from the Web of Light'* indicate that the major Ray of Creative activity, the third of Mathematical Activity that governs the Mother's department (the third Logos) had to be born from this Web if the form could fruit.

The number 108 (9 x 12) of the phrase *'The Seven were not yet born'* is the sacred number for Hindus and Buddhists, as explained in volume 5A of *A Treatise on Mind.* The number signifies the totality of any body of manifestation. It is the number of major *nāḍīs* both above and below the diaphragm, as well as being a significant number in relation to the internal constitution of the Head lotus. This number for instance relates to the 105 Kumāras, plus the three of the abstract Triune Deity, who came to our planetary Scheme to establish Shambhala (the planetary Head centre) on earth at the time of Individualisation of humanity. The 'Seven were not yet born' because the Head centre and associated *nāḍīs* were not yet established.

The number 9 x 12 signifies the twelfth Initiation, here taken to represent the degree of attainment of a solar Logos, the conveyor of the twelve zodiacal energies to the solar system.

Finally, the numbers of the complete phrase *'the Seven were not yet born from the Web of Light'* add to 12, signifying that the twelve petals of the Heart centre were not yet activated, and with the Heart not functioning no embodied Life could exist. The Hierarchical energies that constitutes this Web, from which emanates the Seven attributes of Life, thus did not exist.

The numerical breakdown of the last two phrases:

> Darkness alone (48, 12), Darkness alone was Father-Mother (120, 30), Svabhavat (24, 6), was in Darkness (49, 22), in Darkness (42, 15), Svabhavat was in Darkness (73 = 10, 28).

The rest of this Stanza is virtually a repetition of the information provided in Stanza 1:5, except that here Darkness is equated with the Father-Mother and 'Svabhavat' is substituted for the phrase *'the Boundless All'*. The meaning of *svabhāva* as the plastic Essence that fills the universe, the root of all things, was given in Stanza 2:1. There it was also equated to *ākāśa*. Because the energy that drives forth the appearance of phenomena was not manifesting, so all was in darkness.

Having dealt with the great evolutionary Entities, the planetary Deities and Regents in their septenary ramifications, and the method by which they would come into manifestation, it is natural that the rest of the stanza will analyse the substance that they will soon inhabit and utilise as the forms of their Bodies (as constructed by the Builders). It is also this substance that originally gave them birth, because 'Darkness is Father-Mother: light their son', to quote H.P.B.[42]

Darkness therefore is the fount of all there is, and from another angle of vision, it is *svabhāva,* for that is what it comes *to be* (for this reason the word is a separated entity in the middle of the sentence), and yet, 'Svabhāvat was in Darkness'. Hidden here is the mystery of the manifestation of Light from where there was once Darkness,[43] which involves the secret of Creation and the mystery of Being, which has already been partly explained.

This is also exemplified by the numbers of the phrase *'Darkness alone was Father-Mother',* which add to 12 x 10, 30, where the number 120 refers here to an earlier time, when there was only ten signs to the zodiac, which terminated in the tenth sign of the zodiac, Capricorn

42 Ibid, Vol. 1, 40.

43 This subject is basically also treated in somewhat explained in Bailey's *Letters on Occult Meditation* in the section on the meditation on colour.

the goat, one of the most mysterious of all the signs of the zodiac. Capricorn is the most material hard, rocky, of all the signs. It governs the mountain load of *karma* associated with three dense planes of perception, as well as the qualities of the angelic kingdom responsible for the manifestation of the various forms that evolve within the confines of *saṃsāra*. It also represents the cosmic mental plane, wherein the forces of Father-Mother reside. Because cosmic Mind was outwardly inactive so all was in Darkness. At the end of our solar evolution there will again be only ten signs as explained in *Esoteric Astrology.*

> Eventually, in some mysterious way, there will be only ten signs of the zodiac again; Aries and Pisces will form one sign, for 'the end is as the beginning.' This dual and blended sign is called in some of the ancient books 'the sign of the Fish with the head of the Ram.' We shall then have

1. Aries- Pisces	6. Virgo- Libra
2. Taurus	7. Scorpio
3. Gemini	8. Sagittarius
4. Cancer	9. Capricorn
5. Leo	10. Aquarius.[44]

The number 30 refers to the perfected expression of the third Ray of Activity and its abstraction into the *pralaya* that caused the manifestation of darkness.

The numbers of the phrase *'Darkness alone'* add to 4 x 12, referring to the sign Cancer the crab, which was earlier explained in this context in reference to the phrase *'Darkness alone filled the Boundless All'*. In relation to the sign Capricorn we have the downward arm of the cardinal cross portrayed, as Capricorn and Cancer are polar opposites. This arm immediately takes on the guise of the 'One Ray' that 'flashed into the Germ', which is found in Cancer. The central spinal column can also represent this descent of energies via the *suṣumṇā nāḍī*, through which the primordial Ray of cosmic electricity can flash, causing manifestation. Cancer is the door into incarnation and mass life, whilst Capricorn is the door of Initiation, 'into the life of the spirit—into the Kingdom of God, the life and purposes of the Hierarchy of our

---

44 Bailey, *Esoteric Astrology*, 213. See also page 159.

planet'.[45] Cancer is the door of opportunity and sacrifice in the prison of material involvement.

The cardinal cross is 'the cross of Life related to Shambhala, the Monad, and the Father aspect of Deity. It governs the path of Initiation and of beginnings, thus the beginning of the cosmic journey into manifestation.

D.K. states that 'at the time that any particular race comes into being both the doors in Cancer and Capricorn stand wide open, being then occultly aligned.'[46] It stands to reason therefore that they also stand open at the time of the birth of any new planetary Chain, Scheme or globe.

The meaning of the Father, Mother and Son were explained in Stanza 1:5. Here Father and Mother are united in the hyphenated word Father-Mother, implying the concept of the Divine Hermaphrodite, of a complete conjugal Union. This is the cause of the emission of the Ray that could fertilise the germ of the Bud Lotus, *mātripadma* that effectively was the Womb of the Mother.

Note that the qualities of the Divine Hermaphrodite are symbolised by the sign Taurus the bull, to which the numbers of the word *'Svabhavat'* (2 x 12) also refers.

The numbers of the phrase *'Father-Mother'* add to 65 (13 x 5), 11, signifying the combined first (11) and third Ray (13 x 5) energies that produce the emanation of the one Ray, the *sūtrātmā* that fertilises the Womb of the Mother.

The numbers of the phrase *'was in Darkness'* add to 7 x 7 and to 22. The number 49 appeared previously with regards the Seven that 'were not yet born from the Web of Light'. Their entire Bodies of manifestation (7 x 7), the Womb of the *mātripadma* (22), were therefore still in darkness.

The numbers of the phrase *'Svabhavat was in Darkness'* add to 7 x 4, which refers to the four cosmic ethers, as well as to the entire body of manifestation. Essentially the number 7 x 4 indicates that *svabhāva* was immersed into the type of abstraction associated with *śūnyatā*.

45 Ibid., 168.

46 Ibid., 169.

Stanza Two part Six

Stanza 2:6 states:

> **These two are the Germ, and the Germ is – One. The Universe was still concealed in the Divine Thought and the Divine Bosom.**

Keynotes: Cancer, *anupādaka.*

The numerical breakdown of the first two phrases:

These two (34, 7), the Germ (40, 13), These Two are the Germ (89 = 17, 26 = 8), the Germ is (50, 14) - One (66, 21).

Cancer the crab is now implicated, which is concerned with incarnation into form and mass movement of energies. The entire Thought-Form of what the universe is to be has now been constructed by the Logos, but not acted upon. Thus 'the Universe was concealed in the Divine Thought'. The symbolism of the 'Divine Bosom', here immediately introduces the imagery of the solar disc, the symbol of material manifestation, needing the outpouring of the energies, the 'milk', that would produce the curdling of *svabhāva.* The plane implicated here upon the upward arc of the rectified wheel is *anupādaka,* as from here pours the 'milk', the Consciousness principle (Love-Wisdom), that nourishes the Lives that will come into incarnation.

The phrase *'These Two'* (17 x 2, 7) refers to *svabhāva* and Darkness, or even to the Father-Mother (the number 17 referring to the reflection of divinity), which emphasises the latent and basic duality associated with the totality of all Being. The Father-Mother also symbolises the Monad-Soul. The number 7 indicates that the two have within them the Seed of the septenary and all of the ramifications of divinity, which can be reflected into manifestation at the appropriate cycle.

In Stanza 2:3, with respect to the phrase *'the Ray had not yet flashed into the Germ',* 'the Germ' (40) was said to signify either the Causal Body, or else the earth Scheme, Chain or globe. Here however, this Germ takes on a new significance, as referring to the Monad or even to the abstracted Logos, Who is unequivocally the Germ of all Being. In this sense the meaning of the Father-Mother can be seen in a new light. During the process of *pralaya* the Seven become the Three and the Three merge into the Two that become fused into the One (Germ), the abstracted Logos. Regarding the evolution of a planetary sphere, the Father-Mother is the union of a positive (masculine) and a negative (feminine) polarised Logos, esoterically we have 'the marriage of the spheres', which produces a Son, the new globe. The main implication of 'the Germ' here however is the relation of *svabhāva* to Darkness. Darkness must evolve into Light within the *nāḍī* system (*svabhāva*) of what must be.

The numbers of the phrase *'the Germ is One'* add to 66, 21, where the number 66 is a shorthand form of the number 666,[47] which signifies the entire creative and evolutionary period on all planes of perception, especially in relation to the making of a humanity. It concerns the sum of planetary evolution. The number 7 x 3 has a similar significance regarding the three dense material planes of perception, or with those associated with the spiritual triad. What is signified is that this Germ is 'One' (16, 7), the Christ principle (16), the cosmic Consciousness that veils the inherent septenary. This is the true source of all manifestation. The two are the abstracted Deity that are integrated as the Son of their union. This Son is the Germ that is the radiant source of all Life and Light. It projects itself via the *svabhāva* into the Darkness.

The numerical breakdown of the third phrase:

> The Universe (56, 11), was still concealed (60, 24), The Universe was still concealed (116 = 100 + 16, 35), was still concealed in the Divine Thought (161, 53 = 8), The Divine thought (87 = 15, 24), in the Divine Thought (101, 29 = 11), Concealed in the Divine Thought (136 = 100 + 36, 37 = 10), The Divine Bosom (70, 25), The Universe was still concealed in the Divine Thought (217 = 200 + 17, 64), The Divine Thought and the Divine Bosom (167 = 14, 50), concealed in the Divine Thought and the Divine Bosom (216 = 24 x 9, 63), still concealed in the Divine Thought and the Divine Bosom (234, 72), as still concealed in the Divine Thought and the Divine Bosom (241, 79 = 16), in the Divine Thought and the Divine Bosom (181, 55), The Universe was

47 The number of the 'beast' of chapter thirteen of *The Revelation of St. John.*

still concealed in the Divine Thought and the Divine Bosom (297 = 33 x 9, 90).

The meaning of *'The Universe'*, which is the result of the swelling of the One, was explained in Stanza 1:6. The number 7 x 8 here implies that this universe constitutes the expression of potent energies on seven multidimensional levels of expression (the 'seven infinities') in every direction the Mind can conceive.

The numbers 2 x 12 and 5 x 12 of the phrase *'was still concealed'* refer to the second and fifth signs of the zodiac, informing us that all the qualities associated with Taurus the bull, the principle of cosmic Desire, and of the second stage of the evolutionary process, associated with the cosmic Egg, was still concealed. Also implicated is the sign Leo the lion, the symbol of the individualised self-conscious Son, a sphere of consciousness differentiated from all other such entities or World-spheres. Such a form was also similarly concealed. Taurus and Leo represent two arms of the fixed cross of the Heavens, the cross of the crucified Christ, which governs the evolution of our present solar system. The Day for the evolution of the Son in manifest space had yet to come.

The word *divine* refers to what pertains to divinity, generally thought of as a supreme Being. It pertains to the sacred and sanctity. The divine esoterically incorporates all entities that act upon the dense form to help effect the liberation of the imprisoned lives therein. The purpose is to bring them into absorption into the Bosom of Deity, so that they can accordingly manifest as Deity. In the complicated phrase here being analysed there are three aspects of the divine implicated:

a. *'The Divine'* (17 x 3, 15) refers to the most abstracted aspect of divinity—the entire source of all (17 x 3) that is to be, ever was, and ever will be. The Father.

b. *'The Divine Thought'* (24, 15) refers to the method of clothing the Divine (a Taurean function, 2 x 12) with images of what is to be, and which can later be projected into manifestation. Here the number 15 indicates the activity aspect of the Mind that produces the Thought. Taurus clothes the Divine Thought-Form and constitutes the substance of the astral plane, cosmically or systemically considered. It is thus identified with the great Mother, the cosmic Egg depicted in many myths, and assists in the formation of the Christ child (the Divine Thought, the Son) in the womb of Virgo and His birth in Capricorn.

c. *'The Divine Bosom'* (70, 25) refers to the formation of a sphere of Logoic Activity from whence the septenaries of space can appear (7 x 10). Within this Bosom manifest the 'seven Eternities', the unconscious pulsation of the Life of the universe. The number 5 x 5 also refers to the principles of Mind, or to the Causal Form, here viewed as this Divine Bosom from which the universe will emanate. This Bosom contains the variegations of the expression of the Divine Thought, expressed as the Mother.

The Divine Thought governs the complete life-span of an entity, the summation of that One's entire being. It is the conceptualisation by the Logos of the totality of the evolution of the Son (or universe) from the beginning to the end, to the attainment of a completely liberated Buddha. The Thought organises all of the energies, cosmic Law, forces and conditionings needed, plus the roles that the entities concerned must play to bring that evolution to conclusion. All of this activity is effectively carried out within the Divine Bosom. The Divine is All that Is.

The numbers of the phrase *'The Universe was still concealed'* add to 7 x 5, referring to the attributes of cosmic Mind (Mahat), hence Divine Intelligence, which was effectively slumbering. There is also the number 100 + 16, referring to the cosmic Christ, which was similarly concealed. The process of 'concealing' and also of 'revealing' necessitates principally the activity of the Mind, for it is the intellect (and its illusions) that conceals, and the light of the mind/Mind that reveals. The entire Dharmakāya Flower of what is to be was thereby concealed.

The act of concealing can also concern Light of such intensity that it prevents the eyes from seeing, thus that Light becomes viewed as Darkness. As a sense organ the eyes (and sight) relate to the qualities of mind/Mind and the Element Fire. For this reason there are the various multiples of the number 5 given in the above phrases.

Concerning *'The Divine Thought',* H.P.B states:

> The *"Divine Thought"* does not imply the idea of a Divine thinker. The Universe, not only past, present, and future — which is a human and finite idea expressed by finite thought — but in its totality, the Sat (an untranslateable term), the absolute being, with the Past and Future crystallized in an eternal Present, is that Thought itself reflected in a secondary or manifest cause. Brahma (neuter) as the Mysterium Magnum of Paracelsus is an absolute mystery to the human mind. Brahmâ, the male-female, its aspect and anthropomorphic reflection, is conceivable to the perceptions of blind faith, though rejected by human intellect when it attains its majority. (See Part II., "Primordial Substance and Divine Thought.")
>
> Hence the statement that during the prologue, so to say, of the drama of Creation, or the beginning of cosmic evolution, the Universe or the "Son" lies still concealed "in the Divine Thought," which had not yet penetrated "into the Divine Bosom." This idea, note well, is at the root, and forms the origin of all the allegories about the "Sons of God" born of immaculate virgins.[48]

When Blavatsky states that 'The "Divine Thought" does not imply the idea of a Divine thinker', what she is trying to establish is that at this stage the 'Thinker' was concealed, slumbering, not yet awake. There was only the 'Divine Thought', conceived here in terms of Brahman, the uncognisable principle, the essence from which all things emanate and to which all things return, that which is 'unborn', immutable. It is the absolute, or ground of the universe, the ultimate principle in Vedic beliefs, attributeless, unmodifyable and does not move. The Thought of what was to be (personified in the function of Brahmā) had not yet awakened.

As Blavatsky states, the idea of the Divine Thought to the human mind has in it the concept of the Thinker, and that Thought about (the universe) and as such has implicated in it the concept of duality. In the Absolute sense such duality does not exist, there is just the One, immutable and indivisible, which 'stretched boundless, infinite, causeless in dreamless sleep' (Stanza 1:8). On that level of Being-Non-Being, the human idea of Thought becomes meaningless, and the idea

48 *The Secret Doctrine,* Vol. 1, 61.

of its transmuted correspondence unknowable. Thus 'the One' remains Absolute, unconditioned, etc.

Thought is non-vocalised Sound, therefore is an expression of the Creative Deity (an aspect of Brahmā, not the Brahman) prior to the act of precipitation and the materialisation of that Thought. We must necessarily liken this to the process of meditation, and are effectively speculating upon the nature of the third Logos, the Creative Deity (the Mother), and the quality of the Son within the Divine Bosom.

The condition associated with the phrase 'There was..... naught save Ceaseless Eternal Breath, which knows itself not' (Stanza 2:2) therefore no longer applies, for the process of Thought implies the ability to Know and to utilise that knowledge in the construction of what is Thought about, and in that Thought the universe was still concealed. The first step of Creation, 'Divine Ideation' is yet to begin, as all still remained in the realm of the Mind, and that in the Bosom of the Mother. It is conceptualised in the eternal Now, but not yet actualised in relation to time. The Will of the Thinker has yet to vitalise the Thought into an active expression.

The number 100 + 36 of the phrase *'concealed in the Divine Thought'* refers to the sign Gemini the twins. Gemini here represents the Temple of the Lord veiling the Holy of Holies, wherein this Thought is concealed. More specifically this sign governs the *chakra* and *nāḍī* system, which was not yet vitalised, hence 'concealed'. What was *'in the Divine Thought'* (101, 11) and yet to be properly projected are the seed *bījas* and the lines of Thought *(sūtrātmās)* that would awaken them into new *maṇḍalas* of expression.

That *'The Universe was still concealed in the Divine Thought'* (200 + 17, 8 x 8) indicates that the universe (here referring to the local part of this universe, the Body of the One about Whom Naught may be Said—200 + 17), or the Lord of Love, was still concealed by the Divine energy (8 x 8) that conditioned the abstraction of the Thought. The number 8 of the phrase *'was still concealed in the Divine Thought'* has a similar significance to the number 8 x 8 above.

The number 72 of the phrase *'still concealed in the Divine Thought and the Divine Bosom'* refers to the sign Virgo the virgin, hence all that is embodied by the great Mother, which was thus concealed.

The numbers of the phrase *'concealed in the Divine Thought and the Divine Bosom'* add to 200 + 16, 12 x 18, 7 x 9, which indicate that this universe in the form of a Cosmic Christ (200 + 16) was concealed within the Divine Bosom (12 x 18). One can speculate that such a One equates with the Hindu concept of Īśvara, meaning 'capable or all-controlling Lord', the personalised Deity. Īśvara, is Brahman with form *(saguṇa brahman),* the world Soul, or Logos, from which incarnation proceeds and to which it recedes. From Īśvara emanates the *trimūrti* of Brahmā, Viṣṇu and Śiva. The number 12 x 18 refers to the expression of the energies of the twelve signs of the zodiac (12) upon the cosmic astral plane, which represents the 'Bosom'. The Lords of these signs have mastered (been Initiated into) the attributes of the cosmic Waters (2 x 9), for which reason their potencies can be perfectly expressed through the cosmic astral to effect conditionings within the cosmic dense realm. The number 7 x 9 here is another way of referring to the seven Creative Hierarchies (as Initiates from a former cycle of endeavour).

The numbers 16, 7 of the phrase *'was still concealed in the Divine Thought and the Divine Bosom'* refers to the consciousness principle, the Son or Christ aspect, Īśvara.

The numbers 14, 50 of the phrase *'the Divine Thought and the Divine Bosom'* emphasise the importance of the Mind (Mahat) in the entire awakening process of the universe, within the 'Divine Bosom' that represents the cosmic astral plane (14) conditioned by it. Similarly the number 55 of the phrase *'in the Divine Thought and the Divine Bosom'* also implies Mahat, cosmic Intelligence in its Will aspect, and all of the forces pertaining thereto, that would cause a universe to come into manifestation, as well as causing the spheroid shape of the 'Divine Bosom' (the Monadic Form). This number also indicates the importance of the *devas,* the Builders of the forms to be, which were 'still concealed', not yet called into activity. What is implied is that these forces were present, but not yet actively manifesting. Without the application of the Will by the Logos the new *manvantara* could not commence. Note that the number 4 x 11 specifically refers to the human stream of evolution, whereas the number 5 x 11 refers to the *deva* stream. The human and *deva* streams are the *piṇgalā* and *iḍā nāḍīs* of manifest expression. All were in existence ('concealed') but not yet actively expressed.

In the past solar system the Mind was evolved and gained pre-eminence. As it was the gain of that solar incarnation all who evolved from it are *manasaputras*, beings of Mind substance, as are the Kumāras. Everything in this solar system is coloured by that Mind. It is inherent throughout Nature, hence we move on from that base to evolve Love-Wisdom.

To finally consider is the complete phrase: *'The Universe was still concealed in the Divine Thought and the Divine Bosom'* (9 x 10, 33 x 9). The number 9 x 10 refers specifically to the perfected Initiate, the Logos of a (non-sacred) planet, as is our planetary Logos. Once these Logoi are awakened they will cause the local universe (the appearance of their bodies of manifestation) to manifest. The number 33 x 9 refers to the events that would result in the eventual Initiation of the Creative Intelligences (*manasaputras*) that will be responsible for all aspects of manifested Life.

Between this Stanza and that of Stanza 3:1 there is a lacuna, where obviously the process of manifestation has begun. The lines of Thought (*antaḥkaraṇas*) that would awaken the seed *bījas* into new *maṇḍalas* of expression have been projected.

Stanza 3:1, which is ruled generally by the sign Scorpio the scorpion, starts with 'the last vibration of the Seventh Eternity'. Between Cancer and Scorpio three signs have transpired, which we can presume deal with the manifestation of the six preceding vibrations. These signs are Leo, Virgo, and Libra. In the early stages of the evolutionary process Leo and Virgo are joined, producing the mystery of the sphinx. This mystery relates to what integrates the masculine and feminine forces to impregnate the Womb of the great Mother with the seeds of Life. The entire philosophy explicated in my book *The Nature and Development of Maṇḍalas,* of the birth of the Dhyāni Buddhas in the Womb of the Consort of the Ādi Buddha, comes to the fore here. The focus now concerns the birth of a solar system rather than just the earth sphere. Libra balances the engendered forces and instigates the new cycles of Life.

6A

Stanzas 3:1 – 3:4

Commentaries Stanza Three

The Stanza begins after a hiatus of information associated with the mechanism of projection of the creative Seed of a Logos that will precipitate a Logoic form (the emanation of a world sphere) into manifestation. The form in question here is that of our present solar system, the central one of three that constitute an esoteric unity. The entire *pralaya* process associated with the other 'six Eternities' are omitted between Stanzas 2:6 and 3:1 because of the virtual impossibility of explaining the true nature of the qualities of these realms during *pralaya* as the related Lives are preparing for rebirth. Stanza three is divided into twelve parts, each of which express the qualities of one or other of the twelve signs of the zodiac that condition the petals of the Logoic Heart centre.

It was earlier seen that the seventh Eternity happened under the auspices of Leo (Stanza 1:8), whilst the Mother refers to Virgo the virgin. The concept of 'the last vibration' however introduces the attributes of Aquarius the water bearer, the polar opposite of Leo. The glyph for Aquarius consists of two wavy lines signifying the conveyance of energies, in this case that of vibration. The exoteric ruler of Aquarius is Uranus, which governs the seventh Ray (of 'the seventh Eternity'), whilst its Hierarchical ruler is the Moon, which in this case veils the 1-4-7 Ray expression. The seventh Ray manifests the Power to cause the outpouring of the cycles of time, the *yugas* of manifestation.

The overriding sign of the first verse is Virgo, the great Mother, as it is Her substance that 'swells' and to expand 'from within without'. This is the result of the Scorpion's 'sting', which moves in an arc to produce a potent effect to the object of impact, and so the substance and Lives inside the Womb are stirred to activity. The 'sting' bears the sixth Ray Martian energy of the Scorpion (the polar opposite of Taurus) and with the recurring jabs of Fohatic energy the Lives begin to 'thrill' in Her Womb,

There is therefore a triangle of signs that come into play as a consequence of the expression of the 'last vibration' (Aquarius) in Stanza 3:1 – Leo, Virgo and Scorpio. Leo embodies the Mahatic effect of the Meditation-Mind of the Logoic Personality, instigating the forces that cause the entities within the Mother to awaken 'like the bud of the lotus' in the new 'Day-be-with-us'.[1] Within that Day the Logos manifests the complete *maṇḍala* of His Body of expression. All constituent forces and entities are then awakened and 'rush' into objective appearance via the martial energy of Scorpio (acting as the Son or consciousness-principle). Scorpio imbues them with the necessary impetus to begin the process of undergoing the trials and tribulations of gaining the next step forward in conscious evolution.

The Scorpionic energy therefore brings into expression the momentum of the Creative Intelligences, each propelled into form at the appropriate cycle. The sixth Ray borne by Scorpio, coupled with the seventh Ray of Aquarius, manifests as a potent combination to impel the new cycle of activity, and to project the Lives therein to manifest their appropriate activity. They are procreative forces, seeds of purposeful potential that the Logos injects into the Mother, causing Her Womb to swell with the genesis of the new cycle. From another perspective the Lives can be viewed as the *saṃskāras* ('genetic imprints') generated in the past cycles of activity that are to be inherited by the awakening Child of the *manvantaric* dawn.

The collective Wisdom of the manifest Creative Intelligences is veiled by Mercury, the Hierarchical ruler of Scorpio. Mercury is

1 Leo governs the Soul, whilst its esoteric ruler is the sun veiling the Heart of the sun or the central spiritual sun, consequently the Meditating Logos draws upon or acts as the Soul to produce the new activity.

esoterically related to the energy of *buddhi*—the enlightened Mind. Mercury wields the caduceus staff, with its entwined serpents, signifying the descent into manifestation, and then ascent of these Creative Intelligences after they awaken *kuṇḍalinī,* the primal heat of the Mother. *Kuṇḍalinī* then spirals through the spirillae of the Logoic physical permanent atom to produce radiant Light (see Stanza 3:6). The Wisdoms of these Intelligences therefore provides Mercury with the major characteristics attributed to it. These Lives find their point of entry into the solar system via the activity of the Mercury Scheme.

Representing the Mother's department, Virgo controls the myriads of *devas* that embody the sum of the form. They are brought into activity when the Solar Plexus centre and also the sum of the Inner Round *chakras* become awakened. This is governed by the work of the Lord of the Jupiter Scheme, the Hierarchical ruler of Virgo. Jupiter is assisted by Mercury, the star of the dawning, who carries the golden energies that vitalise the awakening Flowers. The manifold Flowers *(chakras)* in the etheric body of the Logos then unfold, and the regulation of the circulation of the *prāṇas* within that web of Life (Stanza 3:12) takes the complete developed Wisdom and Love of the Lord embodying the Solar Plexus centre. Watery cosmic astral energies are projected into Jupiter via the agency of Scorpio. *Manasic* energies from the Logoic Mind via Leo also manifest, to form the basis of Jupiter's Wisdom, allowing Him to rightly direct *prāṇas* throughout the sum of the Inner Round of the solar system.

The general outline of the verses of Stanza Three

There are seven stanzas to Cosmogenesis, therefore it can be presumed that each relates to the manifestation of conditionings upon one or other of the planes of perception. Stanza one thus relates to the formation of the plane *ādi,* the first cosmic ether, wherein all the Lives that will embody the form are fully abstracted in the permanent atoms stored there. When the time comes for the instigation of a new *manvantara* the presiding Logos sends a Ray to activate these atoms, and the impetus of the energies awakens the Life streams, which then 'thrill' with activity. The remaining six Stanzas show how the Life-streams come to thus thrill to produce the manifest forms of Life known to us.

The second Stanza relates to the plane *anupādaka,* where the consciousness bearing elements that will eventually play a role in the new *mahāmanvantara* are organised. The Lords of Life proceed to take their appointed roles and the way is prepared for the descent of the Monads that will inform the forthcoming kingdom of Souls.

The third Stanza directs the process to the *ātmic* plane, from whence the *karma* of the entire incarnation process comes into being. From here the *deva* Builders responsible for the manifestation of the phenomena of the material world come into play. They are the 'Universal Mind' of Stanza 1:3, hence the active manifestation of the Ah-Hi. The Mother's department then swells in preparation for the birthing of the All.

Stanza 3 is also an elaboration of Stanza 2:3 at the time when 'the hour' strikes.

If we take each of the twelve verses of Stanza 3 to embody the attributes of one or other of the twelve petals of a Head lotus that are awakened in turn, then each of these verses generalise the function of a particular sign of the zodiac. The verses also explain the formation of a Logoic sphere of activity. They manifest in an apparently linear fashion, but in reality there is great mutability and overlapping of activity. Also, as stated earlier, the general focus of Stanza 3 is the *ātmic* plane, hence the first Outpouring, but we will see that within the context of this Outpouring Stanza 3:3 introduces the effect of the second Outpouring. From this perspective Stanza 3:3 is also basically governed by the second Ray of Love-Wisdom. Stanza 3:2 is consequently ruled by the first Ray of Will, which starts the process of world formation. Stanza 3:1 is concerned with the cosmic astral plane, the cosmic Waters that surrounds the cosmic foetal Life that is the newly forming world (or solar) sphere, which at this stage is the Virgin-Egg.

The Heart centre, and its equivalent as the twelve petals of the Head lotus, is subdivided into five non-sacred and seven sacred petals. The twelve statements are also conditioned by this paradigm, where the first five verses cosmically govern the attributes of the five non-sacred petals, and the remaining seven verses the attributes of the seven sacred petals. In this case these 'non-sacred petals' convey the five attributes of cosmic *prāṇa (ākāśa),*[2] as wielded by the five Dhyāni Buddhas

2 These forms of *ākāśa* are explained in my book *Esoteric Cosmology and Modern Physics.*

(Kumāras), and signify the five liberated Hierarchies that are briefly explained in *Esoteric Astrology*. In speaking of 'liberated Hierarchies' the concern is with five streams of Life that passed through the human conditioning in the last solar system.

Note here that the concept of 'sacred' and non-sacred' is reversed, where five petals are effectively the 'sacred' ones, dealing with energisation of the evolving forms, and the remaining seven are 'non-sacred', because directly concerned with the mutability of evolving life within *saṃsāra*. The energies pouring through *ākāśa* represent the Waters of the Womb, whilst the activity associated with the remaining petals represents the evolving foetus. From a higher perspective, the seven systemic planes manifest as the foetus. The cosmic astral plane is then the Water of the Womb, and the cosmic mental plane creates the Thought-Form, the ring-pass-not that contains it all.

The overall conditioning sign of Stanza 3:1 is Virgo and the activity within the Womb of the great Mother, established via the substance of the seventh cosmic astral sub-plane. This Stanza incorporates the effect of the first of the Creative Hierarchies, the energy of which is given by D.K. to be that of 'Intelligent substance',[3] which in the Stanza is termed 'Infinitude'. The organisation of this substance comes under the auspices of the second of the Dhyāni Buddhas, Akṣobhya, rather than from Vairocana. One reason being that this Stanza is concerned with projecting the sum of the Watery energies from the cosmic astral plane via its seventh sub-plane into the systemic domain (the seven sub-planes of the cosmic dense physical plane). This is an effect of Akṣobhya's Mirror-like Wisdom. Another reason is that the objective for this solar evolution is the development of Love-Wisdom, which is esoterically Watery in nature. The projection of the energies of the cosmic Waters via the impetus of Virgoan purpose causes the Mother to swell, 'expanding from within without'. The Watery *ākāśa* therefore is pre-eminent in this solar system, of which the others are subdivisions. This Hierarchy draws energies from the third cosmic astral sub-plane.

Stanza 3:2 is conditioned generally by the attributes of the sign Libra the balances, effecting the Meditation process that causes the vibration to sweep along. The sweeping movement projects the elements

3 The energies of the liberated Hierarchies are taken from *Esoteric Astrology,* 34.

of Life into the cosmic Womb, signified by the seven systemic planes (the cosmic dense physical plane) via the first cosmic etheric sub-plane *ādi*. This Stanza therefore manifests the Aetheric *ākāśa* via *ādi* in the form of the vibration that sweeps along as the 'swift wing'.

The 'feathers' of this wing convey the forces of the five types of *ākāśa* and their subdivisions as they descend down the planes signifying the cosmic ethers. The seven spirillae of the Logoic physical permanent atom is thereby vivified, and this constitutes the work of the first of the manifest Creative Hierarchies, titled 'Divine Flames, Divine Lives'. The energy is drawn from the seventh cosmic astral sub-plane, and the fifth of the liberated Hierarchies governing the 'Mass Life' preparing to enter cosmic dense physical space. They are impelled into manifestation by means of the application of Logoic Will. The Lives here implicated will also reverberate to effect the streams of sentient life that will play their roles in the three worlds of human evolution, causing the evolutionary progress of the five kingdoms in Nature: the mineral, plant, animal, human and the liberated Lives (including the *devas*).

The Aetheric *ākāśa* is the seed conveying the other cosmic ethers, and is wielded by the All-accomplishing Wisdom of Amoghasiddhi. Amoghasiddhi's Wisdom and Power is needed to master the attributes of the cosmic dense physical plane. His energy instigates the expansion of the 'bud of the Lotus', starting from the plane *ādi*. Libra the balances helps the projection of the necessary cycles of accomplishment. Here the Logoic Mind, taking the sum of the effort of the Dhyāni Buddhas into account, utilises the *karma* from past cycles of expression (adjudicated by Libra) to awaken the germ of the new Life with the appropriate energies.

Stanza 3:3 relates to the expression of the Airy *ākāśa,* projected by the martial impetus of Scorpio the scorpion, which causes 'the Eternal Egg to thrill' and the condensation of 'the World-Egg'. The focus is the second cosmic etheric sub-plane, *anupādaka*. The Airy Element is the general medium of expression of all five cosmic *prāṇas,* the *ākāśas,* consequently the Fiery Element seeded in Stanza 3:2 is now embellished with the streams of the Creative Hierarchies that will inform systemic space. They are generally conditioned by the second Ray of Love-Wisdom and bring into manifestation the Consciousness-principle via the second Outpouring. The second Ray purpose produces the fields of testing in this solar evolution. The incoming Lives bring with them the various intensities of Light generated in former aeons of evolutionary attainment. The energy is drawn from the sixth cosmic astral sub-plane, and is empowered via the Equalising Wisdom of Ratnasambhava acting via the second cosmic ether, *anupādaka*. His energy is needed to rightly control the flow of the potency of cosmic Love that manifests via this most Watery sub-plane of the cosmic astral plane. The associated liberated Hierarchy upon that plane is the fourth, designated as 'Desire for Duality' by D.K. This 'Duality' is the interrelation between the liberated Lives upon the cosmic astral plane, and those now to incarnate into systemic space. The Law of Attraction rules this purpose, to eventually abstract the gain of the experiences of the incarnating Lives into the Unity represented by the Logoic Thought upon the cosmic mental sub-planes.

Stanza 3:4 explores the overall effect of the energies of Sagittarius the archer, whose arrows intensify the Fiery *ākāśa* manifesting upon the *ātmic* plane, the third cosmic ether. They cause 'the three to fall into the four' via the first Outpouring proper. The appearance of the five planes of Brahmā[4] are specifically emanated, whereon is enacted the *karma* of human evolution. This happens as an expression of the third Ray of Mathematically Exact Activity. The work of the Mother and the *deva* kingdom is therefore exemplified as the Lesser Builders begin to manifest their assigned functions. These Builders draw from the energies of the third Liberated Hierarchy – 'Light thro' knowledge' and the fifth cosmic astral sub-plane. This *deva* Hierarchy therefore specifically reflects the energy of cosmic Mind into manifestation, producing all of the associated karmic implications. This work comes under the auspices of Amitābha and his Wisdom of the Discriminating Inner Vision. The Creative forces of Logoic Mind hence build the forms of what must be, whilst Amitābha's Wisdom ensures that the manifestation is in accordance with the Logoic Plan.

This Stanza is specifically concerned with the manifestation of Logoic Purpose via the four higher *ātmic* sub-planes. Each of the odd numbered planes of perception is dual. *Ādi* has three abstracted and

4 Counting from *ātma* down.

four concreted. *Ātma* manifests its reflection as four abstracted and three concreted. The mental plane reverses this with three abstracted and four empirical sub-planes. The physical plane has four etheric and three dense sub-planes. The twelve subsidiary Stanzas of Stanza three takes this arrangement into account. For the plane *ādi,* the fact that the fifth 'liberated' Creative Hierarchy is 'on the verge of liberation'[5] implies that a part of this Hierarchy still occupy the three highest sub-planes of *ādi,* whilst the Divine Flames mainly occupy the four lower sub-planes. In Stanza 3:4 the first Outpouring happens via the four higher sub-planes of *ātma,* whilst the three lowest sub-planes contain the mount of residual substance that 'remains'. The differentiation between the three abstract and four empirical sub-planes of the mental is well explained in my *A Treatise on Mind* series, as well as the etheric and concrete sub-divisions of the dense physical plane.

Stanza 3:5 signifies the store of substance needing converting into the elements of mind during the evolutionary process. It also signifies the impact of the first Outpouring of cosmic Mahatic substance upon the mental plane, whereupon the transformation and transmutation of substance happens. This is conditioned by the energies of Capricorn the goat. Capricorn embodies the substance of the Darkness of *saṃsāra,* the general material substance of the space that is enacted upon, of the primal, elemental attributes of mind *(manas),* which is impacted upon by the Logoic Mind. This interrelation generates light, and the entire process happens in the domain ruled by Capricorn, the lord of the mount of *manasic* substance, wherein is enacted the karmic interplay of the interrelation between the evolving forms. One must master and climb this substance of mind/Mind if one is to be Initiated into the Mysteries of being/non-being, to penetrate the veils of the Darkness upon cosmic levels. One then Knows the attributes of cosmic Mind that causes the appearance of things in cosmos.

The impact of Mahatic energies upon the higher mental plane via *buddhi* is effectively the lowest descent of the direct Power of Logoic Mind. The resonance of that Mind, via the five types of *ākāśa* manifest in its Earthy form under Capricornian influence, and affects the planes

5 *Esoteric Astrology,* 34.

of human evolution from the higher mental plane. The projection of the energies of cosmic Mind, that consolidate all of the above to effect the happenings of the concrete sub-planes of the cosmic dense physical plane, happens under the auspices of Amitābha's Wisdom.

The above concern is with the dissemination of the substance of the planes, rather than specifically the controlling Lives governing the plane of perception.

Stanza 3:6 describes the general effect of the sign Aquarius the water bearer, which governs 'every drop of the ocean of Immortality' that manifest via the *buddhic* plane. Upon *buddhi* exists the bulk of the *chakra* and *nāḍī* system of the Logos (the higher correspondence to the Inner Round and the centres below the diaphragm). These energies reflect 'the three' so that they fall as 'the four' constituting the embodied form: the higher and lower mental plane, the astral plane and the etheric double wherein exists the reflected *nāḍīs* underlying the appearance of things.[6] This process is governed by the fourth Ray of Harmony overcoming Strife. *Buddhi* is the Watery conveyor of the five *prāṇas*.

The second liberated Hierarchy ('Unity thro' Effort') projects its power through the fourth cosmic ether, and by utilising the *chakras* thereon can influence the appearance and evolution of the sum of manifest space, *saṃsāra* as we understand it. The governorship of *buddhi* esoterically is by the fourth Creative Hierarchy, humanity, 'the Initiates', also styled 'Lords of Sacrifice' (who are ruled by the sign Scorpio) by D.K. They reflect the attributes of the second of the Liberated Hierarchies into dense manifestation. A direct affinity with the conditionings associated with Stanza 3:3, whereon the Monadic Life is externalised can also be considered.

Humanity directly bears the reflected attributes from the cosmic astral plane, conditioned by the qualities of Akṣobhya and directed by the fifth of the liberated Hierarchies. The human Soul consequently is a direct embodiment of the principle of Love, which conditions their purpose. Human Souls (the kingdom of the Sambhogakāya Flower) however are manifest upon the higher mental plane and they bear

---

6 The physical form is not considered a principle, rather is an automaton of the energies pouring through the etheric, hence is not included in this list.

the brunt of the energies of the Dhyāni Buddhas, who condition their subsequent activities.[7] Aquarius is the energy distributer for this activity.

The energy utilised by the fourth Creative Hierarchy is given as 'Mantrikashakti, the WORD made flesh, Speech'.[8] This means that a major objective of human evolution is to eventually discover the mantras, the words of Power governing the forces of Creation utilised by the Logos and the higher Creative Hierarchies. Such knowledge will allow humanity to work seeming miracles in the realms of form, to transmute substance, and to transform mind into sublime states of cosmic Consciousness.

Stanza 3:7 is governed by the sign Pisces the fishes and the conditionings governing the kingdom of Souls upon the higher mental plane, hence the principle of rebirth. Vairocana's Dharmadhātu Wisdom is reflected from the level of the Logoic Soul to condition this plane of perception, and the subsequent moulding of dense substance so that it eventually meets the requirements of the grand Logoic Plan for that *manvantara*. The attributes of this 'Soul' are reflected by the highest of the liberated Creative Hierarchies, simply termed 'Intelligent substance' by D.K. The attributes express the Law of Identity, explained in the last chapter of my book *Meditation and the Initiation Process*. The Hierarchical ruler of Pisces, Pluto (bearing first Ray energies), helps project the zodiacal wheel in a retrograde fashion, to condition *saṃsāra* so as to produce the birthing of each new zodiacal cycle and the termination of its purpose. Thus the wheel of the zodiac turns within the Mother's Womb, the attributes of which are found in the symbolism of the aspects of this long verse. The fifth Ray conditions the mental plane in general.

As this Stanza is now focussed upon the domain of the Soul, so the awakened disciple (the Lanoo, here therefore an Initiate of the third degree) can be shown certain mysteries pertaining to cosmic evolution and world formation, as depicted in these Stanzas. The objective also is to awaken in the Lanoo *buddhic* vision, hence the use of the term 'Behold'.

---

7 See my book *The Buddha Womb and the Way to Liberation* for detail concerning this relationship.

8 *Esoteric Astrology*, 35.

The higher mental plane is the bearer of the Earthy *ākāśa* into manifestation. One could also consider that this plane represents the first sub-aspect of this *ākāśa,* the lower mental plane its second sub-aspect, the astral plane its third sub-aspect, the four ethers the fourth sub-aspect and the dense physical as the most concretised form of this cosmic energy.

Stanza 3:8 depicts the effects of the sign Aries the ram, signifying the energy of the Will and of initial beginnings that impregnates the Germ with light. The impact of Mahatic energy upon the lower mental plane is also directed via the first of the seven Creative Hierarchies, the Divine Flames (whose energy is 'Parashakti, supreme energy'), as an effect of their work with the substance of the cosmic physical plane. They project the Aetheric *ākaśa* to the system, and this Fiery energy impacts the substance of the lower mental plane so that it manifests in accord with the Logoic Mentation, the Plan for that *manvantara.* When reflected upon the lower mental plane this Power is conditioned by the All-accomplishing Wisdom of Amoghasiddhi. His energy is needed to help convert the cosmic 'black dust' that is the substance of this plane, so that it can be incorporated into the structure of human thoughts. Humanity will thus imitate in a distorted, highly reified manner the Thought-Forms of a Logos.

Leonine energy from the Divine Flames energises the mental plane with a reified Fire via the fifth Creative Hierarchy, 'Makara, the mystery' who embody substance of the human personality. This Hierarchy are still working towards their liberation. The attributes of the substance they wield, and the conditioning energies of these *devas* is governed by Capricorn the goat. The creative energy assigned to them is 'Ichchhashakti, the Will to manifest', which is facilitated by the first Ray aspect of Aries.

This Stanza focuses upon the lower mental plane, but specifically in terms of the path of ascent of the mind of the enquiring aspirant, who has awakened the light within the Darkness. The aspirant upon the upward Way is consequently asked appropriate questions to help develop his/her abstract reasoning. The development of the powers of mind/Mind comes under the mode of activity the fifth Ray of Science, whilst the mastery of the substance of *saṃsāra* necessitates the development of the attributes of the Will, as governed by Aries, the first of the signs of the zodiac. Aries drives the impetus to move all forwards and upwards to heights supernal. It also rules the emanation of the abstract Mind to cause the beginnings of things. The Will here is also an aspect of the seventh Ray (Uranus, the Hierarchical ruler of Aries), as all seven Ray methods and attributes must be mastered as one battles the material domain. On this plane humanity manifest their esoteric purpose, which is to convert the base substance, the Elemental Lives, into units of mind. Humanity are consequently Lords of Sacrifice (referring to our Monadic forms). Humanity inverts the substance of the three lower planes, so as to bring the lives of the form to liberation (the plane *buddhi).* Such activity is governed by Scorpio, which conditions the testings of Initiation, as aspirants battle to overcome the substance of these planes. To do so they must develop the first Ray Arian impetus to master the impediments of the path before them.

Stanza 3:9 is governed by the attributes of the sign Taurus the bull, who embodies the Waters of the cosmic astral plane in general ('the Water of Life in the great Mother'), hence also its reverberation upon the systemic astral plane. Humans utilise the first Ray impetus of Vulcan, the esoteric and Hierarchical ruler of Taurus in terms of personality will, to project the self-focussed images desired by the individual, plus the creative imaginings of the mind, ruled by Venus, the exoteric ruler of Taurus, to create the conditionings of the astral plane for them. They have created Watery miasmas under the auspices of Taurean impulses, and the desire impulses of its polar opposite, Scorpio, manifesting via the sixth Ray.

The sixth Ray that generally governs this Stanza facilitates reception of the concrete mental substance to the Watery energies from the cosmic astral plane conveyed by Pisces (a Water sign). The martial sixth Ray energy and the Will or Power of the first Ray therefore work together as a unit to accommodate the potency of the impact of the energies of the Logoic Mind that conditions the turning of the great Wheel. (Also considered in terms of *pratītyasamutpāda,* as explained in the fourth volume of *A Treatise on Mind.)*

The Equalising Wisdom of Ratnasambhava also governs the astral plane, in order to assist humanity to control the Lunar Lords that constitute the substance of this plane of perception. Ratnasambhava here works with the third sub-aspect of Earthy *ākāśa,* which facilitates the crystallisation process. It also helps engender the attributes of the mind upon the upward cycle via loving, magnetically attractive attitudes of humanity. (Ratnasambhava also condition the evolutionary process under the law of Love.) The entire field of desire and attachment and all other forms of emotional thinking and glamour must be mastered. The energy of the Lunar Lords is given by D.K. as 'Kundalinishakti, the energy of Matter'. We know *kuṇḍalinī* to be the inherent Fires that sustain the form, which humanity must learn to rightly release, if they are to be liberated from *saṃsāra.* By mastering the Lunar Lords humanity can transform the primal energies unifying the Elemental Lives (the last of the Creative Hierarchies) and so mentally control the material forms we see all around us.

The sign attributed to the Lunar Lords (who clothe our mental-emotions) is Sagittarius. The Sagittarian impulse conditions them mainly because of the disastrous activities of humanity upon the moon Chain and Atlantis, where their massed wilful desire precipitated this energy upon the Lunar Lords. Much of the sexual misery on earth has its foundation here. Most of this *karma* will be rectified with the advent of the new age and the appearance of the sixth Root Race.

Stanza 3:10 depicts the attributes of Gemini the twins, under whose auspices the *deva* kingdom 'spin a web' of the *nāḍī* system, the webs of Life for the new form. The systemic astral-etheric plane now comes into view. Gemini projects the higher, living vitality, into the Blinded Lives that the *devas* rightly organise. The complete externalisation of the first Outpouring via the energetic impetus of the sixth Ray can thereby manifest.

Both this Stanza and Stanza 3:11 (directly dealing with the etheric domain) are concerned with the crystallisation of the originating cosmic Fires to cause the appearance of the elementary substance of the mineral kingdom. *Kuṇḍalinī* is the means whereby the Elementary Lives are organised by the crystallised Fire, integrating the Anu's *(aṇus),* the elementary atoms, into the atomic Elements known to scientists.[9] The

9 See the later chapters of *Esoteric Cosmology and Modern Physics* for detail of this process.

devas (the Agnisuryans and Agnichaitans) utilise the energies from the Lesser Builders to build upon a mass scale the forms found in the three worlds of human livingness. The *karma* of the lives evolving in the material domains is thereby moulded. The governing sign of the Lesser Builders (the third Creative Hierarchy) is Libra the balances, whilst *jñānaśakti,* the 'force of mind', is their conditioning energy. The impact of the work of Lesser Builders is first upon the mental plane, and then reverberates via the astral to cause the conditionings of dense form. This allows aspects of cosmic Mind to reach right down to form the mineral kingdom via the agencies of the astral and etheric *devas* that are the bearers of increasingly reified aspects of Mahat. The third *(manasic)* sub-aspect of Earthy *ākāśa* under the auspices of Ratnasambhava and the sixth Ray energising potency is utilised to produce this consolidation process of substance into forms.

Stanza 3:11 continues with the externalisation process, under the auspices of Cancer the crab (the gateway to birth) and its sixth Ray Neptunian energies (whereby the Waters are appropriately distributed), Neptune being the esoteric and Hierarchical ruler of Cancer. Here the sixth Ray works in conjunction with the seventh (that governs this Stanza in general) in order to cause the precipitation of the mineral kingdom. The combination of the dual Rays assists in the objectivity of the etheric-physical domain. 'The great Day' of the new *mahāmanvantara* thus manifests. The incorporation of the tenth and eleventh Creative Hierarchies into the physical universe, as well as the process of their mastery, is taken into account in this Stanza. This work happens under the power of Amitābha's Wisdom, with the fourth sub-aspect of Earthy *ākāśa* assisting in the reflection of the energies of the four cosmic ethers into their physical counterparts.

Stanza 3:12 is governed by the attributes of the sign Leo the lion, the sign of individuation, which controls the Earthy Fires of the mind, with its separative, concretising attributes. Leo is ruled exoterically, esoterically and Hierarchically by the sun (which veils certain planets). Leo conditions the evolutionary process by seeding the elementary attributes of self-consciousness (instinct) of the evolving Lives, each of which reflect aspects of 'the Self-Existing Lord'. This causes the appearance of the final concretion of material substance, the atomic

Life of the mineral kingdom, hence the manifestation of the Elemental Lives, the twelfth Creative Hierarchy.

The third Ray of Mathematically Exact Activity generally rules the physical domain, as it also veils the import of all the Rays of Mind. This Ray is needed by the Lords of Life to externalise the material domain and to sustain its activities for the needed duration of time, so that its purpose can be accomplished. The Elemental Life comes under the field of embrace of the energy distribution of Aquarius (the polar opposite of Leo). There is no *śakti* assigned to them, but the work manifests under the fifth sub-aspect of Earthy *ākāśa*, and Amitābha's Wisdom.

The sum of the forces of the liberated Hierarchies working via humanity, as presented in Stanza 3:6 (under Aquarius, the polar opposite of Leo), is now brought to bear upon this elementary Life, to lift up their sentience to the higher dimensions, by being incorporated as the substance of mind.

Before delving into the explanation for this section, Tabulation VI from *Esoteric Astrology*[10] needs to be provided, where the orthodox, esoteric and Hierarchical planetary rulers to the signs of the zodiac are given. The orthodox planetary rulers are those traditionally assigned to a native born in the respective sign. They are part of the great illusion, and in time become superseded by the esoteric ones, after the turning about in the seat of consciousness has occurred in the disciple. The disciple is no longer focussed downwards into the materialism of *saṃsāra,* but rather upwards towards the Soul and the liberated domains. The Hierarchical rulers govern the Life of the awakened Initiate (from the third Initiation onwards), where the Monadic aspect and the energies streaming from Shambhala condition his/her consciousness and activities.

For the purpose of analysing these stanzas therefore, mainly the Hierarchical rulers to the various signs of the zodiac need to be used, as they condition the evolutionary process and the formation of our solar system. In doing so some of the reasons why they were so assigned can be revealed. The qualities associated with the planetary Schemes, especially with respect to the *chakras* they embody in the solar system can be studied to assist comprehension.

---

10 *Esoteric Astrology,* 68.

Constellation	Orthodox	Disciple	Hierarchical
Aries	Mars	Mercury	Uranus
Taurus	Venus	Vulcan	Vulcan
Gemini	Mercury	Venus	The Earth
Cancer	The Moon	Neptune	Neptune
Leo	The Sun	The Sun	The Sun
Virgo	Mercury	The Moon	Jupiter
Libra	Venus	Uranus	Saturn
Scorpio	Mars	Mars	Mercury
Sagittarius	Jupiter	The Earth	Mars
Capricorn	Saturn	Saturn	Venus
Aquarius	Uranus	Jupiter	The Moon
Pisces	Jupiter	Pluto	Pluto

Table 2. The Planetary Rulers governing the Constellations

In connection with the Hierarchical rulers of the signs we see that Ray one governs Vulcan and Pluto, relating Taurus to Pisces. Ray two governs the Sun and Jupiter, relating Leo to Virgo. Ray three governs the Earth and Saturn, relating Gemini to Libra. Ray four governs Mercury and the Moon, relating Scorpio to Aquarius. Ray five governs Venus via Capricorn. Ray six governs Neptune and Mars relating Cancer to Sagittarius, and Ray seven governs Uranus, ruling Aries. It should be noted that the Moon and the Sun but veil other planetary influences. As D.K. states in the case of the Moon:

> The moon is a dead form; it has no emanation at all. That is why the moon is spoken of in the ancient teachings as "veiling either Vulcan or Uranus."[11]

11 Ibid., 13.

Concerning the sun D.K. states:

> The three aspects of the Sun (as dealt with in *The Secret Doctrine*) are of importance at this point, because influences flowing through and from them bring the entire subjective and latent world consciousness to the fore and produce eventually (at the final revelation and liberation) the full expression of the consciousness of Deity. This can be called divine sensitivity, the universal mind or the divine plan or purpose. Words are inadequate to express that of which the highest initiate as yet knows but little. These three aspects of the Sun are the factors which bring consciousness to the birth and make the ultimate goal attainable; they make all forms of consciousness possible because these are rooted in the Sun (symbolically speaking) and are an inherent aspect of the greater whole.
>
> 1. The physical Sun—the anima mundi; the animal soul. Multiplicity.
> 2. The heart of the Sun—the human soul and the divine ego. Duality.
> 3. The central, spiritual Sun—the divine consciousness. The will of the whole. The awareness of God. Unity.
>
> As you have been told, the Sun veils certain hidden planets, and in the case of Leo, the two planets through which the Sun focuses its energy or influences (like a lens) are Neptune and Uranus. The "heart of the Sun" employs Neptune as its agent, whilst the central, spiritual Sun pours its influences through Uranus.[12]

Stanza Three part One

Stanza 3:1 states:

> **.....The last vibration of the seventh Eternity thrills through Infinitude. The Mother swells, expanding from within without like the bud of the Lotus.**

Keynotes: Virgo, seventh cosmic astral sub-plane, the cosmic Waters, Akṣobhya.

The numerological breakdown of the first sentence:

---

12 Ibid., 295-296.

> The last vibration (69, 24, Taurus), the seventh Eternity (89, 17), the seventh Eternity thrills (124, 25), thrills through Infinitude (135, 15 x 9, 27 = 3 x 9), the seventh Eternity thrills though Infinitude (224, 44), the last vibration of the seventh Eternity (170, 44), the last vibration of the seventh Eternity thrills (205, 52), the last vibration of the seventh Eternity thrills though Infinitude (305, 71 = 8).

As stated, the overall conditioning sign of Stanza 3:1 is Virgo and the activity within the Womb of the great Mother, established via the substance of the seventh cosmic astral sub-plane.

The meaning of *'the seventh Eternity'* was explained in Stanza 1:1. The phrase *'The last vibration of the seventh Eternity'* thus concerns the last or final rhythmic oscillation of the 'slumbering' solar or planetary Personality upon the cosmic astral before incarnation into the cosmic etheric plane, and therefore dense physical involvement. *'The seventh Eternity'* thus refers to the process of precipitation of substance from the seventh sub-plane of the cosmic astral to the cosmic dense physical plane.

Concerning *'the Seventh Eternity'*, H.P.B states:

> The seemingly paradoxical use of the sentence "Seventh Eternity," thus dividing the indivisible, is sanctified in esoteric philosophy. The latter divides boundless duration into unconditionally eternal and universal Time and a conditioned one *(Khandakāla)*. One is the abstraction or noumenon of infinite time (Kala); the other its phenomenon appearing periodically, as the effect of *Mahat* (the Universal Intelligence limited by Manvantaric duration). With some schools, Mahat is "the first-born" of Pradhāna (undifferentiated substance, or the periodical aspect of Mulaprakriti, the root of Nature), which (Pradhāna) is called Maya, the Illusion. In this respect, I believe, esoteric teaching differs from the Vedantin doctrines of both the Adwaita and the Visishtadwaita schools. For it says that, while Mulaprakriti, the noumenon, is self-existing and without any origin — is, in short, parentless, Anupadaka (as one with Brahmam) — Prakriti, its phenomenon, is periodical and no better than a phantasm of the former, so Mahat, with the Occultists, the first-born of Gnāna (or *gnosis)* knowledge, wisdom or the Logos — is a phantasm reflected from the Absolute NIRGUNA (Parabrahm, the one reality, "devoid of attributes and qualities"; see Upanishads); while with some Vedantins Mahat is a manifestation of Prakriti, or Matter.

> (b) Therefore, the "last vibration of the Seventh Eternity" was "fore-ordained" — by no God in particular, but occurred in virtue of the eternal and changeless LAW which causes the great periods of Activity and Rest, called so graphically, and at the same time so poetically, the "Days and Nights of Brahmā."[13]

The word *vibration* is defined as an oscillating or periodic motion of a fluid, of air or an elastic body where its equilibrium has been disturbed. The numbers of the phrase *'The last vibration'* add to 24, 15, where the number 24 also appeared earlier in reference to the word Svabhavat, the plastic essence that fills the universe, and also to the phrase 'The Alaya of the Universe'. What concerns us here is 'the last vibration' of the cosmic Waters, which condenses to become the *devamātri* that form the substance *(svabhāva)* of the cosmic ethers. The number 24 refers to the second sign of the zodiac, Taurus the bull, which constitutes the great Womb of Being *(hiraṇyagarbha).* In this respect 'the last vibration' is synonymous with the final labour pain of the cosmic Mother (in the guise of the cosmic Cow) that brings about the parturition of the visible universe. The number 3 x 5 has reference here to the Will of cosmic Intelligence (Mahat) that causes the flow of the Eternities right to the manifestation of the 'last Vibration'.

The numbers of the phrase *'the seventh Eternity'* add to 17, 8, indicating that everything is permeated with the Presence of Deity (17) that manifests as the fundamental spiral-cyclic motion (8) associated with the circulation of energy within each Eternity, and which links them together. Each Eternity can be conceived as an unbounded sphere, and when stacked upon each other seven times, like one eight above another, effectively makes a spinal column.[14] This column is surmounted by the Head centre – the ineffable Mind of 'God' that permeates and controls all. Everything is concerned with the effect of energy interplay.

The numbers of the phrase *'The seventh Eternity thrills through Infinitude'* add to 200 + 24 (Taurus) or 7 x 32, 44. The number 7 x 32 implies that this Eternity, like that of the other Eternities, is an expression of Logoic Love. This means that the entire process of the

13 The S.D., Vol. I, 62.

14 This imagery but provides a basic idea of a far more transcendental process.

energy that thrills through the infinitude is an act of Logoic Compassion meant to advance all Lives caught up in the sweep of the motion one stage further upon their evolutionary journeying once Incarnation proceeds. Akṣobhya's Mirror-like Wisdom is expressed to effect this purpose, and also for the reasons explained in the general outline. These Lives, being former liberated members of a human kingdom (signified by the number 44), are brought into objectivity within the Womb of the great Mother once the energy 'thrills' them into activity. The Womb consists of cosmic astral and etheric substance (governed by the sign Taurus).

The word *thrills* means to affect with a sudden wave of keen emotion or excitement, to produce a tremor or tingling sensation throughout the body. The energy associated with this vibration stirred into action, or vivified (awakened), the myriads of Creative Intelligences, the *devamātri,* Ah-Hi, Dhyān Chohans, and so forth. All of the forces constituting the immanent Body of manifestation of the cosmic Logos are activated. The vibration manifests like a contagious harmonising melody that the great Ones listen to, reverberate the Sound with added strains to their subordinates in order to produce the needed activity. The modified melody also awakened the human Monads, to direct them into their next Round of service. Collectively all are symbolised by the number 44, hence the numbers of the phrase *'The last vibration of the seventh Eternity'* adds to 44 (as well as to the number 17 x 10). The number 4 x 11 implies that this 'seventh Eternity' manifests as the Logoic *nāḍī* system, from which all the energies in systemic space are derived, allowing the incarnating Logos (17 x 10) to establish His seat of Power via that which 'thrills'. The vivification of the *chakras* of Deity on the cosmic ethers happens as a consequence of this 'last vibration'. The quaternary of the form nature can thereby be established. Also the fourth (earth) Scheme in the solar septenary is where the lowest point of descent of the energy that 'thrills' occurs. The fourth globe then appears, wherein terrestrial life is possible. The number 17 x 10 refers to the expression of the absolute Power of Deity throughout a complete sphere or cycle of *manvantaric* activity (the number 10).

Here the relationship of Taurus to Scorpio (whose significance was explained above) is that of a horizontal line, signifying the feminine principle in Nature, bisecting the sphere of the zodiacal Womb. It represents the cosmic Egg that will be fecundated by the masculine principle, the descending energies of the Eternities from the higher cosmic spheres. Inevitably the approaching crescendo of this seventh Eternity will impregnate this Egg, producing the appearing phenomena upon the cosmic dense physical plane. Taurus supplies the field of Desire, the feminine principle that represents the Womb within which the divine Child is to be formed. Scorpio provides the cyclic energetic impulses (the continuous injection of Desire-filled Lives) to effect every change in the Womb. The injected Lives form the substance and organs of this growing cosmic Child.

The numbers of the phrase *'thrills through Infinitude'* add to 3 x 9 and to 100 + 7 x 5, 15 x 9. The number 3 x 9 here refers to the Will of the cosmic Soul which generates the originating impetus of rebirthing, that permeates cosmic Fire (from the Mind of Deity – 100 + 7 x 5, 3 x 5 x 9), and causes all the Laws pertaining to the manifestation of every atom in space. The process is thereby set in motion that will eventually assist the resultant evolving streams of human consciousness to be Initiated into aspects of that Mind. Primal substance is consequently mastered by those involved. The Impulse of the energy of cosmic Mind (Mahat) permeates all with Logoic purpose, which *'thrills through Infinitude'*. This energy is projected in the form of the Kumāras (15 x 9) that will inevitably establish Logoic Head centres for every circumscribed domain of Logoic planetary or solar spheres of Activity. All is emanated as an activity of cosmic Mind (7 x 5, or more specifically symbolised by the number 305 of *the complete phrase)* so that all attributes of the units of consciousness evolving through manifest space can eventually embody Mind. The number 305 implies that the Creative Word (Mahat) of the third Logos (300) is expressed.

The numbers 15 x 9 and 3 x 9 also refer to the *deva* triads that thrill through Infinitude to help produce the evolution of substance into units of consciousness.

Here also is implied that the 'last vibration' of this 'seventh Eternity' eventually impacts upon the substance of the systemic mental plane, the lowest reach of a Logos. From here nevertheless the entire formed domain can manifest, as explained in chapter one and in my book

Esoteric Cosmology and Modern Physics. As the energy that 'thrills' passes from the *buddhic* plane (which can also be symbolised by the number 44) to the mental so then the projection of the Creative Thought from the Mind of Deity can express, sustain, and then abstract the entire *mahāmanvantara.* The cosmic mental plane (and its astral expression), from which all proceeds, can be considered infinite in that it is dimensionless, having no boundaries other than the 'limits' of the greatest cosmic Mind. Naught therein however is eternal, for all conceptions and Thought Forms have a beginning and an ending.

The numbers of the phrase *'the seventh Eternity thrills'* add to 31 x 4 and to 5 x 5. The number 31 x 4 implies that this Eternity is an expression of the Will of Deity, the purpose being to establish a Throne or Seat of Power (Shambhala). When projected via the four cosmic ethers this Will galvanises into activity the substance of the mental plane (5 x 5) and the condensation of cosmic 'black dust' in the manner described in my book *Esoteric Cosmology and Modern Physics.* This energy also establishes lesser seats of Power (31 x 4) on the mental plane, the formation of the kingdom of Souls via which the entire creative play concerning the redemption of this 'dust' can be made possible.

The number 124 also adds to 100 + 24, which refers to the sign Taurus. As well as what has been explained it should be noted that within the Womb of the great Mother (embodied by this feminine sign) primeval matter *(mūlaprakṛti)* can be wrought as the 'food' for the evolving man-plants. Thus Taurus is the harbinger of all the creation myths associated with the various cow Goddesses upon this earth (despite astrologically being called a bull). The constellation holds the Pleiades, the seven Sisters, upon its back, who are primarily concerned with the formation of stellar and planetary spheres, as was explained in my book *The Constitution of Shambhala.* The thrill of the 'seventh Eternity' therefore impels the activity, mantric Songs, and *deva* Potentates from this constellation to impact upon the nebulae wherein suns are born.

The numbers of the phrase *'the last vibration of the seventh Eternity thrills'* add to 200 + 5, 52. The numbers refer to the Mahatic impetus (5) of the compassionate meditation of a Logos (200) that sends this final vibration (mantric emanation) to produce the appearance of a new *mahāmanvantara* for the duration of a great Day or Year of Brahmā

(52). The cycles of time are therefore instigated. There are 52 weeks to a solar year, which symbolises the duration of this Eternity, in terms of cosmic evolution, or the phases of a night of Brahmā.

The numerical breakdown of the last two phrases:

> The Mother (49, 13), The Mother swells (67 = 13, 22), expanding from within (112 = 7 x 16, 31), from within (63, 18), from within without (98 = 49 x 2, 26 = 8), expanding from within without (147 = 49 x 3, 39) like the bud (43, 25), the bud of the Lotus (66, 30), the Lotus (30, 12), the bud (24, 15), like the bud of the Lotus (85 = 17 x 5, 40), expanding from within without like the bud of the Lotus (232, 79 = 16).

The meaning of *'the Mother'* and Her relationship to the Father and the Son was explained in Stanza 1:5, as well as in Stanza 2:3 in relation to the *mātripadma*. The numbers of this phrase add to 7 x 7, 13. The Mother thus embodies all of the various septenaries and their subdivisions associated with the many categories of manifested life. The activity of each septenary expands from their bud stage to their floral expression by means of the *devas* that embody the substance of it all. The number 7 (the powers of which appear often in this Stanza) refers to all septenaries of expression, the seven stages of the evolutionary process, and to the various *chakras* in the body, that in the early stages of evolutionary development also take the form of buds that eventually expand to fully opened lotus blossoms. The number 13 refers to any sphere of activity *(chakra)* in the Body of Deity, which can 'swell from within without'.

To *swell* means to slowly expand, as for instance water or air filling a balloon, to puff up or inflate (as with pride). It can also refer to a gradual increase of loudness or volume of sound.

The numbers of the phrase *'the Mother swells'* add to 22, 13. Every sphere of activity (13) associated with the planetary or solar *chakras,* here taking the guise of the Mother, swell, thereby undergoing the expansion signifying the manifestation of divine Activity. The number 22 refers to the zodiacal (or Hierarchical) and Planetary energies and all the related entities that form the substance of the Womb of the Mother. They cause the swelling, as the various lives come in with these forces to expand the Womb, as governed by the sign Virgo. These forces (as well as the *karma)* are gathered within a contained form upon the seventh cosmic astral sub-plane and are organised by means of the Love-Wisdom of the Ah-Hi that are called into active manifestation. In relation to this, Jupiter, governing this second Ray, is the Hierarchical ruler of Virgo.

The numbers of the phrase *'expanding from within'* add to 100 + 12, 7 x 16, 31. Here the number 7 x 16 refers to the seven planetary (or solar) Logoi, the *chakras* in the Body of the embodying Logos, who cause the expansion process as they prepare for active manifestation. Each Logos is a cosmic Christ (16), embodying the seeds for the awakening of a Heart centre (100 + 12) for an entire planetary dispensation. The number 31 refers to the Will, the first Ray energy of deity that initiates this expansion. The planetary Logoi must exert their Wills if they are to produce spheres of influence through which to incarnate.

The number 7 x 9 of the phrase *'from within'* refers to the Initiates (9) that will embody the awakening *chakras,* and whose activity causes them to swell from within as the Lives that are incorporated within their bodies of manifestation evolve. The *chakras* expand with the initiation of each new cycle via their agency. They channel the Light of the consciousness or Son aspect (symbolised by Jupiter) that evolves in time and space. The swelling process quickens as these Light bearing agents increasingly command the activity of the *chakras.* Descent into incarnation always signifies the opportunity to undertake Initiation by all concerned, which can be viewed as an expansion of the consciousness and auric state of the Initiates.

The phrases *'from within without'* and *'expanding from within without'* numerologically add to powers of the number 7, (7 x 7 x 2 and 7 x 7 x 3). This informs us that the expanding process happens as a consequence of the activation of the septenaries governing Nature. They manifest in increasing diversity and number as the cycles of Life come into expression. All are activated by the reverberating 'thrill' of 'the seventh Eternity', whose Sound awakens each septenary from their former *nirvāṇic* slumber. The number 49 x 3 also refers to the expansion from within without of the septenaries on all three major levels of expression (Spirit, Soul and matter) associated with material evolution.

The second phrase also provides the number 3 x 13, which refers to the activity cycle of each Logoic sphere. This expansion process effectively lasts for three quarters of the entire *manvantara,* wherein the material or Mother aspect, the five lesser Ray qualities associated with the evolution of Mind, are developed. (Thirty-nine being three quarters of the number 52 that signifies the entire great year of evolution.) After that the epoch of the Son (the second Ray cycle of Love-Wisdom) comes into play, whereby the transformation and transmutation of the evolved *saṃskāras* are effected upon the upward way of abstraction and eventual Monadic return.

The numbers of the phrase *'like the bud'* add to 5 x 5, 7. The number 5 x 5 refers to the higher mental plane, wherein resides the causal form of the Soul, which in the early stages of its development is a bud lotus, which slowly opens as the necessary characteristics are developed by the personality aspect rayed down into the realms of the form. Each *chakra* similarly awakens as the principle of Mind (5 x 5) increasingly manifests its activity.

Concerning the expansion of the Soul-form ('egoic body') D.K. states:

> At the early stages after individualisation, the egoic body has the appearance of a bud. The electric fire at the centre is not apparent, and all the nine petals are closed down upon the inner three; the orange colour has a dead aspect and the three points of light at the base are just points and nothing more; the triangle which is later seen connecting the points is not demonstrated. The surrounding sphere is colourless and is only to be appreciated as undulatory vibrations (like waves in the air or ether) reaching barely beyond the petal outline.
>
> By the time the third Initiation is reached, a wondrous transformation has transpired. The outer sphere is palpitating with every colour of the rainbow, and is of wide radius; the streams of electrical energy circulating in it are so powerful that they are escaping beyond the periphery of the circle, resembling the rays of a sun.[15]

What applies for the human unit, or the Sambhogakāya Flower, can always be transposed in a transmuted form to Logoi.

---

15 Alice Bailey, *A Treatise on Cosmic Fire,* 763. See also page 823 for an illustration of this Soul form.

The numbers of the phrases *'the Lotus'* and *'the bud of the Lotus'* add to 30, 6.6 (12) and to 66. The number 30 refers here to the ring-pass-not, the delineation of the boundaries of form, of the kingdom of 'God' within which the divine Child evolves, causing the expansion of consciousness that develops from 'within without'. The Mother works within this boundary to build all of the attributes of this Child, once the twelve petals of the Heart centre are awakened. The Heart is needed to contain the qualities of the Love-Wisdom generated by the evolution of the Son in incarnation. The lotus can also be considered to embody the united substance of the forms of the twelve Creative Hierarchies. It remains in bud form in preparation to embody manifest space, whence it begins to flower.

The number 66 refers to the *maṇḍala* based on the hexagrams of expression that govern the patterning of all manifest life. It signifies the empowerment of the Sacral centres that build and vitalise evolving forms of the incarnating Lives. It is a shorthand form of the no 666 that appears at the end of chapter thirteen of the *Book of Revelation*. There it is said to be the number of man, which can be interpreted also as a planetary or solar Logos actively involved in incarnate expression.

The numbers of the phrase *'like the bud of the Lotus'* add to 17 x 5, 4 x 10. The no 17 x 5 refers to the five liberated Hierarchies that embody attributes of the Mind of a Logos, or to the five Kumāras (the five Dhyāni Buddhas). They are responsible for the projection of the five Elements of Mind into systemic space, and later from the *ātmic* plane down. The five sense-consciousnesses in Nature evolve from the Kumāras. Through the transmutative activities of humanity the sense-consciousnesses eventually develop into the Wisdoms of the Jinas (Dhyāni Buddhas). The entire philosophy of such development was provided in my *Treatise on Mind*. The expression of their Wisdoms via the establishment of a Shambhalic seat of Power causes this *mātripadma* to 'swell from within without', once evolution proceeds and humanity evolve their innate capabilities. The five non-sacred petals of a Heart centre accommodate the evolution and eventual transformation (mastery) of the associated *prāṇas*. One can also consider the five non-sacred planets in the chart of solar evolution, which take the attributes of the constitution of Brahmā in the solar system.

The number 4 x 10 refers to the fourth principle *(buddhi)* wherein reside the *chakras* in the Body of Deity. It is also the number signifying our planetary Scheme, Chain or globe, the human Kingdom (the fourth in Nature) and of the solar Logos (which is of the fourth order). During the early stages of evolution they can all be pictured in the form of bud lotuses, which 'swell from within without'.

H.P.B's essential commentary:

> The expansion "from within without" of the Mother, called elsewhere the "Waters of Space," "Universal Matrix," etc., does not allude to an expansion from a small centre or focus, but, without reference to size or limitation or area, means the development of limitless subjectivity into as limitless objectivity. "The ever (to us) invisible and immaterial Substance present in eternity, threw its periodical shadow from its own plane into the lap of Maya." It implies that this expansion, not being an increase in size — for infinite extension admits of no enlargement — was a change of condition. It "expanded like the bud of the Lotus"; for the Lotus plant exists not only as a miniature embryo in its seed (a physical characteristic), but its prototype is present in an ideal form in the Astral Light from "Dawn" to "Night" during the Manvantaric period, like everything else, as a matter of fact, in this objective Universe; from man down to mite, from giant trees down to the tiniest blades of grass.
>
> All this, teaches the hidden Science, is but the temporary reflection, the shadow of the eternal ideal prototype in Divine Thought — the word "Eternal," note well again, standing here only in the sense of "Æon," as lasting throughout the seemingly interminable, but still limited cycle of activity, called by us Manvantara. For what is the real esoteric meaning of Manvantara, or rather a Manu-Antara? It means, esoterically, "between two Manus," of whom there are fourteen in every "Day of Brahmā," such a "Day" consisting of 1,000 aggregates of four ages, or 1,000 "Great Ages," Mahayugas. Let us now analyse the word or name Manu. Orientalists and their Dictionaries tell us that the term "Manu" is from the root *Man,* "to think"; hence "the thinking man." But, esoterically, every Manu, as an anthropomorphized patron of his special cycle (or Round), is but the personified idea of the "Thought Divine" (as the Hermetic "Pymander"); each of the Manus, therefore, being the special god, the creator and fashioner of all that appears during his own respective cycle of being or Manvantara. Fohat

> runs the Manus' (or Dhyan-Chohans') errands, and causes the ideal prototypes to expand from within without — viz., to cross gradually, on a descending scale, all the planes from the noumenon to the lowest phenomenon, to bloom finally on the last into full objectivity — the acme of illusion, or the grossest matter.[16]

With respect to the above quotation it can be added that H.P.B. can state that the expansion of the bud lotus 'was not an increase in size' because the originating Logos circumscribed an area of space, establishing a 'ring-pass-not' within which the entire play of *saṃsāra* ('the bud') is to be effected. The area of space to be mastered is established from the beginning, nevertheless there is a growth outwards from a bud form of a lotus to fill this space, and the auric radiance of its emanatory influence inevitably stretches far into cosmic space.

The concept of throwing 'its periodical Shadow from its own plane into the Lap of Maya' is esoterically veiled in the symbolism of the 'fall of the three into the four'. Fohat, the dynamic energy of cosmic Ideation, is the basic *prāṇa* of cosmos. It is a Fiery force (*śakti*) emanating via the cosmic astral plane, a threefold energy (cosmic electricity) that impacts upon the three higher systemic planes, precipitating what is latent (*mūlaprakṛti*) into activity as the demonstration of material power. The energising expression of the Divine Thought of the third Logos (Brahmā) produces the activity of the seven Systemic planes of perception. Indeed, it is the cause for their manifestation. This energy therefore 'runs the Manus' errands', to awaken the Head centres of what must come to rule all under the auspices of the progenitor Manu, the Manu being the Father of the Race or embodied attribute to come. The 'ideal prototypes' then are the images of deity (the Heavenly Men, Logoi, or their Causal Forms) in the form of the Humanity that must expand 'within without' to embody the Mind-space of what is possible to contain in each expanded Head lotus.

The numbers 200 + 32, 16 of the complete phrase *'expanding from within without like the bud of the Lotus'* implies that this lotus expands when the Love-Wisdom or Christ principle evolves within the manifest form. The energies can be reflected from above down, but specifically

---

16 The S.D., Vol. 1, 62-63.

from within without, when looking inwards relates to the attainment of the higher dimensions of perception by way of the Heart, Love-Wisdom being reflected thereto by means of Akṣobhya's Mirror-like Wisdom. The nature of the expression of the quality or intensity of this energy causes this expansion. The principle of Love is at-one with the substance of cosmic astral Space. It is literally the All-that-Is.

Stanza Three part Two

Stanza 3:2 states:

> **The vibration sweeps along, touching with its swift wing** *(simultaneously)* **the whole Universe, and the Germ that dwelleth in darkness: the darkness that breathes** (moves) **over the slumbering Waters of Life.**

Keynotes: Libra, Aetheric Element, the first Ray, first cosmic ether - *ādi,* Amoghasiddhi, Divine Flames, reflecting the fifth Creative Hierarchy. The fourth Eternity.

The numerical breakdown of the first two phrases:

The vibration (62 = 31 x 2, 17), sweeps along (46, 10), the vibration sweeps along (108, 27), Touching with its swift Wing (128 = 32 x 4, 29 = 11), its swift Wing (61, 16), The whole Universe (83 = 11, 20), touching with its swift Wing the whole Universe (211, 49).

As stated, Stanza 3:2 is conditioned generally by the attributes of the sign Libra the balances, of the effect of the Logoic Meditation process that causes the resultant energy to sweep along the vast reaches of cosmic Space. The 'sweeping' projects the elements of the cosmic Womb into the seven systemic planes (the cosmic dense physical sub-planes) via the plane *ādi.* The first of the incarnated Creative Hierarchies, the Divine Flames are awakened thereby. They reflect the energies and purpose of the fifth liberated Creative Hierarchy into manifestation.

The concept of 'touching' indicates contact with something material, in this case with the substance of the cosmic dense physical plane.

Stanza 3:2 also introduces a triangle of energies associated with the western quadrant of the zodiac: Libra the balances, Scorpio the scorpion and Virgo the virgin. The Scorpionic impulse energises the projection of the forces and Entities constituting the cosmic Womb that are swept into activity. The energies from the exoteric and esoteric ruler of this sign, Mars the god of war, are utilised, plus the mediatory effect of Mars' Hierarchical ruler, Mercury. This martial force pierces 'the Germ' with Logoic Purpose. The 'swift wing' of this motion signifies Kalāhaṃsa, the bird of space and time, which represents the process that awakens the *karma* of those within the Womb (governed by Virgo), as wielded by Libra the Balances. (Saturn, the lord of *karma* being the Hierarchical ruler of Libra.) The instigation of the new cycle therefore reveals the *karma* of the past, as the Light bearing forces (the Creative Hierarchies) are awakened from their slumber. Being the adjudicator of the law Libra holds in its embrace all that is contained in the coming cycles of expression (symbolised by the feathers of the wing of this bird) that will awaken the evolving form.

This *karma* is stored in the spirillae of the Logoic physical permanent atom, which is symbolised by 'the Germ' in this verse. Libra controls the rate of release of the qualities of energies *(saṃskāras)* contained in the spirillae. The feathers of this wing can also be considered the main spirals of this atom (viewed in terms of the energies moving through time), each possessing subsidiary spirals capable of attracting to them the corresponding substance *(svabhāva)* of the Mother, so that the required form can be built.

In this triangle the energies of Scorpio represents the Son, Libra the Father aspect and Virgo the Mother of what is to be. The martial energies of Scorpio therefore activates the Heart centres of the Lives to be awakened from slumber via the materialising energies of the seventh cosmic astral sub-plane. This activation is accomplished by means of *sūtrātmās,* each of which is projected by the symbolic 'sting' of Scorpio. With the Heart centre established the remaining six major *chakras* of the informing Lives will in turn be awakened. The meditating One in Libra weaves the pattern of the integrated Lives of the Ah-Hi, the bearers of Mind. Each Heart centre becomes a vehicle of compassionate concern, projecting the *bodhicitta,* which here is an effect of Scorpionic energy.

This is the guarantor that all will inevitably tread the Bodhisattva path to liberation.

Libra is responsible for activating the Throat in the Head, Scorpio the Heart in the Head, and Virgo the outermost tier of petals, the Solar Plexus in the Head centre of the embodying Logos for that Womb.

The meaning of the term *vibration* was explained in Stanza 3:1, whilst the numbers of the phrase *'the vibration'* add to 31 x 2, 17. The number 31 x 2 refers to the reflection (2) into manifest space of the Will (31) of the Deity (17) that instigated the vibration.

The word *sweeps* means that something is moved with swiftness, force, etc., to touch or come in contact with (a surface) in the manner of a brush. The Mind's energies move to cause the sweeping motion of that which it contacts, the manifest space of the external universe. Part of the work of the awakened Divine Flames concerns vivifying the spirals and spirillae of the physical permanent atom with the Lives and energies needed for the new Logoic Incarnation. They work with the fifth liberated Creative Hierarchy under the auspices of the potency of Amoghasiddhi's All-accomplishing Wisdom. Amoghasiddhi's Wisdom drives forward this sweeping motion so that the various spirals of the atom are rightly imbued according to what needs to be expressed at any specific cycle *(yuga)*. Divine Will must be utilised in order to bring into manifestation all that must be. The incoming *saṃskāras* (the Lives bearing the needed attributes for the manifesting cycle) must be appropriately timed and rightly directed in order to produce what is desired and to mitigate any possible negative effect.

The numbers 108, 27 of the phrase *'the vibration sweeps along'* relate to the establishment of the entire compliment of a planetary or solar Head centre (Shambhala), wherein the vibration sweeps, to awaken all of the attributes associated with its various petals. The Divine Flames awaken and energise this centre at the beginning of time and coordinate its construction with the aid of the Lipikas. The five tiers of this centre manifest in order to accommodate the down flow of energies from the five liberated Creative Hierarchies, with the fifth, signified by 'Mass Life' by D.K. overshadowing the expression of the outermost tier of the Head centre, which I have termed 'the Solar Plexus in the Head'. The establishment of the Head centre is in conjunction with the foundational

Base of Spine centre, upon which all rests, to command the various factors of Logoic incarnation. At first however, the Head centre acts as a Solar Plexus centre, dealing primarily with the effects of the cosmic Waters. The number 27 here implies that the laws associated with the Element Fire (wielded by the Divine Flames), which are needed to create the material realm and its qualities, sweep into manifestation as part of the moving meditation of the presiding Logos. What *'sweeps along'* (10) therefore, in terms of this Fiery energy, are the forces and Entities (Minds) that will produce evolutionary perfection. All of the factors the 'germs', the Lives 'slumbering' within the spirals and spirillae[17] of the atomic structure awaken, once these two centres are awakened to direct the process.

This being the fourth Eternity, so *ādi* acts as a mirror, reflecting the Mahat (literally Logoic *kāma-manas)* of the triad of the three lower liberated Hierarchies to awaken the 'slumbering' Lives in cosmic etheric Space.

In the form of a Solar Plexus centre the *sahasrāra padma* (Head lotus) is able to accommodate the Watery energies from the cosmic astral plane pouring into it as a consequence of the sweep of this vibration. Concerning this centre I stated in *An Esoteric Exposition of the Bardo Thödol* that:

> The Solar Plexus tier, consisting of 8 x 96 = 768 petals, governs the expression of Fiery-Earthy *prāṇas*. The major consciousness-aspects associated with material plane living are processed here. These *saṃskāras* flow to and from the Knowledge petals of the Sambhogakāya Flower. This fifth level conveys the energy of the Dhyāni Buddha Amoghasiddhi.[18]

The *wing* is an organ of aerial flight and thus relates to the Element Air associated with the *buddhic* plane. Movement in that realm (of the intuition) is indeed swift, instantaneous. A wing is a material sheaf that flies in the air, and thus refers to the substance of the Minds of the Divine Flames and the lower Creative Hierarchies, which flies in the immensity of cosmic etheric space.

---

17 The basis of the *nāḍī* system of what is to be.

18 Balsys, *An Esoteric Exposition of the Bardo Thödol,* (Universal Dharma Publications, Sydney), 428.

The numbers of the phrase *'its swift wing'* add to 16, 7, suggesting that this 'wing' is a Thought-Form embodying the energies of the cosmic Christ (here the Creative Hierarchies), which had seven major 'feathers', relating to the seven planes, the seven Schemes and their various sub-planes, etc.

The feathers of the 'wing' signify the descent of spiral-cyclic energies to lower octaves of expression. They carry with them the energies that will qualify the spheres of influence associated with any of the Lords of the Schemes, Chains and related septenaries in their bodies of manifestation. Smaller feathers carry the energy input of smaller cycles of expression. They therefore delineate time, and can be considered to be the embodied function of certain *devas.* Thus the image of a wing is formed through the interrelation of many such cycles, directing cosmic energies, which vivify and bring into active expression all manifest Life. A *buddhic* permanent atom is also in the form of spiral-cyclic motion.[19] The interrelation of spiral eights can also be esoterically constituted in the form of chains of *vajras,* which convey the wisdom of the Dhyāni Buddhas into manifestation. They represent the expression of the spiral-cyclic energy of the greater and lesser Builders manifesting the form, and to do so they must 'touch' that form. Each such figure is part of a larger one.

The mode of functioning of the Lipikas, the Lords of *karma,* is also implied here, in how they organise space in accordance with the blueprint of karmic purpose.

The numbers of the phrase *'touching with its swift wing'* add to 128 (8 x 16, 32 x 4), 11. The number 8 x 16 informs us that the energy body of the Christ actually does this 'touching'. This energy builds a Seat of Power in manifestation for the demonstration of the Love-Wisdom principle (32 x 4). This means that the 'wing' is but the conveyor of the Consciousness that en-Souls the form. This Christ principle effectively represents the descent of the Creative Hierarchies into manifestation. They are projected from *pralaya* into manifestation via the impetus of Scorpio by means of spiral-cyclic motion. (This work is explained in Stanza 3:3.) Each Hierarchy appears via one or other of the planetary spheres that are thus established. (Though there is an overlapping of

19 See *A Treatise on Cosmic Fire,* 531.

cycles and smaller cycles within the greater ones to be considered.) There is an appropriate sequence of expression through time for the appearance of each Creative Hierarchy. The *wing* therefore signifies the mode of manifestation of the vivifying Lives that 'touch' the forms they will inhabit, as part of the evolution process. This is similar to the way the human Soul appropriates the material sheath of a personal-I for each incarnation. The atoms of substance utilised are borrowed, they are not a permanent fixture.

As they descend and touch, the wings activate the *kuṇḍalinī* (the energy of the Mother) that integrates the atoms of substance into a coherent form, sustaining the Life of that body of manifestation. *(Kuṇḍalinī* provides the sustaining internal heat.) The number 11 refers to the projection of the *sūtrātmā*, the Life link, which allows this 'touching' process to be accomplished. Of the five senses that of touch is directly related to the sixth Ray, facilitating the Watery experiences of sensation and attachment to things through desire.

H.P.B. adds the word 'simultaneously' to the process of touching with the 'swift wing' in an endeavour to try to describe the instantaneous nature of this process of descent of divinity.

The meaning of *'The Universe'* was explained in Stanza 1:6 and thus needs no elaboration. This universe was said to be a cosmic Christ, a 'Son of Necessity'. By the numbers 11, 20 of the phrase *'the whole Universe'*, we see that this universe manifested via an energy field, the source of the first and second Ray dispensations, a powerhouse of Light and Love. The concept of 'universe' must be thought of philosophically and multidimensionally. The atoms, cellular constituency and organs of a human unit can also be considered a universe to an individual sentience incorporated within it. Similarly the body of manifestation of a Logos constitutes a universe for the Lives evolving through it. The level of expression of the Logos concerned is the question here. It is best to limit one's vision to THAT Logos, whose body of manifestation incorporates the visible stars in the night sky, and within which the constellations of stars that our sun is part of the constitution of one of the *chakras*.

The numbers of the phrase *'touching with its swift wing the whole Universe'* add to 200 + 11, 7 x 7. The significance of the number 11 was given above, whilst the number 200 refers to the Consciousness-principle that is instantaneously conveyed by this 'swift wing'. The number 7 x 7 refers to the subdivisions of the feathers of this 'wing', plus the subdivisions of what is touched. It implicates the formation of the sum of the seven Rounds of evolution carrying with them the Hierarchies of Lives that are to inform the manifestation of the appearing forms (the Chains and globes of evolutionary expression).

The numerical breakdown of the last two phrases:

> the germ (40, 13), the germ that dwelleth (88, 25), in darkness (42, 15), the germ that dwelleth in darkness (130, 40), dwelleth in darkness (77, 23), The darkness that breathes (89 = 17, 26), the darkness (43, 16), breathes over (6.6.), breathes over the (6.6.6), the slumbering Waters (86 = 14, 23), Waters of Life (58, 13), The slumbering Waters of Life (121, 31), the darkness that breathes over the slumbering Waters (199, 55), the darkness that breathes over the slumbering Waters of Life (234, 63).

The *germ* is a *bindu,* a collection of seed points *(bījas)* for manifest space, that is circumscribed as a sphere of activity, a corporeal body (the earth). It is the Germ of all manifest activity. This Thought Form *(bindu)* takes the form of human, earth, solar or atomic spheres, each of which can be considered 'germs'. We saw above that this 'germ' is effectively the Logoic physical permanent atom.

The numbers of the phrase *'the germ'* add to 40, 13, as also the phrase *'The germ that dwelleth in darkness'* (which also adds to 10 x 13). The number 40 here refers to the embodiment of the fourth principle, the quaternary, the throne of God, the Base of Spine *chakra*, each of which can be considered the *germ,* a place from which the *maṇḍala* for the entire Body of manifestation can evolve. This number also symbolises our earth sphere or Scheme, and can even refer to the solar Logos, or a humanity. It can signify the seed of *śūnyatā* at the heart of every form, or atom. The number 10 x 13 refers to the ability of this Germ to evolve, to produce complete evolutionary perfection (10) of the point within the sphere (of the twelve petals of a Heart centre). The form considered at this stage is however in darkness, yet to awaken. The esoteric significance of this *darkness* was explained in Stanza

1:5 with respect to the phrase: 'Darkness alone filled the Boundless All'. There it was said to relate to pure Spirit (that veiled by *śūnyatā).* That description however, was taken from the point of view of below up. Now our vision is from above down – to the darkness of matter, of substance divorced from realms of ineffable Light. The number 13 x 10 also refers to the ten planetary Schemes or spheres of evolutionary activity in a solar system, each of which can be likened to a germ. They are *chakras* in the body of the Logos.

This *'germ that dwelleth in darkness'* is differentiated from 'the whole universe', it is an addition to it, though part of it. This germ is also the seed to its own universe, a microscopic reflection of the whole. The two are connected by means of the vibration of the 'swift wing' that comes to touch, hence incorporate, it. The germ in the darkness of Earthy substance is thereby activated and can then respond to the Light of the universe. A smaller universe (such is the human unit) evolving within a greater universe, and that within an even greater One, etc., is the way of cosmic evolution.

The term 'whole' means what is singular, complete in its entirety, which this germ must evolve to become, yet it already contains this 'whole' in its constitution. Each germ can also be considered an atomic unit, a *chakra,* or aspect thereof, in the Body of the presiding Logos. All manifest spheres, from the greatest to the lowest, can be considered germs that *'dwelleth in the darkness'* (77). 'Darkness' here is thus viewed from a vaster, higher perspective than is normally considered. The number 77 informs us that this the germ undergoes repeated incarnations within the seven (cosmic) planes of perception, of seven sheaths, the totality of being\non-being. Each incarnation signifies an awakening from slumber.

Darkness is also the darkness of ignorance, which must be conquered and turned into the various Wisdoms of the Jinas as each germ unfolds in space.

By the numbers 42 and 15 of the phrase *'in darkness'* we see that what is 'in darkness' is the entire zone of manifest space (6 x 7) wherein intelligent *(manasic)* activity (3 x 5) will evolve to shed various tonalities and intensities of light to overcome the darkness of the levels of ignorance.

The numbers of the phrase *'the germ that dwelleth'* add to 5 x 5 and to 8 x 11. The number 5 x 5 indicates that this germ exists upon the higher mental plane, thus signifies the individuality of the Sambhogakāya Flower, hence a human Life-stream. Our vision has consequently moved from *ādi* to the human domain. The Soul is the true 'germ that dwelleth in darkness', for it is a projection of the Father energy and is able to eventually return to its source in a full blaze of glory. It rays down a *sūtrātmā* into the womb of a mother to vitalise the seed of a new child, into which it incarnates at the time of first breath when the *chakras* are activated. The 8 x 11 here refers to the 'swift wing' of the energy of Life that vitalises the heart of each Lotus bearing the expression of the attributes of consciousness. It represents the chains of 'eights' constituting the *nāḍī* system, which allow the expansion of the germ to its full potential.

The numbers of the phrase *'the darkness that breathes'* add to 17 and to 8, indicating that this 'darkness' is the 'breath of God', or rather the 'Spirit of God' that moved 'over the face of the waters', in the opening statement of the book of Genesis. Here we have a similar statement, as this darkness also breathes, or moves over the (slumbering) Waters. Breath energises with *prāṇic* vitality, of which there are five types embodying the attributes of the five Elements.

When this phrase is carefully analysed in context with the previous one, then we see that there are two aspects to this darkness:

a. That which breathes.

b. That which contains the germ.

That which breathes is an emanation from the *ātmic* plane[20] (the domain of the Mother) via *buddhi* (the Airy Element). That which contains the germ is the higher mental plane. As Stanza 3:2 deals primarily with the vibration that sweeps via the plane *ādi* we see that the lowest reflex of its energies manifests upon the higher mental plane. This Stanza in general deals with the emanation of what is called elsewhere as the first Outpouring.[21] Technically it should be called the

20 From a higher cosmic perspective this view of darkness could also be considered to refer to the *ātmic* plane that embodies the Womb of space-time.

21 See my book Med*itation and the Initiation Process,* 277-284.

third Outpouring, where the term 'third' is not viewed in terms of time, but rather in terms of the quality of energy. The focus therefore is the *ātmic* plane (Stanza 3:4) and the formation of the planes of perception (the major spirals of the Logoic physical permanent atom), as signified by the symbolism of the phrase 'the three falling into the four'.

The energies from *ātma* impact upon the mental plane, which is the cosmic dense physical, that represents the darkness of material substance to an incarnating Logos. What is therefore also implied by the term 'darkness' is the substance of the dual mental plane, or of *buddhi* in terms of what a downward focussed human mind cannot perceive. Prior to the appearance of minds that can conceive anything the substance of this plane of perception is dark, not comprehended. The objective of the sweep of the 'swift Wing' is to produce the containers of mind, human units, that will comprehend things through generating light (the Fires of Mind) within this Darkness. The extent of the ignorance thereof is thereby revealed. Another aspect already discussed concerns the transformation of primal substance, cosmic dust, into light bearers. Putting this information in context with the phrases of this verse, where the Scorpionic impulse provides the Fire to light the wick of the lamp of mind, we have in terms of the inversion process of the cosmic energies:

1. The vibration sweeps	*ādi*
2. The swift Wing	*anupādaka*
3. Touching the Universe	*ātma*
4. The darkness breathes (moves)	*buddhi*
5. The germ that dwells	higher mental plane
6. Darkness	lower mental plane
7. The slumbering Waters	astral plane
8. The slumbering...Life	physical plane

One must remember here that the focus of Stanza three is the *ātmic* plane, therefore at this stage the Lives and planes below *ātma* in the list are in potential, described in terms of 'slumbering', and 'the germ that dwells', as they are not yet active. The vibration has moved to 'touch the Universe', signified by the store of *karma* held upon *ātmic* levels, but the spiral-cyclic motion must yet activate that *karma* in terms of a phenomenal appearance. The *maṇḍala* that forms will however serve to precipitate all of the appropriate forces to produce the ordained phenomena. There is also a reciprocal movement upon mental levels to reflect what is forming upon *ātma*, and at the appropriate moment the impetus will manifest there to cause the appearance of the material domain. *Manas* reflects *ātma,* whilst the dense physical is an expression of what transpires upon the mental plane.

The numbers of the phrase *'breathes over'* add to 6.6., and the continuation in *'breathes over the'* provides us with 6.6.6., the number 666 signifying the material universe, the body of manifestation of any Logos, into which the five *prāṇas* are imbued by means of this breathing process. Here the number relates to 'breathing over' that which is material in nature, or else the slumbering Watery Lives within the systemic domains, symbolised by the number 6.

From the above list we see that *'the slumbering Waters'* refers to the astral plane, as is verified by the number 14 of this phrase. However, the systemic astral plane is non-existent until after the advent of humanity, who will create its conditionings via desire and the creative imagination. Until then it exists as a zone of energisation, therefore the Watery *deva* lives (the Agnisuryans) that will energise it are 'slumbering' at this stage, as they have not been called into activity.

The number 13 of the phrase *'Waters of Life'* refers here to the Lives embodying the Creative Hierarchies (spheres of self-contained activity) that will flood the entire sphere of Logoic activity (13). The Waters are the energies manifesting through the fourth cosmic ether *(buddhi)* that impact upon the astral plane. These energies are an expression of the cosmic Blood of Deity, the Life giving principle animating all forms, from the atomic up. Similarly, terrestrial *prāṇa* is the Life giving vitality for all manifest Lives. Implicated also with this phrase is the sign of the water bearer, Aquarius, who pours the Waters of Life into all those involved with manifest activity. Its exoteric ruling planet is Uranus (governing the seventh Ray of Ceremonial Magic). Uranus was the deity who ruled the primordial waters of space in the Greek mythology. The lowest of the twelve Creative Hierarchies, 'the Elemental Lives', the

'Baskets of Nourishment'[22] are governed by this sign. They embody dense substance, and are the bases through which the other Hierarchies work to utilise physical phenomena. They have not yet been activated to inform the dense physical plane, therefore no physical forms could be appropriated by the greater Lives.

H.P.B's essential commentary:

> The idea of the "breath" of Darkness moving over "the slumbering Waters of life," which is primordial matter with the latent Spirit in it, recalls the first chapter of Genesis. Its original is the Brahminical Nārāyana (the mover on the Waters), who is the personification of the eternal Breath of the unconscious All (or Parabrahm) of the Eastern Occultists. The Waters of Life, or Chaos — the female principle in symbolism — are the vacuum (to our mental sight) in which lie the latent Spirit and Matter. This it was that made Democritus assert, after his instructor Leucippus, that the primordial principles of all were atoms and a vacuum, in the sense of space, but not of empty space, as "Nature abhors a vacuum" according to the Peripatetics, and every ancient philosopher.
>
> In all Cosmogonies "Water" plays the same important part. It is the base and source of material existence.[23]

The numbers of the phrase *'The slumbering Waters of Life'* add to 11 x 11, 31, which implicate the first Ray energies of Deity. These energies animate the central dynamo of energy situated at the Heart of every being, which contain the combined first and second Ray energies that are the expression of the cosmic Waters. They are the cause, sustaining power, the destructive and regenerative potency of the Life of all beings. The number 11 x 11 also signifies the energies causing *pralaya,* plus the *antaḥkaraṇas* that interrelate all lives therein that are 'slumbering'. We also have the cosmic *nāḍī* system, the lowest of the seven Eternities, wherein the associated Lives are 'slumbering'. The concept of 'slumbering' simply means that these Lives are not active upon the physical domain but can be active upon the higher dimensions, as in a dreaming state for humans. In such cases the human

22 See Alice Bailey, *Esoteric Astrology,* 35.

23 *The Secret Doctrine,* Vol. 1, 64.

units are active astrally, though their physical forms are sleeping. Thus though 'sleeping' at this stage the 'slumbering Lives' were preparing for active incarnate existence.

From the above listing the phrase *'the darkness that breathes over the slumbering Waters'* refers to the *ātmic* plane, which is implicated by the numbers of the phrase (5 x 11). The 'breathing over' these slumbering Waters is the expression of the Will of the Logos projecting the *antaḥkaraṇas* of Divine Activity to all groups of Lives to awaken the slumbering ones. The objective is to gain complete mastery (adeptship) over the substance of mind by converting it to Mind (5 x 11). As the dense physical realm is a direct effect of causes emanating from mental realms, so as this conversion happens, it then causes the dense substance to 'etheralise', to be abstracted into the ethers.

Finally, the numbers of the *complete phrase* add to 16 x 9, 7 x 9, which refer to the cosmic Christ (16 x 9) into which all Life (of the Creative Hierarchies) is abstracted during a solar period of deep sleep. He represents the 'Son' aspect of Deity, being the Lord of Life awakening His *chakras* (7 x 9) with the Consciousness principle ('the Waters of Life') in the process of Breathing over (fecundating) the Mother (the 'slumbering Waters') who contains the Germ of manifest activity in her Womb. The entire process of this awakening represents an Initiation process (9) for the Logos, and the activity of the awakening Christ principle is explained in Stanza 3:3.

Stanza Three part Three

Stanza 3:3 states:

> **'Darkness' radiates Light, and Light drops one solitary Ray into the Waters, into the Mother Deep. The Ray shoots through the Virgin-Egg, the Ray causes the Eternal Egg to thrill, and drop the non-eternal** *(periodical)* **germ, which condenses into the World Egg.**

Keynotes: Scorpio, Airy Element, the second cosmic ether – *anupādaka,* the second Ray, Ratnasambhava, Divine Builders, reflecting the fourth Liberated Hierarchy – 'Desire for Duality'. The fifth Eternity.

The numerical breakdown of the first three phrases:

> Darkness radiates Light (89 = 17, 26 = 8), radiates Light (61 = 7, 16), Light drops one solitary Ray (127, 46), One solitary Ray (71 = 8, 26), into the Waters (60, 15), the Waters (38, 11), Light drops one solitary Ray into the Waters (187 = 16, 61 = 7), Light drops (56 = 7 x 8, 20), into the Mother Deep (92 = 11, 20), the Mother Deep (70, 16).

The esoteric significance of the term *Darkness* was explained above and also in Stanza 1:5 with regards the phrase *'Darkness alone filled the Boundless All'*. H.P.B.'s earlier comment is that 'Darkness is Father-Mother; Light Their Son'.[24] The sign that comes into prominence in this verse is Scorpio the scorpion, which energises the second, Monadic plane of perception, *anupādaka*. Upon this plane Shambhala is established upon earth, allowing the incarnation of human Monads. Consequently they come into incarnation under Scorpionic influence. The combined activities of the human Monads and the Lords of Shambhala (or its correspondence on other planetary spheres), cause the radiation of Light to overcome the Darkness of the new sphere, at first under the auspices of the second of the manifest Creative Hierarchies, the Divine Builders. These Builders build the Monadic form and its habitation upon *anupādaka*.

After the appearance of the plane *anupādaka* by the first Outpouring, which establishes the planes of perception that organises the Virgin-Egg, the second Outpouring can begin. This Outpouring manifests via a solitary Ray that is projected into 'the Mother Deep'. The second Outpouring causes the appearance and vitalisation of the *chakras* (ruled generally by Mercury, the Hierarchical ruler of Scorpio) that will govern the evolution of consciousness in the body of manifestation of the new form. This is similar to the process of the foetus forming in the womb of the mother. At this stage the *chakras* are but *laya* centres[25]. They

24 *The Secret Doctrine,* Vol. 1, 40.

25 A *laya* centre is a point of disappearance, a zero-point, or a point in substance where every differentiation has temporarily ceased. It is a seed that can be used by a creative entity to project a body of manifestation. It is an unpotentised point of potential power waiting for its cycle of activity, when it will manifest its potential. For

are activated by the 'solitary Ray', which brings with it the Builders of the form, the Virgin-Egg that becomes the World Egg. This activity is via the potency of the scorpion's 'sting', which represents the process of the generation of Light.

Anupādaka represents the fifth Eternity, thought of in terms of locality and not as a sequence of time. Being the 'fifth', the reverberation of the energies of the third liberated Creative Hierarchy ('Light thro' Knowledge') also manifest upon this plane. This Hierarchy convey the energy of cosmic Mind, which means that the Divine Builders can utilise with equal faculty both the Airy *ākāśa* and Mahat in their Creative endeavours.

The polar opposite of Scorpio is Taurus the bull (whose Hierarchical ruler is Vulcan), who conditions the substance of 'the Mother Deep' (the cosmic astral plane), and also embodies the Womb that is represented by the various 'Eggs' of this Stanza. The Scorpionic energy consequently conditions the activity within the Mother, causing the manifestation of the sentience and consciousness of the embryonic Life forms, causing 'the Eternal Egg to thrill'.

Mercury, governing the fourth Ray of Harmonising Beauty overcoming Strife, assists Scorpio to work via the Airy Element, and as stated in the synopsis, the Airy Element is the general medium of expression of all five cosmic *prāṇas,* the *ākāśas.* The Fiery Element that was seeded in Stanza 3:2 is consequently appropriately energised for the informing streams of the Creative Hierarchies that will inform systemic space. They are generally conditioned by the second Ray of Love-Wisdom and bring into manifestation the Consciousness-principle via the second Outpouring. The second Ray purpose produces the fields of testing in this solar evolution. The incoming Lives bring with them the various intensities of Light generated in former aeons of evolutionary attainment. The energy is drawn from the sixth cosmic astral sub-plane, and is empowered via the Equalising Wisdom of Ratnasambhava acting via the second cosmic ether, *anupādaka*. His energy is needed to rightly control the flow of the potency of cosmic Love that manifests via this most Watery sub-plane of the cosmic

---

example, the seed that grows into a flower. *Laya* centres can be seen as *chakras* that have not yet been awakened, as part of the planetary, systemic or cosmic *nāḍī* system.

astral plane. The associated liberated Hierarchy upon that plane is the fourth, designated as 'Desire for Duality' by D.K. This 'Duality' is the interrelation between the liberated Lives upon the cosmic astral plane, and those now to incarnate into systemic space. The Law of Attraction rules this purpose, to eventually abstract the gain of the experiences of the incarnating Lives into the Unity represented by the Logoic Thought upon the cosmic mental sub-planes.

The meaning of how *'"Darkness" radiates Light'* (17, 8) has already been explained. Light is an expression of the third (Activity) aspect of Deity. It concerns the awakening of the energies of the mind, which at first resides in darkness until ignorance is overcome. The process will incrementally cause the appearance of the radiant luminosity of the clear light of Mind. The number 17 indicates that the process of the generation of Light will eventually create a Logoic sphere out of the darkness. (The empowering of the personality aspect of Deity that will inevitably see the blazing luminosity of a sun formed out of the darkness of primal cosmic dust.)

To radiate means to emit or to spread rays of light or energy around from a centre. That which esoterically *'radiates Light'* (16, 7) is the awakened Son of the Father-Mother, and as the radiance increases in scope and intensity, then eventually there is the appearance of a (cosmic) Christ. The Christ (the conscious aspect) is the 'Light of the world', or the universe, depending upon the level of interpretation. Consciousness (Love-Wisdom) evolves from the darkness of deepest matter, from a state of ignorance to the most intensified energies of the Spirit aspect. It evolves into the conscious mediator's, Christ's, Ah-Hi, Dhyān Chohans, the cohorts of loving Intelligences that are capable of creating world spheres. The number 7 refers to the seven subdivisions of the One fundamental Ray, or the seven primordial Rays of Light, the Aeons (etc.).

The numbers of the phrase *'One solitary Ray'* add to 8, informing us that this Ray is composed of pure energy, moving in spiral-cyclic motion. It is coloured by a fundamental hue, which we know also consists of seven sub-hues. Also, from above we know that this Ray represents the manifestation of the second Outpouring of the Consciousness principle via the plane *anupādaka*. Its purpose is the evolution of Love-Wisdom in the solar system, and as stated with it comes the outpouring of the seven Creative Hierarchies that will be ensconced in the solar form.

To *drop* means to cause something to fall down, especially by releasing hold of it. The force of gravity then plays its appropriate role. This implies that the 'solitary Ray' was held by the Logoic Will in potential until the time came to release it. There is a direct line of descent for this Ray. The existence of a force akin to gravity, possessed by the Waters (of the 'Deep'), to which the Light is attracted, is also implied. The physical laws are an affect of subjective considerations, not a cause. The darkened, blinded lives constituting dense substance thrill with the light that helps liberate them from thrall. This attractive force at first acts as a light sink, and later as its generator. Light itself is substance and has 'weight' and 'falls' to the lower denser planes of perception. The Ray travels through multidimensional space and the dimensions of time as it moves through the Virgin-Egg. As it does so it brings with it the Consciousness-principle with which the principle of mind can progressively see what is veiled in the Darkness.

The Ray is 'dropped' according to Logoic planning, but there is an adventitious effect as to what happens to it when acted upon by the Watery world that accommodates its intrusion. Light is the substance of consciousness, the demonstration of the reason behind the appearance of things. There can be no manifestation of light therefore without the thought structure of the Mind/minds that move 'it', or causes it to manifest. There are also elements (the dark brotherhood) that are resistant to, or oppose, the manifestation of light.

Even the rays emanating from a sun or from terrestrial fire are inherently aspects of the Fires of mind/Mind, of the Fiery Elementals embodying the radiance. The light from the stars is but the reified outward manifestation of the Minds of Logoi. Other forms of light are either created as a consequence of human minds, or directed by the *devas,* the units of Intelligence commanding Nature. The phenomenon of light necessitates sentience or consciousness to register its existence, thereby gaining awareness as a consequence. Light moves into an arena of darkness, which it illuminates, but such illumination needs intact senses to perceive it and to gain from its expression.[26]

---

26 The subject of light in relation to consciousness was treated in some depth in my *Treatise on Mind,* to which the reader should refer for further insights.

The numbers of the phrase *'Light drops'* add to 7 x 8, 20, and 11. These numbers indicate that the Primordial Ray dropped by this Light possesses the seven sub-rays of pure energy (7 x 8) and consists of the intense first and second Ray energies (20, 11) conveyed from Shambhalic levels in cosmos. The number 10 of the phrase *'Light drops one solitary Ray'* signifies that it will produce evolutionary perfection. The number 10, written as ⦶ signifies the descent of the *sūtrātmā* into/as manifest space. Thus is begun the ten stages of the evolutionary process, explained in volume 5A of *A Treatise on Mind.* The radiation of light indicates the formation of a solar sphere from Darkness.

The numbers of the phrase *'into the waters',* 60, 15, appeared previously in the phrase *'darkness radiates'.* They refer to the totality of all substance that is fluid and mutable, and specifically the Watery astral domain (60).

The number 11 of the phrase *'the Waters'* indicates that these Waters are an expression of the *nāḍī* system of Deity, which is but an extension of the one Ray. The *nāḍīs* convey into Systemic space the Waters of the cosmic astral ocean in the form of *ākāśa* via the four cosmic ethers. They find their lowest reflex in the substance of the astral plane. The energies expressed via the *nāḍīs* are but an expression of Logoic Love and Wisdom.

The numbers of the phrase *'Light drops one solitary Ray into the Waters'* add to 16, 7, the meaning of which was explained previously regarding the phrase 'radiates Light'. The objective of this Ray is obviously to cause the appearance of a Christ (the consciousness-aspect) in time and space via the septenaries of manifestation.

The meaning of *the Mother* was explained in Stanzas 1:1 and 1:5. Here the phrase *'the Mother-Deep'* (70, 16) is equated with the Watery depths of the Mother's Womb, to *ātma,* and thence via the planes of perception established by means of the first Outpouring to the highest of the three lower sub-planes of the cosmic dense physical realm (the mental plane). These three (the mental, astral and dense physical planes) are the planes of gross illusion, the Darkness wherein this Ray of light must express itself if the material world is to be sustained and made to evolve. The human bearers of mind must evolve within these planes so as to eventually learn to project the Light of Love and Wisdom to convert the *māyā* of things into the Real.

The number 16 here refers to all the spheres of expression (the Womb of the Mother) wherein the Christ-consciousness (the Son), the boon of the second Outpouring, may flower and grow. The number 7 x 10 refers to those spheres, as *laya* centres, still in Germ or egg form. They are the *chakras* in the solar form, the bodies of manifestation of various planetary Logoi, and thence within each such Logos. One can also think in terms of the appearance of the seven Creative Hierarchies to awaken these centres within the Logoic form.

The numbers 20, 11 of the phrase *'into the Mother-Deep'* refer to the energies of the first two Rays (borne by the highest of the Creative Hierarchies), being the constituency of the primordial Ray that is dropped into the Mother–Deep, as previously explained. The Mother provides the third Ray of Activity.

The numerical breakdown of the fourth phrase:

> The Ray (32, 14), The Ray shoots through (99, 27), The Virgin-Egg (77, 23), Through the Virgin-Egg (120, 30), Shoots through the Virgin-Egg (144, 36), The Ray Shoots Through the Virgin-Egg (176, 50).

H.P.B.'s essential commentary states:

> The solitary ray dropping into the mother deep may be taken as meaning Divine Thought or Intelligence, impregnating chaos. This, however, occurs on the plane of metaphysical abstraction, or rather the plane whereon that which we call a metaphysical abstraction is a reality.[27]

When analysing the structure of this verse then the Darkness that radiates light represents the energy of the first Logos governing the Will expression of the first Outpouring upon the plane *ādi* for a planetary or solar system. The 'one solitary Ray' that is emitted is projected into 'the Waters', here signifying the substance of the plane *anupādaka*. This Ray can therefore be seen to effectively facilitate the establishment of the appearance of human Monads (meaning 'one, singular') upon this plane. 'The Mother Deep' refers to the *ātmic* plane, the domain of the third

---

27 The S.D. Vol. 1, 64.

Logos, the Mother of the *karma* and associated phenomena of the planes of activity governed by the evolution of the attributes of mind/Mind. The 'Virgin-Egg' relates to the establishing of a Seat of Power upon the plane *anupādaka* by a Logos from which the proceedings concerning the manifestation of a world-sphere can manifest. The incarnation process of all manifest Life can consequently begin. The evolution of this Life is embodied and directed by the first three Creative Hierarchies of the seven that are incarnate in the solar form.

The Virgin-Egg represents the establishment of the four cosmic ethers, the point of externalisation of which is the fourth cosmic ether *(buddhi),* signifying the attributes of *śūnyatā*. It is 'virgin' in the sense that it remains unaffected by phenomena, *saṃsāric* substance, untainted by mind and associated material activity. Through it the Ray can pass without being modified, yet *śūnyatā* is the support or base for all *saṃsāric* activity. This happens via the *śūnyatā-saṃsāra* nexus explained in the first three volumes of *A Treatise on Mind.*

The word *egg* refers to the reproductive body laid externally by birds (and many reptiles), and internally by mammals. It contains the germ of the future adult life, whilst its esoteric relation to the atom on all levels of perception and the intricate *nāḍīs* of our subtle bodies has already been provided. The number 77 of the phrase *'The Virgin-Egg'* is a shorthand notation for the 777 incarnations, for which this Egg is therefore responsible. Thus as well as referring to the Logoic *nāḍī* system, this Egg can also refer to the Monadic aspect, with the Ray coming from the Logoic Mind. Being virgin, this Egg is unmodified, unadulterated etc., as is the Monad. From the perspective of human evolution the Monad is the cause of our periodic incarnations via the Soul form. From the *nāḍī* system, cosmic or human, the material form can materialise.

The term *shoot* means to cause to move rapidly with force in a given direction, as an arrow, to fire a bullet etc. It also can refer to being emitted as a ray of light that passes rapidly onwards. Note the difference between the terms *drop* and *shoot*. The first refers to that which is material, allowing it to be dropped,[28] which is the consideration from

28 For instance in Alice Bailey's *Telepathy and the Etheric Vehicle* (Lucis Publishing Company, New York), 26, D.K. states: 'Light is subtle substance. Upon a beam of light can the energy of Mind materialise'.

the cosmic astral perspective, however, by the time the cosmic ethers, the 'Virgin-Egg' is reached, it has become pure energy, and 'shoots through' instantaneously to effect the material domain.

The numbers 32, 14 of the phrase *'The Ray'* verify that this Ray brings into objectivity the consciousness or second Ray aspect (the Christ principle) via the cosmic astral (14), which governs the manifestation of light to overcome ignorance by generating wisdom. From the present perspective the Christ principle refers to the projection of the Creative Hierarchies into manifestation.

The symbol of the descent of this Ray (⦶) also represents the threefold *iḍā, piṇgalā* and *suṣumṇā nāḍīs* housed in the spinal column, which delineates the form that must come to be. Esoterically it depicts the divine Hermaphrodite. From the central spinal column radiates the entire *nāḍī* and nervous system that vitalises the entire being. These *nāḍīs* can also be thought of in terms of the Divine Flames *(suṣumṇā),* the Greater Builders *(piṇgalā)* and the Lesser Builders *(iḍā).*

This Ray carries the Thought Form of the Logos for the *maṇḍalic* expression of the incarnating Monads, who are 'Virgin-Eggs' upon the second sub-plane of the cosmic dense physical. The Ray shoots through these 'Eggs' because there is no resistance. The actual Creative process starts on the plane *ātma,* the third plane from above-down. There this Ray activates the necessary substance that will allow building the *maṇḍala* of what is to be via the *devas*. The Ray also incorporates the activity of the Monads to Ray down an aspect of themselves onto the higher mental plane, to cause the 777 incarnations of the human Soul.

The numbers of the phrase *'The Ray shoots through'* add to 99, 27, which indicate that the objective of the Ray is to cause the Initiation process of all the Lives that will come into active manifestation. These numbers can also be thought in terms of the *deva* triads associated with the Greater and Lesser Builders.

The numbers of the phrase *'through the Virgin-Egg'* add to 12 x 10, 4 x 30, 30. The number 12 x 10 refers to the tenth sign of the zodiac, Capricorn the goat, who governs the mountain load of *karma* associated with the incarnation process and the dense material world. As stated by D.K. in *Esoteric Astrology* Capricorn is the first and last sign of the zodiac in the early stages of evolution, when there were only ten signs to the zodiac. This relates to a stage when the Shambhalic correspondence acts as a Solar Plexus centre, hence when primarily the *deva* kingdom were active upon the cosmic ethers (4 x 30) to cause the formation of the attributes of *saṃsāra.* What shoots through the Virgin Egg therefore, is the seed or germ associated with the turning of the wheel of the Law. The first cyclic impulse of the zodiacal wheel turns to impact upon the sign Cancer the crab, the gateway to birth and the polar opposite of Capricorn.

The number 30 refers to the third Ray of Activity as expressed by the Logos, which is needed to construct a ring-pass-not, or outer boundary, around any sphere of influence (Thought Form) to be embodied by the Life force. Here the outer boundary is that of a planetary or solar Heart centre, which represents the Virgin-Egg. The Ray of activity passes through this Egg to produce the Seat of Power (4 x 30) for the work of the Builders that will produce the form through which all can incarnate.

The number 12 x 10 also refers to the tenth Creative Hierarchy. They are denoted as Makara the Mystery, who are found incarnate on the lower mental plane. The purpose of this Ray then is to 'shoot through' to this domain to awaken this order of *devas* (the Agnishvattas) so that the sum of the corporeal activity that forms the lowest of the planes of perception can commence. This necessitates the organisation of the cosmic 'black dust' that has been incorporated into the ring-pass-not of the Logos, which constitutes the virgin substance within of this Egg. It is the substance of the Womb of Life.

The numbers of the phrase *'shoots through the Virgin-Egg'* add to 12 x 12 and to 3 x 12. The no 12 x 12 symbolises the sum of manifest Life, as governed by the twelve Creative Hierarchies. This is symbolised in the book of Revelation as the 144,000 of 'all the tribes of Israel' who were 'sealed with the seal of God' on their foreheads.[29] It implicates the categories of all manifest Life that come under the jurisdiction of the twelve petals of the Logoic Heart.

This number also refers to the sign Pisces the fishes, which relates to bondage in the form. The two fishes (Soul and matter) are yoked together and swimming in the waters of sensation until final liberation from all contact with matter occurs. The bond then breaks. At the

29 Rev. 7:3–5.

primeval dawning of the evolutionary arc it thus signifies the process wherein the 'fish' become bonded. Pisces heads the list of the twelve Creative Hierarchies, and therefore its characteristics are embodied in the energy that shoots through the Virgin-Egg to impregnate the Eternal Egg. This process then starts the entire wheel of the twelve signs of the zodiac turning, bearing with them their associated cosmic potencies.

The number 3 x 12 refers to the third sign of the zodiac, Gemini the twins, the polar opposite of Pisces. Gemini governs the etheric double, and all relationships between the pairs of opposites in any body of manifestation. It expresses the energies that are pumped through the form by means of the Heart. At this stage it is the cosmic, not the lower, ethers that are vitalised.

The numbers of the *complete phrase* add to 88 x 2, 44 x 4, 22 x 8, 11 x 16, and to 5 x 10. These numbers indicate that the energies that pass through the cosmic ethers ('the Virgin-Egg', the Womb of time and space) are responsible for awakening and energising the sum of the attributes pertaining to *saṃsāra.* They bring with them the complete expression of the zodiacal and planetary energies, as well as from other cosmic sources, needed to awaken and to vitalise the seeds of all Life within the Womb of Being (8 x 22). The purpose is to incorporate the potency of the cosmic Christ into the forming space (11 x 16) so that consciousness bearing units can evolve therein.

The number 44 refers to the development of a humanity, here with a specific reference to the planetary Logos of the earth Scheme, which is the fourth in the solar system. When multiplied by 4 then the establishment of the Logoic Seat of Power is implied, which manifests as 'the Eternal Egg'.

The number 50 implies that this Ray of Light is a projection from the Mind of a cosmic Logos to activate the seed of the creative impetus.

The numerical breakdown of the remaining phrases:

> the Eternal Egg (64, 19), to thrill (42, 15), the Ray causes the Eternal Egg to thrill (152, 53), causes the Eternal Egg to thrill (120, 39), the non-eternal Germ (86, 23 = 5), drop the non-eternal Germ (112, 31), the World Egg (61, 25), condenses into the World Egg (118, 37), which condenses into the World Egg (151, 43 = 7).

This Egg (an ovum bearing the characteristics of its parents, the seed of all corporeal Life) is here said to be eternal, lasting forever. It is eternal because it underlies the form and far outlasts the births and deaths of the corporeal entities it embodies. From it emanates the streams and rivers of the vicissitudes of Life, the denizens of the various kingdoms of Nature, of which esoterically there are five main categories; mineral, plant, animal, human and the divine (including the *devas).* Consequently it is the world Soul *(anima mundi),* of which the human Soul on the higher mental plane is the reflection. The number 8 x 8 of the phrase *'the Eternal Egg'* indicates that this Egg is a body of pure energy, thus this world Soul is the containment of the energies of the four cosmic ethers upon the *buddhic* plane, of which *śūnyatā* is technically the fourth sub-plane.

H.P.B.'s essential commentary:

> The Virgin-egg being in one sense abstract Egg-ness, or the power of becoming developed through fecundation, is eternal and for ever the same. And just as the fecundation of an egg takes place before it is dropped; so the non-eternal periodical germ which becomes later in symbolism the mundane egg, contains in itself, when it emerges from the said symbol, "the promise and potency" of all the Universe. Though the idea *per se is,* of course, an abstraction, a symbolical mode of expression, it is a symbol truly, as it suggests the idea of infinity as an endless circle. It brings before the mind's eye the picture of Kosmos emerging from and in boundless space, a Universe as shoreless in magnitude if not as endless in its objective manifestation. The simile of an egg also expresses the fact taught in Occultism that the primordial form of everything manifested, from atom to globe, from man to angel, is spheroidal, the sphere having been with all nations the emblem of eternity and infinity — a serpent swallowing its tail. To realize the meaning, however, the sphere must be thought of as seen from its centre. The field of vision or of thought is like a sphere whose radii proceed from one's self in every direction, and extend out into space, opening up boundless vistas all around. It is the symbolical circle of Pascal and the Kabalists, "whose centre is everywhere and circumference nowhere," a conception which enters into the compound idea of this emblem.

The "Mundane Egg"[30] is, perhaps, one of the most universally adopted symbols, highly suggestive as it is, equally in the spiritual, physiological, and cosmological sense. Therefore, it is found in every world-theogony, where it is largely associated with the serpent symbol; the latter being everywhere, in philosophy as in religious symbolism, an emblem of eternity, infinitude, regeneration, and rejuvenation, as well as of wisdom. (See Part II. "Tree and Serpent and Crocodile Worship.") The mystery of apparent self-generation and evolution through its own creative power repeating in miniature the process of Cosmic evolution in the egg, both being due to heat and moisture under the efflux of the unseen creative spirit, justified fully the selection of this graphic symbol.

The "Virgin Egg" is the microcosmic symbol of the macrocosmic prototype — the "Virgin Mother" — Chaos or the Primeval Deep. The male Creator (under whatever name) springs forth from the Virgin female, the immaculate root fructified by the Ray. Who, if versed in astronomy and natural sciences, can fail to see its suggestiveness? Cosmos as receptive Nature is an Egg fructified — yet left immaculate; once regarded as boundless, it could have no other representation than a spheroid. The Golden Egg was surrounded by seven natural elements (ether, fire, air, water), "four ready, three secret."[31]

The numbers of the phrase *'The Ray causes the Eternal Egg to thrill'* add to 100 + 52, 8. The number 52 refers to the entire *mahāmanvantara*, the solar year wherein this Egg manifests its activity of 'thrilling'. To *thrill* means vibrating, a tremulous excitement, or to affect or cause to become affected by shivering, throbbing or tingling. Esoterically we have the vivification of the spirillae of this atom/Egg with the spiral-cyclic energy (8) conveyed by the Ray.

This tremulous excitement manifests throughout the etheric Body of Deity (the subtle correspondence to the nervous system), and the various spirillae (planes of perception) of the Logoic permanent atom. The reverberation of this thrill causes the building of the form nature, as symbolised by the numbers of the phrase *'to thrill'*, which add to 6 x 7, 15. These numbers indicate the active expression of the Mind

30 In later editions of the S.D. the term used here is 'World-Egg'.

31 S.D., Vol. 1, 64-65.

to vivify the *maṇḍalic* pattern associated with the various planes and sub-planes of manifest space (6 x 7).

The process of this thrill, when impacting upon the substance of the higher mental plane, causes the appearance of the Sambhogakāya Flowers of humanity. This is symbolised by the phrase *'drop the non-eternal Germ'* (7 x 16, 31), where the number 7 x 16 refers to the seven main Ray subdivisions of this 'Germ', viewed not just in terms of the kingdom of Souls, but to the subdivisions of the various streams of Life that come into manifest existence. From the Ray and sub-ray categories of this kingdom eventually evolve the corresponding Ray departments of the Ashrams of the Masters of Wisdom. The 'non-eternal Germ' of material plane activity represents the *nāḍī* system, from which a body of manifestation ensues. The World Egg represents the appearance of the physical seed, the ovum or world sphere, such as the earth, that represents the newly evolving Life upon the physical plane.

The 'dropping' of this Germ is the effect of the original expression of the Will of Deity (31), and as stated above, the concept of 'dropping' involves something possessing weight, material in nature, passing through Airy substance, thus allowing it to appear in form. What is 'dropped' is what remains from the Ray after it has passed through the Eternal Egg. The Will is needed to direct the forms that appear in the dense physical realm, to sustain the illusion of it all for the nominated cycles of activity. The number 7 x 16 also relates to the awakening of the seven *chakras* in the manifest form. From a higher perspective we have the externalisation of the seven Creative Hierarchies that inform the Logoic *chakras*. There is also the demonstration of the seven Ray energies that manifest via this non-eternal Germ to awaken the consciousness-principle. The Christ aspect thus comes into manifestation as the Rounds of Life manifest through the seven spirillae of this atom.

'The non-eternal Germ' can also be considered to be the etheric double, which becomes the externalised anchor for this Ray of the Thought of Deity. The etheric body becomes the means whereby an entity can express itself in dense physical substance. Prior to the actual appearance of a dense form the energies vivifying the *nāḍīs* are primarily the astral condensate of *manas,* hence the numbers of this

phrase add to 14, 5. (The *nāḍī* system can also signify the physical permanent atoms of the appearing forms.)

The numbers of the phrase *'causes the Eternal Egg to thrill'* add to 120, 13 x 3, where the number 120 refers to Capricorn the goat, who represents the substance of the material domain, of the will-to-manifest therein, whilst the number 13 x 3 refers to the divine activity causing the appearance of the various spheres of influence of those that are to incarnate. Capricorn also represents the domain of mind/Mind, whose Thought projection causes this *'Eternal Egg to thrill'*.

To *condense* means to make dense or more compact, or to condense a gas or vapour into a liquid (which is what is implied in this Stanza). What *'condenses into the World Egg'* (118) is the complete externalisation of the energies of the first Outpouring via the *ātmic* plane, causing the appearance of the five planes of Brahmā, whereon we create *karma,* experience it, and then finally annul what was expressed. The number 100 + 18 refers to a sphere of activity whereby Initiation can be undertaken. Here the second Initiation is implied, mastery of astral plane phenomena upon the downward spiral. Eventually dense incarnation (18 = 3 x 6) is possible, as the sum of *saṃsāra* needs to be mastered.

'The World Egg' (5 x 5, 7) refers to the material globe, the sphere of activity of a planetary or solar Logos (7). The higher attributes of this Egg are found into the qualities of the Soul upon the higher mental plane (5 x 5). From here emanates the ability to experience the three worlds of human livingness (the mental, astral and dense physical) whereon all human *karma* is generated and lived out. The number 7 refers to the septenary subdivisions of the spheres of activity of the World Egg, and also to the final manifestation of the seven planes of perception constituting the cosmic dense physical plane. This number thus implies the subdivisions of the fertilised ovum, whilst the Egg reminds us that the ideal form is spherical in nature, as is the Head, the thinking agent of a human unit, and the Sambhogakāya Flower. This spheroid form is also found in the cosmological symbol of the serpent biting its own tail.

The phrase *'which condenses into the World Egg'* (151, 7) refers to the activity of the energies of the triune Logos (100 + 17 x 3) which produces this 'condensing' process.

Stanza Three part Four

Stanza 3:4 states:

> *(Then)* **The three** *(triangle)* **fall into the four** *(quaternary).* **The radiant Essence becomes seven inside, seven outside. The luminous Egg** *(Hiranyagarbha),* **which in itself is three, curdles and spreads in milk-white curds throughout the depths of Mother, the Root that grows in the ocean of Life.**

Keynotes: Sagittarius, the Fiery Element, the third cosmic ether – *ātma,* specifically the four higher *ātmic* sub-planes. Amitābha, the Lesser Builders, reflecting 3rd Liberated Hierarchy – 'Light thro' knowledge'. The sixth Eternity.

The numerical breakdown of the first phrase:

> The three fall (57 = 12, 21), the four (39, 12), fall into the four (74, 20), the three (44, 17), the three fall into the four (118 = 10, 37).

This verse deals with the next stage of the manifestation of the new solar system. It is concerned with the main thrust of the first Outpouring via the plane *ātma* assisted by the one-pointed focus of the energies of Sagittarius the archer, and the energies of Mars, the Hierarchical ruler of this sign. Sagittarius fires his arrows towards a perceived goal, and in this case it represents the outpouring of the substance that causes the formation of the planes of perception, specifically those from the plane *ātma* down (the five planes of Brahmā), whereon is enacted the *karma* of human evolution. As stated previously this happens as an expression of the third Ray of Mathematically Exact Activity. The work of the Mother and the *deva* kingdom is therefore exemplified as the Lesser Builders begin to manifest their assigned functions. These Builders draw from the energies of the third Liberated Hierarchy – 'Light thro' knowledge' and the fifth cosmic astral sub-plane. This *deva* Hierarchy therefore specifically reflects the energy of cosmic Mind into manifestation, producing all of the associated karmic implications. This work comes under the auspices of Amitābha and his Wisdom of the Discriminating Inner Vision. The Creative forces of Logoic Mind hence build the forms of what must be, whilst Amitābha's Wisdom ensures that the manifestation is in accordance with the Logoic Plan.

This Stanza is specifically concerned with the manifestation of Logoic Purpose via the four higher *ātmic* sub-planes. In Stanza 3:4 the first Outpouring happens via the four higher sub-planes of *ātma,* whilst the three lowest sub-planes contain the mount of residual substance that 'remains'.

The Rāja Lords governing the activities of the planes of perception now fully come into active manifestation. They are a direct expression of the organising aptitude of the Logoic Mind, and their substance is needed for the building of the forms. Consequently 'the three fall into the four' and 'milk-white curds' are 'spread throughout the depths of Mother'. The Watery Element is now in the process of congealing, 'curdling', with the application of the reifying forces of Mahat, under Amitabhā's guise, because the Building forces are now called into action. The Womb of the Mother is appropriately activated, as the forces reach 'the depths of the ocean of Life'.

H.P.B.'s essential commentary of the first phrase:

> The use of geometrical figures and the frequent allusions to figures in all ancient scriptures (see Purānas, Egyptian papyri, the "Book of the Dead" and even the Bible) must be explained. In the "Book of Dzyan," as in the Kabala, there are two kinds of numerals to be studied — the figures, often simple blinds, and the Sacred Numbers, the values of which are all known to the Occultists through Initiation. The former is but a conventional glyph, the latter is the basic symbol of all. That is to say, that one is purely physical, the other purely metaphysical, the two standing in relation to each other as matter stands to spirit — the extreme poles of the ONE Substance.
>
> As Balzac, the unconscious Occultist of French literature, says somewhere, the Number is to Mind the same as it is to matter: "an incomprehensible agent;" (perhaps so to the profane, never to the Initiated mind). Number is, as the great writer thought, an Entity, and, at the same time, a Breath emanating from what he called God and what we call the ALL; the breath which alone could organize the physical Kosmos, "where naught obtains its form but through the Deity, which is an effect of Number."[32]

32 S.D., Vol. 1, 66-67.

So far three Elements have been expressed through the cosmic ethers, the cosmic Waters, and its Aetheric and Airy aspects. Next comes the Fiery Outpouring through *ātma* that allows the establishment of the fifth Element (Earth) via the higher mental plane, which will be the focus of information from Stanza 3:5 on. These Elements are expressed via Gemini (the polar opposite of Sagittarius) who governs the establishment of the etheric web via which these Elements will manifest. They are incorporated into the 'milk white curds' and are the forming substance constituting them.

From a normal perspective the five Elements incorporate the five planes of Brahmā, when considering these planes cosmically our focus is however the Elements as subdivisions of the cosmic Earthy Element. In considering the four cosmic ethers then the *prāṇas (ākāśa)* flowing through them convey the Elements as subdivisions of the cosmic Waters. From this perspective *ādi* expresses the Aetheric aspect of *ākāśa, anupādaka* the Airy aspect, *ātma* the Fiery aspect, *buddhi* the Watery and the higher mental plane the Earthy.

We thus have:

1. *The Radiant Essence,* governed by Aquarius the water bearer, as an expression of the Aetheric aspect of the cosmic Waters, which is here conceived as the Essence of this 'Water'. This radiance represents the effect of the quality of the Logoic Mentation as it establishes itself to organise the substance of the cosmic dense physical plane by manifesting the seven planes of perception via the first, atomic sub-plane, *ādi.* Here the glyph for Aquarius, consisting of two wavy lines, signifies the reflection of the energies from the mental sub-plane of the cosmic astral plane (the higher band of energies) into the plane *ādi* (the lower band of energies). The energies then become expressed in a reified fashion via *ātma.* This Essence establishes the *maṇḍala* for the kingdom of 'God' (Shambhala), a Logoic Head centre, in a triune form. Upon the plane *ādi* is established the Throat in the Head. Upon *anupādaka* we have the Heart in the Head, and upon *ātma* is established the Solar Plexus in the Head (the outermost tier of petals of the Head lotus). Leo the lion, the polar opposite of Aquarius, empowers the Individuation of the Head lotus.

2. *The Luminous Egg (hiraṇyagarbha),* governed by Taurus the bull, expresses the dispensation of the Airy aspect of the cosmic Waters (hence the attributes of *ākāśa* in general) into the solar manifestation. This allows the establishment of the Logoic Head centre upon the second highest cosmic ether *(anupādaka).* This represents the proper incarnation of the Logos in the form of this Luminous Egg. The Egg represents the totality of the ring-pass-not of any Logoic form that manifests in the solar system, as symbolised by the glyph of the sign Taurus, which represents the arc of the psyche evolving out of the containment of a sphere of activity, which the Egg represents. The Heart in the Head allows the projection of Logoic Love to control the evolutionary development of the sum of the evolving form. The Luminous Egg is therefore the sphere of Love-Wisdom that circumscribes all that is to be in this solar system. The Logoic Heart centre is consequently also established at this stage. Scorpio, the polar opposite of Taurus, vitalises the luminosity of this Egg.

   Taurus is normally considered an Earth sign and Scorpio a Water sign, but from the above perspective Taurus is seen as the ruler of the substance of the cosmic astral plane in general, (the Mother's department) hence bears the sum of its *prāṇas* into manifestation, which is projected via the Airy disposition. Scorpio is the means of projection of these Watery-Airy *prāṇas.* The Pleiades that are carried upon the back of Taurus are responsible for the Earthy building potency. Governing the Deva Builders the Pleiades condense the cosmic Waters into the substance of the cosmic dense sphere, thus building the form of the Egg. They cause the placement and appearance of the Logoic form.[33] The Eye of the Bull, Alderbaran manifests a Fiery disposition, the directive Forces energising the Builders.

3. *The depths of the Mother.* The general dissemination, or embodiment, of the cosmic Waters in the solar form is generally governed by Pisces the fishes. Taurus builds the sphere, and Pisces bonds the Lives that are to evolve to that sphere. 'The depths' represents the elementary substance that is organised into the evolving forms

33 This subject was explained in *Esoteric Cosmology and Modern Physics.*

by the Love of the Mother. This is the substance of the Mother's Womb, governed generally by the sign Virgo, the polar opposite of Pisces. Within the depths of the Mother is found the fishes of the embodied personality form (the Lives) swimming in the waters of sensation, which is established by means of the projection of the *sūtrātmā* from the higher to the lower self. The *sūtrātmā* bonds the higher three to the lower three that manifest via the appearance of this fourth principle *(buddhi)*. The *chakras* below the diaphragm centre are thus established upon the fourth ether.

4. *The Root that grows* represents the germ of material plane activity, whereby the Fiery Element evolves and is disseminated in the solar form, as governed by Capricorn the goat. The purpose is to develop the abstract Mind by the evolving units of sentience, and then consciousness, ensconced as 'the four', who will thereby eventually master the sum of *saṃsāra*. The 'four' evolve the five as a consequence. Capricorn also governs the *manasic* activities of the *deva* Builders that rightly organise the substance of the evolving forms. This is a power bequeathed by Venus, who embodies the fifth Ray, and who is the Hierarchical ruler of this sign. The solar Throat centre is thereby established upon the third ether. This Root grows through the gateway of incarnation of the massed Life, as governed by Cancer, the polar opposite of Capricorn. Capricorn is spoken here as Fiery because though it is considered an Earthy sign, governing the most material, rocky aspects of the evolutionary process, this Earthy-ness is in reality crystallised Fire, hence Capricorn is represented as the mountain of mind/Mind.
5. The formation of the *milk-white Curds* is governed by Sagittarius the archer, who fires the Fiery arrows of *ākāśa* to help condense the elementary Earthy forms of 'the Root that grows'. This is done by means of projecting the energies from *ātma* into the *nāḍī* system being established,[34] and whose qualities are ruled by Gemini the twins (the polar opposite of Sagittarius). The above energies work via the fourth ether and specifically by the *chakras* established thereon (the immortal brother) as the ethereal substance of space curdles.

---

34 The lines of light of the *nāḍīs* can be viewed as the arrows fired by the Archer.

This inevitably causes the precipitation of the Earthy Element from the (material) Fiery substance wielded by Capricorn. The precipitation happens via the establishment of the *nāḍī* system in the three worlds of human livingness. (The mortal brother.) This allows 'the Root' to grow into the Tree of Life. The accomplishment of this process is indicated by the symbolism of Stanzas 3:4 to 3:11. From this we can see that the purpose of Sagittarius in Stanza 3:4 is to drive the Logoic Thought via *ātma* through to conclusion in Gemini. From here the material world can consequently materialise. Gemini veils the cosmic Christ, the conscious Lives, who are then integrated as 'every Drop of the Ocean'. The Base of Spine/Sacral centres can consequently appear to accommodate the appearing form upon the physical plane.

6. The initial impetus of the Logoic Mind (Mahat) that causes the fall of 'the three into the four' is conveyed by the sign Aries the ram, who governs initial beginnings. (The Hierarchical ruler being Uranus, which governs the seventh Ray dispensation, hence the materialising power of this Ray and of its cyclic activity.) The entire process is an effect of the meditation of the Logos, a consequence of His *dhyāna,* (governed by the attributes of the sign Libra the balances, the polar opposite of Aries). The initial rarefied Fire of the Logoic Mind is eventually expressed as the crystallised Fire of the material substance of the cosmic dense physical plane by means of the above process.

In this way the energies of the signs of the zodiac gradually condition the early formation of the solar form. The interrelation between the Elements governing the signs could also be noted in the above. They are the Airy triad of Libra, Aquarius and Gemini, the Earthy triad of Taurus, Virgo and Capricorn, the Watery triad of Scorpio, Pisces and Cancer, finally the Fiery triad of Aries, Leo and Sagittarius. All of these Elements are consequently but attributes of different energy states that are denominated in terms of the Elements because of their respective qualities relative to each other. Things are viewed differently from different levels of perception.

Following from point five above the outline for the remaining chapters can be further clarified as follows.

Stanzas 3:4 to 3:11 are concerned with the process of the reification of the Fiery substance of the Logoic Mind via the Waters into the Earthy Element conveyed in the cosmic dense physical domain. In Stanza 3:4 the plane *ātma* represents the plane governing the materialisation of this process. It consequently represents a first Ray activity of the projection of the first Outpouring by Sagittarius the archer.

In Stanza 3:5 the Sagittarian impulse projects the Fiery *ākāśa* under the auspices of Amitābha's potency. This potency is reinforced by the *manasic* power of Capricorn that condenses the Logoic Thought (Stanzas 3:4 – 3:11), hence 'the Root remains', 'the Light remains', etc. This Thought, reiterated by the Lesser Builders, causes the projection and awakening of the massed Lives (Oeaohoo) in manifestation.

In Stanza 3:6 under the Sagittarian impulse the Watery *ākāśa* is expressed into dense manifestation ('every drop of the Ocean of Immortality') via the *buddhic* plane. The Waters convey the Love-Wisdom principle, which must be reflected into manifestation. This energy causes the appearance of the kingdom of Souls upon the higher mental plane, where this form of *ākāśa* clothes the substance of the Causal form. This happens under the auspices of Akṣobhya, whose potency upon the cosmic astral plane is here expressed. The fourth Ray governs the dispensation of this fourth cosmic ether, which acts as a mirror, reflecting the potency of the cosmic Waters into dense manifestation. The substance of the potent energy found upon the *buddhic* plane necessitates stripping bare all *saṃsāric* attributes upon the upward Way by those gaining enlightenment and who enter into the Void of *śūnyatā*. Therein the intensity of the energies that will be experienced must be borne, as empirical thoughts cannot be sustained under the potency of *śūnyatā's* energies. This force also acts as a transmutative agent, causing the eventual manifestation of the Void Elements upon the upward way of the returning Jīvas. What is experienced upon *buddhi* then is the collective Awareness of the Lives, Oeaohoo, incorporated in cosmos.

The higher energies impact upon and incorporate the prima matrix of the cosmic 'black dust' found upon the lower mental plane, allowing the planes of *saṃsāric* activity to appear. This happens via Aquarian influence, which, in this case, the higher band of the glyph for this sign represents the energies passing through the higher mental plane, and the lower band the substance of the lower mental.

In Stanza 3:7 Sagittarius projects the first Outpouring via the first sub-aspect of the Earthy Element (Earthy *ākāśa).* It utilises the combined power of Vairocana's Purpose and Amoghasiddhi's All-accomplishing Wisdom (reflected from the plane *ādi)* to organise the primal substance of the higher mental plane so that the entire evolutionary process of the incarnating Lives can be accomplished. The governing Ray is the fifth of Science, but is also effected via the martial sixth Ray energies from the Watery Womb of substance, governed by Pisces the fishes. The sixth Ray makes the activity of the 'black dust' of the mental plane more mutable, Watery. It softens the inherent materialistic aspects of the fifth Ray, so that 'Oeaohoo, the Younger' can evolve. The added first Ray potency from *ādi* allows the Logos to master the sum of the sub-planes of the cosmic dense physical plane through manipulating and moulding the 'mineral' content of this domain with the assistance of the inherent attributes of this Earthy Element. The externalisation process that produces the dense physical, as humans presently understand it, is an automatic reflex of the forces that shape the mental plane, a subject adequately explained in my earlier writings.

Stanza 3:8 concerns the enquiring mind of an evolving human kingdom under the auspices of the fifth Ray of Scientific Aptitude. Humanity ascend up the planes of perception by utilising the Arian impetus of the will to overcome, to conquer or to master. What needs mastering represents the lower mental plane. Here the developed empirical mind is assisted to think more inclusively, rather than separately, by the second sub-aspect of Earthy *ākāśa*, which is expressed as the substance of this plane. There is a long aeonic evolutionary process whereby cosmic dust evolves over the course of a solar evolution or two to eventually manifest the attributes of a humanity that can 'think' and to use the will.

Stanzas 3:9 and 3:10 can be considered a unity, as effectively at this stage the astral plane is non-existent, hence the objective for the first Outpouring at this level concerns the projection of the third (more *manasic)* sub-aspect of the Earthy Element by the Sagittarian archer to build the etheric substratum of the dense physical domain so as to reflect the attributes of the four cosmic ethers. This sub-Earthy aspect facilitates the development of the mind to assist in controlling the Watery substance of the astral domain (which is *piṅgalā* in nature). This sub-aspect assists in awakening *iḍā nāḍī* attributes that mainly materialise to form the dense physical domain.

Scorpionic force via Taurus (the two are polar opposites) and the second Ray are also reflected from the plane *anupādaka* via Ratnasambhava's Equalising Wisdom to help control the Watery substance.

Scorpio precipitates the cosmic astral Waters to energise the movement of the Lives via the seven main *chakras,* producing the Rounds of evolution. The Waters embody the planetary and zodiacal potencies that vitalise everything coming into being with the various *prāṇas* sustaining their activities.

Because of their association with the cosmic astral plane Taurus and Scorpio naturally facilitate the appearance of the Watery astral dispensation, and the later development of a humanity's creative imagination and emotional activity that cause their heaven and hell zones. The martial Scorpionic sixth Ray potency (coupled with the Sagittarian Will) is tempered by the effect of Ratnasambhava's Wisdom. The sixth Ray facilitates the downpour of cosmic astral energies, but also intensifies the emotional intensities of humanity, providing the testing ground for firstly the development of desire-ambition and later of affection, aspiration and then Love. The sixth Ray acts as the precipitating energy that projects the elementary Lives into dense physical forms, the atoms of substance.

The astral-etheric planes are governed by Taurus and Gemini, the first Ray (via Vulcan in Taurus) and the third Ray (via the earth in Gemini), with which 'Father-Mother spin a web'. The first Ray provides the driving Will, and the third Ray the mathematically exact Activity to accomplish the task. The entire *chakra* system can thereby be built that governs the earthy terrain, via which the lesser streams of Lives constituting the kingdoms of Nature can incarnate.

Stanzas 3:9-10 and 3:11-12 are concerned with the inherent dualism of the sign Gemini, of the immortal and mortal brothers, where Stanzas

3:9-10 concern the activity of the 'immortal brother', the web that is spun. Stanzas 3:11-12 are consequently concerned with the effect of what was thus created, the web of Life that expands and contracts, according to the types of energies that affect it. The mortal brother is concerned with the realm of incarnation, evolution, sickness, disease and death, which is fully expressed in the embodied form. Stanza 3:12 deals with the consequences of the energies passing through the ethers.

Stanzas 3:10 and 3:11 are concerned with the appearance of the physical plane (in its etheric subdivision) under the auspices of Gemini the twins (hence via the third Ray). This is assisted by the Mahatic input of Amitābha's Discriminating Inner Wisdom, which draws its materialising potency from the *ātmic* plane. Also the third sub-aspect of Earthy *ākāśa* of Stanza 3:10 allows the energies of the Mother to project Her *manasic* force to cause the final concretion, the most material sub-plane, of the substance of the Womb. This is the consequence of sending 'Fohat to harden the atoms' in Stanza 3:12. The 'Child' is consequently born. Using this energy the Mother builds with the outpouring of the third Earthy sub-aspect (Stanza 3:10), the fourth Earthy sub-ray (Stanza 3:11), and the fifth Earthy sub-ray (Stanza 3:12). These aspects facilitate the work of the *deva* builders, whose activities are generally governed via them. They are the reflected attribute of the Mother's energies that initially manifested via the third plane of perception, *ātma*. Stanza 3:10 is governed generally by the sixth Ray, and Stanza 3:11 the seventh Ray. Together these Rays wield a potent materialising potency for the appearance and hardening of the atoms of substance.

In Stanza 3:12 the effect of the forceful projection of the Will (first Ray) upon the higher mental plane by the Logos causes the final, most material appearance of a world-sphere, the seventh emanation of the first Outpouring, governed by the third Ray generally. The potency of the Ray combination of these two Stanzas manifests via Leo, the sign of individuation, conditioning the manifestation of the forms, from the appearance of atomic to animal life.

The qualities of the triune Deity are thereby reflected into the microcosm. This emanation concerns the fall of the triangle ('the three'), which becomes a square ('the four'), as soon as matter is formed and regulated. When another factor is add to the triangle, it geometrically becomes a square, the form is thus objectively differentiated from the cause, yet both are integrated by the middle principle *(śūnyatā)* that is Void of both, and yet is the mechanism of integration. It is the mirror that allows the One to be reflected into the other.

The geometric foundation of this process was explained in chapter three of *Esoteric Cosmology and Modern Physics,* hence the reader needs to refer to that chapter for detail. With respect to Buddhist philosophy the act of causation of phenomena by the creative Logos concerns the projection of the image held steady in the Mind of the 'all creating King' (Vajrasattva)[35] into the planes of expression.

The process of manifestation proceeds from the third – the Mother (the lowest expression of the Abstract triune Deity). She expresses Herself as the fourth principle, the manifest universe, and this principle is symbolised by a square. This 'square' is esoterically incorporated as the content of Her 'Womb'. It is constituted of the mental, astral, etheric, and dense physical space.

In terms of the meditation process there are three aspects to consider. First there is the Thought (or Will-to-Be), the Father. Next the Word (or the Sound which amalgamates all into a coherent shape), which represents the activity of the Son, and finally the Breath, which is the movement, the Mother demonstrating the various activities in the totality of the body of being. They are archetypal, but together they project a Thought-form by imbuing the matter, the omnipresent Waters of Space, with the qualities of Deity. The Thought and Word are instantaneous with the Movement that produces the material universe.

The creative process unfolds to externalise the material world, and this world tends to reproduce itself as countless different forms, all reflecting (in differing degrees) the triune qualities of Deity. The 'square' therefore is illusory, and though it has a momentarily reality it has no permanence, symbolising the transitory material world. It is an arbitrary medium between the archetypal and what is projected into objectivity. This is also symbolised by the word Jehovah of the Old Testament, or Jod-He-Vau-He: 'I AM THAT I AM'.[36] He represents the creative principle inherent in the solar system.

35 A phrase explained with respect to Buddhist philosophy in volume two of *The Treatise on Mind.*

36 *Exodus 3:14.*

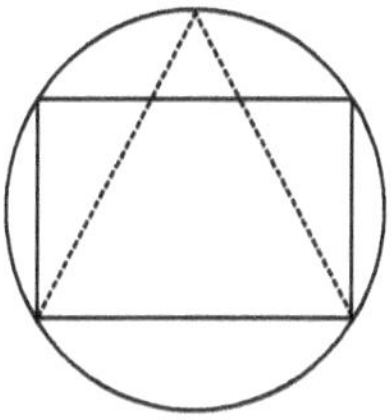

Figure 8. The fall of the three into the four

It can be said metaphysically that the material world tends to reproduce itself in terms of the smallest geometrical shape – another triangle (or rather triangles) for every form via the process of birth, expansion and death. This then mirrors the qualities of Deity.

The involutionary process described until now is associated with the Consciousness-stream, hence the emanation of the twelve Creative Hierarchies. The descending energies for instance of the tenth Creative Hierarchy ('Light thro' knowledge') reverberates from cosmic astral levels to the systemic lower mental plane to activate the tenth Creative Hierarchy (Makara the Mystery, the Crocodiles), the *devas* constituting the substance of mind.

The Hierarchies represent the Lives and units of mind/Mind that en-Soul the substance that comes into existence by means of 'the fall of the three into the four'. The formed realms thereby appear, to thrill with Life. The lower Lives gain the fifth principle through their consequent evolution. Humanity utilises the *manasic* substance of the lower tenth Creative Hierarchy to reason and think with, but must learn to bridge the gap in consciousness symbolised by the separation of the triangle to the square through building the *antaḥkaraṇa* (the consciousness-link) and so reside at the *śūnyatā-saṃsāra* nexus. The meaning of this nexus and its attainment was explained in detail in the first five volumes of *A Treatise on Mind*.

Having this background in mind the meaning of the numerical implications to Stanza 3:4 can now be analysed.

The numbers of the phrase *'the Three'* add to 44, 17, which direct our focus to the triune Logos, in particular to the governance of the earth Scheme, symbolised by the number 44. The 'three' stand as a template allowing comprehension of the nature of the whole. In the case of our planetary Scheme there is the triune Logos: the Avatar of Synthesis, the Spirit of Peace and the Mother of the World. Sanat Kumāra and the Three Buddhas of Activity stand as 'the Four', where the dynamic Word from 'the Three' manifests via the fourth to be directed into manifestation.[37] The Three Buddhas of Activity, Ray down the material aspect of themselves into the three worlds of human livingness to do so.

The concept of falling implies that that what falls has weight, is material in nature (similar to the meaning of the word 'dropped'). However here our consideration is not a Ray of Light, but rather a triad of Beings and their energies.

The numbers of the phrase *'the Three fall'* add to 7 x 3, 12, where the number 7 x 3 can refer to this Trinity, and also the domains that they fall to. Each of the Three can embody a septenary of energies and forces. The number 12 refers to the Heart centre that is awakened as they do so. This Heart contains the energies and Lives constituting the twelve Creative Hierarchies. They pour through the Three and effectively do the actual 'falling', to embody the sum of what must be. The conditionings on the higher mental plane then become a matrix of Light, the 'Womb of the Mother' *(mātripadma),* the 'Germ', into which 'the Three' esoterically 'fall' to cause the formation and conditionings of a kingdom of Souls. Amitābha's energies helps produce their phenomenal appearance. From another perspective 'the Three' also represent the three Outpourings, which organise the primeval substance *(mūlaprakṛti)* that is condensed to form the dense physical plane, as well as the Lives utilising that substance as their sheaths and the consequent evolutionary growth to liberation.

The numbers of the phrase *'the four'* add to 13 x 3, 6.6., where the number 13 x 3 refers to the cycles of activity that condition the appearance of the four, whilst the number 6.6. refers to the actual appearance of the formed world associated with 'the four'.

The numbers 11, 20, of the phrase *'fall into the four'* refer to the first and second Ray energies that cause the projection of the three to

---

37 The nature of and interrelation between these great Ones was explained in *The Constitution of Shambhala.* There it was shown that Sanat Kumāra was a unique Individuality, a cosmic Avatar, greater than the position indicated in the *maṇḍala,* Who expresses within Himself the attributes of 'the Three'.

cause the quaternary. The process of this 'fall' depicts a concealed mystery. What falls evolves added characteristics, which is accomplished by this substance coming into contact with the consciousness aspect and to be incorporated by it. They consequently evolve into vectors of light. The substance of the form, the lunar lives, the *lunar pitṛ (pitris),* must develop into their solar prototypes *(solar pitṛ)* encountered on the higher mental levels, who convey the energy from the Heart of the Sun, in the form of radiant *prāṇa.* (A lower interpretation of the phrase 'Radiant Essence'.) The *solar pitṛ* embody the substance of our Sambhogakāya Flowers.

The Feet centres of a Logos stand upon the dense physical substance of the cosmos (the mental plane) from which the Logos can extract information concerning that realm. This is accomplished by means of the streams of *prāṇas* emanating from the toes, which find their externalisation in the planetary Solar Plexus centre (the ten petalled lotus). The *devic* lives governing *saṃsāra* thereby receive information from the sum of the dense Body of the Logos.

These *prāṇas* carry with them what was rejected from a former cycle, the stored mineral, plant and animal Life that now have a chance to evolve further. The *karma* of the past thereby emerges. The incorporated *virgin* substance of the new cycle is integrated with these three kingdoms, as they represent the past attainment of the Logos. They are the base reservoir of experience that will help carry the momentum of the new cycle forward. By means of empathy of vibration the pristine substance can be integrated with the gain of the past and be directed by the overriding Thinker.

The Base of Spine centre directs the elementary mineral *prāṇas* of the new Round, the nature of the expression of the Earthy Element, which can be viewed as a quaternary, a pentad or septenary. The septenary can be considered as the expression of the downward pointing triangle of the Sacral centre integrated with the four petals of the Base of Spine centre. (These two centres are united in this manner.) The four petals of the Base of Spine centre are also responsible for the *prāṇas* that feed the evolutionary growth of the four objective kingdoms of Nature, viewing them in relation to their physical plane expression. The Sacral centre is the directing centre for plant-like *prāṇas,* and the Solar Plexus centre for the animal-like *prāṇas*. The appearance of a human kingdom instigates the awakening of the Heart centre. All *prāṇas* are circulated through the system by the Splenic centre. Thus is established the corporeal universe forming our dense physical world, the enveloping Watery domain and the all-embracive Fiery spheres of experience. The primal substance is thus triune, an expression of the third aspect of Deity, and consequently bears the quaternary or Son aspect, the consciousness factor, which incorporates 'the four', which from this perspective is the awakening human kingdom.

The number 100 + 2 x 9 of the phrase *'the three fall into the four'* has a reference to the fact that the human Hierarchy ('the four') are termed 'the Initiates', whilst 'the three' refers here to the spiritual triad *(ātma-buddhi-manas)* that 'fall' into the higher mental plane to cause the appearance of the kingdom of Souls, the Initiates. The associated number 10 refers to the totality of any Body of manifestation via the ten stages of the evolutionary process.

The numerical breakdown of the second to the fifth phrases:

> The radiant Essence (71, 17), seven inside (53, 8), the radiant Essence becomes seven (117, 27) becomes seven inside (79 = 16, 16), The radiant Essence becomes seven inside (150, 33), seven outside (50, 5), The luminous Egg (68 = 17 x 4, 34 x 2; 23), in itself (40, 13), in itself is three (79 = 16, 25), which in itself is three (112, 31).

'The radiant Essence' (17, 8) is the essence of being, the energy (8) that manifests through the etheric Body of Deity (17). It is radiant because it is the pure energy of Light, expressing the divine Will in the form of the intensity of its radiation, and Love that denotes its quality. A radiatory emanation is the aura determining the quality of the life of an entity, and which expresses the eventual phenomenal appearance. Here however it more than just radiant, it is also the essence of Being/Non-being. This energy is aptly symbolised by the wavy bands of the sign Aquarius. What concerns us here is what the Water Bearer dispenses into the Logoic manifestation from cosmic astral levels (or ultimately from the domain of the Logoic Soul) via the Sagittarian impulse. Its dynamic impetus vitalises the atomic structure of all the

Lives that 'thrill'. It also eventually liberates one from the thrall of bondage to the form. It can therefore be equated with the energy of *bodhicitta* that vitalises the Heart centre with compassionate purpose.

Concerning the radiant Essence H.P.B states:

> "The radiant essence curdled and spread throughout the depths" of Space. From an astronomical point of view this is easy of explanation: it is the "milky way," the world-stuff, or primordial matter in its first form. It is more difficult, however, to explain it in a few words or even lines, from the standpoint of Occult Science and Symbolism, as it is the most complicated of glyphs. Herein are enshrined more than a dozen symbols. To begin with, the whole pantheon of mysterious objects, every one of them having some definite Occult meaning, extracted from the allegorical "churning of the ocean" by the Hindu gods. Besides *Amrita,* the water of life or immortality, *"Surabhi"* the "cow of plenty," called "the fountain of milk and curds," was extracted from this "Sea of Milk." Hence the universal adoration of the cow and bull, one the productive, the other the generative power in Nature: symbols connected with both the Solar and the Cosmic deities. The specific properties, for occult purposes, of the "fourteen precious things," being explained only at the fourth Initiation, cannot be given here; but the following may be remarked. In the "Satapatha Brāhmana" it is stated that the churning of the "Ocean of Milk" took place in the Satya Yug, the first age which immediately followed the "Deluge." As, however, neither the Rig-Veda nor Manu — both preceding Vaivasvata's "deluge," that of the bulk of the Fourth Race — mention this deluge, it is evident that it is not the "great" deluge, nor that which carried away Atlantis, nor even the deluge of Noah, which is meant here. This "churning" relates to a period before the earth's formation, and is in direct connection with that other universal legend, the various and contradictory versions of which culminated in the Christian dogma of the "War in Heaven," and the fall of the Angels.[38]

Concerning the phrase *'The radiant Essence becomes seven'* (117, 27), the numbers 13 x 9, 3 x 9 imply the attainment of the Initiation process (for the Logos concerned), whilst the number 3 x 9 can also refer to the Soul of manifest Life residing on the higher mental plane (in the

38 S.D. Vol. 1, 67-68.

form of 'the Eternal-Egg') from which emanates the material universe. The 'Radiant Essence' is thus incorporated into/as the Sambhogakāya Flower, the Son in incarnation, who is fecundated with Amitābha's Discriminating Inner Wisdom. This Essence thereby empowers the Heart of manifest Life. It is an aspect of the Ray that has been projected into the Soul from the Monad.

When analysing the phrases *'seven inside'* and *'seven outside'* the question immediately asked is 'inside and outside of what?' The statement that starts with 'the Luminous Egg' implies that it is this Egg which is the concern here. Another interpretation would be the newly formed solar sphere at a period of time when all still remains subjective. In order to properly assess the question one needs to analyse the entire verse as a unit. When done so then seven main factors appear, which can be related to the seven planes of perception that form inside the new solar system.

1. The radiant Essence – *bodhicitta* first appearing upon the plane *ādi,* though its main expression is upon *anupādaka.* It is the cosmic astral energy, the source of Love to the system, which drives all forward to an enlightened conclusion.
2. The Luminous Egg – the Womb of the consciousness-bearing principle. It is the World Soul that contains the radiant Essence, becoming a radiant sun for a world sphere. For a Logos this Egg manifests upon the plane *anupādaka.* It carries the germs of the Monadic Life that will establish the appearance of a human kingdom. To do so the Monads manifest a reflection of this Egg upon the higher mental plane in the form of our Souls.
3. The depths of the Mother – which constitutes Her Womb upon the *ātmic* plane, thence the five planes of Brahmā.
4. The energy that causes the curdling and spreading—*buddhi.*

5a. The depths of the Ocean – the higher mental plane.

5b. The Root that grows – *manasic* substance upon the mental plane.

6. Growing in the depths – of the Waters, the astral plane.
7. The Ocean of Life – the etheric/dense physical plane, plus the sum of the Lives that evolve in the systemic Waters, that appear in all of the abovementioned planes. All are linked by the Watery principle (Divine Love).

As 'the Luminous Egg' is said to be triune this appears to preclude it from being that into which the radiant essence manifests as a septenary. However we know that 'the three fall into the four', making a septenary. If this Egg is thus said to be the solar form (where H.P.B.'s note states it is *hiraṇyagarbha)* then it can also be viewed as a septenary.

Hiraṇyagarbha is derived from the Sanskrit roots *'hiraṇya',* meaning imperishable substance, golden, plus *'garbha',* womb, embryo, is literally the 'golden womb' or 'golden egg' from which the manifested universe came into being.[39] It is also a name of Brahmā in the Purāṇas, who was said to be born in water or from a seed that became this golden egg.[40] Within this egg the abstracted Brahman, while remaining transcendent, manifested as Brahmā, the Creative Deity of the Hindu *trimūrti* (Śiva, Viṣṇu, Brahmā). After a year in the egg, through the power of thought he bisected it. We then have the appearance of the heavens and earth, with the sky in between, the eight cardinal points and the Waters.

The online encyclopaedia, Wikipedia succinctly summarises the various Creation Myths of Hinduism:

> Matsya Purāna (2.25-30) gives an account of initial creation. After Mahāprālaya, the great dissolution of the Universe, there was darkness everywhere. Everything was in a state of sleep. There was nothing, either moving or static. Then Svayambhu, Self-manifested Being arose, which is a form beyond senses. It created the primordial waters first and established the seed of creation into it. The seed turned into a golden womb, Hiraṇyagarbha. Then Svayambhu entered in the egg.
>
> The Nārāyana Sūkata exclaims that everything that is, visible or invisible, all this is pervaded by Nārāyana within and without.
>
> The Īśvara Upanisad says that the universe is pervaded by Īśvara (God), who is both within and without it. He is the moving and the unmoving, He is far and near, He is within all these and without all these.
>
> The Vedānta Sūtra further states that Brahman is That from Whom this Universe proceeds, in Whom it subsists, and to Whom, in the end, it returns.
>
> The Samkhya school holds that there are only two primary principles, Puruṣa and Prākṛti, and creation is only a manifestation or evolution of the constituents of Prākṛti due to the action of Puruṣa's Consciousness.

39 See the *Rig Veda* for detail.

40 According to *Manu* (1:9).

The Mahābhārata states that Nārāyana alone was in the beginning, who was the pious of principles of creation, sustenance, and dissolution (also known as the Hindu Trinity of Brahmā, Viṣnu and Śiva) - the Supreme Hari, multi-headed, multi-eyed, multi-footed, multi-armed, multi-limbed. This was the Supreme Seed of all creation, subtler than the subtlest, greater than the greatest, larger than the largest, and more magnificent than even the best of all things, more powerful, than even the wind and all the gods, more resplendent than the Sun and the Moon, and more internal than even the mind and the intellect. He is the Creator, the Father Supreme.

The Manu Smriti says: In the beginning, all this existence was one undifferentiated, unmanifested, indefinable, unarguable and unknown in every way. From this condition arose the Universe of 'name and form' (Sanskrit: nāmarūpa), through the medium of the Self-existent Creator, Svayambhu.

The numbers of the phrase *'becomes seven inside'* add to 16, 7. The number 7 here is self-explanatory. When observing the numbers of the phrase *'seven inside',* which add to 8, referring to the spiral-cyclic energy, then we see that these seven refer to the seven primordial Rays, and the seven Ray Chohans that distribute their energies into planetary manifestation. There are also the seven planes of perception, the seven Regents before the Throne of 'God', all septenaries in Nature, the purpose of which is to evolve the Christ principle (the number 16). Their qualities are reflected in the seven *chakras* within a person.

By the number 50 of the phrase *'seven outside',* we see that all is a direct expression of the Mind of the cosmic Logos from which emanates a similar, though higher vaster septenary, such as the seven stars of the constellation of which our sun is one.

The phrases *'seven inside'* and *seven outside'* can also refer to the energies of the Pleiades, the seven Sisters, who's activities and forces are invoked to help cause the appearance of phenomena. Those who are 'outside' relate to the Sisters active within the constellation, whilst those 'inside' relate to the *deva* agents (the Rāja Lords) within the appearing form, embodying the Fiery attributes of Mind (50) to effect the necessary appearances of the formed world, as will be explained here and in the rest of stanza three. The basic doctrine concerning these

Sisters is found in chapter three of *The Constitution of Shambhala,* Part 7B, and also elaborated in *Esoteric Cosmology and Modern Physics.* Of them Electra governs the manifestation of Manas (Mahat) upon the plane *ādi* in the form of cosmic electricity, termed 'radiant Essence' in this Stanza. Maia builds the conditionings upon the plane *anupādaka.* Celaeno, the 'black', governs the conditionings within the Womb of the Mother, represented by the plane *ātma.* Alcyone, the great divider of the Waters of Life, governs the work via the plane *buddhi.* Merope governs the formation of the mental plane and the evolution of the attributes of mind/Mind. Taygeta, the 'beloved daughter' births the functioning of the Watery astral plane. Sterope is the means for the particularisation of the highest energies to cause the conditionings appearing as the world of forms.

The numbers of the phrase *'The radiant Essence becomes seven inside'* add to 150 = 15 x 10, 25 x 6, 5 x 30, 3 x 50, and to 33. The number 33 refers to all the Creative Intelligences constituting the totality of a planetary or solar sphere of activity. They convey the Fiery nature that is the basis to this radiation, and they come under the jurisprudence of the five Kumāras (the Dhyāni Buddhas) – 5 x 30. The number 3 x 50 infers that the external septenary is reflected internally upon all three levels (Spirit-Soul-matter) of this Egg. The number 150 exemplifies the fact that the radiance is the effect of the Mind in action, the interplay between Mind and Spirit regarding the evolution of the form nature. This level of expression is that of the Shambhalic correspondence of any Logos that is established at this time in the form of a 'Radiant Egg', into which will incarnate the informing Lives that will administer to the Rounds of the evolutionary process. When the 'three fall into the four', thus making the material universe, the four (in this case the four cosmic ethers) then get overshadowed by the three representing the triune Deity (3 x 50). We thus have the appearance of what allows the evolution of a thinker, man.

This number also refers to the way that the Pleiades manifest their activities upon the planes of perception via the expression of the three *guṇas: rajas, sattva* and *tamas.* They are the fundamental qualities or triune attributes of manifesting energies, being dynamic *(rajas),* active *(sattva),* or relatively inert *(tamas).* Cosmic Mind (Mahat) is thereby utilised to mould the primal substance of the planetary or solar form to produce the appearances of what is to be.

Spirit (the Life principle) and matter interact and blend, the result is the Fires of the mind, of intelligence, and this allows the seven *(chakras)* to be awakened. The complete powers of all these centres can then eventually be developed. The mind consequently becomes liberated as Mind via the activity of the human bearers of these *chakras*. As this is accomplished then the fifth principle effectively evolves into the two, Will and the Christ-force (Love-Wisdom), which is the essence of the five, and which thus perfectly embodies the seven. This Christ-force is the radiant Essence that is veiled by Mind.

On a planetary or solar scale the perfected five, who embody the attributes of the Mind of the Logos (the planetary Head centre), and who are Lords of the various kingdoms in Nature, thus project the energies from the seven *chakras* within their respective bodies of manifestation. (For a solar Logos the *chakras* become the planetary Schemes.) Each *chakra* contains various Monadic or Soul groupings that correspond to its related qualities, which become the *anima mundi,* the Soul of all manifest Life (the number 25 x 6).

The manifestation of the seven primordial Rays by means of the radiant Essence effectively causes the formation of the archetype (or Soul) of all that is later to become active in the realms of form. The inner and outer seven form the sum of the body of manifestation of any particular planetary or solar Logos. The radiant Essence is the expression of the Spirit aspect (the Monad), but is projected into the 'seven inside, seven outside' by means of accomplished Mind (the Christ force). It sustains and vitalises the form and is akin to the *prāṇa* in our bodies.

At this level of cosmic evolution, one of the wavy bands of the glyph of Aquarius represents the energies of cosmic astral space and the other to the energies contained in the four etheric sub-planes of the cosmic dense physical.

The term *luminous* means being shining, brilliant, illuminated, full of light, or enlightened. All these qualities are expressions of the light of the mind/Mind. Note the difference in the intensity of energy expressed between the terms 'luminous' and 'radiant', where radiance signifies a more intense type of energy than being luminous. Hence luminance implicates the awakening Mind or the Soul aspect, whereas radiance to that pertaining to the spiritual triad *(manas, buddhi, ātma).*

The number 17 x 4 of the phrase *'The luminous Egg'* relates to the quaternary nature of Deity, the Seat of Power of the Logos, from whence all else emanates, thus it is the germ of all corporeal Life. This Seat is established upon *anupādaka,* but incorporates the substance of the four cosmic ethers. At this stage the Logoic Egg is luminous rather than radiant because the reference is to the early evolutionary stage before the manifestation of the full expression of what is to be. Because 'The luminous Egg' is the physical seed of the projected form it expresses the quaternary. Through it the Logoic trinity manifests, which is then expressed as a septenary, as the third (the Mother) is inherently a pentad of expression. (The symbolism of the five original heads of Brahmā.) This pentad embodies the attributes of cosmic Mind, as represented by the Mind-born sons of Brahmā, the Kumāras. There are said to be four exoteric and three esoteric Kumāras. They can also be considered the four faces of Brahmā, with the fifth being the central overshadowing head that represents the esoteric three. This head was later cut off (i.e., made subjective) by the wrath of Śiva.

The numbers 16 and 25 of the phrase *'in itself is three'* refer to the world-Soul – 'the luminous Egg', which in itself is triune, as are the nine major petals of the Soul. There are three tiers of three petals each around a central bud of three veiling the Śūnyatā Eye.

The number 40 of the phrase *'in itself'* refers to the Throne upon which the triune Logos sits, explained above.

The numbers of the phrase *'which is in itself three'* add to 7 x 16 and to 31. The number 7 x 16 refers to the seven *chakras* (Schemes of planetary spheres[41]) whereby the expression of the Christ energy awakens the consciousness-principle in any body of manifestation. Each of these *chakras* can also be considered 'luminous Eggs'. Each is essentially triune, as is all manifest Life (the central seed bearing area, the petals and the stem). Each 'luminous Egg' is the seed of an entire world or solar sphere, a direct product of the Will of 'God' (31).

41 They are generally subjective, with one generally manifesting objectivity, as is the case of the earth for the earth Scheme.

The numerical breakdown of the last two phrases:

> curdles and spreads (66, 21, 1.1.1), milk-white curds (67, 22), throughout the depths (96, 24), the depths (42, 15), The depths of Mother (88, 25), throughout the depths of Mother (142, 34), spreads in milk-white curds (109, 37), curdles and spreads in milk-white curds (147, 48), spreads in milk-white curds throughout the depths (205, 61), spreads in milk-white curds throughout the depths of Mother (251, 71), curdles and spreads in milk-white curds throughout the depths (243 = 27 x 9, 72), curdles and spreads in milk-white curds throughout the depths of Mother (289, 82), the Root (38, 11), the Root that grows (79 = 16, 25), the ocean (35, 8), the ocean of Life (70, 16), in the ocean (49, 13), the Root that grows in the ocean (128, 38), the Root that grows in the ocean of Life (163, 46).

The formation of the *'milk-white curds'* is governed by Sagittarius the archer, who fires the Fiery-Watery arrows of *ākāśa* to condense the elementary Earthy forms of 'the Root that grows'. This is accomplished by means of projecting the energies from *ātma* into the *nāḍī* system being established, whose qualities are ruled by Gemini the twins (the polar opposite of Sagittarius). The *deva* Builders are consequently called into action. The above energies work via the fourth ether and specifically by the *chakras* established thereon (the immortal brother) as the ethereal substance of space curdles. This inevitably causes the precipitation of the Earthy Element from the (material) Fiery substance wielded by Capricorn. Myriads of *devas* stream into activity to cause the precipitation of 'things'. This happens in the three worlds of human livingness (the mortal brother) via the established *nāḍīs*. The 'the Root' can then grow into the Tree of Life.

The curdling and spreading 'in milk-white curds' is explained in *A Treatise on Cosmic Fire*. D.K. starts at the third stage of the form building process, which he calls 'the Nebulous'. The first two stages can be considered the instigation of a ring-pass-not (upon the plane *ādi)* and the establishment of the 'Golden Egg' *(anupādaka)* within which the form building happens. His concern is with the process that will eventuate the earthy world, hence he speaks concerning the *'Pitris' (pitṛ),* the 'Fathers'.[42] Lunar Pitris are the elemental forces of the lower three Creative Hierarchies that build the forms in which we all reside. The term 'lunar' refers to the lower domains, the psychic realms, hence these *pitris* are the fathers of the periodic sheaths of humanity. When transposing the concept to the level of a solar system the term *pitṛ,* can be elevated to a higher level, as the great building *devas,* the Divine Flames and the greater and lesser Builders. D.K. states:

> This work of form-building proceeds under definite laws, which are the laws of substance itself; the effect is the same for human, planetary and solar vehicles. The different stages might be enumerated as follows:
>
> 1. *The Nebulous.* The stage wherein the matter of the coming sheath begins to separate itself gradually from the aggregate of plane substance, and to assume a nebulous or milky aspect. This corresponds to the "fire-mist" stage in the formation of a solar system and of a planet. The *Pitris of the Mist* are then active as one of the many subsidiary groups of the three major groups.[43]

For the genesis of the curdling process one must look to the fourth of the liberated Creative Hierarchies, governed by the sign Gemini the Twins, and whose energy is described as 'Desire for duality' in the tabulation of the Creative Hierarchies of Bailey's *Esoteric Astrology.*[44] This Desire (literally the power from the sixth cosmic astral sub-plane) manifests via the force of the Sagittarian impetus upon the *ātmic* plane impelling the Lesser Builders to help curdle the primal substance thereon by utilising *jñānaśakti,* the force of Mind. The curdling happens in a Watery environment, which the cosmic astral energy provides, whilst the primal substance of the *ātmic* plane represents that which curdles. (The *ātmic* plane being the apex of a downward pointing pentagram, where the sixth astral sub-plane is the right foot and the seventh astral sub-plane is the left foot.) The associated *pitṛ* of this plane are then activated to build the forms wherein the *karma* of the new cycle can be

---

42 There are many levels of expression of these progenitors.

43 T.C.F., 783. The rest of these stages will be explained below.

44 Pages 34-35.

expressed. This *karma* from cosmic sources manifests via the two feet of this inverted pentagram and can be considered to be projected by the third of the liberated Hierarchies, governed by the sign Taurus the bull, with the energy given as 'Light thro' knowledge'. As previously stated, Taurus embodies the Creative function of the seven Sisters. The focal point for their activities is the *ātmic* plane, from which the first Outpouring manifests properly.

From this we can see that under the auspices of Virgoan energy Stanza 3:1 concerns the activation of the substance of the great Mother to produce an 'expansion from within without', with the assistance of the work of the first liberated Creative Hierarchy. The associated energy is that of 'Intelligent substance', necessitating the awakening of all the slumbering Lives in the great Deep (ruled by Pisces) so that they can play their appointed roles in the creation of the form that is to be. This happens under the auspices of the third Ray of Mathematical Exact Activity.

Stanza 3:2, deals with the sweeping of the vibration to awaken the Germ dwelling in the darkness under the influence of Libran energy, which brings into activity the work of the second liberated Creative Hierarchy. The governing sign is the martial potency of Aries the ram, and the fourth Ray expression, to produce 'Unity thro' effort' – the integration of all the forces in 'the whole universe' to produce the birthing of the new Logoic form.

Stanza 3:3 concerns the work of the third liberated Creative Hierarchy, governed by the sign Taurus the bull, wielding the fifth Ray energy that expresses the development of 'Light thro' knowledge' to achieve the radiation of light from out of darkness. This is gained by bringing to the fore the *karma* of whatever is to be accomplished by means of Mind via the projective 'sting' of Scorpio. The two 'feet' of the inverted pentagram are thereby 'stung' into activity. The right foot, the fourth liberated Creative Hierarchy, signified by Gemini effects the Watery substance, the curdling process, whilst the left foot, the fifth liberated Creative Hierarchy, ruled by Cancer, governs the activity of the manifestation of the substance that curdles, hence the activities of the *pitṛ*. The activities of both feet find their apex in the 'head' upon the *ātmic* plane, from whence the first Outpouring proceeds. This is the concern of Stanza 3:4.

The right and left hands of this inverted pentagram are represented by the first two incarnated Creative Hierarchies, where in terms of energy expression, the left hand is represented by the Divine Flames, utilising *paraśakti,* the supreme energy (of cosmic Mind) and the right hand, the Divine Builders, utilise *kriyaśakti,* the 'Materialising ideal'.

The energies from the highest three of the liberated Hierarchies esoterically 'fall' into the lowest three planes. The highest of the Hierarchies, whose energy is 'Intelligent substance', eventually impacts upon the mental plane to activate the tenth Creative Hierarchy, Makara the mystery. The second of these Hierarchies, whose energy is 'Unity thro' effort', conditions the activities of the *lunar pitris* upon the astral plane. The energies from the third of the liberated Hierarchies 'falls' into the seventh plane and conditions the activities of the Elemental Lives, indicating thereby the outermost reach of the work of the Pleiades.

Continuing with the work of form building D.K. states:

> 2. *The Inchoate.* Condensation has set in but all is as yet inchoate, and the condition is chaotic; there is no definite form. *"The Pitris of the Chaos"* hold sway, and are characterised by excessive energy, and violent activity, for the greater the condensation prior to co-ordination the more terrific are the effects of activity. This is true of Gods, of men, and of atoms.[45]

This brings us to the plane *buddhi,* which bears the brunt of the impact of the energies of the four cosmic ethers in general. Stanza 3:5 effectively explains this stage of the appearing form. *Buddhi* is literally the plane of reflection of the higher three into the lower three.

The Capricornian impetus of Stanza 3:5 consolidates the establishment of all the links *(sūtrātmās)* into the form so that incarnation is possible. All chaotic, activated energies must be determinedly controlled and held in situ by Logoic Mind so that they can be rightly pulsed into manifestation at the appointed cycles by means of the power of the seventh Ray (which comes into activity in Stanza 3:6). Stanza 3:5 reflects the forces of the inverted pentagram into the formed domains, emanating thereby the Fiery principle that represents

45 Ibid, 783-784.

the concretion of Logoic Mind. The reflection continues in Stanza 3:6 producing complete concretion (from a Logoic perspective) in Stanza 3:7, presented as the third stage of the form building process by D.K.

> 3. *The Fiery.* The internal energy of the rapidly congregating atoms and their effect upon each other produces an increase of heat, and a consequent demonstration of the spheroidal form, so that the vehicle of all entities is seen to be fundamentally a sphere, rolling upon itself and attracting and repulsing other spheres. *"Pitris of the Fiery Spheres"* add their labours to those of the earlier two and a very definite stage is reached. The lunar Pitris on every scheme, and throughout the system, are literally the active agents in the building of the dense physical body of the Logos; they energise the substance of the three planes in the three worlds, the mental, the astral and the dense physical planes of the system. This needs much pondering upon.[46]

The main effects of the impact of the liberated Hierarchies analysed in the previous statements was via the plane *ātma,* with a reverberation upon the three lowest planes. In this way everything becomes imprinted by the impact of cosmic Mind (Mahat). The domain of the abstract Mind contains the impression of all this activity. Another inverted pentagram of energies now forms from the top five of the seven Creative Hierarchies in active expression. Here the Divine Flames upon the plane *ādi* expresses the left foot of the pentad. These 'Flames', whose assigned colour is orange, project the impact of cosmic Mind (the fifth Ray) to delineate the ring-pass-not of the planetary sphere and its radiant essence. This activity comes under the impress of the sign Leo the lion, which is the sign of Individuation. Leo brings into expression the entire solar form, a sun Son with its panoply of light, heat and motion.

The 'Divine Builders, the Burning sons of desire', upon the plane *anupādaka* represent the right foot. The colour assigned to them is blue, here signifying the second Ray veiling the sixth Ray, hence they project into manifest space the cosmic Waters, as derived from the sixth sub-plane of the cosmic astral. They bring into manifestation the materialising energy of the great Mother. This incorporates the Monadic Life, via which the Soul-forms of humanity come to find their proper

46 Ibid, 785.

roles. The seven laws of group evolution can now also play their roles in determining the progress of all travelling through the solar form ('the Eternal Egg'). They consequently organise the liberated Human and Deva Lives that are to govern all that evolves in the Womb of the Mother. This activity is conditioned by the sign Virgo the virgin, who builds the Womb and helps condition the Watery substance therein, for the incarnation of the Conscious Lives that are to inform the All.

The Lesser Builders upon the plane *ātma* (which governs the general activities of the *devas)* represent the left hand and the energies of the great Mother within the Womb of space-time. The energy assigned to them is the emerald green of the third Ray of Mathematically Exact Activity, and they draw their purpose from the seventh cosmic astral sub-plane. This represents the crystallising forces of cosmic Mind that project the qualities of the five Dhyāni Buddhas into the planes of Brahmā, wherein the appearing Lives shall incarnate. Libra the balances facilitates the necessary meditation that will allow the Builders to project their energies at the right cycles of the turning of the wheel of the zodiac. The term 'the Triple Flowers' that D.K. also accords to this Hierarchy indicates the rulership of the lower three Hierarchies, which are technically below the threshold of Awareness of the established Logoi. These 'Flowers' represents the *deva* triads that en-Soul the lower kingdoms of Nature. The phrase also refers to the forces that produced the appearance of the kingdom of Souls upon the higher mental plane.

The human Hierarchy (the Monads) esoterically reflect upon the *buddhic* level the attributes of the above energies into 'the deep'. They govern the dissemination of the Waters of cosmic Love, hence are the right hand of this pentad. They do this by being 'Lords of Sacrifice', the Initiates that robe themselves with that substance in order to produce liberation, via the yellow Ray of Harmony in the midst of the Strife and the chaos of the appearing substance. Scorpio the scorpion produces the necessary testing cycles needed for humanity to master the Watery astral substance, and so to purify the Waters as a mode of ascent to the domain of the cosmic Waters. They must learn the right control of speech *(mantrikaśakti)* to master the *deva* substance into which they have incarnated and which binds them to material form.

All of these energies are focussed upon the Head of this pentagram,

Makara the Mystery, upon the lower mental plane. The purpose is to rightly organise the integrated primal 'black dust'[47] of the system and so build it into the appearing forms in such a way that it evolves the kingdoms of Nature. Incorporated at this level is also the remainder from a former evolutionary cycle, already tainted with the *karma* of that activity. Stanza 3:7 onwards deals with this stage in evolution. Makara represents the substance to be converted, hence is the focus of the energy of Love-Wisdom (the indigo blue of the assigned colour) from the sum of this inverted pentagram. They are an expression of the most crystallised energies of cosmic Mind, as wielded by the sign Capricorn the goat, the mountain of mind/Mind.

The involutionary substance which is worked upon, and which must be transformed into units of consciousness by all of the above forces and entities, are represented by the last two of the Creative Hierarchies, the Lunar Lords (the Sacrificial Fires), ruled by Sagittarius, and the Elemental Lives (the Blinded Lives), ruled by Aquarius. D.K. states that the signs governing the Lunar Lords and Elemental Lives are in the wrong order for an esoteric reason, which will correct itself in time. This will affect the Ray colouring too. The reason for this is the disastrous happenings upon the moon Chain, which was somewhat explained in Volume 7B of *The Constitution of Shambhala*. The widespread promulgation of sex magic at the time, and other abuses of the desire impulse was as a consequence of en-Flamed first Ray potency that was prematurely generated and which acted against the evolutionary goal of the then Lord of that Chain. The result was that this energy then came to colour the Lunar *pitris,* a condition that has carried right through to our present cycle. Because these *pitris* embody the substance of our desire-emotions this has intensified the desire-attachment to sensual pleasure of humanity and has produced war-like emotions, necessitating the development of the Will-of-Love to break free from this Watery dominance. This has made the path to enlightenment and consequent liberation much more difficult for humanity, (causing much accelerated pain and suffering for them) but has also quickened the evolutionary

---

47 That substance which is incorporated upon *ātmic* levels is a consequence of solar evolution, whilst that incorporated upon the lower mental plane is a consequence of the evolution of the planetary spheres.

paths of those who can do so, because of the added development of the needed Will. The added red of the Will is a gain that normally would have been slated for the development in a considerably later cycle.

The effect of this aberrant evolution has also meant that the needed mode to control the substance of the dense physical plane is by means of the seventh Ray of ceremonial magic. Divine alchemy is thereby facilitated, assisted by the rightly developed force of the Will. Scientific Materialism however has prematurely discovered the way of the empirical will to control substance, related to the use of atomic weaponry, as well as modern warfare techniques, dangerously placed in unenlightened hands. The aberrant use of the will has also been used by the lords of Dark Face to control the world's finances, every important form of governance and the propaganda methods of the mass media. Dire consequences can be expected in our civilisation as a result.

The significance of Stanza 3:6, where darkness vanishes, is brought to fruition by means of the activity generated by the Builders. The Lives can rush on to the prepared forms, from the Aquarian store of the consciousness principle.

The next stage of the form building process presented by D.K. concerns the condensation of the systemic Waters.

> 4. *The Watery.* The ball or sphere of gaseous fiery essence becomes still more condensed and liquefied; it begins to solidify on its outer surface and the ring-pass-not of each sheath is more clearly defined. The heat of the sphere becomes increased and is centralised at the core or heart of the sphere where it produces that pulsation at the centre which characterises the sun, the planet, and the various vehicles of all incarnating entities. It is an analogous stage to that of the awakening of life in the foetus during the prenatal stage, and this analogy can be seen working out in the form-building which proceeds on every plane. This stage marks the coordination of the work of the two higher groups of lunar Pitris, and the *"Pitris of the Dual Heat"* are now intelligently co-operating. The heart and brain of the substance of the slowly evolving form are linked. The student will find it interesting to trace the analogy of this, the watery stage, to the place the astral plane holds in the planetary and systemic body, and the alliance between mind and heart which is hidden in the term "kama-manas." One of the profoundest occult mysteries will be revealed to the consciousness of

> man when he has solved the secret of the building of his astral vehicle, and the forming of the link which exists between that sheath and the astral light in its totality on the astral plane.[48]

This stage is presented in Stanza 3:9, governed by the sign Taurus the bull, where the onrushing cosmic Desire to build, to procreate, and to sustain the drive of consciousness becomes fully expressed, when the vehicles for their containment have been produced. Logoic Mind is infused with Desire to see the purpose for the manifestation through to its conclusion. The twilight period of solar evolution has arrived.

Stanzas 3:10 and 3:11 are concerned with the building of the etheric web, which D.K. explains as below.

> 5. *The Etheric.* The stage is not to be confined to the building of the physical body in its etheric division, for its counterpart is found on all the planes with which man is concerned in the three worlds. The condensation and the solidification of the material has proceeded till now the three groups of Pitris form a unity in work. The rhythm set up has been established and the work synchronised. The lesser builders work systematically and the law of Karma is demonstrating actively, for it should be remembered that it is the inherent karma, colouring, or vibratory response of the substance itself which is the selective reaction to the egoic note. Only that substance which has (through past utilisation) been keyed to a certain note and vibration will respond to the mantram and to the subsequent vibrations issuing from the permanent atom. This stage is one of great importance, for it marks the vital circulation throughout the entire vehicle of a particular type of force. This can be clearly seen in relation to the etheric body which circulates the vital force or prana of the sun. A similar linking up with the force concerned is to be seen on the astral and the mental planes. *"The Pitris of the Triple Heat"* are now working synthetically, and the brain, the heart and the lower centres are co-ordinated. The lower and the higher are linked, and the channels are unimpeded so that the circulation of the triple energy is possible. This is true of the form building of all entities, macrocosmic and microcosmic. It is marked by the active co-operation of another group of Pitris, termed *"The Pitris of Vitality"* in connection with the others. Group after

48 Ibid., 784-785.

> group co-operate, for the three main bodies are distributed among many lesser.[49]

Concerning the mode of appearance of the dense physical form D.K. states:

> 6. *The Solid.* This marks the final stage in actual form building, and signifies the moment wherein the work is done as regards the aggregating and shaping of substance. The greater part of the work of the lunar Pitris stands now accomplished. The word "solid" refers not solely to the lowest objective manifestation, for a solid form may be ethereal, and only the stage of evolution of the entity involved will reveal its relative significance.
>
> All that has been here laid down as to the progressive stages of form construction on every plane is true of all forms in all systems and schemes, and is true of all thought-form building. Man is constructing thought-forms all the time, and is following unconsciously the same method as his Ego pursues in building his bodies, as the Logos follows in building His system, and as a planetary Logos uses in constructing His scheme.
>
> A man speaks, and a very diversified mantram is the result. The energy thus generated swings into activity a multitude of little lives which proceed to build a form for his thought; they pursue analogous stages to those just outlined. At this time, man sets up these mantric vibrations unconsciously, and in ignorance of the laws of sound and of their effect. The occult work that he is carrying on is thus unknown to him. Later he will speak less, know more, and construct more accurate forms, which will produce powerful effects on physical levels.[50]

Stanza 3:12 is concerned with this stage of development. Continuing now with the consideration of Stanza 3:4.

The word *curdle* means 'to change into curd, thicken coagulate'. Note that milk-white is opaque, not transparent, and thus relates to what is material, dense. A curd is the coagulated or thickened part of milk as distinguished from the whey or watery part. This 'Luminous Egg' thus thickens or coagulates primal matter in the cosmic dense realms of

49 Ibid., 785-786.

50 Ibid., 786.

perception. It is milk-white because it is unadulterated, pure, unsullied, devoid of evolved characteristics, undifferentiated by any particular Ray colour, yet it is the seed or bearer of them all. The Milky Way, billions of stars in our galaxy, resemble milk-white curds when seen at night.

The numbers of the phrase *'curdles and spreads'* add to 66, 7 x 3, 1.1.1. These numbers refer to the sum of material Life, the manifested realms, of everything coming from the Womb of the Mother. We know that this curdling process commences upon the *ātmic* plane (3 x 7) and spreads to the lower planes of perception (66). As it spreads it obviously thickens. *Antaḥkaraṇas* (1.1.1) are projected by the Will of the primal Logos to cause the condensation, then to control and integrate the chaotic diverse elements into the *maṇḍala* of the form that is to be. The 'Pitris of the Mist' here manifest in the form of a aetheric Fiery-Mist, organised by the Creative Intelligences, who are the Lesser Builders upon this plane. The objective is to produce the condensation of the cosmic Watery energies that will curdle the primal substance of this plane, righty organising it to fill the confines of the appearing *maṇḍala* of manifestation. The substance becomes more dense, concrete, tangible, to complete the primal substance appearing as the planes of perception, filling the volume of the delineated space. The Creative Intelligences hold sway over the activity of the condensation until the form has been built.

The number 22 of the phrase *'milk-white curds'* refers to the zodiacal and planetary energies responsible for all manifest Life. These forces condition the Womb of the great Mother. Their energies begin to permeate the curds, moulding them with the characteristics required by the Logos, which presently exist only in potential. They must yet interact and produce the various colourings to be evolved as they undergo evolutionary change.

The number 6 x 7 of the phrase *'the depths'* refers to the *maṇḍala* of the hexagram, the lower planes of perception to which these curds spread.

The numbers of the phrase *'throughout the depths'* add to 96 = 8 x 12 and to 2 x 12. These numbers refer to the eighth and second signs of the zodiac, Scorpio and Taurus. Taurus represents the activity of the Pleiadian Mothers to project their forces 'throughout the depths' to produce the curdling process. Scorpio, whose ruler is Mars, governs the materialising energy that helps project cosmic astral energies responsible to churn the curds. The number 96 also refers to the *chakras* that will appear throughout the depth to organise the movement of the energies. The curds can also be conceived as the manifestation of the loci of the appearing *chakras* and the forms that will be attracted to them.

The numbers of the remaining phrases concerned with this curdling process add to 109, 27 x 9 and 8 x 9. The number 100 + 9 refers to a new cycle of Initiation activity to produce vehicles for the appearance of the kingdom of Souls (27 x 9). Eventually many of these 'curds' take the shape of these nine-fold Causal forms. (Referring to the nine main petals of each Soul.) The Sambhogakāya Flower is effectively a third degree Initiate (3 x 9) existing upon the higher mental plane. Myriads of Soul-groups and angelic triads (group-Souls, 8 x 9) consequently appear, preparing to take their appointed roles in the new form. They are the basis of that which en-Souls Life. The milk-white colouring being the general admixture of their various Ray energies.

'The Mother', as the third, Activity aspect of the Trinity, has been explained above. The numbers 100 + 6 x 7, 25 of the phrase *'throughout the depths of Mother'* imply that these depths manifest in terms of all the various septenaries governing incarnate Life. As these curds appear they instantaneously differentiate in terms of the qualitative distinctions between them, thus the planes of perception appear (6 x 7), up to the formation of the higher mental plane (25). At this stage all is still subjective, as the substance of the systemic dense physical still needs to be incorporated. Puruṣa (the en-Souling principle) is still in the process of manifesting His domain. The world-spheres are yet to appear. The number 88 of the phrase *'the depths of Mother'* implies the spiral-cyclic motion manifesting simultaneously through innumerable force vectors to produce this curdling 'throughout the depths'. The complete mastery of the Creative process thus manifests, allowing Deity to project energies into the depths of Space ('the Mother'). The number 88 also equals 4 x 22 and 2 x 44, referring to the falling into 'the four' of the planetary and zodiacal energies of cosmos.

The number 48 of the phrase *'curdles and spreads in milk-white curds'* refers to the sign Cancer the crab, thus the process that eventuates into myriads of beings (massed Life) reincarnating into the curdling form that is steadily growing in the depths of the Womb of the Mother.

The numbers 7 and 200 + 5 of the phrase *'spreads in milk-white curds throughout the depths'* refer to the appearance of the septenaries of Life instigated through the Compassionate Activity of the Logoic Mind (200 + 5) via this curdling and spreading activity. This Mind of the Mother, as indicated above, manifests via the attributes of Amitābha's Discriminating Inner Wisdom. When the numbers of the phrase *'of Mother'* are added then the resultant number (200 + 17 x 3) refers to the divine activity of the triune Logos producing this effect.

The numbers of the *complete phrase* add to 10, which refers to the totality of Being, specifically the etheric form, to which the dense physical form is but an automaton.

The main meaning of *'the Root'* was explained in Stanza 2:1 in relationship to the phrase 'The Producers of form from no-form, the root of the world – the devamatri and svabhavat'. They were 'the Builders, the luminous Sons of manvantaric dawn'. They are the liberated Logoi coming back into manifestation, the solar *devas*, as well as the symbolic 33,000,000,000 Creative Intelligences, the sum of the *deva* Hierarchy, as incorporated in the twelve Creative Hierarchies. In that Stanza I stated that *'the Root'* implies the source from which everything else stems. These Builders are therefore the Roots of the world Tree, the emanating source of the Life from which the nourishment and strength must come to support the Life of the entire world system, to anchor it firmly in cosmos. It is not surprising therefore that the numbers of the phrase add to 11 and 2, which indicated the first and second Ray qualities that have this function. The number 11 also refers to the *antaḥkaraṇas* and *nāḍīs* (symbolised by 'the root') that grow the world Tree.

The numbers of the phrase *'The root that grows'* add to 16, 25. The number 16 informs us that the Germ of the Christ-consciousness, in the form of the Soul aspect (the number 25), is able to spread this root throughout the depths of *'the ocean'* of Logoic Mind (7 x 5).

The numbers of the phrase *'the ocean of Life'* add to 70, 16. These numbers refer to the septenaries governing all manifest Life, to the beings that evolve from awakening the seven *chakras* in the body of the Logos. This implicates therefore all of the seven planes of existence in the cosmic physical plane. Together they embody 'the ocean of Life', to the 'depths' that is the present focus of our view. Therein the Christ-consciousness (16) must eventually evolve. What is *'in the ocean'* (7 x 7) similarly refers to the various septenaries and their subdivisions associated with all Being.

'The Root that grows in the ocean' (128, 38) is the Seat of Power of the principle of Love-Wisdom (32 x 4). This principle is borne by the man-plants, humanity, who grow in the Watery dispensation. When the numbers of the phrase *'of Life'* are added, then the number 100 + 7 x 9 is obtained, signifying the Initiation process, thereby making this the Root of the Initiation Tree, which all that reside in this ocean of Life must learn to climb as they ascend to their Father's domain.

6B

Stanzas 3:5 – 3:7

Stanza Three part Five

Stanza 3:5 states:

> **The Root remains, the Light remains, the curds remain, and still Oeaohoo is One.**

Keynotes: Capricorn, Amitābha, Fiery Element. Three lower sub-planes of *ātma.*

The numerical breakdown of the Stanza :

The Root (38, 11), The Root remains (72, 18), The Light (44, 17), The Light remains (78, 24), The curds (35, 8), The curds remain (68 = 17 x 4, 14), Oeaohoo is One, (64, 19), still Oeaohoo is One (82, 28).

A new solar *manvantara* has begun with the first Outpouring proper. This signifies the development of the new qualities that will be indigenous to this solar system, governed by the second Ray of Love-Wisdom, rather than that of the third Ray of the old system. The three higher Creative Hierarchies that have been dealt with so far are products of the former solar system, but the remaining parts of Stanza three deal with the evolution of new streams of Life that will have their roots firmly planted in this solar system, hence will be appropriately conditioned by its second Ray purpose. The qualities developed in the former solar system will nevertheless continue to play their part in this present one, and are incorporated in 'the Root'. All are attributes of Oeaohoo, signifying the Logoi of the planetary Schemes in general, and specifically to the planetary Schemes that will bear the five indigenous streams of human evolution that will evolve in this solar system, of which our present humanity is the fourth. Humanity is the obvious focus of these stanzas.

Stanza 3:5 is deceptively simple. It prompts us to immediately query as to why the Root, Light and curds remain as a consequence of the fall of the three into the four. This is because Consciousness, symbolised by the seven 'vowels', Oeaohoo, exists in time and space and so can ask such questions. The curds are the vehicles of Consciousness, the Light is the substance that expresses Consciousness, and the Root (of the 'man-plant') is the mechanism of its growth. The theme concerning the nature of Consciousness being One with these three aspects is appropriate in this fifth verse of Stanza three. Up till now only three aspects of Oeaohoo have appeared, the first of the seven Creative Hierarchies, the Divine Flames, who thereby have a direct bearing upon the curds, organising them into activity. Next the Greater (Divine) Builders assist with the dissemination of Light into the system, and finally 'the Root' is an extension of the work of the Lesser Builders, and signifies the first Outpouring that establishes the five planes of Brahmā via which the lesser Creative Hierarchies evolve.

The 'curds remain' because they have developed into the forms of the human Soul, the 'Light remains' and is further developed by means of the evolution of the Souls, and 'the Root' remains because it is the basis of all further evolutionary growth of the kingdoms of Nature that have awakened because of it. 'The Root' is an outpouring of the highest of the three lower sub-planes of *ātma,* Light is projected via the sixth of these sub-planes and 'the curds' are an emanation of the seventh sub-plane

As stated earlier this Stanza is concerned with the Capricornian impetus, which consolidates the establishment of all the links *(sūtrātmās)* into the form so that incarnation is possible. The Stanza signifies the store of substance needing converting into the elements of mind during the evolutionary process. This is effected by means of developing Amitābha's Discriminating Inner Wisdom, which governs the dissemination of the Fires of Mind (Mahat). This Wisdom consolidates all of the above to effect the happenings of the concrete sub-planes of the cosmic dense physical plane.

Capricorn embodies the substance of the Darkness of *saṃsāra,* the general material substance of the space that is enacted upon, of the primal, elemental attributes of mind *(manas),* which is impacted upon by the Logoic Mind. This interrelation generates light, and the entire process happens in the domain ruled by Capricorn, the lord of the mount of *manasic* substance. Therein the karmic interplay of the interrelation between the evolving forms happens.

The impact of Mahatic energies from *ātma* is primarily upon the higher mental plane via *buddhi,* and is effectively the lowest descent of the direct Power of Logoic Mind. The resonance of that Mind, via the five types of *ākāśa,* manifest in its Earthy form under Capricornian influence, and affects the planes of human evolution via the mental plane.

Upon the upward way the disciple must master and climb this substance of mind/Mind in order to be Initiated into the Mysteries of being/non-being, to penetrate the veils of the Darkness upon cosmic levels. The Initiate then Knows the attributes of cosmic Mind that causes the appearance of things in cosmos.

The sum of *manasic* substance ruled by Capricorn must be determinedly controlled and held in situ by Logoic Mind so that the aspects of Mind can be rightly pulsed into manifestation at the appointed cycles by means of the fourth Ray mirror that is activated in Stanza 3:6. The mechanism of the emanation of Mind/mind is the expression of the seven voweled Word, Oeaohoo in the form of the Logoic Will to hold manifest Space in situ as an incarnate form. Stanza 3:5 thereby reflects the forces of the inverted pentagram explained in chapter 6A into the formed domains. This pentad emanates the Fiery principle (Oeaohoo) in a form that condenses and concretes the energies of Logoic Mind. The beginning of the condensation process is explained in Stanza 3:6 and the reified externalisation of Logoic Mind is described in Stanza 3:7.

The meaning of *'the Root'* has been explained in Stanza 3:4. It remains in the form of its essential primordial integrity, even though it grows in space and time. This is because in the Monadic form it stays as the undifferentiated, singular, primordial source of the manifesting phenomena. The phenomena that grows, that continually changes and transforms, is the illusional substance signified as *saṁsāra*. The number 72 of the phrase *'The Root remains'* here refers to the ideal life span of any entity. 'The Root' is a direct expression of the Father-Mother – the emanating source or foundation of being, but remains within the conditionings of the Womb of space-time, symbolised by the sign Virgo the virgin (governed by the number 72). 'The Root' represents the Father aspect, but the substance within which this Root grows, and within which it remains, is that of the Mother. 'The Root' then represents the intricate *nāḍī* and *chakra* system, from which the material universe (the Mother) stems. This *nāḍī* system develops into the Initiation Tree, hence the way of liberation into cosmic space. It thus represents the way of return.

The *chakras* represented here are those of the solar Logos, established upon the *buddhic* plane, to which Stanza 3:6 refers. The *chakras* are emanations of the seven voweled Word, which governs the dispensation of the planetary systems that come into objectivity. Capricorn signifies the concreting, reifying energies moving through the cosmic ethers to cause the appearance of things via the *chakras*.[1] As *ātma* is the third cosmic ether, so the Logoic Throat centre is established here, which Sounds out the seven voweled intonation of the appearance of the seven *chakras,* here indicated by Oeaohoo, which is One.

'The Light remains', not only in the form of the Rays of the sun that sustains and nourishes the evolution of all within the embrace of the solar ring-pass-not, but also because it is the Light generated by the evolving units of consciousness. It can be considered the conscious enlightened intermediary that binds or sustains all that is visible. It is the effect of the Mind of Deity or of liberated enlightened Beings. They bind everything into the coherent unity of a solar or planetary form. It relates the Root to the Curds and sustains the entire evolutionary play,

---

1 Note that the Head lotus of a human unit is established upon the first ether, the Heart centre upon the second ether, the Throat centre upon the third ether, and the centres below the diaphragm, plus the Inner Round of minor *chakras* are upon the fourth ether. This arrangement is a reflection of the expression upon the cosmic dense physical plane.

being the nourishment that causes the Root to grow, yet is the objective of evolution to produce. It is the Son in space and time.

'The Light' (44) is a direct expression of the Son aspect of Deity (a humanity, 44), the conscious mediator that is a product of the relationship between the Root and the curds. It is emanated from the One and is evolved by the other (humanity).

'The curds' (7 x 5) are a direct expression of the Mother aspect, the primordial substance that forms the field in which the Root grows. This substance is that of the domain of the mind/Mind (7 x 5). We saw earlier that one of the meanings of the curds is that they represent that which condenses into world or solar spheres. Energy drives them to congeal the basic Mind stuff (7 x 5) that 'remains' (from the former solar evolution). This substance is therefore now brought into play in this present solar evolution. The elementary Lives that were in *pralaya* are now activated, they come into manifestation as the first subray of the Earthy *ākāśa,* and generally directed by Amitābha's Wisdom. Human Lives come into manifestation under the auspices of the fourth Ray, brought into expression via the activities of the Morning Sons of Glory who evolved in the early Mercury Scheme. Nature in general however is under the auspices of the third Ray, which governs the expression of Stanzas 3:4 and 3:5.

The number 24 of the phrase *'the Light remains'* refers to the second sign of the zodiac, Taurus the bull, who governs the Eye of illumination that must be opened in order to see this Light, and later the all-seeing Eye awakens. Taurus clothes the divine Thought with the substance of Light and generates the entire onrushing push that moves the wheel of the zodiac onwards upon its appointed course, cycle after cycle, until the great mountainous heights of Initiation can be scaled in Capricorn and liberation from the bonds to the Waters of *saṃsāra* achieved in Pisces. This number also refers to the twelve Creative Hierarchies plus the twelve signs of the zodiac, which act as the Soul aspect of all Life manifest in the solar system. They are the prototype subjective Light bringers to all that is manifest. Seven of these Hierarchies (directed by the Taurean Eye) are brought into active manifestation via the emanation of the seven voweled mantra, Oeaohoo. The Hierarchies are the Light bringers, the Consciousness-aspect embodying the appearing forms.

The Earthy triad Capricorn-Taurus-Virgo (who govern the expression of the *deva* Lives) lay the foundation for the appearing forms, the curds, from which the Light evolves.

The number 17 x 4 of the phrase *'the curds remain'* indicates that the Seats of Power for the establishment of each world-sphere 'remains', so that the Rounds and Schemes of the evolutionary play can manifest. They become the foundation of all Life.

Regarding the term *Oeaohoo* H.P.B. states:

> OEAOHOO is rendered *"Father-Mother of the Gods"* in the Commentaries, or the SIX IN ONE, *or the Septenary Root from which all proceeds.* All depends upon the accent given to these seven vowels, which may be pronounced as *one,* three, or even seven syllables, by adding an "e" after the letter "o". This mystic name is given out, because without a thorough mastery of the triple pronunciation it remains for ever ineffectual.[2]

Though H.P.B. had to be guarded concerning this mantra in her day, considering also that very little background knowledge was available to explain it, much more can now be revealed. First, it should be noted that the vowels veil well-known key mantric syllables from the Tibetan Buddhist perspective. Her statement that 'All depends upon the accent given to these seven vowels, which may be pronounced as *one,* three, or even seven syllables' is correct. Being vowels they relate to the appearance of the Son in manifestation, the expression of the seven Creative Hierarchies that are incarnate. There are also five key mantric syllables veiled in the name Oeaohoo, which introduce the attributes of the Fire's of Mind into the forming systemic space that are borne by the Sons of the solar Logos.

First there is the 'O', signifying the Aūṁ—the Word of Creation, embodying the triune energies of the Mother, in which case the work of the *deva* (angelic) kingdom dominates. This Sound governs the period of time that establishes the seat of Power of a Logos, and the sum of the governing planetary Hierarchy. The five esoteric *laya* centres of the Logos from the Head/Ājñā centres to the Sacral/Base of Spine centres are established, allowing the appearance of all corporeal forms. The

2 The S.D., Vol. 1, 68.

governing plane is *ātma*. The Aūṁ represents 'the three' that 'fall' into the 'four'. When the Aūṁ is viewed as a trinity, then the remaining four syllables form a septenary with it.

The 'e' refers to the syllable Hrīḥ,[3] the organising note in *saṃsāra* upon the higher mental plane. It sets into motion the tremulous vibration that attracts the substance of space to the *laya* centres, allowing the Son to incarnate into the preparing form. There is consequently the process leading to the Individualisation of a Humanity. The Throat centre in the solar system is first stimulated, producing a strong reciprocal response in the Sacral centre to effect the process of manifestation. The Hrīḥ activates the *devas* that provide a mechanism for 'the three' to fall into *saṁsāra*.

Concerning this seed syllable Govinda states:

> 'H' is the sound of the breath, the symbol of all life; 'R' is the sound of fire ('RĀṀ'). The 'Ī' being the vowel of the highest intensity or rate of vibration, stands for the highest spiritual activity and differentiation. The aspirated after-sound *(visarga),* following the 'Ī', though being written in the Tibetan script, is omitted in pronunciation, so that the seed-syllable could be rendered phonetically 'HRĪ' (as is often done).[4]

He further states

> As a sound-symbol HRĪḤ means far more than hinted at by its philological associations. It does not only possess the warmth of the sun; i.e., the emotional principle of goodness, compassion and sympathy – but also the power of illumination, the quality of making things visible, the faculty of perception, of direct vision. HRĪḤ is a mantric solar symbol, a luminous, elevating, upwards-moving sound composed of the prānic aspirate (H), the fiery R (RAṀ is the seed syllable of the element 'fire') and the high 'i'-sound, which expresses upwards movement, intensity, etc.[5]

---

3 Hrīḥ is pronounced H-reee, as the ḥ is silent.

4 Lama Anagarika Govinda, *Foundations of Tibetan Mysticism* (Samuel Weiser, Maine, 1982), 183, *fn* 1.

5 Ibid., 231.

The remaining three syllables are the familiar Āḥ, Aūṁ, Hūṁ relating to the process of gaining liberation from *saṃsāra,* representing the response from the awakening 'Son'. The Aūṁ and Hrīḥ therefore represent the downward focus of the Compassionate Intent of the Creative Logos. The world-sphere is consequently formed (the emanation of the Aūṁ), into which 'the Root' is planted, by means of the emanation of the Hrīḥ, which also signifies completion, accomplishment. The resultant evolving life of the 'man-plant' eventually produces the appearance of a Son – the aspiring aspirant seeking liberation from *saṃsāra.* The Āḥ, Oṁ, Hūṁ then become part of the mechanism *(dhāraṇī)* of release. Much could be said concerning these mantras. Govinda summarises its potency succinctly:

> The 'OṀ-ĀḤ-HŪṀ'...corresponds to the three principles of 'Body' *(kāya;* Tib.: *sku),* 'Speech' *(vāk;* Tib.: *gsuṅ)* and 'Mind" *(citta;* Tib.: *thugs),* which – after the unification of all psychic qualities and forces of the meditator – are transformed into:
>
> 1. The principle of the all-embracing universal body ('OṀ'), realized in the Crown Centre;
> 2. The principle of all-embracing, i.e., mantric speech (Tib,: gzuṅs) or creative sound ('ĀḤ'), realized in the Throat centre;
> 3. The principle of the all-embracing love of the Enlightened Mind (bodhi-citta; Tib.: byañ-chub-sems) of all Buddhas ('HŪṀ'), realized in the Heart Centre.[6]

With reference to Oeaohoo we have:

A = Āḥ, the Word of Abstraction, the breathing in of all the forces of the creative Mind, so that the context of the *maṇḍala* of what is to be can be empowered with the appropriate forces and elements – the dynamic Word of the Father. It signifies the ending of the third Ray cycle and the beginning of that dominated by the second and first Rays, when the Spirit aspect can begin to directly utilise the form. The Āḥ signifies the control of all the forces of the lower mind, and their transformation, so that they can be projected upwards to the abstracted domain.

6 Ibid., 185.

The following 'O' here is the Oṁ, which concerns the control of the Breath via contemplative absorption in the Head lotus. All of the procreative forces (the Creative Hierarchies) are drawn together, aligned and empowered with the energies, imagery and mantra to fulfil their purpose. The Oṁ sustains the universe of forms (the *maṇḍala)* for the necessary cycles of expression, so that their purpose can be accomplished. It signifies the consciousness-building activity of the Son. Its potency is later utilised to control the often turbulent and volatile Watery domain of the human psyche. The emotions and desires must quieten, be refined and then transformed into the Heart based qualities productive of the various Jina Wisdoms. The Oṁ awakens consciousness, liberating it to express itself freely in multi-dimensional space. Its energies work to awaken one to becoming a conscious factor of a Creative Hierarchy.

Finally, the 'hoo' is the Hūṁ, the resultant gain of the liberation process, the final accomplishment of an awakening response from the liberating ones upon the path of return. This concerns the consequent out-breathing of the mantric expression via the way of the Heart. The Hūṁ represents the complete mastery of the entire bodily manifestation, so that the liberating Bodhisattva path becomes the leitmotiv for existence. It assists the transmutation of all base elements into spiritual gold.

Taking all five seed syllables into account the relation of the Aūṁ to the Hūṁ can be viewed as the serpent of time consuming its own tail. Here the Aūṁ concerns the descent or appearance of time, and the Hūṁ its vanquishing. The aspirate of Aūṁ (ṁ) merges into the Hūṁ.

The Oeaohoo signifies the mode of the evolution of consciousness in our solar system. Therein there are five indigenous human streams (the bearers of this consciousness) that will come into manifestation as a consequence of the emanation of mantric Sound by the solar Logos. Four have manifested and one is yet to appear. The first of these is the humanity of the Venus Scheme. This Scheme came in as an emanation of the *Aūṁ* and the establishment of the solar Base of Spine/Sacral centres, and their link to the Head/Ājñā centres. This humanity consequently are an emanation of the Creative Fires (the process of the descent of the *iḍā nāḍī* stream) of the Logos. *The Secret Doctrine* calls the representatives of this humanity on our earth 'Lords of Flame'.

The Mars Scheme humanity awakened the potency of the Sacral – Solar Plexus centre on the path of descent of the attributes of the *piṇgalā nāḍī* of the human consciousness stream. The emanating sound was *Hrīḥ*.

The third human stream developed upon the third Chain and Round of our earth Scheme (the moon Chain). The moon Chain humanity further developed the Solar Plexus potency and awakened properly the lower *manasic* attributes on the path of the ascent of the *iḍā nāḍī* attributes of the human consciousness stream. The emanating sound was *Āḥ*.

The purpose of the present earth Chain's humanity is to properly awaken the Heart centre, and thus to find their true esoteric home *(buddhi/śūnyatā)*. They work to fully awaken the attributes of the *piṇgalā nāḍī* stream on the path of ascent of the principle of Love-Wisdom of the human consciousness stream. The emanating sound is *Oṁ*.

The fifth and final human stream, who will develop in the fifth Round and Chain of our earth Scheme is to fully awaken the creative potency of the Throat centre by blending the *iḍā prāṇas* with those of the Heart centre. The aim is to thereby offset the possible development of dark brotherhood characteristics, which an undue emphasis of Throat centre development will produce. Theirs is the path of return to the Father via the plane *ātma*, hence to reside in *dharmakāya*. They esoterically work to awaken the potency of the *suṣumṇā nāḍī* for the human consciousness-stream and to lead the humanity into the new solar system in the form of the Builders who will creatively build the new forms therein. The emanating sound is *Hūṁ*.

These five seed *bījas* can also be considered expressions of the Creative Word of the five Kumāras that embody the evolution of the various kingdoms of Nature constituting *saṃsāra*. They are the summation of the Personality expression of a planetary or solar Logos.

The path of Initiation provides the keys for the correct notes of these seed syllables. There are higher as well as lower levels to the use of all of these mantras. The Initiate of the first degree learns to collect his/her forces by means of the mind, to utilise them in creative endeavour and to master aspects of his/her personality concerning physical plane livingness. Aspects of the creative potency of the Aūṁ thereby come under sway. The Initiate of the second degree begins to rightly use the Oṁ to master the proclivities of the desire-mind, to enter properly into the domain of meditative visualisation. Many are the images that must be understood and correctly interpreted in the subjective domains of the psyche entered into. The Initiate of the third degree has learnt to concentrate all aspects of mind (the use of the seed syllable Āḥ) to master the concentration needed to produce any form of creative output needed in meditation. He/she seals this accomplishment through the ability to intensify the Fires of Mind to produce their highest most vibrant abstracted notes via the Āḥ, Oṁ, Hūṁ.

Oeaohoo can be diagrammed thus:

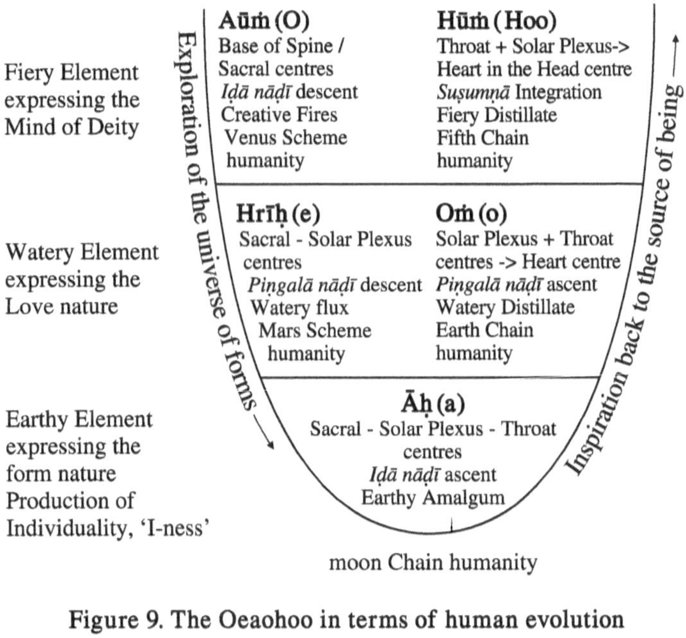

Figure 9. The Oeaohoo in terms of human evolution

The Initiate of the fourth degree has learnt to pacify all aspects of mind to produce the serene equilibrium of the Heart via compassion to master the Oṁ and to resonate the Hūṁ. The fifth degree Initiate fully awakens the Heart in the Head centre (Huṁ), the Throat in the Head (Āḥ), and the Solar Plexus in the Head (Oṁ). Sounding the Hrīḥ awakens *antaḥkaraṇas* to the Monad that increasingly rules the Initiate. Finally, the Aūṁ allows the integration of all five levels of the Head lotus in creative mastery of everything connoted by *saṃsāra*. It provides command of the categories of the *devas* that embody substance of the five planes of perception. Thus there is the appearance of a Master that is adept of the subray line that determines his/her disposition.

The Oṁ is the Word mainly expressed by the human kingdom, the Aūṁ by the angelic. Eventually the Initiate gains complete mastery of the Mysteries pertaining to the Oṁ, where the path that leads from the systemic to the cosmic Waters is produced. All is thus concealed in the correct pronunciation of the Oeaohoo, which produces the Chohan, an Initiate of the sixth degree. The mantra Oṁ Maṇi Padme Hūṁ: Hrīḥ then sounds out in its completeness.

From a higher perspective, the Oeaohoo is the Word of the abstracted Logos, (Who embodies a World Soul) sounded in its entirety, from the beginning to an ending of an entire evolutionary period. It embodies all the planes of manifestation, the septenaries of the Schemes, Chains, globes and Rounds of expression, yet remains aloof from what appears. The Soul aspect (the Ālaya of the Universe) is inclusive of all manifest things, and yet still remains One, indivisible, intrinsic on its own plane of Being, whereas the evolving forms appear, disintegrate and reappear again and again. What it embodies is far less than the sum of its Being, as Kṛṣṇa, who expressed this Soul aspect for humanity, stated in the Bhagavad Gītā:

> Having pervaded the whole Universe with a fragment of Myself, I still remain.[7]

The number 8 x 8 of the phrase *'Oeaohoo is One'* refers to the fact that the sum of these streams of consciousness are linked by spiral-cyclic energy and manifest through time as part of an organic whole.

The number 7 x 4 associated with the phrase *'still Oeaohoo is One'* refers to the fourth cosmic ether, *buddhi*. Therein exists what remains after the manifest universe has ensued. From it the world Soul emanates, the embodied Christ principle (of which the vowels constituting this name are expressions). This plane is also the esoteric home of the fourth kingdom of Nature, humanity. The Root, Light, the curds and Oeaohoo manifest as a quaternary, 'the four' into which 'the three' has fallen.

---

7 Annie Besant, *The Bhagavad-Gita* (G.A. Natesay & Co, Madras, fourth edition, 1922), 151.

'Oeaohoo is One' with them, esoterically the fourth principle, the factor of consciousness that links 'the One' to 'the other'. The Light relates to the Fiery principle (the evolution of intelligence), the curds here to the Watery principle, the Root to the Earthy and Oeaohoo to the Airy. Oeaohoo is literally the *prāṇas* of Life, the *jīvas* that are carried by the Light, that are embodied by the curds and that grow into the Tree of Life as the Root sprouts in the cosmic soil. The term 'One' here is capitalised because it conveys the principle of Divinity that is the Life of all that IS. Here it conveys the Aetheric Element. We see therefore that Oeaohoo is conveyed by all of these Elements, it is 'One'.

H.P.B.'s essential commentary, in relation to the phrase 'still Oeaohoo is One':

> This refers to the Non-Separateness of all that lives and has its being, whether in active or passive state. In one sense, Oeaohoo is the "Rootless Root of All"; hence, one with Parabrahmam; in another sense it is a name for the manifested ONE LIFE, the Eternal living Unity. The "Root" means, as already explained, pure knowledge *(Sattva),* eternal *(Nitya)* unconditioned reality or SAT *(Satya),* whether we call it Parabrahmam or Mulaprakriti, for these are the two aspects of the ONE. The "Light" is the same Omnipresent Spiritual Ray, which has entered and now fecundated the Divine Egg, and calls cosmic matter to begin its long series of differentiations. The curds are the first differentiation, and probably refer also to that cosmic matter which is supposed to be the origin of the "Milky Way" — the matter we know. This "matter," which, according to the revelation received from the primeval Dhyani-Buddhas, is, during the periodical sleep of the Universe, of the ultimate tenuity conceivable to the eye of the perfect Bodhisatva — this matter, radical and cool, becomes, at the first reawakening of cosmic motion, scattered through Space; appearing, when seen from the Earth, in clusters and lumps, like curds in thin milk. These are the seeds of the future worlds, the "Star-stuff."[8]

Stanza Three part Six

Stanza 3:6 states:

> **The Root of Life was in every drop of the Ocean of Immortality**

8 The S.D., Vol I, 68-69.

(Amrita), **and the Ocean was radiant Light, which was Fire and Heat and Motion. Darkness vanished and was no more. It disappeared in its own essence, the body of Fire and Water, of Father and Mother.**

Keynotes: Aquarius, *buddhi.* Watery conveyor of the five *prāṇas.* fourth Ray, fourth cosmic ether. Akṣobhya, Human Hierarchy, reflecting the second Liberated Hierarchy – 'Unity thro' Effort'. The seventh Eternity.

The numerical breakdown of the first phrase:

The Root (38, 11), every drop (56, 11), Life was in every drop (100, 28), The Root of Life (73, 19 = 10), every drop of the Ocean (103, 22), The Ocean (35, 8), The Root of Life was is in every drop (150, 42), Life was in every drop of the Ocean (147, 39), The Root of Life was is in every drop of the Ocean (197, 53 = 8), of Immortality (68, 14), the Ocean of Immortality (103, 22), every drop of the Ocean of Immortality (171, 36), Life was in every drop of the Ocean of Immortality (215, 53), The Root of Life was in every drop of the Ocean of Immortality (265, 67).

Though the meaning of the phrase *'the Root'* was previously explained as the seed of the totality of Being, Oeaohoo, there can also be such considerations as 'the Root' of the 'man-plant'. In Stanza 3:4 the phrase was 'the Root that grows in the midst of the ocean of Life', in Stanza 3:6 it is 'The Root of Life' that existed in 'every drop of the Ocean of Immortality'. The focus is then upon the concept of 'Life', with 'the Root' relating to the Lives existing within the manifest form. This direct teaching is in contradistinction to what humans incarnate in the material realms normally identify with Life. They view the living form as being alive and lose sight of what incarnates into it, that organises and utilises the form for a purpose. Each form, each 'drop', bears the seed of Life (the Spirit aspect) within it. Though the appearance of phenomena in *saṃsāra* concerns transience, evolving life, sickness and death, the reality is that underlying it all is the rebirthing principle, bequeathing immortality[9] – and that is Life.

9 Blavatsky has Amrita *(amṛta)* here, which signifies the deathless state, ambrosia, flowing from the Heart lotus when *kuṇḍalinī* has been awakened. A purified,

The next sign to consider is *Aquarius the water bearer,* whose glyph consists of two wavy bands, signifying two types of mutable flowing energies. Our vision consequently moves from consideration of the primary consequences of activating the *ātmic* plane, through to the fourth cosmic ether *(buddhi),* whereon the *chakras* below the diaphragm of the Logos exist. From here the causative energies pass to the higher mental plane, from whence they cause the appearance of *saṃsāra.* This process is symbolised by the phrase 'the fall of the three into the four', where the energies constituting 'the three' represent the upper band of the glyph of Aquarius *(ātma, buddhi, manas)* and 'the four' the lower band of the appearing phenomena from the lower mind down. The higher mental plane consequently receives the impact of the cosmic Waters reflected in terms of the Law of Synthesis by the second Liberated Hierarchy – 'Unity thro' Effort' via the Mirror-like Wisdom of Akṣobhya. The energy from these Waters is then depicted as 'the Ocean of Immortality' in this stanza, whilst Aquarius facilitates their distribution into the cosmic dense physical plane. Consequently, via the higher mental plane, the principle of Love-Wisdom, cosmic Love, can effect the appropriate changes in the three planes of human evolution, signified by the term *saṃsāra.*

The 'Ocean of Immortality' is thus the energy from cosmic astral sources that flows through the four cosmic ethers and which impacts upon *saṃsāra* via *buddhi.* The governing Ray is the fourth, which produces harmony in the midst of Strife, and the (human) Lives from former cycles upon the seventh Eternity now awaken to continue their evolutionary journey. On *buddhi* we have the beginning of the formation of things, the energies manifesting via the 'mirror' that cause the appearance of the human Soul, the Sambhogakāya Flower upon the higher mental plane. The higher *manasic* impulse thus instigates new cycles of expression, the downward spiral of Life, projecting the energies of divinity into manifestation.

The second liberated Hierarchy ('Unity thro' Effort') projects its power through the fourth cosmic ether, and by utilising the *chakras*

---

transmuted mixture of the *saṃskāras* that formerly produced ego-clinging. *Amṛta* is the Water of Life, the ambrosial drink *(soma)* of the gods. According to the Purāṇas, Ramāyāṇa and Mahābhārata, it came from the cosmic ocean of milk that was churned in a contest to produce it between the *devas* and *asūras.*

thereon can influence the appearance and evolution of the sum of manifest space, *saṃsāra* as we understand it. The governorship of *buddhi* esoterically is by the fourth Creative Hierarchy, humanity, 'the Initiates', also styled 'Lords of Sacrifice' (ruled by the sign Scorpio) by D.K. They reflect the attributes of the second Liberated Hierarchy into dense manifestation. The human Soul consequently is a direct embodiment of the principle of Love, which conditions their purpose. A direct affinity with the conditionings associated with Stanza 3:3, whereon the Monadic Life is externalised can also be considered.

From the context of solar evolution the formation of the kingdom of Souls upon the higher mental plane happened first in the Venus Scheme (in the third Round via the *Aūṃ).* This necessitated the purveyance of the Fiery Element, drawing upon cosmic Fire from the central Spiritual Sun. Aries, a Fire sign, consequently started that new cycle, to plant 'the Root of Life', but this Root is vitalised by the 'Ocean of Immortality' via the sign Aquarius the water bearer, who pours forth this immortality from His urn. These energies come from the Heart of the Sun. 'Radiant Light' brings into perspective the energies of Capricorn (governing the previous Stanza) and the illumination that happens upon the mount of Initiation. This mount refers to the energies upon the higher mental plane that produce the Individualisation of a human kingdom (which represents an Initiation for the Logos in Whose body of manifestation it occurs). Human units can then evolve by means of the appearance of the kingdom of Souls. Capricornian energies impacting upon the Aquarian Waters help generate the energies causing the radiance of the physical sun. This is an expression of the rulership of the sum of *manasic* substance, both subjective (Aquarius) and concretised (Capricorn). The nuclear fire that lights up the sun and sustains all life in the solar system is thereby a product of the externalised Logoic Mind.

As three planetary Schemes in the solar system bore the fruit of human Individualisation upon them, one can deduce that the influences of Aries, Leo (the polar opposite of Aquarius) and Capricorn were prominent in each Scheme respectively.

a. The Venus Scheme that was impressed with cosmic Fire via Aries. This then sets the keynote of the humanity evolving through that Scheme—the 'Lords of Flame'. During this time the systemic mental plane came into existence. The energies from the central spiritual sun were drawn upon. This set in motion the *iḍā nāḍī* line of development. The term 'Fire' in Stanza 3:6 relates to this development.

b. *The Mars Scheme* that was impressed with the Waters of cosmic Love via Leo, which directs solar Fire. This set the stage for their *piṅgalā* line of development. The systemic astral plane was consequently established, with the Atlantean type of dispensation at its height being the goal for that ancient epoch. The term 'Heat' in Stanza 3:6 relates to the development of the internal vitality in this humanity that sustained their sex drive, psychic vitality, and the emotions.

c. *The earth Scheme* was activated under the auspices of Capricorn, and the moon Chain became a zone for Individualisation in a similar manner that happened in the last solar system, which was by means of a long, slow, gradual course of development. The physical sun had by now developed the intensity of the blaze of light that we presently experience. Motion is the keyword provided in this Stanza for the development of this humanity, here signifying that complete mobility and agility of living in physical plane forms was the main development. The moon Chain humanity were mainly polarised in their etheric/physical forms, the Mars humanity in their astral/etheric forms, and the Venusian humanity in their mental/etheric forms. In the earlier two Schemes (Vulcan and Mercury) a period of early formative physical plane activity manifested wherein conditionings existed that allowed two human streams from the former solar system to be established and so complete their evolutionary development.

d. The present earth humanity is conditioned by the sign Scorpio, a Water sign, and is principally concerned with the testings for Initiation to transmute the phenomena of Capricornian substance, and to master the sum of the Watery nature (the astral domain) by means of the development of Mind. They consequently sum up in their attributes the accomplishments of their forebears in the earlier Schemes. As earlier stated the energy utilised by this humanity is given as 'Mantrikashakti, the WORD made flesh, Speech'.[10] This

10 *Esoteric Astrology*, 35.

means that a major objective of human evolution is to eventually discover the mantras, the words of Power governing the forces of Creation utilised by the Logos and the higher Creative Hierarchies. Such knowledge will allow humanity to work seeming miracles in the realms of form, to transmute substance, and to transform mind into sublime states of cosmic Consciousness.

e. The next humanity will be conditioned by Sagittarius, a Fire sign. The Sagittarian Will is needed to quickly project this humanity towards achieving the Logoic goals for this *mahāmanvantara*.

The phrase *'every drop of the Ocean'* (103, 22) refers to the various world spheres, the Lives of the higher Creative Hierarchies, as well as the human Causal forms, as all imbibe the Waters of the cosmic astral Ocean. Each can be considered a Thought-Bubble within the Logoic Mind, constituted of *deva* substance. They are the condensed 'drops' of the energy from the cosmic ethers in the field of *māyā,* and in the higher mental plane take the shape of Causal forms. Each atom of dense physical substance can also be considered to embody such a 'drop', containing its own seed, or 'Root of Life'. Each drop of this Ocean is a Womb (22) of planetary and Hierarchical energies from which evolve the forms that must gain experiences in the material domains. This substance will thereby eventually be transformed into mind-stuff. The first phrase of this Stanza therefore refers to the consequences of an animal kingdom having undertaken the Individualisation process in the abovementioned planetary Schemes, wherein the overshadowing Monadic Life (the 'Ocean of Immortality') could project a Ray or 'Root' towards the higher mental plane. There it will eventually meet the embryonic *manasic* aspiration of the animal units, allowing the Solar *devas* to build the Causal forms upon this abstracted domain of mind.

Every drop is also that of self-contained energy, which permeates the energies of any of the seven *chakras* in the Body of Being. It takes the complete expression of seven centres to form the ovoid or drop, as hinted at by D.K.:

> According to the position assumed by the man, he is seen as a symbol of the cross and is then fourfold (the two legs being considered as one lower limb) or, if separated, as fivefold, and has been then considered

> as the symbol of the five-pointed star. This fivefold nature of the dense physical body is brought about through the fact that only five centres primarily are really active in average man up to the third Initiation; all are there, and all are vitalized, but only five in this fivefold normal evolution are dominant. The force emanating from these five, therefore, sweeps the dense substance into a close aggregation. As two of the centres are not functioning as actively as the other five, an ovoid is not formed as in the case of the etheric, astral and mental sheaths. The fivefold shape of physical man is the result of the fivefold direction of force currents from five centres.
>
> It might be interesting also to point out that the interaction of the energy of the solar Pitris and of the lunar Pitris produces a very definite effect upon the lower group of lunar Pitris, and is one of the means whereby they will eventually reach the stage at which the solar Pitris are. This (if fully realised by man) will bring him to a very careful control of his sheaths, and to a close attention to the direction in which his force or energy is turned. He is responsible for the work of aiding in the evolution of substance, being himself a manasaputra.[11]

By the number 100 of the phrase *'Life was in every drop'* we see that Life will guarantee the perfected result of every aspect of the entire evolutionary process (100). The progress of that evolution is indeed Life itself. Once an entity attains and perfectly masters a quality, that quality is then embodied, and it can then be projected downwards as the force of Life to these that must yet attain it. This Life proceeds from the *buddhic* realm, the etheric substratum of manifestation (7 x 4). The 'Life' that *'was in every drop of the Ocean'* is that of the energies of the Heart centre (12), whether systemic, animal or human. It conveys the blood *(prāṇa)* that vitalises the All ('every drop in the Ocean'), sustaining their activity. Once the human Soul was Individualised then evolutionary perfection became the goal for each and every human unit.

The word *immortality* means unending existence or fame, that which is imperishable, endless, or deathless. The term refers esoterically to that or those who know no death, are thus not involved with the rounds of perpetual incarnation in the formed world. It therefore refers to a quality possessed by the liberated Ones that reside on the four cosmic ethers,

---

11 T.C.F., 790-791.

or the higher cosmic planes. The numbers 103 and 22 of the phrases *'the Ocean of Immortality'* and *'every drop of the Ocean'* indicate that this 'Ocean of Immortality' consists of the various zodiacal and Hierarchical energies that embody the sum total of manifest Being. These energies empower every Life-stream to undertake the cycles of activity (103) and so eventually gain immortality through conquering all of the forces incorporating *saṃsāra* by mastering its challenges. Each Buddha, as a 'world conquerer', has evolved thus. The experience of the *dharmakāya* and of identification with the Monadic sphere of Life (each Monad being triune, manifesting as an Eye) is what esoterically connotes the gaining of immortality. The number 103 here refers to the triune organisation of this Eye.

The *sūtrātmās* from the main trunk of the Root of Life split off into myriad lesser streams of spiral-cyclic motion (the number 8) to incorporate 'every drop', every embodied form, into the One integral Ocean of duration that is called Life. The consequence is a hylozoistic universe. Nothing is inanimate, inert, even though substance appears so to the mundane consciousness of the unawakened human. Because the substance of Mịnd (50 x 3, of the phrase *'The Root of Life was in every drop')* incorporates all in its embrace, so all is geared to awaken the empirical mind (200 + 15, 13 x 5) upon the path of liberation from the thrall of repetitious recycling. This Life is the bringer of the elixir of immortality *(amṛta)* consumed by the victorious Initiates, the perfected Ones (100). The Root manifests in the form of *iḍā, piṇgalā* and *suṣumṇā nāḍīs,* which subdivide into the minor rootlets of the *nāḍī* system.

We can also think in terms of 'Rootlets' associated with the three above planetary Schemes, whereby *manas* can be developed by the evolving kingdom of Souls that have come to exist in their domain. This Root can thereby extend itself deep into the substance of the cosmic dense physical soil, to extract the sum of the 'nutrients' therein by means of the man-plants that are consequently made to grow. Here Venus, the 'earth's alter ego' or Soul aspect, manifests the attributes of the *suṣumṇā nāḍī,* Mars the *piṇgalā nāḍī,* and the earth Scheme the *iḍā nāḍī.*

The number 3 x 12 of the phrase *'every drop of the Ocean of Immortality'* informs us that each drop (here the drops are the en-

Souling Lives) in this Ocean is infused with the energy of *buddhi,* the functions of which are governed by the sign Gemini the twins. Gemini veils the energy of the cosmic Christ, of the principle of Love that is carried by the Life via the ethers. This is obtained in the adytum of the sacred temple administered to by the Holy Ones; the Initiates that manifest the purity of Life, rituals, meditation and *dhāraṇīs,* necessary to have mastered the Life process. All three streams of evolving human Lives (that are organised according to the twelve zodiacal potencies of the petals of a Heart lotus) will inevitably Know what Life IS once they can gain access to the sacred precincts of the adytum.

The numerical breakdown of the next three phrases:

> radiant Light (60, 15) The Ocean was radiant (73, 19) The Ocean was radiant Light (102, 30), which was Fire (69, 24), Heat (16, 7), Motion (32, 5), which was Fire and Heat (95, 32), Fire and Heat and Motion (97, 25), which was Fire and Heat and Motion (137, 38 = 11), Darkness vanished (65, 20), was no more (42, 15), Darkness vanished and was no more (117, 36), Darkness vanished and = 10.10.1.

We know light to be the substance of the mental plane, and when it is radiant then it indicates that the quality of the substance manifests an intensity of energy synonymous with enlightenment. The focus therefore is upon the higher abstracted levels of the mental plane.

The number 60 of the phrase *'radiant Light'* refers to the sign Leo the lion, ruled by the sun, and is the sign of individuation, of self-consciousness, plus the Soul aspect of manifested Life. Our focus therefore is upon that which en-Souls Life – the Souls that manifest in the form of the 'drops' in 'the Ocean of Immortality'. From them ensue the Lives evolving in the three planes of human livingness. Leo (the polar opposite of Aquarius) thus becomes the focal point of the activity of the emanation of Fire and Heat and Motion. Leo is governed by the sun upon all three levels of expression: the physical sun, the Heart of the Sun and the central Spiritual Sun. Its energy is utilised in the Individualisation process to produce the spheres of the Sambhogakāya Flower on the higher mental plane, which are literally suns on this plane of perception. It governs the activity of the solar *devas* as they construct the Causal form. This, plus the orange hue of these forms, provides the reasons why the human Souls are styled 'tawny lions basking in the sun'.

This Light is also the result of the active interaction between Darkness (Spirit) and substance on every level of perception, from this interaction the Light evolves as conscious evolution. It is only perceptible if there is a field of interaction (the number 60 also indicates the desire principle) and a perceiver (the number 5 x 3, hence intelligent activity) to perceive it, otherwise it remains in darkness. We thus have the mode of causing attachment to pleasurable and illusory things, plus the consciousness that gains from experiencing such attachment, which is the hallmark of human Life in *saṃsāra*.

The number 10 of the phrase *'the Ocean was radiant'* signifies perfection, the complete sphere of radiation. It also implies the totality of the cosmic ethers, which convey the *prāṇas* that cause the radiance. The source of luminosity had thus appeared through which the actual birth of the corporeal form could be experienced. It signifies the vivification of the *prāṇic* triangle of Deity and thus the consequent vitalisation of all the various cells and organs in His Body with the Living Light of the incarnating Souls. The focus here is via the activity of the Sacral centre. The vitalisation with *prāṇic* energy as directed from the Sacral centre provides a coherent unity to the form so that the principle of desire (the number 60) could produce its inevitable results in *saṃsāra*. Without this vitalisation directed by an overshadowing Soul the Ocean would consist of scattered atoms with no conscious organisation or progressive direction. Once the seven *chakras* that exist in the ethers begin to convey lighted substance then this guaranties further evolution as an integral entity, a unity in time and space. The *chakras* thus awaken. First the Base of Spine centre is established to organise the scattered elements into a form, then the Sacral centre comes into expression to vitalise the entire form with living Light. Each solar sphere can be viewed as such a centre.

The *'the Ocean was radiant Light'* (120, 30) once the outer periphery of the kingdom of God, the ring-pass-not circumscribed by any Logos for a particular Incarnation (30), had been established. Within each such form, constructed also by lesser Hierarchies of illumined Beings (102), the *maṇḍala* of the entire 'Web of Light' explained in Stanza 2:5 could be formed. Light then radiates out to fill all dark recesses of space via the empowerment of the higher mental plane. The spheres of limitation for each evolving form, governed by the law of Economy, set the laws in motion by means of which all could interrelate and gain evolutionary experience.

Fire is the substance of the mental realm, an expression of the Mind of 'God'. When therefore 'radiant Light' is equated with Fire, the reference is to the auric sphere generated by each Causal Body on the higher mental plane. They demonstrate solar Fire, from which emanates the Light that illumines the three worlds, and which infuses Life into the etheric body. Mind and *prāṇa* are expressions of each other. (An often repeated truism.) Light, the effect of the interaction between Spirit and substance on the higher mental plane, is then conveyed as *prāṇa* in the dense form via the etheric body.

In examining the terms Darkness, Light, Fire, Heat and Motion there is a descending order of expression with respect the planes of perception they can be related to. First, as already explained, Darkness can be viewed as being an expression of *ātma-buddhi*. Light has its expression on all the planes of perception, though its phenomena in the form of solar Light first manifests upon the higher mental plane. We then have the astral light, the light of the sun and other forms of light upon the physical plane. Fire, heat and motion relate esoterically to the three planes of human evolution. Fire is the substance of the mind and specifically of the lower mind, sustaining the realm of ideas and concepts. The substance of mind *(citta)* burns to create the light of understanding, of illumination. Heat is sustained in the etheric form, such as is *kuṇḍalinī,* and Tum-mo, the inner heat that warms and produces the activity of the dense form. This heat also has its expression in the middle, astral body, as D.K. pointed out:

> The blending of the three fires, the merging of the three Rays, and the co-operation of the three Logoi have in view (at this time and within this solar system) the development of the Essence of the cosmic Lord of Love, the second person in the logoic trinity. Earlier it was not so, later it will not be, but now is. When viewed from the cosmic mental plane these Three constitute the PERSONALITY OF THE LOGOS, and are seen *functioning as one.* Hence the secret (well recognised as fact, though not understood) of the excessive *heat,* occultly expressed, of the astral or central body of the triple personality. It animates and

> controls the physical body, and its desires hold sway in the majority of cases; it demonstrates in *time and space* the correspondence of the temporary union of spirit and matter, the fires of cosmic love and the fires of matter blended. A similar analogy is found in the heat apparent in this second solar system.[12]

It should also be noted in this respect that the astral body is a practical unity with the etheric body for normal evolutionary expression. The passion, desires and creative imagination of humanity has produced the habitation of humanity on the astral plane, but this is only a temporary phenomena.

Motion is specifically what governs all activity upon the dense realm (and of a *manvantara*, which is the dense appearance of a Logos). Constant periodic motion and mutable activity characterises *saṃsāra*, specifically what relates to its dense aspect. Such activity allows the accumulation of experiences, causing an intelligence to react to its transient phenomenon to seek what is non-mutable, hence the *nirvāṇic* peace found upon *buddhi.*

It was also earlier stated that the term Fire refers to the Individualisation of the humanity upon the Venus Scheme. Heat then refers to the Individualisation of Mars Scheme humanity, and Motion to the Individualisation of moon-Chain humanity. Darkness then can have a reference to the appearance of the humanity upon the Vulcan Scheme, when the sun had not yet generated its full quota of light. Light therefore here can refer to the appearance of humanity upon the Mercury scheme, when the morning sun had gained its brilliance. Finally, darkness also refers to the expression of Life upon the earth Scheme, the lowest point of inversion of the spheres of activity of a solar Logos, wherein the darkness of ignorance is to be converted to Light on a mass scale. This necessitates the development of the will by the evolving humanity over time and the projection of the *antaḥkaraṇas* to the higher dimensions. Darkness then vanishes. This process is signified by the number 11 of the phrase *'which was Fire and Heat and motion'*.

The numbers 24, 15 of the phrase *'which was Fire'* refer to the second sign of the zodiac, Taurus the bull and to the intelligence (15) that is the fuel of this Fire. Once each humanity is established then the

12 *T.C.F.*, 64.

energy of Taurus comes to the fore to clothe the sum of the context of the civilisations that arise. As shall be shown in the next stanza, this is the major energy that conditions the evolutionary progression of each humanity. It inexorably turns the zodiacal wheel onwards, so that wisdom can be the inevitable gain for all. Taurus represents the opened Eye of illumination hid within the Causal form. The Eye of the bull directs the Fiery energy to help build the Light Body of the Logos. This is also seen in the guise of the 'four and twenty elders' that sit around the throne of Deity.[13] These Dhyān Chohans clothe the Thought Form emanating from this Throne with the embodied Light of the energies of the four cosmic ethers impacting upon the higher mental plane, that are then projected into the realm of substance. These Elders are thus responsible for conveying Hierarchical energies into the form. The Fire of cosmic Mind (directed via Aries) thus passes through this Eye to regulate the attributes of the evolving form (governed by Taurus) via the agency of intermediaries associated with the expanding petals of a Head lotus. Thus the wheel of the zodiac is caused to turn, and as it is set in motion it generates heat. Heat is the expression of the fire that is fuelled by dense substance. It is a product of the 'whole creation' as it 'groaneth and travaileth in pain together'[14] along its evolutionary course. It is an expression of the Mother, of frictional energy and its abrasive journeying in the realms of substance.

'The Root of Life' is also seen as the downturned horns of the Ram projecting energies from the domain of cosmic abstract Mind to impregnate 'every Drop' of the Ocean with the Immortality of its Presence. The energy of Aries thus impels every evolving form within that Ocean to start their evolutionary journeying.

Motion can be considered as triune, as all else. We have:

Types of energy:

Forward progressive	(first Ray)	the Father aspect,
Spiral-cyclic	(second Ray)	the Son aspect,
Rotary	(third Ray)	the Mother aspect

---

13 *Rev. 4:4.*

14 *Romans 8:22,* 'For we know that the whole creation groaneth and travaileth in pain together until now'.

These three types of motion indicate the sum of the entire evolutionary path, an entire Day or Year of Brahmā. They are the vehicle of the radiatory energy of heat, Fire and the movement (of the mind) that allows one to perceive things. The perception of things generates heat. Fire, heat and motion therefore signify the essence of the substantiality of *saṃsāra,* the gain of which is radiatory activity, and the quality thereof is Light, the expression of consciousness.

Concerning *Darkness*, H.P.B. has this to say:

> The essence of darkness being absolute light, Darkness is taken as the appropriate allegorical representation of the condition of the Universe during Pralaya, or the term of absolute rest, or non-being, as it appears to our finite minds. The "fire," "heat," and "motion," here spoken of, are, of course, not the fire, heat, and motion of physical science, but the underlying abstractions, the noumena, or the soul, of the essence of these material manifestations — the "things in themselves," which, as modern science confesses, entirely elude the instruments of the laboratory, and which even the mind cannot grasp, although it can equally as little avoid the conclusion that these underlying essences of things must exist. Fire and Water, or Father [footnote given, See "Kwan-Shai-Yin"] and Mother, may be taken here to mean the divine Ray and Chaos...According to the tenets of Eastern Occultism, DARKNESS is the one true actuality, the basis and the root of light, without which the latter could never manifest itself, nor even exist. Light is matter, and DARKNESS pure Spirit. Darkness, in its radical, metaphysical basis, is subjective and absolute light; while the latter in all its seeming effulgence and glory, is merely a mass of shadows, as it can never be eternal, and is simply an illusion, or Maya.
>
> Even in the mind-baffling and science-harassing Genesis, light is created out of darkness "and darkness was upon the face of the deep (ch. i, v. 2) — and not *vice versa.* "In him (in darkness) was life; and the life *was the light of men,"* (John i. 4).[15]

Darkness vanished into the Light of Day, the dawn of a new *manvantara,* the realm of conscious and material activity, which occludes the intense Light of the Spirit. Also, 'Darkness vanished' in the Light provided by Leo upon the abstracted domains of the Mind, whereon the kingdom of Souls are established.

15 Ibid., 69-70.

From the perspective of this Stanza Darkness can also refer to the Vulcan Scheme. Its 'vanishing' thus refers to the dematerialising of its dense form, so that its densest sheath is composed of etheric substance. That is why no planet can presently be seen between Mercury and the sun.

The numbers of the phrase '*was no more*' add to 13 x 5 and 6 x 7. The number 13 x 5 refers to the five sense-consciousnesses, and the engendering of the light of the mind by humanity, thereby vanquishing the darkness of ignorance over time. Eventually the spheres of influence governing Space, manifest the Wisdoms of the five Dhyāni Buddhas, thereby producing a domain of boundless Light. *'Darkness vanished'* (20, 11) thereby, as is also signified by the first Ray attributes of the numbers 10.10. The number 6 x 7 of the phrase '*was no more*' refers to the sheaths of an incarnate personality, which must eventually be mastered, filled with light for darkness to vanish. They dematerialise, enter into *pralaya,* similarly also the Rounds, Chains and Schemes of evolution. The planetary globes come into objectivity and disappear again in succession, therefore *'Darkness vanished and was no more'* (100 + 17, 3 x 12). Here the third sign of the zodiac, Gemini the twins, is implicated, which governs the etheric body. Its energies therefore help to etherealise material space, so that the objective form disappears. In terms of a planetary system the Will of a Logos (100 + 17) eventually abstracts the concrete form of a globe into the fourth cosmic ether *(buddhi).* The darkness of the concrete form thus vanishes. It is obvious at any rate that Darkness cannot stand in the presence of the Light that is generated as a consequence of the evolutionary process, which is the purpose of the appearance of the radiance of a sun.

With respect to the terms Fire, Heat and Motion it would be useful to quote a little from *The Introductory Statements* of the T.C.F., under the heading 'Fires in the Macrocosm'. D.K. first speaks of the three major cosmic Rays: 'The Ray of intelligent action', 'the Ray of intelligent love', and 'the Ray of intelligent will'. He then states:

> These three expressions of the divine Life may be regarded as expressing the triple mode of manifestation. First, the objective or tangible universe; second, the subjective worlds or form; and thirdly, the spiritual aspect which is to be found at the heart of all. The internal fires that animate and vitalise shew themselves in a twofold manner:

First as *latent heat.* This is the basis of rotary motion and the cause of the spheroidal coherent manifestation of all existence, from the logoic atom, the solar ring-pass-not, down to the minutest atom of the chemist or physicist.

Second, as *active heat.* This results in the activity and the driving forward of material evolution. On the highest plane the combination of these three factors (active heat, latent heat and the primordial substance which they animate) is known as the 'sea of fire,' of which akasha is the first differentiation of pregenetic matter. Akasha, in manifestation, expresses itself as Fohat, or divine Energy, and Fohat on the different planes is known as aether, air, fire, water, electricity, ether, prana and similar terms. It is the sumtotal of that which is active, animated, or vitalized, and of all that concerns itself with the adaptation of the form to the needs of the inner flame of life.

It might here be useful to point out that *magnetism* is the effect of the divine ray in manifestation in the same sense that electricity is the manifested effect of the primordial ray of active intelligence. It would be well to ponder on this for it holds hid a mystery.

The fires of the mental plane also demonstrate in a twofold manner:

First, as the *Fire of Mind,* the basis of all expression and in one peculiar occult sense the sumtotal of existence. It provides the relation between the life and the form, between spirit and matter, and is the basis of consciousness itself.

Second, as the *Elementals of Fire,* or the sumtotal of the active expression of thought, showing itself through the medium of those entities who, in their very essence, are fire itself.

These dualities of expression make the four necessary factors in the logoic quaternary, or the lower nature of the Logos viewing His manifestation from one esoteric angle; esoterically, they are the sumtotal of the logoic quaternary, plus the logoic fifth principle, cosmic mind.

The divine spark does not as yet manifest (as do the other two fires) as a duality, though what lies hidden in a later cycle, evolution alone will disclose. This third fire, along with the other two, make the necessary five of logoic evolutionary development and by its perfected merging with the other two fires as the evolutionary process proceeds is seen the goal of logoic attainment for this greater cycle or period of this solar system. When the primordial ray of intelligent activity, the divine ray of intelligent love, and the third cosmic ray of intelligent will meet, blend, merge, and blaze forth, the Logos will take His

> fifth initiation, thus completing one of His cycles. When the rotary, the forward, and the spiral cyclic movements are working in perfect synthesis then the desired vibration will have been reached. When the three Laws of Economy, of Attraction, and of Synthesis work with perfect adjustment to each other, then nature will perfectly display the needed functioning, and the correct adaptation of the material form to the indwelling spirit, of matter to life, and of consciousness to its vehicle.[16]

With respect to the statements that '*magnetism* is the effect of the divine ray (the second Ray) in manifestation' and 'electricity is the manifested effect of the primordial ray of active intelligence' it should be noted that the intervening substance is that of the degree of resistance between these two factors by the mind. As it does so, so the phenomenon of Light is generated.

The above also explains the qualities that established the five planes of Brahmā into which the three aspects of Divine Life are reflected.

a. Latent heat, rotary motion, sustaining physical plane activity. An effect of the Ray of Intelligent Action.

b. Active heat, elementary spiral-cyclic motion, the foundation of the astral plane, which esoterically is an energy distributor (of the sea of Fire) before the appearance of the desire principle of humanity. An effect of the Ray of Intelligent Love.

c. Elementals of Fire, sustaining the substance *(citta)* of the lower mental plane. The beginnings of forward-progressive motion when these Elementals are tamed and directed. An effect of the Ray of Intelligent Will.

These three levels embody the attributes of Logoic *kuṇḍalinī,* the internal Fire that sustains the activity of the form and integrates it into a coherent unity. They therefore represent the forces of the Mother. *Kuṇḍalinī* is consequently awakened when the energy of the Father *(dharmakāya)* descends. When this is done it liberates the Son, who in meditation deep has acted as a channel for the desired union of 'Father and Mother'.

16 T.C.F., 41-45.

d. The Fire of Mind upon the higher mental plane, the relation between Life and form, Spirit and matter, represents the effect of the energy of electricity, of Intelligent Action, whose reflex manifests as the physical plane where the Fires of Mind is positive and the latent heat of the physical plane is the negative expression.

e. The plane *buddhi,* which expresses the magnetic energies of the Divine Ray, that will inevitably refine the Fires of manifestation as it draws their substance to it. This is the potency behind the *śūnyatā-saṃsāra* nexus, explained in depth in *The Treatise on Mind.*

f. The Intelligent Will (Fohat), the cosmic Fire of Logoic Mind (the *dharmakāya)* that manifests via *ātma* and is reflected into manifestation via *buddhi.* Fohat ('the divine spark') stimulates all of the Fires, intensifying their blaze until eventually all is consumed in illuminating Light. Then Darkness vanishes 'and was no more'.

The numerical breakdown of the final three phrases:

It disappeared (64, 10), its own essence (53, 17 = 8), It disappeared in its own essence (131, 32), disappeared in its own essence (120, 30), own essence (7.7.), Fire and Water (61, 16), the body of Fire (75, 30), the body of Fire and Water (107, 35), of Father (43, 7), Father and Mother (75, 12), of Father and Mother (87, 15).

The activity outlined in these phrases refers to the evolutionary process, whose consequence is gaining the enlightened Mind, hence the overcoming of ignorance. As humanity as a whole become enlightened, so then the energies brought to bear upon the material domain will work to etherealise the substance thereof. The darkness associated with the material domain will 'disappear in its own essence', as *pralaya* ensues. First there is the intensification of spiral-cyclic energy (8 x 8 of the phrase *'it disappeared')* to cause the above effect, whilst the number 8 of the phrase *'its own essence'* also refers to the energy Body of Deity.

The word *essence* means the essential, fundamental nature or characteristic of a thing. There is therefore the unusual paradox that both substance and Light ('the body of Fire and Water') are equated with the essence of Darkness. This is not just a mere play on words, but refers to the esoteric fact that the substance of the three worlds of human livingness is darkness from the higher perspective, whilst Light evolves into greater intensities of energy expression, of the first and second Ray aspects of Deity. (The numbers 100 + 31, the first Ray, and 32, the second Ray, of the phrase *'it disappeared in its own essence'.)* This essence becomes Darkness for those eyes that have not the capacity to gaze upon the intensity of the Light.

The essence of the disappearing darkness is Light. Darkness is found at the centre of any sphere of embodied Light, in the form of the Jewel in the Heart of the Lotus. Darkness manifests as Light (which is therefore the Son of Darkness), and Light in its turn moves to overcome the material darkness.

The phrase *'its own essence'* also directly related to 'the body of Fire and Water', to the mental and astral planes of perception, when the atoms of dense physical substance are abstracted thereto, as explained above, and also detailed in my book *Esoteric Cosmology and Modern Physics.* The alchemical process is hinted at here, where the *prima materia,* the virgin substance is liquefied and made volatile.

The number 22 of the phrase *'in its own essence'* indicates that darkness is absorbed in the essence of the zodiacal and planetary energies that constitute the solar Womb at the onset of *pralaya.* By undergoing repetitious cyclic incarnations (the number 7.7. of *'own essence')* all lives then transform this darkness into a body of Light. Light at first manifested in the form of *'the body of Fire'* (25 x 3), wherein cosmic Fire is implicated, as all was permeated with the substance of Logoic Mind. The Water is that of the cosmic astral plane, of the cosmic Christ (16), (the Soul-aspect, the 'Light of the World'[17] of a human Life-stream) who embodies the union of *'Fire and Water'.* Also, after the globes and Chains etherialise they are abstracted into the astral plane (Water), and into the mental plane (Fire) at the end of the solar evolution. The term Water here can also refer to the sum of the energies that manifest through the etheric form as an ocean of energies.

The first Scheme in our solar system to have 'disappeared' thus was by means of the liberating activity of Vulcan's humanity. They were disciples and Initiates from the former solar system, hence the need for physical plane incarnation was comparatively brief for them.

---

17 *John 8:12.*

As only the higher Initiations needed to be accomplished so ignorance quickly vanished, the Mysteries concerning the Darkness of the cosmic mental plane were learnt, thus this form of Darkness also disappeared. The intensity of the downpour of energies consequently transformed the atoms of substance, and thus the gross form of the entire Scheme also disappeared. All human units will undergo a similar process, no matter what Scheme they originate from.

The numbers of the phrase *'Father and Mother'* also add to 25 x 3, which here refers to the triune Logos and their reflection in manifestation in the form of the three Buddhas of Activity. They are responsible for the dissemination of the energies of Deity (of the totality of the Elements, Fire, Water and Earth) into the three lower planes of perception. This is done via the higher mental plane wherein resides the Causal form (of 'the Son'). This is 'the body of Fire', for it is moulded from the substance of the mental plane. From this perspective the 'body of Fire and Water' is the personality nature into which darkness vanished, as each human unit evolves the intelligence to overcome the darkness of ignorance.

'Father and Mother' here infer a duality which existed before the appearance of 'things', as in the opening chapter of the book of Genesis before the appearance of the Son (Light – consciousness). Darkness, the undifferentiated Spirit aspect, disappeared into the Womb of the Mother, which then became the seed or germ of Light.

'Father and Mother' can be considered a Divine Hermaphrodite, relating to the second stage of evolution that produces the splitting of the Divine Egg. The Thought Form is circumscribed by the Fiery Mind of the Father and embodied by the Watery substance of the Mother, whilst Darkness becomes the germ of latent activity. This produces another interpretation of the symbol ⊙. The normal interpretation (from below up) is to view the central dot as the Throne of Deity, and the circumference as the bounded sphere of forthcoming activity. What is outside this sphere represents the Darkness that lies beyond the then focus of activity.

The numbers of the phrase *'the body of Fire and Water'* add to 107 and to 7 x 5, where 100 + 7 refers to the body of expression in which the various septenaries *(chakras)* can find active expression. Darkness therefore has 'disappeared in its own Essence', within the confines of the personality form. It is contained within the seven *chakras* that express the sum total of consciousness. The number 7 x 5 refers to the mental plane, reminding us again that everything produced on the lower planes has their source here.

What comes of or from the Father aspect of Deity is indicated by the numbers of the phrase *'of Father',* which add to 7, referring to the sum of the Logoic Body of manifestation, with its various septenaries of expression.

The number 15 of the phrase *'of Father and Mother'* refers to the activity of Divine Intelligence productive of the evolution of the bearers of mind within the circumscribed form that overcome the darkness of material space. This is the cause for the circumscription of a region of space by Father-Mother.

Stanza Three part Seven

Stanza 3:7 states:

> **Behold, O Lanoo! The radiant Child of the Two, the uparalleled refulgent Glory, bright Space, Son of dark space, who emerges from the depths of the great dark Waters. It is Oeaohoo, the Younger, the * * *** *(whom thou knowest now as Kwan-Shai-Yin).* **He shines forth as the Sun, he is the blazing divine Dragon of Wisdom. The Eka is Chatur** *(four),* **and Chatur takes to itself Three, and the union produces the Sapta** *(seven)* **in whom are the Seven which become the Tridasa** *(the thrice ten),* **the Hosts and the Multitudes. Behold him lifting the Veil, and unfurling it from east to west. He shuts out the above, and leaves the below to be seen as the great illusion. He marks the places for the Shining Ones** *(stars),* **and turns the upper** *(space)* **into a shoreless Sea of Fire, and the One manifested into the great Waters.**

Keynotes: Pisces, the higher mental plane, fifth Ray, first sub-aspect of Earthy *ākāśa*, Vairocana and Amoghasiddhi. The kingdom of Souls, reflecting the first Liberated Hierarchy – 'Intelligent substance'.

The numerical breakdown of the first seven statements:

> Behold, (28, 10), O Lanoo (27, 9), The radiant Child (73, 19), Child of the two (67, 22), The radiant Child of the two (113, 32), the two (28, 10), The unparalleled refulgent Glory (133, 25), refulgent Glory (77, 14), bright Space (54, 18), dark space (33, 15), Son of dark space (57 = 12, 21), who emerges (55, 19), the depths (42, 15), emerges from the depths (103, 31), who emerges from the depths (122, 41), dark Waters (39, 12), the great dark Waters (78 = 6 x 13, 24), the depths of the great dark Waters (132 = 66 x 2, 42), from the depths of the great dark Waters (157, 49), emerges from the depths of the great dark Waters (193, 58), who emerges from the depths of the great dark Waters (212, 68).

This Stanza brings us to the sign Pisces the fishes, whose Hierarchical ruler is Pluto that wields first Ray energy that can carve deep into the concreted Logoic substance. Pluto helps project the zodiacal wheel in a retrograde fashion, from right to left, (the precession of the equinoxes) of the great illusion, once a humanity builds the encapsulating thought-forms in the world of *māyā.* This conditions *saṃsāra* so as to produce the birthing of each new zodiacal cycle and the termination of its purpose. Thus the wheel of the zodiac turns within the Mother's Womb, the attributes of which are found in the symbolism of the aspects of this verse. This precession conditions human evolution until they tread the path of Initiation, in which case the zodiac is rectified to the left to right motion that governs the realms of enlightened being and solar evolution as a whole.

The higher mental plane is now activated, whilst the fifth Ray of science, of *manasic* activity, conditions the mental plane in general, hence this cycle overall. This Ray governs the appearing forms of activity of the *māyā,* whereas Pluto signifies the higher potency emanating from Logoic domains. Coupled with this is the fact that Amoghasiddhi's All-accomplishing Wisdom is utilised to rightly carve, to master the substance of the entire material world. Amoghasiddhi's power is reinforced by the potency of Vairocana's Dharmadhātu Wisdom from the highest sphere of Logoic Mind (the domain of the Soul) to ensure that the cosmic dense physical manifests totally in accord with Logoic Purpose for that *mahāmanvantara.* Amoghasiddhi's Wisdom is essentially an expression of the seventh Ray of Ritual Activity and Cyclic Power, which facilitates the utilisation of the Earthy *ākāśa* that also conditions this Stanza. One could also consider that the higher mental plane represents the first sub-aspect of this *ākāśa,* the lower mental plane its second sub-aspect, the astral plane its third sub-aspect, the four ethers the fourth sub-aspect and the dense physical as the most concretised form of this cosmic energy. The *karma* for the entire material domain can thereby be rightly projected to produce the desired outcome, according to the Logoic Meditation for the evolving forms. Here the ancient *karma* of the mind is reaped, and also the new can be planted in the Logoic soil of the higher mental plane. This plane signifies the densest manifestation of phenomena from the perspective of a Logos.

Upon the higher mental exists the conditionings governing the kingdom of Souls, hence the principle of rebirth. The attributes of the Logoic Soul are reflected into manifestation by the highest of the liberated Creative Hierarchies, simply termed 'Intelligent substance' by D.K. The attributes express the Law of Identity, explained in the last chapter of my book *Meditation and the Initiation Process.*

As this Stanza is now focussed upon the domain of the Soul, so the awakened disciple (the Lanoo, here therefore an Initiate of the third degree) can be shown certain mysteries pertaining to cosmic evolution and world formation, as depicted in these Stanzas. The objective also is to awaken in the Lanoo *buddhic* vision, hence the use of the term 'Behold'. He/she beholds the meaning of the entire turning of the great zodiacal Wheel, and of the entire history of humanity, as well as visualising the sum of the esoteric doctrines.

The main period of evolutionary history is now to be born, signified by 'bright Space', which will herald the solar noonday sun. Within the zodiacal Womb of Pisces and the appearance of this sun, Taurus pushes the signs of the zodiac around their course in the heavens. All of the signs are consequently found expressed in Stanza 3:7. This period covers the evolution of the fourth Round, and thus of the earth evolution that we are presently experiencing, wherein the Lanoo is found. The term Lanoo refers to a student *(chela)* of an enlightened one. Much can be revealed about this period, therefore Stanza 3:7 is large, presenting preparatory information that will be elaborated in Stanza four, which deals entirely with our earth Scheme. Being the fourth Scheme out of seven it acts as a mirror, reflecting the qualities of all the others. As the earth is the fourth globe of the fourth Chain of the fourth Scheme so it embodies the functions of the fourth Ray mirror. Consequently our tiny globe facilitates the ability to observe all of the characteristics of the universe.

Esoterically, to *'behold'* (7 x 4), to be able to vision the scene before us and upon the inner domains, necessitates awakening the third Eye. To do so, one must uplift one's consciousness to the highest plane possible, and from that lofty height to visualise the panorama desired. In this case the Initiate is asked to visualise via the plane of at-onement, of enlightenment, the fourth plane of perception (7 x 4), *buddhi (śūnyatā).* This is important because such perception allows the Lanoo to make the calculations to 'learn the correct age of thy small wheel', by reaching 'the fourth "Fruit" of the fourth path of Knowledge' (Stanza 6:7), which represents the gain or purpose for the present humanity upon our earth globe within the fourth Scheme in the solar system.

By the numbers of the phrase *'O Lanoo',* which add to 3 x 9, we see that he is an Initiate, specifically one that has attained the third Initiation. The phrase is also a device to inform us that this Stanza refers to the stage in the evolutionary process that the present humanity has attained and disciples have evolved that could thus question and also to appropriately vision.

Once the Initiate is able to project his mind onto the *buddhic* level and vision thereon, then he will be able to view the etheric form of the solar Logos, which is *'the radiant Child'* (10) from one perspective. This phrase can also refer to the planetary Scheme, as well as the kingdom of Souls upon it. It is 'radiant' because of the quality of the mental aura developed. The *'child of the Two'* (22, 31 x 2) refers to the Son of the 'Father and Mother', as well as to 'the body of Fire and Water'. Who such a 'Son' is, is determined by what exactly we take as 'Father and Mother' to represent. As our focus is upon the solar Logos, and following the logic so far presented, we can conclude that this 'Son' is the planetary Logos of our earth Scheme. Our planetary Logos is radiant because He bears the accomplishment of a former evolutionary attainment, the attributes of the Will or Power of Deity (31 x 2) and projects them into manifestation. Also, this fourth Scheme is radiant because it bears the purpose of the forces manifesting via the fourth ether (explained in Stanza 3:5) into manifestation by means of the zodiacal and planetary energies (22) that constitute the sum of the form that is the child of the two.

The numbers 100 + 13, 32 of the phrase *'The radiant Child of the Two'* refer to the sphere of activity established by our planetary Logos, plus the energy of Love-Wisdom He bears (32), which will also be evolved by the humanity upon this Scheme to become the 'radiant Child'. This present humanity's leitmotif is to fully express the second Ray attribute, which is the purpose of the present solar Incarnation. Though the members of the former planetary evolutions had developed this quality, it was not the main onus of their evolutionary expression, rather it was the enlightened Mind. Buddhic perception is an addendum that was to be developed later by most members of these former human streams. However for our present humanity this is what they must accomplish as a unit upon our earth globe. Most of our present humanity are considered second Ray Monads that consequently are preconditioned to attain this 'Fruit', whilst those of the former epochs are mainly third Ray Monads.

Members of our present humanity are also the Sons of 'Fire and Water'. 'Fire' was the accomplishment of those of the Venus Scheme, 'Water' was mastered by those of the Mars Chain, whilst those of the moon Chain failed in their task to master the Earth Element. 'Fire and Water' consequently is a preconditioned gain from the former evolutionary epochs, of the Instructors of the present humanity. Earth's humanity are thereby esoterically considered 'Sons' of their Teachers.

The word *glory* refers to the ability to shine, radiate, or to manifest splendour. It can refer to the praise, honour, or high distinction accorded by common consent to a person or thing, the honourable fame coming from the highest achievement. Glory brings or gives renown, resplendence. Esoterically it refers to the divinity in a person, an emanation of Light that proceeds from beings of sanctity, and is the generation of the aura around one, generally taken as a circle of golden light around the head or body. To give glory therefore means to provide an aura, an ineffable radiance, allowing one to eventually be registered as an omnipotent sun, the central light-bearing dynamo to manifest being.

These are all predominantly fourth or second Ray qualities, generated by the radiance that emanates from light (a fifth Ray attribute). Together they can be equated with the Christ-energy, thus Christ-Jesus stated He was the 'Light of the world'.[18]

'Refulgent Glory' (77) is the consequence of having successfully undertaken the symbolic 777 incarnations, to thereby awaken all of the petals of the *chakras*. With the Head lotus awakened an illumined, enlightened being appears with a consequent effulgent radiant aura. When such glory is 'unparalleled', then it implies that not only is the Head lotus awakened, but that it now receives the highest energies possible – that from the Monad. Logoically, the manifestation of *'the unparalleled refulgent Glory'* (100 + 33, 25) establishes a planetary Head centre. In this case, Shambhala upon the earth, allowing the various streams of Creative Intelligences (100 + 33) to preside over building the necessary forms for humanity to develop. Such activity allows Logoic Glory to manifest.

This epithet of 'glory' is especially significant for the One who embodies the fourth globe of the fourth Chain of the earth Scheme, because thereby the full splendour of the solar Logos can be demonstrated via His complete body of manifestation. Here the term 'glory' also refers to the extent of the domain that is encompassed by means of the Creative Eye of the Logos. It represents the field of expression of His body of manifestation. Because our planetary Scheme manifests as the lowest extent of the reach of the solar Logos, the establishment of the Seat of Power of our planetary Logos means that now the entire physical domain of the space initially circumscribed by the Thought of the solar Logos can be fully claimed. Once a sufficient number of the present humanity have gained their 'fourth Fruit' then this *'unparalleled refulgent Glory'* will be an established fact for both the planetary and solar Logos.

The attributes of the sign Taurus the bull comes to the fore here. He embodies the functions of the third Eye, as well as the substance of the complete body of manifestation of the Logos. (Exoterically Taurus rules the manifestation of the homestead.)

18 *John 8:12*.

The earth Chain humanity is governed by Scorpio, the polar opposite of Taurus, hence must master the entire field of desire, selfishness and self-interest. This is especially so regarding the pursuit of pleasurable experiences and the material comforts of the home environment that have caused so much woe to the planetary condition. Such attributes can be contrasted with the main qualities of the former moon Chain humanity (ruled by Capricorn), who are now generally in positions of power all over the planet. This former humanity are divided into two broad camps. One group consists of the serried ranks of the dark brotherhood (though rarely recognised as such by the deluded humanity they ruthlessly manipulate) that govern the material plane affairs of much that is connoted as the present civilisation. Their keynote is personal ambition, materialistic power, manipulative scheming to control all via all avenues of government, and the ruthless cornering of the power that the amassing of money wields. The other group are the members of the white brotherhood, the caring intelligentsia, aspirants and disciples to the Masters of Wisdom that have evolved to generate group glory and Love-Wisdom, by passing the respective Initiation testings (ruled by the sign Capricorn). In between them lies the bewildered and long suffering average humanity, that are the pawns of the materialistic schemes of one group, and a field of service for the other.

The meaning of the word *Space* was given in Stanza 1:1 in relation to the phrase 'The Eternal Parent (Space)'. There it was stated that Space is an Entity and was associated with the word 'God'.

We can view *'dark space'* (33) in terms of the primordial substance of the universe (the 'Darkness alone' of Stanza 1:5) within which each solar Logos carves out a domain, a sphere of activity to be conquered by Light. Dark space may act as a medium via which light may travel, but is not yet organised by the light source in such a way that it manifests in the form of a radiant sun. It may be likened to the hypothetical 'dark matter' and 'dark energy' of modern physicists. It therefore is the background substance not included as the *manvantaric* cycle of a solar Logos. Yet within the domain of the *maṇḍalas* circumscribed by solar Logoi as Their bodies of manifestation there is also the arena of dark substance (the basis of ignorance) that is slated to be converted during that cycle of activity. Because of that conversion process we can see that 'bright Space' is the 'Son of dark space'. 'Dark space' is the substance of cosmic Mind before being activated by coherent Logoic Thought.

This substance contains the seeds of intelligence (33), the primal Fiery Elementals that will eventually evolve into Creative Intelligences, once they have been incorporated within the ring-pass-not of a manifesting planetary Logos. *'Bright Space'* (54, 18) then represents the evolved Light bearers, the Initiates (2 x 9), Chohans, Dhyānis (6 x 9, signifying the energy Body of the Monad) that manifest the basis of Logoic 'unparalleled refulgent Glory'.

Astrologically 'bright Space' can be viewed to be symbolised by Aquarius the water bearer, where the wavy lines of its glyph symbolise the energy dispensation of the compassionate Ones (Bodhisattvas) that emanate Glory. The Water they pour from the urns of their Heart centres is that of the liberating activity that is their purpose. This is symbolised by the number twelve of the phrase *'Son of dark space'* (3 x 7, 12), signifying the Heart of Life from which such activity emanates.

'Dark space' is ruled by Virgo, the great Mother, and is the *deva* substance of her Womb, from which the Light-bearing Child is born. Darkness here need not be black, but can also refer to deep indigo blue. 'Dark space' is also the general substance *(citta)* of the mental plane (15), of which the phenomenal appearance of things in the manifest world is the reflection. From here the Creative Intelligences (33) evolve to eventually manifest in the form of the substance constituting 'bright Space'. The *devas* of the form thereby become *arūpa,* solar *devas.*

The number 3 x 7 informs us that his 'Son' is an expression of the qualities of the spiritual triad, *ātma, buddhi, manas,* the energies conveyed by the eighth to tenth Creative Hierarchies (the number 12). The number 3 x 7 also refers to a triad of astrological forces, Taurus, Aquarius and Virgo, where the Eye of Dangma (Taurus) reveals and circumscribes the arena of the sphere of 'dark space' to be acted upon by the Lords of Life (Aquarius). If we include the other astrological sign so far mentioned (Capricorn) then the three Earth signs are included (Taurus, Virgo and Capricorn) that are acted upon (in the form of versions of 'dark space') by the three different levels of the Waters of Life being poured forth by Aquarius:

1. The energies of the physical sun – Virgo, of the *devas* that come into activity to organise substance and to build the forms that will eventually evolve into conscious units.
2. The energies of the Heart of the sun – Taurus the domain of activity that becomes the home environment of the Logos. Logoic Desire comes into play to bring forth the conscious units that will evolve the wisdom associated with this sign. The solar *devas* consequently build the Causal forms of humanity. Thus we have the appearance of all the material comforts needed by those that evolve within this sphere and which provides the sustenance and needed attributes that the solar children must evolve by.
3. The energies of the central Spiritual Sun – Capricorn, where the sum of *karma* and materialistic activity must be mastered upon the mount of experience, so that liberation can be gained and the Door to Monadic Life be opened.

The numbers 6 x 7, 15 of the phrase *'the depths'* refer to the ocean of substance, the entire material realm (6 x 7) as governed by the *maṇḍala* of the hexagram, and to the minds (15) that evolve in it.

That which *'emerges from the depths'* (103, 31) is the entire sphere of activity (103) instigated by the Will of the Creative Deity (31) producing the birthing process governed by Cancer the crab. The new incarnation of the planetary Logos thus commences, causing the mass Life governed by this sign to appear into objectivity. It should also be noted that the phrase 'the depths' also hints at the sign Cancer, to the watery environment of a crab, from which it emerges to forage on the shoreline of a ocean or estuary, generally at the dawn or dusk of a new day. With respect to this the entire phrase *'who emerges from the depths of the great dark Waters'* (200 + 12, 14) veils the qualities of the three Watery signs. We thus have:

a. *The depths* – Cancer the crab and the appearance of the sum of the *maṇḍala* of the world of form.

b. *Dark Waters* – Scorpio the scorpion, referring here to the depths of the swamp wherein resides the nine-headed Hydra that embodies the sum of the personality allurements in *saṃsāra*. The disciple must battle the Hydra in this sign upon the path of Initiation and rise triumphant, by sinking to his knees in humbleness, raising the monster away from the swamp into the air, as did Hercules.

c. *The great dark Waters* – Pisces the fishes, referring here to the sum of *saṃsāra* wherein the bonded 'fish' swims. It is linked by means of its bond to the Monad, which 'swims' in the Waters of the cosmic astral ocean.

The number 14 above refers to the second plane, the astral, whilst the number 200 + 12 refers to the Christ, the consciousness principle that emerges from 'the Depths' as a consequence of passing the tests of Initiation. It can also refer to the Logos who emerges from the depths of the cosmic astral ocean to establish a Seat of Power upon the 'dry land' of systemic (cosmic dense) space.

The number 5 x 11 of the phrase *'who emerges',* with respect to our earth Scheme, refers to the Lords of Flame who, with Sanat Kumāra, establish Shambhala. If our focus is upon the Initiation process, through passing the tests in Scorpio, it refers to those that consequently master all attributes of the Waters, thereby becoming Masters of Wisdom. The number also refers to the Fiery principle, the bearers of mind/Mind that emerge from out of the depths of the Waters.

The number 100 + 22 of the phrase *'who emerges from the depths'* refers to the constituency of the Womb of the Creative Logos that thereby come into objective manifestation.

The number 3 x 13 of the phrase *'dark Waters'* refers to the activity cycle wherein exist the conditions of the swamp of emotional and desire entanglements, which must consequently be mastered if one is to emerge from 'the depths'. This number refers to that period in time when the third Ray cycle dominates, with the evolutionary emphasis therefore being the life in the form. If 'dark space', refers to the mental plane (or the substance of Logoic Mind), then the phrase 'dark Waters' refers to the astral plane, to the period of activity when the Watery energies condition evolutionary space, specifically once humanity have evolved their desire and emotional attributes, generating the types of activities that muddy up the Waters and make them 'dark'. (Before that the systemic astral realm did not exist.)

"The great dark Waters', 6 x 13, 2 x 12) relates to the cosmic Waters, here referring to the Waters in which Pisces the fishes 'swim'. Pisces contains the Door to the cosmic eighth sphere, wherein the Darkness, the dark brotherhood of the former evolutionary space, plus the 'failures' of that system who did not make the evolutionary grade (also symbolised by the number 13 x 6) await release to continue their evolution according to the auspices of *karma*. They must also be granted opportunity to evolve according to the law, to play their appointed roles at the appropriate cycle. The prisoners of time are released to play their roles in time. They represent the unregenerate *saṃskāras* of the Logos that must yet be converted. The Logos is thereby a 'Son of Necessity' (see Stanza 1:6).

The number 12 x 2 refers to the sign Taurus the bull, governing the substance of the Waters of cosmic astral space, thus the principle of cosmic Desire that conditions the evolution of the Hierarchies of Lives that travel through it. Taurus is literally the cosmic Womb or Egg *(hiraṇyagarbha)* within which the forces of the above Watery trinity are contained.

The Waters are also dark because the qualities of Light have not yet evolved to reveal their intensities and qualities therein, the Christ has not yet risen. One can also look to the night sky and its darkness to represent these 'dark Waters', within which are innumerable pinpoints of light that are spheres of 'bright Space'.

The numbers 66 x 2, 6 x 7 of the phrase *'the depths of the great dark Waters'* directly imply the substance of the material world, the sum of the Bodies of manifestation (the lesser Lives) of the Logoi that evolve in the depths of the Waters. These Lives are collectively the form of the Christ-Child that must eventually make the return journey to cosmic astral space. 'Bright Space' is then the result. This is the accomplishment of the evolutionary journey of a Humanity in 'the depths of the great dark Waters' that evolves the illumination of enlightenment. Eventually all beings stand within the confines of their Monads.

The number 7 x 7 of the phrase *'from the depths of the great dark Waters'* refers to the various septenaries that emerge from these depths, the bearer of the seven *chakras* (or centres of Light) and their sub-centres, with the complete expression of the related energies. All seven

Rounds, Chains, globes, etc., thus emerge from the depths. Specifically however, with respect to the higher mental plane, the numbers relate to the Ray and subray groupings of the kingdom of Souls that emerge from these 'depths'.

The numerical breakdown of the eighth to eleventh phrases:

> It is Oeaohoo (59, 14), The Younger (57, 6.6., 12), The * * * (15, 6.6.6), He shines forth (73, 19), shines forth (60, 15), as the Sun (26, 17), the Sun (24, 15), shines forth as the Sun (86, 32), He shines forth as the Sun (99, 36), the blazing divine Dragon (116, 26), Divine Dragon (68 = 17 x 4, 14), he is the blazing divine Dragon (139, 31), Dragon of Wisdom (73, 19), divine Dragon of Wisdom (109, 28), The blazing divine Dragon of Wisdom (157, 40), he is the blazing divine Dragon of Wisdom (180, 45).

It was earlier shown that the vowel sounds of *Oeaohoo* refer principally to the manifestation of the seven Creative Hierarchies. The name can also refer to the composite of five mantric seed syllables that govern the five steps of the evolutionary process whereby the Wisdoms of the Dhyāni Buddhas are eventually gained by the aspiring units of consciousness. *Oeaohoo* thus determines the entire evolutionary milieu. As an Entity it stands as the Compassionate emanation of a solar Logos in the overall scheme of things, and as such its general qualities can astrologically be governed by the sign Aquarius the water bearer, who directs the Waters of the cosmic astral Ocean (Love) into manifestation. Here however, it is qualified by the appellation 'the younger', which thereby allows us to assign an Identity to the younger Oeaohoo, as our planetary Logos, who reflects the attributes of the solar Logos into our earth Scheme.

There is therefore a juxtaposition of two Logoi, one overshadowing the other, seen astrologically as the sign Gemini the twins, where the solar Logos becomes the older, overshadowing immortal brother, and our planetary Logos the mortal one. The interrelation produces a unique Temple of the Mysteries concerning solar evolution, that can be gained by the Initiated ones qualified to preside at the adytum of this temple. It veils the energies of the cosmic Christ, whose portals leading to the Heart of the Sun can be opened.

The Secret Doctrine then omits the true name of our planetary Logos. This name cannot be provided exoterically because of the inherent dangers to those who would prematurely invoke its potency. Premature revelation could invoke His gaze, bringing with it a consequent downpour of energies upon those not prepared to bear them. Nevertheless we can now be provided with some of His characteristics, starting with the phrase *'He shines forth'* (10), which informs us that He does so in the form of the ten planetary Chains (seven exoteric and three synthesising ones) that constitute His Form, and that it is His etheric Body that 'shines'.

The energy of this radiance is fired by Sagittarius, illuminating the target area with Logoic Thought constructs. The complete radiance of the sun however is Leonine. This is verified by the numbers 60 (5 x 12) of the phrase *'shines forth'*. The number 60 also refers to the Sacral centre of Deity that is responsible for the manifestation of that form. This centre supports the internal heat that energises the vitality (the health aura) of the form and its magnetism. There is also the conveyance of *prāṇa* through the *nāḍīs* that are responsible for the subjective radiance of the entity, depending upon the state of evolution of the *prāṇas.* To be able to shine 'forth as the Sun' necessitates a high stage of evolutionary attainment, and when the numbers 99, 36 of the phrase *'He shines forth as the Sun'* is taken into account then the implication is that the being in question here is Sanat Kumāra, the 'One Initiator' (9 x 11), 'the Silent Watcher', the 'Youth of Endless Summers'. He is the Avatar of the Logos of our earth Scheme. This One will be explained in detail later, the introduction suffices here.[19] That He takes the semblance of a sun also implies that He is a Chela of the solar Logos, and therefore esoterically travels the same cosmic Path as that One. (The number 36 refers to the sign Gemini the twins, already treated above.) That He is a Logos is signified by the number 17 of the phrase *'as the sun'*.

With respect to the above Blavatsky provides an explanatory footnote to the missing true name of the Logos: 'Whom thou knowest now as Kwan-Shai-Yin'.[20] This is the Chinese rendering of Avalokiteśvara,

19 See my book *The Constitution of Shambhala* for an explanation of this great One in context to the manifestation of a planetary Head lotus.

20 The S.D., Vol. 1, 71.

the downward-looking Lord of Compassion, who has gained the result of the entire evolutionary process, but sees the struggles of those still incarnate in the manifest realms and has vowed to never cease striving until all sentient Beings have be liberated. All Logoi are Lords of Compassion, choosing to incarnate to liberate those entities that form part of their Bodies of manifestation. Sanat Kumāra represents the ideal prototype of such Ones.

The numbers of the phrase *'shines forth as the sun'* add to 32, referring to the Love-Wisdom energy of Deity, which is the central animating dynamo of this sun. There is thus active Love and Wisdom manifested as compassion and directed by the animating Will of Deity via the agency of a physical form, its Sacral centre, which provides the physical and subjective radiance that sustains the Lives evolving within the solar form.

The numbers of the phrase *'The Younger'* add to 12, as well as to the number 6.6.6., when the number 6 of the following 'The ***' is added. The number 6.6.6. was earlier explained to signify the body of manifestation of a Logos. The number 12 informs us that Sanat Kumāra embodies the 'younger' or subsidiary Heart centre, via which pours the qualities associated with the twelve Creative Hierarchies into the planetary manifestation. There is thus an implication of the direct overshadowing of a greater Heart centre over another, to produce a cosmic alignment that places the solar Logos in an ideal position to be able to influence planetary affairs regarding the evolution of the earth humanity when necessary. This safeguarding is important, considering the failure of the moon Chain, plus the fact of the second Ray Monadic qualification of most of this humanity, which is the same Ray line governing the solar Logos, thus facilitating the line of approach to influence planetary affairs.

H.P.B's essential commentary:

> "Bright Space, son of dark Space," corresponds to the Ray dropped at the first thrill of the new "Dawn" into the great Cosmic depths, from which it re-emerges differentiated as Oeaohoo, the Younger (the "new LIFE"), to become to the end of the life-cycle the germ of all things. He is "the Incorporeal man who contains in himself the divine Idea," — the generator of Light and Life, to use an expression

of Philo Judæus. He is called the "Blazing Dragon of Wisdom," because, firstly, he is that which the Greek philosophers called the Logos, the Verbum of the Thought Divine; and secondly, because in Esoteric Philosophy this first manifestation, being the synthesis or the aggregate of Universal Wisdom, Oeaohoo, "the Son of the Son," contains in himself the Seven Creative Hosts (The Sephiroth), and is thus the essence of manifested Wisdom. "He who bathes in the light of Oeaohoo will never be deceived by the veil of Maya."

Kwan-Shai-Yin is identical with, and an equivalent of the Sanskrit *Avalōkitēshwara,* and as such is an androgynous deity, like the Tetragrammaton and all the Logoi of antiquity. It is only by some sects in China that he is anthropomorphized and represented with female attributes, when, under his female aspect becoming Kwan-Yin, the goddess of mercy, called the "Divine Voice." The latter is the patron deity of Thibet and of the island of Puto in China, where both deities have a number of monasteries.[21]

The numbers of the phrase *'the Sun'* add to 2 x 12, referring to the zodiacal and Hierarchical energies that together constitute the blaze of energies that can be seen in the form of the Sun. This illumination is facilitated by the energies of Taurus, the second sign of the zodiac, and the Eye of illumination. It represents the integrating substance causing the radiation of the sun and the rest of its body of manifestation, producing the one great 'home environment' between Oeaohoo the greater and the lesser Logos.

Concerning the Dragon, H.P.B states:

The "Dragon of Wisdom" is the One, the "Eka" (Sanskrit) or Saka... The "One" and the Dragon are expressions used by the ancients in connection with their respective Logoi. Jehovah — esoterically (as Elohim) — is also the Serpent or Dragon that tempted Eve, and the "Dragon" is an old glyph for "Astral Light" (Primordial Principle), "which is the Wisdom of Chaos." Archaic philosophy, recognizing neither Good nor Evil as a fundamental or independent power, but starting from the Absolute ALL (Universal Perfection eternally), traces both through the course of natural evolution to pure Light condensing gradually into form, hence becoming Matter or Evil... The primitive symbol of the serpent symbolised divine Wisdom and

21 Ibid., Vol. 1, 71-72.

Perfection, and has always stood for psychical Regeneration and Immortality. Hence — Hermes, calling the serpent the most spiritual of all beings; Moses, initiated into the Wisdom of Hermes, following suit in Genesis; the Gnostic's Serpent with the seven vowels over its head, being the emblem of the seven hierarchies of the Septenary or Planetary Creators. Hence, also, the Hindu serpent Sesha or Ananta, "the Infinite," a name of Vishnu, whose first Vahan, or vehicle, on the primordial waters is the serpent.[22] Yet they all made a difference between the good the bad Serpent (the Astral Light of the Kabalists) — between the former, the embodiment of divine Wisdom in the region of the Spiritual, and the latter, Evil, on the plane of matter.[23] Jesus accepted the serpent as a synonym of Wisdom, and this formed part of his teaching: "Be ye wise as serpents," he says. "In the beginning, before Mother became Father-Mother, the fiery Dragon moved in the infinitudes alone," *(Book of Sarparajni).* The Aitareya Brahmana calls the Earth Sarparājni, the "Serpent Queen," and "the Mother of all that moves." Before our globe became egg-shaped (and the Universe also), "a long trail of Cosmic dust (or fire mist) moved and writhed like a serpent in Space." The "Spirit of God moving on Chaos" was symbolised by every nation in the shape of a fiery serpent breathing fire and light upon the primordial waters, until it had incubated cosmic matter and made it assume the annular shape of a serpent with its tail in its mouth — which symbolises not only Eternity and Infinitude, but also the globular shape of all the bodies formed within the Universe from that fiery mist. The Universe, as also the Earth and Man, serpent-like, periodically cast off periodically, serpent-like, their old skins, to assume new ones after a time of rest...The "Dragon" was also the

---

22 Blavatsky's footnote here is: 'Like the *logoi* and the Hierarchies of Powers, however, the "Serpents" have to be distinguished one from the other. Sesha or Ananta, "the couch of Vishnu," is an allegorical abstraction, symbolizing infinite Time in Space, which contains the germ and throws off periodically the efflorescence of this germ, the *manifested* Universe; whereas, the Gnostic *Ophis* contained the same triple symbolism in its seven vowels as the One, Three and Seven-syllabled *Oeaohoo* of the Archaic doctrine; *i.e.,* the One Unmanifested Logos, the Second manifested, the triangle concreting into the Quaternary or Tetragrammaton, and the rays of the latter on the material plane'.

23 Blavatsky's footnote here is: 'The Astral Light, or the Æther, of the ancient pagans (for the name of Astral Light is quite modern) is Spirit....Matter. Beginning with the pure spiritual plane, it becomes grosser as it descends, until it becomes the *Maya,* or the tempting and deceitful serpent on our plane'.

> symbol of the Logos with the Egyptians, as with the Gnostics. In the "Book of Hermes," Pymander, the oldest and the most spiritual of the Logoi of the Western Continent, appears to Hermes in the shape of a Fiery Dragon of "Light, Fire, and Flame."[24]

In this lengthy quote H.P.B relates the dragon to the evolution of the serpent. The nature of the evolution of a dragon can be considered if we take a desirable *saṃskāra* of a consciousness-attribute, or rather, a bundle of five that are related to the five sense-consciousnesses. Then if we view the evolution of the *saṃskāra* over time we see that it manifests a serpentine motion and grows from inception, the point of the tail of a serpent, to manifesting an increasingly thicker body as various attributes of mind are evolved. Eventually a head is formed with decidedly Fiery *prāṇas*. Then as the Airy Element is incorporated the moving serpent grows 'wings'. Myriads of such moving *saṃskāras* over time eventually show the stage of evolution of the consciousness-stream concerned. Upon the Initiation path, and the consequent liberation of *kuṇḍalinī,* there is the appearance of the mythical Fiery breath of a dragon. In a human unit the process is completed at the fifth Initiation. A Master, specifically along the Rays of Mind, is consequently given the acronym 'Dragon of Wisdom'. The breath of the dragon manifests in the form of Mahat (Universal Mind, cosmic Intelligence).

This brief outline relating such a development for a human kingdom has its parallel Logoically. The movement of Logoi over time can therefore also be viewed as that of large Dragons flying through cosmic space. Also, within their bodies of manifestation dragons of all colourations and sizes exist. They have a special relation to Logoic *kuṇḍalinī,* and can be considered a highly specialised class of *deva.* One should also consider the esoteric reasons why the constellations Draco and Fornax are so named.

Esoterically, serpents refer primarily to the *prāṇas* producing *siddhis,* or to *kuṇḍalinī,* so a dragon is accordingly one that has mastered those energies. He can perfectly express the Fiery Element in the form of the Fiery Breath of Life. He is the Master of Wisdom and embodies the qualities associated with the five realms of Brahmā in such a way

24 Ibid., Vol. 1, 73-74.

that control the substance and entities in the formed realms in any way willed. The dragon is the moving dynamo of the Fiery principle governing the entire evolutionary process in the material realms.

The specific *'Dragon of Wisdom'* (10) concerning us here is that of our planetary Logos, who has manifested a Throne or Seat of Power for our planetary Scheme (10).[25] What differentiates Him from other Dragons is that He is a *'The blazing divine Dragon'* (100 + 16), whilst the numbers of the phrase *'divine Dragon of Wisdom'* add to 100 + 9, 4 x 7). Here the number 4 x 7 refers to the fourth or earth Scheme. The other numbers relate to Sanat Kumāra being styled 'the One Initiator', and that he is a cosmic Christ (100 + 16). The term *divine* concerns that associated with or derived from 'God', who's Purpose Sanat Kumāra manifests for all Life on earth. He is a special dispensation, an Avatar, thus *'Divine Dragon'* (17 x 4) of the Logoic Soul of our planetary Scheme, and in the esoteric doctrine is styled 'the Silent Watcher' for all pilgrims upon the Initiation path (100 + 9). There is a Spiritual triad – the Avatar of Synthesis, the Spirit of Peace, and the Mother of the World, that represent the Trinity, via which the presiding Logos works. Sanat Kumāra represents the mechanism of the 'fall' of the above Three into 'the Four' for our planetary dispensation (symbolised by the number 17 x 4). There is a reflected three Kumāras, the Buddhas of Activity, via which this process of the 'fall' manifests so as to condition the Lives evolving within the material domain.[26]

The number 17 x 4 thus refers to the fact that this 'Divine Dragon' embodies the sum of the Personality nature of Deity via Sanat Kumāra. He comes with His three brothers, the Buddhas of Activity, Who become the four Kumāras that constitute the Throne of the abstract Logos. What comes 'of Wisdom' is the perfect expression of the Fires of the Mind, embodied by the 'Divine Dragon', the Personality aspect of Deity.

The number (100 + 13 x 3, 31) of the phrase *'he is the blazing divine Dragon'* implies that this Dragon is the embodiment of the sum of the Creative activity within the confines of the planetary sphere,

---

25 One should note here that all forms are mind/Mind conditioned, hence upon the inner realms the dragon form is but an expression of the Creative powers of the Mind that creates such a form as a body of expression.

26 Detail of this information is provided in my book *A Constitution of Shambhala*.

that causes world formation and the evolution of the lives upon it. He bears the potency of active manifestation through the use of the Logoic Will (31). This fundamental first Ray quality intensifies the blaze of the Dragon. Sanat Kumāra projects many *antaḥkaraṇas* from cosmic sources to help salvage the situation upon the earth to try to overcome the disastrous events upon the moon Chain. Intensified energies are needed to help produce a blazing forth of divinity in the minds of those that are stricken with darkened *prāṇas* from misdeeds hearkening back aeons ago. The dark brotherhood upon this earth will inevitably be defeated with the impact of this rectifying blaze of Fiery Divine Breath. Its transforming Might will produce the new era. The process nevertheless is one of slow, though increasingly quickening, conversion of the dark mind-set. The final major battles of conversion upon our earth globe will properly begin from the ending of the present fifth Aryan cycle, and will produce its final conclusion in this solar cycle in the next (fifth) planetary Chain.

The number 40 of the phrase *'the blazing divine Dragon of Wisdom'* indicates that he is the Logos for the fourth globe (the earth) of the fourth Scheme and its humanity, which is also ruled by this number.

The numbers 180 = 9 x 20 and 45 of the phrase *'he is the blazing divine Dragon of Wisdom'* indicates his role as the One Initiator (9 x 20) for all that are walking the path of developing Love-Wisdom (20) upon our planet, and as such is the Master of Masters (9 x 5) of the sum of our planetary Hierarchy.

Astrologically the constellations Draco and Fornax are directly associated with the dragon. Also two of the signs of the zodiac can be considered to be thus associated. The first is Capricorn, under the auspices of the crocodile (and Makara) that lives both in the water and land. This reptile embodies the qualities of *kāma-manas* and represents the early stage of the evolution of the dragon, where the Watery quality must be mastered by the evolution of the Fires of mind/Mind. *Manasic* Fire is then ruled by Capricorn, and all of the attributes of the mental plane, from systemic to cosmic Mind (Mahat) are implied. Capricorn represents the substance of the body of the dragon and the fuel of its Fiery Breath.

Next is Libra the balances. In this case the dragon's body is curled around the upright stand of the balances (which symbolises the central spinal column), with the dragon holding the fulcrum of the balances in its mouth. It thereby determines the *karma* of the left and right pans, of the outcome of the battle between the way of Love and that of mind. A proper equilibrium can then be produced, and that is the evocation of Wisdom. Libra stands as the adjudicator between Draco, which can be considered to wield cosmic Fire, and Capricorn, which governs what can be considered crystallised Fire. The associated plane is *ātma,* ruling the sum of the planes of Brahmā. Libra holds the key to the liberation of the mind and the right containment of Fire. Thus a Dragon of Wisdom comes under the rule of this sign.

When the appellation 'blazing' is considered, then the concern is with an advanced stage of development, signifying the intensification of the Fires caused by the liberation of *kuṇḍalinī.* The energies from the Fire signs are then utilised, where the Arian impetus (the polar opposite of Libra) awakens and fans the Fire. Sagittarius directs its purpose, and Leo embodies the complete extent of its blaze, as an embodied sun. Draco represents the repository for the dragon lore and Lives, but draws the Fires from Fornax the Furnace that causes the blazing forth of Mind in all of its attributes.

The four main Elements from a cosmic perspective are expressed in these four Fiery signs:

- Draco – a source of cosmic Intelligence (Mahat) demonstrates the Airy principle of this quaternary, hence manifests the 'home' for the dragon kingdom. (They have wings and can fly.) The Airy Element fans the Fires of Mahat and refines its attributes, so that the Breath of the dragon emanates a transforming force, as well as its inherent Creative potency.

- Fornax – expresses the Fiery Element, and represents the place wherein cosmic *kuṇḍalinī* is generated, which feeds the Fiery Breath of the dragon kingdom, the inherent Power of their Lore.

- Libra – adds the Watery flux that allows it to balance the Fires and so demonstrate the cosmic Law of *karma,* the Way that will inevitably express the Compassionate might of Logoi.

- Capricorn – represents the means of the empowerment of Earthy Fires in the cosmic landscape.

So far all twelve of the signs of the zodiac have appeared in this Stanza. Firstly we considered the three Earth signs (in relation to the phrase 'Son of dark space') that help to establish the appearance of the phenomena of the Chains and globes of a Scheme. Next was introduced the three Water signs, who manifest their outpourings of the streams of Life. (They are seen in the phrases 'the depths', 'dark waters' and 'great dark waters'.) They are the empowering energies that will embody the forms created by the Earth signs. They also represent the astral Waters enveloping the Earthy Element. Finally we have the appearance of the Airy and Fiery signs. These signs relate to the qualities to be developed by the evolving human kingdom via the mind, and then the higher principles that produce enlightenment.

The expression of the three signs governing the Fiery Element has been provided above. Of the Airy signs Aquarius is seen governing the functions of 'bright space' and Oeaohoo the younger, whilst Gemini governs the general interrelation between Oeaohoo the older and the younger. Libra is the balance interrelating all of the signs.

One can also look to the early stages of the evolution of the Root Races. Following from the sign Pisces. Aries starts the new cycle with the Fiery inception of Adamic man. The second Hermaphroditic Root Race is then governed by the sign Taurus the bull in the form of the fertilised egg, *hiraṇyagarbha,* the splitting into two of the zygote. Gemini governed the early formative period of the Lemurian Root Race, when they were primarily still etheric in constitution and struggling to master the proclivities of the dense form. With respect to this, and concerning the astrological conditionings governing the Individualisation process of the earth humanity, D.K. states:

> I earlier gave a hint upon which definite astrological computation could be based when I gave the time of the "Great Approach" of the Hierarchy to our planetary manifestation when individualization took place and the fourth kingdom in nature appeared. I placed that stupendous event as happening 21,688,345 years ago. At that time the Sun was *in Leo.* The process then initiated upon the physical plane and producing outer physical events took approximately 5,000 years to mature and the Sun was *in Gemini* when the final crisis of individualization took place and the door was then closed upon the animal kingdom.

> It has been stated that Sagittarius governs human evolution, as the Sun was in that sign when the Hierarchy began its Approach in order to stimulate the forms of life upon our planet. *Sagittarius, however, governed the period of the subjective approach.*
>
> The Sun was *in Leo* when physical plane individualization took place as a result of the applied stimulation.
>
> The Sun was *in Gemini* when this Approach was consummated by the founding of the Hierarchy upon the Earth.[27]

We would then have the Watery signs and Taurus, governing the early Atlantean period, with Leo manifesting at the end of the Atlantean cycle to produce the birth of the Aryan Root Race. Sagittarius governs the main aspects of the mental development of the fifth Root Race wherein the attributes of the will of mind are developed. Sagittarius fires its Fiery arrows of mind towards the mount of Initiation in Capricorn, wherein the divide between the forces of the dark brotherhood and the white brotherhood is resolved. Presiding over the general process is the sign Scorpio, producing the many tests of this fourth Creative Hierarchy, who are titled 'the Initiates', 'Lords of sacrifice'.[28] Libra cyclically turns the wheel of Life during the entire process to assist in the mastery of meditative pursuits, of understanding the law of *karma* and its rectification upon the mount. We see therefore that the entire play of the path to enlightenment is focussed upon the western quadrant of the zodiac.

The numerical breakdown of the ninth to the thirteenth phrases:

> The Eka is Chatur (59, 23), takes to itself Three (74, 29), Chatur takes to itself Three (100, 37), The union (43, 16), the Sapta (27, 9), produces the Sapta (65, 20), the union produces the Sapta (108, 36), The Seven (35, 8), The Tridasa (42, 15), The seven which become the Tridasa (135, 36), in whom are the Seven (87, 24, 5.5. 6.6.), in whom are the Seven which become the Tridasa (187, 52), become the Tridasa (67, 22), which become the Tridasa (100, 28), the Sapta in whom are the Seven (114, 33), the union produces the Sapta in whom are the Seven (195, 60), the Sapta

27 *Esoteric Astrology*, 63-64.

28 Ibid., 34.

in whom are the Seven which become the Tridasa (214, 88), the union produces the Sapta in whom are the Seven which become the Tridasa (295, 88), the Hosts (33, 15), the Multitudes (51, 15), the Hosts and the Multitudes (94, 31).

The Sanskrit numbers given imply the significance of 'the fall of the three into the four'. The Rounds, Chains and globes of earth evolution are implicated, as well as the septenaries that manifest in formed space.[29] The use of this language here, as all else in *The Secret Doctrine,* is not arbitrary. In this case it is a device bringing our vision from the end of the Atlantean epoch to the present era when Sanskrit is being used.

First there is the concept of the one in four, marking the first stage of the evolutionary process, wherein the four cosmic ethers are constructed, which channel the energies from the cosmic astral plane into systemic space (the cosmic dense physical plane). Next there is a further descent of 'the four', whereby the three lower planes are incorporated and the four etheric subdivisions of the physical plane come into activity.

Another way of interpreting these numbers is that *'the Eka'* refers to the triune planetary Logos, whereas *'Chatur'* is the fourth point, namely Sanat Kumāra. He then manifests via the three Buddhas of Activity. This makes the septenary, which is the foundation of the establishment of Shambhala. (Signified by the number 108 of the phrase *'the union produces the Sapta'.*) Shambhala becomes the vehicle for the second Ray dispensation that is the purpose of our solar Logos, which produces evolutionary perfection once attained, as signified by the number 100 of the phrase *'Chatur takes to itself Three'.*

The phrase *'The Eka is Chatur',* (the One is Four) thus instantly directs our vision from the overall picture of a Logoic sphere of influence throughout space and time (the moving serpent evolving into a Fiery Dragon of Wisdom) to that associated with his Head centre – the Throne of 'God'. Therein resides 'the One' that is 'the Four', the four Kumāras or Elohim that support and constitute the Throne upon which the One sits. Together they are responsible for the sum of manifestation (the four kingdoms, four Elements, plus the fifth the Soul aspect) in the four

---

29 See chapter 7 of *Esoteric Cosmology and Modern Physics* for an in-depth geometrical analysis of this fall.

directions in space. The One plus the Four produce the five Kumāras that embody the manifest qualities of the Mind of 'God' which is projected into/as the formed universe. (To which therefore, the number five governing this phrase refers.) From the perspective of the *chakras*, *'the Eka'* relates to the Head centre and Chatur to the four petals of the Base of Spine centre. When the two are aligned and integrated within the Thought-Construct of the Logos, the seven centres then come into existence to play their roles in evolutionary space.

When seeking the cause of manifest space, we look at the quaternary nature of Deity that is overshadowed by the One, the triune abstract Deity, which makes the esoteric seven.

Once the throne of 'God' (the base *chakra*) is established the embodied Deity is then seen in His integral form. The intensified energy from the spiritual triad can then be projected downwards into formed space and be anchored therein. This is implied by the numbers of the phrases *'takes to itself Three'* (11), and *'Chatur takes to itself Three'* (100). These numbers refer to the projection of the *sūtrātmā* (11) bearing first Ray energies from the spiritual triad via *buddhi* to cause the appearance of the complete body of manifestation (the *nāḍī* system) of the Logos. A complete zone of influence (100) thereby appears, such as a Scheme or globe, via the Three (e.g., the Buddhas of Activity) that are responsible for the evolutionary development of the kingdoms of Nature that will evolve within the established form.

When all of the numbers of the statements *'Eka is Chatur'*, *'and Chatur takes to itself Three'*, are observed then we get 8.1.8.1.8.2.8.8.11, implying the evocation of *kuṇḍalinī* (8.8., 1.1.), plus the emanation of spiral-cyclic energy that awakens the consciousness-bearing principle in the emerging world-sphere. This process is also an effect of the energies of the sign Scorpio the scorpion, who generally rules this Stanza and stage in the evolutionary process. The Scorpion 'stings' into activity cycle after cycle of evolutionary activity, whilst the sixth Ray via Scorpio provides the energies, the *ākāśa/prāṇa* that vitalises the sum of the activity of world formation. This is the effect of the reification of the Earthy *ākāśa* under the guidance of Amoghasiddhi's Wisdom.

The fall of the Four of the Throne of Deity into the three of manifest space bring into manifestation the seven Ray departments of Life. Here the appearance of the Seven Creative Hierarchies are implicated *('the Sapta',* from this perspective).

'The Sapta' (27, 9) are also the seven planetary Logoi (numerologically viewed as Initiates), the Regents of the seven Rays that produce the body of manifestation of a solar Logos. They find their reflection in the seven Regents of the Chains to a planetary Scheme. They are also the seven Kumāras, where there is an exoteric four united with the esoteric three.

'The Union' (16) is that between Eka and Chatur, Chatur and Three, which then links Eka to Three. The Eka and Chatur make the pentad of the Logoic Mind, the five Dhyāni Buddhas and their correspondences in planetary or solar manifestation. They are the conduits for the expression of Mahat into manifestation. The fall of the four into the three then express the potency of Mahat upon the mental plane. The sum of these forces impact upon the cosmic dense physical substance that is signified by the lower mental plane. The Idea-forms of what is to Be is sculpted thereon by the Logoic Mind.

From a lower perspective the statement *'Chatur takes to itself Three'* is translated as the 'fall of the three into the four', where the middle, fourth principle, reflects the Three into the three embodied principles, as the illusional fourth principle, the *māyā* of the phenomenal appearance that all are ensconced in.

Astrologically the sign Gemini the twins is also indicated, where Eka, the One, becomes the immortal brother, and 'Three', (here the reflection of the higher triune unity) becomes the mortal brother, united by Chatur (the four). Here Chatur becomes the Holy of Holies, the Door to the Mysteries of Initiation. Gemini also brings to the fore the Initiation process, here specifically the formation of the kingdom of Souls (the veiled Christ in the human form – 16), which possesses three main whorls of petals. The numbers 8.2.8.8.2, etc., of the phrase 'Chatur takes to itself Three' can also be interpreted from this perspective in terms of the potency of the second Ray of Love-Wisdom, which is the objective of this Incarnation process of the Logos.

The numbers 108 (Sagittarius) and 36 (Gemini) of the phrase *'the union produces the Sapta'* astrologically verify this Individuation process of a Logos. By the number 108 we have the implication of the simultaneous establishment of the kingdom of Shambhala, from which emanates 'the Sapta', the seven Rays, Spirits before the Throne, the seven Root Races of evolution etc., of our planetary evolution.

The numbers of the phrase *'produces the Sapta'* (13 x 5, 11, 20) refer to the first and second Ray energies, plus these of the Brahmā aspect (13 x 5), which are responsible for the emanation of the various septenaries.

Having established the planetary Head centre (Shambhala), the rest of the body of manifestation then forms, governed by the sign Taurus of the phrase *'in whom are the Seven'* (24, 5.5. 6.6.). Taurus (24) governs the principle of Logoic Desire and of the substance that is built into the Logoic construct, of the entire *manvantara* that now commences, as signified by the number 52 of the phrase *'in whom are the Seven which become the Tridasa'*. The numbers 5.5. and 6.6. are also incorporated in this phrase *('in whom are the'),* which relate to the interrelation between the mental and astral planes, or of the mind and its relation to the precipitating energies of desire.

The phrase *'the Seven'* (7 x 5) refers not only to the seven planetary Schemes and the seven *chakras* of planetary manifestation, but to the seven Creative Hierarchies, which inform the sum of solar space with Life. They also have their correspondences within our planetary Scheme. All thereby become clothed in consciousness (7 x 5), which is the basis of the evolution of the man-plant. They *'become the Tridasa'* by reflecting planetary and zodiacal energies (the number 22 of this phrase) into manifestation by means of the associated Creative Intelligences, the hierarchies of *deva* workers.

The numbers of the phrase *'the Seven which become the Tridasa'* add to 27 x 5, 36. The number 36 in relation to the sign Gemini has been explained above, whilst here it can refer to the fact that 'the Seven' refer to the functions of the mortal brother, and the *tridaśa* refer to the 'immortal brother', who are directly concerned with governing the attributes of the manifesting form. The number 27 x 5 refers to the ramifications of the forces of Mahat (5) to the sum of the Initiated bearers of Mind (27), where the number 27 refers to the third degree Initiate who has mastered the attributes of the higher mental plane. These bearers of Mind are also expressed as the *tridaśa*. Concerning them H.P.B. states in her footnote:

> "Tri-dasa," or Thirty, three times ten (30), alludes to the Vedic deities, in round numbers, or more accurately 33 — a sacred number. They are the 12 Adityas, the 8 Vasus, the 11 Rudras, and the 2 Aswins—the twin sons of the Sun and Sky. This is the root-number of the Hindu Pantheon, which enumerates 33 crores, or over three hundred millions of gods and goddesses.[30]

There is no need to enter into the minefield of philosophic speculation based upon the varying accounts of these deities from the Vedas, hence I shall posit only a basic esoteric interpretation. The reader can enter into further study if so desired. The Ādityas are the twelve sons of Āditi, the infinite shoreless expanse of space. She can also be equated with *devamātri*, the Mother of the gods. The Ādityas thereby represent the major gods of the Hindu pantheon. They can also refer to the twelve signs of the zodiac. The Vasus are hosts, or vehicles (of consciousness) embodying the eight directions of space. The Rudras are aspects of Śiva, as the destroying and regenerative forces in Nature. The Aśvins are twin deities of the Vedas that appear in the sky before dawn in a golden carriage drawn by horses and have similar attributes as the twins Castor and Pollux of Gemini. They represent the reincarnating principle preparing the associated beings or forces to descend through the open gate of the next sign, Cancer.

The list is provided esoterically in the order given because first there is the circumscription of a ring-pass-not for the Logoic form, thereby creating a Womb of space and time. This Womb is delineated by the twelve zodiacal influences that condition the formation of Life within the enclosed space. Next are the eight arms of the cross of direction in space (the Vasus), determining which way the energies can flow. (This number can also be viewed in terms of the eight main *chakras,* if the dual Splenic centre is counted as one.) Evolving within this Womb are the 11 + 1 destroying and regenerative forces that produce the changes needed by consciousness to grow. One is added to the eleven Rudras according to whether the Rudra are allied to the mortal brother (Castor) or the immortal one (Pollux). This is determined by the factor of the 'fall of the three into the four'. These twelve forces can then be related

30 The S.D., vol. 1, 71. Note that a *crore* is 10,000,000, hence 33 *crore* is 330,000,000.

to the twelve planetary Regents ascribed esoterically or Hierarchically to the signs of the zodiac.

The numbers of the phrase *'the Tridasa'* add to 42, 15, informing us that the symbolic 330,000,000 Creative Intelligences symbolised by the term *tridaśa* are units of consciousness (15) in the process of evolving Mind as a consequence of the opportunity provided by the appearance of evolutionary space (6 x 7). They then incorporate *'the Hosts and the Multitudes'* (31)[31] of all the intelligent (15), as well as the lesser lives yet to evolve self-consciousness. All are but an expression of and directed by, the Will of the Logos (31).

The term 'hosts' means large bodies of people, or forces marshalled for war. The number 33 of the phrase *'the Hosts'* indicates that the Creative Intelligences are indeed implied here. They take unto themselves bodies of manifestation consisting of lesser evolved entities, *'the Multitudes'* (51, 15). The hosts are Intelligences, whilst 'the multitudes' are the entities constituting their external forms, the active embodiments of mind (15), as everything is infused with innate intelligence. The number 17 x 3 informs us that the multitudes represent the sum of the Body of activity of Deity.

The number 33 of the phrase *'the Sapta in whom are the Seven'* indicates that they produce the *tridaśa,* the symbolic 330,000,000 Creative Intelligences. The phrase *'the union produces the Sapta in whom are the Seven'* (60, Leo) concerns the Leonine function that embodies the 'I am' principle governing the evolution of mind in Nature, plus the appearance of the kingdom of Souls upon the higher mental plane. The numbers of the remaining two phrases, *'the Sapta in whom are the Seven which become the Tridasa'* and *'the union produces the Sapta in whom are the Seven which become the Tridasa'* are 200 + 14 and 88. The number 88 simply indicates that they are all expressions of the downward spiralling energies that sustain the duration of the *mahāmanvantara* that has appeared to accommodate the evolving

31 Note that in the text there is no comma between the word 'tridasa' and the phrase 'the Hosts and the Multitudes', but needs one both grammatically and numerologically. In the earlier listing of the Stanzas Blavatsky, on page 29 of *The Secret Doctrine,* has in capital letters: 'in whom are the Seven which become the Tridasa (or the Hosts and the Multitudes)'.

phenomena of the activity of 'the Multitudes'. The number 200 + 14 (2 x 7) refers to the reflection of one septenary from cosmic astral realms ('the Sapta') into manifest space ('in whom are the Seven') to produce the evolution of Love-Wisdom (200).

The numerical breakdown of the next two phrases:

> Behold him lifting (90, 18), the Veil (36, 9), lifting the Veil (77, 14), Behold him lifting the Veil (126, 27), unfurling it (61, 7), from east to west (55, 28), unfurling it from east to west (116, 35).

A new clause or section of Stanza 3:7 is now entered, starting with the word 'behold', because it asks us to refocus our vision to cosmic etheric space, thus to receive a new set of images concerning this 'divine Dragon of Wisdom'.

A veil is a transparent piece of cloth used to hide, conceal or disguise a person or thing. Esoterically it is a sheaf of substance (that which veils) that prevents the entry of light so that no one can properly see what is behind it. The early evolutionary epochs have to be shielded from the intensity of the Light of cosmos, otherwise the evolving Lives would be destroyed by the energy impact. The process of unveiling the barriers, the etheric webs, protecting 'the Hosts and the Multitudes' therefore happens slowly over the course of evolutionary time. This happens through the Initiation process, eventually attained by all, from the Logos down, and so the Light of the central Spiritual Sun will inevitably manifest in the depths of matter. (Thus the numbers of the phrase *'Behold him lifting'* add to 90, 18, signifying various levels of Initiation undertaking.) This allows the Logos to See therein, because the Darkness will then vanish and 'be no more'. This is synonymous with the act of lifting the veil. Conversely the Multitudes will then also envision the Logoic domains.

The number 3 x 12 of the phrase *'The Veil'* signifies the Etheric Body of the Logos (governed by the third sign, Gemini the twins). This also refers to the webs of etheric substance between each major *chakra,* preventing premature awakening of the *siddhis* associated with these flowers. Each *chakra* must therefore be rightly awakened under the law, and the (alchemical) process accomplished that will sufficiently refine the substance by burning away the obscuring webs.

Because it is the Dragon of Wisdom that lifts the 'Veil', so our vision must be focussed to view events from the perspective of the Shambhalic domains. It implies that Masters of Wisdom have evolved from evolutionary space that can do so. This implies that they have contacted the types of energies and Lives that the Logos works with.

The number 77 of the phrase *'lifting the Veil'* refers to the 777 incarnations, by means of which one can eventually evolve the qualities needed to lift the veils of the etheric web that bar entrance into the higher domains. For human units it concerns taking the fourth or higher Initiations, to which there are Logoic correspondences. This necessitates bringing into manifestation the intensity of energies that will burn away, to refine and transmute this veiling substance. It thus concerns the evolution of the ability to master the substance of the veil, to reveal what it hides. We are therefore asked to envision the process concerning the beginning of the entire course of evolution in the material domain right through to the end attainment for the purpose of repeated incarnations.

The numbers 14 x 9, 3 x 9 of the phrase *'Behold him lifting the Veil'* inform us that the process of lifting this Veil really only begins after the third Initiation (the first cosmic Initiation) is reached, signifying mastering of the material domain by means of Mind. The Initiate will then be poised to attain the fourth Initiation to enter into cosmic etheric space, producing the vast revelations that the overcoming of dense material substance will provide. The Initiate of the third is identified with the Sambhogakāya Flower, which veils the higher *arūpa* (formless) domains. The veil of the Temple of the Soul must be rent at the fourth Initiation, providing access to the 'Father's kingdom' of the Spirit.[32] The process of the original Logoic impulse will thereby be reversed. The Initiate can then travel to cosmic astral space by following the Way of Monadic return (14 x 9). When the Logos lifts the Veil it brings into manifestation an increasing amount of Light from cosmic astral sources, the intensity of the energies rents the substance of the etheric web of His sheaths, allowing escape by the Lives imprisoned within His body of manifestation. *Pralaya* then ensues.

---

32 *Matthew 27:51.* 'And, behold, the veil of the temple was rent in twain from the top to the bottom; and the earth did quake, and the rocks rent'.

The direction *west* refers to the direction outwards into manifestation, the field of service, via the gain of the entire evolutionary process, to which the sun must shine as it rises in the east and sets in the west. The *east* then refers to the Heart centre, the awakening of the energies from the Heart of Life that must enlighten and liberate the west. The general course of the evolutionary process is thus implied here. The number 7 of the phrase *'unfurling it'* implies the seven-layered nature, the material sheafs, planes of perception, constituting this veil, which must be unfurled layer by layer. It must be effectively unfurled seven times seven times (viz., the seven days of Creation in Genesis) before the task can be completed.

The numbers 30, 7 x 3 of the phrase *'east to west'* refer to the outer periphery of the kingdom of 'God', the ring-pass-not or sphere of activity bounded by the Creative Intelligences that constitute the Logoic Body of manifestation (30). This is related to the direction east, signifying the bounds of the expression of Divine activity. The number 7 x 3 refers to the three dense material sub-planes into which a Logos is endeavouring to manifest Light, thus the direction west, which becomes the sphere of liberating activity.

The number 5 x 11, 7 x 4 of the phrase *'from east to west'* refer to the perfected expression of the Fires of Mind by means of this unfurling process, conveying of complete Adeptship upon those that travel east to west. As the concern is with a Dragon of Wisdom, the energy that causes this unfurling is his Fiery Breath *(ātma),* and this must be accommodated in the Minds of those that are to obtain liberation from the ring-pass-not of the embodied form. Adeptship of Mind (5 x 11) then allows one to pass through cosmic etheric space to the cosmic Paths at the appointed time. (The *nirvāṇees* must presently wait until the sixth Initiation, however the fifth is the true accomplishment of the 'burning ground' of this Fiery Breath.) The number 7 x 4 refers to the *buddhic* plane which veils the nature of the cosmic space revealed by this unfurling process.

The numbers 100 + 16, 7 x 5 of the complete phrase *'unfurling it from east to west'* refers both to the Christ principle (16) that is evolved through the process of unfurling this veil, plus the fact that it is a cosmic Christ (100 + 16) that unfurls it. This is accomplished through the development of the mind (7 x 5) and then the evocation of wisdom. The result of this entire lifting and unfurling process is the vivication of a Planetary Head centre, a new Shambhala, by 'the Multitudes' that evolve out of the 'great dark Waters'. (The descent of the New Jerusalem upon the material domain, as explained in my book *The Constitution of Shambhala.)*

The numerical breakdown of the next two phrases:

> He shuts out the above (72, 27), the above (33, 15), the below (36, 9), leaves the Below (55, 19), the great illusion (78, 24), to be seen (31, 22), to be seen as the great illusion (111, 48), seen as the great illusion (96, 33), leaves the below to be seen (86 = 14, 41 = 5), leaves the below to be seen as the great illusion (166, 67 = 13).

Having introduced the general vision of the entire evolutionary process, of the purpose for the establishment of the form and repeated incarnation, the process of the formation of the Logoic sphere of activity can now be observed. Being shut out means that one is prevented from entering a particular type of environment, atmosphere or habitat, such as a room. It can also signify an inability to incarnate into a corporeal form.

As it is *'the above'* (33, 15) that is shut out, so the dense corporeal form of Deity concerns us here (that which is 'below'). It implies the entire gamut of evolution dominated by the material world and its Life. The energies of the spiritual triad ('the above') would produce a much too destructive intent upon the Life of the evolving form if expressed too soon, thus it is shut out. The number 33 refers to the Creative Intelligence constituting Shambhala, the sum of what is above and expressed in the form of the energy of the Triad. The process of the Creation of the various spheres of active Life has finished, thus the intensity of that energy is diminished, shut out, allowing those within the forms to pursue their appointed evolutionary progression.

The concept of 'shutting out' implies the use of a Door. The Doorway to the path of incarnation into matter consequently closes. By the closing of this Door the opportunity for any new Monads to find scope for evolutionary play (incarnation) for that particular solar or planetary cycle is shut, the quota for Incarnation into the planetary sphere has been achieved. Another Door will inevitably open, which produces Initiation into the domain of Life upon the path of ascent.

'The below' (36) refers to everything below the four cosmic ethers, governed by Gemini. This concerns the sum of *saṃsāra* and *māyā*, *'the great illusion'* (24 = Taurus, 13 x 6). The nature of this illusion, plus the mechanism of gaining liberation, is well explained in *A Treatise on Mind,* therefore little needs to be further explained, except in reference to the numbers of the various phrases. The numbers 24 and 13 x 6 refer to the sum of the field of desire, thus the desire for material comforts, sexuality, and for pleasurable things, governed by the sign Taurus the bull. The number 13 x 6 refers to the *maṇḍala* based upon the hexagrams delineating the Womb of Nature, the six-petalled lotus, the Sacral centre, which vitalises the entire form, and of attraction to other forms, thus the many relationships producing karmic entanglements with ever-changing phenomena.

The sign Gemini indicates that *'the above'* refers to the immortal brother, here representing all of the *chakras* above the diaphragm. The diaphragm here can be considered to be the fourth cosmic ether *(śūnyatā)*. Effectively then, everything concerning the evolution of mind into Mind (signified by the number 5 x 11 of the phrase *'leaves the below')* can be considered 'the below'.

The pronoun 'He' here refers to 'the Dragon of Wisdom' (governed by the sign Libra), indicating fields of activity stemming from the meditation-Mind. The numbers 72 = 6 x 12, 9 x 8, 27 of the phrase *'He shuts out the above'* would normally refer to the sign Virgo the virgin, thus to the entire material domain, for which 'the above' is shut out by means of the generation of the complete body of manifestation of the Logos, of all the sheaths (veils) of substance. Here the number 9 x 8 also refers to the Dragon as a high Initiate, who has the capacity to thus shut 'out the above' so that a proper evolutionary environment can be obtained for the streams of Life within the Womb of the great Mother (Virgo).

The number 72 also refers to the ideal life span of any incarnate being, for which duration the 'above' is shut out, for then, when a Buddha appears (an Initiate of the sixth or higher degrees) the Door has opened for entry for Life in the cosmic astral plane. This is the consequence of the path of Initiation (27), allowing the incarnate Lives to fully enter into the 'above'. Those from below who have attained the third Initiation (3 x 9) begin to truly pierce the Veils, which will allow the 'above' to be envisioned. Here also is implied the significance of the phrase *'to be seen'* (31, 22), which indicates the evolutionary process of being able to see and to develop the will to overcome (31) the vicissitudes of the *māyā* that is the way to liberation from *saṃsāra.* It takes much evolutionary time to be able to see the true nature of *'the great illusion',* the Womb of space and time (22). The disciple must then learn to project the *antaḥkaraṇas* to all the higher centres above the diaphragm, and eventually into cosmic space. (Signified by the number 111 of the phrase *'to be seen as the great illusion'.)* The numbers of this phrase also add to 48, referring to the sign Cancer the crab. Cancer is the open door of incarnation into the regions 'below', *saṃsāra,* but also represents the beginning to the ascent along the path of Initiation, signified by Capricorn, its polar opposite.

The numbers 14, 5 of the phrase *'leaves the below to be seen',* refer to the astral and mental planes, which are left 'to be seen' by the evolving lives in *saṃsāra.* We also have the number 7.7. appearing in the phrase *'be seen',* again informing us that the great illusion is what is experienced via the 777 incarnations of any entity. Everything associated with those incarnations are illusory, a constantly changing play of effects prompted by past causes that must work themselves out according to the various Laws of conservation of energy and its conversion from one form to another.

Next to be considered is the sign Scorpio the scorpion, of the phrase *'seen as the great illusion'* (96, 33), indicating the many tests, temptations, the various forms of human culpability and emotional nastiness (the stings of the Scorpion) that the intelligences (33) evolving through the *māyā* are engaged in. This entire Scorpionic play governs *saṃsāra.* Scorpio also governs the nature of the turning of the petals of the *chakras* (symbolised by the number 96). The *chakras* are not just viewed as those governing the human unit, but also their correspondences in Nature. The consequence of their awakening will allow the enlightened One to truly know that all is 'seen to be the great illusion'. The third Eye (possessing two lobes of 48 petals each) will have awakened, providing far-sighted vision into the domains of 'the above'.

The numbers of the complete phrase *'leaves the below to be seen as the great illusion'* add to 100 + 66, where the number 66 speaks for itself as the number par excellence signifying the 'great illusion', of the entire material universe, everything embodied as the form or incarnated into the form. The number 666 is the number of 'the beast' of the Book of Revelation, which is 'the number of a man'.[33] Here also is veiled the significance of the sixth Ray function, which generally governs people's activities in *saṃsāra*.

Finally, it should be noted that the signs of the zodiac mentioned in this section are those associated with the bottom half of the zodiacal wheel: Taurus, Gemini, Cancer, Leo, Virgo and Libra. The exception is Scorpio, to which they all lead, because the tests of discipleship are applied there, that if passed provide the revelations that lead to the upper section of the wheel, 'the above'. Initiation upon the summit of the mount of the entire material world in Capricorn is then accomplished.

The numerical breakdown of the remaining phrases:

> He marks (30, 12), the places (35, 8), He marks the places (65, 20), the shining Ones (76, 22), The places for the shining Ones (132, 33), He marks the places for the shining Ones (162 = 18 x 9, 45 = 9 x 5), The upper (46, 10), a shoreless sea of Fire (88, 34), sea of Fire (48, 21), a shoreless sea (47, 20), into a shoreless sea of Fire (110, 38), turns the upper into a shoreless sea of Fire (176 = 2 x 88, 50), The One (31, 13), manifested into the great Waters (126, 27), into the great Waters (84, 21), The One manifested (73, 19), the great Waters (62, 17), The One manifested into the great Waters (157, 40).

To *mark* is to make a line or object that serves to indicate position. What is here implied is the extension of the line to produce divine geometrisation, the projection of the blueprint for the future positioning of those ('the shining Ones') that will gain the objective of the entire evolutionary journey.

---

33 *Rev. 13:18:* 'Here is wisdom. Let him that hath understanding count the number of the beast: for it is the number of a man; and his number is Six hundred, threescore and six'.

The number 30 of the phrase *'he marks'* bears this out, as it relates to the divine activity that circumscribes the ring-pass-not of a Logoic sphere, hence the entire *maṇḍala* of what is to be. Also, the activity of marking the places refers to the function of Sagittarius the archer (which follows after the sign Scorpio), where 'the places' refer to the various targets the Archer fires his arrows to. The act of pulling the bow string to produce the required tension of energy to fire the arrows, plus measuring the distance of the target and its overall shape (the bull's eye), all symbolise this activity, as also do the numbers, 11, 20 and 13 x 5 of the phrase *'He marks the places'*. They relate to the use of the first, second and third Ray energies (of the 'target') to delineate the places for 'the shining Ones' (the enlightened). It concerns the future, when they have also developed these Ray qualifications as par the process of gaining enlightenment. The future is an integral expression of the Thought-Form of the Creative Deity. Everything was conceived of in Meditation since before 'the foundation of the world'.

The number 7 x 5 of the phrase *'the places'* refers to the domain of the abstract Mind where the 'shining Ones' that have mastered Mind will reside. The phrase therefore refers to the manifestation of the Hierarchy of Light upon the higher mental plane. Thus are established the places for all of the Ray Ashrams and their eventual fields of activity.

The term *shining* means emitting or reflecting rays of light, to glow brilliantly and to manifest in an elegant fashion. We see therefore that *'the shining Ones'* (22, 13) are those that emit their own Light, who reflect the radiance from the Head centre, or from their higher selves, specifically from the Monad. The generation of Light is the effect of the process of enlightenment, thus the 'shining Ones' are the enlightened, or the Causal forms of humanity. From a cosmological perspective, they are Lords of Shambhala, who embody planetary or solar spheres. (Blavatsky's footnote relates them to stars.) The number 22 here refers to the various planetary or solar Logoi, which en-Soul the form – the Regents of expression of planetary and zodiacal energies to any system. The number 13 refers to the various spheres of activity that these entities embody.

The phrase *'the shining Ones'* refers to those that have gained illumination after having climbed the mountain of Initiation (signified by the sign Capricorn the goat, that follows after Sagittarius). They are therefore Masters of the material domain and have developed radiant, shining auras.

The numbers of the phrase *'He marks the places for the shining Ones'* add to 18 x 9, 9 x 5. All Masters of Wisdom (9 x 5), Chohans, Logoi (18 x 9), the stars in the sky, have passed various Initiations, thus are similarly endowed. The entire path of Initiation is therefore implicated, from the first cosmic Initiation (the systemic third) to that which makes a Logos. All is planned and foreordained in the meditation of this Dragon of Wisdom. The stage is thus also set for the evolution of our spiritual Hierarchy and their final destination (in the stars).

The numbers 66 x 2 and 33 of the phrase *'the places for the shining Ones'* refer to all of the Logoic bodies of manifestation (66 x 2) and to the zones for activity for all the active Intelligences (33) within the confines of a solar form. Each can also be considered a 'shining One'. Each of these zones would be complete unto itself, a self-enclosed sphere of attainment, cells within the *maṇḍala,* the sum of which constitutes His body of manifestation. Each zone is a shining or radiant cell of Light within the One (boundless) sphere of Light that is the Logoic Meditation process. One must also look to the Causal forms of the kingdom of the Sambhogakāya Flower similarly as 'shining Ones'. They can also be considered Creative Intelligences, whose places are 'marked out' upon the higher mental domains.

'The upper' (10) is that which 'is above', here referring to what is above the material domain ruled by the mind, thus signifying the realm of the spiritual Triad, to the sum of the etheric Body of the Logos (10), the formless realms. *'The One'* here refers to the Monad that resides in this 'upper' domain. Its appearance is a direct expression of the manifest Will of the Logos, and this Will is expressed as dynamic Electricity, for as stated below; 'Electricity is an Entity'. Cosmic Electricity can be considered the expression of the Fiery *prāṇas* of the Logoic Mind (Fohat). The concern therefore in the last two paragraphs of Stanza 3:7 is the path of Monadic return. The 'shoreless sea of Fire' *(ākāśa)* is the domain of the cosmic astral ocean ('the great Waters') within which the Monad resides. We can see, by the juxtaposition of these two phrases, that these Waters are the essence of Fire. They are effectively the medium or flux whereby the energies of cosmic Mind can mould or adapt the crystallised Fire of the dense form to become the vehicle

of the Divine Prototype. It is so adapted so that what is known as Life can evolve from it.

Concerning *'the sea of Fire'* H.P.B. states:

> The "Sea of Fire" is then the Super-Astral *(i.e.,* noumenal) Light, the first radiation from the *Roo*t, Mulaprakriti, the undifferentiated Cosmic Substance, which becomes *Astral* Matter. It is also called the "Fiery Serpent," as above described. If the student bears in mind that there is but One Universal Element, which is infinite, unborn, and undying, and that all the rest — as in the world of phenomena — are but so many various differentiated aspects and transformations (correlations, they are now called) of that One, from Cosmical down to microcosmical effects, from super-human down to human and sub-human beings, the totality, in short, of objective existence — then the first and chief difficulty will disappear and Occult Cosmology may be mastered. All the Kabalists and Occultists, Eastern and Western, recognise (a) the identity of "Father-Mother" with Primordial *Æther,* or *Akāsha* (Astral Light); and (b) its homogeneity before the evolution of the "Son," cosmically *Fohat,* for it is Cosmic Electricity. "Fohat hardens and scatters the seven Brothers;" (Book III. Dzyan); which means that the primordial Electric Entity — for the Eastern Occultists insist that Electricity is an Entity — electrifies into life, and separates primordial stuff or pregenetic matter into atoms, themselves the source of all life and consciousness. "There exists a universal *agent unique* of all forms and of life, that is called Od, Ob, and Aour, active and passive, positive and negative, like day and night; it is the first light in Creation". (Eliphas Lévi's Kabalah): — the first Light of the primordial Elohim — the Adam, "male and female" — or (scientifically) ELECTRICITY AND LIFE.
>
> (c) The ancients represented it by a serpent, for "Fohat hisses as he glides hither and thither," in zigzags. The *Kabalah* figures it with the Hebrew letter Teth ט, whose symbol is the serpent which played such a prominent part in the Mysteries. Its universal value is nine, for it is the ninth letter of the alphabet, and the ninth door or the fifty portals, or gateways, that lead to the concealed mysteries of being. It is the magical agent *par excellence,* and designates in Hermetic philosophy "Life infused into primordial matter," the essence that composes all things, and the spirit that determines their form.[34]

34 Ibid., 75-76.

Fire is the natural Element associated with the Mind. In this case the concern is with cosmic Fire, which is a boundless (shoreless) sea of Fiery energy, the ineffable Mind of 'God', which encompasses the furthermost stretches of the universe. For this reason the numbers of the complete phrase *'turns the upper into a shoreless sea of Fire'* add to 5 x 10, implying the perfected expression of the Mind. The numbers also add to 2 x 88, whilst the numbers of the phrase *'a shoreless sea of Fire'* add to 88, plus 17 x 2. The number 8 x 11 here refers to the complete expression of Logoic *kuṇḍalinī* in terms of its consciousness-engendering aspect (Fohat), which is the sustaining Power behind the emanation of the Christ-energy in Nature (2 x 88) when expressed in terms of compassion. This Fiery quality is the base substance constituting Shambhala, and its correspondences throughout space. The number 17 x 2 refers to the reflection of the energies of Deity into manifestation.

Also to consider is the qualities of the sign Aquarius in the phrase *'a shoreless sea'*, Aries in the phrase *'sea of Fire'*, and Pisces in the phrase *'the great Waters'*. They thus complete the turning of the wheel of the zodiac. The wavy bands for the glyph of Aquarius aptly symbolise the nature of the endless duration of the boundless Electrical Fire that is an expression of the Mind of the cosmic Logos (Fohat). It also indicates the positive and negative polarity of electrical phenomena, of the concept that it is moving from a positive dynamic source towards a negative, receptive polarity. Every star system or planetary body that may express the role of being receptive to a positive source can be considered a 'shore' whereby this energy is absorbed. Such a body then colours it with its own integral qualities before reemitting it into the general sea of energies.

From this perspective then, *'a shoreless sea'*, embodying the collective first and second Ray energies of all stars (11, 20) is a sea of intensified Electrical energy, a direct expression of the Will and Love-Wisdom of Deity. It refers to the fact that despite these little islands of receptivity exist there is no final destination for these energies, a shoreline, for them to pound upon and be absorbed. There is however an 'ultimate boundary', the ring-pass-not of the Logoic Mind. The concept then is that the multidimensional universe is infinite, boundless, stretching further than the mind can imagine. The number 10 x 11 of the phrase *'into a shoreless Sea of Fire'* implies the above, plus indicating all lines of energy interrelationships *(antaḥkaraṇas)* between the stellar spheres in the Sea that constitute the dynamics of the motions of its 'waves'. The concept implicates the *prāṇas* coursing through the *nāḍī* system of cosmic Space.

That this is a *'sea of Fire'* indicates that it is directed by the Minds of the various Logoi constituting cosmos. It is therefore criss-crossed with streams of Thought travelling from one source to another. Thought being the means of communication and mode of sending qualified energies governing the nature of the Thought-streams. Here Aries represents each Logoic Will that projects its Thought emanations to others, as well as embodying the qualities of the general emanation of the Element Fire. It governs the focussed Mind concentrating upon the object of meditation along any of the seven Ray lines, which are veiled by the seventh Ray energy of the Hierarchical ruler of this sign, Uranus. These Rays can also be viewed in terms of the seven qualifications of Mind found upon the cosmic mental plane that are collectivised under the term *ākāśā,* and the *ātmic* plane, when impacting upon the shores of the systemic space of the solar system. The seven sub-planes of the mental plane, from the highest to the lowest, can be considered as:

The Clear Light of Mind
Soul consciousness
The abstract Mind
The contemplative mind
The empirical mind
Desire-mind
Concretised mind

The higher three are collectivised under the term abstract Mind (which can be considered a positive energy field), and the lower four under the phrase, the empirical mind (thus a negative or receptive energy field to the abstract domain), as explained in my former writings. They all have their transmuted Logoic correspondences that are symbolised by the phrase 'a shoreless sea of Fire'. This Fire therefore is not homogeneous, thus consists of many different energy qualifications.

The term 'Waters' is a generic term for substance on all levels of perception, and when applied upon cosmic levels from the perspective of those ensconced in the cosmic dense physical plane that substance is inherently 'Fiery' (Fohat), even though from the Logoic perspective it may demonstrate as Watery. Specifically the cosmic astral/etheric substance is implied by the term, the ethers being the container for all energies manifesting through them.

Continuing the thread of the passage of the zodiac from Sagittarius to Aquarius, we see then that the phrase *'the great Waters'* refers to the sign Pisces the fishes. Inevitably the 'fish' swimming in the waters of sensation breaks its bonds to the 'dark Waters' to be able to swim in 'the great Waters'. These Waters are 'great' because they express the Loving Will (31 x 2) of the Logos (17). The Waters therefore represent cosmic astral space, within which the Logoi exist. Each *nirvāṇee* that breaks the ties with the earth Scheme becomes such a 'One manifested into the great Waters' when they travel upon their cosmic path. They will eventually become the Avatars of a later cycle. (This path is also ruled by Pisces under the first Ray impetus of the Lord of death, Pluto, the esoteric and Hierarchical ruler of Pisces.)

The number 4 x 12 of the phrase *'sea of Fire'* refers to the fourth sign of the zodiac: Cancer the crab, who governs both the open door into incarnate life, as well as that into ineffable Life (being one of the arms of the cardinal cross). It is the primary Watery sign in the zodiac and what is implied here is that the 'sea of Fire' is the electrical potency that embodies the cosmic astral plane. It is projected downwards to the realms of the Triad to manifest in the form of systemic *prāṇa*. There is also a direct descent of Fiery energy from Capricorn, the polar opposite of Cancer, thereby reflecting Logoic Mind into manifestation. Thus is the Creative process enacted.

Upon the attainment of their complete evolutionary impulse, with the consequent gain of Mind by those evolving out of the dense realms, so this 'sea of Fire' is also accordingly propagated by the generation of Mind from mind. It is thus fuelled by every enlightened being, each *nirvāṇee* returning to the central Spiritual Sun.

The numbers 14 x 9, 3 x 9 of the phrase *'manifested into the great Waters'* refers to the *nirvāṇees,* the liberated Initiates (9) that journey into the Waters of the cosmic astral ocean (14). Each Logoic Causal Form (Initiates of the cosmic third Degree) also incarnate therein in the form of their 777 Incarnations, via the Logoic forms (solar Logoi) that undergo experiences in 'the great Waters'.

The numbers 7 x 12, 7 x 3 of the phrase *'into the great Waters'* refer to the seventh sign of the zodiac, Libra, which governs the turning of the entire wheel of *saṃsāra,* the cycles of being/non-being and the expression of the law of *karma* that governs the activity (7 x 3) of all that live in 'the great Waters'. The number 7 x 3 here also refers to the triune nature of the all these Lives. They are three in One, such as is the Eye of the Monad.

The number 40 of the complete phrase *'the One manifested into the great Waters'* can refer to our solar Logos (a Logos of the fourth order), as well as to our planetary Logos, who is the fourth out of the seven, or even to the human kingdom, which is the fourth in Nature. Each is a unitary entity that embodies an entire *maṇḍala* of expression when travelling through space. The *nirvāṇees* that find their liberation in the Waters of cosmic astral space have evolved from the fourth Creative Hierarchy, 'the Initiates', that are humanity.

6C

Stanzas 3:8 – 3:12

Stanza Three part Eight

Stanza 3:8 says:

> **Where was the Germ, and where was now Darkness? Where is the Spirit of the Flame that burns in thy Lamp, O Lanoo? The Germ is That, and That is Light; the white brilliant Son of the dark hidden Father.**

Keynotes: Aries, lower mental, ascent, the fifth Ray, Amoghasiddhi. Second sub-aspect of Earthy *ākāśa*. Makara the mystery.

The numerical breakdown of the first to the fourth phrases:

Where was the Germ? (79 = 16, 25), The Germ (40, 13), Where was now Darkness (83, 29 = 11). Where is the Spirit (94, 22), the Spirit (52, 16), the Flame (34, 16), the Spirit of the Flame (98, 35), the Flame that burns (67, 22), burns in thy Lamp (66, 21), Where is the Spirit of the Flame (140, 41), The Spirit of the Flame that burns (131, 41), Where is the Spirit of the Flame that burns (173, 47), Where is the Spirit of the Flame that burns in thy Lamp? (219, 66), the Flame that burns in thy Lamp (113, 41), Oh Lanoo (27, 9), Thy Lamp (32, 14), The Spirit of the Flame that burns in thy Lamp (177, 60).

This Stanza is concerned with the attributes of the lower mental plane after humanity have appeared and are upon the process of ascending to the higher domains. This is signified by the questions to the Lanoo, who must seek out intelligent responses to what is enigmatical. The process of ascent necessitates the development of the will to overcome, as ruled by the first sign of the zodiac, Aries the ram, which generally governs this Stanza. The mental plane governs the fifth Ray of Science.

Aries drives the impetus to move all forwards and upwards to heights supernal. It also rules the emanation of the abstract Mind to cause the beginning of things. The Will here is also an aspect of the seventh Ray (the Hierarchical ruler of Aries), as all seven Ray methods and attributes must be mastered as one battles the material domain. On this plane humanity manifest their esoteric purpose, which is to convert the base substance, the Elemental Lives, into units of mind. Humanity are consequently Lords of Sacrifice (referring to our Monadic forms). Humanity inverts the substance of the three lower planes, so as to bring the lives of the form to liberation (the plane *buddhi).* Such activity is governed by Scorpio, which conditions the testings of Initiation, as aspirants battle to overcome the substance of these planes. To do so they must develop the first Ray Arian impetus to master the impediments of the path before them.

As previously stated the impact of Mahatic energy upon the lower mental plane is also directed via the first of the seven Creative Hierarchies, the Divine Flames (whose energy is 'Parashakti, supreme energy'), as an effect of their work with the substance of the cosmic physical plane. They project the Aetheric *ākaśa* to the system, and this Fiery energy impacts the substance of the lower mental plane so that it manifests in accord with the Logoic Mentation, the Plan for that *manvantara.* When reflected upon the lower mental plane this Power is conditioned by the All-accomplishing Wisdom of Amoghasiddhi. His energy is needed to help convert the cosmic 'black dust' that is the substance of this plane, so that it can be incorporated into the structure of human thoughts. Humanity will thus imitate in a distorted, highly reified manner the Thought-Forms of a Logos.

Leonine energy from the Divine Flames energises the mental plane with a reified Fire via the tenth Creative Hierarchy, 'Makara, the mystery' who embody substance of the human personality. This Hierarchy are still working towards their liberation. The attributes of the substance they wield, and the conditioning energies of these *devas* is however governed by Capricorn the goat. The creative energy assigned to them is 'Ichchhashakti, the Will to manifest', which is facilitated by the first Ray aspect of Aries.

The second sub-aspect of Earthy *ākāśa* is expressed, which helps overcome the natural concretising, reifying, separative aspects of the mind.

All incidents leading to the One that 'manifested into the great Waters' produce the onset of *manvantara* via the (primordial) Element *(ātma)*. The questions now asked of the Lanoo consequently relate to the reverse of this process, the production of enlightenment and thus *pralaya* of the appearing form as the enquiring mind reaches out to awaken Mind. The Initiate then resides in the higher dimensions of perception. The process of *pralaya* concerns the dematerialisation of substance, hence mergence into the four ethers. Such etherealisation happens as a consequence of the meditation process of an aspiring consciousness that strives to gain access to the higher domains, from which there is a consequent down flow of energies. This heightens the energy level of the sheaths incarnated into. The Fires of Mind ('the Spirit of the Flame') consequently consumes the form in the burning ground of the Initiation pyre. The internal motion of each atom of substance moves from rotary to spiral-cyclic and then fourth dimensional. The form can then no longer be sustained, the Life escapes to a higher octave of expression and the form dematerialises.

There are various couplets, governed by the sign Gemini the twins, veiled in this Stanza. They manifest where one part of the couplet refers to the immortal brother and the other to the mortal one. The analysis reveals seven of these that appear in a progressive manner, from the conquering of darkness to the manifestation of brilliant light. These couplets are consequently governed in turn from the seventh to the first Rays. The immortal brother stands in the form of the Soul or Spirit (the Monad, or *ātma-buddhi-manas),* and the mortal brother acts as the person or form in relation to it. Gemini governs the entire etheric body via which the appearing form, projected by Arian energy, must appear.

Note the correlation between these questions and those given in Stanzas 2:1 and 2:2 associated with the plane *anupādaka,* the plane of residence of the Monad, which can be considered to be *'the Germ'* that is the subject of the first question. The present series of questions are effectively extensions of the earlier ones. These questions also bring our thinking from the unfathomable distant past to the present, the eternal Now, the time zone wherein the disciple is to reside.

The first question concerns *'the Germ'* (40, 13) of Light and Consciousness, the immortal brother to Darkness, which is consumed as the Germ grows. The governing Ray for the couplet of the Germ versus Darkness is the seventh of Ceremonial Magic and Ritualistic endeavour. The process of the growth of 'the Germ' is therefore ruled by the law of cycles, of successive days and nights. From incarnation to incarnation does 'the Germ' grow.

The meaning of the phrase *'the Germ'* was given in Stanzas 2:5 and 3:2, where it was stated that it can refer to the germ of the solar system, the earth Scheme, or even the jewel in the heart of the Sambhogakāya Flower, or of any *chakra* or atom. In relation to our earth Scheme, the Germ can refer specifically to the fourth Round of the fourth globe (40, 13). It can also refer to any other Scheme or solar system, as well as to the existence of the human Monad, hence the fourth kingdom in Nature.

The phrase *'Where was the Germ?'* (25, 16) therefore asks the disciple to seek for the heart or source of all Life, thus to inevitably be centred in his/her fundamental Being. By the numbers of this phrase 'the Germ' referred to here is specifically that of the central jewel in the Sambhogakāya Flower on the higher mental plane (5 x 5), which is the seed of the Christ-consciousness (16). The entire evolutionary play is indicated wherein the evolved self-conscious humanity are slowly brought to that degree of attainment whereby the Germ of their own inner Light and its radiance can be revealed to them.

The question *'where was now Darkness?'* (11) is answerable by analysis of the term 'Darkness', which was explained in Stanzas 1:5 and 2:1. From the highest perspective it refers to being ineffable Light, Darkness being the next step of the disciple's journeying to pierce the veils of what it reveals. The lowest expression of darkness is ignorance. The relation of the highest to the lowest, the alpha and omega of being/non-being is implicated by the number 11. It signifies the building of the *antaḥkaraṇa* from here (ignorance) to there (ineffable Light) in one unbroken succession of revelation.

The next couplet to consider is *'the Spirit of the Flame'* (7 x 7 x 2, 7 x 5) and *'the Flame'* (17 x 2, 16). We know that this Flame refers to the light of the mind (7 x 5) that burns the substance of *saṃsāra*. It is the expression of the emerging divinity within *('the Germ')* – 17 x 2, and the evolution of the Christ-principle (16). 'The Spirit' of this Flame is then the emerging divinity that manifests in the form of the seven Ray attributes (7 x 7 x 2) governing all of the septenaries of Nature. The associated Ray is the sixth of Devotion-Aspiration, which increases the rate of burning of the Flame according to the intensity of the devotion or aspiration applied to seeking liberation from *saṃsāra*.

Then there is *'the Flame that burns'* (22, 13) and *'thy Lamp'* (32, 14). This couplet is governed by the fifth Ray of Scientific endeavour, via logical deduction and reasoning by the mind. It is the flame of the substance of the mind that burns. As it does so it consumes the energies of the Womb of Nature (22) that has been experienced. Empirical knowledge is first gained by obtaining comprehension, and later wisdom is developed. This allows the nature of the interrelation of the planetary and zodiacal energies constituting the Womb of constant periodic activity to be envisaged. This Flame also burns in each *chakra*. The *chakras* can therefore be considered as lamps that awaken to bear the evolving consciousness. The lamp then is the container of that mind, which exoterically is the brain, but esoterically is also the Soul (32) that garners all experiences *(saṃskāras)* from each incarnation, and which resides in the abstract domains of Mind.

The couplet of the Teacher asking the questions and the student is governed by the fourth Ray of Beautifying Harmony overcoming Conflict. This Ray governs the general human condition, and their striving to gain release from *saṃsāra* by realising *śūnyatā* (the fourth plane of perception). This necessitates passing Initiation tests upon the path to enlightenment, thus the phrase *'O Lanoo'* adds numerologically to 3 x 9. Here the Teacher represents the immortal, and the Lanoo the mortal brother.

The third Ray of Mathematically Exact Activity is veiled in the couplet of the phrase *'the Germ is That'* (7 x 9, 2 x 9). The term 'That' refers to the Seat of Power of a Logos, the quaternary upon which the triune Logos sits. It can be viewed also as the Base of Spine centre that supports the entire manifestation. It is therefore the foundation for the establishment of a Head lotus, the Shambhalic correspondence of any Logoic form. The associated plane is *ātma*. It thereby becomes the complete glorious flower that the Germ grows into, and so stands as the immortal brother. The numbers of this phrase refer to the Initiation process, the reaching out for the Light of the central Spiritual Sun that causes this Germ to grow out of the soil of *saṃsāra*.

The next phrase, *'That is Light'* (52, 16), refers to the second Ray of Love-Wisdom (governing present Monadic evolution) and the second plane of perception, *anupādaka*. The concept of the generation of Light out of the entire evolutionary process, a *mahāmanvantara* (52), is obvious enough once a Seat of Power has been established to do so. This Seat of Power has thereby evolved into a brilliant Son/Sun, a Christ in manifestation (16), which then becomes the immortal brother to that material construction upon which 'the One' sits upon. The Light emanates from 'That', it is the radiance of the Love that is the foundation of all that IS and is not.

In the final phrase the first, or destroyer, Ray of Will or Power and the highest plane of perception *(ādi)* is implicated in the couplet indicated by the juxtaposition of *'the white brilliant Son'* to *'the dark hidden Father'*. This Son, the planetary Logos, abstracts His principles into the plane *ādi,* and the Logoic physical permanent atom therein, where He prepares for the next cycles of incarnate experience to begin. The objective of a solar evolution has ended for those participating in the *manvantara*. Riding upon the first Ray impetus they must seek out their purpose in cosmic space as they travel upon their cosmic Paths within the abstraction of the Space of the 'dark hidden Father'. *Pralaya* thereby ensues for what was manifest, as the form, signified by 'That', no longer serves the purpose of holding the liberated unit.

Concerning these questions H.P.B. states that:

> The answer to the first question, suggested by the second, which is the reply of the teacher to the pupil, contains in a single phrases one of the most essential truths of occult philosophy. It indicates the existence of things imperceptible to our physical senses which are of

> far greater importance, more real and more permanent, than those that appeal to these senses themselves. Before the Lanoo can hope to understand the transcendentally metaphysical problem contained in the first question he must be able to answer the second, while the very answer he gives to the second will furnish him with the clue to the correct reply to the first.[1]

Note the similarity between the numbers of the phrases *'the Spirit'* and *'the Flame'*, both add to 16, as both are aspects of the Christ energy. The difference is that 'the Flame' is the dense sheath of 'the Spirit', its external manifestation. It reflects the attributes of Deity (17 x 2). 'The Spirit' on the other hand embodies those attributes for the complete length or great Year in the life of Brahmā. 'The Flame' burns for the life span of 'the lamp', the Causal Body that exists in the Lanoo, or for the life of the *chakras* whilst incarnate. *'The Spirit of the Flame'* is then essentially the Monadic aspect (17), a direct expression of the Head centre of Deity.

The numbers of both the phrases *'where is the Spirit?'* and *'the Flame that burns'* add to 22, informing us that the Spirit is in the Flame and is expressed via the ten planetary and twelve zodiacal energies (22) associated with any body of manifestation. The sum of their energies manifests as the burning Flame.

The number 100 + 13 of the phrase *'The Flame that burns in thy Lamp'* refers to any circumscribed sphere of activity, such as a *chakra,* which can contain the fuel that burns in the form of this Flame of consciousness. The Flame can then be made more intense, ethereal, by improving the quality of the fuel, until eventually the fuel is so refined that 'the Spirit of the Flame' is revealed. The substance that does the actual burning is indicated by the numbers of the phrase *'burns in thy Lamp'*, which add to 66, 7 x 3. These numbers refer to the sum of the material domain, of the manifest Body of the Logos (66), specifically that of the three worlds of human livingness (7 x 3), hence of the process of the transformation, refinement and transmutation of *saṃskāras* that occurs as a consequence of burning this fuel.

---

1 Ibid., 77.

The numbers of the complete phrase *'Where is the Spirit of the Flame that burns in thy Lamp'* also add to 66, implying that the student must find this 'Spirit' throughout the Body of manifestation of the Logos. Everything is infused with divinity, and as such must burn in the crucible of the mind/Mind in order to produce the revelations that lead to liberation.

The numbers 60 and 100 + 77 of the phrase *'The Spirit of the Flame that burns in thy Lamp'* have similar implications, but with the added information that the answers will come as the 777 incarnations are trodden. The *'Spirit of the Flame'* will then burn as a consequence of the production of the awakening of all the tiers of petals of the Head centre at the third to the fifth Initiations. All of the petals of the *chakras* in the body of manifestation will be en-Flamed when 'the Spirit of the Flame' liberates *kuṇḍalinī*. The number 60 relates to the Sacral centre (a six petalled lotus) and Base of Spine centre relationship, which is the 'lamp' wherein the *kuṇḍalinī* is generated. This Fire then rises up the spinal column, awakening all of the centres in turn, and finally turns the Head lotus into a blazing furnace. Only then can this 'Spirit of the Flame' be considered to be truly burning in 'the Lamp' that is the Head centre, to infuse the sum of the space that is the embodied form.

The question *'Where is the Spirit of the Flame?'* is answered numerologically by the number 140, as it refers to the ocean of Fiery energies manifesting via the cosmic astral plane (10 x 14). This energy emanates from the various Logoi travelling through cosmic astral space. There are also the energies of 'the seven Spirits of God'[2] (7 x 20), who are the planetary Logoi, as well as the rulers of the seven planes of perception that constitute systemic space. The 'Spirit of the Flame' has therefore manifested Itself as the essential Nature of all that is, the expression of the Fiery Will upon all dimensions of perception and in all embodied forms. The number 100 + 31 of the phrase *'the Spirit of the Flame that burns'* implicates the potency of the first Ray of Will or Power, to complete the understanding of what constitutes this 'Spirit'.

Effectively, the 'Spirit of the Flame', 'The Flame' itself, as well as 'the Lamp' are triune aspects of the energy from the Mind of 'God'.

---

2 *Rev. 4:5.*

They represent the projections of that Mind on three different levels of expression, that relating to the Father, Son and Mother aspects of Deity.

The number 11 of the question '*Where is the Spirit of the Flame that burns?*' informs us that this Spirit is concealed as part of the integral etheric Body of Deity. The question is asked because the Monadic aspect ('the Spirit') had incarnated in the form during solar evolution. Once comprehended the question allows, or rather posits, that the disciple builds *antaḥkaraṇas* to that Spirit via the planes of perception by burning the Fuel in his/her own 'Lamp'. Once the projections have been made by the mind/Mind then the disciple can travel the way of these *antaḥkaraṇas* to liberation in cosmic astral space. The process allows one to be Initiated into the Mysteries of being/non-being. The numbers of the phrase '*O Lanoo*' consequently add to 3 x 9.

The numerical breakdown of the last two phrases:

> The Germ (40, 13), The Germ is That (63, 18), That is Light (52, 16), the white brilliant Son (99, 27), The dark hidden Father (97, 25), hidden Father (66, 12), Son of the dark hidden Father (121, 31), The white brilliant Son of the dark hidden Father (208, 55).

Here we are told that '*the Germ is That*', where That refers to the undefinable, inexplicable aspect of Deity that is the foundation for any Logoic body of manifestation. By the number 7 x 9 of this phrase 'That' represents the qualities of a (cosmic) Christ in incarnation, the gain of the entire evolutionary process. Such a One can then truly say 'I am That I am'.[3] 'That' is then identical with the Spirit aspect that has unfolded in space and time.

The phrase '*the Germ is That*' refers to the evolution of the originating Germ that grows to eventually encompass what embodies all of Space, whilst the phrase '*That is Light*' (52, 16) refers to the embodied expression of That (or 'Darkness') in the form of Light. 'The Germ' has evolved into That, an abstracted cosmic Christ that manifests Light, illuminating all beings in the far reaches of the universe. The numbers of phrase '*The Spirit*' also add to 52 and 16. Here then an evolutionary progression is implied involving the gain of an entire *mahāmanvantara's* (52) purpose. 'The Germ' evolves into That, which

3 *Exodus 3:14.*

is a Logoic Seat of Power, and That animates the 'white brilliant' Light of the Son in incarnation, a cosmic Christ (16). Light then manifests for a complete 100 years duration of the Life of Brahmā.

'The white brilliant Son' (9 x 11, 3 x 9) is the embodiment of Light, specifically that of a solar Logos in active manifestation (99), or else the Logos of a sacred planet. Their whole Body is full of Light. The number 3 x 9 refers to the Sambhogakāya Flower, which can also be considered a 'white brilliant Son of the dark hidden Father' (the Monad). The Soul of Life is the true Christ principle that en-Souls all incarnating forms. White light means 'spotless, pure, unadulterated light', and implicates also the blended seven Ray colourings, as well as all of the septenaries in Nature.

The numbers of the phrase *'hidden Father'* add to 66, 12, implying that the Father, the Spirit or Monadic aspect, is hidden in the sum of the form (66), and activates the principle of Life conveyed by the Heart centre (12).

The numbers 16 and 25 of the phrase *'the dark hidden Father'* verify that this 'Father' can also be considered the Soul or Christ aspect hidden within all embodied Life.

The term 'dark' in reference to the Causal form is interesting, because this Flower is usually spoken of in terms of solar Light, as it is the conscious intermediary between Spirit and matter. It implies that the view is from the perspective of the Acolyte embodied in his/her personality vehicle, where the Soul manifests the attribute of Father to the personality life, and is dark, hidden, incomprehensible to the intelligence that perceives it not. It is yet to be discovered (as a powerhouse of Love and Wisdom) to fully enlighten the disciple at the attainment of the third Initiation (3 x 9).

The numbers 11 x 11, 31 of the phrase *'Son of the dark hidden Father'* refer to obtaining the first Ray qualities of Deity, which is the gain of liberation via the ability to project *antaḥkaraṇas* (11) to the Father (the Monad). It thereby reveals His awesome Presence as a vehicle of the most intense form of Light. The evolutionary gain of the disciple is thus compared by these phrases to that of a Logos of a sacred planet. The higher interpretation thus relates to a similar relationship between those governing a planetary sphere and the Lord of a solar system.

The number 5 x 11 of the phrase *'The white brilliant Son of the dark hidden Father'* informs us that such an entity eventually becomes an Adept, a perfected Master of the mind/Mind and thus of the entire material world. All exists within the Mind of the cosmic Creative Logos. The appearance of the phenomena of cosmos is but part of the meditative play in that Mind so that another Logoic principle *(saṃskāra)* can be mastered. Once mastered *pralaya* can ensue, in preparation for mastering the next quality the Logos deems worthy of developing. When all of the forces are brought into play to do so in the Mind of That One, so then a new *mahāmanvantara* can ensue, as the Logos focuses upon the forming Images in His Mind, and commences upon reflecting that Image *(maṇḍala)* into objectivity.[4] The remaining verses of Stanza three therefore deal with the process of the activation and descent of the Logoic Thought-Form into objectivity.

This stanza continues under the auspices of Amoghasiddhi, who also generally governs Stanza 3:7,[5] because now disciples have evolved from *saṃsāra* that can utilise the All-accomplishing Wisdom and the Will power derived from Aries to overcome the darkness of materialism in its entirety. There is also a trinity of signs under Aries appearing in Stanza 3:8. First the sign Gemini, interrelating all of the dualities explained earlier. Gemini governs the manifestation of etheric space, and also presides over the inherent duality of etheric versus dense physical space. It thus represents the Mother aspect of this trinity.

Next is Aquarius in the phrase 'the white brilliant Son', who as the prototype Bodhisattva (of whom the Lanoo is the reflection), dispenses the Waters (Logoic Desire, systemic Love-Wisdom) of the cosmic astral ocean into manifestation. Aquarius thereby represents the Christ-principle,

---

4 See my book *The Nature and Development of Maṇḍalas* for detail, remembering always the adage 'as above, so below'.

5 The rulership of the Stanzas from 3:7 down are considered in terms of pairs. First, Stanzas 3:7 and 3:8 are concerned with *saṃsāra,* the Earthy domain, governed by Amoghasiddhi's All-accomplishing Wisdom. Next is that related to the generation and mastery of the Watery domain, governed by Ratnasambhava's Equalising Wisdom. (Stanzas 3:9 and 3:10.) Finally that related to the generation and mastery of the Fiery domain, governed by the Discriminating Inner Wisdom of Amitābha. There is a process of descent and ascent of human awareness and its ability to conquer implied in these assignments.

whose Fiery-Watery energies guides all Lives immersed in *māyā* to liberation. It empowers the liberating energy of purposeful resolve *(bodhicitta)* that inspires all upon the Bodhisattva path to perpetually reincarnate so that the little ones can be rightly educated and liberated. Gemini then represents the methodology of the targeted ones (via Sagittarius, its polar opposite) to administer to the Temple of Life.

Finally, the sign Capricorn indicated in the phrase 'the dark hidden Father', governing the qualities of cosmic Mind, and thus the formulations of the *maṇḍala* building that eventually become expressed via Gemini. The dualism of Gemini allows it to manifest the functions of the Mother (the mortal 'brother') fecundated by the Father (the 'immortal brother'), to give birth to the Son (the appearance of the *maṇḍala* of space-time of *saṃsāra),* and then interrelate the Son to the Father. Revelation of the nature of such activity is the purpose of the Mysteries veiled within the sacred precincts of the Temples Gemini governs. Capricorn signifies the awakened Initiate that has mastered all of the testings associated with Scorpio (which governed the previous stanza). Aquarius signifies the resultant gain of the enlightened consciousness, and Aries projects that accomplishment to new heights of Revelation.

The esoteric and Hierarchical rulers of Capricorn are Saturn and Venus, those of Aquarius are Jupiter and the Moon (veiling Vulcan and Uranus), whilst those of Gemini are Venus and the Earth. The Hierarchical Venus of Capricorn, reflecting the manifestation of cosmic Mind, produces the appearance of systemic Mind via Venus, the esoteric ruler of Gemini. The activity via Uranus in Aquarius channels all seven Ray aspects of Logoic Mind in the form of the dispensation of the Water Bearer. This Mind is consequently tempered by the Waters. The activity that awakens the perceptions happens upon the earth (the Hierarchical ruler of Gemini), and upon the path of aspiration and Initiation on the return journey (via the testings in Scorpio). The awakening of Mind via the influence of Aquarius reveals the hidden Mysteries of the Father, and the nature of the Love-Wisdom (Jupiter) of the Son. This necessitates the development of the Will (Vulcan), manifesting in the form of the Will-to-Love in the disciple. Vulcan is also the esoteric and Hierarchical ruler of Taurus, who pushes the cycles of accomplishment through the zodiac as a consequence of onrushing Logoic Desire.

The disciple's aspiration eventually becomes the will to liberate, which evolves the Divine Will (via Aries) whereby the reality of 'the dark Hidden Father' can be revealed. From Gemini to Capricorn the attributes of seven signs (including Capricorn), must be trod and thoroughly experienced to comprehend the nature of the hidden Mysteries in Capricorn, and then expressed via the fluid Mind of Aquarius. A new cycle of service work can then be embarked in Aries, after having terminated the old shell of 'darkness' in Pisces. Taurus represents the gain of it all (the awakened Wisdom-Eye), and with that Eye directs a new cycle onwards to its conclusion.

Concerning the above H.P.B. states:

> In the Sanskrit Commentary on this Stanza, the terms used for the concealed and the unrevealed Principle are many. In the earliest MSS. of Indian literature this Unrevealed, Abstract Deity has no name. It is generally called *"That" (Tad,* in Sanskrit), and means all that is, was, and will be, or that can be so received by the human mind.
>
> Among such appellations, given, of course, only in esoteric philosophy, as the "Unfathomable Darkness," the "Whirlwind," etc. — it is also called the "It of the Kalahansa, the Kala-ham-sa," and even the "Kali Hamsa" (Black swan). Here the *m* and the *n* are convertible, and both sound like the nasal French *an* or *am*, or, again, *en* or *em (Ennui, Embarras,* etc.) As in the Hebrew Bible, so many a mysterious sacred name in Sanscrit conveys to the profane ear no more than some ordinary, and often vulgar word, because it is concealed anagrammatically or otherwise. This word Hansa, or esoterically "hamsa" is just such a case. Hamsa is equal to a-ham-sa, three words meaning "I am He" (in English); while divided in still another way it will read "So-ham," "He (is) I" — Soham being equal to Sah, "he," and aham, "I," or "I am he". In this alone is contained the universal mystery, the doctrine of the identity of man's essence with god-essence, for him who understands the language of wisdom. Hence the glyph of, and the allegory about, Kalahansa (or hamsa), and the name given to Brahma (neuter), later on, to the male Brahmā, of "Hansa-vahana", "he who uses the Hansa as his vehicle." The same word may be read "Kalaham-sa," or "I am I" in the eternity of Time, answering to the Biblical, or rather Zoroastrian, "I am that I am."[6]...

6 Ibid., 77-78.

(T)he symbol of Hansa (wether "I," "He," Goose or Swan) is an important symbol, representing, for instance, Divine Wisdom, Wisdom in darkness beyond the reach of men. For all exoteric purposes, Hansa, as every Hindu knows, is a fabulous bird which, when given milk mixed with water for its food (in the allegory) separated the two, drinking the milk and leaving the water; thus showing inherent wisdom—milk standing symbolically for spirit, and water for matter[7]... The "Swan or goose" (Hansa) is the symbol of that male or temporary deity, as he, the emanation of the primordial Ray, which is made to serve as a Vahan or vehicle for the divine Ray, which otherwise could not manifest itself in the Universe, being, antiphrastically, itself an emanation of "Darkness" — for our human intellect, at any rate. It is Brahmā, then, who is Kala-Hansa, and the Ray, the Hansa-Vahana.

As to the strange symbol thus chosen, it is equally suggestive; the true mystic significance being the idea of a universal matrix, figured by the primordial waters of the "deep," or the opening for the reception, and subsequently for the issue, of that one ray (the Logos), which contains in itself the other seven procreative rays or powers (the logoi or builders)[8]...Appearing with every Manvantara as Narāyan, or Swayambhuva (the Self-Existent), and penetrating into the Mundane Egg, it emerges from it at the end of the divine incubation as Brahmā, or Prajāpati, the progenitor of the future Universe, into which he expands. He is Purusha (spirit), but he is also Prakriti (matter). Therefore it is only after separating itself into two halves — Brahmā-vach (the female) and Brahmā-Virāj[9] (the male), that the Prajāpati becomes the male Brahmā.[10]

---

7 Ibid, 79.

8 Ibid, 80.

9 Virāj (Virāṭ), sovereign, splendid, the macrocosm, the manifested universe. Also the universal Man, cosmic Mind (Mahat), the son of Brahmā. In the Liṇga and Vāyu Purāṅas Brahmā is said to have divided his body into two parts, one half being male and the other half a female (Vāch). Virāj, the early universe, was created from the female. The *Rig-Veda* makes Virāj spring from Puruṣa (the universal Soul or heavenly Man), and Puruṣa spring from Virāj. Virāj is incorporated as all male beings, and Vāch (speech, the creative Word, the power of mantric Sound), is incorporated as all female forms. As Śata-rūpā she is the goddess of a hundred forms.

10 Ibid., 80-81.

H.P.B. uses the symbolism of Kalāhaṃsa, which governs the in and outbreathing of time *(kāla),* to depict the 'divine hidden Father'. The reason being that the Lord of time lies outside of the creation of the phenomena of all manifestation, and yet is the cause of it. Being outside the cognisance of those evolving within the phenomena, this One then is 'dark', 'hidden'. The symbol of the swan in flight (Brahman) is provided because it possesses two wings, symbolising the *iḍā* and *piṅgalā nāḍīs,*[11] plus the main body of the bird *(suṣumṇā).* It flies high above the material manifestation and yet can land upon the Waters of sensation, the source of Love-Wisdom to our system. The feathers of the wing symbolically manifest in the form of spiral-eights that delineate the cycles of time (the work of Brahmā). The egg that is laid when on land symbolises the World Egg.

The 'Swan' or 'Goose' also aptly symbolises the Soul that flies high above the waters of sensation associated with *saṃsāra,* and yet can also land upon the earth or alight upon the Waters of the astral plane via the activities of its incarnate personality. It is the Lord of time with respect to the cycles of karmic expression of the personality, instigating its birthing and also the moment of death. It lays the 'Golden Egg' of enlightenment in the awakening personality as it aspires upwards to the light of the Sun. The idea can also be extended to the macrocosm, i.e., to the solar or planetary Causal Form, as depicted above in Blavatsky's commentary.

Stanza Three part Nine

Stanza 3:9 states:

> **Light is cold Flame, and Flame is Fire, and Fire produces heat, which yields Water, the Water of Life in the great Mother** *(Chaos).*

Keynotes: Taurus, astral plane, sixth Ray, third sub-aspect of Earthy *ākāśa*, Ratnasambhava.

The numerical breakdown:

---

11 Here the *iḍā nāḍī* can be considered as Brahmā-vach (the female) and *piṅgalā nāḍī* as Brahmā-Virāj (the male).

Cold Flame (35, 17), Light is cold Flame (74, 29 = 11), Flame is Fire (58, 22, and 10, 1, 11), Fire produces heat (83, 29 = 11), yields Water (51, 15), which yields Water (84, 21), the Water of Life (72, 18), the great Mother (73, 19), Life in the great Mother (110, 29) the Water of Life in the great Mother (159, 42).

The process leading to the precipitation of the Watery substance within the Womb of the great Mother can now be considered. The seed of the 'dark hidden Father' (Light) has been implanted in that Womb so that the embryo can grow. This produces the process of the condensation of the Fiery substance of Mind (from the domain of the abstract Mind to the empirical) to produce the Waters. The appearance of the astral plane comes under the auspices of Taurus the bull. It is an Earth sign, as the driving impetus of the bull is to turn the zodiacal wheel that produces the crystallisation of the Fiery energies of the Logoic Mind via its Watery phase within the Womb of time and space. Taurus conditions the substance *(mūlaprakṛti)* of systemic space, the result of the Desire of the Logos, to produce the Germ of what is to be for all that are to incarnate.

By embodying the Waters of the cosmic astral plane in general ('the Water of Life in the great Mother') its reverberation upon the systemic astral plane can manifest. As previously stated, humans utilise the first Ray impetus of Vulcan, the esoteric and Hierarchical ruler of Taurus in terms of personality will, to project the self-focussed images desired by the individual, plus the creative imaginings of the mind, ruled by Venus the exoteric ruler of Taurus, to create the conditionings of the astral plane for them. They have created Watery miasmas under the auspices of Taurean impulses, and the desire impulses of its polar opposite, Scorpio, manifesting via the sixth Ray.

The sixth Ray that generally governs this Stanza facilitates reception of the concrete mental substance to the Watery energies from the cosmic astral plane conveyed by Pisces (a Water sign). The martial sixth Ray energy and the Will or Power of the first Ray therefore work together as a unit to accommodate the potency of the impact of the energies of the Logoic Mind that conditions the turning of the great Wheel. (Also considered in terms of *pratītyasamutpāda,* as explained in the fourth volume of *A Treatise on Mind.)*

Stanza 3:8 dealt mainly with the energies of the Father-Son, whereas Stanza 3:9 concerns the conditions of the Womb of the great Mother as governed by the work of the creative Logos, Brahmā. Via the sixth Ray manifest the energies that condition the activities productive of the condensation of the Waters, and the appearance of the concrete form. The Equalising Wisdom of Ratnasambhava also governs in order to assist humanity to control the Lunar Lords that constitute the substance of this plane of perception. Ratnasambhava here works with the third sub-aspect of Earthy *ākāśa,* which facilitates the crystallisation process. It also helps engender the attributes of the mind upon the upward cycle via loving, magnetically attractive attitudes of humanity. (Ratnasambhava also condition the evolutionary process under the law of Love.) The entire field of desire and attachment and all other forms of emotional thinking and glamour must be mastered. The energy of the Lunar Lords is given by D.K. as 'Kundalinishakti, the energy of Matter'. We know *kuṇḍalinī* to be the inherent Fires that sustain the form, which humanity must learn to rightly release, if they are to be liberated from *saṃsāra*. By mastering the Lunar Lords humanity can transform the primal energies unifying the Elemental Lives (the last of the Creative Hierarchies) and so mentally control the material forms we see all around us.

The sign attributed to the Lunar Lords (who clothe our mental-emotions) is Sagittarius. The Sagittarian impulse conditions them mainly because of the disastrous activities of humanity upon the moon Chain and Atlantis, where their massed wilful desire precipitated this energy upon the Lunar Lords. Much of the sexual misery on earth has its foundation here. Most of this *karma* will be rectified with the advent of the new age and the appearance of the sixth Root Race.

At this stage of evolution *mūlaprakṛti* (or the term *svabhāva* could best be used[12]) is Fiery-Watery, designated as *'cold Flame'*. The anachronistic phrase *'Light is cold Flame'* (11),[13] brings our vision to the higher mental plane, as the energy of the abstract Mind, the Clear Light of Mind, is literally *'cold Flame'* (7 x 5, 17). This is because its

12 *Svabhāva* as the self-becoming plastic essence underlying manifestation, equated with *ākāśa,* was explained in Stanza 2:1.

13 It is anachronistic, because fire is normally experienced as heat.

energy qualification is the serenity of the meditation-Mind, which is cool, reflective, absorbed in dispassionate atemporal observations. From this perspective then, the bird of time and space *(kalāhaṃsa)* has projected the *antaḥkaraṇas* (11) downwards in the form of cold Flame, in order to set the *maṇḍala* in motion of what is to appear.

'Cold Flame' can also be considered to be the light emanated from the spiritual realms at the *śūnyatā-saṃsāra* nexus, as signified by the number 11 above. This number is also found in the phrases *'Flame is Fire'* (10.1.11) and *'Fire produces heat',* where the first two words each add to 11. These numbers veil a mass of downward moving forces, not just the energy of Logoic Desire-Mind, but also of the accompanying Entities that are to incarnate into the Womb of the Mother as its forming embryo.

There is also the fundamental first and second Ray energy of the Light realised at this nexus. It sustains the 'Jewel in the Heart' of each Lotus *(chakra).* Heat is the effect produced when energy impacts upon the inertia of the substance that conditions the activity of this Womb. The work of form building thereby manifests. From the above perspective Heat is the expression of the Mother, 'cold Flame' the Father, and Fire is the Son. Fire is the result of the electrical exchange between Father-Mother. Light is a product of the Fire, an extension of the Flame. It is an expression of the energies conveyed by the twelve Creative Hierarchies that become incorporated into the schema as 'the Waters of Life'. All three aspects of Deity are interrelated by *sūtrātmās* or *antaḥkaraṇas* (11). All are fundamentally potent expressions of energy on their own respective levels. All is permeated with the One Life.

The number 11 x 10 of the phrase *'Life in the great Mother'* implies that the objective of this Life in the Mother is to develop the first Ray energy of Will of Power, and project the *antaḥkaraṇas* from systemic to cosmic space. (Pain and suffering associated with this Life produces the will to overcome.) For Life to be projected into 'the great Mother' it requires that expression of the Will of Deity in the form of the *sūtrātmā,* which vivifies the permanent atoms. The appropriate substance that is incorporated into the material form is thereby attracted to them.

The view from the perspective of the order given for the terms in this stanza concerns the impact of Light upon the primal substance *(mūlaprakṛti)* in the Womb of the great Mother. This substance exists upon the mental plane, the cosmic dense physical, and represents the 'black dust' that must be incorporated into any Logoic manifestation. It must become redeemed and transmogrified into man-plants.

Light (streaming from various constellations and suns in cosmos) is then the primary seed implanted into the Womb to set the entire chain of events of world-formation into motion. Light can be considered consisting of Rays bearing Consciousness-attributes, of an originating Thought-Form from a Logoic Mind. It possesses qualities, Ideas, that impact upon substance, or that influence other Logoi and liberated Beings.[14]

'Cold Flame' is then the way this Thought-Form impacts upon the higher mental plane of a new solar sphere, causing a ring-pass-not delineating the extent of what will later be known as *saṃsāra*. Fire is the effect of this organising 'Flame' upon the primal substance, causing rotary motion, friction, compression and combustion. That Fire produces heat is obvious enough, however here we see that Water is the product. This Water obviously is not physical plane water, however it could be so construed if the substance heated contains moisture, which condenses out. This is not the case with the primal dust. The Water is fluidic, volatile substance, sentient Life streams that evolve to en-Soul the prima matrix. We thus have the appearance of the myriad forms of Life in the Womb of the great Mother.

We are provided with a septenary of terms in this verse. This septenary must be viewed in terms of the conditioning Womb from whence emanates the 'Child', all of the Lives that evolve through it. This cosmic astral plane projects its primal substance, 'the Water of Life', into this Womb in the form of the *prāṇas* manifesting via the four cosmic ethers. (From this perspective this Womb is conditioned by the sign Taurus.) These *prāṇas* are an expression of *ākāśa*, the 'sea of Fire'. This represents the Manasic energies of the Logoi, the general cosmic Humanity that travel through the cosmic astral plane, thus manifesting a Watery Atlantean disposition from their perspective. The relation to general cosmic Humanity provides the appellation 'fourth order' (hence 'Atlantean') for our solar Logos, who is part of the population of such Logoi. The list provided depicts the planes of perception to

14 Its relation to consciousness was explained in *A Treatise on Mind*.

systemic space, as well as the process of evolution of the Lives within that space. It also depicts the Watery environment of the Womb of the great Mother, where the term 'Watery' at first represents the energies *(ākāśa)* conditioning that Womb from the cosmic astral plane. 'Cold Flame' is the energy that manifests from this astral domain through *ākāśa*. Later comes the Watery disposition of systemic space, the astral plane experienced by humans. We thus have:

Term	**Plane**	**Element**
The great Mother	*ādi*	
Water of Life	*anupādaka*	
Cold Flame	*ātma*	Aether
Light	buddhi	Air
Fire	mental	Fire
Water	astral	Water
Heat	dense	Earth

The number 10 of the phrase *'the great Mother'* indicates that this Mother is a self-contained sphere of activity. She is great for she embodies all forms in our solar system, or earth sphere, on their journey to evolutionary perfection. Here we see that her Womb consists of the substance *(devas)* of the entire systemic space, of the seven planes of perception, from the plane *ādi* down. The Watery expression manifesting via the cosmic astral plane can then be accommodated in systemic space. The *bījas* of the Lives to evolve through the Womb of the solar sphere can consequently be awakened. Being the Mother the concern is also with the activities of the Builders *(deva* and human), specifically the first three Creative Hierarchies, the Divine Flames, upon the plane *ādi*, the Greater Builders upon the plane *anupādaka,* and the Lesser Builders upon the plane *ātma*. From the above tabulation therefore we see that the Greater Builders convey *'The Water of Life',* whilst 'cold Flame' represents the energies of the Lesser Builders.

'The Water of Life' (72, 18) therefore represents the substance of the second plane of perception, *anupādaka,* which directly conveys the Watery energies of the cosmic astral plane that activates the spirals of the Logoic physical permanent atom with the general informing Lives that will condition and guide all the streams of Life. These Lives will

evolve to become the Christ–child of a solar evolution. This Water is therefore Life Itself, pure unadulterated Love, the instigating Source of the quality known as consciousness in systemic space. It nourishes Monadic evolution. The number 6 x 12 refers to the sixth sign of the zodiac, Virgo the virgin, who carries the 'Water of Life' in Her Womb, from which eventually will emerge the Christ-child. This Water fills the Womb of Being (Mother Nature) within which we live and come to be. The number 72 also refers to the ideal life span of any incarnate entity, the evolutionary progress that produces the appearance of a Buddha, then an Initiate of the eighth degree (72 = 9 x 8).

Water is sensation, the fluid intermediary between the Fiery substance of the mental plane and the substance that is enacted upon, that 'burns'. (All are the embodiments of differing types of angelic Intelligences.) The burning of this elementary fuel is the heat engendering capacity, which in turn produces the evolution of conscious differentiation. Water thus is the substance of conscious evolution, seen at first as the appearance of the quality of streams of sentient Lives. It thereby becomes the Element associated with the astral plane. 'Heat yields water', for out of the heat-engendering friction, the pain of struggle to overcome inertia, comes understanding, adaptation, the ability to flow and be moulded, the experience of sensation, feeling, and thence desire. It is the expression of those entities (the eleventh Creative Hierarchy, the *lunar pitris)* that embody dense material substance. It incorporates also therefore the members of the twelvth Creative Hierarchy, the 'blinded lives' and 'baskets of nourishment'. Water is the life-giving principle to all embodied forms.

The numbers of the phrase *'yields Water'* add to 17 x 3, 15, 6, referring to the activity aspect of Deity (17 x 3), which produces the evolution of intelligence (15) in the realms of Watery substance (6). It 'yields water' for one must become sensitively attuned to sensation before one can react consciously to it, thereby affecting the Waters. The nature of this attunement produces the field of desire, thus the complete gamut of human experiences in *saṃsāra*. Humanity first evolves an astral plane before the mind can be properly developed. Water must then be consumed in the Fire. This all comes under the auspices of the Activity cycle of the Logos.

In this stanza the term Water concerns the conditioning energy of the cosmic astral plane that emanates via its correspondence to our systemic *ātmic* plane in the form of *'cold Flame'*. Cold Flame incorporates the lines of interrelated karmic interactions between the cosmic astral plane and the basic *manasic* substance of the Lives evolving within the Womb of time and space. Consciousness therefore is the most elementary quality of this substance. This Fiery form of the Element Water then manifests in the five subdivisions associated with the Rays of Mind. These Rays manifest in terms of the Sense-Consciousnesses of the Logos, and cause the evolution of consciousness within the embodied forms.

The numbers of the phrase *'which yields Water'* add to 84 (Libra), 21. The entire statement *'Fire produces Heat, which yields Water'* comes under the general influence of Libra the balances. Libra regulates the cyclic outpouring of the Fire from the Logoic Mind, according to the cadence of the mantric sentence governing the entire process. These cycles then help produce the many internal changes within the Womb for the appearance of Water. The Hierarchical ruler is Saturn, which governs the directive impulse of the *karma,* the *saṃskāras* that are awakened at the appropriate cycles. Libra's influence therefore is general and pervasive. All happens under the auspices of Virgo ('the Great Mother'), who bears the sum of the Watery substance within the Womb wherein the foetus develops. She thus en-Souls the process associated with building the form of the Divine Child, under the second Ray impulse of its Hierarchical ruler, Jupiter, according to mantric directives that the turning of the great wheel of the zodiac provides.

One can also consider the sign Aquarius, who symbolises the attributes of the *'the Water of Life'*, which is esoterically Fiery in nature, vitalising the blood stream that feeds the foetal development with the nourishment it needs. Via its Hierarchical ruler Uranus, bearing seventh Ray energies, Aquarius thereby oversees the development of consciousness within the Sons of Mind that are also called 'Flames' (Stanza 7:7), a term that has a general application for all the Creative Hierarchies. The seventh Ray helps to particularise all of the karmic cycles governed by Libra for the foetal development, so that the Mother's objective is accomplished. The two wavy bands of the glyph of Aquarius introduce here two other signs in relation to the expression of the Waters. First is the sign Taurus the bull, embodying the attributes of the higher band, the Waters from the cosmic astral plane, governed by Taurus. The second sign is Scorpio the scorpion, who governs the nature of the Watery dispensation of the evolving Lives within the Womb. Scorpio, a Water sign, governs the general evolutionary development of humanity. Aquarius pours the Waters from one to the other.

The mechanism of interrelation is via the fourth Earthy *ākāśa* under the auspices of Ratnasambhava's Equalising Wisdom. The fourth Ray function allows the energies of the cosmic Waters to be effectively reflected into its systemic counterpart to nourish the Life in the great Mother. In the juxtaposition between Taurus and Scorpio the entire field of desire-attachment and sexuality (governed by these signs) and their eventual rectification needs Ratnasambhava's Wisdom to produce a positive outcome as the cycles come and go via Libra's purpose.

Virgo, Libra and Scorpio govern the western quadrant of the zodiac, the expression of outwards to the field of service representing humanity, which is the focus of activity for all of these energies. Cold Flame, Light, Fire, Water and Heat, the five Elements, are the consequence of the interrelated activity of these signs.

When looking to the Elements normally attributed to the signs mentioned, then we see that the Fiery Element is omitted. We have Libra, Virgo, Aquarius, Taurus and Scorpio, to whom are ascribed Air, Earth, Air, Earth and Water respectively. In this schema the Fiery Element is provided by the general Arian dispensation of the previous Stanza, and manifests as the 'cold Flame' of Stanza 3:9, which is distributed via Aquarius. We are also told that 'Light is cold Flame', which is expressed as the Airy attribute of Aquarius via the fourth cosmic ether, *buddhi*. The 'Water of Life', 'cold Flame' and Light then impact upon the higher mental domain to cause the formation of the kingdom of Souls, under the auspices of Leo the lion, a Fiery sign. Humanity consequently develop the Fiery Element as they evolve the attributes of the lower mental plane, and struggle with the consequences of Water and heat. The formation of the systemic astral plane is consequently formed by the creative emotional response of human activity in the dense material world wherein there is much friction and strife, pain and suffering, symbolised in this Stanza under the term 'heat'. Here also can be considered the manifestation of the five sense-consciousnesses and of the way that they gather experiences, to be correlated and assimilated by the mechanism of the physical brain.

The Elements attributed to these senses are: hearing—Earth, touch—Water, sight—Fire, taste—Air, and smell—Aether.

A Treatise on Cosmic Fire provides a list of the higher correspondences of these five senses, providing information that could be extrapolated for Logoic development if carefully meditated upon. As it is a process of descent of energies, form building, and consolidation of forces for the congealing of primary substance, the order of the senses provided is opposite to that for those incarnate and evolving on earth. We must learn to ascend to subtler domains of perception, to dematerialise the substance of our sheaths to relinquish all attachments to form, whereas increasing materialisation is needed for Logoi that wish to incarnate. D.K. states:

> In the final perfection of this third sense of sight, the term used is the wholly inadequate one of *realisation.* Let the student study carefully the lowest and highest demonstration of the senses as laid down in the tabulation earlier imparted, and note the occult significance of the expressions used in the summation.

Hearing	Beatitude.	This is realised through the not-self.
Touch	Service.	The summation of the work of the Self for the not-self.
Sight	Realisation.	Recognition of the triplicity needed in manifestation, or the reflex action of the Self and the not-self.
Taste	Perfection.	Evolution completed through the utilisation of the not-self and its realised adequacy.
Smell	Perfected Knowledge.	The principle of manas in its discriminating activity, perfecting the inter-relation between the Self and the not-self.

> This all concerns the perfected, realised Personality.[15]

15 T.C.F., 200. See also pages 188-189.

The phrase 'Recognition of the triplicity needed in manifestation, or the reflex action of the Self and the not-self', would normally refer to the trinity of Spirit-Soul-form. Here however we can look to the qualities of the three western signs of the zodiac that are exemplified in this verse: Virgo, Libra and Scorpio. Virgo is the Spirit of the Womb in the depth of its magnitude. Libra is the process that en-Souls the various attributes of its form, and Scorpio battles with what has been en-Souled to free the Life from its encasement of substance.

Because the overall sense governing astral plane phenomena is Touch, so we can see therefore that the theme of 'The summation of the work of the Self for the not-self' concerns the Bodhisattva ideal applied to the role of salvaging the elementary Lives through sacrificial activity in their domain. To do so the Logoi must be able to touch the realms wherein these lesser Lives abound with the energies of Their Presence. The purpose is to manifest the acts that will enable these Lives to 'see', thereby to consciously strive to attain the qualities needed to exist in the higher domains of liberation. Touch also incorporates the process of sexual interactions, the interrelation between the polarities of Life, in order to produce the appearance of the form. Upon the path of ascent, touch concerns contact with the substance of the higher dimensions of perception and the Lives therein.

Correlating the above tabulation to the information provided in this verse we see therefore that the qualities of 'the perfected, realised Personality' provide us with a close approximation of the qualities of the Logoic Personality, when that One's Senses are extended into manifestation. We can then extrapolate the information concerning the five senses in the order provided below.

Hearing (Beatitude) cosmically concerns the uplifting of all Lives incorporated within the sheaths of the incarnate Logos. It necessitates listening to the beat of Secret Mantra from cosmic mental levels via the cosmic astral to the seven manifest Creative Hierarchies. The mantras heard carry a Watery disposition into dense manifestation. One should note that water is a better medium for carrying sound than air. Hearing relates to manifesting the All-accomplishing Wisdom of Amoghasiddhi, thus to the overall grounding into *saṃsara* of the remaining four sense-Consciousnesses. All mantric sounds of the various Logoi are heard and integrated into a unified *maṇḍala* of activity. The cascades of Sound then activate torrents of vast Watery *devas* to help precipitate elementary substance via moving vortices and whirlpools of organising purpose.

The mode of such manifestation is via 'cold Flame' *(ākāśa)*. The mantras are Heard via the plane *ādi*, drawing its energies from the third cosmic astral sub-plane. It instigates the rotary motion of the *maṇḍala*, and the associated activity releases energy, which in the primary stage of expression externalises in the form of heat, (thus the infra-red portion of the electro-magnetic spectrum) upon the mental plane. We have the primal appearance of solar or world-spheres, embodying at first latent and then active heat, that then blazes into Fire. Thus is the *karma* instigated of what is to be incorporated into the budding form growing in the Waters. The Nutrients that are incorporated in the form (via cosmic Blood, the 'Water of Life') are seen in terms of the energies from the constellations and the zodiac, collectively, the *chakras* in the Body of THAT Logos. The integration of all these energies and their inevitable expression in the field of Service is expressed by D.K. in terms of the word 'Beatitude'.

The cosmic sense of *Touch* via the plane *anupādaka* draws cosmic Watery Purpose from the fourth cosmic astral sub-plane, as an expression of the quality of 'Service' producing the sum of Bodhisattvic activity manifesting in the domain of the Logoi concerned. Touch organises the substance and Lives that are to incarnate into the new form ('the not-Self'). They are therefore moulded into the shapes or forms desired by the Logos. The Mirror-like Wisdom of Akṣobhya comes into expression. The form that appears that is Touched or moulded by the energies of cosmic Love-Wisdom that manifests via *anupādaka* mirrors the image created in the Logoic Mind. These energies are utilised by the Greater Builders to build the domain of Shambhala, from which directive purpose can proceed. The energies of this Service manifests in the form of the Light of the seven Ray modes of activity.

Light is the conveyance of all the cosmic forces so that they can be used as a Tool for the building of the desired consciousness-bearing forms. Light is projected into active manifestation via an embodied self-governing agent. Light therefore is the vehicle of Conscious transmission from the Soul or Logoic Mind that garners the experiences from the engagement with appearing phenomena. Light consequently represents the *saṃskāras* of awareness directed from one organising centre (sphere of consciousness) to another. With respect to a human unit we have the mechanism of transmission *(antaḥkaraṇas)* from the consciousness of a human unit to the various petals of the Sambhogakāya Flower. Light then carries the quality of the expression plus the nature of what has been experienced. Similarly we cognise and know about things because of the light that strikes objects, which then passes through the retinas of our eyes to the brain. The brain interprets the energy qualifications in terms of the images that are 'seen'. Empirical knowledge accumulates in this way.

Light manifests through the four cosmic ethers via the *chakras* and *nāḍīs* therein to impact upon the substance of the cosmic dense physical plane, the systemic mental, in order to mould or manipulate its substance, according to the Will/Desire (mantric Sound) of the Divine Thinker.

Fire is the result of the impact of Light upon dense substance, facilitating the sense of *Sight* to see the detailed minutiae of all aspects of the *manasic* form to be built in compliance with the Image upon the cosmic mental plane of what is to exist. Fire produces the cogent Realisation of the orchestrated beauty of the entire panorama that comes into manifestation. The streams of Creative Intelligences can then flow through the established *nāḍīs* to play their appointed roles. This happens via the plane *ātma,* drawing from the fifth cosmic astral sub-plane. Thus manifest the organs and organelles of the foetal Child to prepare for the birthing by being awakened from *pralaya*. The Discriminating Inner Wisdom of Amitābha is activated to produce the diversity of all that is to appear.

The *Watery* expression manifests from the sixth cosmic astral sub-plane via the plane *buddhi* in the form of the sense of *Taste*. It is an expression of the Equalising Wisdom of Ratnasambhava, and prepares the fully formed foetus for incarnation, after ensuring that all attributes of the child are integrated and functioning with one unitary purpose to produce the Perfection of what is to be. The subtle discriminating ability accorded to this sense is used to ensure complete compliance with the ideal.

The sixth astral sub-plane is the major energy qualification of the cosmic astral plane, and its energy translates as *bodhicitta* (the driving force of the enlightened Mind, or Love-Wisdom) upon our systemic planes. It is the basis to the Bodhisattva vow, being the expression of the Meditation-Mind that sees all as an integral unity, therefore the Knowledge that one can only progress along the upward Way if the entire body of manifestation (the 'Child') is brought along with one. Spiral-cyclic motion is evolved and works to produce evolutionary perfection, hence D.K. provides the quality of 'Perfection' for this sense and then states that it concerns the completion of evolution 'through the utilisation of the not-self and its realised adequacy'. This comes as a consequence of right discrimination by the human units constituting the Christ-Child, allowing them to reject what hinders their journey to liberation. From a Logoic perspective therefore, taste and smell (the two minor senses) represent qualities garnered from experiences wrought from those that have evolved in systemic space, that have gained perfection, and brought with them the attributes that can be subtly discerned by means of these two senses.

The term *Heat* Logoically refers to the expression of the cosmic sense of *Smell,* producing 'Perfect Knowledge'. The Flames of the Logoic Mind are activated to awaken the petals of the foetal force centres upon the mental plane. The heat comes as a consequence of the impact of Logoic Mind that works to organise the primal substance, the black dust of the mental plane. *Kuṇḍalinī* is consequently generated, and thereby becomes the central integrating energy that unifies all atomic substance with one inherent purpose, one unified Flame in the Womb of the great Mother. Once the form has incarnated then this unifying Fire of the Mother becomes hidden in the concretised form, but is responsible for the maintenance of its internal heat, and the integrating coherence of the Life of the form. Concerning the term 'heat' D.K. states:

> The internal fires that animate and vitalize shew themselves in a twofold manner:
>
> First as *latent heat.* This is the basis of rotary motion and the cause of the spheroidal coherent manifestation of all existence, from the logoic atom, the solar ring-pass-not, down to the minutest atom of the chemist or physicist.
>
> Second, as *active heat.* This results in the activity and the driving forward of material evolution. On the highest plane the combination of these three factors (active heat, latent heat and the primordial substance

> which they animate) is known as the 'sea of fire,' of which akasha is the first differentiation of pregenetic matter. Akasha, in manifestation, expresses itself as Fohat, or divine Energy, and Fohat on the different planes is known as aether, air, fire, water, electricity, ether, prana and similar terms. It is the sumtotal of that which is active, animated, or vitalized, and of all that concerns itself with the adaptation of the form to the needs of the inner flame of life.[16]

The energy to mould the most concrete aspect of the cosmic dense physical plane is drawn from the seventh cosmic astral sub-plane, which carries the silver-white Light of which our seven Rays are subdivisions. The entire teaching anent these Rays manifesting through the cosmic dense physical plane, and the overcoming of its resistance to evolutionary change provided in the esoteric philosophy then applies. Such resistance produces the heat content found in the extra-spirals of the Logoic physical permanent atom. The All-accomplishing Wisdom of Amoghasiddhi governs this entire output. The subtlest of the senses, *smell,* is involved because only the most refined of the sense-impressions are transmitted from the spheres of sensation (the cosmic dense form) to the experiencing Logoic Consciousness. Hence the entire evolutionary process must be taken into account, the way to the liberation of the 'Son', whereby right discrimination, refinement, and consequent transmutation of substance is required. Once liberation is achieved then a *nirvāṇee* is released from the thrall of bondage to systemic space. Each such returning one represents the perfume of the Flower stimulating the *saṃskāras* of olfactory awareness for the presiding Logos. One should also note the quality of the radiance and intensity of the light with respect to the type of information conveyed (the 'perfected Knowledge' associated with this sense-consciousness).

The number 22 of the phrase *'Flame is Fire'* implies that the entire Womb of Nature is infused with Flame, the conscious Lives that govern the evolution of substance through time. The Lives are conditioned by the ten planetary and twelve zodiacal Potencies. This Fire sustains all Logoic spheres of activity (13).

Concerning this Stanza H.P.B. states:

16 T.C.F., 41-44.

> All these — "Light," "Flame," "Hot," "Cold," "Fire," "Heat," "Water," and the "water of life" are all, on our plane, the progeny; or as a modern physicist would say, the correlations of ELECTRICITY. Mighty word, and a still mightier symbol! Sacred generator of a no less sacred progeny; of fire — the creator, the preserver and the destroyer; of light — the essence of our divine ancestors; of flame — the Soul of things. Electricity, the ONE Life at the upper rung of Being, and Astral Fluid, the Athanor of the Alchemists, at its lowest; GOD and DEVIL, GOOD and EVIL...
>
> Now, why is Light called in the Stanzas "cold flame"? Because in the order of Cosmic evolution (as taught by the Occultist), the energy that actuates matter after its formation into atoms is generated on our plane by Cosmic heat; and because Kosmos, in the sense of dissociated matter, was not, before that period. The first primordial matter, eternal and coeval with Space, "which has neither a beginning nor an end," is, "neither hot nor cold, but is of its own special nature," says the Commentary (Book II). Heat and cold are relative qualities, and pertain to the realms of the manifested worlds, which all proceed from the manifested *Hyle,* which, in its absolutely latent aspect, is referred to as the "cold Virgin," and when awakened to life as the "Mother." The ancient Western Cosmogonic myths state that at first there was but cold mist which was the Father, and the prolific slime (the Mother, Ilus or Hyle), from which crept forth the Mundane snake-matter, *(Isis,* vol. i., p. 146). Primordial matter, then, before it emerges from the plane of the never-manifesting, and awakens to the thrill of action under the impulse of Fohat, is but "a cool Radiance, colourless, formless, tasteless, and devoid of every quality and aspect." Even such are her first-born, the "four sons," who "are One, and become Seven," — the entities, by whose qualifications and names the ancient Eastern Occultists called the four of the seven primal "centres of Forces," or atoms, that develop later into the great Cosmic "Elements," now divided into the seventy or so sub-elements, known to science.[17]

The number 6 x 7 of the phrase *'the Waters of Life in the great Mother'* directly refers to the sum of manifest substance of the sixth of the seven planes of perception, the Watery astral plane.

---

17 Ibid, Vol. 1, 81-82.

Stanza Three part Ten

Stanza 3:10 states:

> **Father-Mother spin a web whose upper end is fastened to Spirit** *(Purusha),* **the Light of the one Darkness, and the lower one to matter** *(Prakriti)* **its** *(the Spirit's)* **shadowy end; and this web is the universe spun out of the two substances made in One, which is Swabhavat.**

Keynotes: Gemini, astral-etheric planes, sixth Ray, third sub-aspect of Earthy *ākāśa*, Ratnasambhava.

The numerical breakdown of the first three phrases:

Father-Mother (65, 11), Father-Mother spin (87, 15), a web (13, 4), upper end (45, 9), Father-Mother spin a web (100, 19), fastened to Spirit (74, 20), whose upper end is fastened to Spirit (154 = 77 x 2, 100 + 6 x 9, 46 37 = 10), spin a web (35, 8), a web whose upper end is fastened to Spirit (167, 50 41), Father—Mother spin a web whose upper end is fastened to Spirit (254, 65 56), the Light (44, 17), the one Darkness (59 = 14, 23, 5), the Light of the one Darkness (115, 43 = 7), the lower one (59 = 5, 23), its shadowy end (58, 13 = 4), the lower one to matter (90, 36), the lower one to matter its shadowy end (148, 49), matter its shadowy end (81, 18, 5.3.5.5).

The tone of this verse is provided by the sign Gemini the twins that governs the etheric web, hence the body of energies *(prāṇa),* from which all Life emanates. The view at first descends to the four higher etheric sub-planes of systemic space via the general Ray line governing this Stanza, the sixth Ray of Devotion, under whose auspices the *deva* kingdom 'spin a web' of the *nāḍī* system, the webs of Life for the new form. The Stanza however states that 'Father-Mother' spin this web. The Father is the directive Will and the Mother represents the *devas* that are impelled to act accordingly. The meaning of the phrase *'Father-Mother'* was also provided in Stanza 2:5 in reference to the phrase 'darkness alone was Father-Mother; Svabhavat'.

The systemic astral-etheric plane now specifically comes into view. Gemini projects the higher, living vitality, into the Blinded

Lives that the *devas* rightly organise. The complete externalisation of the first Outpouring via the energetic impetus of the sixth Ray can thereby manifest.

As stated earlier, both this Stanza and Stanza 3:11 (directly dealing with the etheric domain) are concerned with the crystallisation of the originating cosmic Fires to cause the appearance of the elementary substance of the mineral kingdom. *Kuṇḍalinī* is the means whereby the Elementary Lives are organised by the crystallised Fire, integrating the *aṇus,* the elementary atoms, into the atomic Elements known to scientists.[18] The *devas* (the Agnisuryans and Agnichaitans) utilise the energies from the Lesser Builders to build upon a mass scale the forms found in the three worlds of human livingness. The *karma* of the lives evolving in the material domains is thereby moulded. The governing sign of the Lesser Builders (the third incarnated Creative Hierarchy) is Libra the balances, whilst *jñānaśakti,* the 'force of mind', is their conditioning energy. The impact of the work of the Lesser Builders is first upon the mental plane, and then reverberates via the astral to cause the conditionings of dense form. This allows aspects of cosmic Mind to reach right down to form the mineral kingdom via the agencies of the astral and etheric *devas* that are the bearers of increasingly reified aspects of Mahat. The third *(manasic)* sub-aspect of Earthy *ākāśa* under the auspices of Ratnasambhava and the sixth Ray energising potency is utilised to produce this consolidation process of substance into forms.

This form of Earthy *ākāśa* allows the energy of the Mind to mould the appearing forms according to the pattern of divine Mentation. Ratnasambhava's Equalising Wisdom harmonises the outer appearing pattern of things in accordance with the nature of the *maṇḍala* imprinted upon the substance. What must be according to the Will of the Father can thereby take shape in the Womb of the Mother wherein the *maṇḍala* of this web is formed.

Normally we think of the twelve signs of the zodiac, but here a hypothetical thirteenth sign is implied – Arachne, the spider, which stands between Gemini and Cancer, and takes the qualities of both. Arachne stands for that which builds the web of Life inside the Womb,

---

18 See the later chapters of *Esoteric Cosmology and Modern Physics* for detail of this process.

the field of space within which the twelve signs of the reversed zodiacal wheel reside. The signs are impacted upon by the energies from the twelve great zodiacal constellations, which project the modalities of Life. The web of all the formative forces conditioning the space that is *saṃsāra* then appears. This web is that of the *nāḍīs* and associated *chakras* underlying the etheric form of manifest space. The etheric substratum bears the forces of the Real. From this appears the great Illusion, the imprint or reflection of the Real. The wheel of the zodiac reverses for humanity when they appear, as they must learn to master that illusion, the *māyā* within which they are caught. They battle this substance to transmute and elevate it to the higher dimensions, thus rectifying the zodiac.

Father and Mother are here united in the hyphenated word 'Father-Mother', implying the concept of the Divine Hermaphrodite, or else of a complete conjugal Union. (The cause of the emission of the 'One Ray' that could fertilise the germ of the bud Lotus, 'Matri-Padma'.) The qualities of the Divine Hermaphrodite is symbolised by the attributes of Taurus the bull. The horns of its glyph represent the psyche that is evolving, or budding (the forces of the Mother) to form the material domain, which is still attached to the circle of the Spirit (the Father).

The phrase 'Father-Mother' also implicates the three Earth signs, where 'Father' refers to the sign Capricorn the goat, the 'Mount of God', signifying the expression of cosmic Mind, the sphere of the Spirit. The 'Mother' embodies the substance that is impregnated, and also the Lives that build the form, as associated with the sign Virgo the virgin, and here representing the budding horns of the Bull moving to embrace the extent of the substance of the sphere that is not yet. Their conjugal union produces the field of cosmic Desire that is Taurus. *Svabhāva* then represents the plastic substance of that field (the etheric domain) as organised by the Creative Word of Father-Mother. Whatever is to be can then incarnate within the illusional forms that come into being in the manifesting space. This Earthy trinity thus conditions the sum of the cosmic dense physical plane.

This brings the Hierarchical planets Venus, Jupiter and Vulcan into play via Gemini, which represents the field of the earth (the Hierarchical ruler of Gemini). Virgo provides the greenery upon which the animals (Taurus and Capricorn) of Logoic desire graze. Venus, representing the discriminative aspects of Mind, governs the mode of activity of the awakening permanent atoms upon the atomic (first) sub-plane of the cosmic dense physical plane of the Logos, and that of the streams of Creative Intelligences. The *saṃskāras* that are to flow through the spirals and spirillae of the Logoic atom are thereby activated. They then draw to them the substance of the periodic sheaths, regulated by Jupiter and the second Ray of Love-Wisdom, who thereby governs the general qualities of the etheric sub-planes in this second Ray Logoic dispensation. (Which conditions the building of the second Ray form.) Vulcan (ruling the first Ray) then utilises the major cosmic sense of Touch to mould the pliant cosmic dense substance (the mental plane) according to the impact of Logoic purpose.

The number 13 of the phrase *'a web'* refers to the underlying geometry governing this web that *'Father-Mother spin'* (15) by means of the use of the active expression of Divine Intelligence (3 x 5). Everything coming into manifestation is an expression of the modifications of that Mind. This concept is exemplified further by the numbers of the phrase *'spin a web'* (35, 8). The number 8 signifies the spiral-cyclic motion utilised to accomplish this spinning process, whist the number 7 x 5 implicates the energies of the Logoic Mind that directs the activity.

The number 100 of the phrase *'Father-Mother spin a web'* refers to the sum of the etheric body of underlying macrocosmic Space. It is the number of the great Perfection that is integrated into the planning of this web, and commensurate with a new cycle of endeavour of what is to be produced.

The web is *'fastened to Spirit'* by means of a *sūtrātmā* (11, 20) which is then extended to incorporate the process of spinning the web. It thus symbolises the properties of the web itself, being the conveyor of intensified energies to the form. The web exists to convey qualified *prāṇic* energy from one part of the organism to another.

As the concern is the systemic etheric web, comprised of the four etheric sub-planes, so the upper end must be interpreted from this perspective. By the number 9 x 5 of the phrase *'upper end'* we see that this end is fastened to the Mind of the Logos. Its purpose is to produce Masters (9 x 5) out of the incarnate Lives (the development of *ātmic* perception). They can then pass on to the 'upper end' of this web through the projection of the required *antaḥkaraṇas*. The number 70 of the phrase *'Whose upper end'* refers here to the septenary of expression that this end consists of, specifically the seven planetary regents, or solar systems of Stanza 2:5. It can refer to the seven cosmic astral sub-planes that can also represent the upper end of this web. Through them the Watery energies of Love and Life then pour through the etheric web to en-Soul and vitalise the structure of the formed space with all that must come to be.

'Spirit' is what embodies the attributes of Deity for a complete length or Great Year in the Life of Brahmā. It is the non-manifest abstracted Archetype that is the cause of manifestation, yet remains aloof from it all. It is the first aspect of Deity. Here Blavatsky relates Spirit to Purusha. Purusha (Puruṣa) essentially refers to the universal Soul, the ideal or cosmic Man (Īśvara). In Sāṇkhya philosophy Puruṣa is pure consciousness, unattached and not related to anything. In Advaita Vedānta it is the supreme Self *(paramātman),* the eternal Witness. The Muṇḍaka Upaniṣad states that Puruṣa is immutable *(takṣara)* and eternal *(para).* It fulfils all things from within without. One can conceive that the upper end of this thread is fastened to the Head or Heart centre of this grand Heavenly Man, but in terms of the actual manifestation of phenomena, the Logoic Splenic centre would actually emanate the thread. This centre embodies the activities of the *nāḍī* system in a human unit.

The numbers of the phrase *'a web whose upper end is fastened to Spirit'* add to 50, consequently we see that this entire process is an expression of the Logoic Mind, which projects the *sūtrātmā* in order to produce the web of 'the universe', at whatever scale we wish to interpret this term 'universe'.

The number 200 + 6 x 9 of the complete phrase, *'Father-Mother spin a web whose upper end is fastened to Spirit',* refers to the Monadic aspect of 'Father-Mother'. From a lower perspective it can also refer to the Dhyānis that establish the Shambhalic correspondence into which a Logos incarnates. All have a myriad links to various stellar spheres, with whom they energetically interrelate. These links then manifest as the various petals of the Logoic Head lotus (and by extension, to the Causal form) into which the *saṃskāras* derived through incarnate Life are abstracted. Abstraction into the Shambhalic Domain represents 'the Spirit' for the lesser Lives evolving within the Womb of the Mother. As they travel up the cord, the *sūtrātmā,* they thereby develop aspects of the Mind of the presiding Logos. The numbers 13 x 5, 11 of this phrase relate to the *nāḍī* system (11) constituting this web, plus the spheres of activity (13 x 5) contained within it.

In the next phrase the meaning of the term Spirit is clarified, as it is equated with the term Light, the first differentiation of Darkness. This Darkness was explained in Stanza 1:5, which states that 'Darkness alone filled the Boundless All'. *'The Light'* then refers to the corresponding phrase in Stanza 2:5: 'The Seven were not yet born from the Web of Light. Darkness alone was Father-Mother, Svabhavat'. In the form of 'the Spirit' we also saw that Darkness is intensified energy that puts into shadow all lesser forms of Light by which we may wish to view it.

The phrase *'the one Darkness'* (5) specifically refers to the darkness of ignorance (the unaware mind), both in the sense of not knowing, as well as in the case of awakening from slumber, because the light of day has a chance to reveal what it will show. From this perspective it is also an attribute of the Mind of Deity, and is 'One' because it is indivisible, universal.

'The Light' (44, 17) is the mechanism of conscious unfoldment that will reveal to the mind/Mind what was formerly veiled, and which conquers ignorance. The process is similar for a Logos as for an individual. These numbers indicate that Light is a direct embodiment of the energy Body of Deity (17, 8), the sum of the energy associated with enlightenment, especially that vivifying the cosmic etheric Body *(buddhi)* and the *chakras* therein (44). Spirit can therefore also be viewed as a generic term relating to the planes of perception associated with that cosmic etheric Form from which the Light that is the salvation of the world emanates.

We see also by reference to Stanza 1:5 that this Light can be equated with the Son, who at this stage had 'not yet awakened for the new wheel'. What is here implied is the subtle vehicle (a light body) of the Son aspect of Deity, His radiant aura. This is seen objectively as a blazing sun in the Heavens (to which the number 44 also refers regarding our solar or planetary Logoi). The sign Leo the lion is astrologically implicated, which is ruled by the sun on all three levels, and signifies the development of self-consciousness, the separative self-willed individual that distinguishes him/herself from all other such 'selves'.

'The one Darkness' then refers to the sign Pisces the fishes, thus to the *pralaya* that comes as a consequence of the ending of things. By the number 100 + 15 of the phrase *'the Light of the one Darkness'* we see that this Light is that of the development of intelligence. It is the Light of the great Day 'Be with Us'[19] for one complete *mahāmanvantara*. The act of spinning is therefore equated with the infusion into the etheric Body of Deity, the Light of the Son, Love-Wisdom, or consciousness, so as to make perfect, or to complete the entire evolutionary process. The number 7 implicates the seven Ray aspects of the one fundamental Ray, as manifested on the seven planes of perception, and the seven Chains, The entire *nāḍī* system of Deity thus comes to be vivified with living Light.

Having analysed the upper end of this web its lower connection, *'its shadowy end'*, can now be considered. By the term 'shadowy' we see that it involves the effect of something material that blocks the approach of light, hence the casting of a shadow. In being 'shadowy' there are many such obstructions, hence the differences between the various forms of obstructions of light must also be viewed. Some are completely opaque, others are partially transparent, others will colour the impacting light with the effect of their own hue. This relates to the myriad different groups of sentient beings constituting formed space, as well as the various grades of human consciousness concerned, from Lemurian humanity right through to the highly illumined Sons of Light. There is thus an apt depiction of the nature of *saṃsāra* in the word 'shadowy', including also its ephemerality. The objects also absorb the impact of the energy of the light rays and retransmit them after adding their own qualities.

The numbers of the phrases *'the lower one'* and *'the one Darkness'* both add to 14, 5. The concept of a mirror-like activity of the Real ('the One Darkness') being reflected into its mirror-image ('the lower one'), the lower darkness is thereby implied. Effectively therefore there is the reflection of the energies of the cosmic astral plane (2 x 7),

19 See Stanza 7:7.

which is the Real, into the etheric web, thence into the systemic astral (and mental) plane, which is the great illusion *(saṃsāra).* The etheric web therefore acts as a mirror for this process, inverting the images concerned. 'Matter', the substance of the mind (5) thus manifests as the lower darkness as a reflection of the Mind of 'God', of Darkness itself. As earlier stated, from a cosmic viewpoint our mental plane is dense substance matter.

'Its shadowy end' refers to the quaternary (13, 4), the foundation or square that supports all manifest space, of the domain of the empirical mind (the 'shadowy end' = 5.5.). Such a mind is 'shadowy' because constantly changing, fickle, in relation to the direction of the light source, or to the generation of thoughts. The thought-form making tendencies of most human thinkers are generally constituted of concrete-minded, mundane, trivial, earthy ideas and images (with occasional flashes of revelation and inspiration) that make them shadowy.

The Earthy Virgoan qualities are here implied, whereupon within the mundane material domains the individual must eventually learn to develop the keen intuitive perceptions and high realisations associated with Mercury, the 'messenger of the Gods', the exoteric ruler of this sign. The shadows are thereby brightened up and eventually eliminated altogether. Solar light then replaces lunar light.

The numbers of the phrases *'the lower one to matter'* and *'the lower one to matter its shadowy end'* add to 90, 36, 148, and 49. The number 90 here implies that a Logos undergoes an Initiation as He/She manifests the process of *manvantara,* which thereby extends the Logoic *sūtrātmā* to the 'shadowy end', causing the formation of world spheres and the evolution of the Lives thereon. Paradoxically, even the dense physical sun and its compliment of planets can be considered 'shadowy' in relation to the domain of the central Spiritual Sun at the 'upper end'. The emanation of the *karma* of various types ('the shadows') to their eventual resolution thus manifests. The number 36 = 3 x 12 here refers to the third sign of the zodiac, Gemini the twins, whose functions in this respect have been provided above.

The number 100 + 48 and 7 x 7 refer to the appropriation of this 'shadowy end' in that the number 4 x 12 refers to the fourth sign of the zodiac, which governs the rebirthing process, whilst the number 7 x 7 symbolises the septenaries associated with all of manifested Life.

The third and fifth Ray aspects of the projection of the Mind that will bring about the appearance of matter as physical plane phenomena is hinted at in the numbers 5.3.5.5 of the phrase *'matter its shadowy end'*. The number 81 = 3^4 of this phrase also implicates that matter is an expression of a quaternary, where every aspect is conditioned by the three *guṇas, sattva* (truth, rhythm), *rajas* (activity) and *tamas* (inertia).

The numerical breakdown of the last two phrases:

> this Web (32, 5), the universe (56, 11), this Web is the universe (98, 17), the two Substances (52, 16), made in One (44, 17), the two substances made in One (96 = 8 x 12, 33), in One (30, 12), spun out of the two substances made in One (135, 45), out of the two substances (75, 21), spun out of the two substances (91, 28), this Web is the universe spun out of the two substances (189, 45), the universe spun out of the two substances (147, 39), the Universe spun out of the two substances made in One (191, 56), in One (30, 12), this Web is the universe spun out of the two substances made in One (233, 62), which is Swabhavat (68, 14), Swabhavat (25, 7).

By the number 32 we see that *'this web'* expresses the Love-Wisdom characteristics of Deity.

By the numbers 7 x 8, 11 of *'the universe'* (explained in Stanza 1:6) we see that the universe is a body of energies (7 x 8) containing lines (a web) of interrelationships (11). The web underlies the knowable universe, and from the esoteric viewpoint the web *is* that universe, for the dense physical form is an automation, an illusional effect of the energies manifesting through the web. The numbers 49 x 2 and 17 of the phrase *'this web is the universe'* inform us that everything this universe is constituted of is a transcendental level after transcendental level of septenaries, which is indeed Divinity Itself (17).

H.P.B's essential commentary:

> In the Mandukya (Mundaka) Upanishad it is written, "As a spider throws out and retracts its web, as herbs spring up in the ground...so is the Universe derived from the undecaying one," (I. 1.7). Brahmā, as "the Germ of unknown Darkness," is the material from which all evolves and develops, "as the web from the spider, as foam from the

> water," etc. This is only graphic and true, if the term Brahmā the "Creator" is, as a term, derived from the root *brih,* to increase or expand. Brahmā "expands" and becomes the Universe woven out of his own substance.[20]

We now enter into the concept of 'substances', implying what is tangible, cognisable. There is however an immense chasm between *'the two substances'* (52, 16, 7), Spirit and matter. Spirit is highly insubstantial from the point of view of those ensconced in matter. Matter on the other hand is a solid concretion or condensation of primal substance. Nevertheless, during the *manvantara* (52) they are incorporated as one by means of the web. The number 16 refers to Spirit, the substance of the (cosmic) Christ, the number 7 to matter, the seven planes of perception within the confines of the cosmic dense realm.

The number 44 of the phrase *'made in One'* implies that they are thus consubstantiated in the body of manifestation of the planetary or solar Logos, cosmic Humanity. This number also refers to the expression of *buddhic* energy (the fourth ether) and all the Wheels (Deities, *chakras)* within that Web that are to capture, integrate, process and express it. They are all interrelated by this spinning process, and thus 'made in One'. Unity is all there is, and energy unites the seemingly separated in time and space.

The numbers 96, 33 of the phrase *'the two substances made in One'* have a similar connotation, but with the added emphasis of the multitudes of Creative Intelligences (33) that are brought into active play by means of the interrelationship of these two substances.

The number 96 refers to the base number of petals to all of the *chakras.* They are force plexus' within the Web, directing energies from one zone or plane of perception to another. Via them manifests the substance that causes the appearance of things. Also implied is the sum of yogic philosophy, and of the two main kingdoms involved in solar evolution, the human and the *deva.* The human stream bears the substance of Love, thus of the qualities of the *piṇgalā nāḍī,* of the way of the Heart, which unites disparaging parts into a unity – the Soul of all Life. The *deva* stream embodies the substance of the appearing forms,

---

20 Ibid., Vol. 1, 83.

of matter, integrated by the qualities of *manas,* which distinguishes one from another, that differentiates and segregates unity into the diversity of parts, producing the many categorisations in Nature needed for sentient entities to develop mind. This constitutes the evolution of the *iḍā nāḍī* stream in Nature. The evolutionary process starts with this differentiation because bearers of consciousness must arise in order to eventually develop the way of the Heart. The *devas* therefore represent the forces of the Mother, whilst the human stream represents the forces of the Son in evolution. What unites them into One is the Father aspect (the *suṣumṇā* stream).

The number 8 x 12 also refers to the sign Scorpio the scorpion, which here indicates the mechanism of directing and moulding the substance into the needed forms by means of the sting of the scorpion. Scorpio also signifies the cosmic Humanity Who are brought into manifest activity, as also the full flowering of a human kingdom. Scorpio is the sign of discipleship and of testing. Thus it represents the means of integrating the *deva* and human kingdoms into a unity (which happens at the attainment of the sixth Initiation). Therefore upon the path of Initiation the individual learns to first master the Elementals governing his/her desire body, then the unruly forces of the emotions. Later there is the path of cooperation with the greater *devas* and eventual marriage between human and *deva* potencies. The entire path to liberation can be thought of in such terms. As for a human unit, so also for a Logos, though upon a far vaster scale.

The numbers 15 x 9 and 5 x 9 of the phrase *'spun out of the two substances made in One'* refer to the Initiates, the Greater (15 x 9) and Lesser Builders (5 x 9). Under the directives of Father-Mother they spin the forms of the appearing Lives into concrete manifestation within *manvantara* by means of the sixth, seventh and third Ray (of Stanzas 3:10 to 3:12) Activity. The human Adept (9 x 5) later evolves from manifestation and works to unravel what was spun, cleansing the *karma* of it all, thereby lessening contact with the material domain upon the upward arc of liberation from it all. Humanity refine, transform and transmute matter so that it is eventually manifested as Spirit, the One. Matter as such is effectively but transient substance, condensed *manasic* energy that cloaks the appearance of 'things', as explained in my book *Esoteric Cosmology and Modern Physics.*

Implicated in these numbers also are the Brothers of our solar Logos, Who together produce the sum of the evolutionary attainment of all entities incarnate in time and space within the confines of the Body of the 'One About Whom Naught May Be Said'.

The number 4 x 7 of the phrase *'spun out of the two substances'* refers both to the four ethers as well as to *manasic* substance. From *manas* comes the quaternary of the lower mind, astral body, the etheric double and the dense body of the embodied form. The interpretation of 'the two substances' here therefore refers to the substance of the cosmic ethers (the embodied Life) integrated with what has been incorporated from primal *manasic* substance *(prakṛti),* because the quaternary emanates from *manas. Prakṛti* then is the 'cosmic dirt' that must eventually be converted into man-plants by means of the evolutionary process. Eventually the place of integration of Spirit and *manas* upon the upward arc of the returning *jīvas* (lives) becomes the *śūnyatā-saṃsāra* nexus.

The number 30 of the phrase *'in One'* implies that all is made in the One sphere of Activity of the cosmic Deity, the ring-pass-not within which the Logos limits His/Her expression for the entire *manvantara.*

The numbers of the phrases *'this Web is the universe spun out of the two substances'* (189 = 21 x 9, 45), *'the universe spun out of the two substances made in One'* (11 and 7 x 8) and of *the complete phrase* (233, 31 x 2) refer to the energies (7 x 8) with which this Web is spun by, plus the *sūtrātmās* that are woven together (11) to spin this Web. Essentially this Web is spun out of the substance of the twelve Creative Hierarchies, the Creative Intelligences (200 + 33) who embody all manifest space with the substance of their forms. The number 7 x 3 x 9 refer to the trinities, the Soul aspect of all that is to BE, manifesting in the form of the septenaries of Life, which interrelate Spirit (9) to matter (3 x 7). All is spun by means of the reflected Will of the Logos (31 x 2) utilised by the Creative Hierarchies.

As earlier stated 'the universe' can refer to the internal or external universe, or a metaphorical one, such as Life in our earth Scheme. The 'universe' manifesting as our solar system is governed by the second Ray of Love-Wisdom, which is the objective of the evolving Lives to engender.

The number 13 x 3 of the phrase *'the universe spun out of the two substances'* indicates that this 'spinning process' (spiral-cyclic motion) is divine Activity that integrates the central Throne or Seat of Power of a Logos to the circumference of the ring-pass-not that is the sphere of limitation within which the fabric of the universe appears and plays its appointed role.

With respect to *svabhāva* I stated in volume 1 of *A Treatise on Mind* that there are two types inferred in Buddhist philosophy, the first being inherent existence, which relates to *mūlaprakṛti,* the basis to *saṃsāra.* The second relates to emptiness *(śūnyatā),* the final nature for every phenomenal appearance. *Śūnyatā* is the substance of the fourth cosmic ether. The term *svabhāva* therefore covers both of these two substances. The number 14 of the phrase *'which is Swabhavat'* refers to the septenaries of manifestation wherein all Lives evolve and the substance of which all Lives embody as their forms. H.P.B has rendered the term Swabhavat in two different ways, as the Sanskrit v sounds like w, hence in Stanza 2:5 the term is spelt Svabhavat, whereas here we have Swabhavat. (Stanza 3:12 provides us with Svābhāvat). There is a numerological difference in the v = 4 and w = 5, and Blavatsky uses either rendering according to what is numerologically important at the time. The numbers of the phrase *'which is Svabhavat'* for instance add to 67, 13, which would simply refer to a sphere of activity, whereas the number 14 provides a better numerological explanation as to what is meant by the term *svabhāva.*

Stanza Three part Eleven

Stanza 3:11 states:

> **It expands when the Breath of Fire is upon it; it contracts when the Breath of the Mother touches it. Then the Sons dissociate and scatter, to return into their Mother's Bosom at the end of the great Day, and re-become one with her; when it is cooling it becomes radiant, and the Sons expand and contract through their own Selves and Hearts; they embrace Infinitude.**

Keynotes: Cancer, the etheric plane, the seventh Ray, fourth sub-aspect of Earthy *ākāśa*, Amitābha.

The numerical breakdown of the first two phrases:

> It expands (40, 13), the Breath of Fire (83, 29), Fire is upon it (71, 17) The Breath of Fire is upon it (125, 35), the Breath (42, 15), when the Breath of Fire is upon it (148, 40), It expands when the Breath of Fire is upon it (188, 53 = 8), it contracts (43, 7), The Breath of the Mother (103, 31), the Mother (49, 13), the Breath of the Mother touches it (142, 43), When the Breath of the Mother touches it (165 = 35 x 5, 48), touches it (39, 12), it contacts when the Breath of the Mother touches it (208, 55).

Stanzas 3:10 and 3:11 are effectively expressions of Gemini, where Stanza 3:10 is concerned principally with the functions of the mortal Brother, the conditional forces underlying the 'creation' of things. Stanza 3:11 provides information on the immortal Brother, namely the consciousness-streams that evolve in the manifest universe. Stanza 3:11 is also conditioned by the sign Cancer the crab, which governs the process of descent into incarnation of the streams bearing the principle of Life. Life must contend with the appearance of phenomena, *saṃsāra* proper. Cancer's sixth Ray Neptunian energies appropriately distribute the Waters, Neptune being the esoteric and Hierarchical ruler of Cancer. Here the sixth Ray works in conjunction with the seventh (that governs this Stanza in general) in order to cause the precipitation of the mineral kingdom. The combination of the dual Rays assists in the objectivity of the etheric-physical domain. 'The great Day' of the new *mahāmanvantara* thus manifests. The incorporation of the tenth and eleventh Creative Hierarchies into the physical universe, as well as the process of their mastery, is taken into account in this Stanza. This work happens under the power of Amitābha's Discriminating Inner Wisdom, bearing the energies of Logoic Mind, which is needed to produce the final concretion of substance into dense forms. The fourth sub-aspect of Earthy *ākāśa* assists in the reflection of the energies of the four cosmic ethers into their physical counterparts. This is a continuation of the strong effects of the sixth Ray that we saw in Stanza 3:10, but now the process is more 'scientifically' applied to produce definite effects.

Cancer is the primary Watery sign in the zodiac. The fearful, scurrying crab symbolically lives at the juncture between the watery and the earthy terrain. The higher correspondence refers to the epoch of transiting from cosmic astral to cosmic physical space. Under the auspices of Neptune the god of the Waters Cancer opens the gates for the downpour of the expression of the cosmic astral Waters, as well as from the Mental impulses (instructions) from its polar opposite, Capricorn ('the Mountain of 'God'). Cancer also plays a similar role with the mass instinctual Elementary Lives that embody the primeval substance that appears at the earlier stages of the evolutionary process. Cancer opens and closes the gates for incarnation for all that have been appropriately prepared to play their roles in the manifestation of systemic dense physical space: the Divine Flames, the Greater and Lesser Builders, and the human Monads.

The concept of 'Breath' implies a certain quantity of subtle, Airy, virtually intangible energy that impacts upon phenomena. This Airy Element conveys the principle of Life, hence this Stanza is primarily concerned with the dissemination of the streams of Fiery Life, the seven Creative Hierarchies, into the prepared (etheric) form, rather than the manifestation of that form itself.

There are two Breaths implicated:

a. 'The Breath of Fire' (11), causing expansion.

b. 'The Breath of the Mother' (7 x 4), causing contraction.

Here the Fire Breather can be assumed to be the Father, the Logos projecting intensified Fiery energy containing the streams of the Creative Intelligences into the young universe, causing the expansionary evolution of its sentient Lives, the kingdoms of Nature, and the consciousness of humanity, to fill the bounds of the sphere of the Thought structure. Expansion via the use of Fiery energy esoterically means the evolution of consciousness, thus the entire evolutionary process is implied.

For a human unit there is a limit to the extent of the expansive process due to the effect of mind because what can be cognised from empirical phenomena is limited. At a certain stage the higher faculties must be developed, leading one beyond the domain of the senses and of the mind that reasons because of them. The Mind consequently evolves by those that can express the Airy aspect of this Fiery Breath. This Airy aspect concerns the refinement, sublimation and liberation of the substance constituting the Mother's Womb, producing the onset of *pralaya,* hence contraction of the form that was. The second Ray of Love-Wisdom is thereby evolved by the conscious Lives to produce the liberation process.

The outpouring of this Airy Element, *buddhi* (7 x 4) is here expressed as *'the Breath of the Mother'.* The awakening of the Airy principle is the response of the incarnate conscious Lives to the impact of the Fiery Breath. That response is the drive to gain liberation from the prison-house of the form, thus to achieve the emptiness associated with *śūnyatā* (which embodies the Airy Element). The activity of *'the Breath'* (42, 15) then produces the most refined attributes of the Mother's substance (symbolised by 6 x 7 and 3 x 5 for its Watery and Fiery characteristics). Through *śūnyatā* also flows the Fiery energy of the cosmic *nāḍīs* that at first produces the expansion process, and later assists in the abstraction of that which was formerly emanated. This implicates the energies associated with *ātma* and the rectification of causative *karma.*

The concept of expansion and contraction is that of breathing in and out. The One that breathes out is the Father, and the breathing in is accomplished by the touch of the Mother's Breath. The associated cyclic recurrence at each level of expression is governed by Libra the balances. This causes the process of the engendering of *karma* (by means of conscious volitions) and its eventual resolution.

This view is opposite to that which is normally given in terms of the Father-Mother relationship, where the Mother is seen as the Creator (i.e., the outward movement) and the Father as the destroyer of the form (the inward movement). The reason for the difference is because with respect to the use of the Breath our focus is upon the outpouring of potent subtle energies dealing with consciousness and its evolution, whereas the above case is concerned with the evolution of the form, the way of expression of matter and its eventual annihilation.

Stanza 3:10 therefore concerns the expansion process of the Fiery expression of Breathing, the involution of energies via the bottom hemisphere of the zodiac. Stanza 3:11 is concerned with the contraction process of substance, its liberation via the exhalation of the Breath of the Mother, thus with the qualities of the upper hemisphere of the zodiac.

The meaning of the concept of expanding was explained in Stanza 3:1 with regards the phrase 'The Mother swells, expanding from within without, like the bud of a lotus'. By The number 40 of the phrases *'It expands'* and *'when the Breath of Fire is upon it'* we see that the embodied form of our planetary or solar Logoi is what expands with the Fires of Consciousness. Also the number 100 + 48 is provided, which refers to the open gate of incarnation through Cancer the crab for the descent of this Fiery energy into systemic space.

The meaning of the term *Fire* and its relation to the *prāṇas* of the mental plane was explained in Stanza 3:6 in relation to the phrase 'The Ocean was radiant Light, which was Fire, and Heat, and Motion'.

The meaning of Breath was explained in Stanza 2:2. Here however we have the phrase *'the Breath of Fire'* (11), where this Fiery Breath is dynamic energy (Electricity), the essence of the quality of the higher mental plane. (This is essentially an *ātmic* expression.) We saw that Breath is an expression of Deity that exists even during *pralayic* sleep, whilst Fire is the Impulse of the awakened Mind, which causes all to come to be. By inference this Fiery Breath (literally a Dragon's Breath) is a product of the Spirit aspect that vitalises the corporeal form of the Son (or Web), causing it to expand, increase in magnitude and evolutionary accomplishment. It is the Web of the universe, 'The Son of necessity' (Stanza 1:6) that expands. The 'Breath of Fire' is also an expression of 'The Eternal Parent' (Stanza 1:1), Space, emanated by the cosmic Adept. The sign Leo the lion governs the expression of the awakening intelligence, the 'I am' principle that comes to know itself and to differentiate, even upon the mass scale of the universe expanding, where myriads of such self-conscious units awaken by means of this Fiery energetic stimulation. The entire universe then thrills with the vibrancy of self-conscious Life.

The numbers 7 x 5 and 125 of the phrase *'the Breath of Fire is upon it'* verify the above with respect to the dissemination of the energy of mind (7 x 5), with the added information that the Head centres (125) of all the Logoi that are to establish planetary and solar Bodies of manifestation now come into active expression. (The number 25 x 5 refers specifically to the five Kumāras, the Dhyāni Buddhas, that embody the Mind aspect of the cosmic Logos.) Fire comes to infuse every iota of all that is. It is the substance of Divinity (17 of the phrase

'Fire is upon it'), the energy of the Spirit that incorporates all in its embrace. The Fire thus is an expression of the energy body of Deity. The term *'upon it'* (32, 5) refers not only to the fact that this Fire energises the web by being absorbed into it, but that it completely surrounds and embraces it at the same time with the Love of Deity (32) that at first manifests in the form of Fiery expansion.

The number 7 of the phrase *'It contracts'* refers to any of the organised septenaries associated with manifest space. The number 7 x 7 of the phrase *'the Mother'* has a similar connotation. (The meaning of 'the Mother' was explained in Stanzas 1:5 and 3:1). The septenaries are also signified by the numbers 7 and 100 + 6 x 7 of the phrase *'the Breath of the Mother touches it'*. We see therefore that this Breath incorporates the entire *maṇḍala* of the form, with its seven subdivisions and Ray qualifications.

The ability to touch something implies contact with a material form, and once touched one comes to truly know that thing, rather than merely imputing its existence (as for instance by means of the sense of sight). We saw earlier that the sense of touch is the predominant one developed in this solar evolution. It relates to the complete expression and cognisance of the Watery Element, thus to the principle of Love-Wisdom *(bodhicitta),* which therefore is the ultimate gain of the expression of this sense.

The contraction process therefore leads one into the Waters of cosmic astral space as the prospective *nirvāṇees* gradually develop this sense to contact (hence touch) and experience increasingly subtler planes of perception. Through this sense one then becomes a resident of the plane contacted. Once consciousness is stabilised upon a plane of perception another higher one can be contacted, and so the process continues until liberation has been achieved from *saṃsāra,* and indeed from the entire cosmic dense physical plane after the seventh Initiation.

The numbers 13 x 3, 12 of the phrase *'touches it'* refer to the activity of the twelve Creative Hierarchies that must thus touch the planes of perception in order to first manifest their spheres of activity (13 x 3) and to later gain their liberation as *nirvāṇees,* thereby contracting the fabric of manifest space. This process of 'contraction' is infinitesimal at first, but gathers momentum as an increasing number of *nirvāṇees* appear.

'The Breath of the Mother' (103, 31) therefore relates to the perfection of the third Ray cycle of activity (103). This Breath represents the first Ray aspect of the third Ray (the Destroyer, the number 31) that results in the liberation and thus expulsion from the formed world of the enlightened beings. These *nirvāṇees* start their journey into abstract space, expulsed in the form of a 'Breath'. This phrase thus refers to the ending of the *mahāmanvantara*, when the many return from whence they came via the Mother's out breathing.

As the Mother also refers to the sign Virgo the virgin, consequently in relation to the phrase *'when the Breath of the Mother touches it'* (100 + 13 x 5, 48), so our focus is upon its esoteric ruler, the Moon, here veiling the first Ray potency of Vulcan. Vulcan's energy must be sought by the aspiring ones, to overcome the pull (addiction) to form *(saṃsāra)* in order to be liberated from it and thus be breathed out. The number 48 refers to the sign Cancer the crab, but it stands here at the northern position of the zodiac, and manifests in the form of the open gate to cosmos. It therefore represents the mechanism of escape by the Lives constituting the expiring Breath of the Mother. A triad of energies is thereby implied between Gemini, Virgo and Cancer. Here Gemini (whose Hierarchical ruler is the earth) represents the field upon which the prospective *nirvāṇees* 'stand' to enter the portals of Initiation and access to the Mysteries of being/non-being. Virgo then awakens the intuitive qualities, the refined intelligence embodied by Mercury, who holds the Caduceus staff, to awaken the latent powers associated with the *chakras* and to access the *devas* (the Mother's emissaries). Virgo also provides the will (Vulcan) to overcome the form and the wisdom (Jupiter) to seek the source of Love by treading the path to liberation. Once the temple work has been accomplished Cancer then opens the gates to experiencing ('touching') the higher planes of perception, until they become the new home of the Initiates concerned.

The number 100 + 13 x 5, or 33 x 5 here refers to the Creative potencies of the Wisdoms of the five Dhyāni Buddhas, as outlined above, that must be accessed if this 'Breathing' process is to happen. These Buddhas/Kumāras embody the 33 *cores* of Intelligent beings associated with manifest space. All beings must develop the prototype Wisdoms before they can be propelled into subjective space with the 'Breath of the Mother' at the ending of all evolutionary journeying.

The numbers 25, 55, 88 and 208 of the phrases *'the Mother touches it'* and *'It contracts when the Breath of the Mother touches it'* refer to the abstract Mind (25) as well as the adeptship of Mind (55) gained through riding the spiral-cyclic-*kuṇḍalinī* motion (8 x 11) to liberation into the cosmic ethers, wherein the principle of Love-Wisdom rules (200 + 8). They leave incarnate Life altogether (via the plane *ātma)* thereby contracting the etheric web, because with every ascended Being there is one less form to vitalise this web. The non-expression of each such unit of force means contraction.

H.P.B's essential commentary:

> The expanding of the Universe, under the breath of FIRE is very suggestive in the light of the "Fire mist" period, of which modern science speaks so much, and knows in reality so little.
>
> Great heat breaks up the compound elements and resolves the heavenly bodies into their primeval one element, explains the commentary. "Once disintegrated into its primal constituent, by getting within the attraction and reach of a focus, or centre of heat (energy), of which many are carried about to and fro in space, a body, whether alive or dead, will be vapourised, and held in "the bosom of the Mother" until Fohat, gathering a few of the clusters of Cosmic matter (nebulæ), will, by giving it an impulse, set it in motion anew, develop the required heat, and then leave it to follow its own new growth."
>
> The expanding and contracting of the Web — *i.e.,* the world-stuff, or atoms — express here the pulsatory movement; for it is the regular contraction and expansion of the infinite and shoreless Ocean of that which we may call the noumenon of matter, emanated by Swābhāvat, which causes the universal vibration of atoms. But it is also suggestive of something else. It shows that the ancients were acquainted with that which is now the puzzle of many scientists and especially of astronomers; the cause of the first ignition of matter or world-stuff, the paradox of the heat produced by refrigerative contraction and other such Cosmic riddles. For it points unmistakably to a knowledge by the ancients of such phenomena. "There is heat internal and heat external in every atom," say the manuscript Commentaries, to which the writer has had access; "the breath of the Father (or Spirit), and the breath (or Heat) of the Mother (matter);" and they give explanations which show that the modern theory of the extinction of the solar fires by loss of heat through radiation, is erroneous.....Contraction develops heat,

> it is true; but contraction (from cooling) is incapable of developing the whole amount of heat at any time existing in the mass, or even of maintaining a body at a constant temperature, etc.[21]

The numerical breakdown of the third to the fifth phrases:

> The Sons dissociate (69, 15), the Sons (28, 10), the Sons dissociate and scatter (102, 21), dissociate and scatter (74, 11, then the Sons dissociate (89, 17), then the Sons dissociate and scatter (122, 23), their Mothers Bosom (87 = 15, 24 = 2 x 12), into their Mothers Bosom (109, 28), to return (41, 14), to return into their Mothers Bosom (150, 42 = 6 x 7), the end of the Great Day (92, 29 = 11), at the end of the Great Day (95, 32), the Great Day (51 = 17 x 3, 15), at the end (32, 14), to return into their Mother's Bosom at the end (182, 56), to return into their Mother's Bosom at the end of the great Day (245, 74), re-become one (55, 19 = 10), one with Her (62, 17) re-become one with Her (101, 29 = 11).

'The Sons' (7 x 4) are members of the fourth Creative Hierarchy (humanity). The fact that they dissociate themselves implies that they have passed the testings for Initiation associated with the sign Scorpio. They dissociate from the human group Soul (on the higher mental plane) after the fourth Initiation and enter into cosmic etheric space.

The number 15 of the phrase *'the Sons dissociate'* refers to the development of intelligence. This concerns the nature of the empirical mind to scatter the thought process into every conceivable direction of mental discursion. Later this process must be tamed and rightly orientated towards abstract thinking on the way to the mastery of mind. The Initiation process then sees to the development of higher perceptions that eventually produce the fourth and later the sixth Initiations, which allow escape (dissociation from the human kingdom) into cosmic space.

To *dissociate* means to separate, the break the union between companions, to think of something as being distinct from something else. Here it refers to the fact that until the sixth Initiation travelling together and in companionship has been the hallmark of the Initiate, and indeed for every group of entities as part of a kingdom of Nature.

---

21 Ibid, Vol. 1, 83-84.

At the fifth Initiation, the victorious Sons of the evolutionary process must make a decision as to which of the various cosmic Paths to travel upon, and thus to 'dissociate' from this world. At the sixth Initiation they will be 'Breathed out' by their Mother and continue the momentum of their awakening into cosmic Space. The dissociation is but an illusion, for nothing is separate in the cosmos. The acts of dissociation are an expression of the Mind, here of the Master, to differentiate one Path from another, and then to travel upon the chosen one. The process of the scattering of the units of the Breath concerns the modes of journeying upon the cosmic Paths.

The number 11 of the phrase *'dissociate and scatter'* refers to the projection of *antaḥkaraṇas* into cosmic space by the perfected Ones, via which they will later travel into the Life of the cosmic astral plane.

The number 17 of the phrase *'then the Sons dissociate'* implies that they dissociate from the human group Soul as they develop the attributes of divinity. *'The Sons dissociate and scatter'* (102, 7 x 3) as they are able to reside in the vehicles of their spiritual triads (7 x 3), which allow access to cosmic Space. They must also develop second Ray qualities (102) to do so. They *'scatter into their Mother's Bosom'* (109, 28) as Initiates of high degree (109). The energy utilised is provided by Sagittarius the archer, who also gives orientation in space. Under the guise of the Archer they fire the arrows of insight to the respective targets, the cosmic centres and star systems, which represent their next School of Learning and testing ground, so that they can undertake even higher (cosmic) Initiations.

The meaning of the term *Bosom* was explained in Stanza 1:2 with regards the phrase 'infinite Bosom of Duration'. It is symbolised by the sphere: ⊙. This symbol implicates the Seat of Power of any Logos. Here *'the Bosom'* is an expression of the universal, revealed Mother, the material universe from which the Sons have evolved. The number 2 x 12 of the phrase *'their Mother's Bosom'* relates to the qualities of the sign Taurus the bull, which governs the (cosmic) astral plane and its conditionings. In this case Taurus veils the significance of *the Seven Sisters,* the Pleiades in the scheme of things. They ride on the back of the Bull and are the cosmic Mothers, the wives of the seven Rishis of the Great Bear (the cosmic Source of the first Ray potency and of the emanation of the seven Rays). These cosmic Mothers preside over the star nurseries of nebulae, such as the Horse Head Nebulae in the constellation Orion.

After the Sons scatter to develop needed skills in the cosmic Landscape many will then find themselves in the Pleiades preparing for the next cosmic Incarnation, wherein they will be the informing Logoi (or constituency of their Head centres) of a future planetary or solar system. D.K. states in *A Treatise on Cosmic Fire* that because our solar system is governed by the second Ray, so the first stop for all the *nirvāṇees* is the star Sirius, the Source of Love within the Body of THAT Logos. They consequently travel to any of the constellations that are the cosmic custodians of planetary and zodiacal energies (signified by the number 100 + 22 of this phrase).

The numbers 3 x 50, 6 x 7 of the phrase *'to return to their Mothers Bosom'* refer to the complete perfection of all aspects of Mind, thus of the qualities developed by a Logoic Head lotus and the great Ones embodying it. The entire entourage of a planetary Logos will thereby be able to return to the cosmic astral domain. This return is also accomplished in the form of the Monad, which is symbolised by the number 3 x 50, because it exists in the form of an Eye, consisting of a pupil, iris and white of the Eye. Each of these possess their own colourations and are capable of utilising the Fiery Energy of the Mind of the Logos, which manifests in the form of an *iḍā, piṅgalā* and *suṣumṇā* expression. The Monad is a true cosmic voyager, and is presently ensconced upon the plane *anupādaka* (the number 6 x 7 counting from below up) in order to master the sum of the cosmic dense physical plane. It is the 'man-plant' planted in the cosmic dense physical 'soil' to evolve needed characteristics. Upon attaining the sixth Initiation the Initiate is thoroughly Identified with the Monad, coupled with the actual gain derived from evolution in the material domain. The cosmic Paths then open up, where the Initiate must decide which path to travel back 'to their Mother's Bosom'. This 'Bosom' can also refer to the stars of the milky way, as the ancient Greeks likened it to the milk that spilt from Aphrodite's breast.

The number 6 x 7 can also refer to the period at the end of the sixth Root Race, when many human groups, in accordance with the laws of group evolution, will begin this return journey.

By the number 2 x 7 of the phrase *'to return'* we see that this journey is for their Monadic aspects to enter again into cosmic astral space. One thus returns by renouncing the *māyā* of systemic space, and to aspire upwards to master the qualities of the various planes of perception until the cosmic Watery domain is reached. The plane *anupādaka* becomes the platform to enter the cosmic Waters.

The phrase *'to return into their Mother's Bosom at the end'* add to 11, 7 x 8, referring to the projected *antaḥkaraṇas* and the spiral-cyclic motion that allows them to travel therein. The numbers of the phrase *'to return into their Mother's Bosom at the end of the great Day'* also add to 11 and to 200 + 45, which refers to the Masters (9 x 5) that evolve as a consequence of the appearance of the second Ray cycle (200).

We know *'the great Day'* (17 x 3, 15) refers to an entire *mahāmanvantara*, signifying the period of divine Activity of a Logos. This is aptly symbolised by the number 17 x 3, during which time the unfoldment and activity (3 x 5) of the mind/Mind reigns supreme. It is a Day in the Life of Brahmā (for a planetary or solar Logos), the Mother aspect of Deity, before the oncoming of cosmic Night ('Darkness alone').

'The end of the great Day' (11) refers to the onset of *pralaya*. It begins with the outpouring of the second and first Ray cycles. The Destroyer first Ray aspect liberates and releases the imprisoned Life. The numbers of the phrases *'at the end of the great Day'* and *'at the end'* both add to 32. This signifies that the time of the second Ray or Love-Wisdom cycle will be in ascendency, heralding the opportunity for the evolved Sons to register their glory and wisdom in the preparation for the return journeying.

The sign Capricorn the goat is implicated in this statement because it is the mount of Initiation, the pinnacle of Earthy achievement, through the attainment of the higher Initiations, signifying mastery of what one is Initiated into. From the summit of the mountain of the material domain one ascends to cosmic space. By the number 5 x 11 of the phrase *'re-become one'* we see that this necessitates the complete mastery of all attributes of mind, to awaken *dharmakāya*, cosmic Mind, thus knowledge of where to travel and what to expect as the outcome of the journey. Inevitably one becomes a Deity within the *'Bosom of the Great Mother'*, and so 're-become one with Her'. This is implied by the first Ray significance of the number 101 and the numbers 31 x 2, 17 of the phrase *'one with Her'*. To become 'One' thus implies abstraction, mergence into the all that in the beginning was 'immersed in Parinishpanna' (Stanza 1:6). (This concerns the ending of the turning of the wheel of the zodiac, as signified by the sign Pisces the fishes, being the effect of Pluto, its Esoteric and Hierarchical ruler.)

The numerical breakdown of the final phrases:

> When it is cooling (83 = 11, 20), it is cooling (60, 15), it becomes radiant (68, 14), the Sons (28, 10), the Sons expand (56, 20), expand and contract (69, 15), Hearts (26, 8) the Sons expand and contract (97, 25), their own Selves (68, 23), their own Selves and Hearts (104, 32), through their own Selves (111, 30), through their own Selves and Hearts (147 = 12, 39), contract through their own Selves (142, 34), contract through their own Selves and Hearts (178, 43), expand and contract through their own Selves and Hearts (216 = 24 x 9, 54), expand and contract through their own Selves (180, 45), the Sons expand and contract through their own Selves (208, 55), the sons expand and contract through their own selves and Hearts (244, 64), They embrace Infinitude (108, 27).

Having finished the sequence of one narrative to conclusion the threads of the main theme following from the expansion of the 'Breath of Fire' and the contraction associated with the 'Breath of the Mother' can be picked up again. The following statement informs us that it becomes radiant when cooling, rather than when the Fire is upon it, in which case it would become hotter, and with increasing heat we would expect a radiatory emanation. It however *cools* with the Mother's Breath and becomes radiant because of the pressure of the energies from the higher domains, as the energies contacted and utilised are Airy and not Fiery. Via the Airy Element is expressed the Waters of cosmic astral space. The Fiery principle of mind is supplanted by the enlightened cool Clear Reason from the higher domains of Mind. Such Mind is abstracting and dispassionate, not tainted by the emotional volatility of the lower domains. The radiance is then the clarified Fiery substance abstracted into the domain of the Waters, producing the intense compassionate auras (of *bodhicitta)* generated by the *nirvāṇees* as they leave the system in increasing numbers after finalising their service work upon the earth.

In Stanza 3:6 it is stated that heat is the expression of Fire that is fuelled by the substance of 'the Ocean of Immortality'. Fire is also an expression of the Mother, of frictional energy and its abrasive journeying in the realms of substance. From this perspective cooling means a non-vitalisation of the Fire that is fuelled by dense substance. This is also the accomplishment of the meditation process, where the process of cooling implies an intensified meditation whereby the Fires of the mind become stilled. Because the mind is no longer active it is thus cooled. The simile of cooling can be found in the fact that when heat escapes the confines of any ring-pass-not or container (here the substance of the great Mother) it cools the rest of the substance in the container.

This produces the seeming paradoxical statement that this cooling vessel becomes radiant, which is answered by the fact that the radiance is the product of the enlightenment. It becomes the radiatory activity of the Sons that are preparing to leave with the Breath of the Mother. As they leave they take the heat of the Fiery substance with them. The cooling process thus produces contraction and an intensification of the radiatory activity of the Entities constituting the Rays of Light and Heat from a brilliant Son (Sun) of Wisdom. Cooling also indicates a changing of colouring from the violet, yellow, orange and green shades of activity to the deep blue of meditative absorption. The radiant Sons leave after they have instructed their Sons in the art of meditation and the abstraction process. The cooling is also the result of the extinction of the Causal forms of the Souls (which are miniature suns) upon the higher mental plane by those undertaking the fourth Initiation.

The numbers 60 (5 x 12), 15 of the phrase *'it is cooling'* refer to the substance of manifest space, the container (the *maṇḍala* of the hexagon, 60) and the mind-stuff (15) it contains, that undergoes this cooling process. The web of the universe can also be considered the container of the mind/Mind. Modern physicists also posit that the universe gradually cools after its initial expansionary process. The number 5 x 12 also refers to the fifth sign of the zodiac, Leo the lion, who embodies the attributes of the mind/Mind, of the consciousness that consequently 'cools' or wanes, as the *nirvāṇees* pass through the open gate of the polar opposite of this sign, Aquarius the water bearer, into cosmic space.[22] The radiatory process is consequently governed by the qualities of the sign Aquarius, whose glyph of two wavy lines aptly depicts the nature of the energy flowing forth. Uranus, the Hierarchical ruler, governing the seventh Ray, implicates the cyclic nature of the outgoing motion of the radiation,

The numbers 20, 11 of the phrase *'when it is cooling'* refer to the radiatory activity of the evolving Sons (their projection and inception of first and second Ray energies as their combined auras) that allow this cooling to be accomplished, as they escape the confines of formed space. This is the activity of the prospective *nirvāṇees* in their roles as Bodhisattvas, residing in the domains beyond mind (the four cosmic ethers).

The number 17 x 4 of the phrase *'it becomes radiant'* refers to the quaternary of the divine Personality (or human unit) that becomes radiant in this manner. This quaternary embodies the four manifest kingdoms of Nature associated with the great Mother as they gradually develop the attributes of divinity. The Throne or Seat of Power of a Logos thus becomes increasingly radiant.

The number 7 x 4 of the phrase *'the Sons'* refers to the Causal forms that en-Soul manifest space, to the fourth kingdom of Nature, humanity. They evolve into the *nirvāṇees* that cause the cooling.

The numbers 7 x 8, 20 of the phrase *'the Sons expand'* imply the development of Love-Wisdom and spiral-cyclic energies that cause the expansion process of the consciousness-principle. Human consciousness expands to embrace the qualities of Deity when the 'Breath of Fire' manifesting from divinity vitalises them. This also concerns the growth of the Ashrams of the Masters of Wisdom that grow in size and stature as increasing numbers develop the necessary attributes to be included in them.

By the number 15 of the phrase *'expand and contract'* we see that what expands and contracts here relates to the qualities of the lower mind. It generally evolves through each incarnation of a personality,

22 Aquarius represents the passageway for Bodhisattvas, whereas Pisces is more specifically the sign of the incoming Avatar, that comes to bring needed attributes to a world sphere.

seen in the context of the lives and deaths happening via the rebirthing principle of the Soul. As enlightenment is gained the empirical, *kāma-manasic* aspect contracts, whilst the enlightened aspects expand. This philosophy is well known, hence needs no further commentary.

There are three methods of growth to enlightenment to produce this expansion and contraction process. First is by the means of one's own consciousness (*'their own Selves'*, 17 x 4) that reacts to all of the external effects of *saṃsāra*. The expansion is via intellectual development and discursive analysis. The external observation of the universe produces knowledge of the Real, of the kingdom of 'God', astrological deductions, and of *dharmakāya*. This is the *iḍā* path to enlightenment and leads to perfection of Mind, the empirical method largely used in Western ontological pursuits and religions. The number 17 x 4 here indicates the quaternary of the Self that mimics what is established as the Seat of Power of a Logos. Thus as one develops the capacity to know 'Self', so then is gained the qualities supporting the Power of an incarnate Logos embodying the material domain. The phrase *'their own Selves'* therefore, refers essentially to the basic mind stuff that the Causal form is composed of. The human Sambhogakāya Flowers represent the substance of the Throne of Deity, via which can manifest the Commands to rule the material domain. These mantric statements intensify the Fiery nature of human minds at the appropriate cycles, allowing the expansion process to proceed through the awakening of divine Knowledge. The expansion is gained as a result of repeated incarnation into the formed realms.

The other method is the way of the Heart, travelling inwards via the Heart centre to realise the internal universe. This is the *piṇgalā* way to enlightenment, and produces liberation via the art of meditation, largely pursued via the Eastern religious approaches. This then produces the contraction process.

The third method involves direct Tantric yoga that incorporates both methods above, but adds strict yogic disciplines, coupled with correct esoteric Knowledge, which is the *suṣumṇā* path, which significantly quickens the liberation path.

When the term *'and Hearts'* is added to the phrase *'their own Selves'*, then the numbers 104, and 32 are obtained. The number 104 is the number of the Lords of Flame that came with Sanat Kumāra to establish the Head centre of our planet. Here it relates to awakening the Heart in the Head centre of aspirants by the above methods. The number 32 refers to the second Ray aspect of Deity, the Love-wisdom that awakens the Heart centre. The phrase *'their own Selves and Hearts'* thus relates to the door of awakening the twelve petalled lotus in the Head, (thus the number 12 of the phrase *'through their own Selves and Hearts')* and the contraction of attachment to the world of form through the engendering of Love-Wisdom. The product is a radiatory emanation that uplifts all related forms into the embrace of the infinite expanse of Beingness that Love represents. Therefore a contraction of mind produces a liberation into the infinite reaches of space through the evolution of Mind. The number 12 also refers to the energies of the twelve Creative Hierarchies that manifest through the twelve petals of the Head centre.

The way of awakening Mind evokes the 'Breath of Fire' to produce an expansion of consciousness. The way of the Heart therefore represents the 'Breath of the Mother' to produce contraction of attachment to *saṃsāra* until eventually *śūnyatā* is experienced. The integration of expansion with contraction implicates the *suṣumṇā* way governing the Bodhisattva path. This establishes the *saṃsāra-śūnyatā* nexus explained in my *Treatise on Mind.*

The numbers 16, 5 x 5 of the phrase *'the Sons expand and contract'* refer to the development of the attributes of mind (5 x 5) to produce the expansion process, and then the principle of Love-Wisdom of a Christ, to produce abstraction (hence contraction) from the domains of *saṃsāra.*

By the numbers 100 + 6 x 7, 17 x 2 we see that those that *'contract through their own Selves'* gain knowledge of or are able to reflect the qualities of Deity (17 x 2) via comprehension of the nature of the sum of the embodied form (6 x 7). Here the number 100 + 6 x 7 refers to the potent energies of the cosmic astral plane. This method can then be contrasted with the meaning of the numbers 16, 7 of the phrase *'contract through their own Selves and Hearts'* where we see that one awakens to the Way of the Christ (16), the principle of Love-Wisdom, along all seven Ray lines (7). There is also the number 111 of the phrase *'through their own Selves'*, implying the ability to project *antaḥkaraṇas* upwards to the domains of divinity in order to receive impressions and energies from the liberated domains that awaken one to the Reality of the subtler domains. The *antaḥkaraṇas* then become the way of escape into cosmic Space.

The numbers of the phrase *'expand and contract through their own selves'* add to 5 x 9 (and to 20 x 9), and when added to those of the phrase *'and Hearts'* then the numbers 6 x 9, and 24 x 9 are produced. This expansion and contraction process will therefore make a Master of Wisdom (5 x 9), who represents the gaining of the perfection of Mind. When the focus is upon the Way of the Heart then is seen that the real effect of expansion after expansion from one field of Revelation in the realm of substance to the next, is to make of one a Chohan, an Initiate of the sixth degree, who has completely Identified with the Monad. This way is what truly liberates, allowing one to travel in the Waters of cosmic astral space, which is the source of Love to our system. Expansion and contraction follow each other with rhythmic succession in terms of the process of birth and death, of breathing in and out one life after the next one. Eventually the Initiation path is trod, which produces of expansion and contraction of awareness states upon increasingly higher spirals of attainment, until a final contraction from *saṁsāra* becomes the force that drives the Initiate out of earth sphere evolution.

This activity upon the Path of Identification with the Source or Heart of Being makes one a Christ, the embodiment of the energy of Divinity for all manifest space. Consciousness expands and then is transcended to become universal Mind, when identification with the material form contracts to zero. This is the way of the Heart, the Love aspect that drives all into the freedom of the Spaciousness of the All that Is.

The number 20 x 9 relates to the Initiation process of the entire Hierarchy of Enlightened Being, the Heart centre of the planetary Logos. Their path lies in an expansive embrace to evolve into the petals of the planetary Head centre (Shambhala). The number 24 x 9 relates to the Initiation of the Elders constituting the Logoic Head centre. Their path lies in a contraction of commitment to dense physical space, thus abstraction into the sum of cosmic astral Space, as signified by the sign Taurus (24), which governs the interrelations between the suns evolving therein. The occupants of Shambhala principally embody the Wisdom aspect (cosmic Mind) via Divine Will of the Love-Wisdom Ray, and will further develop Love on top of what is already considered 'perfect' from the perspective of those incarnate in systemic space.

Those embodying the Logoic Heart centre (Hierarchy) are embodiments of the Love-Wisdom Ray, and are endeavouring to expand to embrace of the attributes of Logoic Mind through increasing receptivity to the Impressions from the Logoic Mentation.

The numbers of the phrase *'the Sons expand and contract through their own Selves'* add to 208, 55, whilst those of the phrase *'the Sons expand and contract through their own Selves and Hearts'* add to 244, 64. The entire process produces gain of the compassionate stance of all Logoi (200 + 8) and takes the entire course of the *mahāmanvantara* to produce the Masters of Wisdom (5 x 11) that are the gain of this evolutionary process. They can project the *antaḥkaraṇas* to cosmic Space and thereby escape the confines of systemic space. That related to the Heart produces the evolution of the Compassionate Mind, which concerns the projection of the spiral-cyclic energies (8 x 8) so that the Selves and Hearts of cosmic Men and Women (200 + 44) can be contacted and experienced.

The concluding statement: *'They embrace Infinitude'* (108, 27) sums up the entire process. Here the pronoun 'They' refers to all that have gained the first cosmic Initiation (3 x 7) onwards. Their journey then leads them to the Infinitude of cosmos, where the sacred number 108 represents the complete awakening of all the petals of the Head lotus of 'The One About Whom Naught May be Said' (That Logos). The observable stars and constellations of the night sky represent the petals of this Lotus. The ontology of cosmos is then thoroughly Known. The significance of the number 108 with respect to the Head lotus was explained in volumes 4 and 5A *(The Nature and Development of Maṇḍalas,* and *An Esoteric Exposition of the Bardo Thödol)* of my Series *A Treatise on Mind.*

Stanza Three part Twelve

Stanza 3:12 states:

> **Then Svabhāvat[23] sends Fohat to harden the atoms. Each is a part of the web. Reflecting the "Self-Existent Lord", like a mirror, each becomes in turn a world.**

---

23 Blavatsky has Svābhāvat here, but I have corrected this and subsequent entries to Svabhāvat.

Keynotes: Leo, dense physical plane, the third Ray, fifth sub-aspect of Earthy *ākāśa*, Amitābha.

The numerical breakdown of this Stanza:

> Then Svabhāvat sends Fohat (83, 20), Svabhāvat sends Fohat (63, 18), to harden the atoms (69 = 15, 24), the atoms (29, 11), Svabhāvat sends Fohat to harden the atoms (132 = 66 x 2, 42), then Svabhāvat sends Fohat to harden the atoms (152, 44), the Web (29, 11), Each is a part of the Web (86 = 15, 32), a part of the Web (59, 23), is a part (1.1.10), the "Self-Existent Lord" (87, 24), Reflecting the Self-existent Lord (141, 33), like a mirror (66, 21, 10.1.10), a mirror (47, 11), each becomes in turn a world (104, 41 = 5), a world (28, 10).

Stanza 3:12 continues from the opening statement of Stanza 3:11, which was associated with the effect of the establishment of the etheric web (governed by Gemini), and the process of incarnation governed by the sign Cancer the crab. Stanza 3:12 is concerned with the actual appearance of the concrete form (the hardening of 'the atoms'), the material universe wherein the human kingdom evolves. This 'hardening' process is caused through utilising Amitābha's Discriminative Inner Wisdom, hence the reifying power of the Mind directed downwards via the fifth and lowest sub-aspect of Earthy *ākāśa*. The appearance of the atoms and their 'hardening' is governed by Leo the lion, who wields the application of the Fiery Element via the activity of Fohat. Stanza 3:11 was concerned with the evolution of the Life aspect, and Stanza 3:12 is concerned with appearance of the forms to contain them. The focus is then the objective appearance of the *permanent atoms* from out of the web of Life.

As stated, Leo is the sign of individuation, which controls the Earthy Fires of the mind, with its separative, concretising attributes. Leo is ruled exoterically, esoterically and Hierarchically by the sun and conditions the evolutionary process by seeding the elementary attributes of self-consciousness (instinct) of the evolving Lives, each of which reflect aspects of 'the Self-Existing Lord'. This causes the appearance of the final concretion of material substance, the atomic life of the mineral kingdom, hence the manifestation of the Elemental Lives, the twelfth Creative Hierarchy.

The third Ray of Mathematically Exact Activity generally rules the physical domain, as it also veils the import of all the Rays of Mind. This Ray is needed by the Lords of Life to externalise the material domain and to sustain its activities for the needed duration of time, so that its purpose can be accomplished. The Elemental Life comes under the field of embrace of the energy distribution of Aquarius (the polar opposite of Leo). There is no *śakti* assigned to them.

The sum of the forces of the liberated Hierarchies working via humanity, as presented in Stanza 3:6 (under Aquarius, the polar opposite of Leo), is now brought to bear upon this elementary Life, to lift up their sentience to the higher dimensions, by being incorporated as the substance of mind.

The final materialising projection of the forms from out of subjective space necessitates direct application of the first Ray energies of the Will of Deity, of the Logoic Thinker. The economy of the spirals and spirillae of these atoms then contain the various streams of Life (in the form of Logoic *saṃskāras*). The nature of such atoms has been dealt with in depth in my book *Esoteric Cosmology and Modern Physics,* to which the reader should refer here.

From an astrological perspective the forces of the Crab's claws effectively hold these atoms in a vice-like embrace for the entire *mahāmanvantara,* whist the energies of Leo externalises their form. Thus is produced the material appearances we know so well in the phenomenon of the universe. The entire body of the Crab represents the (inverted) mechanism (the Sacral-Gonadal-Base of Spine centre interrelation) that allows the opening and closing of the doors of incarnation for the respective Lives that are to experience life in the cosmic dense physical plane, whilst Leo causes the differentiation of the forms that manifest.

Stanza 2:1 provided the meaning of the term *svabhāva*, where it was said to refer to the plastic essence from which all material things can be said to emanate. This substance is utilised by the *devamātri*, the 'Gods' that are the various Intelligences in the universe, on whatever plane it is found.

Concerning *Fohat* H.P.B. states:

> "Fohat hardens the atoms"; *i.e.*, by infusing energy into them: he

scatters the atoms or primordial matter. "He scatters himself while scattering matter into atoms." (**MSS.** commentaries).

It is through Fohat that the ideas of the Universal Mind are impressed upon matter. Some faint idea of the nature of Fohat may be gathered from the appellation "Cosmic Electricity" sometimes applied to it; but to the commonly known properties of electricity must, in this case, be added others, including intelligence.[24]

She stated earlier that:

Fohat runs the Manus' (Dhyan Chohans') errands, and causes the ideal prototypes to expand from within without — viz., to cross gradually, on a descending scale, all the planes, from the noumenon to the lowest phenomenon, to bloom finally on the last into full objectivity — the acme of illusion, or the grossest matter.[25]

Also from the Proem:

The "Manifested Universe," therefore, is pervaded by duality, which is, as it were, the very essence of its EX-istence as "manifestation." But just as the opposite poles of subject and object, spirit and matter, are but aspects of the One Unity in which they are synthesized, so, in the manifested Universe, there is "that" which links spirit to matter, subject to object.

This something, at present unknown to Western speculation, is called by the occultists Fohat. It is the "bridge" by which the "Ideas" existing in the "Divine Thought" are impressed on Cosmic substance as the "laws of Nature." Fohat is thus the dynamic energy of Cosmic Ideation; or, regarded from the other side, it is the intelligent medium, the guiding power of all manifestation, the "Thought Divine" transmitted and made manifest through the Dhyan Chohans, the Architects of the visible World. Thus from Spirit, or Cosmic Ideation, comes our consciousness; from Cosmic Substance the several vehicles in which that consciousness is individualised and attains to self — or reflective — consciousness; while Fohat, in its various manifestations, is the mysterious link between Mind and Matter, the animating principle electrifying every atom into life.[26]

---

24 Ibid., Vol. 1, 85.

25 Ibid., Vol. 1, 63. See also Stanza 5:2, where further information shall be presented.

26 Ibid., Vol. 1, 15-16.

D.K., states:

Akasha, in manifestation, expresses itself as Fohat, or divine Energy, and Fohat on the different planes is known as aether, air, fire, water, electricity, ether, prana and similar terms. It is the sumtotal of that which is active, animated, or vitalised, and of all that concerns itself with the adaptation of the form to the needs of the inner flame of life...[27]

The fundamental fact that should here be emphasised is that AGNI, the Lord of Fire, rules over all the fire elementals and devas on the three planes of human evolution, the physical, the astral, and the mental, and rules over them not only on this planet, called the Earth, but on the three planes in all parts of the system. He is one of the seven Brothers (to use an expression familiar to students of the *Secret Doctrine)* Who each embody one of the seven principles, or Who are in Themselves the seven centers in the body of the cosmic Lord of Fire, called by H. P. B. "Fohat." He is that active fiery Intelligence, Who is the basis of the internal fires of the solar system. On each plane one of these Brothers holds sway, and the three elder Brothers (for always the three will be seen, and later the seven, who eventually merge into the primary three) rule on the first, third and the fifth planes, or on the plane of adi, of atma and of manas. It is urgent that we here remember that They are fire viewed in its third aspect, *the fire of matter.* In Their totality these seven Lords form the essence of the cosmic Lord, called in the occult books, Fohat.[28]

In looking at the matter from the standpoint of fire the idea may be grasped a little through the realisation that the latent fire of matter in the atom is brought into brilliance and usefulness by the action of the personality Ray which merges with this fire and stands in the same position to the permanent atom in the microcosm as Fohat does on the cosmic plane. The fire is there hidden within the sphere (whether the sphere systemic or the sphere atomic) and the personality Ray in the one case, and Fohat in the other, acts as the force which brings latency into activity and potentiality into demonstrated power. This correspondence should be thought out with care and judgment. Just as Fohat has to do with active manifestation or objectivity, so the

27 Bailey, T.C.F., 43-44.

28 Ibid., 65-66.

personality Ray has to do with the third, or activity aspect in the microcosm. The work of the third aspect logoic was the arranging of the matter of the system so that eventually it could be built into form through the power of the second aspect. Thus the correspondence works out. By life upon the physical plane (that life wherein the physical permanent atom has its full demonstration) the matter is arranged and separated that must eventually be built into the Temple of Solomon, the egoic body, through the agency of the egoic life, the second aspect...[29]

These major seven planes of our solar system being but the seven subplanes of the cosmic physical plane, we can consequently see the reason for the emphasis laid by H. P. B. upon the fact that matter and ether are synonymous terms and that this ether is found in some form or other on all the planes, and is but a gradation of cosmic atomic matter, called when undifferentiated mulaprakriti or primordial pre-genetic substance, and when differentiated by Fohat (or the energising Life, the third Logos or Brahma) it is termed prakriti, or matter.[30]

We proceed now to take up the consideration of *the Ruler of Fire, AGNI,* and are brought to the study of the vitality that energises and the Life that animates; to the contemplation of the Fire that drives, propels, and produces the activity and organisation of all forms. The realisation of this will reveal the fact that what we are dealing with is the "Life and the lives," as it is called in the *Secret Doctrine*; with Agni, the Lord of Fire, the Creator, the Preserver, and the Destroyer; and with the forty-nine fires through which He manifests. We are dealing with solar fire per se, with the essence of thought, with the coherent life of all forms, with the consciousness in its evolving aspect, or with Agni, the sumtotal of the Gods. He is Vishnu and the Sun in His glory; He is the fire of matter and the fire of mind blended and fused; He is the intelligence which throbs in every atom; He is the Mind that actuates the system; He is the fire of substance and the substance of the fire; He is the Flame and that which the Flame destroys.

Students of the *Secret Doctrine* when they read carelessly are apt to consider Him only as the fire of matter and omit to note that He is Himself the sumtotal—and this is especially the case when they

29 Ibid., 72-73.

30 Ibid., 118.

find that Agni is the Lord of the mental plane. [88] He is the animating life of the solar system, and that life is the life of God, the energy of the Logos, and the manifestation of the radiance which veils the Central Sun. Only as He is recognised as Fohat, the energy of matter, as Wisdom, the nature of the Ego and its motivation, and as essential unity, can any due conception be arrived at as to His nature or being. He is not the solar Logos on the cosmic mental plane, for the egoic consciousness of the Logos is more than His physical manifestation, but *Agni is the sumtotal of that portion of the logoic Ego which is reflected down into His physical vehicle; He is the life of the logoic Personality, with all that is included in that expression.* He is to the solar Logos on His own plane what the coherent personality of a human being is to his Ego in the causal body...[31]

Agni is Fohat, the threefold Energy (emanating from the logoic Ego) which produces the solar system, the physical vehicle of the Logos, and animates the atoms of substance. He is the basis of the evolutionary process, or the cause of the psychic unfoldment of the Logos, and He is that vitality which ultimately brings about a divine synthesis in which the form approximates subjective demand, and after being consciously directed, and manipulated, is finally discarded. This is the goal for the Logos as it is for man; this marks the final liberation of a human being, of a Heavenly Man and of a solar Logos...[32]

Note that the statement by D.K. above that the 'work of the third aspect logoic was the arranging of the matter of the system so that eventually it could be built into form through the power of the second aspect' has a direct bearing to Stanzas 3:10 and 3:11. Stanza 3:10 deals with the Logoic third aspect, whilst Stanza 3:11 deals with the second aspect. By extension, the Power of the Logoic first aspect is reflected into the subject of Stanza 3:12.

From the above we see that Fohat can be considered to be divine Fiery Energy of cosmic Intelligence, that as Stanza 5:2 states, 'runs circular errands'. It is the spiralling motion that is congruent with the evolution of consciousness, the way of movement of Fiery energy throughout the cosmic dense physical plane, causing the sum of the constituency

31 Ibid., 601-03.

32 Ibid., 610.

of the Logoic Personality. Fohat is the coalition of Intelligent forces through which cosmic Ideation, or cosmic Intelligence, impresses upon substance, thus forming the various worlds of manifestation. It is the electric, vital Power, which, under the Will of the Creative Logos, unites and brings together all forms, giving them the impulse to be, manifesting as karmic law. Consequently Fohat is the basic energy *(prāṇa)* of cosmos. It is a Fiery force (*śakti*) emanating from the cosmic astral plane, a threefold energy manifesting via the three higher Systemic planes precipitating what is latent (*mūlaprakṛti*) into activity as the demonstration of material power. It is the energising expression of the Divine Thought of the third Logos (Brahmā) that produces the activity of the seven Systemic planes of perception. It is the cause for their manifestation. It can be considered the expressed power of Lord Agni. It is cosmic electricity in its primordial essentiality. Literally it is the Fiery electrical energy that is the basis to the Creative potency from the Mind of the embodying Logos, and which emanates as the Breath of Light. It is the expression of that dynamic Will that translates as electrical phenomena in all its diversifications, when conveyed through the medium of the *nāḍī* system of etheric space. Fohat is the driving Fiery force of the enlightened Mind in action, and ā*kāśa* is the substance that is moved by this electrical Wind. It can be viewed as Monadic Ideation, the energy of Logoic Thought, in its creative, sustaining or destructive aspects.

Fohat is ever-present and active from the primordial beginnings of a *manvantara* to *pralaya,* and becomes quiescent or latent, sleeping until the next *manvantara.*

Stanza 3:11 depicted the nature of evolutionary attainment of consciousness within a solar system or the earth sphere under the general effect of the second Ray, which produces the efflux of the escaping *nirvāṇees* as they develop the Will to do so. They can then experience the Infinitude associated with attaining the higher cosmic Initiations. The seventh Ray governing this Stanza is concerned with the precipitation of astral energies via the etheric needed for form building. Stanza 3:12 refocusses our vision to the process of world formation.

The fact that *'Svabhāvat sends Fohat'* (63, 18) implies that Svabhāvat is here *considered an Entity.* We can conceive of One that governs the manifestation of the etheric web, thus with the mode of manifestation of the cosmic dense physical plane (hinted at by the number 7 x 9 of this phrase, referring to an Initiate of the seventh degree that rules formed space). From this perspective Svabhāvat also organises the substance of Kṣiti, the Deva Lord of the Element Earth. Fohat, in the form of 'the Breath of Fire', is then called to *'harden the atoms'* (24, 15). The 'atoms' here represent the permanent atoms of the Logoi and are concerned with dense incarnation. Substance *(mūlaprakṛti)* is to be attracted to them from the cosmic stores contained in the nebulae of dust, which is then incorporated in the spirals of the atoms. The increasing densification of this primal substance hardens them. Via this process the Will of the first Logos impacts upon substance to form the material universe.

The number 2 x 12 implicates the sign Taurus the bull, and the Pleiades. Under the auspices of Amitābha's Wisdom Taurus clothes the Divine Thought with the entire field of the substance of Logoic Desire. The energy of Fohat can however be considered to be governed by the Fiery Arian impetus to build the Purpose into the new Logoic dispensation by hardening 'the atoms' so that new Life can evolve. The instigation of a new zodiacal cycle for an entire world period is thereby implied. The energy of Leo produces the vast diversity of the combinations of these atoms, of the elements and chemical compounds experienced upon the physical domain.

The role of the Pleiades in Building the forms from primal cosmic 'black dust' that Logoi incarnate into was detailed in *The Constitution of Shambhala* part 7B, and *Esoteric Cosmology and Modern Physics,* hence needs no repetition here.

By the numbers 20, 11 of the phrase *'Then Svabhāvat sends Fohat'* we see that Svabhāvat utilises considerable Will and Love-Wisdom to contact and direct Fohat and His emissaries so that the new *maṇḍala* of expression can awaken, according to the Logoic Plan for the new cycle. All informing Lives must be contacted and integrated into the developing syzygy of Spirit and matter so that consciousness can evolve. At this stage the work of the Fire *devas* are preeminent so that the desired form can take shape upon the mental plane wherein the primal substance and the incarnating forces of the Logos are integrated.

The number 11 indicates that *'the atoms'* in question are constituted of lines of interrelation, the spirals and sprillae that via numerical associations can attract to them energy affiliations (colours attract like colours and hues) that will clothe these permanent atoms with form. This then allows all Lives to awaken from *pralaya.*

To *harden* means to make firm and hard, to solidify, or to become fixed, firmly decided in opinion or ideas. Here the term refers to the energy of the cosmic Thinker projecting set or determined Thoughts to the Creative Intelligences or the Monads embodying the forms, to again project Themselves into/as manifest Space. The forms are 'hardened' with the down pouring of the qualities of the congealing substance of *svabhāva* by means of the energy of Fohat.

That we are reminded that these atoms are *'a part of the Web'* (14, 5) signifies that the concern is still primarily with the attributes of the four ethers, through which the energies of the cosmic astral plane must flow (14). The Web implicates the qualities of the sign Gemini, which follows after the sign Taurus in the sequence of the incarnation process.

That *'each is a part of the Web'* (32, 14) refers to the sequence of Svabhāvat, Fohat and the atoms. This 'Web" consists of the four ethers, whose substance is embodied by Svabhāvat. Fohat is the materialising energy directed by Svabhāvat from the highest of the sub-planes of the cosmic dense physical plane, *ādi,* and which manifests via the *iḍā nāḍī* stream of the odd numbered planes, 1,3,5 and 7. In this guise *svabhāva* manifests a dual attribute of being both the Watery substance of the cosmic astral (14) plus the effect of its condensation into the cosmic dense physical domain to become the primary energy circulating through the spirals of the permanent atoms. This energy conveys the Love-Wisdom from Deity (32) that supports the activity of the second Ray solar system. Love-Wisdom is carried by Fohat, though modified with the attribute of a reifying Intelligence to 'harden the atoms'. A hylozoistic universe is consequently the result. All attributes of the appearing form are thereby impacted upon and incorporated by the Mind of the Logos. Note that the numbers of the phrase *'is a part'* add to 1.1.10., which indicate the sequences of *sūtrātmās* (Thought projections by the Creative Intelligences) needed to produce this effect.

The number 22 of the phrase *'part of the web'* refers to the cosmic and planetary energies carried by Fohat.

The *tanmātras,* the essence of the five Elements, emanate from Fohat. Fohat breathes the Fire of *ākāśa* into the Monadic Life that are established upon the plane *anupādaka.* Fohat is the energy that organises the principle of Life so that it can play its role in the *mahāmanvantara.* Effectively we can think of it as the moving Mental energy of the Eye of the Logos directing what is to be accomplished. At this stage of evolution energies from the left Eye are implicated, utilising therefore Mahat *(manas* cosmically considered) to organise the substance of the form.

The atoms begin to be 'hardened' from the plane *ātma,* the third cosmic ether. From here the karmic ramifications of the substance to be incorporated into the web is sorted, and the sum of the associated *deva* Life can be gathered and directed to play their roles at the appointed cycles. *Ātma* thereby becomes the plane of the expression of *karma* and then of its resolution. All happens as directed by the Manas from the Logoic Eye, making *ātma* therefore the lowest reflex of *dharmakāya.* What is expressed upon mental levels simply becomes the automaton of the karmic impress from *ātma.*

The fourth cosmic ether *(buddhi)* acts as a mirror reflecting the above, which is but the Will of *'the "Self-Existent Lord"'*[33] (2 x 12, 15) preconditioning the *māyā* of the concreted domains, known to us as *saṃsāra.* This Lord is the presiding Logos that governs the entire Incarnation process of the metaphorical universe (here representing the solar system). The concept of 'Self-Existing' implies the qualities of Leo the lion, who governs the development of self-consciousness, the self-centred personality, and also of the luminous orb of the sun (the ruler of this sign), thus the vitality emanating from it. Leo therefore governs the mode of the appearance of the various Logoi, directing the energies that harden the atoms via Fohat (symbolised by the number 15).

The term 'Lord' also signifies the embodiment of the Wisdom principle, which the Logoi reflect into manifestation. The term thus refers to one who is ruler or Master of a Domain, and here this domain is that of the cosmic physical realm, whilst Taurus the bull (24) governs

---

33 The Sanskrit term being *svyambhū,* meaning 'self-generated, self-evolving, being of itself, self-existent, or self-manifesting. *Svyambhū* represents the primordial beginnings of the solar system from the womb of Āditi. *Svyambhū* is a name applied to Brahmā issuing from the abstract essence of Brahman.

the general energies (Wisdom, Compassion) manifesting via that realm. This *'Self-Existent Lord'* can be equated with 'the Eternal Parent', mentioned in Stanza 1:1, who causes the manifestation of a (planetary) Head centre. (The number 24 also refers to the four and twenty Elders associated with the innermost tier of such a sphere of activity.) Fohat is therefore sent to do His 'errands' from such a centre.

The numbers of the term *'Self-Existent'* add to 50, informing us that it is self-existent because it embodies the qualities of cosmic Mind (Mahat). To be self-formed, self-made, self-existent, implies the use of Mahat to sustain its own existence, to project its Self as a corporate Entity (the functioning of the sign Leo the lion). The Mind-nature segregates, separates, discriminates and sustains manifest Existence. H.P.B's reference to this term is that it is 'Primeval Light'.[34] It is the Light that is an expression of the Fires of the Mind of an Entity.

From the above we can perceive the qualities of the triune Logos:

- 'The Self-Existent Lord' – the Father aspect, the Will to accomplish instigating the course of the new solar incarnation.
- Svabhāvat – the Son aspect providing the luminous substance of Light, governed by the Love-Wisdom that clothes the *maṇḍala* of the Logoic form.
- Fohat – the Mother that manifests the activity of the driving momentum of Mind to weave all aspects and forces into the appearing form.

This trinity is then mirrored into the substance of the higher mental plane so that as the minds of humanity evolve they can eventually reflect the image of the qualities of deity. The rubric of what is to be has been inscribed into the base substance from which all else evolves. A *mirror* is a polished surface, which reflects an image. It is usually silvered on one side, and darkened on the other, allowing oncoming rays of light to be reflected according to the angle of incidence. Here the 'silvered' surface faces the domain of the Real and the darkened side faces the substance of the ever-changing *māyā* that is the basis for evolution in

34 Ibid., Vol. 1, 85.

formed space. The analogy is of course not exact because of the nature of the angle of incidence and reflection of a normal mirror happens on one side only, whereas esoterically the mirror reflects that which is above into the below.[35]

The phrase *'Like a mirror'* (66, 3 x 7, 10.1.10) refers to the substance of the embodied form of the Logos, which acts like a mirror reflecting the attributes of the Logos into manifest space. The numbers of the phrase *'a mirror'* add to 11, which with the number 10.1.10 indicates the myriads of *sūtrātmās/antaḥkaraṇas* travelling to and from formed space mirroring the attributes of the Real into the illusion and then back into the Real by the ensconced Lives. Here specifically the domain of the abstract Mind acts as such a mirror. The mirror also indicates the astral plane, because in its unadulterated form it is a mirror, reflecting the attributes of the mental plane into the dense physical. Once humanity incorporates this substance by utilising their creative intelligence then they build the associated images with their desire-minds. Thus we have the creation of the heaven and hell states afflicting humanity. Such activity becomes the basis for the illusions associated with *saṃsāra* and the addictive nature of people's desires. These implications are conveyed by the numbers 66 and 3 x 7 of this phrase, which symbolise the sum of the attributes of *saṃsāra*. The way of mastering *saṃsāra* is to begin to project *antaḥkaraṇas* along the way of descent of the energies that were reflected from the mirror. In doing so the aspirant drives the energy of Fohat back to whence it came. Humanity thereby develop the attributes of a Logos.

The hardening of the atoms (the concretion of substance) therefore produces the dense physical plane via the mirror upon the abstracted mental plane. Here then is seen the objective appearance of the worlds of sensation and of experience. (The expression of the Womb of space and time as associated with the sign Virgo the virgin.)

The process of Svabhāvat sending Fohat to 'harden the atoms' causes the appearance of a world-sphere, implicating the emanation of the seven planes of perception, plus the unfoldment of the signs of the zodiac from Aries to Virgo, thus with the early evolutionary experience.

---

35 The attributes of a mirror are detailed in *Esoteric Cosmology and Modern Physics*, as well as in *A Treatise on Mind*, in relation to the Mirror-like Wisdom of Akṣobhya.

The number 33 of the phrase *'Reflecting the "Self-Existent Lord"'* refers to the Creative Intelligences that are responsible for the formation of manifest space. Each embodies a sphere of self-contained activity that reflects the qualities of this Lord. These Creative Intelligences constitute the Head Centre of any established Logos, thus are responsible for the sum of manifest space. The Web thereby expands to capacity, precipitating the formation of World-spheres. The specific Hierarchy implied here is the tenth, Makara (the Agnishvattas), who embody the substance of the mental plane. They are incorporated with the Lunar Lords and Elemental Lives as the trinity of material plane manifestation.

The numbers 66 x 2 and 6 x 7 of the phrase *'Svabhāvat sends Fohat to harden the atoms'* refer to the vitalisation of all the planes of perception and their sub-planes (6 x 7) with the hardening process brought by the materialising activity of Fohat. This Fiery whirlwind thereby becomes increasingly slower and sombre hued, causing the materialising of the Lives, elementary forces and atoms (66 x 2). The incarnating Monads are also infused with Logoic Desire (6 x 7) to reflect their expressions (human Souls) into manifestation. The fiat is Sounded by all the integrated Sun/Sons in abstract space, producing condensation and crystallisation of the related Thought-Forms.

The numbers 44, 100 + 52 of the complete phrase *'Then Svabhāvat sends Fohat to harden the atoms'* refer to establishing the Seats of Power of the Lords that will come into manifestation (4 x 11) for the duration of an *mahāmanvantara* (100 + 52). They also project various links to similar Logoi in cosmos for mutual support and interrelated energisation (4 x 11), producing a web of interrelationships. The focus is upon the Logos of our earth, of the fourth Scheme of the solar system, or of the solar Logos, which is one of the fourth order. However, the passage refers generally to all Sun/Sons, the members of cosmic Humanity travelling together in the universe. With the establishment of these centres, within the etheric *maṇḍalas* the vitalisation (expansion) of the Web is complete.

'A world' (7 x 4, 10) then is an extension of the etheric web so that it establishes a connection, the *śūnyatā-saṃsāra* nexus, that allows the primeval substance of space to be incorporated into the Logoic *maṇḍala*. The world, a sphere of existence circumscribed by a ring-

pass-not (10), exists so that human consciousness (7 x 4) can evolve from out of its substance, to conquer dark space by overcoming ignorance. The number 104 of the phrase *'Each becomes in turn a world'* thus refers to the cosmic fourth kingdom (cosmic Humanity) that manifest Logoic Seats of Power, each viewed as world spheres. As such a world our earth is the mirror that allows comprehension of the way of the evolution of the rest of such spheres, and of the universe in general. This theme is then elaborated in the rest of the Cosmogenesis section of *The Secret Doctrine.*

Appendix

Keynotes of Stanzas 1 to 3 from the *Book of Dzyan*[1]

STANZA I

Stanza one relates to five cosmic astral sub-planes focussed via the plane *ādi* generally, and contains the 'blueprint' of the attributes of the Stanzas that follow, according to numerical affiliation.

Stanza 1:1

Pisces, third cosmic astral *(ātmic)* sub-plane, the emanative cosmic *karma*. Intelligent substance.

> **The eternal Parent** *(Space)*, **wrapped in Her ever invisible robes, had slumbered once again for seven Eternities.**

Stanza 1:2

Aquarius, fourth cosmic astral *(buddhic)* sub-plane. Unity thro' effort.

> **Time was not, for it lay asleep in the infinite Bosom of Duration.**

Stanza 1:3

Capricorn, fifth cosmic astral sub-plane, Father – the first Eternity. Light thro' knowledge.

---

1 Provided in Blavatsky's *The Secret Doctrine* 1888 version, pages 27–35. As Blavatsky used capital letters in the Stanzas, I have taken the liberty to incorporate lower case lettering. The Stanzas are in bold letters, whilst the words bracketed are Blavatsky's own comments. The references to the Creative Hierarchies are from Alice Bailey's *Esoteric Astrology*.

> **Universal Mind was not, for there were no Ah-Hi** *(celestial beings)* **to contain** (hence to manifest) **it.**

Stanza 1: 4

Sagittarius, sixth cosmic astral sub-plane. Son – the second Eternity. Desire for duality.

> **The seven Ways to Bliss** *(Moksha or Nirvana)* **were not. The great causes of misery** *(Nidana and Maya)* **were not, for there was no one to produce and get ensnared by them.**

Stanza 1:5

Scorpio, seventh cosmic astral sub-plane. Mother – the third Eternity. Mass Life, veiling Christ.

> **Darkness alone filled the Boundless All, for Father, Mother and Son were once more one, and the Son had not awakened yet for the new Wheel and his pilgrimage thereon.**

Stanza 1:6

Libra, *ādi* - the fourth Eternity. The first cosmic ether. The focal point of Stanza one. Divine Flames.

> **The seven Sublime Lords and the seven Truths had ceased to be, and the Universe, the Son of Necessity, was immersed in Paranishpanna** *(absolute perfection, Paranirvana, which is Yong-Grub)* **to be out-breathed by that which is and yet is not. Naught was.**

Stanza 1:7

Virgo, *anupādaka* - the fifth Eternity. The second cosmic ether. Divine Builders.

> **The causes of Existence had been done away with; the visible that was, and the invisible that is, rested in eternal non-being, the one Being.**

Stanza 1:8

Leo, *ātma* - the sixth Eternity. The third cosmic ether. Lesser Builders.

> **Alone, the one form of Existence stretched boundless, infinite, causeless, in dreamless sleep; and Life pulsated unconscious in universal Space, throughout that All-Presence which is sensed by the 'Opened Eye' of the Dangma.**

Stanza 1:9

Cancer, *buddhi* - the seventh Eternity. The fourth cosmic ether. Human Hierarchy, the Initiates.

> **But where was the Dangma when the alaya of the universe** *(Soul as the basis of all, Anima Mundi)* **was in paramartha** *(Absolute Being and Consciousness which are Absolute Non-Being and Unconsciousness)* **and the great Wheel was anupadaka?**

STANZA 2

The general focus of Stanza two is upon the plane *anupadāka.*

Stanza 2:1

Gemini, *anupadāka-ātmic* plane.

> **.....Where were the Builders, the luminous Sons of manvantaric dawn?.....In the unknown Darkness in their Ah-Hi** *(Chohanic, Dhyani-Buddhic)* **paranishpanna, the Producers of form** *(rupa)* **from no-form** *(arupa),* **the root of the world—the Devamatri and Svabhavat, rested in the bliss of non-being.**

Stanza 2:2

Taurus, *buddhic* plane.

> **.....Where was silence? Where were the ears to sense it? No! There was neither silence, nor sound; naught save ceaseless, eternal Breath** *(Motion),* **which knows itself not.**

Stanza 2:3

Aries, higher mental plane.

> **The hour had not yet struck; the Ray had not yet flashed into the Germ; the Matri-padma** *(mother lotus)* **had not yet swollen.**

Stanza 2:4

Taurus (rectified), *buddhi.*

> **Her Heart had not yet opened for the One Ray to enter, thence to fall as three into four in the lap of Māyā.**

Stanza 2:5

Gemini, *ātmic* plane.

> **The Seven (Sons) were not yet born from the Web of Light. Darkness alone was Father-Mother, svabhavat; and svabhavat was in Darkness.**

Stanza 2:6

Cancer, *anupadāka.*

> **These two are the Germ, and the Germ is – One. The Universe was still concealed in the Divine Thought and the Divine Bosom.**

STANZA 3

Stanza three relates to the *ātmic* plane in general, Stanza 1:3, and to universal Mind.

Stanza 3:1

Virgo, seventh cosmic astral sub-plane, Akṣobhya, cosmic Waters. The third Eternity.

> **.....The last vibration of the seventh Eternity thrills through Infinitude. The Mother swells, expanding from within without like the bud of the Lotus.**

Stanza 3:2

Libra, *ādi,* Aetheric Element, first Ray, first cosmic ether. Amoghasiddhi, Divine Flames, reflecting the fifth Creative Hierarchy. The fourth Eternity.

> **The vibration sweeps along, touching with its swift wing** *(simultaneously)* **the whole Universe, and the Germ that dwelleth in darkness: the darkness that breathes (moves) over the slumbering Waters of Life.**

Stanza 3:3

Scorpio, *anupādaka,* Airy Element, second Ray, second cosmic ether. Ratnasambhava, Divine Builders, reflecting the fourth Liberated Hierarchy – 'Desire for Duality'. The fifth Eternity.

> **'Darkness' radiates Light, and Light drops one solitary Ray into the Waters, into the Mother Deep. The Ray shoots through the Virgin-Egg, the Ray causes the Eternal Egg to thrill, and drop the non-eternal** *(periodical)* **Germ, which condenses into the World Egg.**

Stanza 3:4

Sagittarius, *ātma,* Fiery Element, third Ray, third cosmic ether. Amitābha, Lesser Builders, reflecting third Liberated Hierarchy – 'Light thro' knowledge'. The four higher *ātmic* sub-planes. The sixth Eternity.

> *(Then)* **The three** *(triangle)* **fall into the four** *(quaternary).* **The radiant Essence becomes seven inside, seven outside. The luminous Egg** *(Hiranyagarbha),* **which in itself is three, curdles and spreads in milk-white curds throughout the depths of Mother, the Root that grows in the ocean of Life.**

Stanza 3:5

Capricorn, Amitābha, Fiery Element. Three lower sub-planes of *ātma.*

> **The Root remains, the Light remains, the curds remain, and still Oeaohoo is One.**

Stanza 3:6

Aquarius, *buddhi,* Watery conveyor of the five *prāṇas,* fourth Ray, fourth cosmic ether. Akṣobhya, Human Hierarchy, reflecting the second Liberated Hierarchy – 'Unity thro' Effort'. The seventh Eternity.

> **The Root of Life was in every drop of the Ocean of Immortality** *(Amrita),* **and the Ocean was radiant Light, which was Fire and Heat and Motion. Darkness vanished and was no more. It disappeared in its own essence, the body of Fire and Water, of Father and Mother.**

Stanza 3:7

Pisces, the higher mental plane, fifth Ray, first sub-aspect of Earthy *ākāśa,* Vairocana and Amoghasiddhi. The kingdom of Souls, reflecting the first Liberated Hierarchy – 'Intelligent substance'.

> **Behold, O Lanoo! The radiant Child of the Two, the uparalleled refulgent Glory, bright Space, Son of dark space, who emerges from the depths of the great dark Waters. It is Oeaohoo, the Younger, the * * *** *(whom thou knowest now as Kwan-Shai-Yin).* **He shines forth as the Sun, he is the blazing divine Dragon of Wisdom. The Eka is Chatur** *(four),* **and Chatur takes to itself Three, and the union produces the Sapta** *(seven)* **in whom are the Seven which become the Tridasa** *(the thrice ten),* **the Hosts and the Multitudes. Behold him lifting the Veil, and unfurling it from east to west. He shuts out the above, and leaves the below to be seen as the great illusion. He marks the places for the shining Ones** *(stars),* **and turns the upper** *(space)* **into a shoreless Sea of Fire, and the One manifested into the great Waters.**

Stanza 3:8

Aries, lower mental plane, ascent, fifth Ray, Amoghasiddhi. Second sub-aspect of Earthy *ākāśa.* Makara the mystery.

> **Where was the Germ, and where was now Darkness? Where is the Spirit of the Flame that burns in thy Lamp, O Lanoo?**

> **The Germ is That, and That is Light; the white brilliant Son of the dark hidden Father.**

Stanza 3:9

Taurus, astral plane, sixth Ray, third sub-aspect of Earthy *ākāśa*, Ratnasambhava.

> **Light is cold Flame, and Flame is Fire, and Fire produces heat, which yields Water, the Water of Life in the great Mother** *(Chaos).*

Stanza 3:10

Gemini, astral-etheric planes, sixth Ray, third sub-aspect of Earthy *ākāśa*, Ratnasambhava.

> **Father—Mother spin a Web whose upper end is fastened to Spirit** *(Purusha),* **the Light of the one Darkness, and the lower one to matter** *(Prakriti)* **its** *(the Spirit's)* **shadowy end; and this Web is the universe spun out of the two substances made in One, which is Swabhavat.**

Stanza 3:11

Cancer, the etheric plane, the seventh Ray, fourth sub-aspect of Earthy *ākāśa*, Amitābha.

> **It expands when the Breath of Fire is upon it; it contracts when the Breath of the Mother touches it. Then the Sons dissociate and scatter, to return into their Mother's Bosom at the end of the great Day, and re-become one with Her; when it is cooling it becomes radiant, and the Sons expand and contract through their own Selves and Hearts; they embrace Infinitude.**

Stanza 3: 12

Leo, dense physical plane, third Ray, fifth sub-aspect of Earthy *ākāśa*, Amitābha.

> **Then Svābhāvat sends Fohat to harden the atoms. Each is a part of the Web. Reflecting the "Self-Existent Lord", like a mirror, each becomes in turn a world.**

Bibliography

Bailey, Alice A. *A Treatise on Cosmic Fire.* New York: Lucis Publishing Company, 1977.

——. *Esoteric Astrology.* London: Lucis Publishing Company, 1982.

——. *Esoteric Psychology I,* London: Lucis Publishing Company, 1977.

——. *Initiation, Human and Solar.* London: Lucis Publishing Company, 1972.

——. *Letters on Occult Meditation.* New York: Lucis Publishing Company, 1978.

——. *The Externalisation of the Hierarchy.* New York: Lucis Publishing Company, 1982.

——. *The Rays and the Initiations.* New York: Lucis Publishing Company, 1970.

Balsys, Bodo. *A Treatise on Mind, Volume 1.* Sydney: Universal Dharma Publishing, 2016.

——. *A Treatise on Mind, Volume 2.* Sydney: Universal Dharma Publishing, 2016.

——. *A Treatise on Mind, Volume 3.* Sydney: Universal Dharma Publishing, 2016.

——. *A Treatise on Mind, Volume 4.* Sydney: Universal Dharma Publishing, 2015.

——. *A Treatise on Mind, Volume 5A.* Sydney: Universal Dharma Publishing, 2015.

——. *A Treatise on Mind, Volume 5B.* Sydney: Universal Dharma Publishing, 2015.

——. *A Treatise on Mind, Volume 6.* Sydney: Universal Dharma Publishing, 2014.

——. *A Treatise on Mind, Volume 7A.* Sydney: Universal Dharma Publishing, 2017.

——. *A Treatise on Mind, Volume 7B&C.* Sydney: Universal Dharma Publishing, 2018.

——. *Esoteric Cosmology and Modern Physics.* Sydney: Universal Dharma Publishing, 2020.

Besant, Annie. *The Bhagavad-Gita.* Fourth edition. G.A. Natesay & Co, Madras, India, 1922.

Bible, *King James Version*, Thomas Nelson Inc., New Jersey, 1972.

Blavatsky, H.P. *The Secret Doctrine. Vol. 1.* Adyar: Theosophical Publishing House, 1888.

Dowsen, John. *A Classical Dictionary of Hindu Mythology, and Religion, Geography, History and Literature*, Munshiram Manoharlal, 2000

Garfield, Jay L. *The Fundamental Wisdom of the Middle Way*, Oxford University Press, Oxford, 1995.

Kalupahana, David J. *Mūlamadhyamakakārikā of Nāgārjuna, The Philosophy of the Middle Way*, Motilal Barnasidass, Delhi, 1999.

Lama Anagarika Govinda. *Foundations of Tibetan Mysticism*, Samuel Weiser, Maine, 1982.

Napper, Elizabeth. *Dependent Arising and Emptiness*, Wisdom Publications, Boston, 1989.

Panda, N. C. *Cyclic Universe,* Vol. 2, D.K. Printworld (P) Ltd., New Delhi, 2002.

Obermiller, E., trans. *The Uttaratantra of Maitreya*, Sri Satguru, New Delhi, 1991.

Wayman, Alex. *The Buddhist Tantras: Light on Indo-Tibetan Esotericism*, Motilal Barnasidass, New Delhi, 2005.

Index

Index

A

Abhaya mudrā, 131
Absolute All, 40–41, 468
Absolute Being, 281–282
Abstract Deity, 508
Adamic man, 474
Adam Kadmon, 316
Adept, adeptship, 57, 60, 68, 159, 161, 162, 182, 183, 218, 262, 264, 267, 484, 506, 536, 542
Adhiṣṭhāna, 32
Ādi, 26, 110, 151–152, 154, 155, 156, 157, 225–226, 242, 289, 293, 333, 336, 337–338, 359, 367–368, 377, 388, 393, 402, 405, 412, 501, 515, 521, 565
Ādi Buddha, 6, 22, 37, 233, 318–319, 330
Āditi, 10, 93, 104, 289–290, 566
Ādityas, 290, 480
Advaita Vedānta, 14–17, 19, 21, 25, 30, 32, 37–38, 40, 45, 94, 205, 282, 301, 348, 530
Aeons, 374
Ageless wisdom, xv
Agni, 560–563
Agnichaitans, 137, 344, 527
Agnishvattas, 137, 380, 569
Agnisuryans, 137, 344, 369, 527
Āḥ, 429, 431, 432
Ah-Hi, 182, 183, 186–187, 190–195, 201, 275–277, 281–285, 334, 354, 360
Aitareya Brahmana, 469
Ākāśa (Akasha), 33–36, 41, 46, 81, 87, 89, 133, 160, 165, 286, 290–293, 294, 309, 320, 334–335, 373, 376, 388, 390, 408, 449, 490–491, 493, 498, 514–515, 521, 524, 560, 563
    Aetheric, 336, 341, 388
    Airy, 336, 373, 388, 389
    Earthy, 338–339, 341, 343, 344–345, 388, 393, 395, 424, 426, 456, 477, 498, 512, 518, 527, 539, 557
    Fiery, 337, 388, 392, 566
    Watery, 388, 392
Ākaśadhātvīśarī, 130
Akṣara, 16
Akṣobhya, 23, 24, 93, 100, 130, 132–133, 134, 145, 335, 339, 350, 359, 392, 435, 436, 521, 568
Ālaya, 157, 266, 267–271, 272, 291–292, 349, 433
Ālayavijñāna, 18, 20–21, 269–270

Alchemy, 415, 452
Alcyone, 405
Alderbaran, 389
Alice Bailey, xiii, 49
All-accomplishing Wisdom, 24, 94, 128, 131, 146, 147, 148–149, 336, 341, 361, 393, 455, 497, 506, 520, 524
Amitābha, 23, 24–25, 93, 104, 130, 134, 137, 138, 145, 147, 337, 339, 344, 345, 386–387, 392, 395, 398, 402, 420, 422, 424, 426, 506, 522, 538–539, 557, 564
Amitāyus, 130
Amoghasiddhi, 23–24, 25, 94, 128, 131, 146, 147, 148–149, 293, 336, 341, 359, 454, 455, 477, 496, 497, 506, 520, 524
Amrita (amṛta), 401, 435–436
Ānanda, 21
Ananta-Nāga, 16
Ancient of Days, 316
Angelic kingdom, 194, 289, 308, 321
Angelic triads, 166, 246, 280, 288, 290, 419
Anima mundi, 75, 121, 137, 147, 224, 268–269, 277, 285, 315, 347, 382, 406
Anirvacanīyā, 16, 25, 28
Ankh cross, 13
Antaḥkaraṇa(s), 14, 54, 57, 58, 59, 62, 64, 77, 85, 89, 110, 116, 122, 123, 132, 143, 180, 194, 198, 219–220, 233, 255, 330, 370–371, 397, 418, 432, 445, 472, 500, 504, 513, 522, 530, 547, 554–555, 556
Aṇu, 105
Anupādaka, 7, 27, 58, 72, 80–82, 86, 133, 144, 145, 148, 154, 156, 157, 232, 244, 245, 252, 265–266, 272–274, 277, 279, 280, 284, 293, 294–295, 323, 334, 336, 337, 348, 368, 371, 372, 373, 377–378, 388, 389, 394, 402, 405, 407, 408, 412, 499, 501, 515, 521, 548–549, 566
Āpaḥ, 33–36, 41
Aphrodite, 548
Apratiṣṭhitanirvāṇa, 24
Aquarius, 66, 153, 171, 175–176, 177, 178, 213–214, 270, 271, 304, 321, 331–332, 339, 340, 345, 346, 369, 388, 391, 400, 406, 414–415, 435, 436, 437, 442, 461, 465, 474, 492, 506–508, 517–518, 552, 558
Arachne, 527–528
Archangels, 44, 227, 249, 292
Aries, 60, 168, 178, 214, 292, 303, 304, 313, 321, 341–342, 346, 391, 393, 410, 437, 446, 474, 492, 493, 496, 506–508, 518, 564, 568
Aristotle, 315
Arūpa, 192, 248, 258, 265, 275, 277, 286, 461
Aryans, 224
Aryāsanga, 268–269
Asat, 16, 26, 29
Ashrams, 64, 65, 67
Astral Light, 315, 316, 357, 416, 444, 468–469
Astral plane, 9, 29, 34, 56, 59, 61, 71, 101, 103, 112, 133, 144, 147–148, 153, 154, 211, 216, 228, 230, 232, 251, 255, 315, 325, 339, 341, 342, 368–369, 376, 385, 393–394, 402, 405, 411, 415, 416, 438, 445, 450, 452, 463, 479, 491, 510, 511, 515, 516, 518, 520, 525–526. *See also* Cosmic astral plane, Waters
Astrological year, 60
Asūras, 436
Asvatantrā, 16, 26, 29
Aświns (Aswins), 480
Athanor, 525
Atlantis, xvi, xvii, 343, 401, 475, 476, 512
Ātma, 27, 67, 76, 81, 85, 101, 112, 125, 144–145, 154, 156, 245, 251, 252, 256, 265, 275, 276, 277, 280, 284, 292–293, 295, 308, 317, 318, 334, 337–338, 356, 367–369, 371, 376, 377, 379, 385, 386, 387, 388, 390–391, 392, 395, 402, 405, 407, 408, 409–413, 418, 423–424, 428, 431, 436, 444, 451, 473, 484, 493,

498, 501, 515, 517, 522, 529, 541, 542, 545, 566
Ātman, 18, 37, 39
Atoms, 545, 556, 557, 558, 562, 564–565, 566, 569
Aūṁ, 192–193, 229, 296, 427–429, 430, 431, 432, 433, 437
Aura, 358, 400, 457, 458, 459, 531
Avalokiteśvara, 466–467, 468
Āvaraṇa-śakti, 17
Avatāra, 227, 552
Avatar of Synthesis, 398, 471
Avidya, 200, 245
Avyākṛta, 16
Avyakta, 33
Awakened, 221–222

B

Bala-śakti, 17, 35
Balzac, 387
Baptism, 62
Baskets of Nourishment, 370
Beatitude, 519, 520, 521
Behold, 454, 456–457
Being, 249–250
Be-ness, 30, 42, 301
Bhagavad Gītā, 433
Bhāva, 200, 245
Bhumisparśa mudrā, 130
Bhūtātmā, 37–38, 39
Bible, 48
Bīja(s), 3–4, 18, 21, 26, 34, 97, 105, 131, 139, 152, 216, 218, 225–226, 305, 328, 330, 365, 431, 515
Bindu, 179, 225–226, 365
Black dust, 210, 341, 352, 380, 392, 393, 414, 497, 514, 523
Black magic, 40
Blavatsky, xiii–xv, 49, 50
Blinded Lives, 286, 343, 414, 516
Bliss, ways of, 155, 195–200, 293–294
Bodhi, 187, 192
Bodhicitta, 9, 27, 57, 81, 113, 114, 293, 360, 401–402, 429, 507, 522, 543, 551
Bodhisattva Path, 7, 430, 507, 554
Bodhisattva(s), 461, 506, 520, 521, 523, 552
Bosom, 144, 146–149, 152–153, 156–157, 171, 175–180, 180, 182, 183–185, 219, 240, 244–245, 249, 251, 255, 266, 323, 326, 328–329, 545, 547–548. *See also* Womb
Bosom of Duration, 152–153, 157, 175–179, 183–184, 266, 547
Boundless, 255
Boundless all, 208, 211, 217–218, 220, 282, 287, 320, 531
Brahmā, 16, 22–23, 24, 25, 35, 36, 39, 40, 41, 44, 46, 58, 61, 67, 72, 74, 79, 83, 84, 87, 89, 100, 101, 102, 103, 119, 149, 160–161, 170, 175, 179, 220, 249, 261, 272, 278, 279, 280, 281, 287, 301, 305, 308, 327–328, 329, 337, 349, 352–353, 356–357, 403–404, 407, 423, 447, 502, 505, 508, 509, 510, 512, 530, 534–535, 549, 563
    planes of, 36, 65, 112, 144, 156, 385, 386, 388, 402, 413, 450, 470–471, 473
Brahman, 15, 16–17, 21, 23, 26, 29–30, 32, 34, 37–38, 44, 46, 47, 83, 87, 89, 93, 96, 100, 101, 205, 209–210, 327, 329, 348, 403, 508, 510, 566
Brahmāśrayā, 16
Brahmā-vach, 510
Brahmā-Virāj, 510
Breath, 2, 3, 5, 13, 30, 35, 42–43, 78, 79, 82, 85–86, 94, 114–115, 121–124, 134, 138–146, 167, 177, 191, 192, 221, 239–241, 243, 294, 297, 299, 300–302, 328, 367, 370, 387, 396, 428, 430, 470, 472, 473, 484, 538, 539–545, 547, 550–552, 554, 563–564
Bright Space, 454, 456, 461, 464, 467, 474
Buddha-essence, 95
Buddha-germ/womb, 4, 18, 25, 95

Buddha-Mind, 20–21, 35
Buddha(s), 7, 8, 22, 31, 37, 97, 159, 166, 168, 187, 229, 272–273, 326, 441, 486, 516
Buddhas of Activity, 75, 199, 233, 265, 313, 398, 453, 471, 476, 477
Buddhi, 6, 27, 58, 69, 70–71, 89, 92, 112, 125, 144, 145, 147, 148, 154, 157, 159, 165, 173, 176, 187, 197, 221, 232, 256, 265, 266, 267, 292, 293, 300, 302, 333, 339, 357, 367–369, 378, 388, 402, 424, 431, 433, 435, 436–437, 442, 444–445, 448, 451, 457, 477, 515, 518, 531, 535, 541, 566
  plane, 58, 88, 133, 146, 152, 168, 169, 171, 174, 184, 210, 228, 238, 239, 266, 269, 282, 286, 294–295, 309, 339, 342, 352, 362, 382, 392, 405, 411, 425, 440, 451, 484, 497, 522
Buddhic permanent atom, 363
Buddhism, logic, 1–2, 6, 18, 37
Builders, 180, 191, 194, 245, 248, 251, 265, 266, 273, 275, 276, 277, 279, 280, 282, 285, 288–289, 295, 296, 299, 320, 334, 380, 386, 389–390, 408, 409, 413, 415, 420, 431, 515, 540

C

Caduceus, 231–232, 544
Cancer, 71, 127, 137–138, 149, 157, 168, 178, 202, 204, 207, 208, 211–215, 248, 265, 266, 272, 311, 321–323, 330, 344, 346, 380, 390–391, 410, 419–420, 462, 480, 487, 488, 494, 527, 538–540, 542, 544, 557, 558
Capricorn, 64–65, 127, 154, 172, 178, 184–186, 195, 207, 211, 214, 241, 265, 270, 272, 320–322, 326, 338, 341, 346, 379–380, 385, 390–392, 408, 414, 422, 424–427, 437, 438, 460, 461–462, 472, 473, 475, 487, 488–489, 494, 498, 507–508, 528, 540, 549
Castor, 480
Causal Body, 4, 65, 147, 181, 253, 323, 439, 444, 462, 502, 505, 510, 562
Causative agents, 194, 223
Ceaseless, 294, 297, 299, 300
Celaeno, 405
Central Spiritual Sun, 332, 437, 438, 442, 462, 482, 494, 501, 533, 562
Chains, 37, 72, 76, 102, 107
Chaitanya, 15
Chakras (centres), 8, 12, 52, 58, 59, 65, 73, 76, 77, 84, 114, 144, 162–163, 164, 184, 205, 212, 222, 224, 235, 240, 241, 243, 247, 257, 262, 270, 283, 284, 306, 310, 311, 318, 319, 339, 353, 354, 355, 357, 366, 367, 372, 377, 384, 390, 394, 406, 407–408, 419–420, 425, 436, 439–440, 453–454, 464, 479–480, 482, 487, 500, 502, 513, 522, 528, 535, 544
  Ājñā (third Eye), 68, 77, 132, 139, 231, 261, 262, 427, 430, 457, 459, 487, 488
  Base of Spine, 12, 110, 140, 203, 210, 257–258, 310, 313, 319, 362, 365, 391, 399, 427, 430, 443, 477, 501, 503, 558
  Diaphragm, 311
  Feet, 399
  Gonad, 306, 558
  Head, 60, 61, 63, 67, 77, 87, 88, 90, 98, 109–110, 117, 118, 132, 137, 176, 196, 204, 207, 210, 243, 263, 267, 283, 286, 311, 319, 334, 349, 358, 361–362, 406, 425, 427, 430, 432, 446, 459, 466, 477, 485, 501–503, 530, 554–555, 556–557, 569
  Heart, 51, 57, 64, 73, 80, 118, 176, 243, 257, 262, 300, 309–310, 311, 354, 356, 360, 381, 398, 400, 401, 425, 431, 440, 442, 467, 484, 505, 530, 554, 555
  Inner Round, 232, 313, 333, 339, 425

Sacral, 74, 110, 124, 306, 313–314, 356, 391, 399, 427–428, 430–431, 443, 467, 486, 503, 558
Solar Plexus, 44, 65, 110, 176, 178–179, 262, 306, 333, 361, 362, 380, 400, 431
Splenic, 314, 400, 480, 530
Throat, 61, 390, 425, 428, 431, 432
Channelers, 49, 50
Chaos, 370, 411, 447, 468–469
Chatur, 454, 475, 476–477
Chit, 15, 21
Chohans, 8, 226
Christ, xviii, 50, 61, 64, 65, 74, 75, 76, 81, 82, 84, 154, 161, 163, 201, 216, 218, 224, 252, 271, 279, 302, 312, 317, 324, 325, 358, 376, 379, 384, 404, 433, 464, 478, 500, 501, 505, 506, 554, 555
child, 109, 112, 167, 178, 241, 326, 356, 464, 516, 523
consciousness, 59, 99, 377, 420–421, 499
cosmic, 66–67, 70, 89, 138, 164, 178, 180, 183–184, 227, 234, 264, 267, 271–274, 288, 297, 326, 329, 354, 363, 364, 371, 374, 381, 391, 442, 452, 463, 465, 471, 484–485, 504–505
force, 406
Christ-Jesus, 459
Cidābhāsa, 38
Circle, 10–11, 79, 93, 94–102
Cit-śakti, 17
Citta, 18, 269, 270, 429, 444, 450, 461
Clear Light, 41, 69, 134, 146, 209, 493, 512
Cold Flame, 510, 511, 512–515, 517, 518, 521, 525
Colours, 73
Consciousness, 12, 31, 37–38, 81, 86, 124–125, 175, 183–184, 190, 193, 209, 219, 230, 250, 252, 270–271, 274, 284, 302–303, 323, 324, 363, 365, 371, 373, 375, 397, 423, 426, 447, 449, 517, 524, 542
absolute, 3, 42–43, 302–303, 340
purpose of, 46–47
Contemplative, solitary, 7
Cosmic
astral plane, 81, 86, 90, 96, 99, 100–101, 113, 133, 137, 146, 152, 153, 155, 156, 158, 168–171, 175–176, 186–187, 196, 198, 213, 237, 239, 241, 242, 251, 264, 273, 282, 284–285, 287, 292, 293, 304, 309–310, 329, 333, 335, 336, 337, 339, 342, 348, 354, 358, 373–374, 376, 379, 386, 388, 392, 394, 402, 409, 412–413, 439, 463, 464–465, 476, 482, 483, 490, 494–495, 504, 514–515, 517, 521–522, 524, 540, 543, 547–549, 554, 555, 563, 565
Blood, 369
Child, 351
dense physical, 112, 166, 282, 335–336, 341, 359, 385, 425, 476, 497, 514, 524, 548, 562, 564
dust, 4, 210, 214, 341, 352, 368, 374, 392, 393, 469
Egg, 39, 102, 105, 241, 325–326
electricity, 358
ethers, 89, 103, 110, 144, 152, 155, 156, 157, 159–160, 168, 194, 239, 248, 261, 274, 284, 286, 291, 306, 319, 339, 348, 362, 369, 373, 378–379, 380–381, 392, 407, 476, 486, 522, 531, 537, 552
Fire, 343, 351, 527
Heart, 257–258
Humanity, 72, 88, 89, 98, 190, 569–570
Love, 88, 171, 196, 337, 373, 413, 436, 438
mental plane, 4, 5, 6, 10, 75, 97, 285, 292, 300, 318, 335, 337, 352, 493
Mind, 6, 37, 43, 66–67, 94, 98,

100, 104, 112, 113, 114, 132, 139, 167, 185, 217–218, 239, 293, 321, 326, 339, 344, 351–352, 373, 411, 413–414, 446, 449, 461, 472, 527–528, 567. *See also* Mind, Mahat
  Paths, xviii, 8, 196–198, 233, 484, 547–548
  Soul, 258, 351
Cosmos, 38, 39, 97
Count of St Germain, 48
Cow of plenty, 401
Creation, 39, 301, 308, 320, 328, 340, 379, 427, 471, 484, 485
Creative Fires, 145, 430
Creative Hierarchies, 64, 66, 75, 77, 98, 106, 136, 166, 167, 171, 174, 187, 198, 219, 227–228, 281, 287–288, 302, 308, 311, 314, 329, 336, 356, 360, 362–364, 369, 373, 377–378, 381, 384, 397–398, 411, 420, 423, 426–427, 439, 461, 465, 467, 478, 479, 513, 515, 520, 537, 540, 543, 554, 569
  fifth, 67, 72, 73, 154, 155, 208, 338, 341, 359, 361, 410
  first, 60, 152, 156, 158, 160, 280, 335, 359, 410–411, 456, 497
  fourth, 63, 69, 70, 71, 155, 196, 252, 337, 339–340, 374, 409–410, 437, 475, 495, 546
  liberated, 152, 340, 356
  second, 57, 68, 153, 181, 339, 410, 436–437
  seven, 107, 187, 195, 341, 412
  sixth, 75
  tenth and eleventh, 344, 380, 397, 411, 414, 516, 539, 569
  tenthe and eleventh, 498
  third, 187, 285, 337, 344, 373, 386, 410
  twelfth, 345, 409, 414, 512, 516, 557
Creative Intelligences, 66, 70, 80, 106, 149, 154, 174, 192, 194, 244, 259, 284, 292, 311, 330, 332–333, 350, 405, 418, 420, 459, 461, 479, 481, 484, 485, 490, 522, 529, 535, 537, 565
Creative Word, 35, 528
Creator, 541
Crocodiles, 397, 472
Cross, 10, 184
  cardinal, 107, 108, 211, 322
  fixed, 13, 107, 271, 325
  mutable, 108
Crucifixion, 70
Curdle, 417
Curds, 152, 387–388, 390–391, 408, 417–420, 423, 425–427, 433–434
Cycles, 57, 126–127, 133, 136, 137, 159, 163, 173, 179, 181–182, 186, 190, 194, 224, 242, 257, 258, 278, 304, 331, 354, 361, 399, 426, 449, 463, 472, 510

D

Dangma, 157, 250, 252, 256, 260–264, 266–267, 269–271, 274, 461, 573
Dark brotherhood, 49, 74–75, 119, 149, 209, 224, 375, 431, 460, 464, 472, 475
Dark matter, 4
Darkness, 79, 118–120, 121, 155, 198, 201, 208–211, 214, 215–218, 220, 238, 267, 282, 305, 316, 320–323, 326, 338, 341, 365–368, 372–376, 424, 443–445, 447–448, 451–453, 460–461, 464, 482, 499, 504, 509, 531–534, 549
Dark space, 460–461, 463, 467, 570
Dark Waters, 462–464, 485, 494
Dawn, 279, 280
Day-be-with-us, 273, 332, 532
Day to Be, 185
Deity, 315
Democritus, 370
Dependent Origination, 19, 200, 245–247
Depths, 462–464
Devachan, 200, 215
Deva Lords, 147
Devamātri, 289–293, 294, 299, 308,

349, 350, 420, 480
Deva(s), 9, 67, 70, 72, 75, 77, 80, 83–84, 108, 109, 111, 112, 122, 126, 134–138, 143, 147, 149, 156, 165, 166, 191, 193, 214, 219, 244, 245, 247–251, 265, 276–277, 279, 288, 292, 296–298, 318, 329, 333, 337, 343, 351, 352–353, 363, 369, 375, 379, 380, 382, 386, 395, 399, 404, 413, 420, 427, 428, 433, 439, 461, 470, 479, 515, 526–527, 535–536, 544, 564, 566
Dhāraṇī(s), 271, 429, 442
Dharma, xv, 2, 95, 187, 241
Dharmacakra, 223
Dharmadhātu Wisdom, 23, 24, 77, 93, 95, 130, 133, 145, 340, 455
Dharmakāya, 10, 17, 20, 26, 28, 35, 37, 66, 67, 72, 77, 81, 84, 95, 97, 100, 105, 110, 112, 113, 130, 147, 187–188, 269, 431, 441, 450, 549, 553, 566
Dharmakāya Flower, 326
Dharmatā, 95
Dhātu, 95
Dhyāna, 168, 239, 256, 391
Dhyāna mudrā, 130
Dhyān Chohans, 179, 191, 201, 273, 350, 358, 446, 559
Dhyāni Buddha(s), 8, 13, 22, 24, 35, 41, 45, 47, 58, 61, 65, 67, 75, 76, 83, 93, 94, 99, 102, 117, 128–131, 136, 142, 146, 166, 227, 233, 249, 261, 268, 269, 270, 273, 293, 308–309, 334–336, 340, 356, 363, 405, 413, 434, 448, 465, 478, 542, 544
Dhyānis, 134
Direction(s), 51–52, 484
Discriminating Inner Wisdom, 93, 104, 134, 145, 337, 386, 395, 402, 420, 424, 506, 522, 539, 557
Dissociate, 546–547
Divine, 325, 471
Divine Bosom, 323, 325–326, 328–329
Divine Builders, 154, 156, 245, 372, 411–412
Divine Egg, 434, 453
Divine Flames, 154, 156, 214, 226, 336, 338, 341, 359, 361–362, 379, 409, 411–412, 423, 497–498, 515, 540
Divine Ideation, 328
Divine Life, 450
Divine Lives, 277, 336
Divine Love, 402
Divine Ray, 450–451
Divine Thinker, 3–4, 327, 522
Divine Thought, 3, 6, 110, 197, 245, 315, 323, 325–329, 357, 358, 377, 468, 559, 563–564
Divine Voice, 468
Divine Will, 112, 117, 132, 209, 299, 361, 377, 508
D.K. (Djwhal Khul), xiv, 48–50
Door, 485–486
Draco, 470, 472–473
Dragon (of Wisdom), 47, 140, 230, 468–473, 476, 482–483, 484, 486, 490, 542
Duhkha, 200, 245
Duration, 181–185, 217, 244

E

Earth globe, Chain, Scheme, xvii, 41, 136, 151, 175, 227, 230, 232, 278, 289, 308, 317, 346, 350, 357, 365, 394, 431, 438, 445, 456–459, 460, 465, 471, 472, 476, 499, 507, 537, 544
Egg(s), 351, 373, 378, 405, 407, 434, 464
Eightfold Path, 200
Eighth sphere, 464
Eka, 468, 476–478
Elders, 68, 169, 446, 555, 567
Electra, 405
Electric fire, 355
Electricity, 450–451, 490–491, 492, 525, 542, 559–560, 563
Elemental Lives, 288, 342, 343, 345, 369–370, 375, 411, 414, 497, 512, 527, 540, 557–558, 569

Elementals of Fire, 449–450
Element(s), 12, 13, 25, 39, 142, 144, 150, 356, 367, 388, 391, 453, 476, 491, 498, 515, 518–519, 525, 566
  Aether, 12, 27, 28, 39, 130, 213, 307, 359, 388, 434, 491
  Air, 27, 28–29, 39, 58, 130, 144, 146, 175, 213, 239, 336, 362, 367, 371, 373, 388, 389, 434, 470, 473–474, 540–541, 550
  Earth, 39, 59, 131, 143, 148, 213, 388, 389, 391, 392, 393–394, 399, 408, 434, 458, 473–474, 557, 564
  Fire, 5, 6, 9, 11, 13, 27, 29, 39, 58, 69, 72, 73, 130, 132, 138, 139–140, 145, 146, 213, 232, 326, 336, 362, 368, 373, 388, 390, 405, 412, 422, 434, 437–438, 444–447, 448, 451, 452, 458, 470, 472–474, 490, 492, 493, 503, 507, 512–514, 516, 517–518, 521–523, 527, 540, 542–543, 550–551, 553–554, 557, 560–561
  Water (see also Waters), 9, 39, 59, 131, 138, 144, 213, 230, 232, 387, 388, 434, 447, 452, 458, 472, 473–474, 507, 512, 516–518, 541, 543
Elohim, 468, 476, 491
Ensnare, 205–207
Equalising Wisdom, 23, 94, 114, 131, 143, 145–147, 337, 342, 373, 394, 506, 512, 518, 522, 527
Essence, 451–454
Eternal Egg, 336, 373, 381–382, 384–385, 402, 413
Eternal Parent, 152, 157–160, 166, 217, 236, 256, 460, 542
Eternal(s), 86–87, 250
Eternities, 167–171
Eternities (seven), 152–159, 162, 175, 182, 183, 185–187, 189, 208, 217, 244, 252, 256, 257, 258, 266, 278, 281, 331, 348–351, 362, 370, 373
Ethers, 124, 176, 183, 314, 384, 390, 402, 416, 444, 483, 498, 526–527, 529, 533, 537, 545, 565
  Fourth. *See* Buddhi
Eve, 315, 468
Ever invisible, 162–164, 166
Evil, 525
Evolution, 127
Existence, 156, 245–247, 250, 252–253, 258, 268
Existents, 19
Eye(s), 3–5, 11, 125, 126, 132, 136, 157, 163, 166, 180–181, 213–214, 216, 221, 241, 252, 261–264, 266–267, 269, 309, 426, 446, 457, 459, 461, 468, 508, 566
  Monadic, 9, 262–263, 441

F

Face, 142
Fall, 312–313
Father, 13, 79, 86, 104, 109–112, 125, 126, 141, 145, 156, 157, 160–161, 186, 198, 202–203, 210, 219, 225, 236, 238, 274, 280, 304, 367, 396, 425, 427, 447, 450, 453–454, 501, 504–508, 510–511, 541, 545
Father-Mother, 160, 186, 210, 220, 250, 252, 279, 316, 320–324, 394, 425, 427, 453–454, 457, 469, 526, 528–529, 536, 541
Father-Son, 512
Feathers, 336, 363
Fiery Elementals, 461
Fiery Life (Lives), 192, 540
Fiery Will, 148, 503
Fire-mist, 409, 418, 445, 469
Flame (cold, hot), 135–137, 147, 498, 500–504, 512–514, 524–525
Fohat, 44, 332, 357–358, 395, 449, 451, 490–492, 494, 524, 525, 545, 557, 558–569
Form, 31–32
Fornax, 470, 472–473
Four conditions, 20

Fourth cosmic ether. *See* Buddhi
Fourth Fruit, 457, 459
Francis Bacon, 48
Fundamental propositions, 42–47
  fourth, 46–47

G

Gabriel, 227
Garba, 83, 483
Garment, 134–135, 137–139
Garuda, 131
Gautama, 8, 254
Gemini, 70, 92, 102, 103, 109, 168, 169, 176, 177, 183–184, 194, 213, 214, 270–271, 275–276, 286, 287, 295–296, 306, 316, 321, 328, 343, 346, 381, 388, 390–391, 394–395, 408, 410, 442, 448, 465, 466, 474–475, 478–480, 486, 488, 498, 506–508, 526, 527–528, 533, 539, 544, 557, 565
Germ, 78, 82–84, 86, 87, 94, 130, 131, 132, 304–306, 310, 323–324, 341, 360, 365–368, 371, 377, 384, 398, 410, 420, 469, 499, 500–501, 504–505, 511, 534
Ghatākāśa, 38
Glory, 458–459, 461
Gnāna, 348
Gnostic's Serpent, 469
God, 18, 37, 39, 61, 68, 73, 74, 139, 161, 184, 188, 222, 227, 263, 311, 387, 443, 460, 484, 553, 562
  Mind of, 27, 349, 444, 477, 503, 533
  Spirit of, 11, 47, 211, 367, 469, 503
  Throne of, 58, 67, 69
Golden Egg, 16, 40, 83–84, 383, 403, 408, 510
Grand Heavenly Man, xiii, 287, 530
Great Bear, 184, 547
Greater Builders, 194, 275, 279–280, 284–286, 292, 379, 423, 515, 521, 536
Group Lives, 5
Guṇas, 17, 31–32, 34, 38, 39, 405, 534

H

Hari, 301, 404
Hearing, 295–298, 519–521
Heart, 111, 137
Heart in the Head, 110, 284, 361, 388–389, 432
Heart of Life, 52, 135, 137, 239, 461, 484
Heart of the Sun, 184, 347, 399, 437, 442, 462, 465
Heat, 9, 442, 444–446, 448–450, 516–517, 518, 523–525, 542, 545, 551
Heavenly Man, 287
Hegel, 44
Helena Roerich, xiii, 50
Hercules, 463
Hermaphrodite, 250, 322, 453, 528
Hermes, 469–470
Hermetic Cross, 11
Hevajatantra, 24
Hexagon, 74, 551
Hexagram, 59, 68, 462
Hierarchical rulers, 345–346
Hierarchy (human), xiii–xiv, xvi, 41, 64, 65, 67, 76, 163, 180, 274, 279, 308, 319, 321–322, 472, 475, 489–490, 555
Hindu religion, 1–2, 37
Hiranya, 83
Hiraṇyagarbha, 25, 35, 39, 44, 83–84, 87, 349, 389, 403, 464, 474
Holy Ghost, 68
Holy of Holies, 328, 478
Horse Head Nebulae, 548
Hosts, 481–482
Hrīḥ, 428–429, 431
Hūṁ, 429–432
Hydra, 62, 71, 75, 270, 462–463
Hyle, 525

I

Icchāśakti (Ichchhashakti), 17, 286,

341, 498
Iḍā naḍī, 59, 108, 230–231, 262, 311, 329, 394, 430–431, 438, 441, 510, 536, 548, 553, 565
Ideation, cosmic, 43–44
Ignorance, 216, 245, 282
Immaculate Conception, 315
Immortality, 440–441
Incarnations, 777, 85, 88, 117, 122, 136, 206, 223, 237, 242, 284, 286, 289, 313, 378, 379, 459, 483, 487
Inchoate, 411
Individualisation, 84, 207, 231, 437, 438, 439, 442, 445, 474–475
Infinite, 176–180, 182, 255
Infinitude, 351
Initiation(s), Initiates, xvi, xviii, 64, 67, 77, 109, 117, 119, 124, 141, 143, 145, 148–149, 166, 182, 185, 187, 192, 207, 228, 232, 271, 288, 298, 321, 354, 387, 400, 413, 421, 424, 426, 431, 433, 442, 455, 457, 461, 470, 471, 478, 482, 486–487, 498–500, 503, 544, 546, 547, 549, 555
- 1st, 59, 228, 233, 431, 556
- 2nd, 62, 67, 147–148, 228, 431
- 3rd, 69, 92, 173, 181, 221, 228, 306, 340, 345, 355, 432, 456, 483
- 4th, 7, 70, 91, 92, 183, 202, 228, 248, 267, 401, 432, 457, 483, 495, 546, 551
- 5th, 71, 228, 294, 432, 450, 470, 483, 547
- 6th, 72, 226, 228, 290, 306, 433, 536, 546–547, 555
- 7th, 74, 228, 293, 543
- 8th, 75, 168, 486, 516
- 9th, 76, 207
- 10th, 76
- 12th, 63, 319
- group, 50

Intuition, 28, 55, 120
Invisible, 247–248
Israel, 66, 380
Īśvara (Ishvara), 16, 22–23, 37–38, 39, 44, 47, 87–88, 93, 104, 115, 138, 167, 179, 301, 329, 403, 530
Īśvara Upanisad, 403

J

Jarāmaraṇa, 200, 245
Jāti, 200, 245
Jehovah, 315, 396, 468
Jesus, 469
Jewel in the lotus, 4, 284, 287, 452
Jinas, 23, 83, 94, 111, 117, 128, 130, 131, 133, 135
Jīvanmukta, 263, 267
Jīva(s), 7, 9, 38–39, 148, 182, 239, 246, 434, 537
Jīvātmā, 37–38, 39
Jñānaśakti, 17, 344, 409, 527
Jod-He-Vau-He, 315, 396
Jupiter, 58, 215, 232, 333, 346, 354, 507, 517, 528–529

K

Kabalah, 491
Kāla, 348, 510
Kalāhaṃsa, 360, 508–510, 513
Kali Yuga, 11, 119
Kalpa(s), 32, 222
Kāma-manas, 61, 199, 267, 415, 472, 553
Karana, 220, 254
Karma, 2, 4, 19, 26, 27, 45, 58, 74, 81, 101, 111, 125, 127, 130, 140, 142, 149, 152, 155, 156, 178, 199, 203, 214, 225, 245, 249, 252, 256, 270, 272, 278, 280, 288, 311, 318, 321, 336, 337, 343, 344, 360, 368–369, 385, 399, 409, 414, 416, 456, 462, 464, 473, 475, 495, 512, 517, 521, 527, 533, 541, 566
Kartrī, 38, 39
Kāya, 429
Keys, three, 56
Khandakāla, 348
Kliṣṭamanas, 146
Kosmos, 2–3, 6, 10, 15, 220, 240,

307, 315, 382, 387, 525
Kriyaśakti, 411
Kṛṣṇa (Krishna), 23, 433
Kṣiti (Kshiti), 564
Kumāra(s), 58, 63, 65, 67, 73, 142, 227, 233, 249, 277, 313, 317, 319, 330, 351, 356, 405, 407, 431, 471, 476–478, 542, 544. *See also* Dhyāni Buddhas
Kuṇḍalinī, 36, 70, 73, 76, 139–140, 145, 333, 343, 364, 435, 444, 450, 470, 473, 477, 492, 503, 523, 527
Kuṇḍalinīśakti (Kundalinishakti), 343, 512
Kwan-Shai-Yin, 447, 466, 468
Kwan-Yin, 468

L

Lamp, 502–504
Lanoo, 79, 92, 340, 456, 457, 497–498, 500, 502, 504
Lap of Māyā, 314–316, 357, 358
Law of Attraction, 9, 212, 213, 337, 374, 450
Law of Correspondences, 235, 278
Law of Economy, 4, 9, 213, 450
Law of Identity, 340, 456
Law of Love, 343, 512
Law of Synthesis, 8, 213, 436, 450
Laws of group evolution, 292, 413
Laya (centres), 96, 372, 377, 427, 428
Lemurian, 67, 223, 474, 532
Leo, 60, 67, 73, 88, 146, 156, 178, 206–207, 214, 227–228, 251, 252, 256, 257, 261, 271, 304, 321, 325, 330, 331–333, 341, 344, 345, 346, 347, 388, 391, 395, 412, 437, 438, 442, 447, 466, 473, 474–475, 481, 488, 518, 542, 551, 557–558, 564, 566
Lesser Builders, 154, 156, 191, 194, 249, 252, 256, 275, 277, 284, 286–288, 292, 337, 344, 379, 386, 392, 409, 413, 416, 418, 423, 515, 527, 536
Leucippus, 370
Liberated Hierarchies, 98–99, 335, 339, 410, 412
Libra, 76, 125, 156, 176–177, 178, 203, 204, 214, 223, 225, 237, 239, 241, 280, 288, 311, 321, 330, 335–336, 344, 346, 359, 360–361, 391, 413, 472–474, 488, 495, 517–518, 520, 527, 541
Life, 7, 9, 15, 31, 121, 139, 157, 211, 218, 251, 257, 259–260, 268, 274, 277, 306, 309, 320, 367, 368, 369, 378, 382, 384, 387, 395, 406, 420, 434, 435, 440–442, 448, 467, 474, 479, 486, 498, 505, 513, 515–516, 520, 530, 537, 539, 557
Light, 4, 6, 8, 15, 79, 94, 120–121, 155, 210, 216, 219, 271, 305, 320, 324, 337, 354, 373–374, 375–376, 398, 423, 425–427, 433–434, 442–445, 447–448, 499–501, 505, 511, 513–515, 518, 521–522, 524, 531, 542
Light of the World, 374, 452, 459
Lipika Lords, 58, 361, 363
Locanā, 130
Locke, 40
Logoic, Logoi, 118, 267, 282
    Causal Body (Soul), 37, 282, 318, 340, 471
    Desire, 54, 68, 133, 155, 197, 292, 296, 309, 462, 479, 507, 513, 569
    Etheric (Cosmic) body, 35–36, 184, 187, 215–216, 226, 266, 267, 383, 400, 482, 490, 531
    Evolution, 19
    Head centre, 63, 81, 116, 156, 169, 195, 271, 274, 279, 284–285, 294, 305, 388, 389, 542, 548, 555
    Heart centre, 265, 331, 380, 556
    Kāma-manas, 362
    Love, 349, 389
    Mentation/Meditation, 258, 341, 359, 388, 456, 497
    Mind, xv, 34, 89, 90, 95–96, 130, 136, 199, 209, 214–215, 225, 289,

336, 338, 342, 378, 381, 387, 391–392, 404, 412, 416, 420, 424, 437, 439, 451, 452, 455, 463, 478, 492, 494, 507, 511, 514, 517, 521, 523, 529–531, 539, 548, 556, 563
Permanent atom, 36, 97, 152, 225, 242, 333, 336, 360–361, 365, 368, 383, 564
Personality, 3, 10, 37
Plan, 194, 337, 340, 387, 564
Solar Plexus centre, 142
Thought, 3, 98–99, 101, 168, 212, 260, 337, 374, 380, 391, 392, 563
Throat centre, 425
Will, 109, 126–127, 136, 139, 142–143, 188, 206, 287, 371, 375, 424, 457, 462, 467, 472, 490, 493–494, 511, 558
Logos, 8, 12, 15, 35, 44, 47, 71, 72, 74, 76, 80–81, 84, 86–87, 90–91, 95–97, 105–107, 108–110, 113, 115, 118, 120, 123, 126–127, 130, 132, 137, 158, 167, 168, 169, 179–181, 185, 188, 192, 199, 208, 210, 216, 224, 230, 233, 239, 250, 258–259, 267, 274, 288–289, 309, 324, 330, 332, 350, 362, 366, 380, 396, 399, 427, 437, 444, 446, 449, 461–462, 465, 468, 469–470, 476, 478, 482, 484, 490, 501–502, 505–506, 524, 529, 533, 540, 553, 562–563
1st, 86, 89, 115, 121, 377, 564
2nd, 86–87, 90, 121, 127
3rd, 66, 72, 87, 90, 101, 121, 124, 297, 319, 328, 358, 377, 561, 563
planetary, 171, 176, 189, 197, 203, 240, 381, 417, 466, 478, 501, 548, 555
solar, 11, 12, 64, 66, 98, 116, 117, 153, 158, 168, 253, 312, 318
Lokas, 161, 289
Lord, 226, 560, 566–567, 569
Lord of Love, 91, 116, 207, 328, 444
Lords of Compassion, 120, 141, 467
Lords of Dark Face, 415
Lords of Flame, xv, 61, 63, 66, 75, 84, 231–232, 279, 430, 437, 463, 554
Lords of karma, 85, 185, 363
Lords of Life, 140, 197, 334, 461, 558
Lords of Sacrifice, 98, 154, 157, 266, 339, 342, 413, 437, 475, 497
Lotus, 307, 356–358
Love, 9, 23, 54, 98, 131, 133, 142, 155, 156, 196, 272, 359, 376, 394, 402, 437, 442, 505
Love-Wisdom. *See* Ray(s), 2nd
Luminous, 279, 406–407
Luminous Egg, 389, 402–403, 407, 417–418
Lunar Fathers, 136
Lunar Lords, 342, 343, 414, 512, 569
Lunar pitṛs (pitris), 136, 288, 399, 409, 411–412, 414–418, 440, 516

M

Mādhyamika, 17
Magnetism, 449–450, 466
Mahābhārata, 404
Mahāchohan, 75, 76, 159
Mahākāla, 23
Mahākalpa, 160, 278
Mahākāśa, 38
Mahāmanvantara, 63, 67, 72, 77, 103, 118, 121, 136, 148, 158, 180, 218, 225, 238, 267, 318, 334, 344, 352, 439, 455, 481, 501, 504, 506, 532, 539, 544, 549, 558, 566, 569
Mahāparinirvāṇa, 239, 272
Mahāprālaya, 39, 403
Mahat, 33–34, 39, 41, 44, 65, 66, 69, 75, 97, 110, 115, 132, 133, 139, 153–154, 159, 166, 185–186, 190, 208, 214, 270, 311, 326, 329, 338, 344, 348–349, 351, 362, 373, 387, 391, 405, 424, 470, 473, 478, 479, 497, 509, 527, 566–567
Mahatmas, 273
Mahāyāna doctrines, 7

Maheśvara, 39
Maia, 405
Maitreya, 8
Makara, 341, 380, 397, 411, 414, 472, 496, 498, 569
Māmakī, 131
Manas, 6, 72, 73, 338, 369, 384, 424, 441, 519, 536–537
Manasaputras, 194, 330
Maṇḍala(s), 14, 22, 23, 72, 96, 115, 116, 121, 124, 130, 147, 156, 194, 223, 226, 328, 332, 356, 365, 369, 384, 388, 418, 430, 460, 462, 486, 490, 495, 506–507, 520, 543, 564, 567, 569
Man-plant, 5, 6, 87, 352, 435, 514, 537, 548
Mantra(s), 228, 279, 284, 296–297, 427–430, 520–521
Mantrikaśakti, 340, 413, 438
Manu(s), 75, 357–358, 559
Mānuśī Buddha, 8, 273
Manu Smriti, 404
Manvantara, 6, 22, 45, 72, 79, 81–82, 83, 84, 85, 86–87, 100, 103, 106–107, 115, 118, 119, 121, 127–128, 130, 131, 133–134, 136–137, 143, 148, 155, 158–159, 161, 166, 170, 182, 184–185, 202, 212, 214, 215, 217, 221, 254, 261, 265, 270, 272, 280, 296, 298, 304, 306, 307, 329, 350, 357, 445, 447, 479, 498, 501, 533, 535–536, 563
Manvantaric dawn, 284–285
Mars, xvii, 59, 71, 216, 230–232, 346, 360, 386, 418, 431, 438, 445, 458
Martanda, 290
Mass life, 154, 155, 208
Master(s), xiv, 48–50, 53, 72, 75, 76, 85, 105, 115, 118, 158–159, 196, 204, 221–222, 384, 460, 463, 470, 483, 490, 529, 547, 549, 552, 555–556
Mātripadma (Matri-Padma), 304, 306–309, 310–311, 313, 322, 353, 356, 398, 528
Mātṛtamāḥ, 34
Matsya Purāna, 403
Māyā, 5, 16–17, 19, 20, 22–23, 25–31, 32–34, 37–38, 44, 89, 92, 94, 96, 111, 113, 114, 124, 128, 157, 164, 179–180, 199, 201, 204–205, 216, 237, 242, 245, 247, 309, 314, 357, 358, 376, 439, 447, 455, 478, 486, 487, 507, 528, 549, 566
Māyāvī, 34
Mayāvirūpa, 21, 287
Melchesidek, 227
Mental plane, 101, 340, 341, 369, 376, 397, 402, 405, 478, 516, 523, 527, 533, 542, 562
    higher, 34, 134, 144, 166, 182, 282, 299, 308, 338, 339, 341, 355, 367, 368, 384, 388, 392, 393, 399–400, 402, 419, 424, 428, 436, 437, 439, 442, 444, 446, 455–456, 479, 490, 514, 567
    lower, 144, 249, 299, 338, 341, 368, 392–393, 450, 497
Mercury, 230–232, 332–333, 346, 372, 373, 426, 438, 445, 360, 533
Merope, 405
Michael, 227
Milk, 152–153, 175, 323, 401, 417–419, 434, 436
Milky way, xvii, 401, 434, 548
Mind (empirical), 18, 28, 159, 173, 188
Mind (liberated), 25, 67, 74, 82, 84, 97, 99, 101, 105–106, 110–111, 115, 123, 125, 126, 128, 134, 136–137, 143, 147, 154, 166, 169, 186, 188–190, 199, 222, 226, 233, 237, 239, 246, 254–255, 261, 270, 277, 282, 297, 302, 304, 306, 308, 313, 325–326, 330, 341, 351, 355, 368, 374–375, 378, 385, 390, 404–406, 410, 424, 426, 432, 438, 441, 444, 458, 471, 479, 483, 492–493, 498, 500, 504, 506–507, 511, 513,

522–523, 529, 531, 540, 548–549, 550–551, 553, 554–555, 559, 561
abstract, xv, 20, 50, 70, 72, 187, 192–193, 282, 293, 342, 390, 412, 447, 451, 489, 493, 497, 512, 568
Clear Light, 41, 512
Fires of, 23, 449, 484
planes of, 76, 81
Mirror, 567–568
Mirror-like Wisdom, 23, 93, 100, 130, 134, 145, 335, 350, 359, 436, 521, 568
Misery, causes of, 155, 197, 201–202
Mohinī-śakti, 17
Moisture, 6, 9
Mokṣa (Moksha), 197
Monadic Eye, 9, 97, 262, 548
Monad(s), 6–7, 8, 27, 31, 39, 45, 72, 81–82, 83, 85, 88–89, 90, 103, 139, 140, 143, 161, 166, 176, 188, 192, 194, 196, 198, 210, 216, 224, 246, 252, 256, 260, 273–274, 279, 285, 306, 322, 323, 334, 350, 372, 377, 378–379, 402, 406, 413, 432, 437, 439, 441, 458–459, 462–464, 483, 485, 489, 490, 495, 498, 499, 502, 505, 516, 530, 540, 548–549, 555, 566, 569
Moon (Chain), 215, 331, 343, 346–347, 414, 431, 438, 445, 458, 460, 467, 507, 512, 544
Morning Sons of Glory, 426
Moses, 469
Mother, xiv, 13, 27, 34, 46, 70, 75, 79, 87, 88, 89, 93–94, 102, 103–104, 108–112, 113, 115, 124–128, 131, 134–135, 138–139, 144, 145–148, 149, 155–156, 157, 159, 160–161, 164, 165–168, 177, 186, 198, 206, 208, 219–220, 224, 236, 240–241, 245, 252, 274, 310, 311, 314, 326, 332, 335, 349, 353–357, 372–373, 390, 396, 412, 419, 427, 446, 453, 504, 506–507, 511, 513, 515, 517, 525, 528, 541–545, 547–552
Womb, 13, 65, 68, 80, 83–84, 90, 98, 102, 108, 109–110, 112, 122, 124, 135, 137–138, 143, 147, 149–150, 159, 162, 181–185, 211–212, 227, 251, 252, 279, 289–290, 305, 306, 313, 322, 330, 332–333, 335, 336, 340, 348, 350–354, 359, 360, 367, 376, 380–381, 387, 390, 393, 395, 398, 405, 413, 418–420, 425–426, 439, 452–453, 461, 480, 486–487, 500, 511–518, 523, 527, 531, 541, 547–550, 568
Mother Deep (depths of), 371–377, 387, 389–390, 402
Mother Nature, 516
Mother of the Gods, 289–290
Mother of the World, 147, 233, 253–254, 398, 471
Motion, 31, 442, 444–446, 448, 542
forward progressive, 446
rotary, 446, 450
Mukta, 267
Mūlaprakṛti, 19, 41, 43, 46, 47, 84, 97, 111, 165, 167, 177, 238, 290–291, 348, 352, 358, 398, 434, 491, 511–512, 514, 538, 563–564
Mūla-Prakṛti Māyā, 16, 17
Multitudes, 481–482, 485
Muṇḍaka Upaniṣad, 530, 534
Mundane Egg, 2–3, 25, 102, 108, 305, 382–383, 509
Mysteries, 232, 453, 465, 491, 504, 507, 544
Mystery Schools, xvi

N

Nāḍī(s), 8, 12, 28, 30, 41, 54, 57, 59, 60, 62, 63, 64, 65, 70, 75, 76, 81, 84, 89, 91, 103, 107, 108–110, 116, 122, 127, 132, 141, 144, 157, 176, 177, 197, 201, 205, 224, 233, 235, 257, 259, 260–261, 266–267, 287, 289, 293, 299, 306, 309–311, 316, 318, 319, 324, 339, 343, 350, 362, 367,

370, 373, 376, 378, 379, 384–385, 390–391, 408, 420, 425, 441, 466, 477, 493, 522, 526, 528, 530–532, 541, 563
Nāgārjuna, 18, 19, 21, 30, 269
Nāmarūpa, 200, 245, 404
Nāra, 16, 35
Nārāyaṇa, 15, 16, 35, 36, 39, 44, 370, 403–404, 509
Nārāyana Sūkata, 403
Nature, kingdoms of, 12
Nebulous, 408–409
Necessity, 236–237
Neptune, 59, 214, 215, 344, 346–347, 539–540
New Jerusalem, 485
Nidānas, 199–200, 245, 247
Nimitta, 301
Nirguṇa, 348
Nirmaṇakāya, 8, 97
Nirvāṇa, 24, 198, 238, 239
Nirvāṇees, 47, 133, 139, 140, 155, 194, 230, 233, 277, 288, 484, 494–495, 524, 543–544, 551–552, 141
Niṣkriya, 38
Nitya, 434
Noah, 401
Non-Being, 249–250
Nowhere, 113, 123–124
Numerical code, 48–77

O

Ocean, 391, 402, 420–421, 439–444, 542, 545
Ocean of Immortality, 392, 435, 436–437, 439, 441–442, 446, 551
Oeaohoo, 392, 393, 423–425, 426–434, 465, 467–469, 474
Oṁ, 30, 429–433
Oṁ Maṇi Padme Hūṁ: Hrīḥ, 433
One Existence, 301
One Initiator, 471–472
One Ray, 311–312, 374–376, 379–380
Ophis, 469
Orion, 548
Outpouring(s), 398
1st, 12, 70, 108, 132, 156, 245, 252, 256, 334, 338, 367–368, 372, 376, 385, 386, 387, 392, 393, 395, 410–411, 423, 527
2nd, 12, 274, 280, 336–337, 372, 373–374, 377
3rd, 140–141
Over-Soul, 45, 268–269

P

Padma, 307
Pālana, 38
Pāṇḍaravāsinī, 130
Para, 530
Parabrahm, 370
Parabrahman, 14–15, 42–43, 46, 47, 86, 93, 94–95, 96–97, 100, 179, 254, 281, 291, 301–302, 348, 434
Paracelsus, 327
Paramārtha, 15–16, 266, 267–268, 272, 274, 281
Paramārthika, 18
Paramātman, 37, 530
Paranishpanna, 241–242
Paraśakti (Parashakti), 341, 411, 497
Paratantra, 268
Paravara, 14
Parent, 152, 160, 166, 236
Parinirvāṇa, 8, 239
Pariniṣpanna, 194, 237–239, 268, 276, 281–282, 284–285, 550
Pascal, 382
Path, 13
Pentagram, 13, 68
Perfection, 519, 523
Periodicity, law of, 4, 45
Permanent atoms, 557, 565
Philo Judæus, 468
Physical sun, 442
Pilgrimage, 224
Pilgrim, eternal, 7–8
Piṅgalā naḍī, 59, 108, 133, 230–231, 262, 329, 394, 431, 438, 441, 510, 535, 548, 553
Pisces, 66, 152, 158, 161, 171, 178,

181, 213, 214–215, 304, 321, 340, 342, 346, 380–381, 389–390, 391, 393, 410, 426, 455–456, 463–464, 494, 508, 511, 532, 550
Pitris (pitṛ), 266, 296, 399, 409–410
Planetary energies, 68
Planetary rulers, 345–346, 481
Planetary Schemes, 366, 478
Planetary Schools, 232
Planet, (sacred/non-sacred), 51, 76, 77
Plasma, Cosmic, 34
Pleiades, 68, 184, 261, 352, 389, 404–405, 411, 418–419, 547–548, 564
Pluto, xvii, 181, 215, 216, 340, 346, 455, 494, 550
Pollux, 480
Power, seat of, 11, 114, 121
Prabhavāpyaya, 253
Pradhāna, 17, 301, 348
Prajāpati, 509
Prajñā(s), 35, 83, 98, 130, 233, 281, 293
Prakṛti, 29, 33, 348, 403, 537
Pralaya, xvi, xvii, 2–3, 32, 38, 39, 46, 79, 81–82, 84, 86, 106, 107–108, 119–121, 122, 126–128, 148, 151, 154, 158, 161, 162, 164–165, 168, 177, 181, 190, 202, 213, 219, 233, 237, 245, 249, 254, 260, 263, 272, 278, 281, 321, 324, 331, 363, 370, 426, 447, 448, 452, 483, 498, 501, 506, 522, 541, 549, 563, 565
Prāṇa(s), 4, 5, 9, 18, 29, 30, 33–36, 41, 51, 58, 76, 81, 86, 111, 142, 143, 144, 146, 160, 192, 214, 225, 239, 283, 292, 309, 318, 358, 369, 389, 399, 400, 440, 444, 466, 470, 472, 490, 542, 563
Prāṇāyāma, 193
Prāṇic triangle, 176, 311, 443
Pratītyasamutpāda, 19, 22, 199–200, 342, 511
Pratyakṣa, 92
Pratyavekṣaṇa-jñāna, 24
Pratyeka Buddha, 7
Pravṛtti-śakti, 17
Presence, 8, 260–261, 264
Primeval Light, 567
Primordial Buddha, 233
Primordial Ray, 376–377, 406
Progeny, 141
Purpose, 117
Puruṣa, 35, 37, 44, 403, 419, 509, 530
Pymander, 357, 470

Q

Quality, 229–230
Quaternary, 204, 315

R

Radiance, radiant, 135, 137, 406–407, 448, 457–458, 550–551
Radiant Child, 457–458
Radiant Egg, 405
Radiant Essence, 388, 399–402, 406
Radiant Light, 437, 442
Rāja Lords, 142, 156, 249, 387, 404
Rajas, 17, 31–33, 405
Rakoczi, 48
RĀṀ, 428
Ratnagotravibhāga, 25
Ratnasambhava, 23, 24–25, 94, 114, 131, 143, 145–147, 337, 342–343, 344, 371, 373, 394, 506, 510, 512, 518, 522, 526, 527
Ray paths, 196–197
Ray(s), 57, 73, 201, 279, 283, 298, 305–306, 310, 314, 384, 444, 477, 524, 532, 551, 558
    1st, 36, 54, 58, 60, 62, 64, 65, 67, 74, 85, 89, 90, 96, 110, 132, 152, 156, 160, 165, 174, 175, 176, 180–181, 186, 190, 192, 194, 198, 201, 206, 208–209, 214, 215, 219, 224, 226, 233, 234, 236, 239, 242, 248, 251, 264, 289, 297, 299, 304–305, 308, 310, 334, 340, 342, 346, 354, 364, 370, 393–395, 398, 414, 429,

446, 448, 450, 455, 472, 479, 489, 492, 494, 497–498, 501, 503, 505, 511, 513, 529, 547, 549, 552, 558
2nd, xiv, 7, 27, 51, 54, 58–60, 61, 62, 65, 66, 67–68, 69–70, 74, 83, 85, 86–87, 88–89, 90–91, 96, 108, 112–113, 127, 137–138, 141, 143, 146, 152, 156, 160, 174, 184, 190, 197, 198, 213, 219, 222, 234, 236–237, 242, 264, 279, 287, 289, 312, 319, 334, 336–337, 346, 354, 358–359, 363–364, 373–375, 379, 392, 394, 398, 406, 414, 420, 422, 431, 446, 450, 467, 472, 476, 478–479, 489, 492, 501, 510, 513, 517, 529, 537, 541, 545, 548–549, 552, 554, 563
3rd, xiv, 27, 36, 58, 63, 66, 70, 96, 102, 139, 142, 149, 152, 159, 160–161, 174, 181, 190, 198, 201, 213, 224, 230, 244, 276–277, 299, 308, 314, 319, 321, 337, 345, 346, 386, 394, 395, 410, 413, 422, 426, 429, 446, 450, 489, 534, 544, 565
4th, 27, 58, 63, 71, 146, 152–153, 174, 201, 213, 215, 346, 373, 392, 410, 413, 426, 436, 457, 500, 518
5th, 58, 73, 154, 185, 201, 213, 340, 341, 346, 390, 393, 412, 455, 459, 497, 500, 534
6th, 27, 59, 74, 155, 197, 201, 213, 215, 230, 332, 342–343, 344, 364, 393, 394, 395, 412, 477, 488, 500, 511–512, 526–527, 539
7th, 28, 59, 76, 137, 155, 202, 208, 213, 289, 295, 331, 342, 346, 369, 391, 395, 415, 455–456, 493, 497, 499, 517, 552, 563
Rays of Mind, 52, 159, 345, 517, 558
Realisation, 519
Ring-pass-not, 95–96, 118, 123, 356, 389, 425, 443, 449, 489, 514, 523, 537–538, 569–570
Ring(s), 79, 94, 95–97, 114–121
Robes, 162–166, 189
Root, 83–84, 86, 130–131, 133, 390, 402, 408, 420–421, 423–427, 429, 433, 434, 435, 437, 439, 441, 446, 491
Root Race(s), 121, 229, 233, 280, 474–475
2nd, 61, 474
3rd (Lemurian), 280, 474
4th (Atlantean), 69
5th (Aryan), 8, 11, 59, 69, 70, 472, 475
6th, 8, 71, 343, 512, 548
7th, 71
Round(s), 150, 162, 223, 313, 365, 384, 394, 399, 427
3rd, 431, 437
4th, 70, 71, 229, 306, 311, 456, 499
5th, 308, 431
Rudra(s), 39, 480
Rūpa, 192

S

Sacred Numbers, 387
Sacrificial Fires, 414
Sadasat, 16, 26, 29
Sagittarius, 63, 178, 195, 204, 212, 213, 337, 343, 346, 386, 390–392, 393, 394, 400, 408, 409, 414, 439, 466, 473, 475–476, 478, 489, 507, 512, 547
Saguṇa brahman, 329
Sahajānanda, 24
Sahasrāra Padma, 362
Śakti(s), 16, 38, 39, 358, 558, 563
Śakyamuni (Shakyamuni), 8
Samādhi, 134
Samatā-jñāna, 24, 131
Sambhogakāya, 97
Sambhogakāya Flower(s), 4, 7, 10, 18, 25, 39, 69, 95, 97, 132, 137, 147,

161, 166, 222, 241, 249, 258, 260, 269–270, 285, 304, 308–309, 339, 355, 362, 367, 384, 385, 399, 402, 419, 436, 442, 483, 490, 499, 505, 522, 553
Samkhya school, 403
Saṃsāra, 1, 17, 18–20, 22, 25, 26–28, 29, 30, 62, 77, 84, 91, 100, 101, 106, 113, 128, 142, 148, 174, 197, 290, 295, 339, 341, 358, 378, 380, 385, 393, 424, 429, 432, 435, 436, 441, 447, 455, 463, 487, 500, 506, 510, 512, 514, 516, 528, 532, 538–539, 553, 554, 566, 568
Saṃsāra-śūnyatā nexus, 36, 92, 147, 188, 239, 269, 299, 378, 397, 451, 513, 537, 554, 569
Saṃskāras, 18–19, 28, 34, 84, 105, 125, 142, 149, 152, 162, 167, 199–200, 223, 245, 270, 278, 284, 332, 355, 360, 361, 464, 470, 500, 502, 521, 529, 530, 558
Sāmyāvasthā, 33
Sanat Kumāra, 63, 73, 227, 233, 398, 463, 466–467, 471–472, 476, 554
Śaṅkara (Shaṅkara), 32
Sāṅkhya, 17, 21, 301
Sapta, 478–479, 481
Sarjanā-śakti, 17
Sarparajni, 469
Sarva, 24, 25
Sat, 21, 26, 28, 30, 42, 44, 327
Śata-rūpā, 509
Sattva, 17, 31–33, 405, 434
Saturn, 58, 232, 346, 360, 507, 517
Satya, 434
Satya Yuga, 119, 401
Scorpio, 77, 139–140, 155, 178, 209, 212–213, 224, 270–271, 330, 332–333, 339, 342, 346, 350–351, 360–361, 363, 368, 373, 389, 391, 394, 410, 413, 418–419, 437, 438, 460, 463, 477, 487, 488, 489, 507, 511, 518, 520, 536, 546
Seal of Solomon, 71, 289, 308, 313
Sea of fire, 449, 490–493, 514, 524
Seat of Power, 92, 106, 118, 124, 127, 131, 136, 179, 224, 243, 256, 305, 318, 350, 352, 363, 378, 380–381, 407, 427, 459, 463, 471, 501, 505, 538, 547, 552, 553, 570
Secret doctrine, xiv–xv
Secret Mantra, 138, 520
Senses, five, 28–29, 295, 297–298, 364, 519–520
Sephira, 289
Sephiroth, 290, 468
Septenaries, 404, 476
Serpent power, 36
Serpent(s), 35, 36, 47, 230–231, 333, 382, 468–469, 470, 491
Service, 519, 521
Śeṣa, 35, 36, 469
Seven-leafed plant, 5
Seven Sons, 317
Shadowy, 532–534
Shambhala, xv–xvi, xviii, 60, 62, 64, 65, 66, 67, 70, 73, 77, 81, 83, 84, 87, 88, 90, 98, 102, 109, 117, 132, 139, 140–142, 143, 165, 193, 201, 204, 219, 226, 244, 249, 262, 279, 284, 317, 319, 322, 345, 352, 356, 372, 388, 459, 463, 476, 479, 485, 489, 521, 530–531, 555
Shekinah, 290
Shining Ones, 488–490
Shoot, 378–379
Siddhis, 23, 25, 107, 470, 482
Sight, 519, 522
Silence, 297–298, 299
Silent Watcher, 466, 471
Silver cord, 255
Sirius, 184, 197, 548
Śiva (Shiva), 22–23, 24, 25, 36, 39, 44, 87, 121, 403–404, 480
Skandhas, 125, 142
Sleep, 154, 156, 158, 162, 168, 171–172, 174–175, 182, 184–186, 189–190, 211, 216, 221, 248, 252, 254–256, 258–259
Slumber, 168–169, 175
Smell, 519, 523, 524

Soham, 508
Solar devas, 461–462
Solar Logos, 406, 425, 427, 430, 431, 459, 460, 465, 467, 476, 495, 505, 535, 537, 562, 569
Solar pitṛ (pitris), 399, 440
Solar Plexus in the Head, 284, 361, 388, 432
Solar system, 278, 345, 386, 422–423
 last, 276, 278, 422
Solitary Ray, 372–373, 375, 377
Son, 125, 146, 155, 156, 157, 160–161, 180–181, 198, 210, 219–221, 224, 226, 236, 245, 252, 274, 279, 312, 313, 325–327, 356, 371, 396, 400, 412, 429–430, 450, 453, 457, 461, 468, 491, 501, 504–507, 524, 536, 542, 546–547, 549, 551–552, 567, 569
Son of Necessity, 155–156, 226, 364, 464, 542
Sons of God, 327
Sons of Manvantaric Dawn, 277, 279–280, 420
Sons of Mind, 517
Sorcerer, 75
Soul(s), 10, 18, 31, 45, 68, 69, 73, 75, 85, 88, 97, 108, 116, 132, 137, 157, 161, 162–163, 165, 171, 181, 182, 184, 188, 190, 207, 220, 224, 231, 237, 253, 258, 266, 267–268, 277, 283, 285, 286–288, 293, 300, 302, 323, 329, 332, 334, 340, 352, 355, 367, 384, 392, 398, 400, 401, 406, 407, 413, 419, 423, 426, 433, 437, 441–443, 447, 456, 478, 481, 500, 505, 510, 518, 530, 537, 546–547, 551, 553, 569
Sound, 296, 328, 350, 396, 427, 509, 520–521
Space, 4, 5, 38, 40, 78, 81, 87, 89, 91, 93, 95, 100, 104, 113, 157–160, 162, 176, 210, 217–218, 235, 240, 257–259, 289–290, 301, 359, 419, 456, 460–461, 493, 501, 525, 547
Sparsa, 200, 245
Spiral-cyclic motion, 14, 52, 73, 74, 76, 90, 99, 120, 124, 127, 145, 159, 199, 219, 235, 240, 257, 263, 293, 298, 349, 363, 374, 404, 446, 450–451, 498, 523, 529, 538, 549, 552, 556
Spirit, 43–44, 45, 161, 165, 405–406, 429, 447, 451, 498, 502–505, 529–531, 535, 537, 542–543, 545, 564
Spirit of Peace, 398, 471
Spirit of the Flame, 503–504
Spirits of God, 503
Spiritual triad, 67, 177, 184, 199, 248, 258, 324, 400, 407, 461, 477, 485, 547
Square, 396
Sri Sankarāchārya, 254
Sṛṣṭi, 32, 38, 39
Stanzas of Dzyan, xv, xvii
Sterope, 405
Sthiti, 32
Sublime Lords, 227, 233–234, 236
Sukhavati, 130
Sun, 5
Sun (physical), 4, 125, 187, 195, 215, 231, 290, 346–347, 462, 466, 468
Śūnyatā Eye, 407
Śūnyatā (shunyata), 17, 21, 23, 26, 27, 28, 30, 47, 80, 91, 99–100, 106, 109, 112, 128, 145, 165, 174, 183, 189, 197–198, 202, 210, 238, 244, 254, 256, 269, 295, 299, 302, 322, 365–366, 378, 382, 392, 396, 486, 500, 538, 541, 554
Surabhi, 401
Suṣumṇā nāḍī, 59, 108, 230–231, 321, 431, 441, 510, 536, 548, 553, 554
Sūtrātmā, 45, 47, 62, 64, 84, 171, 285, 287, 299, 310, 318, 322, 328, 360, 364, 367, 376, 390, 423, 441, 477, 513, 529, 533, 537, 565, 568
Svabhāva(t), 19, 21, 26, 89, 254, 273, 290–292, 299, 316, 320, 322–324, 349, 360, 420, 512, 528, 531, 538, 558, 563–565, 567–569

Svabhāvikāya, 97
Svādiṣṭhāna chakra, 124. *See also* Chakras (centres), Sacral
Svayambhu, 273, 403–404, 509, 566
Swan, 510
Swastika, 11, 12
Sweeps, 361–362
Swell, 353–354
Symbols, 10–14, 55–56

T

Takṣara, 530
Tamas, 17, 31–32, 405
Tanmātras, 566
Tantric yoga, 553
Tapas, 35
Tārā, 131
Taste, 519, 522, 523
Tat, 30
Tathāgatagarbha, 4, 18–19, 20, 25, 31, 95
Tathatā, 95
Tattva, 24, 25
Tau, 10–11, 13, 14
Taurus, 57, 65, 68, 90, 109, 118, 133, 136, 168, 169, 178, 180, 213–215, 241, 242, 261, 270–271, 291–292, 296, 298, 302, 304, 309, 321, 322, 325, 342, 346, 349, 350, 352, 373, 389, 391, 394, 410, 416, 418, 426–427, 445, 446, 456, 459, 461–462, 464, 468, 475, 479, 486, 488, 508, 511, 514, 518, 528, 555, 564–566
Taygeta, 405
Temple, 92, 168, 483
Teth, 491
Tetragrammaton, 468, 469
Tetraktis, 316
THAT (Logos), xvii, 10, 76, 93, 104, 158, 240–241, 364, 396, 504, 508, 521, 548
The four, 163, 166, 295, 312–313, 338–339, 358, 368, 387, 397–400, 403, 419, 423, 433, 436, 471, 476, 478, 480
The One, 79, 89, 92–97, 104–106, 111, 113, 120, 161, 190, 203, 220, 235, 251, 293, 311, 325, 328, 434, 476–477, 490, 501, 536–537, 541, 556
Theosophical Society, xiv
The three, 96, 163, 166, 268, 295, 312–313, 324, 337, 368, 376, 387, 391, 395, 397–400, 403, 405, 423, 433, 436, 471, 476, 478, 480
Thor's Hammer, 10, 11
Thought, 99
    construct, 37, 98
    Divine, 44, 352
    Form(s), 115, 145, 180, 363, 365, 446, 489, 506
Three times, 22–23, 32, 39, 89, 90, 96, 101, 174, 189, 220, 242, 287
Thrills, 350, 352, 383–384
Throat in the Head, 361, 388, 432
Throne(s), 92, 116, 240, 365, 407, 453, 476–477. *See also* Seat of Power
Time, 172–175, 181–182, 185, 198, 230, 243, 304, 348, 469, 510
Touch, 364, 366, 519, 520–521, 543–544
Transfiguration, 69
Tree of Life, 391, 434
Tridasa (tridaśa), 479
Trikāya, 187
Trimūrti, 22, 39, 87–88, 89, 94, 113, 329, 403
Trinity, 315, 398
Triple Flowers, 413
Tṛṣnā, 200, 245
Trumpet, 298
Truth(s)
    Conventional, 19–20, 268
    Seven, 226–229, 233–234
    Ultimate, 19–20, 268, 272
Tum-mo, 444

U

Unconsciousness, 258
Unicorn, 185

Universal Matrix, 357
Universal Mind, 154, 176, 186–190, 195, 198, 201, 259, 334, 470, 555, 559
Universal Soul, 3–4, 509
Universe, xvii, 40, 43–46, 93, 111, 187, 211, 219, 220, 234–236, 240, 268, 273, 275, 323, 325–327, 364, 469, 530, 534, 537, 545, 551, 557, 559, 570
    creation of, 32–33, 254, 277, 296, 326, 404
Upādāna, 200, 245, 301
Upādāna kāraṇa, 17
Upādhi, 38, 43
Uranus, 59, 290, 331, 342, 346–347, 369, 391, 493, 507, 517, 552

V

Vāch, 509
Vāhana, 131
Vairocana, 22, 23–25, 93, 129–130, 131, 145, 293, 335, 340, 393, 455
Vaishnavas, 301
Vajras, 363
Vajrasattva, 22, 24–25, 37, 233, 396
Varada mudrā, 131
Vasus, 480
Vayus, 59
Vedanā, 200, 245
Vedānta Sūtra, 403
Vedas, 480
Veil, 482–484, 487
Venus, 11, 59, 185, 230–232, 342, 346, 390, 430, 437, 438, 445, 458, 507, 528–529
Vibration, 349, 361
Vibuddha, 24
Vidhātā, 38
Vijñāna, 200, 245, 269, 270
Vikṣepa-śakti, 17
Virāḍ (Virāj), 33–35, 39, 509
Virgin-Egg, 334, 372–373, 375, 378–382, 383
Virgin Mother, 383
Virgo, 75, 108, 118, 156, 167, 175–177, 203, 213, 241, 244, 245, 251–252, 326, 328–329, 330, 331–332, 333, 335, 346, 348, 354, 360–361, 390–391, 410, 413, 425, 427, 461–462, 486, 488, 516–518, 520, 528, 533, 544, 568
Visarga, 428
Visible, 247–248
Visishtadwaita school, 348
Viṣṇu (Vishnu), 16, 22–23, 24, 35, 36, 44, 87, 103, 121, 403–404, 469, 561
Viśvavajra, 131
Vivarta-vāda, 32
Voice of Silence, 295, 298
Void, 18, 20–21, 31, 47, 80, 174, 238, 269, 392. *See also* Śūnyatā (shunyata)
Void Element(s), 18, 20, 21, 26, 27, 34, 291, 392
Vulcan, 214, 215, 342, 346, 373, 394, 438, 445, 448, 452, 507, 511, 528–529, 544
Vyakta, 33
Vyāvahārika, 16

W

War in Heaven, 401
Watchers, 278
Waters, 34, 36, 41, 91, 100, 103, 158, 196, 211–215, 298, 310, 329, 342, 349, 357, 362, 375–377, 389, 392, 396, 400, 403, 412–413, 415, 418, 426, 436, 461, 463–464, 485, 490, 492, 493–495, 507, 510–511, 516, 518, 521, 539, 549, 551
    face of, 11, 367
Waters of Life, 369–371, 405, 461, 513, 515–516, 518, 521, 525
Watery Devas, 521
Watery Lives, 369
Ways to Bliss, 155, 207
Web, 333, 343, 388, 394–395, 483, 526, 528–531, 534, 537, 542, 545,

557, 564–565, 569
Web of Light, 316, 318, 322, 443, 531
Wheel(s), 221–223, 226, 272–273, 275, 286, 311, 342
Will. *See* Ray(s), 1st
Will-of-Love, 414–415, 507
Will-to-Be, 396
Will-to-Manifest, 306
Wing, 362–365
  swift, 336, 360, 366, 368
Womb. *See* Mother, Womb
Word(s), 140, 144, 159, 188–189, 227–228, 232, 266, 296, 340, 351, 396, 427, 438, 509, 528
World Egg, 305, 373, 384–385, 510
World Soul, 68, 75, 121, 329, 382, 402, 433
World Tree, 133, 289, 420

Y

Yātana, 200, 245
Yin-yang, 193, 195
Yogācāra, 6, 268
Yogācāra doctrine, 17–18, 33, 85, 238, 269
Yogin, 140
Yoginī, 140
Yugas, 117, 119, 136, 149, 162, 237, 331, 361

Z

Zero, 13, 310
Zodiac, 51, 60, 61, 62, 66, 68, 118, 137, 161, 177–178, 181, 185, 186, 207, 214, 215, 243, 283, 304, 316, 321, 340, 345, 380–381, 413, 446, 455, 481, 488, 492, 494, 517, 527–528, 564
Zodiacal year, 70, 72

About the Author

BODO BALSYS is the founder of The School of Esoteric Sciences. He is an author of many books on subjects centred on Buddhism and the Esoteric Sciences, a meditation teacher, poet, artist, spiritual scientist and healer. He has studied extensively across multiple traditions including Esoteric Science, Buddhism, Christianity, Esoteric Healing, Western Science, Art, Politics and History. His advanced esoteric insights, gained through decades of meditative contemplation, enable him to provide a rich understanding of the spiritual pathway toward enlightenment, healing and service.

Bodo's teachings can be accessed via the School of Esoteric Science's website:
http://universaldharma.com

For any other enquiries, please email
sangha@universaldharma.com

About Universal Dharma Publishing

Universal Dharma Publishing is a not for profit publisher. Our aim is make innovative, original and esoteric spiritual teachings accessible to all who genuinely aspire to awaken and serve humanity. The books published aim in part to provide an esoteric interpretation of the meaning of Buddhist *dharma* with view of reformation of the way people perceive the meaning of the related teachings. Hopefully then Buddhism can more effectively serve its principal function as a vehicle for enlightenment, and further prosper into the future. A further aim is to provide the next level of exposition of the esoteric doctrines to be revealed to humanity following on the wisdom tradition pioneered by H.P. Blavatsky and A.A. Bailey.

www.ingramcontent.com/pod-product-compliance
Lightning Source LLC
Chambersburg PA
CBHW031956220426
43664CB00005B/46
* 9 7 8 0 6 4 8 7 8 7 7 0 9 *